AF328520

A PUBLICATION OF THE PAUL SACHER FOUNDATION

**Utopia, Innovation, Tradition
Bruno Maderna's Cosmos**

Edited by Angela Ida De Benedictis

Cover: Bruno Maderna, *Giardino religioso,* for orchestra,
score, p. 2, section B
(© 1973 by Ricordi, Milan; 132049)
with kind permission

Translations from Italian:
Sally Davies (texts by Michele Chiappini, Carlo Ciceri,
Paolo Dal Molin, Angela Ida De Benedictis, Leo Izzo,
Veniero Rizzardi, Maurizio Romito, Nicola Scaldaferri,
Claudia Vincis, Benedetta Zucconi)
James Imam (Introduction by Angela Ida De Benedictis)

Copy editing: J. Bradford Robinson, Alexa Ahern

Design and typesetting:
Büro für Buchgestaltung Sibylle Ryser, Basel
Reproduction: Bildpunkt AG, Münchenstein/Basel
Setting of musical notation: Notengrafik Berlin
Fonts: Sabon, Gotham
Paper: Munken Lynx 100 gm^2
Printed by Gremper AG, Basel/Pratteln
Bound by Bubu AG, Mönchaltorf
Printed in Switzerland

First published 2022
The Boydell Press, Woodbridge, UK
ISBN 978-1-83765-030-9
The Boydell Press is an imprint of Boydell & Brewer Ltd
PO Box 9, Woodbridge, Suffolk IP12 3DF, UK
and of Boydell & Brewer Inc.
668 Mt Hope Avenue, Rochester, NY 14620-2731, USA
www.boydellandbrewer.com

UTOPIA, INNOVATION, TRADITION
BRUNO MADERNA'S COSMOS

Edited by
Angela Ida De Benedictis

The Boydell Press 2022

9 INTRODUCTION

STAGING AND PERFORMING SOUNDS: A GLANCE THROUGH THE LAST THEATRICAL WORK

19 **ANGELA IDA DE BENEDICTIS**
Delving into Bruno Maderna's *Satyricon*:
The Looking Glass World of
Storytelling, Performance Interference,
and Authorship

59 **BENEDETTA ZUCCONI**
"In the Beginning Was the Word":
The Sung Text as a Unifying Element in
the Composition of Bruno Maderna's
Satyricon

BUILDING SOUNDS: THE COMPOSER

87 **CARLO CICERI**
Space in Maderna's Last Orchestral
Works

115 **PASCAL DECROUPET**
The Unity of Musical Practice:
Bruno Maderna and His "Shaping Form"
as Composer and Performer of
Experimental Orchestral Music

CREATING SOUND: THE MUSIC BEYOND/WITHOUT THE STAGE

141 **NICOLA SCALDAFERRI**
"A Walk Through a Musical Garden":
Compositional Paths in Maderna's
Late Works

171 **LEO IZZO**
Narrating with Sounds:
Bruno Maderna's Music for Radio and Film

REINVENTING SOUNDS: DIALOGUES WITH MUSIC OF EVERY EPOCH AND STYLE

193 **MICHELE CHIAPPINI**
The Writing of the Interpretation:
Notes on Bruno Maderna's Arrangements

227 **BENEDETTA ZUCCONI**
Analysis and Synthesis in Bruno
Maderna's Creative Process:
Don Giovanni and Other Mozart Scores

245 **LEO IZZO**
Bruno Maderna and His Arrangements

ACROSS BORDERS: THE CONDUCTOR AND THE INTERPRETER

277 **MAURIZIO ROMITO**
"This Bruno Looks Like Fiorello":
Maderna in the U.S.A. (1965–72)

299 **ANNE C. SHREFFLER**
Maderna Goes to Tanglewood:
The Role of American Networks in
the Origins and Reception of
Venetian Journal and *Satyricon*

SEARCHING FOR ROOTS: THE DEVELOPMENT OF A STYLE

331 **VENIERO RIZZARDI**
Venice to Europe:
Bruno Maderna Before and After 1948

357 **CHRISTOPH NEIDHÖFER**
"La révolution dans la continuité":
The Presence of the Past in Bruno
Maderna's Creative Process (1948–55)

STAGING AND PERFORMING TEXTS: A GLANCE THROUGH EARLY DRAMATURGICAL AND VOCAL WORKS

383 **CLAUDIA VINCIS**
The *Studi per "Il Processo" di
Franz Kafka*, and Their Stage Sources

415 **PAOLO DAL MOLIN**
Maderna and the Poets, 1938–48

443 CHRONOLOGY OF BRUNO MADERNA'S WORKS

451 SELECTED BIBLIOGRAPHY

455 INDEX

INTRODUCTION

ANGELA IDA DE BENEDICTIS

Introduction

> It is, indeed, easier to feel the penetrating
> and mysterious *charme* of M. Mallarmé
> than to define and analyze this *charme*.
> (François Coppée, 1842)

In every field of knowledge, in every artistic sector, there are figures who have changed the course of their discipline, with fundamental works and thoughts that challenge the achievements of their predecessors. There are equally revolutionary figures who innovate with a constant sense of doubt, tirelessly interrogating and dialoguing with the past, and building bridges between epochs as they advance inexorably toward the future. These artists, who see continuity as the real catalyst for progress, construct often invisible networks around them – innovative and propulsive undercurrents of thought (both technically and aesthetically) that are revealed mainly in the works of others: of "satellite" friends and colleagues who, in a given moment of their personal and artistic experience, have crossed paths with and entered the orbit of these "creative cosmoses." The full complexity of these figures and the great influence they have had on the artistic, cultural and social worlds around them often becomes clear long after their deaths, as historical and academic knowledge advances, interpretive tools are refined, and notions and categories once taken for granted are subject to a continuous process of reevaluation.

All of this can be perceived in the artistic and personal life of Bruno Maderna (1920–73) and in the critical and public reception of his works. Fifty years after the composer's death, this and many other aspects continue to evade unambiguous interpretation, offering glimpses of an (everlasting) artistic existence that is yet to be discovered, reflected on, and understood. Within the context of twentieth-century music, or indeed in the broader arc of the history of Western music, Maderna's life and output can be seen as a cosmos in perpetual motion, within which one can recognize, quoting Jean-Paul Sartre on a different topic, an "extraordinary example of the whirligigs of being and appearance, of the imaginary and the real."[1] A whirlwind in which, in Maderna's case, a range of elements collide and intermingle. These include aspects of his private and professional lives, both as a composer and conductor; the contemporary reception of his work; and the narration and interpretation of his creative biography in the immediate aftermath of his death. What has followed in recent years is a process of critical reconstruction of facts and contexts based on a large corpus of new and newly appraised documentary sources. The present volume comes in the wake of this exegetic process.

---

1   Jean-Paul Sartre, *Saint Genet: Actor and Martyr* (New York: George Braziller, 1963), p. 611.

The first of these whirlwinds owes to an apparent privilege: scholarship on Maderna flourished in Europe well ahead of – and in some cases more extensively than – that of other prominent composers of his generation, such as Luciano Berio, Pierre Boulez, Luigi Nono and Karlheinz Stockhausen (see the "Selected Bibliography on Bruno Maderna" on pp. 451–54). This privilege owes to an extraordinary and, in some ways, tragic biography, marked by Maderna's complex experience as a child prodigy and an orphan (who was "adopted" by the fascist regime even before he found a definitive guardian) and by his premature death following many frenetic years on the cusp of much longed-for "stability."[2] All of this helped to create the myth of Maderna as an unruly genius.

Born in Venice on 21 April 1920, Maderna died in Darmstadt on 13 November 1973. In those 53 years he seems to have lived many lives, all of an intensity inversely proportional to the brevity of an existence condensed into salient moments of an "Age of Extremes."[3] First, the most challenging period, which was dominated by Fascism, the War and the Resistance; then, the most exhilarating, during the post-war reconstruction, which Maderna lived with an awareness and enthusiasm owing to his precocious maturity. It was a time of both economic and artistic recovery, of exciting musical experimentation full of hope for a brighter future. Readers of this volume will find only a few references to the first of Maderna's lives – that of the child prodigy, the "Toscanini in short trousers,"[4] who in 1932 conducted Verdi, Wagner and Beethoven in theaters including La Fenice in Venice and the Arena di Verona. Instead, we have focused on the transformation that took place from Brunetto Grossato the wunderkind to the young, then mature and affirmed, composer and conductor, Bruno Maderna.[5] Of the many vortexes that whirl around the history and critical reception of the artist and his works, we have chosen to focus mainly on the composer's search for his own identity (as an artist *and* as a man), his own innovative musical language, his own peculiar and protean search – both as a composer and conductor – that

---

2   Various letters and notes written in the year preceding Maderna's death clearly reflect his desire for a new phase of professional and family life: "... my work life unfolds at a dizzying speed. Concerts, composition, plans for the future, commitments, teaching, interviews, travel. In short, there is no more time for private life. [...] I hope to work like this for only two or three more seasons. Then, I want to organize my life more calmly, and devote more time to writing music"; letter to Irma Manfredi, 18 August 1972, Italian original published in Bruno Maderna, *Amore e curiosità: Scritti, frammenti e interviste sulla musica*, ed. Angela Ida De Benedictis, Michele Chiappini, and Benedetta Zucconi (Milan: il Saggiatore, 2020), p. 634.

3   A reference to what has now become a slogan deriving from the title of Eric Hobsbawm's book *The Age of Extremes: The Short Twentieth Century, 1914–1991*, first published by Michael Joseph, London, in 1994.

4   "Toscanini in calzoncini corti": quote taken from an article signed with the initials E.R., "Un minuscolo direttore d'orchestra in Salone. Brunetto Grossato" [A tiny conductor in the Salon: Brunetto Grossato], *Il Veneto*, 7–8 October 1932.

5   On the change of surname, from the paternal (Grossato) to the maternal (Maderna), and the vicissitudes of his youth – namely his illegitimate birth (official records state that Maderna was "the child of an unknown father"; his mother's early death when he was only four years old; the case of a fosterage conditioned by the regime's interference, before the definitive passage to the guardianship of the person who was to become, for all intents and purposes, his adoptive mother (Irma Manfredi) – literature on the musician remains confused and often based on "memories of memories" that are sometimes neither documented nor documentable. See, among others, Raymond Fearn, "Toward a Biography," in Id., *Bruno Maderna* (Chur: Harwood, 1990), pp. 327–35, and various texts listed in the "Selected Bibliography" here on pp. 451–54.

followed the paths furrowed by music of every era and genre. The decision has been taken to do so in a plural way, indulging the multifaceted nature of Maderna's "cosmos" with an equally variegated range of interpretive and methodological approaches rooted in research, study and the re-reading of archive sources.

This choice emerged almost naturally, and is linked with knowledge of a further vortex (or a short circuit) that has shaped the posthumous reception of an artist who, during his lifetime and after his death, was a real magnet of interests. He is a musician about whom much has been said and written, but whose works continue to be performed too infrequently (and performances are indeed limited to rather a small portion of his catalog). If we ask why Maderna's works are discussed more frequently than they are played, one might suggest that this may depend on the contiguity of the two facets of his professional (and, indeed, creative) personality: composing and conducting. More often than not it was Maderna himself who conducted his own works (see the "Chronology" on pp. 443–50), and since he was notoriously reluctant to definitively set his scores in stone, subsequent conductors have frequently refrained from performing them. Such an attitude stems from an interpretive bias that – while anchored in the reality of compositions that indeed need to be given a fixed form in faithful yet reproducible scores in order to facilitate their circulation – does not take into account the poetic, aesthetic and ethical principles of Maderna's creative horizon. Maderna's entire output can be seen as a single, uninterrupted work in progress, within which the unfixed and non-definitive nature of the individual composition is a reflection of a truly liberal and anti authoritarian character. Such a complex corpus requires equally complex methodologies of textual analysis, interpretation and performance practice. Failure to embrace this complexity, along with the aforementioned fascination with Maderna's biography, have contributed to the relative absence of his music from the concert stage, giving rise to a further paradox whereby it has been easier to feel Maderna's "penetrating and mysterious *charme*" than to define and fully understand the reasons for this *charme*.[6] This book arises from the desire, and the necessity, to appropriately retrace and interpret some of the salient stages of Maderna's opus, in an overall effort to reknit some of the threads that form the dense weave of the composer's output. The essays featured here are the fruit of years of research conducted by the individual authors at the Paul Sacher Foundation in Basel and other international archives. They form individual tiles in an interpretive mosaic that has been created in an effort to go beyond the anecdotal power of a charme which, not infrequently, has led music built on pillars of rigor, freedom and concerted choice to be dismissed as music forged out of "disorder," "fragments" and "chance."

One important lesson that can be drawn from the study of an artist like Maderna is that of the importance of doubt when dealing with ecdotic and philological issues. Researchers, performers and commentators who engage with Maderna's music must go

---

6 This is a liberal paraphrase of the citation used in the opening, taken from the editor's "Introduction" in Mallarmé's *Œuvres complètes*, ed. Bertrand Marchal (Paris: Gallimard, 1998), p. ix (original: "Il est, en effet, plus aisé de sentir le *charme* pénétrant et mystérieux de M. Mallarmé que de définir et d'analyser ce *charme*").

beyond the existing evidence and established knowledge. A fresh critical approach requires a thorough study of the sources and a reevaluation of previous notions that were frequently formed by an uncritical perpetuation of information acquired with ethnographic (*via* oral histories) rather than musicological methods. Some of the essays included in this volume constantly dialogue – sometimes implicitly, sometimes explicitly – with studies and interpretations dating from a period spanning the 1970s to the present day. In some cases, this provides clarification; in others, new interpretations are added to preexisting ones. In others still, new stories that have not yet been told, or that have remained on the periphery of the dense landscape of existing commentary, are narrated. The individual texts are not arranged according to a strict chronology, nor do they follow a thematic outline based on aesthetic or biographical considerations. However, they do reflect the main stages of Bruno Maderna's artistic journey, synthesized and recounted "polyphonically" according to the various investigative perspectives chosen by the various authors, and arranged according to a solid structure, as the reader will discover from the index.

As indicated in the title of this volume, the various contributions relate to three macro themes: "Utopia," "Innovation" and "Tradition." These thematic focuses are distributed across seven chapters and arranged according to a precise mirror structure (1→2→3→4←5←6←7), in which the macro themes follow one another, echo one another and fit together in ever different ways, homing in on various aspects that form part of Maderna's creative world. Thus, the seven chapters and individual essays contained within them are interconnected in a mutual game of echoes – chapters 1↔7 / 2↔6 / 3↔5 – based on a mirror (or "inverse") chronology and a thematic affinity that is also reflected in the titles chosen for the individual sections. At the center of this specular grid, there stands a single chapter (Ch. 4) which, unlike the others, is formed of three texts – and not just for the sake of symmetry. We intentionally refrain here from illustrating the various aspects of the individual essays, offering the reader the pleasure of exploring and discovering the different contents, interpretive approaches and methodologies according to his or her own knowledge, curiosity and desire to dig deeper. In this introductory note we wish instead to linger on the question of how the concepts of Utopia, Innovation and Tradition underpin Maderna's entire artistic journey – whether as a composer, conductor or promoter of cultural events – and why they form the foundation stones of this volume.

These concepts will be encountered in the chapters that deal more specifically with the relationship between music and text – Ch. 1: "Staging and Performing Sounds: A Glance Through the Last Theatrical Work," and Ch. 7: "Staging and Performing Texts: A Glance Through Early Dramaturgical and Vocal Works." These chapters are arranged in a mirror image, with Satyricon, Maderna's last stage work, placed in "dialogue" with the composer's first vocal and theatrical projects from the late 1930s and the 1940s. Reference to the three key concepts can also be found in the chapters delving into the musical workshop of this "craftsman" of sounds, in which the mature composer searching for new timbral and formal solutions in the 1960s and '70s (Ch. 2: "Building Sounds: The Composers") is counterposed with a young Maderna grappling with the compositional experiments of his early years and his serialist period shared with the composers of the "Darmstadt School" (Ch. 6: "Searching for Roots: The Development of a Style"). A mix of utopia, innovation and tradition can also be perceived in Maderna's artistic experiences in different contexts such as the radio and television (Ch. 3: "Creating Sounds: The Music Beyond/Without the Stage"), or in geographical locations outside of Europe (primarily the U.S.A.) where it was often impossible to draw a line between the conductor of the music of others, and the composer conducting his own works (Chapter 6: "Across Borders: The Conductor and the Interpreter"). But it is in the central chapter, which forms the axis on which the entire book pivots (Ch. 4: "Reinventing Sounds: Dialog with Music of Every Epoch and Style"), that the three concepts find a true synthesis and a sort of culmination, with an analysis of how Maderna established specific forms of dialogue – via transcription, interpretation and reelaboration – with the music of the European classical and popular traditions. The heart of this chapter contains a kernel of central importance: Maderna's relationship with Mozart's music, which was a constant presence throughout his life. His dialogue with Mozart's operas discloses new patterns and reflections of the Tradition-Innovation-Utopia triad, revealing the timelessness of Maderna's musical journey: he *thought* and *lived* music without borders; he *made* music in the ethical (more than the aesthetical) sense of the term. For Maderna, Mozart's music, and, indeed, all music – "from Monteverdi to today" – can be considered "all contemporary," because it always has been (and always will be) a form of expression that reflects the society that produced it.[7]

In many of the essays collected here, the reader will therefore recognise an attempt to combine documentary information with the literary-cultural context of the specific period under review. Similarly, readers of this volume, whether specialists of twentieth-century music or people who are new to this area of interest, will perceive not only the multifaceted nature of the artist and the resulting plurality of the interpretive challenges posed by analyzing his work and thought, but also the interdependence of the individual themes. Whether these pages are read in a linear way, from the first to the last essay, or at random, the reader will encounter a number of central questions relating to the "Maderna cosmos" that intertwine and illuminate one another. Some of these come close to forming a continuum: the fluid and often controversial issue of performative authorship (especially wherever Maderna conducted his own works); the complexity of his holistic vision of music, seen as a whole in which his composing is reflected in his conducting and vice versa; and, finally, the difficulty of interpreting scores that are often modular and in which the main concern is the sound, rather than the sign (the notation). Maderna's sound is conceived with notational and graphic configurations that even today defy unambiguous interpretation.

It is with this central and open issue that we welcome the readers to explore the following pages at their own pace and with their own preferences, remembering that this collection of essays is not aimed at resolving question marks or exhausting an area of

---

7   The citations are taken from two separate interviews, "In dialogo con Maderna tra Milano e Venezia. Estratti da *Un'ora con Bruno Maderna (II)*" (1969–70), and "Intervista con Günter Engler" (1970), both from Maderna, *Amore e curiosità* (see note 2), p. 200 ("Per me tutta la musica che va da Monteverdi fino a oggi è soltanto la musica contemporanea" [For me, all music from Monteverdi to today is simply contemporary music]), and p. 367 ("La musica è sempre espressione della società contemporanea" [Music is always the expression of contemporary society]).

study that we hope will be ever richer and more deeply researched in the coming years. Above all, we hope that this volume can contribute to a better understanding of a story: that of the life and work of Bruno Maderna. This Story is made of many multifaceted and often elusive stories that are narrated here exclusively with reference to documented facts, and with a critical and scientific rigor that, in the ancient yet pertinent words of Isidore of Seville, differentiate between "true deeds that have happened" (*historia*), "things that, even if they have not happened, nevertheless could happen" (*argomentum*), and "things that have not happened and cannot happen" (*fables*).[8] We have sought refuge here in the last of Isidore's categories, in the hope that, as a result of this collective effort, new lines of research on Maderna's work can emerge tomorrow from the conviction (or the demonstration) that music and the sources that transmit it must be *listened to* before being discussed.

Many institutions and experts have contributed to the creation of this volume in various ways, by offering suggestions, advice, and access to sources. Each author gives acknowledgements, with gratitude, in their individual chapters. My personal thanks go to my colleagues of the Scholarly Staff of the Paul Sacher Foundation; among them, I'm deeply indebted to Matthias Kassel, for having followed and assisted all the preparation phases of this volume, and to Simon Obert and Florian Besthorn, for their generous re-reading of the proofs. A grateful thought also goes to all the librarians of the Foundation and, in particular, to Carlos Chanfón.

I am profoundly thankful to Caterina, Claudia and Andreas Maderna for the constant and invaluable support and for the greatest gift a researcher can receive: unconditional trust. Warmest thanks go to the translators, Sally Davies and James Imam, and to Talia Pecker Berio, for her support during the final preparation of this introductory note. To all authors – "from A to Z," to paraphrase Maderna: Michele Chiappini, Carlo Ciceri, Paolo Dal Molin, Pascal Decroupet, Leo Izzo, Christoph Neidhöfer, Veniero Rizzardi, Maurizio Romito, Nicola Scaldaferri, Anne C. Shreffler, Claudia Vincis and Benedetta Zucconi – I am grateful for their dedication during the research phases and the patience they have shown during the various (and prolonged) phases of preparation of this volume. A special thought goes to one of them in particular – Carlo Ciceri, one of my first students who soon became an enthusiastic colleague and a dear friend, who died prematurely during the last stages of proofreading. It is to him that I wish to dedicate this volume, in memoriam, as a serene choral farewell, remembering the "radiations" (*Ausstrahlungen*) of his joyful and generous smile.

---

8   Cfr. Isidore of Seville, *Etymologiae*, ed. Stephen A. Barney et al. (Cambridge: Cambridge University Press, 2006), I.xli–xliv, p. 67.

CAVEAT

Documents and manuscripts from Bruno Maderna's bequest kept at the Paul Sacher Foundation in Basel are always indicated with the initials "PSS-BMC" (Paul Sacher Stiftung – Bruno Maderna Collection). Unless otherwise specified, they are to be considered unpublished.

The reference to the "Examples" (images and figures) contained in the individual contributions is highlighted for the first occurrence in bold type and with an arrow **(→EX. 1)**. For subsequent occurrences, the full reference is used (Example 1) if it is contained in the text, or abbreviated (Ex. 1) if placed between brackets.

STAGING AND PERFORMING SOUNDS: A GLANCE THROUGH THE LAST THEATRICAL WORK

ANGELA IDA DE BENEDICTIS

Delving into Bruno Maderna's *Satyricon*
The Looking Glass World of Storytelling, Performance Interference, and Authorship

> The vast canvas of Petronius' famous satirical masterwork presents a tumultuous image of life in the Rome of the Emperor Nero. It is a work of endless comic and savage detail, rich in character and contrast, without narrative continuity, an "action painting" of life lived with vulgarity, cruelty and an unforgettable intensity.
>
> In Maderna's delicious *collage,* our musical history parades past us as if we were watching the last supper of all western culture – and the frieze of Petronius has found a new life for the theatre.
>
> *Our* stage realization has evolved using the *improvisational and aleatoric* techniques of the *score.* An *ordering* of the varied narrative elements has been found and the sung music has been given visual and dramatic counterpoint through the presence of seven servants/slaves, mimes and clowns who give us the feel of the other half of society.
>
> We hope that we have, in a fresh and modern idiom, found a way to present a dream-like mosaic of life of both the Roman past and the present day.

This is how Ian Strasfogel presented Maderna's latest stage work in the program notes printed for the Dutch premiere on 16 March 1973 (→ **EX. 1**).[1] His words are the starting point for what is meant to be a round trip through the history of *Satyricon,* in an attempt to find answers not only to questions that are still open today, but also to new doubts that have never been raised before. In the first stages, which look back, we will dwell on the re-reading of some interpretive facts that are well-rooted in the work's history and then try, through the filter of new awareness and recently unearthed documents, to establish some fixed points in a timeline that still requires clear definition. The need for a temporal (re)orientation stems from the analysis of the various ambiguities and inconsistencies surrounding the data and circumstances of some of the developmental stages in its genesis; the hectic days that accompanied its first staging and the performances that immediately followed; and, again, the editorial history of the work. The resulting misunderstandings

---

My sincere thanks to Ian Strasfogel for being such a patient and generous interlocutor in all phases of this research, which began way back in 2011. My heartfelt gratitude – for their help in finding materials, information, and sometimes for just being there to answer endless questions – must also go to Maria Maddalena Novati (NoMus, Archives of the Studio di Fonologia della Rai in Milan) and Maurizio Romito, cherished friends as well as invaluable colleagues; to Marco Mazzolini (Ricordi), an attentive interlocutor; to Ilaria Di Luzio (RAI, Italy) and Henk van de Pol (NOS, Holland); and to Caterina Maderna and Claudia Maderna-Sieben for their support and their memories shared with rare altruism.

1   Example 1 only reproduces the first page of the program, consisting of a bifolium with four pages. The original in English quoted here (printed on p. 3) follows the Dutch translation (p. 2). Emphasis is mine.

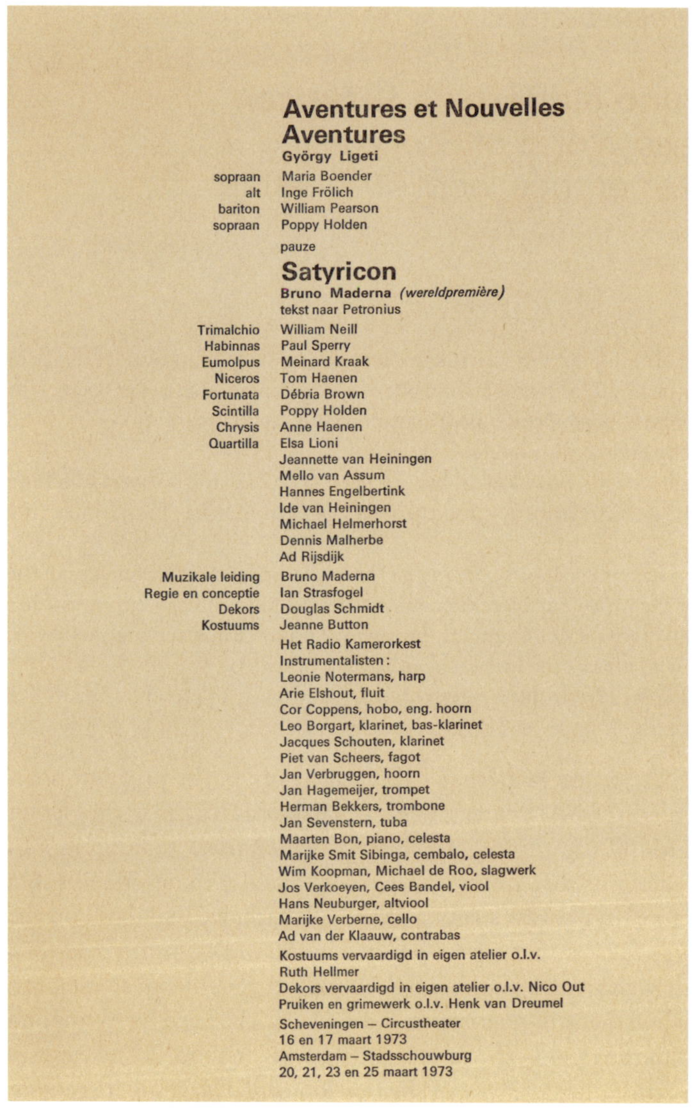

EX. 1   Concert program for the world premiere of *Satyricon* (p. 1); PSS-BMC.

have, in turn, had a tangible impact on concepts that often prove tricky when applied to Maderna and his works: those of "authorship" and "version" (within the field of the performance).

The emphasis added in the opening quote indicates the milestones that have guided the various stages of this journey. These are key concepts which are closely linked to each other and regard: *a)* the authorship of the main performance versions known to date, *b)* the actual degree of "improvisation and aleatory" – in the sense of the open nature – of the work, and, as a consequence, *c)* the structure of *Satyricon*'s printed score and the ordering of its internal parts established by the author (reconnecting with point *a* in a never-ending circle).

As will be seen, the in-depth study of these thematic nuclei will show how *Satyricon* is a paradigmatic case study in the field of distortion and/or interference phenomena in the performance history of a work.

Mobility and Performative Authorship: Some Preliminary Remarks

Satyricon's complexity and its peculiar fascination owe much to the fact that, in form and content, it is a sort of "swan song" created by Maderna in the last year of his life. Indeed, not only is it one of his last works for the stage but, quite simply, it is one of his last compositions and one of the last conducted by himself.[2] The crucial question we wish to readdress here is something that has long been accepted as an undisputed fact: namely, the matter of the "performative authorship" of each of the realizations of *Satyricon* drawn up by its author, in different forms and contexts, in the short period of time that separates the first stage performance from Maderna's premature death. This period barely covers eight frenzied months, from 16 March to 13 November 1973, during which artistic planning was often hampered by the times and conditions dictated by disease.

In these circumstances, the scope of this piece of biographical information assumes considerable importance and affects the ever-changing manifestations of that very authorial "intent," which, in the last difficult stages of its existence, was determined to give specific forms and/or different performances and publishing structures to one of the author's own works that had been conceived in a modular and open way. And, in so doing, it plowed a furrow that would set a predetermined course for the whole tradition of the work (i.e. its reception, execution, exegesis, and theoretical and aesthetic interpretations), indelibly conditioned by that "authorial" stamp.

In medias res…

Studies have already shown that the disorder that apparently reigns in many of Maderna's works is actually a form of entropy often induced retrospectively or conditioned by the persistence of notions of often unreliable or anecdotal origin. They show how his papers – and his own compositional trajectory – speak, on the contrary, of a "moving continuity"

---

2   *Satyricon* would be followed only by the Concerto No. 3 for oboe and orchestra, dedicated to the oboist Han de Vries and conducted by the composer himself on 6 July 1973 in the Concertgebouw in Amsterdam; see, in this book, the "Chronology of Bruno Maderna's Works," p. 448. See also Bruno Maderna, *Amore e curiosità: Scritti, frammenti e interviste sulla musica*, ed. Angela Ida De Benedictis, Michele Chiappini, and Benedetta Zucconi (Milan: il Saggiatore, 2020), pp. 516 and 806. In his last concert, held in London on 5 November 1973 with the London Symphony Orchestra just over a week before his death, Maderna did not conduct his own works but pieces by Schoenberg and Bartók (the concert can be heard on the CD *Bruno Maderna's Last Concert*, Stradivarius 10071, 1993).

in what is actually a far stricter and more conscious planning than one might imagine of musical works that are often interconnected and open to multiple readings, uses, and references.[3]

As far as *Satyricon* is concerned, it has already been pointed out on several occasions that the choice of this particular text falls within a fertile time frame for the reception of Petronius in the fields of music and cinema and also publishing, a time frame dating back to the end of the 1960s and the first half of the following decade.[4] Nonetheless, apart from the particular moment in which Maderna's work is set – that is, in the wake of the long wave apparently set in motion by Federico Fellini's *Satyricon* (1969) – it should be noted that Maderna's acquaintance with Petronius's classic had started long before the 1970s. On more than one occasion, he spoke of how he had been wanting to make a musical adaptation of *Satyricon* "since before the war" (in fact, some documents allow us to backdate his study of Petronius to the second half of the 1930s).[5] Even after its world premiere, in July 1973, Maderna once again pointed out that *Satyricon* had indeed been commissioned by Hans de Roo (superintendent of Amsterdam's De Nederlandse Opera-stichting), but that this request was really only a "catalyst" since "I've been wanting to do something about it" for a long time.[6]

---

3   Regarding the alleged chaos of Maderna's papers, see the focus of the introduction by the editors in Maderna, *Amore e curiosità* (see note 2), pp. 17–50: 21–26. With specific reference to the works of the 1960s and 1970s, let me take the liberty of also referring to my "'Qui forse una cadenza brillante': Viaggio nel *Venetian Journal* di Bruno Maderna," *Acta Musicologica* 72, no. 1 (2000,) pp. 63–105; "*Ausstrahlung*, ou la textualité brisée d'un hymne à la vie," in *à Bruno Maderna*, ed. Geneviève Mathon, Laurent Feneyrou, and Giordano Ferrari, vol. 1 (Paris: Basalte, 2007), pp. 287–317; and "Materiali parziali o strutture fungibili? Nuove prospettive filologiche su *Honeyrêves, Don Perlimplin* e *Serenata IV* di Bruno Maderna," *Il Saggiatore Musicale* 18, nos. 1–2 (2011), pp. 139–72.

4   See, among others, Susanna Pasticci, "La presenza del *Satyricon* sulla scena culturale degli anni Settanta, da Maderna a Pasolini," *Musica/Realtà* 91 (2010), pp. 77–126: 111–26; and, in this book, the essay by Anne C. Shreffler, "Maderna Goes to Tanglewood: The Role of American Networks in the Origins and Reception of *Venetian Journal* and *Satyricon*," pp. 299–327: 311. Alongside the various Petronian revivals (from Fellini to Sanguineti, Polidoro, Pasolini, and others) cited in all the studies conducted to date, we should add the title of a further radio adaptation made by Giorgio Gaslini in 1970: *La cena di Joe Trimalchio*, a "dramatic madrigal" presented at the 22nd edition of the Prix Italia; see my "Art à la radio – art pour la radio: réflexion sur le Prix Italia, suivies d'un panorama des éditions 1949–1970," in *Musique et dramaturgie: Esthétique de la représentation au XXe siècle*, ed. Laurent Feneyrou (Paris: Publications de la Sorbonne, 2003), pp. 657–700: 697.

5   The first reliable document regarding this dates back to 1939: a letter from Mons. Charles Spence sent to Maderna from Cincinnati (Ohio) on 5 March of that year, in which the distant friend remembers "the wonderful [...] unforgettable evenings" spent together in Rome reading and discussing "the classics (Petronius etc.), philosophy, religion" and more, finally asking "Do you still read the Latin authors?" (PSS-BMC); excerpts published in Maderna, *Amore e Curiosità* (see note 2), p. 557. The quotation in the text is taken from Maderna's answer to Piet Hein van de Poel during an interview about *Satyricon* ("it's an idea I had since before the war. It would have been a great job then"; ibid., pp. 318–25: 321). See this same interview (pp. 320–21) for the composer's explicit remarks about the independence of his theatrical experiment from Fellini's *Satyricon*.

6   Quote taken from an interview Maderna gave to Hans Heg for Dutch television, recorded on 4 July 1973, published in Italian in ibid., pp. 223–26: 225 (for more on this interview see p. 755). When de Roo himself was questioned about the matter, he admitted that, regardless of the commission, the "idea" for the subject was Maderna's alone, who worked on it "very carefully" (as de Roo states in a documentary for Dutch television, *Terug naar Maderna*, by Hans Heg and René van Gijn, produced by NOS in 1983). Also see, in this book, the essay by Anne C. Shreffler on p. 310. On the formalization of de Roo's request see below.

The chapter by Benedetta Zucconi that follow in this book concentrates on the centrality of the text throughout the entire creative process of *Satyricon*. Suffice it here to point out that almost all the choices, be they formal or structural or ones that regard both compositional techniques or the work's multilingualism, are visibly made on the text and influenced by its contents. On the basis of an earlier and much wider selection of textual passages from different editions of the Petronian classic in several languages (Latin, Italian, English, French, German), Maderna's final choice mainly focuses on moments taken from the episode of Trimalchio's Banquet.[7] The composer nevertheless takes the liberty of drawing other passages or characters from different sections of the novel and/or changing some parts with respect to the literary source (think, for example, of the character of Criside, who in Petronius has nothing to do with the Banquet; or to the long story dedicated to the Widow of Ephesus [*La matrona di Efeso*], a metanarrative digression placed in another section and, though entrusted in the original to the philosopher Eumolpus, assigned by Maderna to the voice of Habinnas).[8] Generally speaking, his choices allow us to deduce that, around the climactic moment of Trimalchio's Banquet – a veritable reservoir of all the staged themes – Maderna focuses on the creation of numbers that are complete in themselves as "sonic portraits" of the individual characters, or the symbols they embody. The typology of the chosen textual excerpts, almost always organized in a monologic form, allows the composer to further represent in music – at times even to exaggerate – the characteristics, excesses, and weaknesses of the individual characters (and of the society they represent), to reveal their true soul and their intentions that are sometimes hidden behind words or left unspoken. Thanks to a clever use of stylistic and formal references, of obvious or simply allusive quotes,[9] by employing refined or brazenly coarse registers, and again by alternating more or less fixed or indeterminate parts within them, Maderna creates individual musical pieces of a mosaic which, reassembled, returns – behind an apparently reassuring smile – an articulated and disenchanted fresco of contemporary society.

---

7   The basic language used by Maderna is English, a contemporary "standard" language, comparable to the Latin of Petronius's era; the use of French openly refers to moments of seduction; Latin creeps into the parts of the philosopher Eumolpus as if to underline his inability to communicate and *prosopopoeia*, while the use of German is reserved for moments of more subtle and cutting parody. The only surviving word in Italian is "*milioni*" (millions), the climax of Trimalchio's delusions of omnipotence in his *Carriera*. In general, as was the case for the use of musical citations, the choice of idioms also becomes the bearer of implicit meanings for Maderna. For the main Petronian sources used and/or consulted by Maderna, see Zucconi's essay (in particular note 10 on p. 61).

8   It should be noted that the entire work of textual selection (which passed through various stages of typing the selected passages, often transcribed in multiple languages) was carried out by Maderna alone. See also below in this essay and note 41.

9   The use of quotations (textual, stylistic, etc.), with which the entire work abounds, is to be read as a true game of acoustic mirrors. This can be traced back to a practical and compositional poetics that goes far beyond the hackneyed label of collage or pop art, in which often – also thanks to a distorted reading of some of Maderna's remarks (see also below and note 49) – much more complex polystylistic and meta-referential procedures tend to be imprisoned. The quote, or allusion, is used here (as it was in *Venetian Journal* and in other works by Maderna) to stimulate or activate precise memory compartments, regardless of whether the listener can grasp all the meanings and implicit references.

	Voices Instruments	Numbering and pages Salabert score	Numb. of sheets	Writing characteristics	Miscellaneous
1	*Trimalchio e le flatulenze*	tenor + 6 instruments	III/pp. 21–23 repeated as it is in: VII/pp. 37–39 reprise instruments only: XVII/pp. 123–25	3	Totally determined notation	24 bars in 2/4
2	*La Carriera di Trimalchio*	tenor + 16 instruments	XII/pp. 66–85	20	Totally determined notation + Aleatory interventions (in determined notation)	99 bars in various meter + various bars from "bis" to "sexties" Finale interpolable ("Vierzehn Millionen")
3	*Trimalchio contra Fortunata*	tenor + 14 instruments	XVI/pp. 114–22	9	Totally determined notation + Inserts of aleatory notation	52 bar in various meter bars "26 bis" and "36 bis"
4a	*Trimalchio e il monumento*	tenor + instruments (Tutti) + choir of all those on stage	XIX/pp. 125–40	16	Totally determined notation + Aleatory inserts on a partially determined basis	From bar 1 to bar 91 in various meter bars "66 bis" "66 ter" and "87 bis"
4b	*Funeral March*	tenor + instruments (tutti)	XX/pp. 141–46	6	Totally determined notation + Aleatory inserts on a partially determined basis	from bar 92 to bar 112 in various meter bars "103 bis" and "112 bis"
5	*Fortunata*	mezzosoprano + 16 instruments	I/pp. 7–20	14	Totally determined notation (voice and instruments) + Proportional and graphic notation (percussion) + Aleatory notation (some instrumental interventions)	98 bars in 4/4
6a	*Fortunata e Eumolpus* **(followed with no interruption by:)**	mezzosoprano/mass + 13 instruments	XIII/pp. 90–107	18	Totally determined notation	72 bars in 4/8
6b	*Eumolpus Fuga*	bass + strings + bassoon	XIV/pp. 108–11	4	Totally determined notation	29 bars in 2/2
7	*La matrona di Efeso*	tenor (Habinnas) + instruments (tutti except tuba)	X/pp. 40–65	26	Totally determined notation + Proportional and aleatory notation + only recited parts	70 bars in various meter + various "bis" and "ter" bars
8	*The Money*	tenor (Habinnas) + 14 instruments	V/pp. 25–32	8	Totally determined notation + finale aleatory notation	34 bars in mixed meter 34bis
9	*Criside I*	soprano + english horn	XII.1/p. 86	1	Determined notation	No indication of meter
10	*Criside II*	soprano + flute	I.3/p. 6	1	Determined notation	No indication of meter
11	*Love's Ecstasy*	4 voices (2s, bar, bass) + flute, B♭ clar., bass clarinet	XII.3/pp. 87–89	3	Totally determined notation	Vocal Quartet: Scintilla, Criside, Niceros and Eumolpos. 12 bars in 4/4
12	*Scintilla*	coloratura soprano with vocalizations + *ad libitum* flute, oboe, B♭ clar.	I.1 /p. 5 Repeated as it is in: XV/p. 113	1	Indeterminate notation (proportional)	
13	*Lady Luck*	soprano (Quartilla) + strings and tuba	VII/pp. 33–36	4	Totally determined notation	16 bars in 4/4
14	*Food Machine*	only instruments	IV/p. 24	1	Ochestral Improvisation with partially determined and graphic aleatory notation	

EX. 2   Synthetic diagram of each of the vocal/instrumental sections of Bruno Maderna's *Satyricon*.

Just like *Ausstrahlung* (1971), the musical structure of *Satyricon* is made up of individual sound modules, which are all of varying lengths and distinguished by peculiar timbric, graphic, notational, and formal characteristics depending on the character and/or the theme to be "represented" in music (money, sex, food, and fate/luck are the themes around which the entire work pivots). In the composer's papers, the final form of these modules is separated into single files originally with no numbering. Instead, in the printed edition published by Salabert in 1974, they are numbered from 1 to 21.[10]

In fact, Maderna's legacy is fourteen musical panels to be performed live (→ **EX. 2**), plus some other parts pre-recorded on magnetic tape and intended to be interpreted each time as sound comments, final curtains, and/or evocative bridges, to be interspersed in a balanced way (due to the significance of the sound content) between the vocal/instrumental numbers, and, for this purpose, to be used to accompany silent actions on stage. For now, let us leave aside these pre-recorded sections on tape and take a closer look at the data contained in Example 2 (where the panels are numbered in a completely arbitrary order, by "character"). It should be noted immediately that two of the vocal/instrumental numbers (nos. 4 and 6 in Ex. 2), initially intended and composed as an inseparable unit, were subsequently divided and numbered separately in the score;[11] on the other hand, *Trimalchio e le flatulenze* (Ex. 2, no. 1) was numbered three times following its reprise in an identical or varied form; just as, in a similar way, the reiteration of Scintilla's part (Ex. 2, no. 12) meant that it was numbered twice in the score.

We shall return to the numbering and order of the individual panels in the score in more detail later. For now, let us just note that, in the wake of a compositional practice consolidated in previous years (to mention just a few titles, apart from the aforementioned *Ausstrahlung*, think of *Juilliard Serenade* or *Venetian Journal*), *Satyricon* as a whole stands as a mobile or modular organism, made up of single pieces which in turn are characterized by different degrees of control (for that, read determination and/or indeterminacy). In his own papers, the composer classifies each number as a specific type according to whether it is "open form," "closed form," "fixed improvisation," or "free improvisation."[12] Let us

---

10   See Bruno Maderna, *Satyricon: opéra, livret d'après Petrone, texte français, allemand et latin de Bruno Maderna* (Paris: Salabert, © 1974, E.A.S. 17.091). The first printed edition reproduces a copyist's manuscript ("R. Goegel," as can be read in ibid., p. 146). The latest edition, dated 1 December 2020, reproduces a mechanical layout and, compared to the first edition, often introduces incorrect information (see below).

11   Their unity (both creative and performative) can be seen in all existing manuscript sources. In the *Synopsis* printed on the occasion of the world premiere (see note 1), complete with the text of the individual parts (sometimes with variations that are found in some drafts prior to the final one), there was still no division between *Fortunata e Eumolpus/Eumolpus Fuga* and *Trimalchio e il monumento/Funeral March*, a feature that only materialized with the preparation of the materials for the printed edition (see below and note 74).

12   See the plan Maderna drew up on fol. 4 of a notepad ("*Schrijfblok*"), used from February 1973 until the final stages of his life and kept among the materials for Satyricon at PSS-BMC (in the original: "OF / forma aperta" (open form), "CF / chiusa" (closed form), "IMPR. / fixierte improvv." (fixed improvisation), and "fr. impr. / freie" (free improvisation). This plan is reproduced in diplomatic form in Claudia Vincis, "À propos de la nature modulable du *Satyricon* de Bruno Maderna: quelques notes sur la genèse du livret," in *L'opéra éclaté: La drammaturgie musicale entre 1969 et 1984*, ed. Giordano Ferrari (Paris: l'Harmattan, 2006), pp. 25–49: 31; and in Benedetta Zucconi, "*Satyricon*" *di Bruno Maderna (1973)* (Università degli Studi di Pavia, 2010–11), p. 92. For a similar elaboration of the concepts of control and/or opening of the internal modules of a composition, see the parts dedicated to *Juilliard Serenade* in the essay by Nicola Scaldaferri in this book (pp. 141–69: 154–59).

look at Example 2 again: some pieces are completely determined and defined in all their parametric and instrumental dimensions (nos. 1, 6a and 6b, 9, 10, 11, and 13); others contain various degrees of indeterminacy or *ad libitum* choices and can be interpreted in various ways in the performative context (nos. 12 and 14); and others present the two spheres of totally determined notation and random inserts, each time coexisting in a different way (nos. 2, 3, 4a and 4b, 5, 7, and 8). According to the notes left by the composer, the single numbers are to be performed linearly from top to bottom, although for some of them internal interpolations or varied reiterations are not excluded (think of the reprise with and without voice of no. 1, or of the interpolation of the finale of no. 2 with no. 11, an idea already outlined by the composer himself in his notes).

On the basis of a literary model that was in itself already fragmentary and polystylistic, Maderna thus comes to conceive a sort of sound "assembly kit" made up of different, heterogeneous, and autonomous pieces. The plot of the work is not defined and "closed" in the traditional sense, but enclosed within a prismatic network of possible relationships between its individual parts. Given the significance of the characters and themes contained in each of the numbers, the overall meaning of the work does not change with respect to a message (that of the moral decline and decadence of an entire society), which remains unequivocal whatever order is conferred on the individual parts of the whole. In a generous manner, Maderna seems to want to provide the performers with a modular material that is designed to stimulate arbitrariness and imagination in order to find dramaturgical arcs that differ every time.

Nonetheless, the performative events and the publishing history of the work – closely intertwined and sometimes obscured by biographical events – leave a question unanswered: does the modular structure of *Satyricon* legitimize its totally "open" interpretation and complete freedom in arranging or combining each of the numbers?

Up to now, the answer has always been yes, based on the observation of the different forms that Maderna himself gave to his work from its very first performance right up to his death. In the name of the variety of these "authorial" creations – four, as we will see in the following pages – some scholars have even seen *Satyricon* as a real "work in progress" where every order is possible and for which, after all, "It is not necessary that all the numbers should be included in every performance."[13]

From here on, the key concept of "author's version" will no longer be in quotation marks. An attempt will nevertheless be made to carry out an in-depth analysis of each of these productions attributed to Maderna, so as to work our way through the numerous

---

13   As stated by Raymond Fearn, *Bruno Maderna* (Chur: Harwood, 1990), p. 236. The nature of a "work in progress" has then been repeatedly affirmed by Geneviève Mathon, in "À propos du *Satyricon* de Bruno Maderna," in *Musique et dramaturgie* (see note 4), pp. 571–93: 573, and again in the essay with the same title she published in 2007 in *à Bruno Maderna* (see note 3), pp. 69–86: 71; by Roberto Fabbi, in "Cena sociale: *Satyricon* e il 'politico,'" *Musica/Realtà* 67 (2002), pp. 83–100: 86–87; and by many others. Benedetta Zucconi – whose vision I share – clearly distances herself from the aforementioned standpoint; she focuses on a terminological confusion in the studies about the work between the concepts of pop art, open work, and work in progress, and sees instead only a partial mobility in *Satyricon* that underlies the realization of an always coherent structure (see pp. 59–62 of the following essay in this book).

uncertainties that still surround the work's history and to provide, if not answers, at least some concrete hypotheses about its mobility. Because the doubt that the preparatory materials insinuate is that, rather, there are dramatic principles and balances to be respected – implicit assumptions that the author did not have time to formalize in a score published only after his death.

A Bit of History … Overture in Brief

Satyricon is one of Maderna's most studied works, and the various analytical and interpretive insights need to be briefly explored to allow the reader a sort of compendium of the major understandings that have crystallized around his vulgate. The specific points examined here mainly concern data relating to a) the author's versions, b) performance chronology and editorial genesis, and c) more generically, to any traces allegedly left by Maderna on the form or performative structure of the work.

The matrix of almost all the studies on *Satyricon* can be seen in a long fact sheet on the work included in the book *Bruno Maderna: Documenti,* published in 1985 (henceforth *BMD*).[14] Various generations of scholars have subsequently drawn information from this source, and its contents are still seen as a sort of milestone in the studies dedicated to the composer. Hence the need here to cite entire passages dedicated to the specific points we intend to highlight.

The fact sheet starts by retracing *Satyricon*'s precursors. The authors report a "first nucleus" already performed in 1971 in Tanglewood (Massachusetts); a "collective work" made with the students of the Berkshire Music Center "under the musical direction of B. Maderna and the stage direction of Ian Strasfogel" (*BMD*, 312). This information comes from an article published in the *Springfield Republican* on 8 August 1971,[15] announcing the imminent public performance of a collective improvisation experiment entitled *Trimalchio,* to which we will return later. We therefore read that:

> The world premiere of the opera was in Scheveningen as part of the Holland Festival, with Maderna himself as conductor and Ian Strasfogel as director, already present **at the American staging.**[16] […] From the recording of this event we deduce the […] **order of the pieces, which corresponds to the one Maderna wanted** for the Salabert edition, published in 1974. The only difference between the first performance and the material available at Salabert concerns the recorded tapes linking the various numbers of the score, seeing that […] **Maderna provided the publisher** with tapes other than that used for the first Dutch performance. (*BMD*, 314)

---

14 *Bruno Maderna: Documenti,* ed. Mario Baroni and Rossana Dalmonte (Milan: Suvini Zerboni, 1985), pp. 312–17. The fact sheet on *Satyricon* was compiled by Rossana Dalmonte and Tiziano Popoli.

15 Article by Roy C. Hammerich, "Defying the Arts: Maderna Proves Committee Can Create Musical Work of Art," reproduced in this book on p. 327 as Appendix 2 in the essay by Anne C. Shreffler. Also see the essay by Maurizio Romito on pp. 285–86 of this book.

16 From here on all emphasis in bold is mine.

Although the score was published posthumously, it therefore seems certain that the author had time to convey his last wishes in that edition, establishing a precise order for the layout of each of the numbers, similar to the one created for the world premiere, and providing a set of magnetic tapes for the pre-recorded parts that reveal further afterthoughts or refinements. It is further stated that:

> In the same spring **Maderna conducted an "oratorial" version of the opera for the Dutch radio station "NOS,"** where no pre-recorded material is inserted (evidently functional to the stage action more than to musical coherence), and where **the sections follow one another uninterruptedly in a completely different order** [...]. Presumably in the same period (and in any case in the same year, 1973), **Lucas Vis conducted the Radio Chamber Orchestra and the same performers in a TV production** for "NOS," whose visual part was conceived by Wilhelmina Holdeman [sic]. This time, too, **the order of the pieces is changed** and there is a greater variety in the use of tapes than in the first performance. (*BMD*, 315)

They then go back to the edition of *Satyricon*'s score, which was prepared in an era subsequent to the various performances just mentioned. The existence of an autograph document (which acquires a fundamental role in the history of the work, and not just its publication history) allows the authors to date these moments to around September 1973:

> His connection with the Salabert publishing house probably began **during the summer of 1973** [...]. In fact, **on a manuscript sheet dated 3 September 1973, Maderna indicates in detail the order** in which the pieces were to appear in the score, which, however, is not assembled in book form, but consists of separate files and sheets, each containing one of the work's numbers. The autonomous [nature] of the pieces allows realizations that vary in the sense of the temporal sequences, **of which Maderna himself experimented with at least three.** (*BMD*, 316)

These author's versions are in all likelihood the one created for the world premiere and the "oratorial" radio version, to which, in retrospect, the "American staging" attempted in Tanglewood in 1971 is added.[17]

On "Author's Versions" and Other Doubts

In the subsequent studies devoted to *Satyricon*, the information highlighted so far is at times tacitly quoted, at others confirmed on the basis of an examination of the archive materials, or yet again further developed or considered in another light. In all cases, scholars consider the number of different structural arrangements Maderna gave to his work

---

17   This essay does not take into account two other versions that Maderna most certainly could not
have followed: namely, the American premiere of *Satyricon* that took place on 5 and 6 August
1973 in Tanglewood (directed by Ian Strasfogel, conducted by Gunther Schuller), about which the
reader can find information in the essay by Anne C. Shreffler in this book (esp. pp. 318–19),
and the revival at Milan's Piccola Scala (directed by Giulio Chazalettes, conducted by Lucas Vis)
on 25 March 1974, in which Maderna was only involved in the embryonic phases of the project
(see below in this essay).

as being either three or four,[18] depending on whether the order Maderna indicated to Salabert for the printed score, or the television one conducted by his assistant (Lucas Vis) with the composer's approval, is considered the fourth author's version. These versions are summarized here in a comparative diagram (→ **EX. 3**).[19]

Likewise, almost all scholars agree on the importance of the autograph document dated "3 September 1973" and its undisputed role as the "matrix" of the order of the published score. Furthermore, it is often referred to the existence of eighteen magnetic tapes prepared for the world premiere (cited in *BMD*, 316), which are different from those the composer later sent to Salabert, even though listening to the recording of the Scheveningen premiere proves beyond doubt that on that occasion (and in subsequent performances) the magnetic tape interventions were limited to five.[20]

More than one uncertainty exists regarding the chronology of the radio and television versions, and also about the score. The only certain fact concerns the dates of the world premiere and of the subsequent performances in Scheveningen, Amsterdam, and Brussels, which cover a period of time ranging from 16 March to 7 April 1973.[21] As can be seen from Example 3, the order of performance at the world premiere – which remained unchanged until the last performance on 7 April – surprisingly corresponds to the one fixed in the Salabert score. What is uncertain, as far as the performances in Holland are concerned, is whether Maderna conducted them all or only some. At the time, in fact, the composer was already very ill, and whether or not he was in Amsterdam

---

18   More specifically, here we refer to, in chronological order: Paola Maurizi, "Il *Satyricon* di Bruno Maderna: Le relazioni con il testo di Petronio," *Esercizi: arte, musica, spettacolo* 9 (1986), pp. 86–90 (esp. p. 87); Fearn, *Bruno Maderna* (see note 13), pp. 217–91 (esp. p. 233); idem, *Italian Opera since 1945* (Chur: Harwood, 1997), pp. 137–46; Fabbi, "Cena sociale" (see note 13); Mathon, "À propos du *Satyricon*" (see note 13); Ingo Gerlach, "Bruno Maderna *Satyricon*: Musikalische Form und politisches Engagement" (master's thesis, Humboldt University Berlin, Philosophical Faculty III, 2004), where on p. 53 we can read about "five different author's realizations"; Geneviève Mathon, "L'écriture dramaturgique dans le *Satyricon* de Bruno Maderna," in *Musiques vocales en Italie depuis 1945: esthétique, relations texte/musique, techniques de composition*, ed. Pierre Michel and Gianmario Borio, Millénaire 3 (Notre-Dame-de-Bliquetuit, 2005), pp. 61–75; Vincis, "À propos de la nature modulable du *Satyricon*" (see note 12); Mathon, "À propos du *Satyricon*" (2007, see note 13); Pasticci, "La presenza del *Satyricon*" (see note 4); and Zucconi, "*Satyricon*" di Bruno Maderna (see note 12). From here on, reference is made to these texts when speaking of "scholars" or "studies" conducted on the work, only remarking on dissimilar interpretations in the notes.

19   The order of the *Première* in Example 3 is deduced from the program quoted on note 1, and listening to the world premiere and various reruns; the numbering from "1" to "17" follows the one present in the *Synopsis* handed out with the theater program (see note 1); it should be noted that it is identical to the numbering of the score (where some numbers are simply further subdivided). The order of the radio version is instead that taken from the commercial recording published by Stradivarius in 1992 (see below, note 23 and Ex. 4). For the television version, the numbers are transcribed on the basis of the analysis of the original NOS video (copy at PSS). For the score, titles and numbers ("1" to "21") are reported exactly as they appeared in the Salabert edition (see note 10).

20   Sound documents kindly provided, along with other materials, by the NOS. The audio of the world premiere does not refer to an official internal recording; the document was sent to me with the following cautionary note: "This recording is originating from a private archive and there is no documentation who sung which roles and so on" (e-mail from Henk van de Pol, NOS, 3 April 2012). The same message further specifies that the NOS archives contain a 16 mm film with excerpts from the world premiere, which, to date, has not been digitized. Audio copies of the world premiere and some performances are also held at the Centro Studi Bruno Maderna in Bologna (see below, note 71).

21   See also the program reproduced here in Example 1 and later in the text.

Première 1973 (*Synopsis*)	Radio Version	Television Version	Salabert Score (© 1974)
1. *Introduction* (tape) [with: • *Criside II* • *Love ecstasy* (only Criside and Niceros)]	1. *Lady Luck*	1. *Trimalchio e le flatulenze*	1. Tape [no. 1] 1.1 *Scintilla* 1.2 *Niceros* ("*lost*") 1.3 *Criside II*
2. *Fortunata*	2. *Trimalchio e il monumento* [with: *Funeral March*]	2. Tape (opening credits)	2. *Fortunata*
3. *Trimalchio e la Flatulenza*	3. *Love's Ecstasy*	3. *Fortunata*	3. *Trimalchio e le flatulenze*
4. *Food Machine* [1]	4. *Scintilla*	4. Tape	4. *Orchestral Improvisation – Food Machine*
5. *The Money*	5. *Fortunata*	5. *La matrona di Efeso* (I)	5. *The Money*
6. *Erotica* (tape)	6. *Carriera di Trimalchio* [2]	6. Tape	6. Tape no. 2 (*Erotica*)
7. *Lady Luck*	7. *The Money*	7. *Trimalchio e le flatulenze*	7. *Lady Luck*
8. *Trimalchio e la Flatulenza* (reprise)	8. *Fortunata e Eumolpus*	8. Tape	8. *Trimalchio e le flatulenze* (reprise)
9. *Awakening* (tape)	9. *Eumolpus Fuga*	9. *Carriera di Trimalchio* • *Love's Ecstasy* • reprise "*Millionen*"	9. Tape no. 3 (*Awakening*)
10. *La matrona di Efeso*	10. *Trimalchio e le flatulenze*	10. *Scintilla*	10. *La matrona di Efeso*
11. *Trimalchio and animals* (tape)	11. *Trimalchio e le flatulenze* (instrumental)	11. *La matrona di Efeso* (II)	11. Tape no. 4 (*Trimalchio and animals*)
12. *Carriera di Trimalchio* [finale "*Millionen*" mixed with: • *Criside 1* • *Love's Ecstasy*] [3]	12. *Trimalchio contra Fortunata*	12. Tape	12. *Carriera di Trimalchio* 12.1 *Criside 1* 12.2 "*Millionen*" 12.3 *Love's Ecstasy* 12.4 "*Millionen*"
13. *Fortunata e Eumolpus*	13. *La matrona di Efeso*	13. *Fortunata e Eumolpus*	13. *Fortunata e Eumolpus*
[with: *Eumolpus Fuga*]		14. *Eumolpus Fuga*	14. *Eumolpus Fuga*
[*Scintilla*]		15. Tape	15. *Scintilla* and Party re-enter
14. *Trimalchio – contra Fortunata*	14. *Lady Luck* (reprise) [4]	16. *Trimalchio contra Fortunata*	16. *Trimalchio contra Fortunata*
15. *Trimalchio e la Flatulenza* (orchestral reprise)		17. Tape	17. *Trimalchio e le flatulenze* (instrumental)
[*silent mime*]		18. *Trimalchio e le flatulenze* (instrumental)	18. *Party returns* (silent mime)
16. *Trimalchio e il monumento* [with: *Funeral March*]		19. Tape	19. *Trimalchio e il monumento*
		20. *La matrona di Efeso* (III)	20. *Funeral March*
17. *Finale* (tape)		21. Tape	21. Tape no. 5
		22. *Lady Luck*	
		23. *[Party returns]*	
		24. *Trimalchio e il monumento*	
		25. *Funeral March*	
		26. *Lady Luck* (reprise) [5] (end credits)	

[1] In the *Synopsis* of the world premiere we read "Tape," but upon listening it becomes clear that it was actually performed live.
[2] Performed from top to bottom, with no final interpolations.
[3] Ends with the apotheosis of "Millionen" performed by all on stage who exit (the recording makes us think of a procession) leaving the stage free for Fortunata e Eumolpus.
[4] Once with chorus and instruments, once only instruments. No. 1 is instead performed, as in the score, by the Quartilla alone.
[5] With choir and instruments. No. 22 is instead performed, as in the score, by the Quartilla alone.

EX. 3   Comparative diagram of four arrangements of *Satyricon:*
the world premiere on 16 March 1973 (and subsequent performances);
radio version; television version; the order published in the Salabert score.

when these performances were given and/or during the recording of the televised version (to eventually check the order) is not of secondary importance. He certainly did not conduct the scheduled repeat performance in Brussels on 7 April, where he was replaced by his assistant Lucas Vis.[22]

It is just as complicated, and indeed an often-overlooked task, to find any connection or direct line between the two versions as it is to work out the actual dates of the radio and TV recordings from the existing bibliography. It is therefore appropriate to take a closer look at each version individually.

Radio version   There is unanimous consensus among scholars on its attribution to Maderna. Likewise, almost all agree that it was realized before the TV version (the only study where this order is reversed will be discussed below).

A CD of this version, called "Concert version," was released in 1992 on the Stradivarius label.[23] The information provided with the CD tells us nothing about the location, origin, or type of the master tape. However, Alberto Cantoni, who curated its release, confirmed that Maderna's widow, Beate Christine Koepnick, provided the record label managers with all the materials for its publication (now held at PSS).[24] Over the years, this source has become a point of reference both for performance practice and for the exegesis of the work, also because it is one of the last examples that sees Maderna in the double role of interpreter of his own works.[25] The printed notes (→ **EX. 4**) offer the following information: the "radio recording" was made in Hilversum (headquarters of the NOS studios) on 24 March 1973; the cast of voices is identical to that of the world premiere; and Maderna conducted members of the NOS Radio Orchestra for the occasion. No hints or further details are given about a possible broadcast date.

A number of scholars have considered the distinctive features of this version as clearly reflecting the author's intention to adapt his work for the radio. In fact, they have been interpreted in terms of a performance that is specifically for the microphone, to be listened to with no scenic action: the shorter length of this version, the lack of any inserts

---

22   The information can be deduced from various documents, including a letter dated 8 April 1973, sent by René van Arenbergh, harpsichordist and former co-prompter at the La Monnaie theater, to Maderna's address in Darmstadt, in which he informs the composer about the enormous success the work had enjoyed the day before. Letter held in PSS-BMC, already cited in *Documenti* (see note 14), pp. 315–16.

23   See Bruno Maderna, *Satyricon*, Opera in one act, Concert version, stereo, Stradivarius, STR 10061 (1992). This is the "oratorial" version quoted in *Documenti* (see note 14), p. 315 (see above in the text). The radio work *Ages* (1972) is also found on the same CD. It is curious to note that, after listening to *Satyricon*'s world premiere (following its live performance on radio), Luciano Berio wrote to Maderna about the possibility of "being able to make a concert version of about 20–25 minutes" (undated letter, PSS-BMC; published almost in its entirety in Pasticci, "La presenza del *Satyricon*" (see note 4), p. 88). Any analogy with this "Concert version" is, however, purely coincidental, as will be clarified later in the text.

24   Telephone communication on 4 April 2012 from Alberto Cantoni (Stradivarius editions) which was also confirmed in the meeting which took place on the following 2 May in Cremona. Cantoni recalls that Maderna's widow personally gave him some tapes and her own notes with some general information about the place, date, and performers of this radio version, while preventing the release of other tapes relating to a "version by Lucas Vis" (see below, n. 77).

25   See also above, note 2.

BRUNO MADERNA
SATYRICON

Opera in un atto da Petronio, riduzione e traduzione di Bruno Maderna - Versione da concerto
Opera in one act based on 'Satyricon' by Petronius; adapted and translated by Bruno Maderna - Concert version
Oper in ein akt aus Petronio; Reduktion und Übersetzung von Bruno Maderna - Konzertfassung
Opera en un acte aprés Petronio; reduction et traduction de Bruno Maderna - Version de concert

1	Lady Luck	1' 30"
2	Trimalchio e il monumento	8' 39"
3	Love's ecstasy	1' 31"
4	Scintilla	0' 51"
5	Fortunata	2' 59"
6	La carriera di Trimalchio	4' 12"
7	The Money	2' 29"
8	Fortunata e Eumolpus	2' 35"
9	Eumolpus Fuga	1' 01"
10	Trimalchio e le flatulenze	0' 54"
11	Trimalchio e le flatulenze (ripresa)	0' 51
12	Trimalchio contro Fortunata	2' 26"
13	La Matrona di Efeso	9' 45"
14	Lady Luck (ripresa)	2' 29"

Trimalchio : **William Neill** - Fortunata : **Debria Brown** - Habinna : **Paul Sperry** - Eumolpo : **Meinard Kraak**
Scintilla : **Poppy Holden** - Criside : **Anne Haenen** - Nicero : **Tom Haenen** - Quartilla : **Elsa Lioni**
Members of the NOS Radio Orchestra, Hilversum
BRUNO MADERNA
Registrazione radiofonica : Hilversum, 24 marzo 1973

EX. 4   Description of the radio version provided with the
Stradivarius CD 10061, 1992 (booklet, p. 24).

on magnetic tape, the ordering of the fourteen passages (Ex. 3); and the particular drama-turgy that derives from it. As an example, let us read the following interpretation, which leads us directly to the TV version:

> In the radio-version, none of the pre-recorded tape material which was used in the stage-version was employed (material which evidently served the needs of this original presentation for music to accompany stage-actions), but in the television version some use was made of tapes. In both radio and television, the sequence of musical numbers differed both from the stage-version [...]. Where in the case of the radio version of the opera we are confronted simply with a version which attempted to present the main musical sections of the work without any scenic action, and therefore without the need for any linking of the numbers of tapes, the case of the television version is of considerably greater interest [...] in studying the ordering of the musical and dramatic material in *Satyricon*.[26]

Television version   Precisely because of its greater degree of completeness, the question has often been asked as to whether or not this TV adaptation by Wilhelmina Hoedeman should be considered as "the 'definitive' version, and as a model for future performances of the opera," even though it was certainly not conducted by Maderna.[27]

---

26 Fearn, *Bruno Maderna* (see note 13), p. 233, where we can also read that "Both the NOS Radio and NOS Television versions of the opera arose from the stage performance of the work in Holland, but were each adapted to the specific needs of the media through which they were presented." All the studies mentioned in note 18 agree on the congruence between the two versions with the specific characteristics of the respective broadcast channels.

27 Ibid., p. 234. But see below, and the document reproduced in Appendix 2 (p. 57), to understand that the answer to this question can only be no.

As clearly indicated in the credits, the performers (singers and mimes) involved in this production are the same as those who appeared in the world premiere (and, therefore, in the radio version), conducted, together with the members of the Radio Chamber Orchestra, by Lucas Vis.[28]

Unlike the radio version, which is never mentioned in the documents of the time, news of this television production can be found in an issue of *Opera Journaal* (the Nederlandse Operastichting magazine) dedicated almost entirely to *Satyricon* and its imminent staging. Among the biographical profiles of the author, collaborators, and performers, plus a foreword by Strasfogel and more, a short paragraph announces that "Maderna's new opera, *Satyricon* [...] will be in the NOS Hilversum TV studios for a special television production to be included in future programming."[29]

A quick glance at Example 3 immediately shows the major difference between this and the other versions. Here, too, the television format seems to be at the basis of the various choices, among which the most obvious are the new arrangement and dramaturgical concatenation of the various parts and some decidedly extreme performative options carried out at the expense of the work's implicit unity (just consider, for example, the subdivision of the long episode of the *Matrona di Efeso* into three parts – nos. 5, 11, and 20 in Ex. 3 – or the subdivision of the interventions of the tapes, interspersed ten times as a final curtain after almost every number).

Until now both the recording and broadcast dates were unknown. Only one study dates the television production between 20 and 25 March. Upon closer examination, however, it becomes clear that this overlaps with the dates of the first repeat stage performances in Amsterdam and that, in fact, this information is unfortunately not reliable.[30] Moreover, the contemporaneity of two different productions of the same work, both made in the same Hilversum studios between 20 and 25 March, one an author's version (radio) and the other conducted by his assistant (TV), would be hard to explain.

And it is precisely this consideration that raises another doubt that only serves to complicate matters even further. As in fact Claudia Vincis has noted, apart from the completely different order of execution, the singers' performances in both the radio and TV versions are surprisingly similar.[31] This is truly puzzling, considering the autonomy of the radio version with regard to the video one. One might think of a case of "performance crystallization" affecting all the singers, who are now well-accustomed to interpreting the

---

28   As well as Hoedeman (television production and direction), the final credits mentioned Jan Heesemans (lighting director), Hans Hulscher (technical manager), and Roland de Groot (costumes and sets), who all had nothing to do with the theatrical production (see Ex. 1).

29   *Opera Journaal* (season 1972–73), no. 7, p. 2; original in Dutch. The foreword to *Satyricon* written by Strasfogel, "Nieuwe impulsen voor het muziektheater" (New Impetus for Musical Theater), p. 2, makes it clear that, at the time he wrote these pages, the work was still in the pipeline.

30   The information is in Vincis, "À propos de la nature modulable du *Satyricon*" (see note 12), p. 25 and n. 3. The scholar obtained the dates from a document kept at the Centro Studi Bruno Maderna in Bologna, associated with the television recording. In actual fact, it is a tampered photocopy of the program reproduced here in Example 1, from which the upper part relating to Ligeti's *Aventures et Nouvelles Aventures* has been removed.

31   Ibid. No other previous study had ever noted the similarity between the two productions, always interpreted and analyzed as completely different versions.

same role for various audio-visual media; or one could think of a "mimetic" approach adopted by Vis with respect to the model already made by the Maestro. Or, as listening would seem to confirm, there is a third possible scenario: it might be the same audio, only edited differently to be used in two different media contexts.

Vincis's interpretation is along these lines: following the timeline provided by the Stradivarius CD and the presumed dates of the TV recording, she inverts the production order of the two versions, putting the TV one first, and assuming a direct line of derivation whereby the radio version was actually "obtained from" the television version.[32]

But if so, how can we explain the fact, confirmed thanks to sound analysis tools, that the audio of the radio version (CD Stradivarius) and that of the TV video are identical? Thus: conducted by Vis, or Maderna? Radio first or, as Vincis suggests, television first? And, above all, with what "authorial" impact on the work's mobility?

Our journey backwards through *Satyricon*'s performative history stops here, right in the midst of a dense forest of doubts. So, let us now set out in the opposite direction, on a different route through the major stages of the history of the work and its chronology.

A Brief Digression (I): August 1971. *Trimalchio* at Tanglewood

We shall not dwell here on the characteristics of the collective experiment of 1971 based on short sequences taken from Trimalchio's Banquet. Nor will we discuss the profound artistic understanding which, starting from that Festival of Contemporary Music in Tanglewood in 1971, was created between Maderna and Strasfogel.[33] Available data and sources are cited by almost all scholars, who agree in seeing the precursor of *Satyricon* in this improvisation laboratory, intended as a totally open form and resulting from a close collaboration between director and musician.[34] Nevertheless, what we wish to examine and verify here are, on the one hand, the peculiarities of the actual stage performance – of the "staging" – of that experiment announced in the program for 8-9 August and, on the other, Maderna's actual participation in that performance in the role of composer and/or conductor. To date, the documents of that time cited as confirmation (Festival brochures or newspaper articles) always refer to announcements or programs where everything is conjugated in the future tense (albeit a near one), and where nothing is said about any actual and concrete performances. On the contrary, a singular document that has recently come to light gives an account written in the past tense and talks about what *eventually*

---

32   Ibid., p. 25.

33   The following summer, the two artists worked together again, always as part of the "Music Theatre Project" directed by Strasfogel at Tanglewood, on a realization of Monteverdi's *L'Incoronazione di Poppea* (performed on 13, 14, and 16 August 1972).

34   The experiment is cited, with more or less emphasis, as a direct antecedent (or as a first version) of the work in all the studies mentioned above in note 18. For further details see also, in this book, the essays by Anne C. Shreffler (esp. pp. 307–10 and note 45) and Maurizio Romito (esp. pp. 285–86). The main source is the article quoted in note 15 (reproduced in this book on p. 327), where Maderna is however mentioned just as Strasfogel's "advisor." See also "The Music Theater Project" in *Tanglewood Music Center Yearbook*, 1971 (https://archive.org/search.php?query=tanglewood%20music%20center%20yearbook%201971, p. 418; consulted 6 January 2021).

was realized. And surprisingly, it revolutionizes various facts that have been handed down over time. It is a memorandum, drawn up by Strasfogel himself close to the end of the 1971 Tanglewood season,[35] whose contents leave no doubt that things went quite differently from what had been expected by the forecasts and announcements. What was to have been a "collective experiment" based on Petronius, quite simply, never came to fruition and was never staged:

> Along with [the preparation of the Satie and Birtwistle scores],[36] work began on a project to involve the composers at Tanglewood with The Music Theatre Project. The plan was to evolve through improvisational sessions, a music piece for inclusion in the Fromm Festival of Contemporary Music. The Feast of Trimalchio was chosen from Petronius' SATYRICON as subject and meetings were held with Bruno Maderna to coordinate compositional matters. It soon became apparent, however, that both singers and composers were far too busy with other activities in Tanglewood to devote enough time to the evolution of such a work. *We abandoned the project with much regret,* since certain efforts of the performers had been so exciting and suggestive of new possibilities in music theatre. Certainly, such work must be done – but as part of a year-round activity.[37]

When questioned more specifically about that unfinished project, Strasfogel then admitted that, in actual fact, it had not gone much beyond the first generic meetings with Maderna mentioned in the memorandum: "Bruno only observed the *Satyricon* improvisations we did at Tanglewood. He never composed, coached or conducted them. He was purely an observer."[38]

Thus, one of the three (or four) of Maderna's "author versions" – the one that has always been surrounded by vagueness – can immediately be excluded.

No compositional or conducting activity was foreseen at Tanglewood that might have given rise to the score of 1973. If anything, that experience as an "observer" helped Maderna to rekindle an old interest and to bring him closer to a character from the Neronian era whose subjects and historical setting were gaining more and more importance in the early 1970s.

35　"The Music Theatre Project – 1971" (photocopy of draft typescript, 4 fols.), drawn up on New England Conservatory stationery (Boston, Mass.). Private archive of Ian Strasfogel (a copy is now also held at PSS). See also the essay by Anne C. Shreffler in this book, p. 310.

36　As regards this see ibid., p. 311, and p. 286 of the essay by Maurizio Romito.

37　Strasfogel, "The Music Theatre Project – 1971" (note 35), pp. 3–4. The emphasis is mine.

38　Private communication (e-mail) from Ian Strasfogel, 27 December 2020. In a previous e-mail of 22 December 2020, Strasfogel also writes that the work he led with the young artists "was strictly *in studio.* The results were clearly incomplete. [...I]mprovisational work takes a great deal of time and the Music Theatre Project had an extremely crowded performance schedule. [...] That's why I never permitted public performances of the *Satyricon* improvisations." In a letter to Maurizio Romito, dated 18 November 2015, Strasfogel had further confirmed: "The piece was absolutely NOT by Maderna," adding that "There was no orchestra, only a piano" (see also p. 286 in this volume).

A Few Steps Between Dates and Certainties: A Little Bit of Chronology

From Tanglewood to the Dutch premiere there were several stages (among others) that, as regards the genesis of the work, should be retraced in their succession:

• On 17 February 1972 Maderna's manager, Sylvio Samama, informed the composer about established agreements with the "Niederländische Oper" for six performances of "Ligeti *Aventures et Nouvelles Aventures* and Maderna *Satyricon*"; the letter also specifies the dates of the rehearsals (expected to begin on 26 February 1973) and the performances, with the premiere already scheduled for 16 March of the following year.[39]

• 12 March 1972 marks the U.S. premiere of *Venetian Journal:* the various sheets of music paper used to draft this work contain sketches (or were reused) for specific parts of *Satyricon*.[40]

• On 24 April 1972 Strasfogel wrote to de Roo informing him about his recent meeting with Maderna in New York and, among other things, that they had discussed some points of the future theatrical project (still called *Trimalchio* by the director), whose staging in Holland is a sure thing. The names of some of the singers to be engaged are suggested, and, in particular as regards the textual subject, Strasfogel offers to compile a "scenario quasi-libretto." (The idea was later abandoned and, as we have already seen, the textual selection was carried out by the composer alone.)[41]

• In fact, the official agreement between de Roo (De Nederlandse Operastichting) and Maderna was signed on 7 July 1972.[42] The work bears the definitive title (*Satyricon*) and its performance, as already announced by his manager in February, is framed within a diptych with Ligeti's *Aventures et Nouvelles Aventures*. The contract confirms that Maderna is due to conduct "six performance-dates," of which two are to be in Scheveningen (March 16 and 17) and four in Amsterdam (March 20, 21, 23, and 25); a seventh date at the Théâtre de la Monnaie in Brussels is left open between 6 and 7 April (the latter was eventually the final one).[43] It is finally specified that rehearsals will begin in Amsterdam on 26 February. (The various handwritten rehearsal schedules drawn up by Maderna himself in the months preceding and just before the premiere reveal that the latter date marks the beginning of Maderna's rehearsals, where an "instrumental reading *Satyricon* in Holland" would indeed have begun, with an assistant, as early as 14 February 1973.)[44]

---

39   Letter sent to Maderna (in Darmstadt) via the Géza de Koos agency (PSS-BMC).

40   See in this regard my "Qui forse una cadenza brillante" (see note 3), passim.

41   Letter from Strasfogel's private archives (a copy is also held at PSS). In a private communication (e-mail dated 22 December 2020), Strasfogel confirmed that as far as the chosen texts were concerned, "Bruno never showed them to me. They are entirely his work [and] I had nothing to do with them."

42   Agreement on De Nederlandse Operastichting letterhead stationery, kept at PSS-BMC (4 fols.). Also see in this book the essay by Anne C. Shreffler on p. 306, note 36.

43   See also below, note 61. These dates can also be read in several of Maderna's agendas and notebooks from 1972–73.

44   See, among others, the notebook "*Stagione 1972–73 / 1973–74*" (PSS-BMC), from which the quotation in the text is taken (datable to November 1972), and the complete rehearsal schedule drawn up by Maderna on fols. 2–3 of the notepad ("*Schrijfblok*") cited in note 12. As will be discussed below in the text, Maderna would have arrived in Holland a week after the beginning of the "instrumental reading" also due to other conducting commitments: on 23 February he had in fact scheduled a symphonic concert in Milan during which, incidentally, he conducted Paul Sperry – the future Habinnas in the opera – in some of Mozart's arias for tenor and orchestra. The dates of Maderna's arrival (25 February) and departure (initially scheduled for 30 March) from Holland have been established by means of a letter signed by J.M.H. Bouwhuis (the de Koos agency secretary), sent to the composer on 20 February 1973 (PSS-BMC).

• In the second half of 1972, Maderna made various notes and sketches dedicated to the future *Satyricon,* mainly relating to the vocal characters. From these we can deduce the following: the role of Fortunata was initially conceived for Cathy Berberian; Giton also appears among the characters (a role to be assigned to a "young contra tenor"); and the multilingual textual mix of English, French, German, and Latin was also almost tailor-made for the individual characters.[45]

• In the meantime, Maderna's career had reached a major turning point: on 31 July 1972, the Salabert publishing house in Paris announced its intention to include Maderna's name in its catalog. As of 22 September, it is now certain that the composer did not intend to renew his contract expiring at the end of the year with the Ricordi publishing house, so as to join Salabert exclusively from 1 January 1973. A "General Agreement" between Maderna and Salabert was signed on 15 November 1972.[46]

• Finally, the official contract for the publication and transfer of all copyrights of *Satyricon* to Salabert, signed and approved by Maderna, is dated 16 January 1973; it follows an exchange of letters between Maderna and his manager, starting from the beginning of December 1972, regarding the work and its premiere in the Netherlands.[47]

Now that we have reached the threshold of 1973, let us take a closer look at the developments of the work in progress.

Back to the Primacy of Doubt…

It is interesting to note that in Maderna's public comments about *Satyricon* – at least in the ones we know – there is often a strong emphasis on the meanings of a stage adaptation of Petronius created "with the means of the theater" (capable of transmitting "just some of the uneasiness I feel about many aspects of our current culture"), or on the relevance or even political significance of its message.[48] Rather surprisingly, its form and openness are never discussed, nor is there any mention of mobility or multiple interpretive paths. The only references to the term "collage" – or, by extension, to "pop art" – intersect when Maderna illustrates the characteristics of the pre-recorded inserts on magnetic tape, meant

---

45 See, among others, the notes in "*Skizzenbuch 6,*" second half of 1972 (PSS-BMC), especially fols. 6, 20 (from which the quotation in the text is taken), and 32 (which allows us to deduce that Berberian was replaced by Débria Brown, a mezzo-soprano à la "Carmen but also high-pitched").

46 See, respectively, the letters dated 31 July and 22 September 1972 from Erica Salabert to Maderna's manager, Samama (PSS-BMC). In the latter, Salabert and Maderna agree on the delivery of three works, including a theatrical work. The date of 15 November 1972 is deduced from the subsequent contract dated 16 January 1973 (cited below in the text). The official announcement of Maderna's move to Salabert was published in *News from Editions Salabert* 1, no. 1 (January 1973), [p. 1].

47 See, respectively, the letters from Constant Minescaut (Salabert) to Samama on 7 and 8 December 1972 (in the latter, he also asks for information on Strasfogel's collaboration in the stage adaptation of the text). All the documents mentioned here are held at PSS-BMC.

48 See the various accounts of the work now collected in Maderna, *Amore e curiosità* (see note 2) and, among these, especially those in "Prima del *Satyricon:* Colloquio con Frans van Rossum" (pp. 312–17; quotation in the text on p. 314), and in "Intervista con Piet Hein van de Poel su *Satyricon*" (pp. 318–25).

to accommodate various types of "naturalistic, sometimes exaggerated" effects, but also "neo-musical effects, or from neo-citationism."[49]

On the contrary, as far as the vocal and instrumental sections are concerned, the correspondence between the heterogeneity of the Petronian characters/themes, and the heterogeneity of the musical styles/registers employed, leads Maderna to speak of a "great musical form," of a "solid structure":

> This fragment [Trimalchio's Banquet] obviously fascinated me thanks to its intrinsic possibilities for visual theater. [...] But the power of that fragment, dramatically speaking, is the comparison of the various social strata and the most diverse spiritual and social currents: we find there, for example, ministers, priests, philosophers, artists, whores, second lieutenants, soldiers, idlers, freedmen, slaves.
> In some of these figures I have tried to fix the most important [musical] currents. And their interdependence determined the great musical form. Each character brings their own musical form with them. As more characters arrive on the scene, the musical form as a whole becomes more complex, just like the general view of the scene. And by balancing all these elements it seems to me that I have also obtained a solid structure.[50]

Besides, an absolute indeterminacy of the work would seem to be in contrast with what the author himself outlined in various schemas or in the substantial notes he drew up especially close to the world premiere. Here Maderna outlines possible dramaturgical concatenations for the already composed pieces, which reveal the work's consequentiality or an overall vision that, in fact, reflects an extremely "solid" dramaturgical structure.[51] Look, for example, at the sketch reproduced in Appendix 1, which – despite the incompleteness or absence of some parts that are presumably still in progress or yet to be composed – is self-explanatory in showing the strength and coherence of the scenic ideas and the narrative development imagined by the author.[52] Other verbal notes, written using

---

49   The quotations come from ibid., p. 319. It is precisely an incorrect interpretation of this excerpt from the interview – published in a first Italian translation in *Documenti* (see note 14), pp. 111–12, and reprinted verbatim in Fearn, *Bruno Maderna* (see note 13), p. 324 –, that gave rise to distorted interpretations on the categories of pop art or collage applied by extension to the entire work. Yet Maderna's words (he spoke in German in the interview) leave no room for doubt: "die Bände sind Collage und sind naturalistische Effekte [...] bis es geht bei einer Ebene neo-Musical Effekte, oder neo-Zitate … was ich mir immer vorgestellt habe, ist was heutzutage man sich als Pop-Art vorstellen kann; in dem richtigen Sinn, verstehen Sie?" The misunderstanding was also caused by the same interviewer van de Poel, who used excerpts from this interview as the basis for a subsequent article ambiguously titled "Bruno Maderna over *Satyricon*: pop-art in muziek"; see the editor's notes in Maderna, *Amore e curiosità* (see note 2), p. 770.

50   As Maderna says in "Prima del *Satyricon*" (see note 48), p. 315.

51   These are various notes and diagrams contained among the materials for *Satyricon* in the notepad mentioned in note 12 and on other loose sheets, some of which are clearly torn from the same pad. It should be mentioned that the notepad was also used after the world premiere. As we will see later in the text, some final pages contain notes that refer to the preparations for the rerun of *Satyricon* at the Piccola Scala in Milan in March 1974.

52   The sketch is discussed and transcribed in diplomatic form in Zucconi, *"Satyricon" di Bruno Maderna* (see note 12), p. 109, which speaks of a "sort of graphic visualization of the dramatic trend" with an initial crescendo (pp. 109–11). A different transcription is also in Vincis, "À propos de la nature modulable du *Satyricon*" (see note 12), p. 33. It should be noted that, in its incompleteness, this sketch shows some similarities with the final layout of the same parts in the Salabert edition (see below and in Ex. 3, from no. 12 onwards).

pens of several colors to better distinguish between the characters, also bring real "stage directions" to mind, and thus it is all the more surprising to see the total absence of any performance or stage directions when one takes a look at the score published by Salabert.[53]

Toward Holland, and Beyond the World Premiere:
a Bit More Chronology

On 26 December 1972, in a letter from New York, the American composer Jacob Druckman told Maderna that he had "recently spent a pleasant evening with Ian Strasvogel [*sic*] and I had a brief chance to look at your *Satyricon* score. It looks fascinating and shocking in its simplicity."[54]

On that date, the "score" to *Satyricon* – in the version published today – was still far from being ready or assembled. In fact, in all likelihood, what Druckman saw was just some single numbers intended for the tenor Paul Sperry – including the long section of the *Matrona di Efeso*, certainly already composed at the end of 1972 – and, with some uncertainty, some of the parts intended for William Neill, the tenor who was to play Trimalchio.[55] The bulk of the work was in fact drawn up by Maderna just before his stay in Holland, and some parts, including the ones destined for Niceros and for Hermeros, even though their dramaturgical or textual profile had been established, never came to be composed.[56] Strasfogel himself has repeatedly confirmed that he was only able to see all the music and texts for *Satyricon* after he got to Amsterdam. The director's diary indicates the date as being 26 February 1973[57] – less than a month before the premiere.

53　It should be noted that sometimes the drafts of Maderna's musical parts contain stage directions or scenographic notes. In an almost final draft of *La matrona di Efeso*, on the sheet marked "Abinna 6" (circled number), after the breath which closes the (totally determined) text section "conjugal fidelity and love," which precedes the aleatoric intervention of bar 19bis (see pp. 45–46 in the score), Maderna writes: "At this point, before continuing, a quarrel could break out that ends in a joke: example: Trimalchio claps his hands to impose a state of calm, a servant furiously plays a trumpet that is interrupted by a loud clash of cymbals. Another servant, startled by the crash of cymbals, drops a pile of dishes on the floor, making even more of a din. A moment of stunned silence, and Trimalchio with a sweet, very polite voice invites Habinna to continue the story" (orig. in Italian).

54　PSS-BMC. Excerpt published in Italian translation in Maderna, *Amore e curiosità* (see note 2), p. 634.

55　In a private communication from 28 December 2020 (e-mail), Strasfogel confirmed that "the only part of the score that I could show Jake Druckman that December evening was the music of the *Widow of Ephesus*." He also remembers that Sperry was the only one to receive his part "before arriving in Amsterdam," whereas William Neill only managed to get "a brief fragment of his part." B. Zucconi also concludes that Trimalchio's parts were the first to be composed in her *"Satyricon" di Bruno Maderna* (see note 12), esp. p. 124, where one can also find further details about the compositional genesis of each of the pieces in the work.

56　See also below in the text. Therefore, the indication "perdu – lost" that appears in the Salabert score in reference to an elusive number "I.2 *Niceros*," written in the "Ordre des Numéros" of the work, should be considered wrong (see also Ex. 3). In a letter sent by Sylvio Samama to the American impresario Sheldon Soffer on 14 February 1973, we still read that "Bruno is busy composing his opera and cannot find peace of mind to answer to your letter" (PSS-BMC).

57　Personal communication from Ian Strasfogel (e-mail of 27 December 2020). As we can read in one of Maderna's notes, a "probable meeting in Amsterdam with Hans [de Roo] and Jan [Strasfogel]" was planned in November 1972, but was later "CANCELED"; see notebook *Stagione 1972–73 / 1973–74* (see note 44).

Maderna must have started rehearsals with the singers and instrumentalists that very day. He had arrived in Holland the day before, directly from Milan, where, among other commitments, he had been working relatively hard (on the tapes for the opera, but not only that) at RAI's Studio di Fonologia. An internal memo, drawn up to inform the various executives of the Milan RAI about the scheduled recording sessions at the electronic Studio in the four-month period from January to April 1973, clearly shows that several dates had been blocked from 8 January to 9 February for "Maderna – Satyricon." A subsequent worksheet, indicating "Studio use for each production," then shows a total of "112 hours" calculated for *Satyricon*.[58] Given that the opera makes use of tapes of more or less recognizable fragments from previous electroacoustic works (from *Le Rire* to *Don Perlimplin* up to the more recent *Tempo libero*), even half of such a huge amount of time would be enough to dispel the idea that the tapes produced for the world premiere were the result of outright improvisation or reuse of tapes that had already been made or assembled in a haphazard manner.[59] Marino Zuccheri, the chief technician at Studio di Fonologia, worked alongside Maderna on the tapes. He remembers those moments as their "last great collaboration," specifying that "he knew he was ill."[60]

On 20 February 1973, a few days before his departure for Holland, the composer received a letter about the television production of the opera:

> Dear Mr Maderna,
> We hereby inform you of our plans to produce a televised version of *Satyricon* which, in all probability, will be shot in the Hilversum Studio.
> Should the recording take place, then the recording schedule will be as follows:
> <u>19 March</u> 9.30-12.30   14.30-16.30   (Sound recording)
> <u>29 and 30 March 1973</u>   (Time to be arranged)   Video recording [61]

In Maderna's agendas, the dates of 29 and 30 March are thus set aside for "Dutch Television" and go to join the six performances of *Satyricon* scheduled between Scheveningen and Amsterdam, as well as a further cycle of lessons at the Conservatory of The Hague, fixed for the days when there were no stage performances (19, 22, and 24 March).[62]

---

58   Both unpublished documents are kept in the RAI Archives of the Studio di Fonologia in Milan ("Orari e pratiche varie Fonologia" folder, available in copy at the "NoMus" association in Milan); the first is dated 23 January 1973, the second 22 May 1973; both are signed or initialed by Luigi Galvani.

59   Thus, among others, Fearn, *Bruno Maderna* (see note 13), p. 233. It should be noted that this essay will not make an in-depth analysis of topics related to the final tapes of the work. Let us just note the existence, at the Studio di Fonologia, of a four-track reel ("Q.024") with content that demands more detailed study of the materials in the publisher's possession. It can nevertheless be confirmed that the taped parts of the world premiere add up to five interventions on magnetic tape, the same number as those delivered to the publisher.

60   In Angela Ida De Benedictis, "... at the Time of the Tubes ... A Conversation with Marino Zuccheri," in *New Music on the Radio: Experiences at the Studio di Fonologia of the RAI, Milan 1954–1959*, ed. Veniero Rizzardi and Angela Ida De Benedictis (Rome: RAI-ERI, 2000), pp. 176–212: 176.

61   PSS-BMC, unpublished, original in German, signed by J.M.H. Bouwhuis (secretary of the de Koos agency, impresario). This is the same letter, sent to the address in Darmstadt, which also confirms the date of the performance in Brussels (7 April 1973).

And so, not only do we now know the exact recording dates of the TV version but, from a comparison with other NOS internal documents, we are also able to date its airing on the "Nederland 2" channel to precisely 6 April 1973.[63] All the documents leave no doubt that the television production should have been conducted by Maderna himself. But the rampant disease had other plans for the composer, also as regards the six stage performances stipulated in the contract and all the other engagements scheduled for the same days. On 12 March 1973, de Roo wrote a formal letter to Maderna's manager:

> This letter is to confirm the verbal agreement made over the phone following Mr. Bruno Maderna's illness.
> As agreed, the contract [signed] on 7 July 1972 will be modified in such a way that Mr. Maderna will at the moment only conduct the world premiere […].[64]

As it happened, Maderna only conducted the first performance on 16 March, leaving immediately the next day for Darmstadt to undergo a cycle of oncological treatments. For all subsequent performances he was replaced by his assistant, Lucas Vis. The "Study project" at the Conservatory instead had to be canceled. Once again it was de Roo who gave Maderna an account a few days later of the second repeat performance, which took place on the evening of his hasty departure:

> The second performance in Scheveningen was also a success. Lucas Vis did it very well. The reviews I've read so far have mostly been very good. In case you are interested, I could send them to you. On the other hand, I could quite understand that all this does not interest you at all.
> Tonight [20 March] is the first performance in Amsterdam. I'll keep you updated on upcoming developments.[65]

---

62   See the note "MARCH 1973" in the notebook "*Stagione 1972–73 / 1973–74*" (see note 44). The same engagements are also noted in another pocket diary of 1973 (PSS-BMC), where Maderna writes "NOS TELEVISION" close to the dates of 29 and 30 March. Maderna should have held analysis lessons at the Conservatory of The Hague as head of "Study Project 1973," dedicated to "Music from the years 1920–1940" (the syllabus is kept in the Archives of the Royal Conservatoire; my heartfelt thanks to Marie Severt, Head of Library, for kindly providing me with a copy and some information given here in note 65).

63   The program aired in the late evening at 10:40 pm. The date is shown on the broadcast sheet housed in the archives of the Nederlands Instituut voor Beeld en Geluid and in various Dutch newspapers published in those days. My thanks to Maurizio Romito for having generously shared the documents collected on this television production in the course of his research.

64   PSS-BMC, original in Dutch. The letter, written on De Nederlandse Operastichting letterhead stationery, was sent to Samama via the de Koos agency and bears a stamped receipt of delivery dated 20 March 1973. The contract had to be changed also to reformulate the economic commitments.

65   Letter dated 20 March 1973, sent to Darmstadt (PSS-BMC), original in German. Enclosed with the letter, de Roo "returned the texts of *Satyricon*" to Maderna (probably those published in the *Synopsis*, corresponding to the typescripts preserved in PSS among the materials for the work). In the archives of the Conservatory of The Hague there is a note attached to the 1973 programs: "The project was canceled at the last moment because of illness and death [*sic*] of Bruno Maderna." Maderna himself, interviewed in the following July in the NOS studios on the occasion of the world premiere of his Concerto No. 3 for oboe and orchestra, recalled: "I only conducted the first, while he [Lucas Vis] conducted the repeat performances and also the television production"; see "Interview with Harmke Pijpers," now in Maderna, *Amore e curiosità* (see note 2), pp. 393–97: 395.

A Brief Digression (II): *Satyricon* on TV. (No Maderna, No Party…)

Maderna, who was in hospital in Darmstadt, also received updates on the "upcoming developments" from Ian Strasfogel, who on 26 March 1973, the day after the last stage performance, drew up a sort of stocktaking of the whole situation, projected, optimistically, toward the future:

> well, yesterday [March, 25] was the final Amsterdam performance of *Satyricon* – a wildly enthusiastic audience gave it once again a standing ovation. We are about to begin the TV filming – which should be fascinating and there is talk of English, American and French productions in the near future. I think your delightful work is really launched on a very active career.[66]

The filming of the TV production, as we have seen, would have taken place a few days later, on 29 and 30 March. And here we learn another certain fact: Maderna's role – even indirectly – in the arrangement of the parts of the work for the television version, and its final staging and dramaturgical conformation, was quite simply non-existent. If we do need to talk about authorship or responsibility, the organization of this version can be attributed entirely to the director Wilhelmina Hoedeman. Her choices, however, were the source of tangible discontent among all the performers, to such an extent that the entire cast peremptorily distanced themselves in a formal written statement on 7 April 1973 (→ **APP. 2, P. 57**).

In fact, the day after the broadcast, which had been aired without their consent, the singers and mimes signed an official letter addressed to NOS's Head of Cultural Programs (reproduced in Appendix 2). One of the points they contested was, let us note, the very fact that the director had "changed into a totally new production – without rehearsal, direction, and even without explanation of the director's concept" – what was actually "a rehearsed, routined [sic], and performed theatrical production."[67]

Radio Version?

While it has been possible to trace all the production and broadcasting documents of the television version, all the records, files, and information bulletins at the NOS say nothing about the recording and broadcasting of the "chamber" radio version of *Satyricon*. The only document that came to light in the Dutch radio and television archives relating to two stereo reels of Maderna's *Satyricon* refers to the audio production file sheet of the television broadcast, made at the Hilversum studios on 19 March 1973 (→ **EX. 5**).

---

66   And he goes on, regretting the fact that he had not taken leave of the composer after the world premiere: "I was sorry not to have said goodbye at the rather hectic opening night party – but you naturally left early before I got a chance. At this point, let me say once more what a joy it was, as always, to work with you and your beautiful music" (PSS-BMC).

67   Letter from 7 April 1973 to Stefan Felsenthal, signed by all the singers and actors of the production (original at NOS; carbon copy – reproduced here – from the private archives of William Neill, with kind permission). Years later, Strasfogel recalled those moments: "the cuts and changes […] in the television version were done entirely on the initiative of the television director, Frau Hoedeman. Alas, she had a very limited talent. Bruno was by then undergoing treatment for his cancer and not available at all. The cast was unhappy working on the television project, and for a while we all thought about stopping it entirely" (private communication, e-mail dated 20 March 2012).

EX. 5   File sheet of the studio recording of *Satyricon* at Hilversum, 19 March 1973 (with kind permission from the Nederlands Instituut voor Beeld en Geluid Archives, NOS).

And it is thanks to this production document for the two tapes – and by listening to them – that various pieces of this complex story can be seen in a new light and recomposed together in a picture that is in some ways unimaginable.

The two reels are in fact the sound recordings ("*Tonaufnahmen*") mentioned in the letter Maderna received from his manager on 20 February 1973.[68] And here a fact of paramount importance immediately stands out, that is, the correction placed near the name of the conductor: on the already filled-out form, we read that the local "Radio Kamer Orkest" should have been conducted by "Bruno Maderna." His name, typed, is clearly recognizable beneath the noticeable handwritten crossing-out done by someone who, at the last moment, notes his replacement with "Lucas Vis." The indication "NIET" (no), always handwritten in the field marked *"Afgewerkt"* (completed, finished), indicates that it is also a work tape, not intended or finalized for any eventual radio broadcasts.

---

68   See above, note 61.

The recording sheet then shows that six numbers were recorded on the first tape ("Band 41229"), whereas the second ("Band 42472") has seven – some of which were repeated with or without voices (no. 10, *Trimalchio e le flatulenze*) and with or without the chorus (no. 13, *Lady Luck*) – making a total of thirteen pieces lasting 38'53" altogether. Also to be noted is the way in which the part of the *Matrona di Efeso* (no. 12) has already been subdivided, which, exactly as in the TV version (Ex. 3), is split into three parts of respectively 2'50", 6'00", and 2'00" each (a playing time which, in the file sheet, is even followed by the exact indication of the bar numbers of the individual parts – "1–19," "19[bis]–62," and finally "62[bis]–70," which correspond to the bar numbers traced in the manuscript score by Maderna, now to be found in the Salabert edition).

A comparison with the order and duration of the pieces of the radio version published on the Stradivarius CD (Ex. 4) – which was supposed to have been recorded a few days later, on 24 March – shows similarities that can hardly be attributed to chance. Not only are the thirteen numbers recorded on the two NOS reels ordered in exactly the same way as the so-called "chamber version," but, upon listening (with the help of sound analysis tools), they turn out to be the same identical pieces.[69]

And so, since we can *undoubtedly* identify the content of these two reels as being what was handed down as a "radio version," it follows that

    a) the conductor of the alleged chamber version is not Bruno Maderna,
       but Lucas Vis;

    b) the date of the recording on the Stradivarius CD is to be corrected to
       "19 March"; and

    c) this recording provided the audio (soundtrack) for the vocal-instrumental parts
       of the television version.[70]

We are still left wondering whether these reels were used *only* or *even* for the television version. This is a question that finds an immediate answer, although first a further misunderstanding must be cleared up: even if we wanted to see any "dramaturgical logic" in the order of recording of the thirteen pieces – aimed at a hypothetical twofold use of the recording *also* as a separate radio version – this order is not attributable to Maderna.

Neither One (a Version) nor the Other (for the Radio)

Clearing up the doubt about the sameness of the audio of the TV production and that of the so-called radio version actually leaves open a second question: how did such a macroscopic misunderstanding come about, that is, the confusion surrounding Vis's execution and its release – with his widow's approval – mistakenly attributed to Maderna. The answer was gradually disclosed during an attempt to resolve the question of the plausibility of an

---

69 The difference with the numbering of the tracks on the CD (where there are 14 instead of 13, see Ex. 4) is given by the division into two tracks of the version with and without voice of *Trimalchio e le flatulenze* (nos. 10 and 11 on the CD vs nos. 10a and 10b on the NOS tapes).

70 This confirms the idea advanced by Claudia Vincis (see above, note 32), but the chain of derivation of the sources is reversed: the audio recording is a prerequisite for the video and not vice versa.

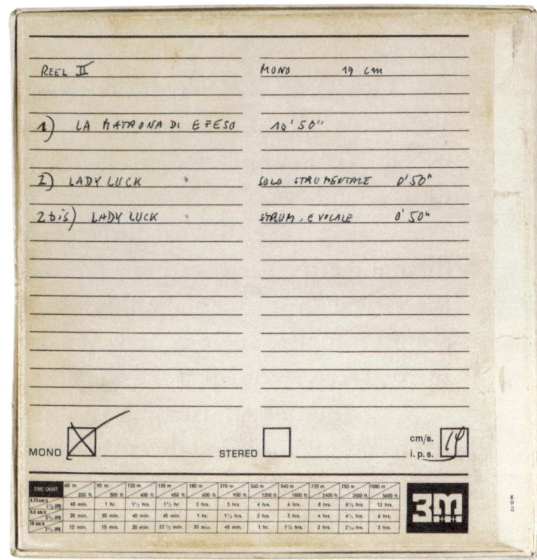

EX. 6   Boxes of two magnetic tapes (*verso*) with list
of sections of the *Satyricon* by Bruno Maderna;
PSS-BMC, "TS 1001" and "TS 1012."

autonomous use of the recording made in the studio on 19 March 1973 as a possible "version" intended for radio broadcasting. In this case, the study involved additional sound sources of *Satyricon* preserved in different archives, giving precedence to the reels preserved in the composer's legacy at the Paul Sacher Foundation, where they were deposited by Maderna's heirs in 1998.[71]

There are three tapes that hand down recordings of the work in Maderna's sound archive. Of these, two contain just the vocal-instrumental parts and make up an inseparable set, as can also be seen from the list of pieces handwritten by the author himself on the back of the boxes (→ **EX. 6**).[72] Various elements, as well as the reels' flanges, make it clear that they are not original master recordings, but copies recorded, among other things, on tapes that had been used previously. A third reel instead contains a copy of the entire audio track of the television production, identical in all respects to what is heard in the

---

71   The reels were deposited by Maderna's heirs four years after the death of their mother, who had kept them at her home (personal communication from Claudia Maderna-Sieben, dated 15 January 2021). It should be noted that the tapes conserved at the Centro Studi Bruno Maderna in Bologna are not taken into account here; this refers to the sources cataloged as "B15," "B16," "B50," and "C1," which turned out to be copies of tapes present in other archives, accompanied by often misleading indications (see above, note 30).

72   These are two "Scotch 3M" tapes (18cm, 19cm/sec., mono, cardboard box), cataloged at PSS-BMC as "TS 1001" and "TS 1012" (see Ex. 6). In a list of tapes compiled by Maderna's heirs between 1996 and 1997, enclosed with the material delivered to PSS-BMC in 1998, these two copies are listed as "Band 3" and "Band 18" (numbering also transcribed on a label that Claudia Maderna-Sieben placed on the *recto* of the boxes reproduced in Ex. 6, together with the date "2.2.96").

NOS video but divided into four clips of various lengths.[73] In this case, the pieces are not listed on the box, but we find just a general handwritten indication (not by the author): "SATYRICON – BRUNO MADERNA."

As can be seen in Example 6, the first of the two reels that make up the set ("Reel I") contains eleven pieces (the numbering from "1" to "10" follows the subdivision into "9" and "9bis" of *Trimalchio e le flatulenze,* recorded twice, with and without voice). The second ("Reel II") has three pieces, numbered from "1" to "2bis" (in this case, too, the numbering derives from a double recording of the second number, *Lady Luck,* with the variant "instrumental only" and "instrum[ental] and vocal"). Once again, there is an almost complete analogy between the order and length of the pieces and the content of the two reels recorded at the NOS (Ex. 5).

And in fact, listening and sound analysis confirm that these tapes are a copy of the recording made in Hilversum on 19 March 1973. The pieces are only distributed differently – using up almost the whole of the first reel, and the rest following on the second – and numbered slightly differently.[74] These were precisely the reels that Maderna's widow entrusted to Alberto Cantoni in the early 1990s and which, in fact, provided the matrix for the Stradivarius record version.[75] In the absence of reliable data on the recording, Beate Christine Koepnick also provided fragments of evidently uncertain memories – where a general amnesia caused Maderna's urgent return to Darmstadt on 17 March to be forgotten, and the non-existent authorial execution in the Dutch studios to be erroneously dated to 24 March. And so, unintentionally and all too easily, the circulation of what, until now, has always been considered the "radio" or "chamber version," conducted by the composer himself, was launched. And this, despite the fact that no indications regarding either the date or the conductor appear on the box of both magnetic tapes or on any other sheet enclosed with these reels.

On closer inspection, the erroneous attribution of its content to Maderna's baton was due to a series of basic assumptions: no one knew about the NOS reels; a "radio version"

---

73 This is an "Agfa-Gevaert" tape (18 cm, 19cm/sec., mono, plastic box), cataloged at PSS-BMC as "TS 1004" ("Band 8" in the list provided by Maderna's heirs and on the label on the box; see above). To be precise, the four segments last respectively 10'40" (from the beginning, *Trimalchio e le flatulenze,* to the end of the first section of the *Matrona di Efeso;* nos. 1–5 in Ex. 3); 13'10" (from the third intervention on the tape to the end of the second section of the *Matrona;* nos. 6–11 in Ex. 3); 14'15" (from the third intervention on the tape to *Lady Luck,* voice only; nos. 12–22 in Ex. 3); and 11'25" (from the laughter preceding *Trimalchio e il monumento* to the end with the choral refrain of *Lady Luck;* nos. 23–26 in Ex. 3).

74 The different numbering on the second reel of the NOS (13 vs 12) depends on the addition, after no. "8" (*Fortunata e Eumolpus*), of a specific number ("9") for the *Eumolpus Fuga* (see Ex. 5, where "fugue" is incorrectly transcribed as "polka"). To note that the playing time of the individual parts remains unchanged in both sets of reels (PSS and NOS); it should be remembered that, as mentioned previously (see above, note 11), the *Eumolpus Fuga* was initially incorporated in the number that bears the name of *Fortunata e Eumolpo,* and that these parts must in any case follow one another without a break.

75 Alberto Cantoni confirmed this during our meeting in Cremona on 2 May 2012. See also note 24. Although the Stradivarius CD specifies that it is a "stereo" recording, sound analysis has shown that the source is clearly mono and that, during the production of the record, a stereo subdivision was only tacitly simulated by carrying out minimal tweaks between the sound levels (low and high) between the two channels. This operation, just like the source of the master tapes and all the remaining information, is not mentioned in the CD.

EX. 7   Autograph list by Bruno Maderna in the notebook "*Schrijfblok*," fol. 32; PSS-BMC.

had already been discussed in the earliest studies on Maderna;[76] and moreover the tapes came from the composer's own private archive. The autograph writing on the back of the reels did the rest: they were understood and cataloged around 1996 as masters or copies of the author's performance, and were interpreted as such in all the studies that were to follow.[77] And as if that were not enough, the misunderstanding about the "author's order" was later strengthened by the existence, in a notebook preserved among the material for *Satyricon*,[78] of an autograph list that refers precisely to the contents of these reels (→ **EX. 7**).

---

76 See above, pp. 28–29, with specific reference to the 1985 book *Documenti* (see note 14), p. 315. We should remember that the very data provided by the editors of the fact sheet on *Satyricon*, for the information on the "oratorial" radio version, drew on the same materials and information received from Maderna's widow.

77 To confirm the misunderstanding which arose in the earliest phases of the organization of the composer's private archive after his death, it should be noted that on the list of tapes drawn up by the heirs in the period prior to the delivery of the material to PSS (see note 72), these reels are included in the first set of sound documents in the chapter "Tonbänder Leitung Bruno Maderna" (tapes conducted by Bruno Maderna). It thus seems even more paradoxical that his widow refused to allow the release of the contents of the third tape (see note 24), attributed – rightly, in this case – to Lucas Vis.

78 This is the same notepad ("*Schrijfblok*") already mentioned in note 12.

But this list, actually, served a different purpose and moves us on a little further in the history of *Satyricon*, that is, close to September 1973 and to the preparatory stages of the revival of the opera scheduled for the following March 1974 at Milan's Piccola Scala.

In such a precarious state of health, Maderna takes up the same notebook he had used at the beginning of the year, just before the rehearsals in Amsterdam. He leaves several blank pages to separate the new notes from the old ones, and dedicates the last three sheets to a sort of diary of the radiotherapy sessions he underwent in September 1973 and to some notes on the revival of *Satyricon*, scheduled for 1974. First, he transcribes by hand the titles and the playing times of each of the pieces contained on the two reels reproduced in Example 6; then, on the next page, he notes (perhaps after having listened to that same sound source) a list of the seven characters in the opera – from Trimalchio to Criside – writing alongside it the names of potential contenders for those vocal parts. (Alongside the part of Niceros, the words "part to be done" immediately catch our attention, further confirming that these pages have never really been lost: quite simply, they were never composed.)[79] In the first half of October, Maderna was supposed to meet the managers of the future Milanese production in Milan;[80] these notes may plausibly be a reflection of this.

One might imagine that, precisely in view of this new revival of *Satyricon* in Italy, Maderna had taken care to request the NOS to provide him a copy of the recordings from the Dutch performances, via the RAI Studio di Fonologia in Milan. In the second half of 1973, the only "official" recording in the Dutch archives was the one made in the Hilversum studio by Vis on 19 March 1973 (Ex. 5).[81] A copy of the two reels was thus sent to the Studio di Fonologia, together with a new "recording report" in which all the data relating to the content were transcribed (→ **EX. 8**).[82] The report carefully and unequivocally pointed out that it was "TV" material.

Compared to the original tapes (Ex. 5), the pieces reproduced in Example 8 were copied in a different order, which actually corresponds to (and finally explains) the one found on the copies owned by the composer (Ex. 6). (In brief, these reels preserved at the Studio di Fonologia were the ones that Maderna himself or a technician from the same Studio used to generate the copies that later came into his widow's possession (Ex. 6) and which, in turn, constituted both the master for the Stradivarius CD – actually,

---

79   The names of the singers (mostly Italian) Maderna put on the list (fol. 33 of the notepad) only partially correspond to the ones finally selected for the cast of the Milanese revival. The two sheets can be dated to September 1973, thanks to the aforementioned hospital notes that neatly come before on fol. 31. It is interesting to learn that in a note on fol. 25 of the same pad, datable between May and June 1973, Maderna defines *Satyricon* as a "musical comedy."

80   See the telegram Riccardo Allorto (Teatro alla Scala) sent to Maderna on 16 September 1973 (PSS-BMC), which refers to the dates of the meeting and mentions, among other things, the performers engaged.

81   See above, note 20.

82   Tapes "Agfa," mono, 38 cm/sec, later cataloged as "Fon. 104" and "Fon. 105." There are no documents in the Archives of the Studio di Fonologia that reveal the exact date of the arrival of the tapes at RAI in Milan. The writing on the recording report and on the *recto* of the boxes is by an unidentified NOS studio technician. The writing on the spine of the boxes "B. Maderna *Satyricon* I Tempo [Fon. 104] / II Tempo [Fon. 105]" is by Marino Zuccheri. Note that the numbering and information on the pieces in Ex. 8 are exactly the same as in the file sheet reproduced in Example 5.

TV   *gegevens bij banden laten*

NEDERLANDSE OMROEP STICHTING TECHNISCHE DIENST RADIO HOOFDAFD. PROGRAMMATECHNIEK

DAGRAPPORT STUDIODIENST   N⁰ 40800

Studiogebouw	hck/eck ck rk	Programma	dag, datum
		Bruno Maderna : „Satyricon"	

INSTALLATIE KOMPLEET EN IN ORDE: ______________________ (Handtekening Programma-technicus)

Tijd	Ruimte	Aard van het programma	Programma-technicus	Opmerkingen — lijntijden — enz.
BAND I				
1.30		1) Lady Luck		
8.40		2) Trimalchio e il Monument		
7.30		3) Love's ECSTASY		
0.50		4) Scintilla - geluiden		
3.00		5) FORTUNATA + Slaju		
4.13	—	6) CARRIERA		
2.35		7) THE MONEY		
3.35		8) FORTUNATA E EUMOLDUS + ? slaju.		
	+	9) EUMOLPUS FUGA		
0.55	aut.	10) TRIMALCHIO E LE FLATULENZE a) met zang		
0.55				b) zonder zang
2.25		11) TRIMALCHIO CONTRA FORTUNATA		
BAND II				
2.50		12) LA MATRONA a) ⑦ – ⑲		
6.00		b) ⑲ – ⑥②		
7.00		c) ⑥③ – ⑦⓪		
		13) LADY LUCK (tutti)		
0.50		a) zonder koor		
0.50		b) met koor		

	Technisch Studiochef	Chef hfd afd. Progr. techn.
Paraaf gezien		
Datum		

Bestemd voor hoofdafd. Programmatechniek

EX. 8   Recording report enclosed with the "Fon. 104" and "Fon. 105" tapes, kept in the Archives of the RAI Studio di Fonologia, Milan (Museo degli Strumenti Musicali, Castello Sforzesco, Milan).

a third-generation copy – and the basis for the autograph list copied in the notebook.) And these two reels kept in the archives of the Studio di Fonologia remove any possible doubt as to whether this recording might be used as an eventual "version" for an autonomous broadcast. To find the answer, all one needs to do is take a look at both the original boxes of the two tapes (→ **EX. 9**), where the following, now blatantly obvious, indication stands out:

"B. Maderna, *Satyricon* / TV-play back band."

Summa summarum: a "radio" or "concert version" never existed. And it was only an incredible chain of misunderstandings that caused a simple recording of a soundtrack, intended as the playback material of a television production, to be published and interpreted to

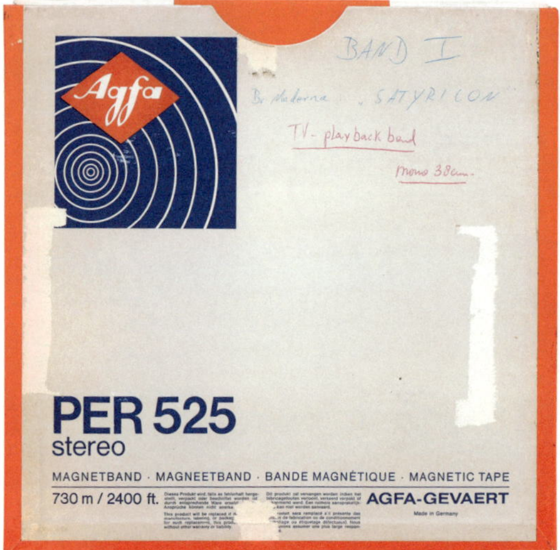
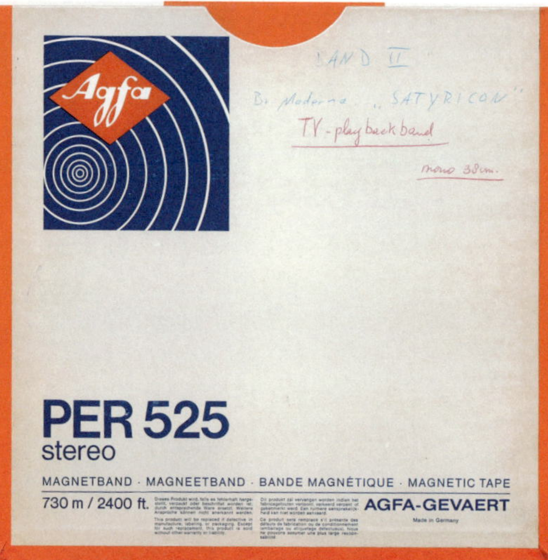

EX. 9   *Satyricon* tapes box "Fon. 104" (*Band I*) and Fon. 105 (*Band II*), housed at the Archives of the RAI Studio di Fonologia in Milan (Museo degli Strumenti Musicali, Castello Sforzesco, Milan).

this day as an "author's version." The very order of recording depended exclusively on management issues and the availability of the soloists and ensembles,[83] also considering that studio time was limited to four hours (Ex. 5). It was precisely that "routined, and performed theatrical production," demanded by the singers in opposition to the formal changes made by the director (see App. 2, p. 57), which allowed Maderna's substitute (Lucas Vis) to record everything quickly, according to a convenient ordering that has nothing to do with any interpretation or dramaturgical elaboration of the parts of the work.

All That Remains Is…

…the score, with its structure derived from a precise *"proposition de Bruno Maderna"* (proposal by Bruno Maderna), as the publisher Salabert noted in the last printed edition, which introduces new information and a mechanical layout that replaces the copyist manuscript published in 1974.[84]

This source allows us to remain in the same orbit of "September 1973," where some of the materials mentioned in the preceding pages have led us. In fact, this is the time period to which almost all the existing studies date the aforementioned manuscript sheet, considered as the basis the author sent to Salabert for the fine-tuning of the edition

---

83 A careful analysis of the order given in the recording sheet (Ex. 5) shows how the solo parts precede the duets, four-part ensembles, and the tutti finale.

84 See above, note 10. Note that in the score published in 1974 there is no mention of the authorship of the order of the numbers as they are set out and indicated in the index.

(→ **EX. 10**).[85] This order, let us note, would provide the last (and only) trace of an "authorial intent" regarding what could *also* be a possible performance order for *Satyricon*.

The emphasis on *also* refers to the already noted uniformity between the final structure established by the composer for the printed edition and the performative structure of the world premiere (→ **EX. 3**). However, one wonders why – considering the much discussed modular and open nature of the work – Maderna presented the publisher with an order that repeats, indeed "freezes," a given order (that of the world premiere), even going so far as to number its internal parts systematically from "1" to "21," and not without inaccuracies (as in the case of Niceros).

The Salabert score was far from ready for its world premiere. On that occasion, Maderna used his autograph manuscript as his conducting score, which was then used by Vis in all the following repeat performances and certainly until its revival in Tanglewood in August 1973.[86] There is no difference between Maderna's autograph score and the score published in 1974 after the composer's death: listening to the recording of the world premiere confirms that not only the order, but the level of editing of the individual parts corresponds almost exactly to the Salabert edition; even on the musical level, nothing performed by either the singers or the instrumentalists differs from the published score.[87]

With this awareness, and since we lack any reliable documentary evidence that allows us to establish exactly *when* Maderna delivered his materials to the publisher,[88] it is useful to go back and examine that "Maderna original" manuscript dated "3 September 1973," that is, the order that would set the final form of the score (→ **EX. 10**). At this point

---

85   PSS-BMC (2 fols., photocopy). The document is cited as "Maderna original of 3 September 1973" in *Documenti* (see note 14), p. 316; Mathon, "À propos du *Satyricon*" (see note 13), p. 572, with diplomatic transcription on p. 592; Gerlach, "Bruno Maderna *Satyricon*" (see note 18), pp. 53 and 74, with diplomatic transcription on p. A7; Vincis, "À propos de la nature modulable du *Satyricon*" (see note 12), p. 25n; Mathon, "À propos du *Satyricon*" (see note 13), p. 70; and Pasticci, "La presenza del *Satyricon*" (see note 4), p. 95. Fabbi, "Cena sociale" (see note 13), p. 87, does not mention the schema itself, but states that the score was prepared "on Maderna's indications." Zucconi, "*Satyricon*" *di Bruno Maderna* (see note 12), p. 24, is alone in advancing the hypothesis that it is not Maderna's handwriting, although she does consider it as an "autograph list […] intended for the Salabert publishing house" (p. 72).

86   See above, note 17. A copy of Maderna's autograph score used for the revival in the USA was recently donated to PSS by Ian Strasfogel. On the drafting level, it is identical to the copy preserved among the materials for *Satyricon* in BMC (see further on in this essay).

87   And this even though in a presentation of the work published just before the premiere, in *Opera Journaal* (see note 29), Strasfogel had stated that some parts had been improvised and, again in the note cited at the beginning of this essay, emphasis was placed on the "improvisational and aleatoric techniques of the score." In actual fact, the only margin of improvisation that can be heard is that implicit in the "programmed alea" common to Maderna's late compositional style, always achieved on the basis of a written track (see above, note 9).

88   Despite several archival search requests sent to the managers of Salabert editions in recent years, only after completion of the first draft of this chapter, has it been confirmed that in the French publisher's archives "there is no trace of the [original] drafts" or other documents that serve to date the deposit of materials at Salabert (e-mail from Bruno Leroy, 18 February 2021). Thus, the only Maderna document known to date regarding the preparation of the printed edition is a generic note, datable to the end of 1972 and written on a loose sheet from "*Skizzenbuch 6*" (see note 45), in which, among the various scores that need to be fine-tuned for printing, the composer scheduled to finish the score for *Satyricon* by "the summer of 1973" (PSS-BMC).

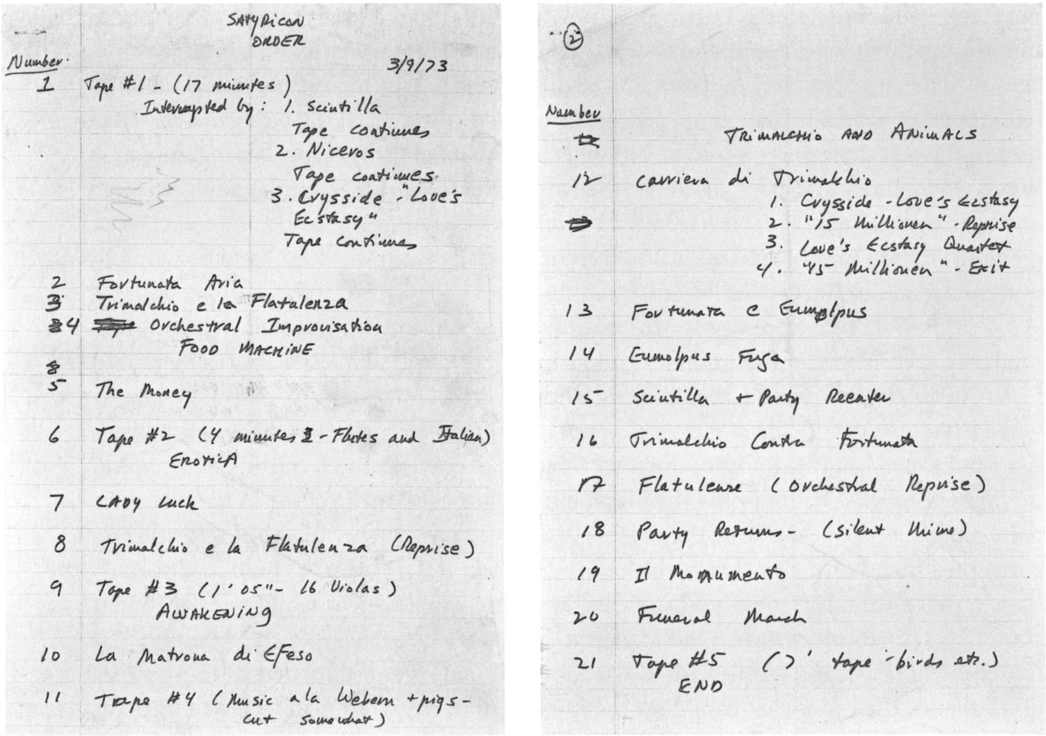

SATYRICON
ORDER
3/9/73

Number

1 Tape #1 - (17 minutes)
Interrupted by: 1. Scintilla
Tape continues
2. Niceros
Tape continues
3. Cryssyde "Love's Ecstasy"
Tape continues

2 Fortunata Aria
3 Trimalchio e la Flatulenza
4 Orchestral Improvisation
FOOD MACHINE
5 The Money
6 Tape #2 (4 minutes - Flutes and Italian)
EROTICA
7 LADY Luck
8 Trimalchio e la Flatulenza (Reprise)
9 Tape #3 (1' 05" - 16 Violas)
AWAKENING
10 La Matrona di Efeso
11 Tape #4 (Music a la Webern + pigs - cut somewhat)

(2)

Number

TRIMALCHIO AND ANIMALS
12 Carriera di Trimalchio
1. Cryssyde - Love's Ecstasy
2. "15 Millionen" - Reprise
3. Love's Ecstasy Quartet
4. "45 Millionen" - Exit
13 Fortunata e Eumolpus
14 Eumolpus Fuga
15 Scintilla + Party Reenter
16 Trimalchio Contra Fortunata
17 Flatulenza (Orchestral Reprise)
18 Party Resumes - (silent mime)
19 Il Monumento
20 Funeral March
21 Tape #5 (?' tape - birds etc.)
END

EX. 10 "SATYRICON ORDER": handwritten sheets dated "3/9/73"; 2 fols., photocopy; PSS-BMC.

in the reconstruction of *Satyricon*'s performance history, the importance of this document is now twofold, since not only does it tell us of the order that the composer gave to his score, but also the one that was repeated in every performance, from the one in Scheveningen to the last one in Brussels.

A first glance already reveals a blunder that has been immortalized ever since the first distant mention of this document (dated 1985):[89] the hand that drew up that handwritten list is simply *not* Maderna's.

The differences or mistakes in the spelling of the titles of the individual parts (one of the many: *Cryssyde* with double "s");[90] the frequent use of words in English, a language little used by Maderna; the use of the "#" symbol next to the numbers of the tapes: all this, and much more, suggests writing characteristics far from European customs. The evidence piles up and seems to lead directly to someone who, on the occasion of the premiere, was

89 See above, note 85.
90 Some inaccuracies in the transcription of the titles of the individual passages are the same to those found in the *Synopsis* printed on the occasion of the Dutch premiere (think for example of "la Flatulenza," see Ex. 3, "Première 1973" column, no. 3).

responsible for the direction and dramaturgy of the opera: Ian Strasfogel. As an American, however, he would have written the date by putting the month before the day, in which case this manuscript should no longer be dated 3 September 1973, but brought forward to 9 March of the same year, that is to say, exactly one week from the premiere of its stage debut. If we accept the aforementioned rehearsal schedule drawn up by Maderna, we would then be close to the start of the "final" stage rehearsals, scheduled from Monday 12 to Thursday 15 March.[91]

"An ordering of the varied narrative elements has been found …": about fifty years after stating these words in the program notes of the premiere (Ex. 1), it is Strasfogel himself who dismisses any doubts in this regard and adds further information as to why that dramaturgical schema was drawn up:

> The document [Ex. 10] is indeed in MY handwriting. It is my plan for the performance order of the opera at its premiere in Amsterdam.
>
> [...] finally it was March of 1973, I was arriving to do my first production in Europe as a young director and I had absolutely no idea of what this opera was. None. I had never seen a note of music, a page of text... [...] I went to the American Hotel in Amsterdam (where Bruno was staying) in the evening of the first rehearsal to get the score, which I had never seen! [...] there was Bruno, and there were piles of music paper [...] "there will be a little *duettino*, a little *quartetto*"... a little this a little that... I could immediately see the sum [...] but it was... very disturbing to me. I finally turned to Bruno and I said: "This is ok, but I will work on an order." I need that list [...], that is, the performance order for Amsterdam.[92]

Far from having been drawn up or entirely thought up for the score, the order in question refers to the dramaturgical organization of the world premiere planned by Strasfogel (*along with* Maderna). We can finally start with a clean slate: on the one hand, the "authorial" vision of the order of pieces printed in the score disappears; and, on the other, some obvious anomalies present in the printed edition are explained.[93] Moreover, the same performance order of the world premiere is put back in the right perspective of a context of shared responsibility ("*our* stage realization"), as is often the case between composer and director in musical theater works.

---

91   This is the rehearsal schedule mentioned in note 44. The schedule covers the dates of all rehearsals (in separate sections, with solos, etc.) between 14 February and 16 March 1973 (the day of the world premiere).

92   The first quotation comes from a private communication (e-mail) from Ian Strasfogel, sent to me on 10 December 2011. The second comes from a long interview Strasfogel gave to Veniero Rizzardi and myself on 17 December 2011 (unpublished).

93   A final word about the case of the piece "I.2 *Niceros*," indicated in the score as lost. As already mentioned, a solo number for Niceros never came to be composed. In the recording of the world premiere, one hears at the beginning the number "Criside II," followed by a version of "Love Ecstasy," performed by just Criside and Niceros (see Ex. 3). Perhaps because this recording was not available or known at the time, and since there was no trace of a solo piece (or of this duet), it was therefore indicated as "*perdu*" by the publisher.

"Besides, when the gods want something done…"

At the end of this journey, we are left with only one of the four performance versions considered to be the author's – the one relating to the world premiere – and this too is only half an authorial version.

The "mobility" of the work thus needs to undergo a profound rethinking, and a single piece of information must be taken into account – one that, yes, undoubtedly has to do with the author: the configuration of the files of the individual parts delivered to the publisher for the finalization of the score. Because, although the existing materials do not allow us to understand *when* Maderna sent his manuscripts to Salabert, they do however permit us to understand *what* he sent, which was the separate vocal/instrumental sections (Ex. 2), collected in single files probably intended to be laid out in the same way. The drafts of each of the files were transcribed by the copyist in charge and, as was customary at Salabert and as stipulated in the contract,[94] sent to Maderna for proofreading in two parts from the second half of October 1973 onwards. The progress of the preparations for the Milanese revival scheduled for March 1974 meant there was no time to be lost. The second tranche of the proofs was sent to the composer by Salabert's Deputy General Manager, Constant Minescaut, on 9 November, along with the following message:

> Dear Maestro and Friend,
> I have just sent you the rest of the proofs of the SATYRICON score so you can make your corrections and send it back to us.
> I hope that my first mailing dated 19 October was well received.
> I am sorry to put pressure on you, but we urgently need your corrections and your "ok for printing" so that we can move on to print the copies and send them to the various organizations that wish to receive them, including the Piccola Scala.[95]

Maderna died in Darmstadt only a few days after receiving this letter, sent together with a score that would neither be corrected nor given an "OK for printing" by the composer. The loose, untouched files were later assembled, numbered in an order wrongly confused as an "author's arrangement," and printed *post mortem*, with the consent of his heirs, completely unchanged from the proofs sent by the publisher.

We will never know if the author saw the sending of those files as a prerequisite for the fine-tuning of a score completely unlike the one we have today.[96] Likewise, only more in-depth research on the tapes will provide answers to questions that are still open

---

94 See above, notes 47 and 10. The printed proofs sent by Salabert to Maderna, along with Maderna's original manuscripts (used as antigraphs) are among the materials for the work in PSS-BMC. The sixteen sections are variously distributed in seven single folders. Only the file for *Trimalchio contra Fortunata* is not included in a folder.

95 Letter on Editions Salabert letterhead paper, sent to the composer in Darmstadt (PSS-BMC; original in French; partially published in Italian in Maderna, *Amore e curiosità* (see note 2, p. 636). The same letter also asks ("trés urgent") for the approval of Flavio Testi's Italian translation of the *Satyricon* texts (later used for the Milanese performance). Minescaut sent Maderna another letter about the Italian texts on 26 October 1973 (PSS-BMC; reproduced in Zucconi, *"Satyricon" di Bruno Maderna* (see note 12), p. 87).

96 Nonetheless, given the current state of research, one hopes that Editions Salabert will give permission for a new critical edition of *Satyricon* that corrects obvious errors and provides for the reproduction of the dramaturgical schemes outlined by Maderna in his papers.

regarding the "definitive nature" of the five tapes held by the publisher. Nonetheless, now that the field has been cleared of some interpretive debris that has accumulated over time, and the work has been relieved of some undue "authorial" burdens, one fact stands out loud and clear: the parts that make up *Satyricon* are to be seen as single planets of a universe, but which – as in *Ausstrahlung* – are well anchored within a "solid structure" and mobile within the limits in which their directionality, or their orbit, is dictated by a *choice* between given elements, and not by *chance*. And at the center of this solid and self-contained system is a star that illuminates and moves the implicit orbits of the individual planets: the text.

Appendix

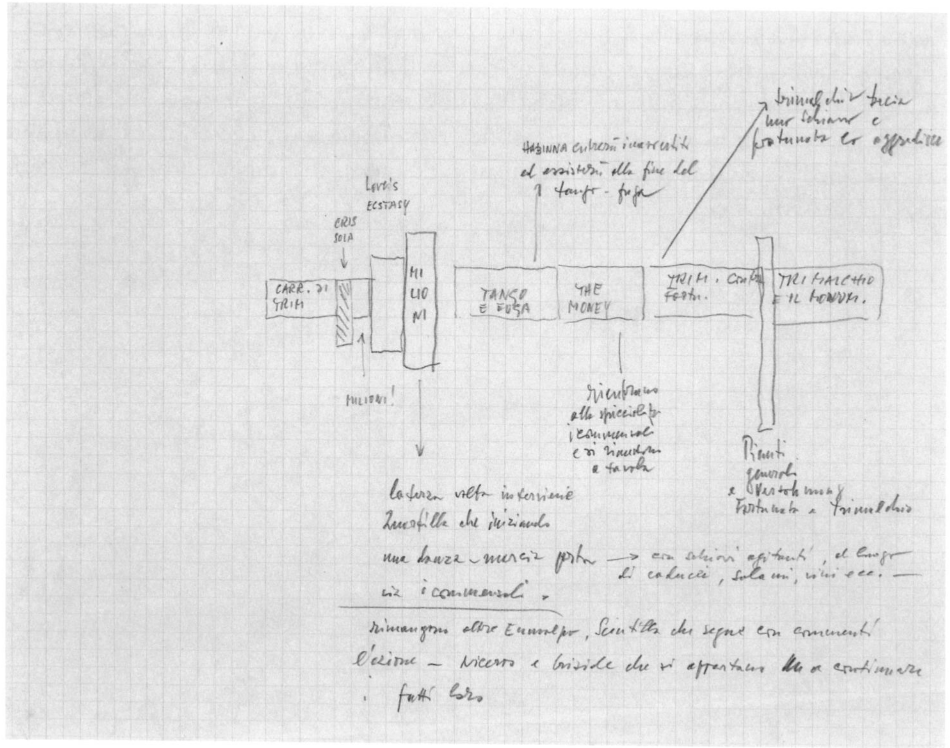

APP. 1   Bruno Maderna, sketch of the dramaturgical evolution
of some sections of *Satyricon;* PSS-BMC.

Mr. Stefan Felsenthal,   7 April 1973
Head Cultural Programmes
Netherland Broadcasting Corporation
Dienst Televisie Programma
Postbus 10, Hilversum
HOLLAND

Re: Satyricon, Director Wilhelmina HOEDEMAN

We the undersigned performers of SATYRICON collectively and of
one accord issue the following:

This was a rehearsed, routined, and performed theatrical production
which was changed into a totally new production--without rehearsal,
direction, and even without explanation of the director's concept.
This is, of course, an impossibility!

We were given no opportunity to approve or even listen to the sound
tapes.

We were given no opportunity to approve or disapprove the costumes,
especially with regard to nudity.

We were expected to work with extras that had no idea of the piece
as a whole; nor could we rehearse with them.

We most vigorously protest:

    1) the use of rotten, filthy food, including calves'eyes, which
       was thrown on us;
    2) having a fire hose turned on us at full force like rioters;
    3) having pails of soapy water thrown on us;
    4) the use of smoke bombs, from which everyone suffered smoke
       inhalation and sore throats and several people became violently ill.
       When one of these bombs actually caught fire, instead of being
       extinguished, the smoke from the fire was fanned into the set!
       Worst of all, our approval was not asked; nor were we forewarned
       of these outrages.

As performers, we all are dependent on our bodies and our voices for
our livelihood, and these abuses jeopardized our health and voices.
Throughout the entire production, and particularly at the end, we
feel that we were treated like stage properties or animals; not as
artists, and certainly not as human beings.

APP. 2   Letter to Stefan Felsenthal, Head of Cultural Programs at NOS,
dated 7 April 1973 and signed by all the singers and actors of the
production; carbon copy from the private archives of William Neill
(with kind permission).

BENEDETTA ZUCCONI

"In the Beginning Was the Word"
The Sung Text as a Unifying Element in the Composition of Bruno Maderna's *Satyricon*

In an interview with Aldo Maranca in August 1964, Bruno Maderna spoke of the relationship between music and poetry in ancient Greece:

> It was a single, indivisible art. It was impossible for the Greeks to imagine it as two parts of a whole. It was a unity. And actually, music had the task of catalyzing the words and the spoken word informed the music of its concepts.[1]

These words are much more than a mere reflection on the artistic legacy of a remote era; in light of Maderna's musical production, they seem to contain a genuine creative manifesto which may have come to its greatest fruition in his last works.

Just seven years after the interview with Maranca, Maderna began composing the central nucleus of *Satyricon,* his last work for musical theater and a modern transposition of the homonymous Latin novel by Petronius Arbiter. He completed the work two years later, in March 1973.[2] The opera is a mixture of languages, styles, genres, and musical quotations, and has until now been ascribed the status of "fragmentation *au carré*" (fragmentation squared).[3] Poised between the concepts of open work, pop-art, and an early postmodernism, Maderna's premature death in November of the same year also played a role in affecting the reading of *Satyricon,* further implanting the idea of it being an unfinished composition.[4]

---

1   "Colloquio con Aldo Maranca," in *Amore e curiosità: Scritti, frammenti e interviste sulla musica,* ed. Angela Ida De Benedictis, Michele Chiappini, and Benedetta Zucconi (Milan: il Saggiatore, 2020), pp. 101–12: 105.

2   *Satyricon*'s premiere took place on 16 March 1973 in Scheveningen as part of the Holland Music Festival, for which Maderna had been commissioned to compose the opera. This version corresponds to the first completion of the work, as well as the only fully authorial one (for further details see, in this book, the essay by Angela Ida De Benedictis, pp. 19–57). The composer's death a few months later (see below) prevents us from hypothesizing about any possible developments of its general structure.

3   Geneviève Mathon, "L'écriture dramaturgique dans le *Satyricon* de Bruno Maderna," in *Musiques vocales en Italie depuis 1945: esthétique, relations texte/musique, techniques de composition,* ed. Pierre Michel and Gianmario Borio, Millénaire 3 (Notre-Dame-de-Bliquetuit, 2005), pp. 61–75: 66.

4   For an in-depth look at the reception of *Satyricon* and the concepts of incompleteness and postmodernism attributed to it, see also Raymond Fearn, *Bruno Maderna* (Chur: Harwood, 1990), pp. 217–91; Geneviève Mathon, "À propos du *Satyricon*," in *à Bruno Maderna,* ed. Geneviève Mathon, Laurent Feneyrou, and Giordano Ferrari, vol. 1 (Paris: Basalte, 2007), pp. 69–82, previously pubd. in *Musique et dramaturgie: Esthétique de la représentation au XXe siècle,* ed. Laurent Feneyrou (Paris: Publications de la Sorbonne, 2003), pp. 571–93); or again Mario Baroni, preface to Nicola Verzina, *Bruno Maderna: Étude historique et critique* (Paris: Harmattan, 2003).

There is no doubt that *Satyricon* defies any analysis that tends to attribute the entire composition to a unitary compositional process or a univocal formal principle. As is known, Maderna makes use of several languages, styles, and compositional methods in the composition of the opera: alongside the massive use of quotations from popular classics, there are stylistic loans from the nineteenth-century operatic tradition, from cabaret, from operetta, and from twentieth-century musical theater (in particular Berg and Weill). And there is more: the stylistic imitations also contemplate the use of acoustic instruments to reproduce the typical sounds of early electronic music, and there is no shortage of parts (such as *La Matrona di Efeso* and *Trimalchio e le flatulenze*) where Maderna takes up dodecaphonic and serial composition again, in order to emphasize specific dramatic situations. In terms of dramatic structure and compositional choices, each of the episodes that make up the work seems to be an autonomous organism in its own right. This idea was further encouraged by the composer's choice to divide the individual pieces into loose-leaf files, a solution the publisher later adopted in the printing of the posthumous score.[5]

However, the study of precompositional materials, sketches, and drafts, in light of Maderna's words about the inseparability of music and text in ancient Greece, allows us to recognize a common feature in the creation of the work, an element of unity in what appears to be a Babel of a composition, that is, the voice and its being the bearer of a semantically connoted text. In fact, the only constant in this great miscellany of styles and compositional solutions, which also, as mentioned before, regards the choice of language (the libretto contemplates the presence of English, German, French, and Latin), is precisely the preeminence of the sung word that guides the process of musical composition. These are the underlying principles that allow us to observe a common working method for more or less all the different pieces of the work.[6]

In the handling of the vocal element, that is to say, in the elaboration of the text and, later, in its rendering in sound, one can recognize a single guiding principle, whose ultimate goal lies precisely in that ancient indivisible union of words and music.[7]

---

5   In some files, in addition to the piece noted in the score, there is also a reference to one or more electronic interventions. For a synopsis of the parts that make up the work (with related titles), as they are laid out in the score, see the essay of De Benedictis on pp. 24 and 30 of this book.

6   Maderna, in an interview on the occasion of *Satyricon*'s premiere, mentions the "magic of language" used in the theater. See "Prima del *Satyricon*: Colloquio con Frans van Rossum," in Maderna, *Amore e curiosità* (see note 1), pp. 312–17: 313.

7   Maderna is certainly not the first who wanted musical theater to return to the classical models of Greek music, and he was not alone in claiming them as a model. Since its origins, there have been a series of similar cases also involving – apart from the well-known examples of Gluck and Wagner – other twentieth-century authors such as Darius Milhaud and Hans Werner Henze (see Silke Leopold, "Singend sprechen – sprechend singen: Versuch einer Antwort auf die Frage, was der Gesang in der Oper zu suchen hat," in *Komponieren für die Stimme: Von Monteverdi bis Rihm: Ein Handbuch*, ed. Stephan Mösch (Kassel: Bärenreiter, 2017), pp. 22–36.

8   Interview with Piet Hein van de Poel on *Satyricon*, recorded on 16 March 1973 on the occasion of the opera's premiere. The translation given here, based on the original recording (in German), differs from the version found in Fearn, *Bruno Maderna* (see note 4), pp. 324–26: 324 ("Interview on Dutch Radio after *Satyricon*, March 1973), which is based on the Italian version "Intervista alla radio olandese NOS dopo *Satyricon*," in *Bruno Maderna: Documenti*, ed. Mario Baroni and Rossana Dalmonte (Milan: Suvini Zerboni, 1985), pp. 111–14. For a new Italian translation see Maderna, *Amore e curiosità* (see note 1), pp. 318–25.

Maderna's words shortly after the Dutch premiere of *Satyricon* are most revealing in this respect: "I don't think at all that this way of composing works for other songs too. It is fine for me especially for Petronius."[8] Not only do these words enlighten us on the compositional choices made for the work as a whole, but they can also be used as a key to understanding how the individual pieces were conceived.[9]

It was Maderna himself who compiled the text for the opera by carrying out a complex work of transcription, translation, and reworking. This fact is certainly not to be taken for granted, since it attests to the very close link between the textual and musical layout, both emanating from the workings of a single mind. And that's not all: the vast amount of autograph materials relating to the composition of the text – currently housed in the Paul Sacher Foundation in Basel – allows one to understand at first glance the complexity of the compositional phases that preceded the preparation of the musical layout, as well as the importance attributed to this first step. Before he started to write the musical part for each of the pieces in *Satyricon,* Maderna carried out extensive work in elaborating the verbal component. The numerous documents speak volumes on his assiduous commitment to this first phase of preparation of the text. His sketches tell us that the choice of passages from Petronius took place in two phases, during which Maderna continuously trimmed down and fine-tuned the chosen texts. After his initial analysis of the episodes, probably in their Italian translation and sometimes in the original Latin version, Maderna then passed to a second phase in which he used editions in English, French, and German to draw up the final multilingual form of the libretto.[10] It is the composer himself who affirms, in the aforementioned interview after the opera's premiere: "For me the text was the main thing – just the text."[11] In a certain sense, the manipulation of the source text through the use of different translations, as well as the stylistic plurality of the subsequent musical choices, signals a continuity with the spirit of Petronius' *Satyricon,* which is also

---

9   Angela Ida De Benedictis has applied similar exegetical operations to *Venetian Journal* and *Ausstrahlung,* in which the author illustrates the unifying principles underlying what are apparently fragmented compositions. The present work aims to follow in the wake of this interpretive line. See therefore Angela Ida De Benedictis, "'Qui forse una cadenza brillante': Viaggio nel *Venetian Journal* di Bruno Maderna," *Acta Musicologica* 72, no. 1 (2000), pp. 63–105; idem, "Scrittura e supporti nel Novecento: alcune riflessioni e un esempio (*Ausstrahlung* di Bruno Maderna)," in *La scrittura come rappresentazione del pensiero musicale,* ed. Gianmario Borio (Pisa: ETS, 2004), pp. 237–91; and idem, "*Ausstrahlung,* ou la textualité brisée d'un hymne à la vie," in *à Bruno Maderna* (see note 4), vol. 1, pp. 287–317.

10   As Maderna himself indicated in his sketches, the reference edition for the Latin text and the Italian translation is Petronio Arbitro, *Il romanzo satirico,* ed. Giovanni Alfredo Cesareo and Nicola Terzaghi (Florence: Sansoni, 1950). However, there are also references to the following Italian editions, used above all as a means of comparison with the Sansoni edition: Petronius Arbiter, *Satyricon: romanzo d'avventure e di costumi,* ed. Umberto Limentani (Genoa: Formiggini, 1912); and Petronio Arbitro, *Satyricon,* trans. Edoardo Sanguineti, illustrated by Bruno Cassinari (Milan: Palazzi, 1969). Instead, the English translation he used is Petronius, *The Satyricon,* trans. William Arrowsmith (New York: Mentor Classic, The New American Library, 1959), whereas, according to Maderna's notes, the French version seems to be Pétrone, *Le Satiricon,* préf. de Jean Dutourd, trans. and notes by Pierre Grimal (Paris: Librairie générale française, 1960). Although he gives no precise references for the German edition, it is most probably Petronius, *Satyrica: Schelmengeschichten,* Latin-German ed. by Konrad Müller and Wilhelm Ehlers (Munich: Ernst Heimeran, 1965).

11   Interview with Piet Hein van de Poel on *Satyricon* (see note 8).

characterized by a multiplicity of languages and styles of diverse origins; on the other hand, this is also consistent with Maderna's poetic path, since he had been making use of the principles of plurilingualism (as well as polystylism) in his works for quite some time: think for example of *Ausstrahlung,* or *Venetian Journal,* composed at almost the same time as *Satyricon.*

The Rhythmic Scansion of the Text as a Starting Point

The complexity of the creative process is evidenced by the number and variety of sketches and drafts Maderna prepared. The heterogeneous nature of these materials makes it difficult to consistently find the same compositional phases for each of the parts that make up the work (let alone the same degree of detail). However, the study of these materials does allow us to observe how Maderna first tries to establish the precise beat of the words for each piece. The first stages of composition are documented by the transcription of the selected texts on staff paper, accompanied by a rhythmic scansion of the syllables with no specified pitch (→ **EX. 1**).[12]

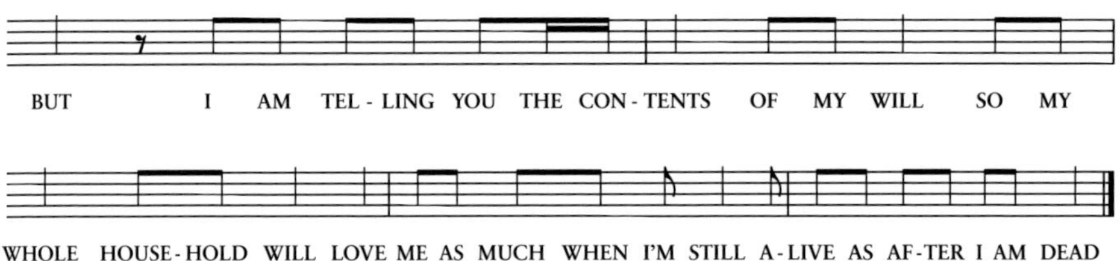

EX. 1   *Trimalchio e il monumento:* transcript of an early draft; PSS-BMC.

He uses this *modus operandi* for the longer pieces in the work, for which there is plenty of material attesting to the compositional moment: *Fortunata, Carriera di Trimalchio, Trimalchio e il monumento/Funeral March, Trimalchio contra Fortunata,* and some sections of *La matrona di Efeso.*[13] Maderna only starts to focus on the musical rendering after he has determined the rhythmic form of the text: he first establishes the pitch of the vocal line, usually integrated on a new staff and placed immediately below the one dedicated to the scansion of the text. Once this operation has been completed, he sets about composing the orchestral part, which in the first phase can be seen to be either in a reduced form of two or three fundamental lines, or as a succession of chords.

---

12   All the musical examples shown here in transcription come from the autograph material kept at PSS or from the edited score: Bruno Maderna, *Satyricon: opéra, livret d'après Petrone, texte français, allemand et latin de Bruno Maderna* (Paris: Salabert, © 1974, E.A.S. 17.091).

13   *Satyricon* was not the first work in which Maderna performed a rhythmic scansion of a text; examples can already be found in his compositions from the late 1940s onwards. See Angela Ida De Benedictis, *Radiodramma e arte radiofonica: Storia e funzioni della musica per radio in Italia* (Turin: De Sono, EDT, 2004), pp. 117–22 and n. 35, p. 118.

It is most likely that the currently available corpus of sketches and autograph materials regarding the compositional process of *Satyricon* is incomplete, due to the absence of any documents that illustrate the aforementioned compositional phases for some of the episodes of the work. Nevertheless, within the existing materials, the preliminary work of rhythmic scansion is applied particularly to numbers of a more declamatory nature, where the main conveyor of meaning is, precisely, the word. On the contrary, the pieces in which this procedure cannot be documented are characterized by a closed musical form, where the stylistic peculiarities of the music enclose the text within a defined framework: take for example *Fortunata e Eumolpus,* structured as a bipartite tango; *Eumolpus Fuga,* whose title comes from the form of the piece itself; the choral *Lady Luck;* or again *Trimalchio e le flatulenze,* in which the text is imprisoned in a series of repetitions of a basic musical motif.

After this constant emphasis on the predominance of the verbal part over the other aspects of the composition, it might sound paradoxical to say that there are some episodes in which the music – understood as a "code" with precise structural and formal conventions – determines the organization of the text itself. However, this is a choice that, once again, starts with or is directly conditioned by the content and structure of the verbal material. Thus, the primary role of the text in the choice of a specific style or a specific form is still confirmed. Take for example, once again, the piece *Eumolpus Fuga,* with its clear parallelism between Eumolpus's reticence toward Fortunata's advances, represented through the reference to the form of the fugue, and consequently also by the semantic ambiguity deriving from the word's double meaning in Italian ("*fuga*" = "fugue" but also "escape");[14] and it is obvious that, in such a context, all the elements of the composition have to converge toward the requirements imposed by this specific contrapuntal writing. It is at this point that the form of the fugue itself becomes a conveyor of meaning just as much as the initial textual content.

Regardless of the presence or absence of sketches that attest to the rhythmic scansion of the text, it should also be noted that there are hardly any musical drafts without vocal lines. The few pages relating only to the orchestral part of the pieces mostly refer to extremely circumscribed passages in which Maderna elaborates specific compositional techniques: this is the case with the serial composition of some moments in *La matrona di Efeso* or the serial procedure of transposition that Maderna applies to the individual motif of *Trimalchio e le flatulenze.* However, this always and only occurs at some point in the process of musical creation in which the connection between the vocal line and a first, even rudimentary, draft of the musical form has already been defined.

---

14   Maderna had already exploited the double semantic meaning of "*fuga*" in the *Fuga "Ignoramus"* ("Ignoramus" Fugue) in the finale of *Venetian Journal,* where it is used both as a compositional solution (also with the further meaning of a model of precision) and, literally, to signify the escape of the protagonist from a psychological and moral dilemma. For more on this, see the essay by Angela Ida De Benedictis, "Qui forse una cadenza brillante" (see note 9), particularly p. 100.

The Rhythmic Scansion of the Text as a Means of Expression

The leading role attributed to the voice in *Satyricon* means that Maderna has to take great care in ensuring that he maximizes not only the musical aspects of the vocal line, but also and above all its verbal content. In the various episodes of the work, even in the aforementioned variety of musical styles, the words are always clearly understandable in both the phonetic and semantic dimensions. Of course, a fundamental element for understanding the text is the precise scansion of its internal stress, which, for Maderna, means paying extreme attention to the relationship between word and music, that is, to the exact subdivision of the syllables within the meter of the composition. As often happens in similar cases, word stress is made to fall on the strong beats of every bar, and preferably at the salient points of the musical fabric, such as for example at the highest or lowest point of a melodic passage. Finally, a correct quantitative proportion is needed to scan the syllables in clearly perceptible musical figures, especially to avoid lengthy passages in which the unity of the discourse could be lost.

Given the fact that Maderna pays great heed to the accentual nature of the verbal text, it may come as some surprise to find an albeit sporadic number of passages in which this aspect seems to have been deliberately ignored. However, a closer look at these cases shows that this particular handling of the text is actually the result of precise compositional choices aimed at seeking specific dramatic and rhetorical effects.

Three emblematic cases are examined below: the first, relating to *Lady Luck*, bears witness to an unusual metric handling of the melodic material and line rhythm; the second, *Love's Ecstasy*, shows a certain poetic license in the use of internal word stress; finally, in *Trimalchio e le flatulenze*, we can observe the unnatural consonantal hyper-connotation of the individual notes.

Lady Luck   In *Lady Luck*, the *"inno morale"* (moral hymn) as Maderna himself called it in the preparatory sketches for the piece, the words of the protagonist Quartilla, marked in the score in a 3/4 rhythm, are extremely dissonant with the hyphenation of the text. In a first and then discarded draft of the piece, Maderna indicates a different, mainly binary, rhythmic scansion[15] (→ **EX. 2**).

Instead, in the latest redaction, identical to the score published later by Salabert, the text is set in a ternary meter, which does not match the metric structure of the verse (→ **EX. 3**).

By proposing a choral harmonization of the song's melody, the string accompaniment (counterpointed by the tuba) further highlights the discrepancy between a background that fits perfectly with the ternary scansion and the metrical restraints of the sung text (→ **EX. 4**).

---

15   This scansion is affected by the presence of a second, metrically regular, descending vocal line with different words (incipit: "I sing of living men, the things they say and do…"), which was then eliminated in the subsequent editions of the piece.

EX. 2   *Lady Luck:* detail of the transcription of a sketch from an early phase; PSS-BMC.

EX. 3   *Lady Luck:* transcription of the vocal line from Maderna's fair copy; PSS-BMC. See also *Satyricon* (Paris: Salabert, © 1974, E.A.S. 17.091).

EX. 4   *Lady Luck:* transcription of bb. 1–4 from Maderna's fair copy (except for the tuba line); PSS-BMC. See also *Satyricon* (Paris: Salabert, © 1974, E.A.S. 17.091).

Apart from undermining the regularity of the scansion, the discordance between the textual meter and the rhythm also leads to anomalies in the musical structuring of the verses: the melodic line of the song does not agree with the 3/4 scansion, thereby contravening the traditional rules that foresee, for example, that the harmonic degrees of tonic and dominant correspond to the strong beats, on which the ascending or descending melodic climaxes should also converge. In *Lady Luck,* therefore, there is no correspondence between the implicit harmony of the melodic line and the metrical factor. In this regard, take the first sentence, which reaches the tonic (F) at the height of the ascent, in correspondence with the first flat syllable of the second hemistich of the first line. However, this does not correspond, as would be expected, to a beat position, but to the second quarter-note of the bar, the weakest beat in the 3/4 time signature. This happens in the first sentence, in which the opening words contemplate the presence of an upbeat quarter-note, thus placing the downbeat on the flat syllable of the line, which is not the subject of the sentence ("we"), but the verb ("think"); furthermore, this insistence on the tonic, which reiterates the note and rhythm of the downbeat, rather than camouflaging the irregular position of the text (as would happen if there were a different scale degree on the second beat of the bar), serves to intensify the contrast. This because it actually brings about the consecutive sequence of two strong tempos, one imposed by the measure and the other by the text and the musical structure, thereby giving rise to what seems to be a hesitation right at the beginning of the piece. Something similar happens a few bars later, in the line "Lady Luck is in heaven" (Ex. 3), where one would expect an accent/strong beat on the words "Luck" and "heaven" in the sequence of long and short syllables; however, against all expectations, the intermediate word ("is") is stressed, once again producing a sense of hesitation.

So, what makes Maderna opt here for an imperfect metrical scansion of the textual and musical material? There is obviously a clear relationship between an unstable formal structure and a text that refers to the transience and uncertainty of human existence.[16] In addition, the sense of uncertainty conveyed by this musical structure is accompanied by an orchestral performance and general musical atmosphere that are at odds with the melody, and which are expressed in the placid and calm solemnity of a seventeenth-century-style hymn. And then again, the imprecise scansion of the text nullifies the authority of the "moral hymn" (which, in Petronius's work of fiction, is after all the brainchild of the churlish freedman Trimalchio): by adopting a procedure that seems to invoke songs invented by children (where metrical accuracy is the first element to disappear), Maderna actually weakens the moral significance of the text, undermining the credibility and force of the character's words. He seems to want to stage a trivialized and coarser version of Horace's *carpe diem,* but also to reveal – as indeed happened in Petronius's novel – the ill-concealed uneasiness of an existential condition that is indeed lucky but marked by the uncertainty of fate. To quote Eric Auerbach:

---

16   Emanuele Senici has identified similar distortion procedures in the finale of Giuseppe Verdi's *Falstaff,* "Tutto nel mondo è burla," another piece whose pompous tones are countermanded by an ironic key; see Emanuele Senici, "Verdi's *Falstaff* at Italy's Fin de Siècle," *The Musical Quarterly* 85, no. 2 (2001), pp. 274–310.

[I]t is easy to understand that a society of businessmen of the humblest origins is particularly suitable material for a representation of this nature, for conveying this view of things. Such a society most clearly reflects the ups and downs of existence, because there is nothing to hold the balance for it; its members have neither inward tradition nor outer stability; they are nothing without money.[17]

Love's Ecstasy   Just as happens in *Lady Luck*, there are several metrical irregularities in the three episodes whose words refer to the title of the poem by Propertius (*Criside I, Criside II, Love's Ecstasy*). However, in this case, the discrepancies no longer regard the phraseological stress, but those internal to the individual words of a text that has been stripped down, so to speak, to just the two words of the title (*Love's Ecstasy*), unchanged in all three pieces. Take for example the vocal line of *Criside II* (→ **EX. 5**).

EX. 5   *Criside II:* transcription of the vocal line from Maderna's fair copy; PSS-BMC. See also *Satyricon* (Paris: Salabert, © 1974, E.Λ.S. 17.091).

The scansion in bars is purely indicative here, as can be seen from Maderna's use of dashed lines: the horizontal nature of the piece and the lack of tonal references greatly weaken the need for a precise scansion. Instead, what stands out is the deliberate and constant inaccuracy in the placement of the tonic syllables. In fact, in none of the six repetitions of the textual parenthesis *Love's Ecstasy* does the stress correctly fall on the first syllable of "Ecstasy"; on the contrary, the second syllable is consistently emphasized from start to finish. And this does not only happen in the passage shown in Example 5: the same procedure is also implemented in *Criside I* and for three voices of the vocal quartet of *Love's Ecstasy* (Criside, Niceros, and Eumolpus), who sing the words of the text, while the fourth voice, Scintilla, only emits inarticulate sounds.

The solutions Maderna adopts to implement this improper scansion all consist in emphasizing the penultimate syllable of the word "Ec**sta**sy," at the same time obfuscating as much as possible the third and last syllable, which should by rights be stressed. First and foremost, although the piece lacks any precise metric indication, and the sound material, even graphically speaking, seems to be detached from the bar subdivisions, the harmonically weak penultimate syllable is always positioned on what is perceived as a strong

---

17   Eric Auerbach, "Fortunata," in *Mimesis: The Representation of Reality in Western Literature*, enlarged new edn., trans. Willard R. Trask, with a new introduction by Edward W. Said (Princeton, NJ: Princeton University Press, 2003), pp. 24–49: 29–30.

beat. On the contrary, proportionally much longer rhythmic values are always assigned to the third syllable, and the concomitance of these two measures means that the latter is perceived, for all intents and purposes, as an upbeat of the last syllable but one. It should also be added that on more than one occasion the unstressed syllable "-sta-" is found at the climax of a melodic ascent, an expedient that, as was already observed for *Lady Luck*, gives particular emphasis to this syllable.

The transparent sound of these three episodes (for example, in *Criside I* and *Criside II* the voice is accompanied by a descant solo instrument) and the extreme simplicity of a text made up of just two words go hand in hand in allowing us to understand these identical words. And it is precisely the sparse textual content that provides the interpretive key for the anomalous metric scansion. These pieces are completely devoid of narrative values, serving rather to circumscribe a situation with an erotic background. In fact, Maderna himself, in his notes, calls them *"atmosfera Ecstasy"* (Ecstasy atmosphere). The imprecise meter, therefore, helps to depict an ecstatic context intended as a blurring of the senses, assisted by other *topoi* of an extra-textual nature, aimed at recalling a Dionysian atmosphere. Think, for example, of the constant use of quite similar chromaticisms within the descant melodic lines, which constantly cross and weave in and out of each other. Or even a choice of timbre that sees the soprano's voice accompanied, in *Criside I* and *Criside II*, by instruments with clear Bacchic associations (english horn and flute respectively), whereas in *Love's Ecstasy* flute, clarinet, and bass clarinet echo the three voices that sing the words.

Trimalchio e le flatulenze   Something quite different happens in *Trimalchio e le flatulenze*, where instead of the metrical inaccuracies of *Lady Luck* and *Love's Ecstasy*, we find a sort of hyper-correctness. Trimalchio's words are carefully divided into syllables, and each syllable is assigned a single note of the musical sequence (→ **EX. 6**).

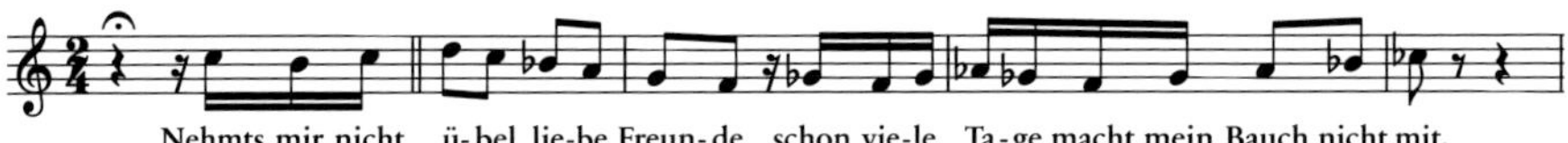

EX. 6   *Trimalchio e le flatulenze:* transcription of bb. 1–4 of the vocal line from Maderna's fair copy; PSS-BMC.

What transforms a perhaps not-so-unusual handling of the text into something quite particular is the very fact that the syllables of the German text, with its wealth of consonant sounds, are made to correspond to short rhythmic values that are mainly sixteenth-notes or at most eighth-notes. German phonetic density is therefore coupled with the brevity of rhythmic musical values. This makes the scansion of the text difficult and not smoothly flowing. And this is further heightened by the choices Maderna makes in terms of the timbre of the accompanying instruments for *Trimalchio e le flatulenze*, deciding on a quintet of mainly dark-timbred woodwinds (bass clarinet, bassoon, trumpet, and trombone) and only one clear timbre (a flute), which, however, has a role to play in terms of "sound-painting." In fact, not only does this choice of timbre serve to make the musical sequence even less fluid, but it also suggests a certain metaphorical and onomatopoeic parallelism between the sound of the instruments and the protagonist's bowel disorders evoked in the title, a practice that Maderna often adopted in his radio works.[18]

The resulting effect is pure comedy: the performer's difficulty in articulating the vocal line immediately relates to the problems Trimalchio is complaining of in the text ("Nehmts mir nicht übel, liebe Freunde, schon viele Tage macht mein Bauch nicht mit"; Don't take this wrong, dear friends, my stomach has been upset for many days); and the very melody itself, literally clogged with consonants, suggests a fitting simile for the protagonist's digestive issues.[19]

Vocal Styles

As stated before, *Satyricon* is characterized by an extreme variety of musical styles. This variety is paralleled by a mixture of different vocal styles, which can be distinguished both in terms of specific emission techniques (sung, spoken, recited, etc.), and also in the distinctive articulation of the vocal lines, which draw on a stylistic palette that includes, among other things, psalmody and recitative as well as lyric lingering and twentieth-century expressive singing. As we shall see, even though the different forms of singing adopted in *Satyricon* are all representative of a specific expressive characterization, they contribute in different measure to the formal definition of the pieces: if in fact the first two stylistic elements analyzed here create a single organism that indissolubly merges the formal structure of the piece and the musical content, the last two (expressive singing and *Sprechgesang*) are mere dramatic solutions that have no effect on the general form.

Operatic Singing   *Fortunata e Eumolpus*, *Eumolpus Fuga*, and *Lady Luck* are episodes that take inspiration from styles of past centuries, and here, quite naturally, Maderna adopts an approach that employs traditional singing, characterized by an operatic style with defined and recognizable melodic lines. However, a similar structure of singing can also be seen in *Criside* (*I* and *II*) and *Love's Ecstasy* as well as *Trimalchio e le flatulenze*. The main peculiarity of this approach is the relevance assumed by the sung melody, which is not there simply to be of service to the text, but actually to help in creating meaning. The degree of autonomy acquired by the melody unchains it from the text and even makes it become the driving element for the construction of meaning. It is no coincidence that the operatic singing style occurs in pieces where the text is ultimately less charged with meaning: the words carry little narrative value, outlining static situations in which the musical element becomes an indispensable tool for the construction of meaning. Finally, we must take into account the fact that the voice is handled in this way mainly in pieces characterized by a closed structure, in which there is a recognizable musical structure and no elements of indeterminacy.

---

18   On this see De Benedictis, *Radiodramma e arte radiofonica* (see note 13), in particular pp. 84–86.

19   Other scholars have identified the comic element of the piece as residing in the combination of a text with a trivial content and the German language, the language of philosophy par excellence; see for example, Roberto Fabbi, "Cena sociale: *Satyricon* e il 'politico,'" *Musica/Realtà* 67 (2002), pp. 83–100: 89.

A traditional operatic melodic vocal line is occasionally manifested in other pieces, but it never influences the formal structure, nor is it ever the only stylistic means used in the piece itself. These are basically points where the voice exploits borrowed traditional melodies, as happens quite often in *Carriera di Trimalchio* and *Trimalchio e il monumento*. A final observation must be made on the linguistic aspect: the aforementioned plurilingualism of *Satyricon* is actually concentrated in those sections mostly sung with a "traditional" vocalism, whereas only English is used for all the other vocal styles described below. This aspect excludes an equal and ultimately indifferent use of the various languages and, instead, establishes a precise hierarchy: English is the true language of the work, the zero degree of content transmission; the use of French, German, and Latin, on the other hand, seems to constitute a rhetorical medium useful for connoting a dramatic context or an inner condition.

Arioso   Then there is a second style of singing that is only slightly different from the one described above, not so much in terms of the singing technique, which once again is of a traditional nature, but for the intrinsic quality of the musical material and for its relationship to the text. This style retains some of the defining characteristics of an arioso,[20] and is mainly found in *The Money* and *La matrona di Efeso,* the episodes sung by the character of Habinnas. Here musical coherence seems to disintegrate in favor of an uninterrupted flow of melodic curves, responding more to needs imposed by verbal narration than to musical contingencies. The musical element is no longer a self-sufficient entity, since it is determined here by the course of the narrative, and it is through the latter that it acquires a complete sense. Obviously, this circumstance alone rejects the use of a style that is in itself closed or that allows for a specific and preordained course of the musical material. We thus no longer have a harmonically structured and codified discourse, but rather a well-composed flow whose only directional element seems to be the verbal content. The musical progression, which is often prone to peaks of lyricism, exploits a model widely used in the works of the early twentieth century, but it is, however, conditioned and generated by the nature of the text, from which its formal construction also derives.[21] It is configured as a sort of organism in which there are also moments of uncertainty, i.e. sections whose insertion within the piece is partially subject to the will of the performer, and therefore to the dramatic contingencies of a specific performance.

"Expressive" Singing   Instead, a sort of expressive singing, which in some ways resembles the vocal nature of the so-called expressionist works, uses different means to seek a correlation between verbal and musical material. Such a style is widely used in *Satyricon,* particularly in episodes like *Fortunata* and *Trimalchio contra Fortunata*, but also in the more animated passages of *La matrona di Efeso.* Even though the voice is still linked to a traditional vocal emission, it acquires an expressive charge that resembles *Sprechgesang,* in which the vocal profile loses its melodic connotation and instead emphasizes the rhythmic element, which has become the peculiar feature of the song. The singing style

---

20 The term is deliberately used improperly, since it relates to a specific aspect of nineteenth-century opera.
21 Consider Arnold Schoenberg's *Erwartung* a paradigmatic example in this respect.

is no longer a consequence or manifestation of what the text describes but, in accordance with the dictates of expressionist poetry, it also becomes the sign of a particular emotional situation or character trait. It is no coincidence that in *La matrona di Efeso* Habinnas abandons arioso for expressive singing only at the emotional peaks of the narrative, that is, to underline the soldier's amazement on discovering the widow inside the tomb, and the woman's final decision to crucify her husband's body to save her lover. It is certainly no chance occurrence that, on both occasions, Maderna chooses to organize the pitch in a serial matrix for expressive purposes, an aspect that will be dealt with later.

"Sprechgesang" and Rhythmic Recitative   It is but a short step from expressive singing to *"Sprechgesang."* In *"Sprechgesang,"* the traditional vocal style is abandoned in favor of an emphatic declamation that calls musical features to mind without really adopting them. Used in short passages in pieces like *Fortunata, The Money, Trimalchio contra Fortunata,* and *Trimalchio e il monumento, "Sprechgesang"* does not appear at points of particular dramatic importance, where, as we have seen, expressive singing is used; rather, it serves to emphasize contrived situations or, more often, to create a caesura in the expressive atmosphere of an episode. Given its sporadic use, it is clear that the use of this vocal technique mainly assumes the function of a rhetorical device, without affecting the general musical structure of the piece.

The same dramatic function is attributed to what could be called a sort of rhythmic recitative in which the enunciation of the text loses any musical connotation, since it is only the words that are stressed. Great use of this style of delivery is found in pieces such as *La matrona di Efeso, Trimalchio e il monumento,* and *Carriera di Trimalchio,* where it assumes different meanings each and every time: if in *La matrona di Efeso* it underlines a meta-narrative (such as the lugubrious quote from Virgil, "Id cinerem aut manes credis sentire sepultos?"),[22] there are plenty of episodes in which this kind of expression is used for openly comic purposes (*Trimalchio e il monumento*), while on other occasions it serves as a caesura between different situations or moods. This is what happens in *Carriera di Trimalchio,* where the alternation between melody and recitative emphasizes the contrast between the outward appearance and the real idea behind Trimalchio's words (→ **EX. 7**).

EX. 7   *Carriera di Trimalchio:* transcription of bb. 4–11 of the vocal line from Maderna's fair copy; PSS-BMC.
See also *Satyricon* (Paris: Salabert, © 1974, E.A.S. 17.091).

---

22   Maderna himself notes in the margin on the typescripts prepared for the selection of the text: "Virgilio, *Eneide* IV, 34" (PSS-BMC).

Trimalchio begins by trying to conceal his pride in a rush of magnanimous humanity ("Once I used to be like you"), and the music seems to play along with him in a childish tune with a descending melody; however, this is suddenly interrupted by the rhythmic recitative, thereby revealing his real, boastful smugness for having been able to rise to the top of the economic pyramid. This is followed by an attempt at mediation, which sees Trimalchio bring the discussion back to a more generic level; but his voice cannot completely mask his real thoughts, and in fact, although the various pitches are defined, they lose all connotations of melody; finally, his real opinion explodes, the final judgment, erupting once again in a burst of rhythmic speech: "the rest is garbage."

Echoes of Serialism

We have already shown how the composition of *Satyricon* does not make use of a unitary compositional principle, but that, on the contrary, from time to time it adopts the style and form most suited to the needs dictated by the verbal content of the text.

Among the various compositional solutions Maderna employs, some serial procedures used at specific points of the opera are extremely interesting. In this context, any talk of "serialism" indicates above all the use of a statistical-combinatorial principle in one or more phases of the compositional process: this can take place at the beginning, thus placing this principle at the basis of the compositional process, but it can also occur in an intermediate stage of elaboration, when a mathematical/numerical type of reasoning is applied to musical material that has already been partially sketched out.

It is important to note that when the serial component is present in *Satyricon*, it seems to be more of a pretext, a suggestion, since Maderna shows on more than one occasion that he is not bound in any way by the very guidelines he himself set up. After he establishes a numerical matrix to order the music, he then proceeds with the decomposition and dissolution of this principle itself, maintaining some operations, but never being obliged in any way to do so. Serial principles seem to be used in *Satyricon* primarily to define a sound universe; once he has achieved this, Maderna frees himself from the constraints of serialism, releasing the musical material from its creative principle.

Satyricon was certainly not the first time that Maderna made such a free use of serial principles. He had already adopted this practice in numerous compositions, even in those in which serialism was not a mere rhetorical artifice but the actual basis of the composition itself, as happens for example in the *Hyperion* cycle and even in compositions back in the 1950s.[23] On several occasions he had declared his aversion to serial rigor when it lacked any expressive purpose. In answering questions about serial music in 1965,[24] while reconfirming the fundamental and irreplaceable role of serialism in post-war

---

23 See Gianmario Borio and Veniero Rizzardi, "Die Musikalische Einheit von Bruno Madernas *Hyperion*," in *Quellenstudien II: Zwölf Komponisten des 20. Jahrhunderts*, ed. Felix Meyer (Winterthur: Amadeus, 1993), pp. 117–48; French trans. as "L'unité musicale de *Hyperion*," in *à Bruno Maderna* (see note 4), vol. 1, pp. 123–61.

24 See Bruno Maderna, "La révolution dans la continuité," in André Boucourechliev, "La musique sérielle aujourd'hui," *Preuves* 15, no. 177 (1965), pp. 28–29.

compositional thinking, the composer was given an opportunity to explain what is almost his own poetic manifesto of serial composition, which is perfectly in line with what he then put into practice in *Satyricon:*

> Do I write series in the "classic" sense of the word? Certainly not: I have my own grammatical system, which derives from the serial principle and which is sufficiently elastic, above all *abstract* enough, to give me all the freedom to represent my musical imagination which is not abstract at all in a thousand ways. The system – and every composer today has his own – must provide a logical basis for thought; it fertilizes this thought, it does not force it in any way.[25]

La matrona di Efeso and *Trimalchio e le flatulenze* are two emblematic but at the same time very different cases of the application of serialist thought within *Satyricon. La matrona di Efeso* is one of the longest and most articulated pieces in the opera in which such procedures are only applied in some specific moments of the narrative, that is, in those of greatest poignancy, while various musical styles are employed in the rest of the episode following a well-structured procedure. Instead, the concept of serial derivation is applied to the whole of *Trimalchio e le flatulenze,* which is a much shorter episode. Furthermore, whereas in *La matrona di Efeso* this principle is set as the basis for the composition of the relative passages, it is used only later in *Trimalchio e le flatulenze* to distort a harmonic and melodic progression that had already been completely and separately drafted. It also has a profoundly different function in the two episodes: in *La matrona di Efeso* the serial echoes seem to be used to underline two points of particular dramatic emphasis, and the serial passages constitute a diegetic element that highlights the pathos of the narrated events. Instead, in *Trimalchio e le flatulenze,* Maderna uses a mathematical procedure to carry out a progressive transfiguration of the sound material that alters the audience's perception of the action on stage, causing a sensation that Susanna Pasticci has identified as a will to generate a sense of "alienation" in the Brechtian sense.[26]

Susanna Pasticci's study provides a thorough description of the serial procedure utilized in *Trimalchio e le flatulenze.*[27] It is therefore worth focusing attention on the serial passages in *La matrona di Efeso,* which to date have never been investigated by Maderna scholars.

As we have already said, some parts of *La matrona di Efeso* are based on a principle of numerical control, whose rules, however, start to be partially circumvented from a certain point in the compositional process onwards. The Milesian tale of the inconsolable widow from the city of Ephesus in Asia Minor tells the story of a woman who, after her husband's death, saves her lover by having the former's corpse hung on a cross. In *Satyricon* the story is told by Habinnas in the third person, but it nevertheless contains several dialogues in direct speech, which are always, however, sung by the narrator. The poignancy of the tale is evident, as is the vein of sarcasm inherent therein. In particular, Maderna

---

25 Ibid. Original in French.
26 See Susanna Pasticci, "La presenza del *Satyricon* sulla scena culturale degli anni Settanta, da Maderna a Pasolini," *Musica/Realtà* 91 (2010), pp. 77–126: 104ff.
27 Further information in ibid., particularly pp. 105–11.

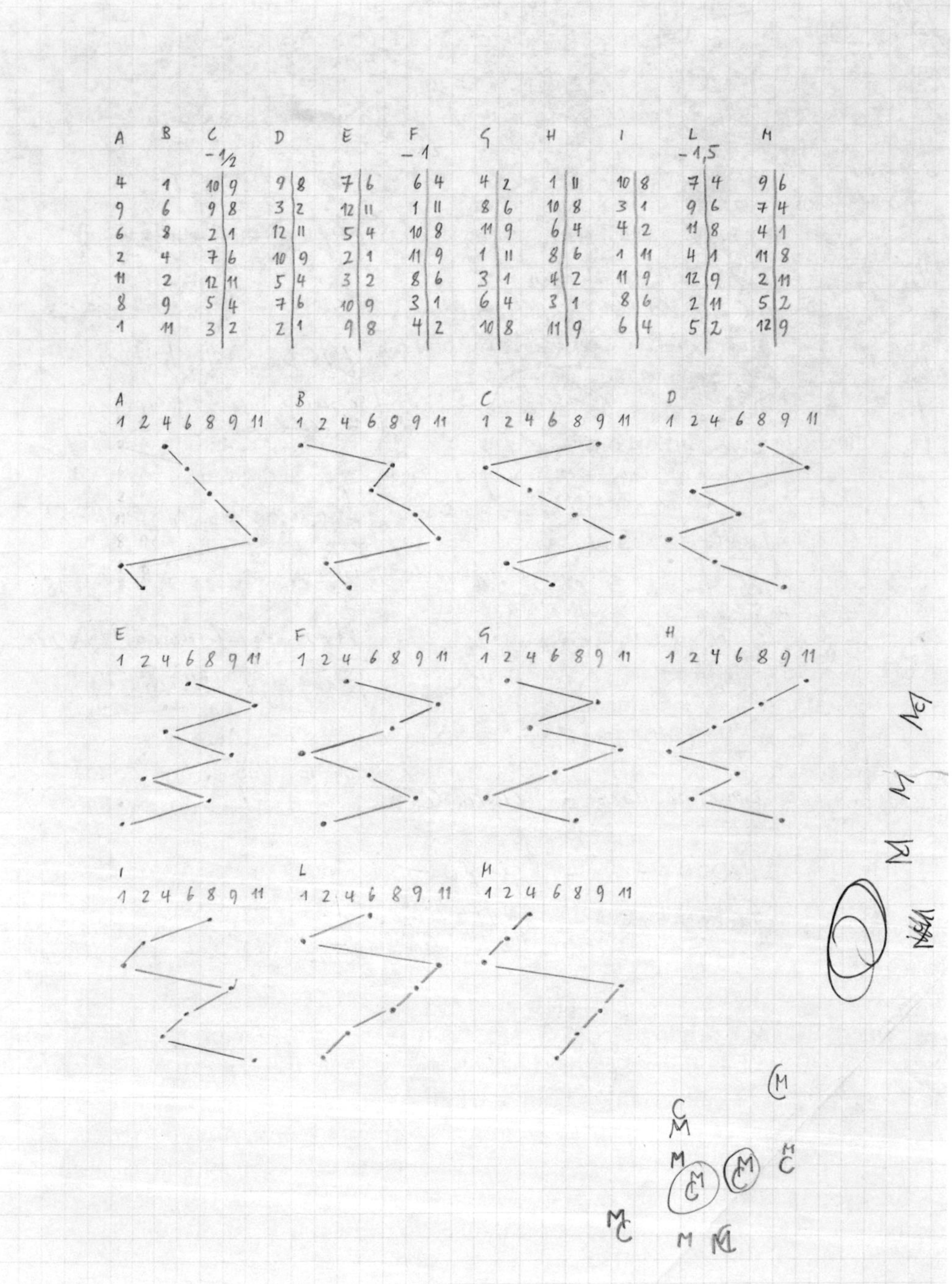

EX. 8   *Satyricon:* sketch with preparatory diagrams for the realization of the serial passages in *La matrona di Efeso;* PSS-BMC.

establishes two points of dramatic climax in the narration of the tale: the first of these corresponds to the moment when the soldier descends into the illuminated tomb and is terrified when he comes across the woman (who will later become his lover), believing her to be a ghost. The second moment is instead related to the woman's exclamation that underpins her brutal final decision: "God forbid, that I should have to see at one and same time the dead bodies of the only two men I have ever loved."[28] In terms of sound, the two passages are remarkable for the great involvement of orchestral sound and for dynamics that oscillate between *forte* and *fortissimo*. In both these sections Maderna carries out a process of musical composition based on the typical numerical grids used in serial music, as can be seen from a diagram preserved in the composer's manuscript collection (→ **EX. 8**).

The diagram is divided into two parts, corresponding to two different systems of visual-graphic representation of pitch and transposition factors. The two macro-systems each report eleven different transpositions (associated with the letters A–M) of the same series of seven sounds, corresponding to a tonal scale of F major (where 1 = A). The first macro-system, i.e. the eleven numerical columns at the top of the page, relates to the first dramatic climax, i.e. the soldier's discovery of the woman, while the second macro-system refers to the woman's exclamation, the second moment of pathos in *La matrona di Efeso*.

The use of the same class of pitches for both episodes highlights an underlying connection between the two moments and underlines their similarities, given not just by a common dramatic emphasis and affinity in orchestral timbre, but also by the sound material and by the compositional technique employed.

The first macro-diagram, as mentioned above, is used for the composition of the first emotional climax. The system comprises eleven utterances (A–M) of the diatonic scale of seven sounds. Each of these statements differs from the others in the position of the individual pitches; starting from statement C, Maderna also undertakes a procedure in which he transposes the pitches of the basic series in ascending order, as indicated in the preparatory diagram, noting the semitones that are required to return to the starting series: first a semitone (see Ex. 8, "-½": C, D, E), then two semitones ("-1": F, G, H), and finally three ("-1,5": L, M). A subsequent sketch makes the effective application of these numerical schemes to the sound material easier to understand (→ **EX. 9**).

Here it is easy to see the eleven vertical utterances of the series, entrusted one for each bar to the wind instruments, as well as the corresponding serial number indicated by Maderna alongside each pitch. The transpositions, indicated by arrows, numbers, and brackets at the top of the system, have already been applied to the sound material here. Furthermore, the sketch also allows us to catch a glimpse of the fact that Maderna actually intends to extend the sound of the piece to the chromatic whole, adding five pitches to the string parts that were missing in the original diatonic series and thereby using up all twelve sounds of the chromatic scale. Whenever a transposition of the series is envisaged, Maderna also plots the additional pitches for the strings, already in their transposed degrees.

---

28 B. Maderna, *Satyricon*, full score (see note 12), *La matrona di Efeso*, bb. 63–66.

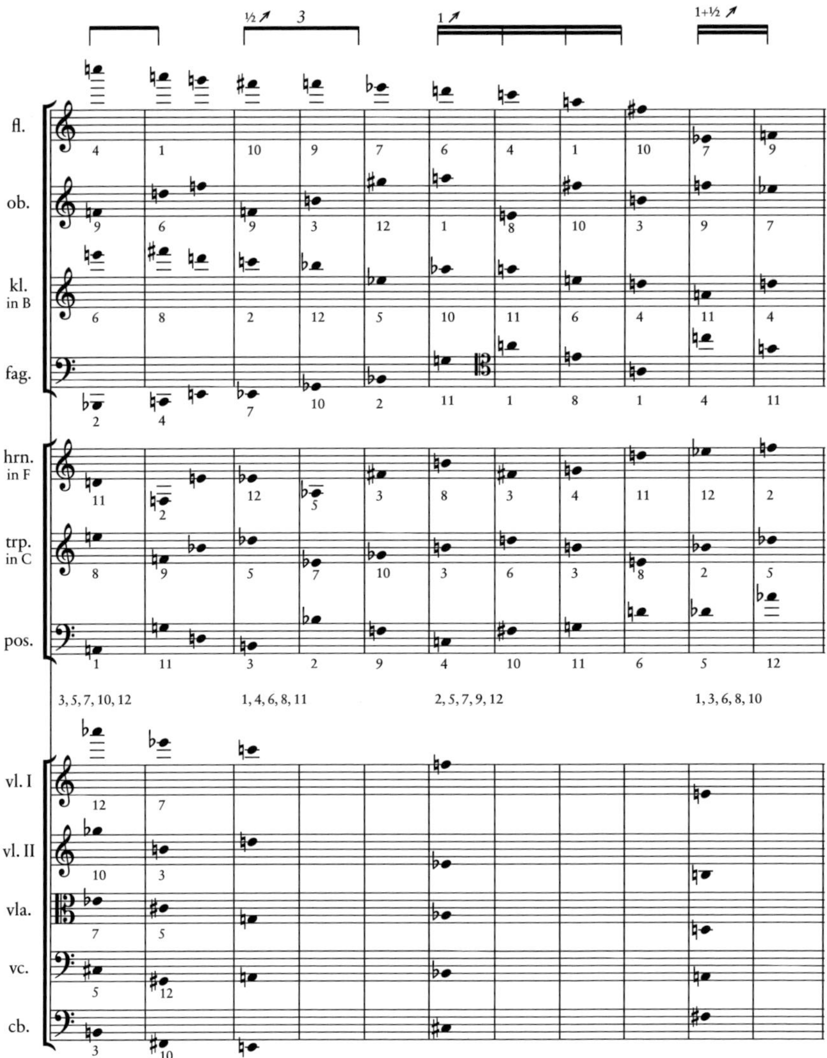

EX. 9   *La matrona di Efeso:* transcription from a preparatory sketch showing
the partial application of the serial layouts of Example 8; PSS-BMC.

In the fair copy by Bruno Maderna (i.e. the antigraph of the score published by
Salabert in 1974), the series for the seven corresponding parts of the wind instruments
(flute, oboe, clarinet, bassoon, horn, trumpet, and trombone) are in line with what was
set out in the previous diagrams (→ **EX. 10**).

However, a look at the sound material as a whole shows a number of significant
differences with the preparatory materials, especially in terms of the handling of the five
pitches assigned to the strings and intended to complete the chromatic whole. First of all,
Maderna eliminates the double bass, entrusting the line to the harp; but this particular
instrument, even though it fills the line initially foreseen for the double bass with other
pitches, already exhausts its enunciation at the beginning of the second bar, when the

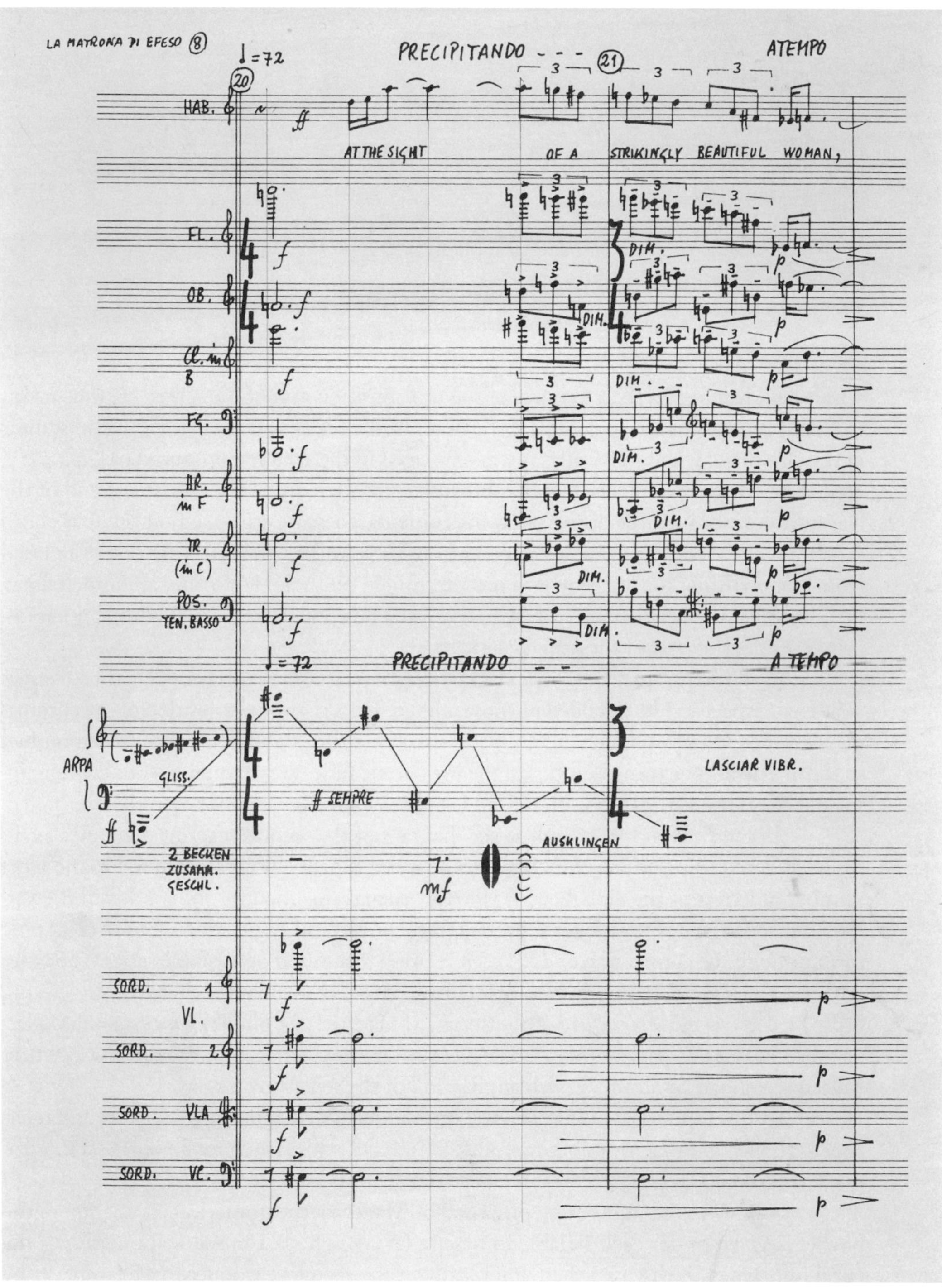

EX. 10 *La matrona di Efeso:* fair copy by Bruno Maderna, bb. 20–21; PSS-BMC.

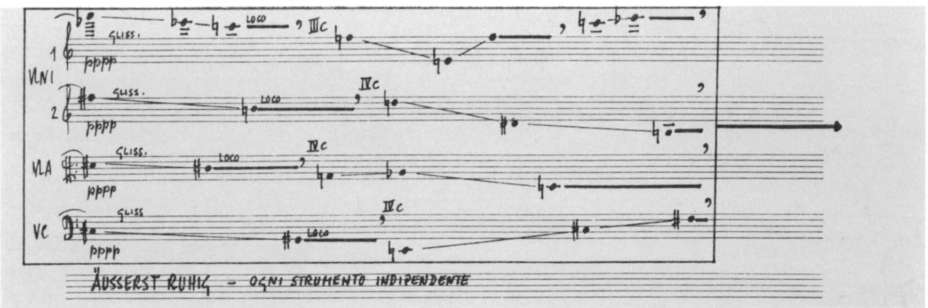

EX. 11   *La matrona di Efeso:* fair copy by Bruno Maderna, b. 21 bis;
PSS-BMC. Details of the string part.

winds have just begun the utterance of the transposition and of the series. He thus seems to abandon any attempt to complete the notes of the series and present all twelve sounds of the chromatic whole vertically, as was envisaged in the sketch reproduced in Example 9. Moreover, the tempo of the strings is broadened to such an extent that at the end of the eleven expositions (A–M) of the wind instruments, they are still fixed on the first chord (pitches 12, 10, 7, and 5; see Ex. 9). Starting from the next bar, the notes are therefore freed from any rhythmic connotation and predetermined mutual relationship and isolated in a box, in which the performance of each instrument, in indeterminate rhythmic notation, is independent of that of the others (→ **EX. 11**).

As the preparatory sketches in Example 9 show, Maderna's original plan thus assumes a different aspect and its intended purpose is altered: if a rigorous exposition of the chromatic whole was initially planned for each vertical chord, the established system is demolished in the final draft; the transpositions of the heptatonic series are maintained but the remaining pitches of the strings are scattered, and thus the established levels are freely interpreted.

As can be seen in Example 8, the diagram of the second macrosystem once again shows eleven transpositions of the heptatonic series, which always correspond to the same number of letters of the alphabet (A–M). Here the arrangement of the sounds in the various transpositions is no longer represented by numerical digits alone, but in a graphic form through the connection of dots, each relating to a sound of the basic series. The latter are set out as it were on the abscissa of an imaginary Cartesian axis, where the underlying ordinate corresponds to the order of utterance of each of the pitches. Once again, Maderna's manuscript materials contain evidence of an intermediate compositional phase, where we can recognize an almost slavish application of the scheme (→ **EX. 12**).

From a numerical point of view ("translating" the heights into numbers and referring to the second macro-system reproduced in Ex. 8), this sketch for *La matrona di Efeso* (→ **EX. 12**) can be represented as a table (→ **EX. 13**).

Following the numbering proposed by Maderna, the numerical translation of the pitches is given under each syllable in base 12 (A = 1). The last numerical line shows the vocal line, which is distinguished graphically in the sketch reproduced in Example 12 by white note heads; finally, the last line shows the correspondence with the letters of the transpositions shown in Example 8.

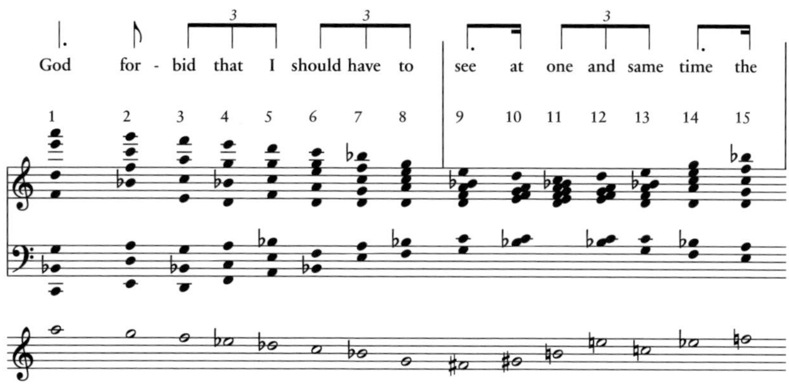

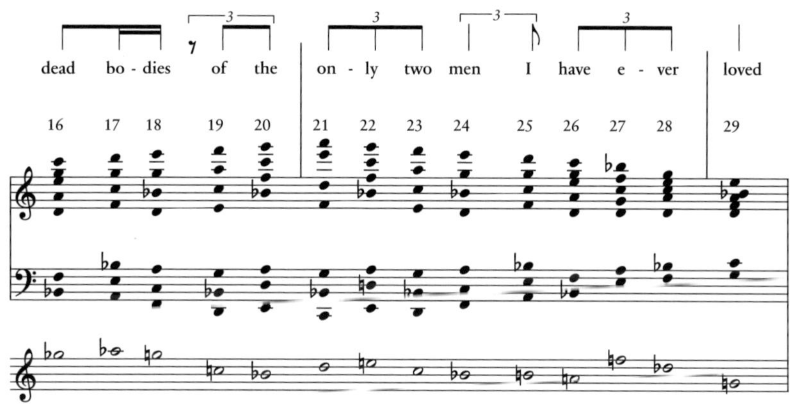

EX. 12 *La matrona di Efeso:* transcription from a preparatory sketch showing the partial application of the serial diagrams of Example 8; PSS-BMC.

1	2	3	4	5	6	7	8	9	10	11	12	13	14	15	16	17	18	19	20	21	22	23	24	25	26	27	28	29
God	for-	bid	that	I	should	have	to	see	at	one	and	same	time	the	dead	bod-	ies	of	the	on-	ly	two	men	I	have	ev-	er	loved

1	2	3	4	5	6	7	8	9	10	11	12	13	14	15	16	17	18	19	20	21	22	23	24	25	26	27	28	29
1	11	9	8	6	4	2	11	8	6	4	6	8	11	2	4	6	8	9	11	1	11	9	8	6	4	2	11	8
8	4	1	11	11	11	9	8	2	1	2	1	2	8	9	11	11	11	1	4	8	4	1	11	11	11	9	8	2
6	9	4	2	4	8	4	4	1	11	1	11	1	4	4	8	4	2	4	9	6	9	4	2	4	8	4	4	1
9	2	8	6	9	1	11	1	9	9	11	9	9	1	11	1	9	6	8	2	9	2	8	6	9	1	11	1	9
11	1	11	1	2	6	6	6	6	8	9	8	6	6	6	6	2	1	11	1	11	1	11	1	2	6	6	6	6
2	6	2	4	8	9	1	2	4	4	8	4	4	2	1	9	8	4	2	6	2	6	2	4	8	9	1	2	4
4	8	6	9	1	2	8	9	11	2	6	2	11	9	8	2	1	9	6	8	4	8	6	9	1	2	8	9	11

1	11	9	7	5	4	2	11	10	12	3	8	4	7	9	10	12	11	4	2	6	8	4	2	3	1	9	5	11
B	?	C	D	E	F	G	H	I	L	M	L	I	H	G	F	E	D	C	?	B	?	C	D	E	F	G	F	I

EX. 13 Numerical translation of the sketch reproduced in Example 12, referring to the serial schemas of Example 8.

EX. 14 *La matrona di Efeso:* fair copy by Maderna, bb. 63–66; PSS-BMC.

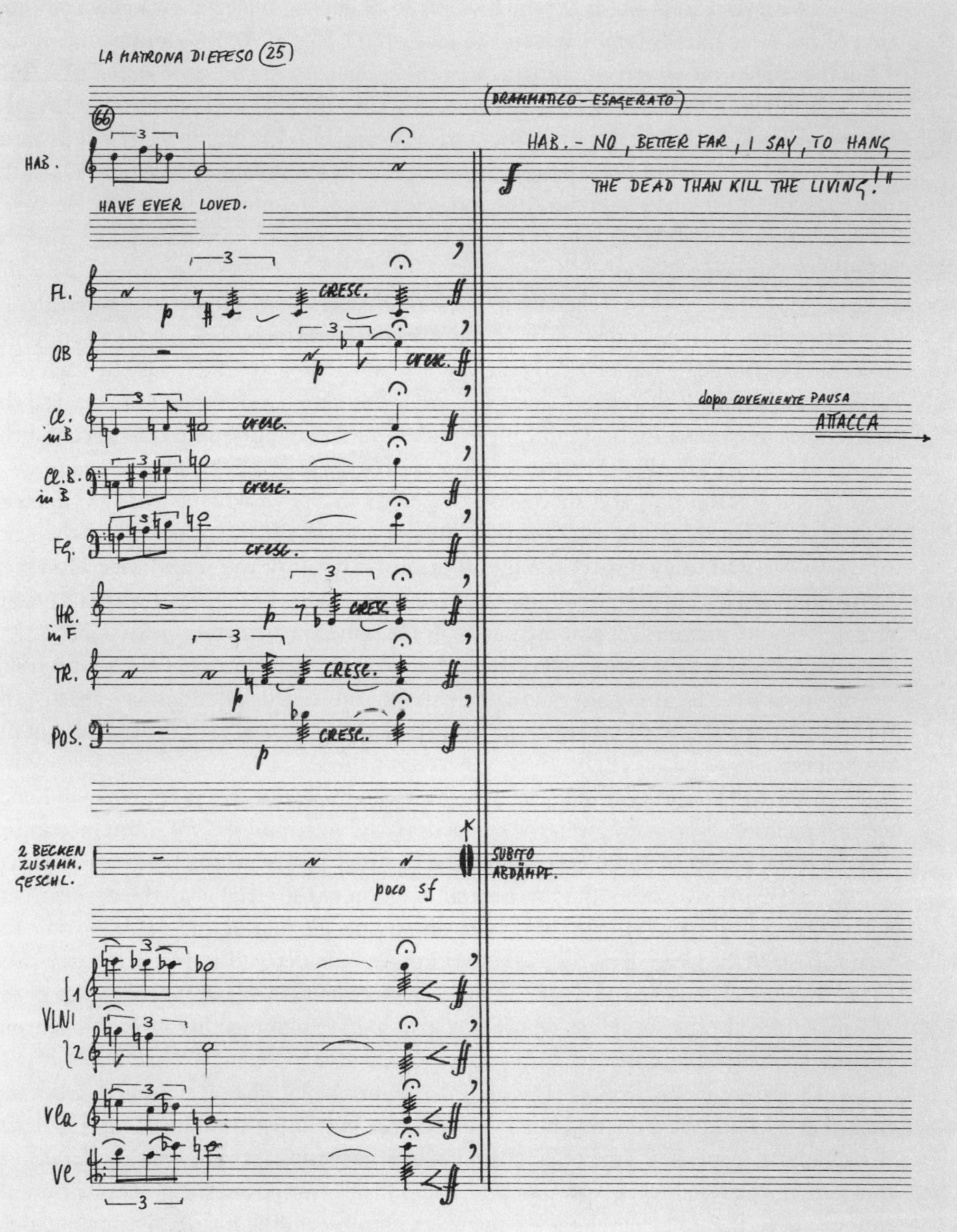

LA MATRONA DI EFESO (25)
(DRAMMATICO - ESAGERATO)
HAB. - NO, BETTER FAR, I SAY, TO HANG
THE DEAD THAN KILL THE LIVING!
HAVE EVER LOVED.
HAB.
FL.
OB
Cl. in B
Cl. B. in B
Fg.
Hr. in F
Tr.
Pos.
dopo coveniente pausa
ATTACCA
CRESC.
2 BECKEN ZUSAMM. GESCHL.
SUBITO ABDÄMPF.
poco sf
VLNI
Vla
Ve

With the exception of A, which seems to disappear, replaced by a new combination of the same pitches (while B seems to take on the role of A), it should be noted that Maderna applies the eleven combinations of the seven chosen pitches in order, first from the beginning up to the M series (occurrences 1–11 in the diagram), then traversing the same path backwards (11–21), and finally starting again and continuing to series I (from 21 to the end), for a total of twenty-nine chords, one for each syllable of the text. Thus, the utterance of all the seven sounds of the series is envisaged under each syllable. However, in the final version of the motif (→ **EX. 14**), Maderna once again partially changes the previously established schemas.

Maderna makes two changes to the sound skeleton of Example 12: first, just as he did in the first serial episode (Ex. 9), he transposes the series by one or more semitones according to the degrees touched by the voice, so as to integrate the vocal line each time within the sounds of the series. There are only a few minor variations compared to the sketch, and only one case of significant variation, near the fourteenth utterance (on the key word "time"), mainly due to the thinning out of the sound (→ **EX. 15**).

The distribution and succession of pitches in the woodwind part are in strict order; but, rather than following the individual sounds of the instruments and their position on the staff, they respect the overall acoustic result of the sound mix. However, by adding harp and strings, Maderna multiplies the sounds of the series without paying attention to the rigorous vertical succession of the same, distorting – at least apparently – the order of serial enunciation. Nevertheless, if we once again consider the sound result of the operation, the amalgam made up of the sounds of the woodwinds – that is, the nucleus carrying the serial progression – is still clearly recognizable in the complex of the timbral mix.

Thus, two aspects of Madernian writing can be seen at this point: first, and once again, the absolute primacy given to the needs of the voice and the vocal line, according to which the sound material is manipulated in order to obtain the best performance; second, the expressive rather than structural function of the serial procedures, which are apparently used as a preliminary outline to obtain specific sounds, but never become the formal basis of the piece. Thus, the serial writing does not determine, but rather is derived from, the textual content and the dramatic context, whereas the formal coherence of the piece is ensured by the vocal line, whose narrative course holds together the heterogeneous parts of *La matrona di Efeso*.

Serialism is thus exploited (as an ordering principle) when it is needed; it is never treated as a self-imposed dogma, but as a useful tool for the generation of sound material (*La matrona di Efeso*) or for the organization of existing material (*Trimalchio e le flatulenze*). In this case, the serial rules correspond to a step in the compositional process, whose results can nevertheless be developed to the point of transcending the serial principle itself. The serial technique becomes a useful tool for the best sound performance of the composition, especially as regards its expressive and dramatic scope. Maderna himself seems to confirm this when, two months after the first performance of *Satyricon*, he affirms:

			-1 semitone					+1 st.		+2 st.			mixed (incomplete)		-1 st.	-2 st.					-1 st.			-1 st.			+1 st	+2 st.
1	2	3	4	5	6	7	8	9	10	11	12	13	14	15	16	17	18	19	20	21	22	23	24	25	26	27	28	29
God	for-	bid	that	I	should	have	to	see	at	one	and	same	time	the	dead	bod-	ies	of	the	on-	ly	two	men	I	have	ev-	er	loved
1	11	9	7	5	4	2	11	9	7	6	8	10	12	2	3	4	6	9	11	1	10	9	8	5	4	2	12	10
8	4	1	10	10	11	9	8	3	2	4	3	4	7	9	10	9	9	1	4	8	3	1	11	10	11	9	9	4
6	9	4	1	3	8	4	4	2	12	3	1	2*	3	4	7	2	12	4	9	6	8	4	2	3	8	4	5	3
9	2	8	5	8	1	11	1	10	10	1	11	11	2	11	12	7	4	8	2	9	1	8	6	8	1	11	2	11
11	1	11	12	1	6	6	6	7	9	11	10	8	7	6	5	12	11	11	1	11	12	11	1	1	6	6	7	8
2	6	2	3	7	9	1	2	5	5	10	6	6	3	1	8	5*	2	2	6	2	5	2	4	7	9	1	3	6
4	8	6	8	12	2	8	9	12	3	8	4	1	10	8	1	10*	7	6	8	4	7	6	9	12	2	8	10	1
1	11	9	7	5	4	2	11	10	12	3	8	4	7	9	10	12	11	4	2	6	8	4	2	3	1	9	5	11
B	?	C	D	E	F	G	H	I	L	M	L	I	H	G	F	E	D	C	?	B	?	C	D	E	F	G	F	I

EX. 15 Numerical transcription of bb. 63–66
of *La matrona di Efeso* reproduced in Example 14,
referring to the serial diagrams shown in Example 8.

I am increasingly convinced that one should not be consistent in life. Especially as a composer, as an artist. I think that one should loathe consistency. Instead, we should try to be as vital and spontaneous as possible, so that we can pander to and best express our body, our psychosomatic being. In my opinion, the notorious serial coherence was one of mankind's greatest afflictions.[29]

If we cast our mind back to those definitions of a fragmentary and disjointed work mentioned at the beginning of this essay, Maderna's compositional choices in *Satyricon* now appear in a completely different light. If we consider the rich variety of compositional choices, one can see that a formal principle is actually clearly present throughout the entire work. Nonetheless, this principle is present more in the compositional process than in the finished result, in other words, in the primary role the composer gives to the vocal part.

Everything starts with the construction of a context or an atmosphere generated by the textual content; once the sound rendering and the relatively most suitable compositional technique for the text in question have been established, this context or atmosphere can then partially overcome the pure intelligibility of the words, or openly contradict it. However, this choice is always a function of an expressive rendering that derives from the content of the text itself. The composition of the various pieces takes place within a field of tension whose opposite poles are marked by the definition of a closed musical form with meaning on the one hand, and a more fluid formal structure on the other, whenever the purely verbal (and not musical) elements of the voice become a conveyor of meaning.

---

29 This is what Maderna had to say on the radio program *Gespräch über Freizeit*, ed. Christof Bitter, 7 May 1973 (original in German). The translation proposed here is based on the original recording (copy housed at PSS-BMC) and differs from the one found in Fearn, *Bruno Maderna* (see note 4), pp. 321–23: 323 ("Conversation about *Tempo libero*"), which is a translation of the Italian version, "Conversazione su *Tempo libero*," in *Documenti* (see note 8), pp. 115–18: 117. For a new Italian translation see Maderna, *Amore e curiosità* (see note 1), pp. 160–66.

Such an affirmation brings to mind the traditional compositional procedures of musical theater, whose lesson Maderna – and this time with no parodic intent – seems to have learned perfectly. Thus, what we see in *Satyricon* is no longer a "fragmentation *au carré*,"[30] or even pop-art, as it has been rashly interpreted eliciting Maderna's words from one of his last radio interviews.[31] Instead, to quote Massimo Mila, we are faced with the "constant presence of the past within the most daring exploration of the future."[32]

---

30 See above in this essay and note 3.

31 Interview on Dutch radio with Piet Hein van de Poel (see above, note 8). For a proper interpretation of the words stated by Maderna see the essay by Angela Ida De Benedictis in this book, note 49, p. 38.

32 Massimo Mila, "Un maestro e i suoi maestri," in *Maderna musicista europeo*, ed. Ulrich Mosch (Turin: Einaudi, 1999), p. 6; first edn. 1976.

BUILDING SOUNDS: THE COMPOSER

CARLO CICERI

Space in Maderna's Last Orchestral Works

> My work of composing comes to an end with rehearsals.
> Bruno Maderna[1]

This essay starts from the assumption that Maderna's last creative period was characterized by his reflection on space. This aspect is particularly evident in the orchestral compositions *Quadrivium* (1969), *Grande Aulodia* (1970), *Ausstrahlung* (1971), *Aura* (1972), and *Biogramma* (1972). In an attempt to provide an efficient means of addressing its vast field of application and also to do justice to the complexity of the underlying compositional thought, the concept will be divided into five main paradigms. The first is *Frontality* which examines the different positions of the musicians on stage; next we have *Projectivity*, in which these same positions are analyzed as a central compositional element that can organize the form, the development of the musical material, and its perspective; the latter is in turn analyzed in terms of its *Extemporaneousness* and in a context of *Ambiguity;* the final paradigm is *Reactivity*, the acoustic reaction of the orchestral space to the presence of a main melodic line.

Frontality

All the aforementioned works are similar in the fact that the orchestral layout is conceived within the orchestral structure itself, that is, on stage, without the audience being considered a physical element therein. This also applies to *Quadrivium*, which has often been misinterpreted in this sense. In fact, at first glance, the position of the instruments as they appear in its score might induce us to envisage a hypothetical rearrangement of the four instrumental groups in the four corners of the hall, around the audience (→ **EX. 1**).[2]

However, not only does this hypothesis lack confirmation in the available sources, but a number of valid reasons point to another interpretation. First of all, although the position of the conductor is not specified in the layout in the printed score, making the

---

1   "Io termino il lavoro di composizione con le prove." From an interview in *Un'ora con Bruno Maderna: Musica, specchio della società*, a documentary by Salvatore G. Biamonte and Giuseppe Sibilla, RAI, Milan-Venice 1969–70, broadcast on 11 October 1971 (quote at 9'10″).

2   See Frédéric Durieux, "*Quadrivium*," in *à Bruno Maderna*, ed. Geneviève Mathon, Laurent Feneyrou, and Giordano Ferrari, vol. 1 (Paris: Basalte, 2007), pp. 143–76. Many thanks to Casa Ricordi, in the person of Marco Mazzolini, for having permitted access to the material and for kindly authorizing the reproduction of extracts from the printed scores of the works in question.

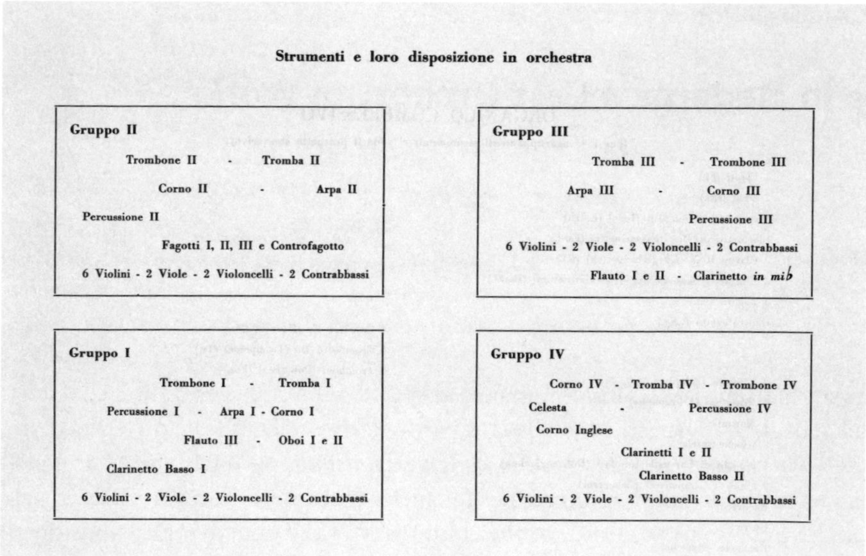

EX. 1   Bruno Maderna, *Quadrivium,* composition of groups I, II, III, and IV; detail from the score (Milan: Ricordi, © 1969, repr. 1976, 131477).

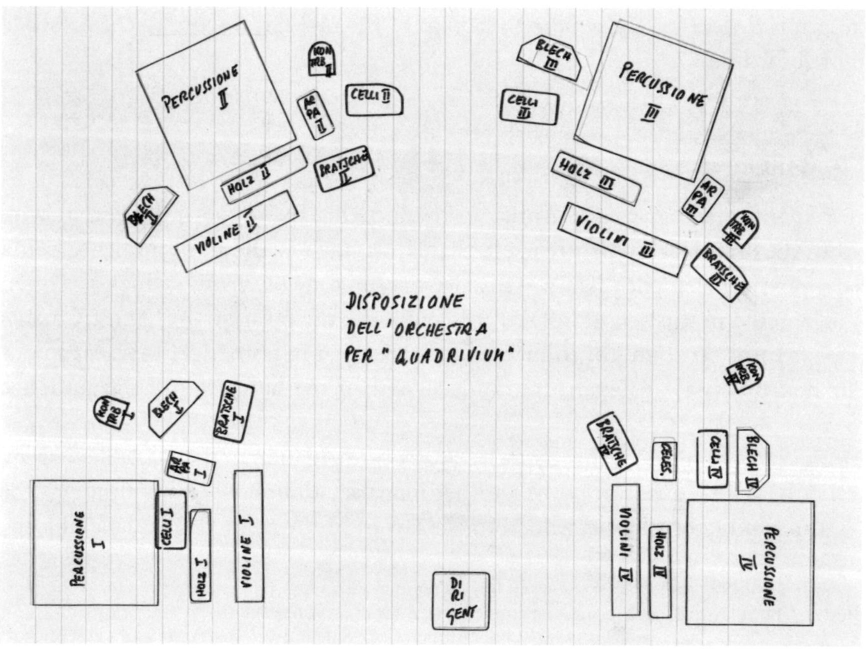

EX. 2   Bruno Maderna, orchestral layout for *Quadrivium;* PSS-BMC.

idea of the dislocation of the groups quite appealing, albeit not easy to control musically, the very indication written in Italian, "Strumenti e loro disposizione in orchestra" (instruments and their layout in orchestra), leaves little room for doubt (where *in* is to be understood as *in the* orchestra *space*). Then, further confirmation comes from a manuscript schema prepared by Maderna and preserved in his legacy,[3] in which both the orchestral layout and the conductor's position (*"dirigent"*) are clearly delineated, with each of the groups seated facing the latter in a semicircle.[4] (→ **EX. 2**)

The symmetrical and essentially homogeneous orchestral layout in *Quadrivium* is a unique case. However, it already provides a clear example of how space functions within the piece as an element that organizes both the musical material and its form.

Ausstrahlung was "conceived as a multitrack tape composed of different elements to be assembled and interpolated at the micro- and macro-structural level,"[5] and here too, the orchestra's seating arrangement is perfectly in line with the modular organization of the macroform. In fact, it is organized in such a way as to make the diffusion of the different sources as analytical as possible. Examples 3 and 4 reproduce two handwritten sheets showing two different orchestral layouts (→ **EXX. 3-4**).[6] The second arrangement was the one eventually adopted.[7]

---

3   The schema is unfortunately missing from the published score. Hopefully, its integration in the not-too-distant future can complete the information on the components of the orchestra and overcome any further misunderstandings relating to the arrangement of the four instrumental groups. I would like to thank the PSS of Basel, and in particular Angela Ida De Benedictis, for all her help and for allowing me access to all the materials useful for writing this article.

4   Among the scarce iconographic sources regarding the first performance of Maderna's works conducted by the composer himself or, more generally, those regarding the layout of the musicians on the stage, the validity of this schema is confirmed by a video recording of the concert performed by the RAI Symphony Orchestra Turin at Venice's Biennale Musica on 4 October 1979. The conductor was Giuseppe Sinopoli and the program included *Grande Aulodia, Aura, Widmung,* and, indeed, *Quadrivium* (source filed at the PSS-BMC). It is interesting to note that while the arrangement of the orchestra for *Quadrivium* in Sinopoli's execution respects the aforementioned sketch (*Grande Aulodia* likewise follows the layout shown in the score), the size of the stage imposed some practical measures. For example, the percussion in *Grande Aulodia* is placed at the back of the stage and not between Strings A and C, a solution which Maderna himself adopted for the concert in Persepolis (see below).

5   Angela Ida De Benedictis, "Scrittura e supporti nel Novecento: alcune riflessioni e un esempio (*Ausstrahlung* di Bruno Maderna)," in *La scrittura come rappresentazione del pensiero musicale,* ed. Gianmario Borio (Pisa: ETS, 2004), pp. 237–91: 274.

6   The composition of the individual groups of strings as indicated in the diagram (Ex. 3) appears on the verso of the sheet.

7   A transcription of the sketch reproduced as Example 4 is published in Angela Ida De Benedictis, "*Ausstrahlung,* ou la textualité brisée d'un hymne à la vie," in *à Bruno Maderna* (see note 2), vol. 1, pp. 287–19: 294.

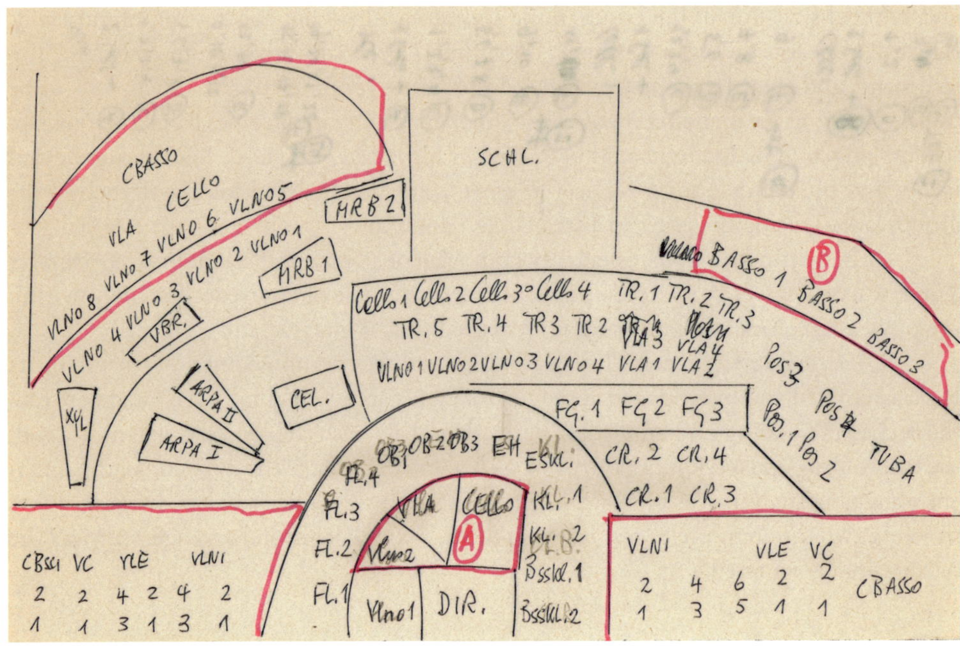

EX. 3   Bruno Maderna, *Ausstrahlung:* sketch showing the first layout of the orchestra; PSS-BMC.

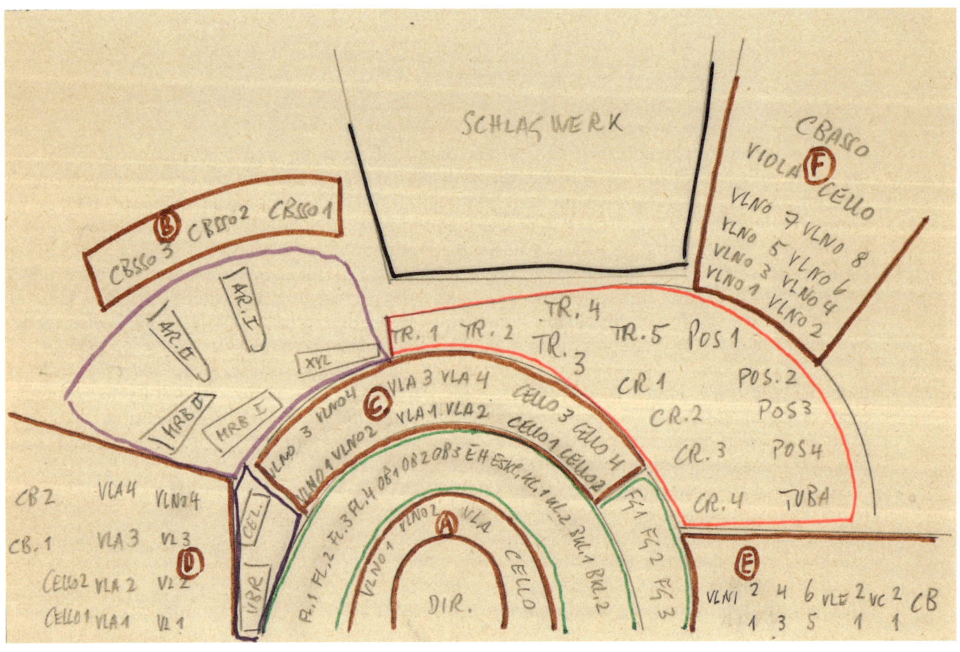

EX. 4   Bruno Maderna, *Ausstrahlung:* sketch with the final orchestral layout; PSS-BMC.

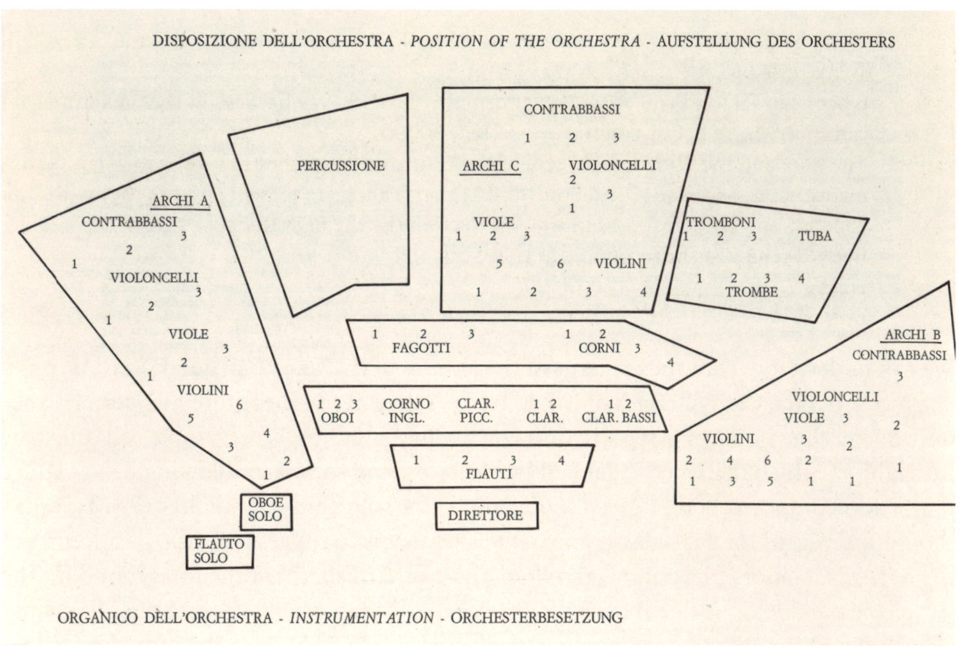

EX. 5　Bruno Maderna, *Grande Aulodia,* orchestra layout; score (Milan: Ricordi, © 1970, repr. 1974, 131648).

Apart from the obvious similarities, we can see the greater separation between the groups in the final version (Ex. 4), mainly because of the creation of the C group of strings and, consequently, the clear definition of the brass group. The inversion of groups B and F does not alter the general role of the strings, which have to "enfold" the orchestra, a role that also appears in the layout for *Grande Aulodia* (→ **EX. 5**), especially in the division of the strings into groups A, B, and C.

There are also clear similarities between the position of the wind instruments and the flute and oboe soloists in the layout for both *Ausstrahlung* and *Grande Aulodia*. Examples 4 and 5 show how the brass and winds are arranged in a similar manner. On the contrary, although the soloists are present in both pieces, their usual position to the far left of the conductor is only clearly indicated in the materials and score for *Grande Aulodia,* and, along with the solo female voice, is not mentioned in the sketches for *Ausstrahlung.* However, photographs documenting the concert of the premiere of *Ausstrahlung* in Persepolis allow us to complete the picture, as they provide irrefutable proof that the position of the two wind instruments was the same in both pieces. A partial explanation as to why the soloists are missing from the *Ausstrahlung* schemas also comes from the letter Maderna wrote to Cathy Berberian on 26 June 1971. Its content is an invaluable aid to understanding several important and otherwise hard to decipher aspects of the compositional process and the general conception of the piece:

Dear Catherine,
Don't be alarmed if you're only getting a small bit.[8] This is the first and the others will arrive little by little as soon as they are finished.
Of course, I'll send you those sung normally straightaway because in the meantime you can study them, because of the intonation, etc.
The flute and the oboe soloists will in the future be "in orchestra." – For this first performance, since Severino [Gazzelloni] and Lothar [Faber] are present anyway, they will flank you, but only sometimes, as in this first section (by the poet Rudaghi).
Bye. I'll send you the second piece this week.
Hugs
Bruno[9]

We can understand from the contents of the letter that the "piece" in question is *Ausstrahlung* no. 5. In fact, Cathy Berberian would be the solo voice of the future first performance on 5 September 1971 in Persepolis, and this is the "small bit" (*pezzettino*), on a text by Rudaghi, in which the voice is flanked by the two wind soloists,[10] allowing us to deduce that it was composed before *Ausstrahlung* no. 2 (for solo voice and orchestra). Maderna's thoughtful regard for the artist is apparent as he seems to suggest that the positioning of the *obbligato* soloists (Severino Gazzelloni and Lothar Faber)[11] in the foreground, to the left of the conductor, is due more to logistical needs than purely musical ones. It should also be noted that the *Grande Aulodia* (dedicated not by chance to the same Gazzelloni and Faber) came before *Ausstrahlung* on the program for the Persepolis concert.[12] This piece already assigned a specific position to the two soloists, and moving them for the rest of the program would probably have proved complex (if not pointless). Added to this was the technical problem of moving the related microphones (see the photos → **EXX. 6-7**): while changing the positions of some of the musicians in the orchestra would only have meant moving the three hanging microphones used to capture and amplify the orchestral mass and pre-recorded sounds on tape – and, probably, even to record the entire event (see below) – it was quite a different matter for the soloists. Relocating them at the center of the orchestra would have involved moving each of their dedicated microphones, or even using a dual microphone setup, one for each piece on the program. Sad to say, we will

---

8   The reference is to Berberian's vocal score, housed in the Cathy Berberian Collection at the PSS.

9   Manuscript letter (original in Italian), sent from Darmstadt, housed in the Cathy Berberian Collection, PSS; published in Bruno Maderna, *Amore e curiosità: Scritti, frammenti e interviste sulla musica*, ed. Angela Ida De Benedictis, Michele Chiappini, and Benedetta Zucconi (Milan: il Saggiatore, 2020), pp. 629–30.

10   This section also includes free or predefined interventions plus some orchestral parts taken from *Ausstrahlungen* nos. 4, 1, and 7. For the structure of the work and the components of the orchestra for each *Ausstrahlung* (seven in all) see De Benedictis, "Scrittura e supporti nel Novecento" (see note 5), pp. 268–69, and idem, "*Ausstrahlung*" (see note 7), pp. 292–93. See these essays also for more details on the magnetic tape (of the four tapes) used in the composition, cited later in the text.

11   It should be recalled, by the way, that it was Koos Verheul and not Severino Gazzelloni who actually performed the solo flute part at the world premiere.

12   The general program for the Festival (PSS-BMC) gives no information about the the concert dedicated to Maderna: the order of the pieces performed can nevertheless be deduced from a letter from Maderna to Irma Manfredi, dated 6 September 1971, kept at the PSS-BMC; original in Italian published in Maderna, *Amore e curiosità* (see note 9), p. 631. Maderna conducted the Orchestre de la Résidence de la Haye.

EX. 6   Positions of soloists and orchestra during the world premiere
of *Ausstrahlung,* Persepolis, 5 September 1971 (photo Gamma, Paris;
copyright: Photo Mali, Charenton); PSS-BMC.

EX. 7   Positions of soloists and orchestra during the rehearsals of
the world premiere of *Ausstrahlung,* Persepolis, 4 September 1971
(speculative date; unknown photographer); PSS-BMC.

EX. 8   Panoramic view of the stage during the world premiere of *Ausstrahlung,*
Persepolis, 5 September 1971 (copyright: Photo Mali, Charenton); PSS-BMC.

never know how Maderna would have solved the "in orchestra" positioning of the solo
flute and oboe "in the future." What we can say, without fear of reading too much between
the lines, is that their positions do find a precursor in the soprano and mezzo-soprano of
the last movement of Gustav Mahler's Symphony No. 2.

The arrangement of *Ausstrahlung*'s sound sources also has to do with the diffusion
of the magnetic tape music and the amplification of the musicians. The lack of any specific
sources related to such aspects means that we can only formulate hypotheses about how
the microphone signals and magnetic tapes were organized in terms of mixer input and
output, based on the recording of the first performance and on the photographic documentation of the stage layout taken during rehearsals and the concert.[13]

In the *mono* recordings that have come down to us,[14] the soloists are always set
in the foreground over a full-orchestra reprise, and the sounds of the magnetic tape are
easily heard. This corresponds to pictures of the stage, which show how each of the three
soloists had their own microphone, while the orchestra had three microphones, on the

---

13   We have no precise details about the rehearsals for the Persepolis concert; the picture in Example 7
      allows us to deduce that they certainly took place close to the premiere, most probably on the
      evening before (maybe also to avoid the heat of the day), that is, on September 4, given the presence
      of a first microphone setup and speakers on the stage.
14   Tape preserved in the PSS-BMC, catalogue number "TS 1084."

left, right, and center of the stage, respectively. It is therefore likely that the *stereo* sound of the magnetic tapes – that is, of the four tapes with pre-recorded voices used in the work – would spread from the two loudspeaker clusters placed high to the left and to the right (easily seen in the photo of the rehearsals, Ex. 7), to be then picked up by the three hanging microphones placed at the center of the orchestra. In fact, if the stereo tracks had only been assigned directly to the four pairs of loudspeakers placed at the foot of the stage, they would probably not be audible on the recording as they are beyond the catchment range of the three microphones located in orchestra (the photos do not appear to show any microphones other than the ones on the stage). The function of these speakers at the foot of the stage might have been to reinforce the general sound of the orchestra, the soloists, and the parts fixed on tape, thereby allowing the sound to reach the back rows of the large amphitheater that had been erected to welcome the audience (→ **EX. 8**).[15]

As far as *Aura* is concerned, no notes revealing a precise layout of the orchestra have come to light among the composer's materials. Likewise, it has not been possible to find any documentary sources attesting to the layout of the Chicago Symphony Orchestra on the occasion of the first performance (24 March 1972). There is thus nothing to suggest that Maderna had decided on any kind of arrangements of the instrumentalists. The only data available to us is the indication in the score, which mentions a specific distribution of the strings in six heterogeneous groups (from A to F).[16] Unfortunately, since we have no manuscript or documentary sources regarding the first performance of *Biogramma*, we can only hypothesize that the strings were divided into two groups (A and B) symmetrically positioned directly opposite the conductor, as indicated in the score.

Projectivity

The most evident characteristic that emerges from the analysis of the orchestral layouts indicated or suggested by Maderna in the compositions discussed here is his quest to establish a close relationship between the location of the sound sources and the construction of the form. Maderna considers the instrumental groups as sound sources whose task is to sculpt the acoustic space (from the stage, where the sounds are generated, to their diffusion in the auditorium). In this sense, Maderna's studies on instrumental layout are more intent on efficiently organizing the orchestral perspective and on "composing the space." The elaboration of compositional strategies that develop a musical rhetoric based on the displacement of sound sources is paid far less attention, almost as if it were inconsequential. Indeed, there is little evidence of an *a priori* structuring of the spatialization of the musical materials. With the exception of the finale of *Grande Aulodia* (see below), to date we only have one sketch relating to *Quadrivium* (→ **EX. 9**), which has three matrices and a diagram that illustrate the four possible ways of organizing the spatialization of musical materials 1, 2, and 3 by assigning them to four instrumental groups (I, II, III, and IV).

---

15   My heartfelt thanks to Alvise Vidolin for his lively dialogue on this matter.
16   See "Instrumentation" in Bruno Maderna, *Aura*, for orchestra, score (Milan: Ricordi, © 1972, repr. 1983, 131960), n.p.

EX. 9   *Quadrivium:* matrices for the spatialization of musical material;
autograph by Bruno Maderna; sketchbook "5" [p. 14]; PSS-BMC.

The fact that the printed score does not record any such distribution of the musical materials suggests that this sketch belongs to an initial phase of reflection on the precompositional material. However, it is also true that the very embryonic stage of this sketch in the creative process could actually testify to how space was considered a fundamental compositional element right from the earliest stages of conception of the work.

The construction of this complex instrumental sound device aims to fill the stage as much and as homogenously as possible. At the same time, it presupposes writing real parts for the orchestra, which, in turn, derives from the structuring of the perspective and the organization of the harmonic planes. In this way, the orchestra becomes a sort of diaphragm that completely or partly expands and contracts and, at the same time, a projective organism that diffuses individual acoustic details, making them perceptible thanks to the physical distance of the sound sources (whatever their asymmetric or symmetric distribution).

For example, the *Quadrivium* finale belongs to this "orchestra-diaphragm" typology (pp. 25–42 of the printed score)[17] and is organized in two distinct sections. The first part, which goes from page 25 to page 32 (bars 184–223), is made up of the slow staggered entrances of the wind instruments and the soloists of the four groups. Starting from the soloists' dynamic "*pp*" and the "*ppp leggero*" of the woodwinds in the background, they all simultaneously perform a long and intense *crescendo*. This leads to the climax in the second section (pp. 33–42), where the strings release the accumulated energy through a long *continuum* of sound, which, from an entrance in "*fff*," gradually proceeds to slowly extinguish the sound. The latter is achieved thanks to an irregular canon of chords that move between the four groups, thereby accompanying the analogous development of the percussion section, in preparation for the coda of the piece with the four solo violins (p. 42). These distinct processes of expansion and contraction are "framed" both physically and musically by two bass clarinets. Physically, because these instruments are in fact placed on either side of the orchestra (in groups 1 and 4 respectively (see Ex. 2); musically, because they are almost given a solo role, which first of all powers the expansion process (from b. 187, they are the only instruments to emerge "*molto f*" in the overall dynamic level of *pianissimo*), only to then accompany the final dissipation, almost in an act of bidding farewell (p. 42).

As a "projective organism," the orchestra is constructed starting from the specific positions of the musicians on stage. This typology aims to offer not only an analytical perception of the timbral counterpoint of the different orchestral families, but also to bring out the polyphonic weave within the same instrumental families. This analytical perception involves numerous sections of the works analyzed here and is particularly effective for those passages in which the orchestra develops homogeneous materials and dynamics. Prime examples are bars 29-98 of Section B of *Biogramma* (woodwinds, horn, and the two groups of strings), bars 107–12 of *Aura* (woodwinds, marimba, and strings), and the last section of *Ausstrahlung* no. 4, particularly bars 27–52 (woodwinds, brass, percussion, and harps).[18]

Instead, the string family offers the majority of examples of the polyphonic weave. This is due both to the large number of musicians involved in this instrumental section, and to the complexity of composing in real parts that follows. This is particularly true for those sections that develop uniform and monotimbric materials through imitative compositional techniques or are based on accumulation or dispersion processes. *Grande Aulodia* offers two explanatory examples in this regard. The first of these is the section that goes from bar 26 to bar 154 (pp. 6–18 of the printed score),[19] in which every group of strings (A, B, C) proceeds by accumulating its internal elements: starting from just three solo cellos, the instrumental totality of each group is reached (bb. 69–76) by means of the progressive addition of the remaining cellos, then the violas, double basses, and finally the

---

17   Bruno Maderna, *Quadrivium*, for 4 percussionists and 4 orchestral groups, score (Milan: Ricordi, © 1969, repr. 1976, 131477).

18   See the following scores: *Biogramma*, for full orchestra (Milan: Ricordi, © 1973, repr. 1974, 131985), pp. 13–14; *Aura*, for orchestra (Milan: Ricordi, © 1972, repr. 1983, 131960), pp. 16–17; and *Ausstrahlung*, for female voice, flute, and oboe obbligati, full orchestra, and magnetic tape (Ricordi, posthumous edn., © 1975, print 1988, 131908), pp. 4–8 (*Ausstrahlung* no. 4).

19   Bruno Maderna, *Grande Aulodia*, for solo flute and oboe with orchestra (Milan: Ricordi, © 1970, repr. 1974, 131648).

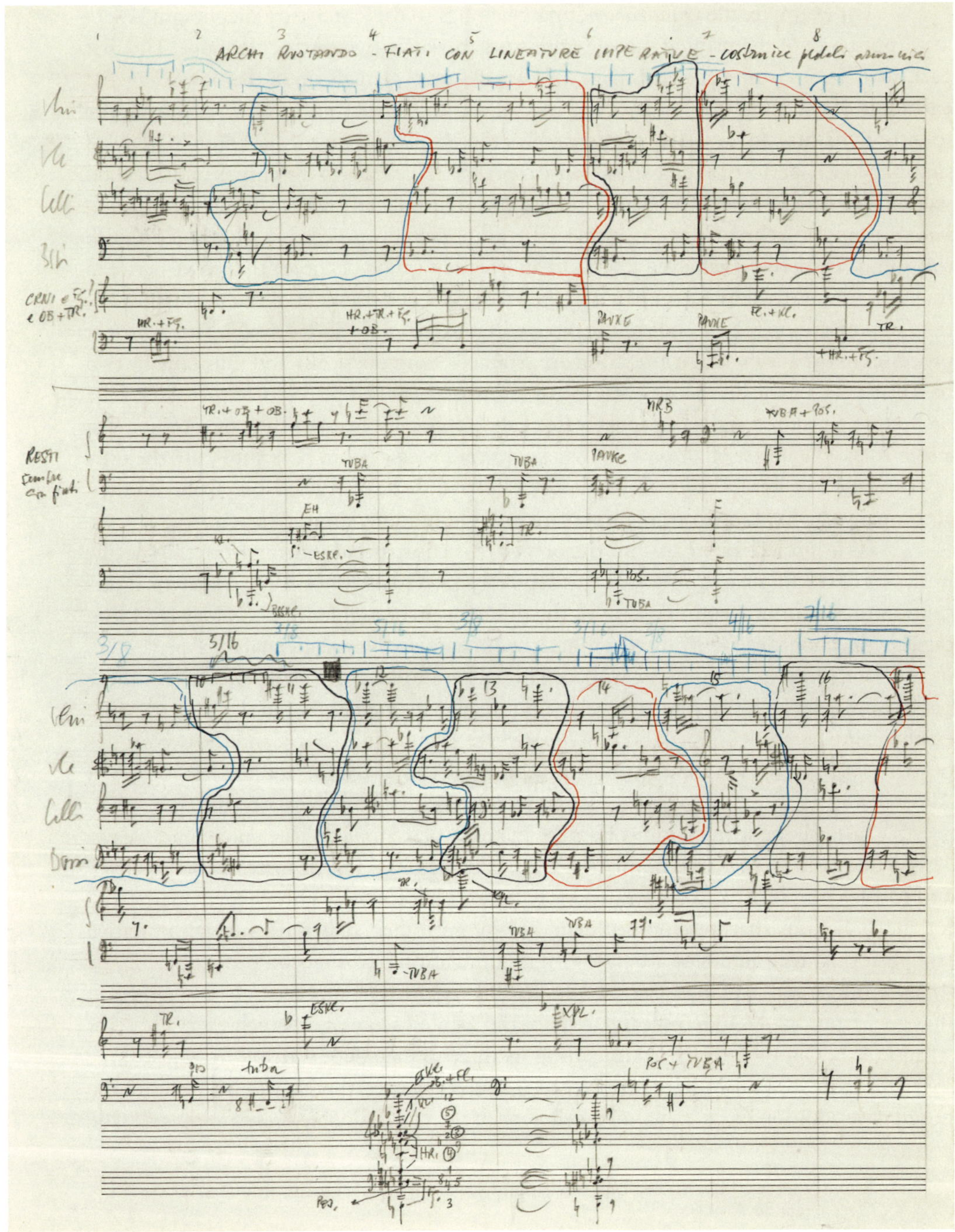

EX. 10 Bruno Maderna, *Grande Aulodia,* preparatory sketch to bb. 101ff.;
PSS-BMC.

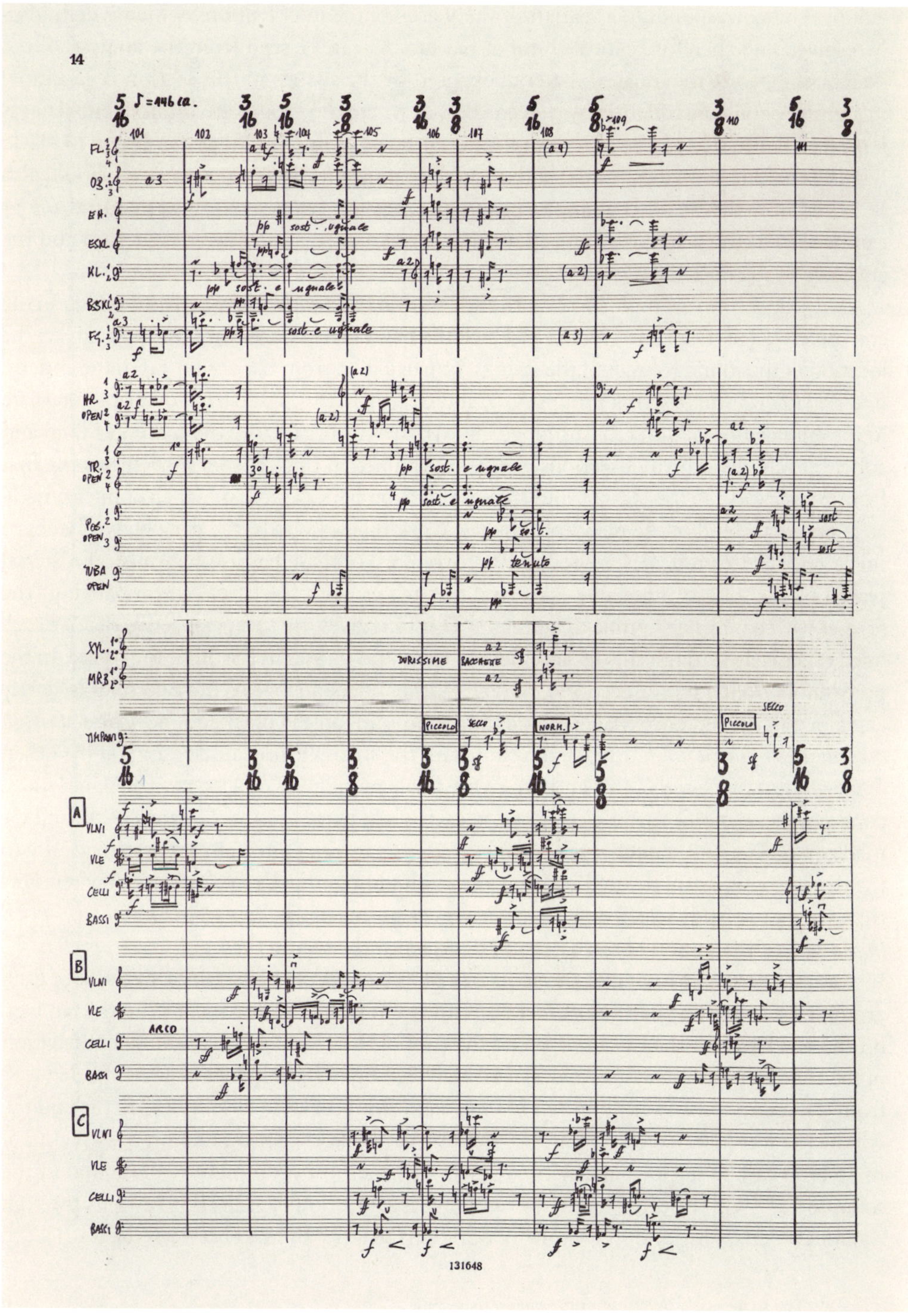

EX. 11   Bruno Maderna, *Grande Aulodia,* score (Milan: Ricordi, © 1970, repr. 1974, 131648), p. 14 (bb. 101–11).

violins. This corresponds to a spatialization of each of the interventions, which is definitively resolved and therefore canceled out at bar 140. As can be seen from the analysis of the sketches (→ **EX. 10**), the musical material exposed by the strings in this section is generated in a unitary and consequential way, regardless of where the groups are located; only later is it projected into space by means of a selection process (group A strings are shown in black, B strings in blue, C strings in red) and one of free rotation ("*archi ruotando*"). It should also be noted how the meter is changed in the final version from the original neutral 3/8 (as can be seen in the printed score → **EX. 11**); as a consequence of the internal rhythm and the entrance of the individual groups.

The second example involves the last section of *Grande Aulodia*, from bar 181 to the end (pp. 28–42 of the printed score), in which the main focus of the composition is in fact the location of the sound sources of the strings. In particular, from bar 205 (p. 34) to the end, we find a spatialization of string groups A, B, and C, which, through partial overlaps, alternate in the enunciation of different sustained chords, thereby organizing the space in a fluid and coherent way. Two distinct sections can be recognized in this chordal movement: the first from bars 205 to 229 (pp. 34–39), and the second from bars 230 to 241, which come immediately before the end of the piece (pp. 40–42). Working backwards, the perspective planes in the latter bars (from b. 230) are reduced to two. Each of these has its own musical material played by the soloists (flute and oboe) and the strings, with the latter "accompanying" the former with barely perceptible dynamics.[20] This thus gives rise to a perspective that is developed exclusively through the displacement of the chord masses in the orchestral space. In the preparatory sketch reproduced in Example 12, the independence of the two roles is clearly explained in the sentence Maderna adds at the bottom: on the one hand, he writes "*fare gli accordi d'archi per il finale*" (make the chords for the strings for the finale), and on the other, "*e inventare il finale con i soli*" (and invent the finale with the solos → **EX. 12**). The upper staves concern the harmonic material assigned to each of the three groups of strings (A, B, and C), made up of 8, 6, and 9 pitch sets respectively. These are attributed almost systematically to the three groups, notwithstanding some octave doubling in both the high and low registers that is certainly freely selected (perhaps this is what is meant by "*fare gli accordi d'archi per il finale*") and the addition of the basses (as indicated at the top on the right: "*tutti con Bassi*"). Instead, the last staff indicates the sequence of entrances of the twenty-three sets of each group, on the basis of a criterion that does not seem to follow any specific matrix. In fact, on the one hand, in the executive phase the twenty-three sets alternate in the enunciation of the chords according to a tempo that is totally left up to the conductor, as can be deduced from the metronome indication "*ad libitum*" and from the note "From here to the end the conductor accompanies the soloists […] taking care that the string section has an aura of mystery. It can be stopped at any time (creating ⌒) almost prompted by the sound of the soloists […]."[21] On the other hand, the temporal organization of each chord evolves through a gradual overlapping and shortening of durations that is stabilized between the fourteenth

---

20   The score reads "Archi sempre *pppppp*" (see ibid., p. 40).
21   "Di qui alla fine il direttore accompagna i solisti […] badando acché la orchestra d'archi sia solo un misterioso alone. Si può fermare in ogni istante (creando delle ⌒) quasi prendesse suggerimento dal canto dei soli […]." Ibid.

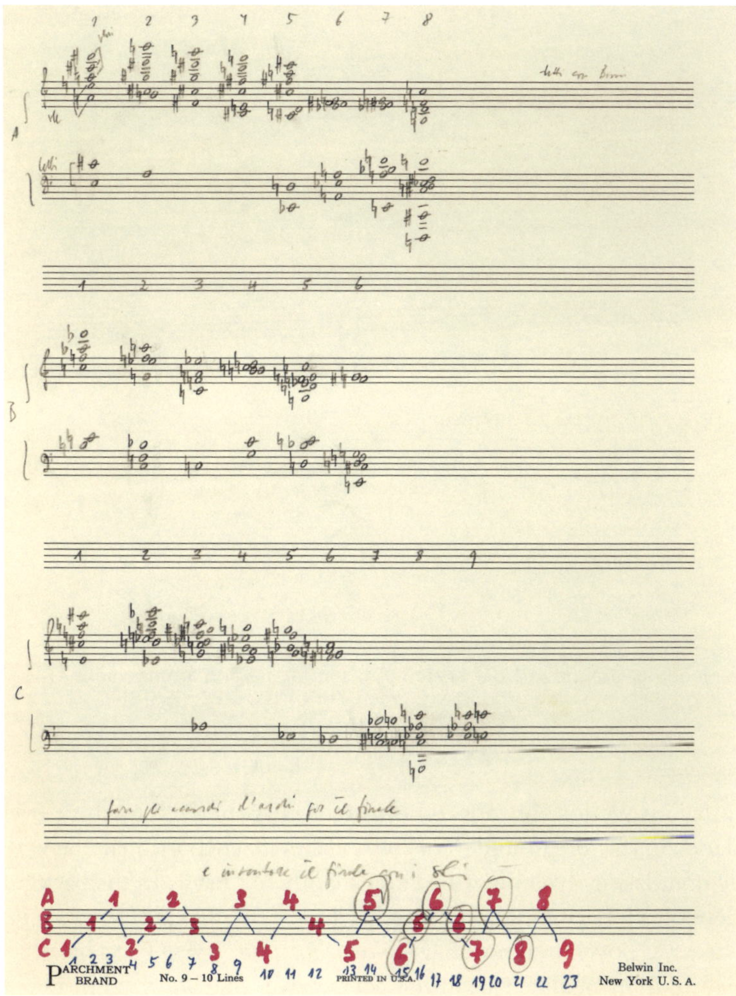

EX. 12　Bruno Maderna, *Grande Aulodia,* sketch of the structure and arrangement of the chord sets of string groups A, B, and C for bb. 230–41; PSS-BMC.

Set No.	1	2	3	4	5	6	7	8	9	10	11	12	13	14	15	16	17	18	19	20	21	22	23
Overlapping	/	0	0	0	1	1	1	2	2	2	3	3	3	4	6	5	4	5	5	6	6	7	$\overset{\frown}{4}$
Duration	8	10	12	16	15	12	11	10	9	8	5	6	8	12	12	12	13	14	16	7	19	$\overset{\frown}{13}$	$\overset{\frown}{4}$

and twenty-first sets (corresponding to those circled in blue at the bottom of the sketch in Ex. 12), only to lengthen once again in the enunciation of the last two sets. Thus, the duration of each set follows an expansion-contraction-expansion dynamic (see table above).[22]

22　The table has the numbers relating to the "overlap" and "duration" fields based on the sixteenth note ($\eighthnote$).

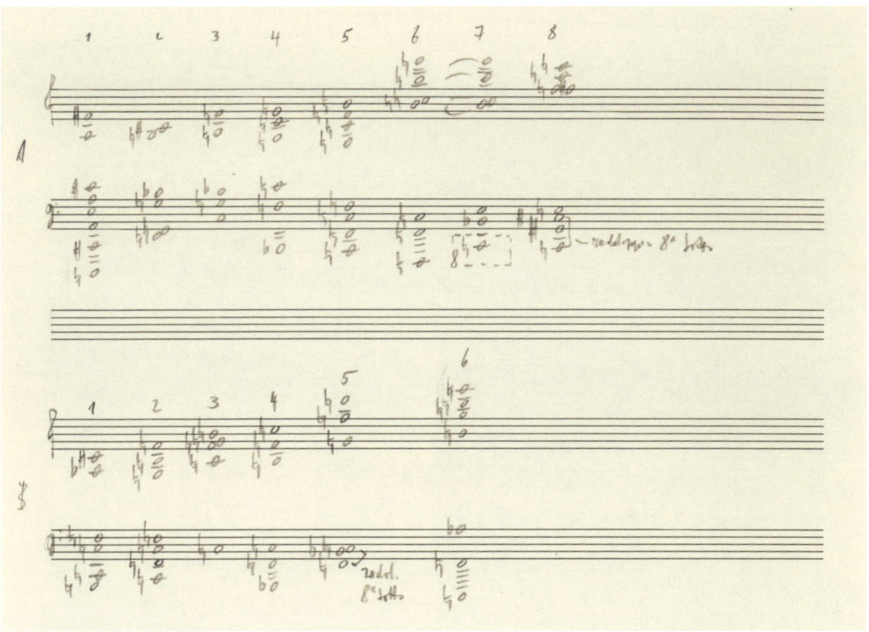

EX. 13   Bruno Maderna, *Grande Aulodia,* sketch of the structure and arrangement
of the chord sets of string groups A, B, and C for bb. 209–29; PSS-BMC.

The previous section (bb. 205–29) is instead characterized by three overlapping
perspective planes: in the foreground the soloists elaborate virtuosic material with agogics
and extremely undulating dynamics (the latter mainly in *f* or *ff*); in the background the
woodwinds develop a long and sinuous melody whose dynamics are *"sempre il più pp possibile"* (always as *pp* as possible), if not as *"pppp come un alito"* (*pppp* like a breath);[23] finally,
the strings play an intermediate role in the perspective, characterized by chord masses
that expand and contract the orchestral diaphragm through dynamics of crescendo-decre-
scendo and with the same pitches as the woodwinds. These chord blocks are pre-arranged
in their harmonic sequence on the *recto* of the same music sheet shown in the previous
example (Ex. 12). As can be seen in Example 13, they have been plotted for each of the three
groups (without giving the order of the respective entrances), and Maderna actually reads
them backwards in the *mise en page* (→ **EXX. 13–14**).

The composition of these bars and that of the string groups D, E, and F in *Ausstrahlung* no. 6 is quite similar (→ **EX. 15**). In fact, there is a clear affinity between the configuration of the musical material used and the arrangement of the groups themselves,
i.e. those placed on either side (D, E) and at the back (F) of the stage, which resembles
the layout for groups A, B, and C in *Grande Aulodia*. Thus, even in *Ausstrahlung* no. 6,
the *continuum* of the chord masses, which repeat the fifty-seven bars *"a volontà"* and

---

23 Maderna, *Grande Aulodia,* score (see note 19), p. 34.

EX. 14   Bruno Maderna, *Grande Aulodia,* score (Milan: Ricordi, © 1970, repr. 1974, 131648); detail of p. 39 with the spatialization of strings A, B, and C (bb. 227–29).

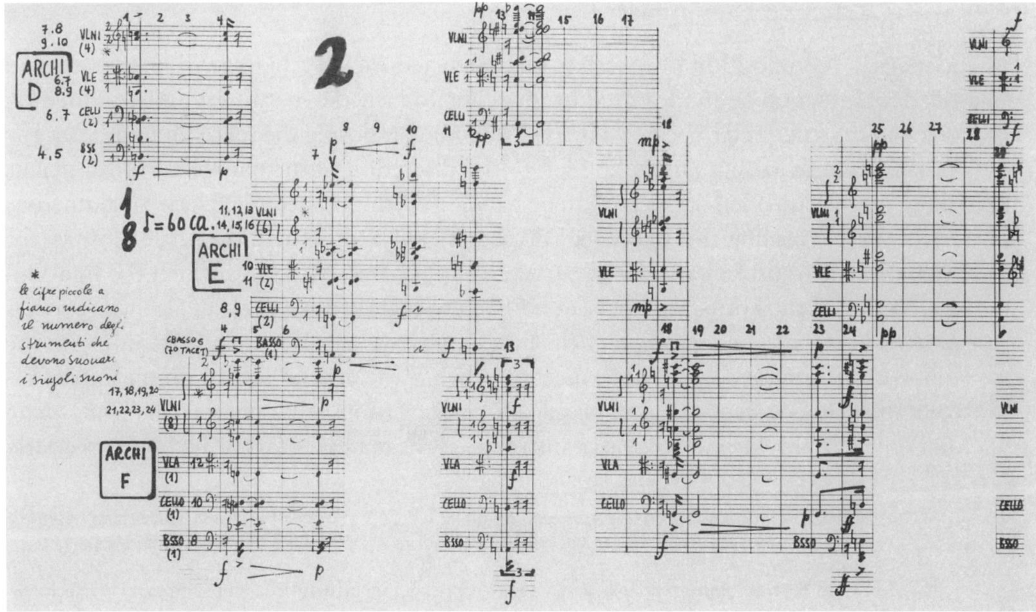

EX. 15   Bruno Maderna, *Ausstrahlung,* composition of groups D, E, and F; detail from the score (Milan: Ricordi, posthumous edn., © 1975, print 1988, 131908), *Ausstrahlung* no. 6, [p. 1].

independently,[24] has a transversal role toward the perspective planes of the instruments that develop its beginning, that is, the soloists (flute, oboe, and voice), tape 1, and the string groups A, B, and C.

The appearance of this material can be traced back to the string section (*"Lento"*) in *Quadrivium*, from bars 118 to 135 (pp. 16–18 of the printed score), even though there are at least two significant differences. First of all, here the chords are not proposed in a synchronic way but formed and unraveled through the gradual addition and removal of instruments belonging to the same group. Second, the four groups of strings (I–IV) are the only instruments in this section and are not related to any other instruments; instead, they organize the orchestral space in an autonomous manner.

Especially in those sections with homogeneous materials, this organization of the perspective and the attention toward the construction of a "perceptive discretion" may also involve those groups whose role is enunciated and exclusively performed in the background. This is the case, for example, with the dissipation in the finales of *Aura* and *Grande Aulodia* (see next section) and that of the wind instruments (*"sempre ppp e legatissimo"* – always *ppp* and *legatissimo*) in the long orchestral section of *Aura* (bb. 223–59, pp. 38–47 of the printed score) that precedes the final improvisation.[25] Finally, the background role is sometimes achieved by means of a transversal and dialectical process with respect to the perspective planes, such as in the fade-outs, organized in families, which articulate the form of *Quadrivium* on page 24B (with solo percussion and strings) and on page 42 (harps and strings).

Extemporaneousness

Maderna's "composition of space" is not entrusted exclusively to writing, or rather to the determination of an idea fixed in the score: in fact, the margins of indetermination given to the interpreter become a further tool for composing the space. In particular, the variations in dynamics and tempo left to the discretion of the conductor or musicians allow the instrumental perspective to be handled extemporaneously. There are numerous indications regarding this in the various scores analyzed here. In the finale of *Aura*, for example, the indistinct and mobile background of the strings, on which the final improvisation of the horns, trumpets, and first flute is grafted (p. 48 of the printed score), is obtained through the repetition of the first sixty-eight bars of the piece according to the following rule in the score: "In the meantime [while the instruments begin the improvisation] the strings start afresh, and play again, one at a time, as a 'cadenza' bars 1–68 – *pppp* and muted."[26] In *Ausstrahlung* no. 1, instead, it is the conductor who "will have to clearly

---

24 Indication found at the end of *Ausstrahlung* no. 6, where Maderna adds that *"il tutto viene ripetuto a volontà"* (everything is repeated at will); see Maderna, *Ausstrahlung*, score (see note 18), p. [2] (*Ausstrahlung* no. 6).

25 The indication *"fiati sempre ppp e legatissimo"* appears for the first time on page 38 and is repeated on almost every page until the end of the section.

26 "Nel frattempo [mentre gli strumenti iniziano l'improvvisazione] gli archi ritornano da capo, uno alla volta, e risuonano liberamente, come in una 'cadenza', le battute 1–68 – *pppp* e con sordina." Maderna, *Aura*, score (see note 16), p. 47.

draw attention to the solo part of the flute and sometimes he can 'accompany it' by high-lighting some particular expression of each group of strings";[27] the strings in turn "must not worry about synchronism, if anything a certain freedom to play 'rubato' is allowed."[28] Likewise, in the last part of Section B of *Biogramma* (bb. 29–98, pp. 13–14 of the printed score), the perspective, which is almost nullified by a general *pp* dynamic, is brought out by both the peculiar timbric properties of each instrument – particularly the wind instruments – and by the explicit invitation to the conductor to organize the general dynamic to his own liking, "with sudden (or gradual) crescendos and decrescendos, highlighting single instruments or groups of instruments."[29] The indication *molto espressivo* also allows each musician a further margin of interpretive freedom. Similar directions are also found in the refrain indicated for the strings at the beginning of *Grande Aulodia*, in a context in which the canceling out of the perspective is brought about by means of a general *pp* dynamic and use of a mute:

> [S]tart afresh from bars 1 to 25. The second time everything is played with the mutes, always in pp but *molto espressivo* and always "Wienerisch" and the tempo will be slowed down to an English Waltz, or rather "Hesitation" because it must always be very *rubato*.[30]

All in all, the background of the strings in the finale of *Grande Aulodia* (bb. 230–41) is characterized not only by the spatial dislocation of the groups, but also by the freedom granted to the conductor both in managing its temporal flow (see above), and also allowing "*tasto, corda, ponticello, vibrato, poco vibrato, molto vibrato, non vibrato*" to alternate *ad libitum*. The dynamic is, however, "*sempre pppppp*," and the soloists are accompanied "with circumspection, ensuring that the string orchestra only lends a mysterious aura."[31]

Ambiguity

We can thus identify the two main types of perspective that coexist in mutual equilibrium: the first is the physical one, peculiar to the instruments on the stage and deriving from the distance between the groups and their internal composition; the second is a more "internal" one peculiar to the act of writing and organized through orchestration.

---

27 "[Il direttore] dovrà mettere in chiara evidenza la parte del flauto solo, e potrà talvolta 'accompagnarlo' mettendo in rilievo qualche espressione particolare dei singoli gruppi d'archi." Maderna, *Ausstrahlung*, score (see note 18), p. 3 (*Ausstrahlung* no. 1).

28 "non devono esservi preoccupazioni di sincronismi, al contrario una certa liberà di suonare 'rubato' è permessa." Ibid.

29 "In generale la dinamica resta *pp*, sebbene molto espressivo. Il direttore potrà, a suo piacimento, articolarla con improvvisi (o graduali) crescendi e decrescendi, mettendo in rilievo strumenti singoli, o gruppi di strumenti." Maderna, *Biogramma*, score (see note 18), p. 13.

30 "da battuta 1 a 25 si fa un da capo. La seconda volta venga suonato il tutto con le sordine, sempre in *pp* ma molto espressivo e sempre 'Wienerisch' e il tempo verrà rallentato a walzer inglese, o meglio 'Hesitation' perché dev'essere sempre molto rubato." Maderna, *Grande Aulodia*, score (see note 19), p. 5. Bars 1–25, played by the strings, fill pp. 2–5 of the score. An "English Waltz," *Hesitation*, also appears in *Venetian Journal*, in section 3II (where the same term appears as a simple expressive reference in section 2A); see Angela Ida De Benedictis, "'Qui forse una cadenza brillante': Viaggio nel *Venetian Journal* di Bruno Maderna," *Acta Musicologica* 72, no. 1 (2000), pp. 63–105: 91 and 93.

31 "con circospezione, badando che l'orchestra d'archi sia solo un misterioso alone." Maderna, *Grande Aulodia*, score (see note 19), p. 40.

EX. 16   Bruno Maderna, *Grande Aulodia,* score (Milan: Ricordi,
© 1970, repr. 1974, 131648), p. 28, bb. 181–84.

EX. 17   Bruno Maderna, *Ausstrahlung,* score (Milan: Ricordi, posthumous edn.,
© 1975, print 1988, 131908), *Ausstrahlung* no. 1, bb. 1–7.

The following two examples demonstrate that the complexity of their relationship leaves room for ambiguity that only a clear and mindful interpretation can resolve.

The first example involves the section of *Grande Aulodia* between bars 181 and 204 (pp. 28–33 of the printed score), in which a material with an irregular canonical sequence of pitches is distributed throughout the space. Maderna assigns the sequence to different instrumental groups, each with its own perspective and with a dynamic never louder than *p*. If we take a detailed look at its development in the early stages, we can identify three levels of organization of the perspective (→ **EX. 16**). The first is entrusted to the woodwinds, placed at the center of the orchestra, who play *"tutti il più pp possibile"* (all as *pp* as possible), in the most indistinct and neutral manner possible (as seems to be suggested by the further indications *"ogni nota accuratamente separate"* (every note distinctly separated) and *"suoni egualissimi"* (extremely equal sounds).[32] The second is made up of strings A and B, positioned at the sides of the stage, which envelop the woodwinds playing in *pp*. Their timbric enunciation can be discerned since they articulate the sound *"un poco vibrando e sostenendo"* (a little vibrating and sustained). Finally, the third level is given by the C group of strings who, let us note, are physically placed behind the woodwinds, at the back of the stage. They play with a much lower dynamic level (only one *p*) marked by a decisive expression with a *"molto vibrando e sost[enuto]"* (much vibrating and sustained sound). Thus, although such indications might lead us to attribute a leading role to the C group of strings, their very position within the orchestral structure would seem to suggest that the different dynamic indications are functional to a realization of perspective levels in which all the strings are placed on the same perceptive plane, albeit with two different kinds of vibrato.

The second example (→ **EX. 17**) concerns the writing for the string groups in *Ausstrahlung* no. 1 and, in particular, interventions *A, B,* and *C,*[33] which are characterized by a complex polyphony of real parts. Although the range and dynamic indications are more or less the same for all three, the way in which the perspective is written attributes an important role to group A, the only one made up of single parts (a string quartet). In fact, from the timbric point of view, it is the only group of strings to play unmuted (see indication "N.B." in Ex. 17), and, simultaneously, the quartet is seated right at the front of the orchestra. The four musicians are thus entrusted with a function of *primus inter pares*, which allows us accordingly to read and interpret their relationship to groups C, D, and E, placed in a semicircle behind them, and to the most distant groups B and F and the three soloists (see also Ex. 4).

Reactivity

The last aspect concerns the orchestral space intended as a place of composition and organization of another virtual space where certain musical materials can resonate. Despite the fact that the prevailing feature of the orchestration of the works considered here is that

---

32 Ibid., p. 28.

33 To avoid any confusion between the nomenclature used in the score for the six string groups (A to F) and the identical one used to define the parts relating to their four interventions in *Ausstrahlung* no. 1 (*A* to *D*; see also Ex. 17), we use normal type for the instrumental groups and italics to indicate the order of these interventions.

EX. 18   Bruno Maderna, *Quadrivium,* score (Milan: Ricordi,
© 1969, repr. 1976, 131477), detail of p. 3 (bb. 33–36).

the musical materials are organized in instrumental families proceeding with a parallel organization, there are a few isolated examples whose exceptionality makes them worthy of mention. One such case occurs in *Quadrivium* (→ **EX. 18**).

The first three solo violins of group I create a background that supports and makes some of the pitches of the xylophone solo resonate in space; at the same time, the first double bass in group IV emerges in the foreground by echoing and developing the initial note (F♯) from the pizzicato of the first cello of group III.

More often, the dialogue between the orchestral families, or between instrumental groups, develops in the presence of a main voice with a melodic trend. This is the case, for example, in Section B of *Biogramma* and has been exhaustively discussed elsewhere.[34] The theme of space here is addressed with regard to the relationship between the roles of the different instrumental families, rather than to the mobility of the sound sources.

---

34 See Alessandro Solbiati, *"Biogramma:* Projet et modalité de réalisation d'une *Weltanschauung,"* in *à Bruno Maderna* (see note 2), vol. 2, pp. 123–42: 138–40.

EX. 19   Bruno Maderna, *Biogramma,* score (Milan: Ricordi, © 1973, repr. 1974, 131985), p. 8, bb. 1–6 of Section B.

EX. 20   Bruno Maderna, *Ausstrahlung,* score (Milan: Ricordi, posthumous edn.,
© 1975, print 1988, 131908), detail of *Ausstrahlung* no. 2, bb. 1–6,
with melodic line marked.

Most of the roles developed by the orchestra already appear in the first four bars of this section (→ **EX. 19**). The foreground melody of the english horn is put in resonance by the A group of strings, which in turn take up all the attacks again, playing muted and *pp;* at the same time, and in an isochronous manner, strings B (also *con sordino* and *ppp*) articulate the background through clusters of pitch sets that rotate around those of the melody. This third role is shared by the celesta and "dirtied" by the vibraphone, playing with a barely audible dynamic level in *pppp* (*"kaum hörbar"*); finally, the glockenspiel assumes an intermediate heterophonic role, executing most of the high notes in the background, almost in a dialogue with the main melody of the english horn.

Instead, the space in *Ausstrahlung* no. 2 is organized through the mobility of the orchestra's response to the melodic line (→ **EX. 20**). If we consider the first six bars, for example, we can identify three roles: in the foreground, the chant of the female voice; the intermediate counterpoint to this chant by the four cellos; and the background of the violins. Among the multiple relationships that are set up between these three roles, let us take a closer look at the one that develops between the melody of the voice and the violin. In other words, we shall focus on how such a relationship is put into perspective through the octavization of the pitches, the dynamic echo (from the *f* of the voice to the *p* of the violins), and the physical position of the musicians. In particular, the singing voice is diffracted by its interaction with the six groups of violins – each of which, as we read in the score, is made up of at least four violins (see Ex. 20: *"4 almeno per parte"*) – thus drawing trajectories that articulate the orchestral space (→ **EX. 21**). The layout of the

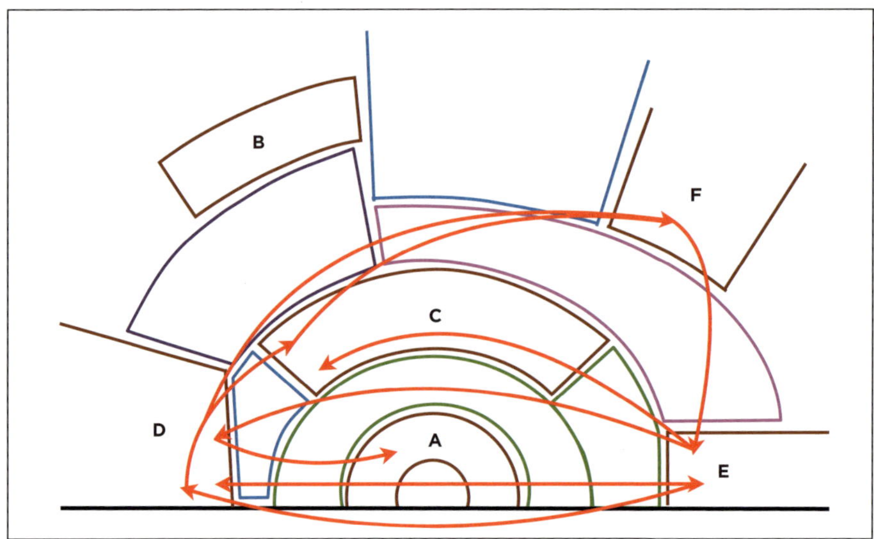

EX. 21   Reconstruction of the diffraction trajectories of the song
at the beginning of *Ausstrahlung* no. 2.

Group	violins 1	violins 2	violins 3	violins 4	violins 5	violins 6
Musicians	1, 2 (A) 3, 4 (C)	5, 6 (C) 7, 8 (D)	9, 10 (D) 11, 12 (E)	13–16 (E)	17–20 (F)	21–24 (F)

six groups, not specified in the score, can be reconstructed from the four parts indicated and summarized in the diagram above (the orchestral group to which each part belongs is indicated in brackets).[35]

In closing, let us just mention the borderline case of the interrelations between the melodic phrases of the soloists and, in particular, the technique of putting in resonance a pitch belonging to a melodic line, so frequently used in both *Grande Aulodia* and *Ausstrahlung*. The relationship between the two wind soloists and the third element, the voice, is particularly interesting in *Ausstrahlung* since the latter is entrusted with a role of alterity not only from the musical point of view, but also from a spatial one. In the final bars **(→ EX. 22)** – sadly absent from the printed score but clearly audible in the recording of the premiere at Persepolis and attested by Cathy Berberian's vocal score[36] – the oboe d'amore enunciates section 5 of *Solo* (with some octave substitutions).[37] Some of the pitches of this melody are echoed (sometimes at a different octave) by the bass flute and the voice, which takes its leave singing with closed mouth (almost as in *Ausstrahlungen* nos. 2 and 5), thus bringing the composition to an end.

---

35   My thanks to Luca Valli for taking the time to discuss this matter with me.
36   Recording preserved in the composer's collection at the Paul Sacher Foundation, which also houses Cathy Berberian's vocal score.
37   For the relationship between *Ausstrahlung*, *Solo*, and *Dialodia* see De Benedictis, *"Ausstrahlung"* (see note 7), pp. 297, 298, and 305.

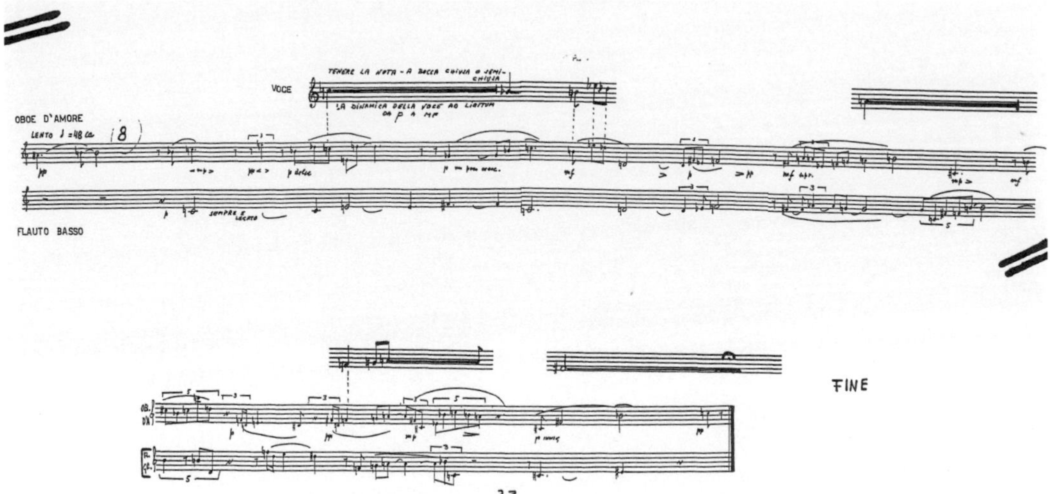

EX. 22   Bruno Maderna, *Ausstrahlung,* finale as it appears in the score assembled by Arturo Tamayo in 1988 for the "limited" Ricordi edition 131908 (ISMN 979-0-041-31908-7; non-commercial use only, based on archive material).

PASCAL DECROUPET

The Unity of Musical Practice
Bruno Maderna and His "Shaping Form" as Composer and Performer of Experimental Orchestral Music

One essential aspect of European post-WWII serialism was the postulate of the reciprocal conditioning of material and form, that is to say, the privileged relation between micro- and macrostructure. This interaction between the different levels of musical structure also directed composers to use studio facilities in synthetic sound production, since these devices seemed to offer them the means to structurally inform sound from the inside, to "compose" it in the most emphatic sense of the word, according to the same determinations as the other acoustic dimensions and further aspects of the music. Among the instrumental scores displaying an almost literal correspondence between the micro- and macrolevels, one of the earliest examples is John Cage's *First Construction in Metal* (1939), where this reciprocity determines the relation between the inner articulation of the first unit of sixteen bars and the whole form of 16×16 bars.[1] This model helped Pierre Boulez to complete his strategies of integral serial composition as realized in his *Structure Ia* (1951), where the intervals within the series are projected onto the level of the series' transpositions (including furthermore a principle of inversion responsible for the linking of the different levels of the structuration).[2] In Karlheinz Stockhausen's *Studie I* (1953), the first electronic music realized by superimposed sine waves in an effort to "compose timbre," the proportion series organizes all the levels, from the number of components per sound and the number of sounds per structure up to the number of sections within the piece. Considering the serial repertoire of the 1950s globally, such linear implications from the basic material to the formal development are typical of the initial attempts, and there exist, according to present knowledge, only a few later examples supporting the idea of an almost "algorithmic" strategy.[3] Indeed, in most cases, supplementary decisions were taken that disrupt any kind of linearity between the levels. Nevertheless, such decisions do not suspend the general idea of reciprocity, since the procedures at the different levels act according to similar strategies, which seemed, for many

---

1   See among others Pierre Boulez and John Cage, *Correspondance et documents,* new edn. by Robert Piencikowski (Mainz: Schott, 2002), p. 74, and James Pritchett, *The Music of John Cage* (Cambridge: Cambridge University Press, 1993), pp. 16–17. For a larger contextualization within the American scene, see Leta E. Miller, "Henry Cowell and John Cage: Intersections and Influences, 1933–1941," *Journal of the American Musicological Society* 59, no. 1 (Spring 2006), pp. 71–80.

2   See Robert Piencikowski, "Structure, que me veux-tu?" in *Théories de la composition musicale au XXe siècle,* ed. Nicolas Donin and Laurent Feneyrou (Lyon: Symétrie, 2013), pp. 867–86, and György Ligeti, "Pierre Boulez: Entscheidung und Automatik in der *Structure Ia,*" *die Reihe* 4 (1958), pp. 38–63.

3   See Pascal Decroupet, "Le rôle des clés et algorithmes dans le décryptage analytique: L'exemple des musiques sérielles de Pierre Boulez, Karlheinz Stockhausen et Bernd Alois Zimmermann," *Revue de musicologie* 98 (2012), pp. 221–46.

of these composers, sufficient to ensure coherence.[4] Let us consider a few examples within the mature serial style, addressing either the possible margin of independent decisions or the presence of micro/macro relations even in aleatoric works, as well as the gap between theoretical formulations by composers and the proper reality in the composed music. In his *Quartetto per archi in due tempi* (1955), Bruno Maderna created a specific relation between the two parts of the score through procedures such as reelaborated transformations and recombination of formerly exposed material.[5] Boulez's *Third Piano Sonata* (1957), namely its central movement *Constellation,* is a prominent example of indeterminacy with regard to the performance, where the completely determined sections provided by the composer can be ordered in different ways for different performances. Nevertheless, all possible arrangements among these sections reproduce on a higher level precisely the same structural combinations (homogeneous presentation, alternation, interlacement etc. of series) that the composer had used to serially elaborate these sections.[6] In his theoretical writings about *Kontakte* (1958–60), namely in his article "Die Einheit der musikalischen Zeit" (the unity of musical time), Stockhausen suggests that the composition as a whole resulted from systematic accelerations of electronic pulse structures, and the sketches for the piece corroborate that this procedure indeed enabled the composer to produce a great number of sounds for this composition.[7] However, the arrangement of the resulting sounds in time was in no way linked to the procedures used during the sound production. Rather, Stockhausen chose and combined his material by taste and intuition, which led Gottfried Michael Koenig to compose an "anti-example" with his own *Terminus* (1962), where the production process rooted in systematic transformations of a basic material has an immediate impact on the resulting form of the piece.[8]

These examples show that the idea of connection between different levels in serial compositions operates in a more general way, based on related qualities rather than on the strict reproduction of quantitative data. Such approaches, oriented toward the resulting sonic qualities, were further stimulated by the experience these composers accumulated in studios for electronic music. While Stockhausen's *Studie I* was "composed at the desk" and afterwards realized in studio, the proper composition of *Gesang der Jünglinge* (1955–56) was preceded by sonic experiments that helped the composer to develop specific structural

---

4   The notion of *analogie* (analogy) is central for Boulez's elaboration of his theory of serial music as formulated in *Penser la musique aujourd'hui* (Geneva: Gonthier, 1963), Eng. trans. as *Boulez on Music Today* (Cambridge, MA: Harvard University Press, 1971). See also Pascal Decroupet, "Comment Boulez pense sa musique au début des années soixante," in *Pli selon pli de Pierre Boulez: Entretien et études,* ed. Philippe Albèra (Geneva: Contrechamps, 2003), pp. 49–57.

5   See Christoph Neidhöfer, "Vers un principe commun: Intégration de la hauteur et du rythme dans le *Quartetto per archi in due tempi* (1955)," in *à Bruno Maderna,* ed. Geneviève Mathon, Laurent Feneyrou, and Giordano Ferrari, vol. 2 (Paris: Basalte, 2009), pp. 323–58.

6   See Pascal Decroupet, "Serial Organisation and Beyond: Cross-Relations of Determinants in *Le Marteau sans maître* and the Dynamic Pitch-Algorithm of *Constellation,*" in *Pierre Boulez Studies,* ed. Peter O'Hagan and Edward Campbell (Cambridge: Cambridge University Press, 2016), pp. 108–38.

7   See Karlheinz Stockhausen, "Die Einheit der musikalischen Zeit" (1961), *Texte zur elektronischen und instrumentalen Musik,* vol. 1 (*Aufsätze 1951–1962 zur Theorie des Komponierens*) (Cologne: DuMont, 1963), pp. 211–21: 211–12; Eng. trans. as "The Concept of Unity in Electronic Music," *Perspectives of New Music* 1, no. 1 (autumn 1962), pp. 39–48.

8   See Elena Ungeheuer, "Analoge Handschriften – Kompositorische Facetten des Kölner Studios für elektronische Musik in den fünfziger Jahren," in *KlangArt-Kongreß 1995,* ed. Bernd Enders and Niels Knolle (Osnabrück: Universitätsverlag Rasch, 1998), pp. 83–95.

strategies in accordance with the sonic properties of given sounds or sound combinations.[9] The Studio di Fonologia Musicale in Milan had been designed from the beginning to allow the composers an almost real-time auditive control throughout all the stages of a realization process.[10] This peculiarity of the technical equipment led composers to develop a specific attitude, resulting in new compositional methods. In his report on *Scambi*, Henri Pousseur described in some detail how he could produce different transformations of his basic material by reacting immediately to the machine's output, so that long sound sequences could be realized in one unique process instead of resulting from numerous operations of tape splicing and synchronization.[11]

Against this background, Maderna's working method in studio, as well as his way of conducting indeterminate scores as documented in video[12] and often regarded (negatively) as "improvisational," appears rather as a logical consequence of a rich experience of aurally based or at least aurally supported compositional strategies.[13] Furthermore, this kind of "freedom" was in no way a simple negation of serial thinking as such, as Maderna pointed out in his answer to André Boucourechliev's inquiry about "serial music" for the periodical *Preuves* in the middle of the 1960s.[14]

The present contribution considers this topic from two different perspectives. The first one concerns Maderna's compositional strategies as documented in the sketches to some of his late compositions for orchestra. It will be shown how Maderna derived more and more specific materials and how he developed sections on the basis of a compact material successively explored through different readings. The second consideration opens with an analysis of Maderna's conducting of Earle Brown's *Available Forms I* (1961), where the conductor is asked to make numerous decisions so as to build the formal dramaturgy of the piece on the basis of the different written sections. Since every section attests a specific "spectromorphological" character,[15] their arrangement (by superimposition or succession) both actualizes multiparametric connection criteria, from strong similarity to maximal difference, and establishes middle- and long-scale formal relations. To conclude, Maderna's late orchestral piece *Aura* (1972) will be briefly considered through the lens of "form-functional spectromorphology."

9   See Pascal Decroupet and Elena Ungeheuer, "Through the Sensory Looking-Glass: The Aesthetic and Serial Foundations of *Gesang der Jünglinge*," *Perspectives of New Music* 36, no. 1 (winter 1998), pp. 87–142.

10   See Angela Ida De Benedictis, "Riflessi del suono elettronico: sinergie e interazioni nell'orizzonte compositivo di Luciano Berio," in *Luciano Berio: Nuove Prospettive / New Perspectives*, ed. Angela Ida De Benedictis (Florence: Olschki, 2012), pp. 293–336.

11   See Henri Pousseur, "*Scambi*," *Gravesaner Blätter* 13 (1959), pp. 36–47 (German) and pp. 48–54 (English).

12   See, among others, *Un'ora con Bruno Maderna: Musica, specchio della società*, a documentary by Salvatore G. Biamonte and Giuseppe Sibilla, RAI, Milan-Venice, 1969–70, broadcast on 11 October 1971 (copy in PSS-BMC).

13   See Angela Ida De Benedictis, "Bruno Maderna e lo Studio di Fonologia della Rai di Milano: musica d'arte e d'uso tra creazione, ricerca e invenzione," *Musica/Realtà* 30, no. 91 (2010), pp. 43–75; and idem, "The Beginning of the Studio di Fonologia Musicale and Bruno Maderna's *Notturno*," in *The Performance Practice of Electroacoustic Music: The Studio di Fonologia years*, ed. Gérman Toro Pérez and Lucas Bennett (Bern etc.: Peter Lang, 2018), pp. 25–41.

14   See Bruno Maderna, "La révolution dans la continuité," in André Boucourechliev, "La musique sérielle aujourd'hui," *Preuves* 15, no. 177 (1965), pp. 28–29; also in *Bruno Maderna / Heinz Holliger: Festival d'Automne à Paris 1991* (Paris: Contrechamps, 1991), pp. 35–36.

15   The term "spectromorphology" was coined by Denis Smalley in his essay "Spectro-morphology and Structuring Processes," in *The Language of Electroacoustic Music*, ed. Simon Emmerson (Houndmills and London: Macmillan, 1986), pp. 61–93. Today it describes a global research area.

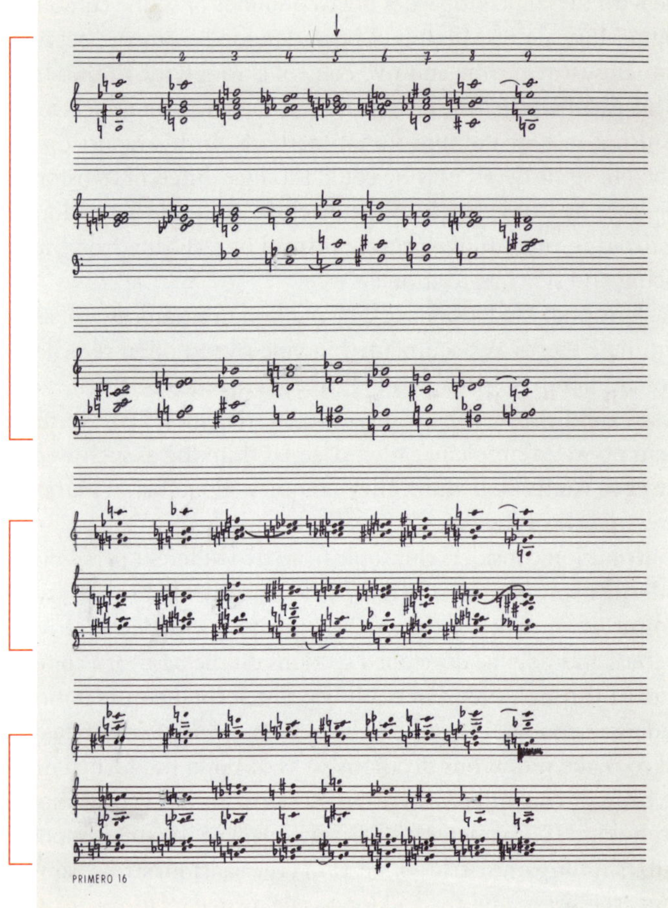

EX. 1   Bruno Maderna, sketch for *Quadrivium* (brass chords); PSS-BMC.

Maderna's Sketches: Derivation and Selective Readings

The identified sketches for *Quadrivium* (1969), preserved in the Maderna Collection at the Paul Sacher Foundation, all concern harmonic fields. Closely related to each other, they at first give insight into the way Maderna produces his material through successive derivations. In a second step, the comparison between such derived materials and the score reveals that he manipulated multiple selective readings of one unique material in order to obtain differently shaped sections. Both these strategies assure at once coherence and variability.

One of the sketches that seems to come first in the compositional process (→ **EX. 1**) shows in its upper part three layers of nine successive four-tone chords each, respectively attributed to trumpets, horns, and trombones. The progressive transformation of the chords conforms to a mirror symmetry with its center in chord 5 (marked by an arrow in

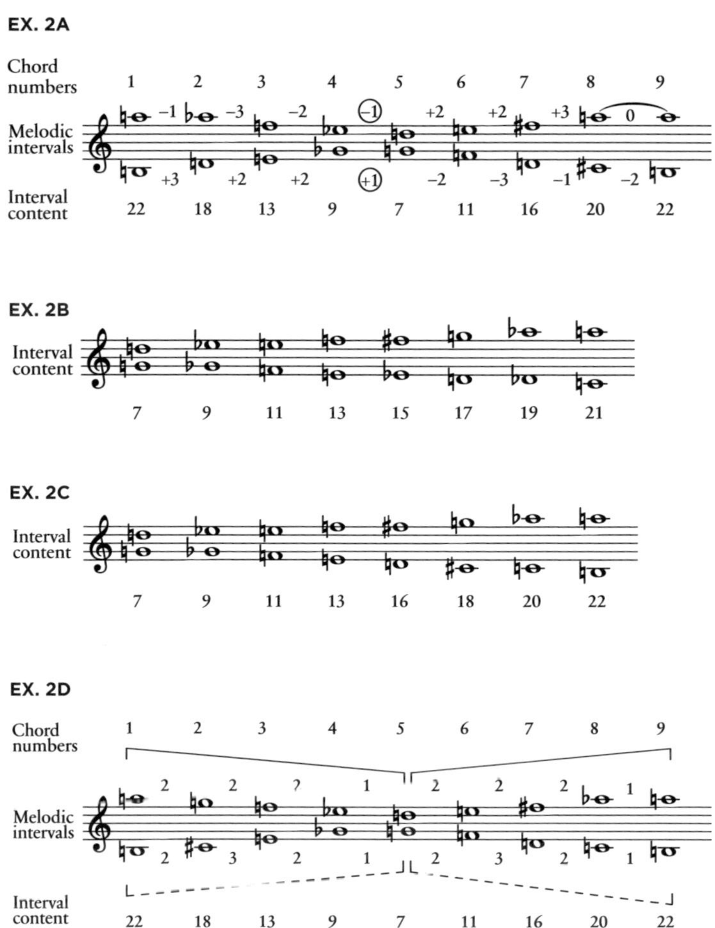

EX. 2 *Quadrivium,* trumpet chords, suggested reconstruction of the derivation process.

Maderna's sketch): in the trumpets, the chords proceed from open to close positions (for 1–5) and back to open ones (for 5–9), while horns and trombones progress according to the opposite movement.

The chords in the trumpets not only appear as the upper layer, but they also form the very point of departure for further steps of derivation. Their inner construction reveals an interaction of the following parameters: registral distribution, chromaticism, and intervallic diversity, both vertically and horizontally. Indeed, when reducing the chords to their outer voices (→ EX. 2A), the aforementioned progression between open and close positions links two identical dyads (B$_3$–A$_5$) at its extremities around the central dyad G$_4$–D$_5$. Considering the vertical extension of each dyad, there is maximal intervallic diversity (with the exception, of course, of the two identical extreme chords): 22-18-13-9-7-11-16-20-22. Placed in ascending order 7-9-11-13-16-18-20-22, these chords seem to highlight an underlying chromatic generator, since both voices progress by widely diverging chromatic lines. But what are the possible reasons for the deviations in the chromatic progressions? If one builds regular diverging chromatic lines departing from the central perfect fifth (→ EX. 2B), the resulting intervals quickly produce interval class repetitions, since in the progression 7-9-11-13-15-17-19-21, 7-17-19 are variants of ic5 and 9-15-21 variants of ic3. To enhance the variety of vertical relations, it is sufficient to enlarge the four last intervals by a supplementary 1 in order to come to Maderna's solution of interval extensions. One easy way to transform the former progression would be to transpose the inferior chromatic line by –1 (→ EX. 2C), leaving the upper line untouched. When combining this intermediate result with the idea of a globally symmetric registral progression (open-close-open), a melodic monotony occurs since in both voices one interval pattern is repeated twice: 2-2-2-1 in the upper one, and 2-3-2-1 in the lower one (→ EX. 2D). Nevertheless, the inferior module shows great diversity, which is a consequence of the skip in the continuity of the descending chromatic line in Example 2c (between E and D). Compared with Maderna's solution in Example 2a, in Example 2d only dyads 2 and 8 are different in pitch (transposed +1), and the melodic module from the lower voice in Example 2d (3-2-1) appears in Example 2a in the upper one. As a consequence of this modification, the condition of maximal diversity in the vertical as well as in the horizontal interval successions seems fulfilled. An additional result from this succession of qualitative decisions is the "serial" relation between these outer voices of the trumpet chords, featuring a retrograde inversion for dyads 1 to 8; the one exception to this principle is the inverse direction of the central circled semitone.

A supplementary aspect consists in the harmonic hierarchy among the interval classes, as can be observed in the process of producing the four-part trumpet chords starting from these voices. First of all, the two sounds that subdivide the extreme (identical) dyads correspond to the first two chromatic derivations from the central fifth, producing in both chords a similarity by inversion: [7-9-6] in chord 1, [6-11-5] in chord 9 ([5] and [6] being the inversion respectively of [7] and [6], while the central [9] and [11] are resulting intervals). These intervals of fifth/fourth and tritone gain a real structural role, as can be easily observed in the other chords.

The first step in which proper "tables" appear consists in the combination of these trumpet, horn, and trombone chords (Ex. 1, upper part, consisting of three systems with "white" notes) to present the chromatic total without any timbral differentiation, summarized on three staves in the lower center of the sketch (fourth system). At the bottom of this page (fifth system) follows a split of the former chordal succession according to a tritone transposition, since the six highest tones and the six lowest ones are transposed respectively a tritone upward and downward.

In a second step (→ EX. 3A), Maderna develops the latter table into a double pair (which he calls "A"), where each twelve-tone chord is now distributed on six staves (containing two sounds each). The second part of this diptych (which for simplicity I call *A-right*, and which is numbered by Maderna as retrograde from 9 to 1) consists in the inversion of the first part, again transposed at the tritone (between the highest tone of column 1 in *A-left*, A$_4$, and the lowest one of column 9 in *A-right*, E flat$_3$). This is followed by table "B," whose highest tritone suggests a transpositional relation with the beginning

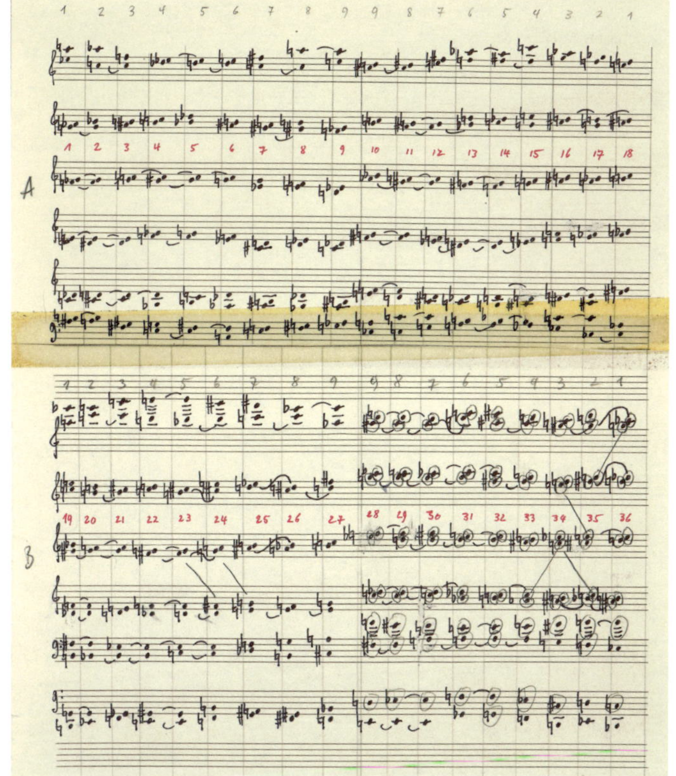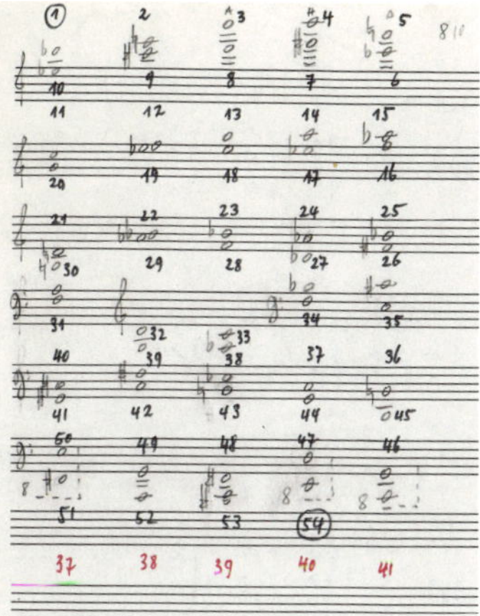

EX. 3   Bruno Maderna, *Quadrivium;* PSS-BMC.

3A (↑)
Sketch rearranging the chords resulting in Example 1 on
six staves into table *A-left* and complemented by a
second table in *A-right;* table B presents an original derivation
starting from the tritone.
3B (↗)
Sketch with complementary chords numbered 37 to 41 (in red).

of table "A," although the initial twelve-tone chord now appears significantly expanded through the registers, its harmonic structure being completely modified. The last chord of table "B" (column 1) presents, in its upper part, a transposed inversion of the initial twelve-tone chord (table *A-left,* column 1). The sequence of figures 1 to 36 of tables "A" and "B" (in red) is prolonged (written with the same red pen) on the bottom of another sketch with chords numbered from 37 to 41 (→ **EX. 3B**). Presented in retrograde from 41 to 1, these chords will serve as the strings' background layer in the last part of *Quadrivium* (pp. 33–42 in the score).[16] Furthermore, Maderna assigns additional numbers from 1 to 54 to each tone of these last five chords (in black ink in Ex. 3b).

---

16   See Bruno Maderna, *Quadrivium,* for 4 percussionists and 4 orchestral groups, score (Milan: Ricordi, © 1969, repr. 1976, 131477).

EX. 4   Bruno Maderna, *Quadrivium:* sketch for filtering procedure;
PSS-BMC.

A Upper part, new version of *A-left* with systematic slurs.
B Central part, selective table with sustained sounds only.
C Lower part, sounds that are filtered out.

In the third step (Ex. 4, which in the original faces Ex. 1 on the inner side of the same double page), the observation of the obtained results seems to have led Maderna to add a supplementary principle that will have significant impact on the derivation of further material. In a new version of table *A-left* (→ **EX. 4A**), Maderna has used slurs to highlight the presence of one identical tone in the same register in successive chords, stressing not only the structural function of common tones, but also the musical value of prolonged sounds (circled in green). The tones that remain in the second table of this page (→ **EX. 4B**) are those fulfilling this principle of prolongation, the unslurred tones being "filtered out" and transferred into the two lowest staves (→ **EX. 4C**).

Starting from this table, Maderna draws a new diptych marked with a circled "B" (→ **EX. 5**), which is the basis for the realization of the brass chords with mixed timbres that appear in the score on pages 27 to 32.[17] The right part of this diptych (chords numbered from 9 to 1) consists in a retrograde inversion with register exchange of the reduced *A-left* table, transposed at the tritone. Putting this complete table in relation to the aforementioned passage in the score, it appears that Maderna must have extracted the sounds according to a serpentine, proceeding from top left to bottom right by groups of two staves (→ **EX. 6**). As a result, the brass chords progressively shift down in register. From time to time, Maderna includes one or another sound from the surrounding staves into a segment in order to create a greater number of figures of three sounds. Indeed, since the brass instruments are distributed into four spatially separated groups,[18] in each group there is only one brass timbre (trumpet, horn, and trombone). The beginning of the process offers a paradigmatic situation, since the first figure opens with the trombone (G) and answers with horn and trumpet (B flat/C). Since the next attack in the reference staves (1–2) is constituted by the dyad D flat/E flat, Maderna takes from a lower staff a supplementary sound (B in staff 3), a procedure he reproduces immediately afterwards to complete the new dyad B flat/D with the A flat from staff 4. An exception of another nature concerns the two positions 9 in the center of the table, where two sounds are added in the sketch in green so as to reach in each part of the diptych an almost complete chromatic segment (F missing in the left part, C and E flat in the right one). Such additions of sounds reinforce the opposition between almost complete chromatic fields at the beginning of the serpentine versus highly selective fields in the second half, as a harmonic complement to the change in register.

The instrumental parts in melodic percussion and woodwinds completing the brass chords up to bar 207 are also based on the table circled "B," drawing on the eliminated sounds (lower staves in Ex. 5). In complementarity with the aforementioned selections within the chromatic total, there is an incidence here on the level of timbral distribution, since the reduction of available tones in the brass (due to the repetitions) entrusts the other timbres with a larger choice of pitches for this second stratum. Moreover, for reasons of acoustic clarification, these figures of short sounds all share a linear figural character (as opposed to the brass chords). The chords resulting from this selection process end in bar 207/2 of *Quadrivium* (p. 29 of the score). From the middle of bar 207 onwards, the spatial sensation changes, since the initially sketched twelve-tone chords (Ex. 1) are presented within the three homogeneous brass timbres, temporally desynchronized. The order of appearance of the material within the music is thus reversed with regard to the assumed derivation process.

The way Maderna deduces such linear figures from harmonic entities can be seen in his sketches for *Ausstrahlung* no. 4,[19] where numerous tables show layered instrumental parts derived from specific chords or chord successions, most of them consisting

---

17   Ibid. The filtering procedure has resulted in a supplementary intermediate sketch (total of five pages, named "A" to "E" at the top of each page).

18   See Example 1 in Carlo Ciceri's essay in this volume, pp. 87–113: 88.

19   *Ausstrahlung*, composed in 1971, consists of seven different parts (or "Ausstrahlungen").

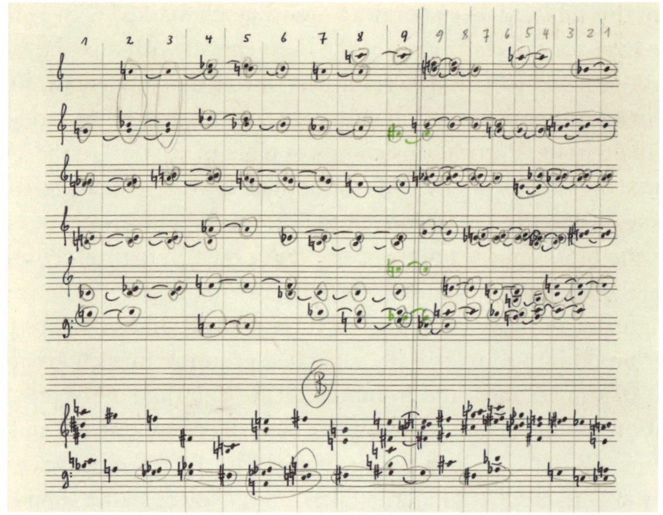

EX. 5   Bruno Maderna, *Quadrivium,* table circled "B"; PSS-BMC.

EX. 6   Bruno Maderna, *Quadrivium,* brass chords for pp. 27–32 of the score; structural reading of table circled "B" according to the three segments of the serpentine (corresponding to staves 1–2, 3–4, and 5–6).

of clusters (the only non-chromatic interval being placed at one edge of the chord). Once again, Maderna uses this material according to principles of selection, both horizontally and vertically. Indeed, what appears continuous in the sketch might be fragmented into separated units, and the number of effective layers in a given passage might also vary from a few to the total number of strata contained in the sketches. Most of these sketches associate a precise instrument with each layer, and parts of this material have entered the score almost unchanged.[20] For the beginning of *Ausstrahlung* no. 4, the selection conforms to supplementary indications found in Maderna's sketch (eventually added in a later stage) (→ **EX. 7**). Indeed, for the four flute parts in bars 1 to 7, he works on the basis of the first four layers (associated instruments: four flutes), while the two marimbas (active only in bars 1–3 and 6–7) take their material from layers 5 to 8 (associated instruments in the sketch: three oboes and english horn). From the end of bar 7 to bar 14, the next four layers (5–8) are now played by the four flutes, while the two marimbas add figures excerpted from later in the same sketch (units 11–16) to enhance the heterophony. In bars 14–18, where the piccolo clarinet joins the four flutes, Maderna uses the remaining five layers of the sketch (associated there with piccolo clarinet and four clarinets). The grouping of figures into units is indicated in the sketch through lines in different colors. In bars 23 to 26 (third page of *Ausstrahlung* no. 4), a partial reading of this sketch page beginning in unit 5 sounds with the originally sketched orchestration. Finally, the complete sketch will be used, with some slight rhythmic variations, on the last page of this fourth *Ausstrahlung*, at bars 45 to 49.

While for *Biogramma* (1972) the only available document classified as such to date is a sketch for the principal melody of Section B,[21] there is another source of interest that can be related to this score and that documents another aspect of Maderna's compositional preoccupations. Contained in his sketchbook no. 4 (pp. [1] to [9] with complementary information on pages [10] and [12]), this source shows Maderna listing morphological observations concerning recordings[22] based on the score of Section C of *Biogramma* (pp. 15–25).[23]

This score section adopts a kind of space notation and only exceptionally conventional rhythmic notation. Indeed, the note heads without any rhythmic indication are supposed to be played *"sempre staccatissimo."*[24] On Maderna's list, there are numerous lines giving divergent indications for the same excerpt, such as *"solo note cortissime"* (which is congruent with the score) as opposed to *"solo note lunghe."* During the recording sessions, Maderna thus modulated his text by modifying the performance instructions in order to achieve different sonic realizations on the basis of one and the same notated material.

---

20 See *Ausstrahlung* no. 4 in the score (Milan: Ricordi, posthumous edn. © 1975, print 1988, 131908).

21 See Bruno Maderna, *Biogramma*, score (Milan: Ricordi, © 1973, repr. 1974, 131985), pp. 11–14.

22 The different "MI" (i.e. "Milano") numbers in the sketches refer to tapes, *"bobine"* recorded or worked at the RAI (Studio di Fonologia). Certain indications in these sketches are in another hand, probably by a technician who assisted Maderna in this task (information kindly provided by Angela Ida De Benedictis).

23 A drawing contained on page [11] of this same sketchbook no. 4, studied by Angela Ida De Benedictis (*Radiodramma e arte radiofonica: Storia e funzioni della musica per radio in Italia* (Turin: De Sono, EDT, 2004), pp. 88–89), reveals the context of this material: the radio play *Ages* (1972).

24 See Maderna, *Biogramma*, score (see note 21) p. 4, first occurrence of this kind of notation in Section A, and p. 12, toward the end of Section B. This indication is not repeated at the beginning of Section C.

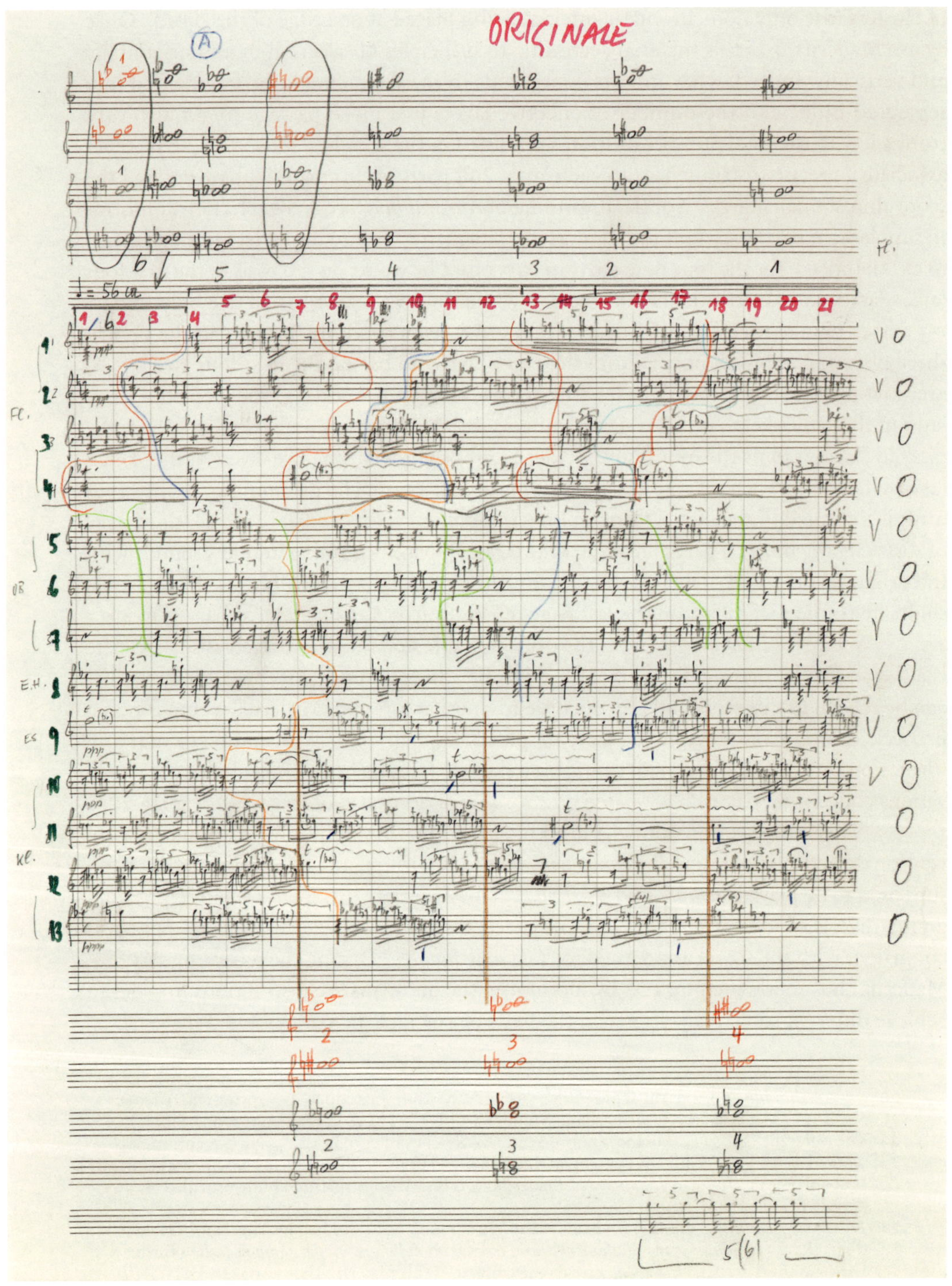

EX. 7   Bruno Maderna, *Ausstrahlung* no. 4, sketch with linear figures;
PSS-BMC.

These qualitative indications concern variable spectromorphological aspects such as duration (long/short), accents and dynamics (diminuendo/crescendo/delicate/dolce), timbre (harmonics/mutes/vibrato), tempo, and other specificities (rarefaction from the middle on/interruption/with final *"volatine"*). These descriptions concern both the sound production and the resulting sound effect: indeed, the conductor has to give specific instructions to achieve the expected textures. This aim conditions the very nature of the descriptions and explains why Maderna does not need other spectromorphological tools to fix his intentions. Beyond the question if he had read or could have read Pierre Schaeffer's *Traité des objets musicaux* (1966), his longstanding experience in electroacoustic music, as well as his practical knowledge of "timbral" categories beyond usual instrumental specifications, have directed him toward similar conceptions.[25]

Maderna as Performer-Composer of Earle Brown's *Available Forms I* (1961)

At the beginning of the 1960s, the discussions among European composers encompassed numerous elements concerning aleatoricism (which was both an inner development of serial thinking as well as a taking into account of experiences accumulated within the New York School since the beginning of the 1950s).[26] But aleatoricism is not synonymous with chance composition, as Brown repeatedly emphasized.[27] When asked by Maderna in 1970 to provide some information on *Available Forms I* for students, he answered:

> My "open-form" work is not to evade compositional responsibility!!!!
> My original motive, in 1951–52, was to create a newly intense poetic exchange and collaboration within the performance (realization) of a work!!!!
> Out of this "motivation" (the performer aspect of me) came an entire new relationship between the composer and performer... yes?? (COMPLETELY different from the fixed performance "chance pieces" of Cage at that time ('52).
> Please point out that the AVAILABLE concept is a music of CHOOSING, not of chance!!!
> I am FOR making esthetic decisions!!!![28]

---

25 Specific reflections on differentiated timbres formed part of Maderna's craft since *Notturno* (1956), where he distinguished numerous *"colori timbrici"* in his sketches. See also Nicola Scaldaferri, *Musica nel laboratorio elettroacustico: Lo Studio di Fonologia di Milano e la ricerca musicale negli anni Cinquanta* (Lucca: LIM, 1997), pp. 89–130.

26 For a detailed historical narrative concerning aleatoricism and indeterminacy in the context of the *Internationale Ferienkurse für Neue Musik Darmstadt*, see Pascal Decroupet, "Aleatorik und Indetermination," in *Im Zenit der Moderne: Die Internationalen Ferienkurse für neue Musik Darmstadt 1946–1966*, ed. Gianmario Borio and Hermann Danuser (Freiburg im Breisgau: Rombach, 1997), vol. 2, pp. 189–275.

27 See John Yaffé, "An Interview with Composer Earle Brown," *Contemporary Music Review* 26, nos. 3–4 (2007), pp. 289–310: 302.

28 Letter from Earle Brown to Bruno Maderna, 9 January 1970 (PSS-BMC). Different excerpts of this letter have been transcribed in Elena Dubinets, "Between Mobility and Stability: Earle Brown's Compositional Process," *Contemporary Music Review* 26, nos. 3–4 (2007), pp. 409–26: 417. Concerning the "fixed performance 'chance pieces' of Cage" see John Holzaepfel, "David Tudor and the 'Solo for Piano,'" in *Writings through John Cage's Music, Poetry, and Art*, ed. David W. Berstein and Cristopher Hatch (Chicago and London: University of Chicago Press, 2001), pp. 137–56.

More generally, Brown gave a rather restrictive definition of "open form," since "[…] to be called open form, a work must have an identifiable content which can then be *formed…* as in *Twenty-Five Pages* or the *Available Forms* works."[29] And to him, the reason for such music was the complete network of interactions during a process of musical communication, as stated in the "Prefatory Note" to *Available Forms I*:

> In *Synergy, Available Forms,* and other works in between, an invitation has been extended in the interest of intensifying the conceivable and inconceivable "process" relationships which are active within and between the steps leading to a realized sound-event: composer – score (graphic implications) – performer(s) – SOUND – and audience.[30]

The premiere of Brown's piece at Darmstadt in 1961 was conducted by Maderna (in two different versions), who also gave a new one the following year[31] and recorded a version for commercial disc in 1966.[32] The following examination tries to clarify how Maderna "actualized" Brown's score (its "graphic implications") by choosing to obtain a specific "SOUND."

So, what is *Available Forms I* about? In the "Prefatory Note," Brown explains how the score is to be used:

1) There are six score pages, each containing four or five events identified by a figure.

2) The conductor chooses an event (on whatever page) to begin with and then continues (events/pages might be repeated or omitted); he gives the musicians an indication concerning the specific page(s) and event(s) to be played; through his gestures, he indicates and modulates the relative speed and dynamic of the events; he is furthermore allowed to modify the instrumentation by selecting the active musicians.

The composed "specific material" the conductor has at his disposal ensures a strong identity for each event, with its own sonority and thus a distinct arrangement of spectromorphological features, resulting from variable combinations of the parameters: sound form (staccato points, tenuto sounds, melodies, chords, etc.), register, and instrumentation, incidentally also dynamics.[33]

---

29 Earle Brown in "Form in der Neuen Musik," *Darmstädter Beiträge zur Neuen Musik* 10 (1966), p. 60.

30 Earle Brown, "Prefatory Note," in *Available Forms I*, score (New York: Associated Music Publishers, 1962).

31 I had the opportunity to study parts of the archive of the Internationales Musikinstitut Darmstadt between 1994 and 1996. The two versions analyzed below (the first version of the premiere in 1961 and the 1962 version) correspond to shelf marks IMD-M-11619 and IMD-M-11653 (imd-archiv.de).

32 First published in the U.S. by RCA in 1967: *The New Music*, RCA Victrola VICS-1239. Other "national" issues were published in the following years in France (*Musica Nova*, RCA France 940.044), Italy (*La Nuova Musica* 1, RCA Italiana MLDS 61005), and so forth. See also Richard Toop, "Their Man in Europe, Our Man in America: Earle Brown and the European Avant-Garde," in *Beyond Notation: The Music of Earle Brown*, ed. Rebecca Y. Kim (Ann Arbor: University of Michigan Press, 2017), pp. 143–44.

33 In the aforementioned letter to Maderna (see note 28), Brown describes the "identity" of the events as follows: "Because of the 'open-form' realization potential (rather than a strict continuity from left to right, in sequence, as in closed score) I have a kind of technique of balancing the <u>content</u> of the events in any one score between different kinds of <u>energy</u> (density of <u>motion</u> through time) potential and <u>color</u> contrasts (instrumentation), and acoustic <u>weight</u> … (a combination of instrumentation and register and interval)." Also quoted in Dubinets, "Between Mobility and Stability" (see note 28), p. 418.

Page	Events	1	2	3	4	5	Supplementary observations
1	sound form	stacc.	stacc.	stacc.	stacc.	tt	
	register	total	total	total	total	–	
	instruments	tutti	tutti	tutti	tutti	–	
2	sound form	stacc.	stacc.	stacc.	ten.	stacc.	
	register	total	low	low to high	central	very high	
	instruments	tutti	low + winds + narim + cb	reson. + strings	winds + strings harm.	reson.	2–3 complementary
3	sound form	mel.	mel.	stacc. reson.	stacc.	–	
	register	central stable	central ascend.	high	total	–	
	instruments	ww + pno + marim + vln	2 cl + tpt	harp + xyl + vla	tutti	–	1–3 complementary
4	sound form	stacc.	ten.	figures	mel. slow	mel. fast	
	register	high	central	cigh	central	central	
	instruments	fl + vln + reson.	ob + bsn + tpt (harmon mute) + vlc harm.	reson.	2 cl + hrn	bcl + trb + timp + vla + cb	1–5 complementary; all instr. of 3 play in 1
5	sound form	stacc.	prolonged sounds + stacc.	iterative chords	ten.	iterative chords + harm.	
	register	total	low-central	high	very high	high	
	instruments	tutti	tutti	reson. + vlc	ww	reson. + vln	
6	sound form	ten.	stacc.	stacc. + mel.	stacc.	–	
	register	central	low	high	low (C)	–	
	instruments	ww + vla + vibra	bcl + reson	fl + reson. + vln	low w + marim + tpt + vlc + cb	–	1–4 complementary

EX. 8   Earle Brown, *Available Forms I,* table with global morphological qualities per event.

The score pages suggest different degrees of relatedness between the printed events, possibly resulting in privileged successions suggested by the spatial repartition on the page (→ **EX. 8**). Page 1 consists of a unique *staccato tutti* almost arbitrarily subdivided into four events. On page 2, four events are *staccato,* but in different registers (with a continuous evolution from low to high in 2+3+5 and complementarity in instrumentation between 2 and 3), while 4 is the only *tenuto* event (one contrasting morphology). On page 3, events 1 and 2 present melodies, events 3 and 4 opposing resonating *staccato* sounds or small groups of short sounds; furthermore, if events 1–3 are complementary in instrumentation, event 4 is a *tutti.* On page 4, each event features a different sound form (displaying the complete scale from *tenuto* to fast melodies: events 2-4-3-1-5), while instrumentation is complementary between all events (except for the resonating instruments present in events 1 and 3); moreover event 3 (containing figures in the melodic percussion instruments) is printed as superimposed on event 2 (*tenuto* chord), which suggests a specific layering representative of all relations between a *tenuto* event as background and one or more figural events in the foreground. Page 5 also presents dissimilar sound forms (with two new types: event 2 – sustained sounds forming chords mixed with resonating sounds; events 3+5 – chords with fast iteration); the global *staccato* sound form (including the iterative chords) is opposed to the *tenuto* chord in event 4. On page 6, the graphic superimposition from page 4 is taken one step further: the *tenuto* chord of event 1 (including dense groups in the vibraphone) hosts two fields with short sounds (event 2: *staccato* in low register, event 3: high resonating sounds combined with a melody and glissandos); event 4 is not superimposed on event 1 and features low and loud *staccato* sounds (in opposition to the soft dynamics in events 2 and 3).

The conductor has a clear responsibility as regards the overall form since his selections and combinations of events will shape the performance in a specific way. On the basis of the overview of global morphological qualities in Example 8, it will appear that the formal features resulting in a specific performance are congruent with both the compositional idea and the score since they transpose on the level of the sonic experience those types of relations Brown has "pre-formed" in the graphic design of his score.

In the following, I will consider three performances of *Available Forms I* conducted by Maderna between 1961 and 1966, presenting different steps in his "playing with the rules." It would be exaggerated to consider them linearly as a one-dimensional evolution from a simple to a complex use of the score; nevertheless, the exhaustive exploration of each page, which can be considered a predominant feature of the premiere, diminishes in the next ones, whereby, with an increasing knowledge of the piece, strictly spectromorphological similarities between events from different pages progressively gain in importance. The tables presenting these versions (→ **EXX. 9-11**) display columns with the successive sections according to the change of score page. The horizontal layers indicate the section, score page, selection of events, and the four major morphological features (sound form, register, dynamic, and density), followed by observations concerning connections between sections, relations between distant sections, and, finally, other considerations on the formal unfolding.

For the first performance (→ **EX. 9**), Maderna presents the score systematically, exploring each page once in complete form; this version ends with a coda combining elements from two pages (1 and 4). Globally, the resulting form can be subdivided into four higher-level parts: part A consists of sections I–II, where successions of events with selective qualities predominate; B is a contrasting *tutti* (section III); C features different possibilities of superimposition of materials (simple in section IV, more complex with an inner transformation in sections V and VI); D is the coda (section VII). Silences isolate the events more often toward the beginning than from part C on, corroborating the difference between event successions (part A) and event superimpositions and transformations (part C). For the first two sections, the unity of each page is manifested by the fact that the first selected event is repeated after all the others have been played. The passage from section I (page 2) to section II (page 6) is realized with the aim of stressing

Timing	0	1'08"	2'09"	3'23"	4'16"	5'40"	6'51"
Part	A		B	C			D
Section	I	II	III	IV	V	VI	VII
Score page	2	6	1	3	4	5	1 4
Events	2–3 ‖ 5 ‖ 4–1 ‖ 2 ‖	4 ‖ 1——| 4 ‖ 3*3–2 ‖ 2–3—|	a—b—*c—‖ a—*b—‖	3 | 2———| 4 ‖ 1—|	3 ‖ 3 ‖ 2———‖ 5— 4—‖ 3–1	2———4———| 1 ‖ 3 ‖ 5———|	a*b ‖ a–b–c ‖ a ‖ a* ‖ a ‖ 3 ‖ 3
Morphology	p p t→p p	p t+p p/m p	p p* p p* p	p m m	p p t+m+p p	t t+p p t/p	p
Register	l–h h m–t l	l l–h l h l t		h m(+h) t	h h m (+h) t	l–h h t h	m–h t t h h h m
Dynamic	*p p p–mf p*	*f p<f p p mf*	*f f f p mf*	*f p (mf)*	*mf pp p mf-f-f (mf) mf*	*mf-f> p–pp f pp*	*pp mf f f p p p pp pp*
Density	m	m m+h m m/l m	h> h> h> m> h	m l h>	l l l (+h) m	m[vd] l h l	m h m h h l l
Interior formal principles	successive presentation of isolated characters	A-B-A B = background sustained chord	most dense clouds	A-B-A B = background melodies	A-B-A B = background transformation sustained chord to melodies	A-B-(A)-B B = background transformation sustained chord to iterative	densification – liquidation
Connections between sections	= staccato groups # register / dynamic	= staccato # group select. vs tutti chord	= staccato # cloud vs isolated sounds	= staccato # groups vs accents/chords	= staccato # isolated sounds vs isolated attacks building up chords	= staccato + sustained # sustained background vs staccato with sustained resonances	
Distant formal relations	assonance with II: end: low staccato groups	assonance with I: end: low staccato groups background type chord	assonance with VII: dense clouds with density decreasing per event	background type melody	background type chord to melody	background type chord to iterative	assonance with III: dense clouds with density decreasing from event to event after *f*
Observations	variable degree of continuity: from strong discontinuity to greater continuity			increasing transformations within background events through successive accumulation			closing function

EX. 9   Earle Brown, *Available Forms I,* formal overview of Maderna's first 1961 version.

a spectromorphological continuity, since the chosen events are both *staccato* with a selective low pitch range (events 2/2 and 6/4). At the end of section II, after an important silence highlighting the similarity in procedure with section I (the restatement of the initial event), Maderna adds further short events from page 6 with even stronger morphological assonances to the end of section I. While the *staccato* is common to all the page changes in this version, section III (page 1), with its *tutti* events, nevertheless marks a perceptible contrast. Since page 6, in its physicality, presents the superimposition of a sustained background (6/1) and supplementary *staccato* events (6/2–3), the idea for part C has been somehow "anticipated." While all sections IV to VI display a kind of inner A-B-A articulation, the qualitative difference between the respective B sections is indicative of a process: background with melodies (section IV), transformation from sustained chord to melodies (section V), transformation from sustained chord to iterative chords (section VI). Globally, the sections are always connected through strong morphological similarities, so that a change in morphology is not revelatory of a change of score page.

The 1962 performance is far longer than the premiere, since Maderna returns to a page more than once (→ **EX. 10**). The first five sections are connected through the idea of a sustained background chord, whose duration diminishes progressively, and whose morphology is transformed into background melodies in section V. The only explicit silence between two background chords separates sections III and IV. Section VI establishes the staccato morphology as a new reference point (prepared during the previous sections), so that the sudden return to a sustained chord to begin section VII marks the only strong contrast in the formal evolution of this version, although this chord appears more to be

Timing	0	0'54"	2'27"	3'00"	4'37"
Section	I	II	III	IV	V
Score page	6	2	6	5	4
Events	1———	4————||5||1||1||1||4— / 2+3 2	1————|| / 4—2—3—4	4————||1-2||3—|2||5|| / 1 select 4—|	2————| / 3||3|| 3————||3|| 1||1-5| / 4————||
Morphology	s	s +p +p p p p p s	s+p	s +p p→s p+s ps ps	p s p m p p
Register	mh	m (lh) l h t t t mh	l-m +h	h +m t mt h l-m h	mh h h+ml
Dynamic	*pp*	*p p p p p p-mf*	*mf*	*p mf pp/p*	*f p mf p*
Density	l	l m m m m l	m	l +m l l l	l l m l
Interior formal principles		A + B B A	A B A	A + B B (echos of A)	A B transforming A
Connection		sustained chord / chord change	sustained chord / chord change	sustained chord / silence before new chord	short sounds / resonating instruments — staccato
Distant formal relations	chord	chord	chord	chord	chord / transformation P → M
Observations	time expansion	accumulations and return to starting point — return to beginning of section / liquidation		forming of chord	accumulation transformation / chord → melody

Timing	5'59"	7'39"	9'23"	9'38"	10'20"	11'29"
Section	VI	VII	VIII (a)	VIII (b)	VIII (c)	VIII (d)
Score page	1 2	6	5	4	+3	4
Events	1-2-3*4 ||1||1||1||1-2-3|| 1||1||1||	1————||1||1————| / 4—3—||3||	1||1—|	1||3————	—| / 1+2————|1————|| / W. +Str. 3 4 4 3	3||3||2 short||1|| chord
Morphology	p (s) p p p p p	s +p p	p p	p p	+m p p p p	p s m
Register	mh mh mh h m mh	mh +l +h h	t	h h	+m h t t h	h mh m
Dynamic	*mf/f p p pp p-f-mf p*	*p <mf> pp p mf pp*	*mf pp*	*mf pp*	*pp p mf*	
Density	h h m h m	l (+m) l l	h m	h l	l m m	l l h
Connection	staccato	contrast / cloud vs. sustain / similarities / dynamics / diminution of density goes on	staccato staccato / resonating instruments		background continues new background strata	staccato –short figures resonating instuments
Distant formal relations	staccato as only remained character (just a small echo of sustain through local fermata)	last occurrence of chord (from beginning)			transformation P → M	short chord (souvenir)
Observations	liquidation liquidation with changes of instruments	time expansion	CODA		time expansion rall. anticipation of end	final liquidation ———

EX. 10   Earle Brown, *Available Forms I,* formal overview of Maderna's 1962 version.

a farewell than a return to a lively presence. Sections II to VII explore the respective score pages exhaustively. If section I – as an introduction – has fixed the "time scale," consisting in long expansions of a single material (this will reoccur in sections VII and VIIIb), section VIII presents a coda with a selective combination of events from different pages. Another feature of this version is liquidation gestures, which occur toward the end of section II (where the return of the initial event 4 is similar to the strategy observed in 1961), as an intermediate rest in section VI (as well as for its end), and for the *staccato* section from the end of VIIIc to VIIId, at the end of the piece. In this "study on the idea of the chord" and its possible transformations (besides the changes between the chords to be found on the different score pages), the initial chord admittedly acts as a hidden refrain (sections I-III-VII), but it is treated differently in each of its occurrences: continuous in section I, with accumulation of *staccato* events in section III, interrupted by silences and transforming into staccato in section VI. The latter morphological transformation is symptomatic of

Timing	0	1'10"	2'29"	3'09"	3'47"
Section	I	II	III	IV	V
Score page	4	1	4	1	2+4
Events	2———‖ 4+1 3 3 3 4——‖ > > > 11	2*‖ 2*‖ 2 1*2–3–4 ‖	5 11 5—|2 ————| > > > 4———|	1–2–3–4	*with accents on entries* 2/4 —————| 4/3 4/3—‖ 4/3——‖
Assonances	chord 4/2		chord 4/2	page 1 *p*	chord 4/2
Groupings of sections	A	B (contrasting but also with common element with A-section)	A		A
Distant formal relations				contrast consisting in cloud of points in low dynamic	
Other sonic peculiarities		1/2 glissando appearing in *p*-version and at the end of *mf*-diminuendo-version	4/5 two times glissando	1/2 glissando distinctly audible	
	figures resonating instruments 4/3 initial signal 4/1 interior		4/1 interior	melodic percussions with metal mallets	4/3 initial signal
Observations		adopts the principle of sustained chords at the end of clouds of points		contrasting interruption	sections V to VIII: transformation process from chord to melody

Timing	4'38"	5'06" (5'51")	6'06"	7'16"	8'12"
Section	VI	VII	VIII	IX	X
Score page	3	4+2	2+3+6	5	1
Events	2————‖ 3–‖ 4—	2/4————‖ 3—| 4/3—— 2/3 3 2————	3/2———————— 2/5— 3/3 1 6/3	4——— 5+3———	1–2–3–4
Assonances	melody	chord 4/2	melody	chord 5/4	page 1 *p*
Groupings of sections	B (strongly contrasting but short)	A			
Distant formal relations					connection with section IV
Other sonic peculiarities			6/3 glissando very prominent		1/2 glissando present, echo effect
		4/3 initial signal			melodic percussions with metal mallets
Observations	a priori: anticipation of VIII reorienting the ABA toward a transformation				

EX. 11 Earle Brown, *Available Forms I,* formal overview of Maderna's recorded version.

the whole version: in section V, the chord is progressively built up and then transforms via a *staccato* layer into melodies. This principle, from *staccato* points to melodies, also joins sections VIIIb and VIIIc.

The version contained on the commercial recording[34] **(→ EX. 11)** presents these same features, but complexly intertwined. Three "structural levels" determine the resulting form: assonances between sections, grouping of sections into higher-level units, and distant relations. Furthermore, Maderna exploited certain sonic characteristics as further markers in the formal development. According to the page changes, this recording consists of ten sections. The formal unfolding is shaped through different degrees of recurrence as well as transformation between materials – categories reminiscent of traditional strategies and common formal functions, such as beginning, development, transition, or end.

---

34 See note 32.

Assonances   The most prominent features within this category are sustained chords (events 4/2, 2/4, and 5/4) and melodies (all taken from page 3). The chords 4/2 and 2/4 appear twice each, as backgrounds for two sections separated both times by one contrasting section, while chord 5/4 sounds only as background for section IX.

A-B-A Groupings of Sections   The close recurrences of chords 4/2 and 2/4 create small ternary forms. The first one (sections I to III) features a contrasting section of similar duration integrating a prominent chordal feature (sustained resonances to end, *staccato* clouds of variable length). The second one (sections V to VII) contains a clearly contrasting middle section (polyphonic melodies as opposed to the chords). Both these A-B-A groupings are followed by a section using the same score page as the respective B section, but with a significant difference from a form-functional perspective. Sections II and IV consist of completely opposed exploitations of the same text, so that their relation is not really identifiable by listening to the recording (strong opposition in dynamics and continuity): while section II connects I and III through a similar morphological feature, section IV marks a first interruption. Section VI is significantly shorter than the surrounding ones and appears *a posteriori* as an anticipation of section VIII, which is the proper goal to reach. The small ternary form is thus absorbed by a larger grouping displaying a directed transformation, by diminishing the duration of the chords and replacing them progressively with melodic features.

Distant Relations   The concluding section X is an evident evocation of section IV, globally treated as an echo and a textural liquidation. The ending, with its increasingly spaced single sounds, is similar to that of section VII, although this gesture is no longer charged with expectation, but only with the intention of extinction through rarefaction.

Two other sonic peculiarities intervene in the formal process. On the one hand, there are the resonating instruments. At the beginning of sections I and V, their marked attacks (based on event 4/3) clearly endorse the role of formal signals, stressing the respective beginnings of the A-B-A groupings. The third and last occurrence of these figures, at the beginning of section VII, creates a disequilibrium within the second A-B-A grouping that corroborates its transformational reorientation. On the other hand, three sections contain glissandos (from events 1/2, 6/3 and 4/5 – in the latter a specific interpretation of the "relative contours" of the winding). The different glissandos do not highlight specific formal functions, but are mere remembrances supporting a feeling of coherence through a play with memory.

Spectromorphology as a Path through Maderna's Forms: the Example of *Aura*

As seen in the previous analyses, Maderna developed specific strategies of stratifying and filtering Brown's material. This last procedure is a common compositional device for Maderna, as the sketch studies for *Quadrivium* and *Ausstrahlung* no. 4 have shown. Beyond the morphological categories discussed concerning *Available Forms I,* there are a few supplementary texture-types most characteristic of Maderna's music, as in *Aura* (1972), where their spectromorphological oppositions are entrusted with syntactical and formal functions (→ **EX. 12**). All the occurring textures can be divided into two categories: polyphonic textures of linear figures (Lines / Type A) or clouds of punctual sounds (Points / Type B).

An overall formal trajectory can be recognized and outlined in its main features, consisting of five main parts: the exposition of two texture-types (sections I–II); a first development of the still isolated textural ideas that leads to an intermediate conclusion ending with texture-type B (sections III–X); a three-part suspension beginning with a fermata in the form of an oboe solo (section XI), followed by the shortest version of texture-type A (section XII: revealing somehow the linear "basic motive") and ending with long, very low brass sounds (section XIII); a second developmental section characterized by an increasing interaction between the two texture-types as well as the regular participation of percussion of indefinite pitch, and culminating in a synthesis built on texture-type A (sections XIV–XIX); a concluding *"improvvisazione"* based on figures similar to those of the oboe solo in section XI, but now assigned to all trumpets and horns before turning over to the solo flute (section XX). The more or less regular alternation of these textural sections is interrupted four times by brief brass inserts (sections IV, VIII, XIII, and XVIII): this function of an added layer is manifest in the score, since all these inserts, from the point of view of bar numeration, consist of so-called "bis" bars that do not alter the continuous numeration within the principal layer.[35] The purpose of these inserts is twofold, since, on the one hand, they create an irregularity within the two developments, and, on the other, they signal the formal function of "point to reach" at the end of each development.

Texture-type A is dominated by the strings, progressively enlarged by melodic percussion instruments, two harps, and unpitched percussion (end of section I). This texture is presented in different variants, from a very dense polyphonic web of highly individual voices that are not intended to be audible per se (A_1 – section I) to a perfect homophony in all participating voices (A_5 – section XII) passing through different stages of polyphonic and melodic clarification in sections III, VII, and IX. Furthermore, A_4 (section IX) includes a first combination of opposed features, since an iterative texture of fast *pizzicato* points (a trait associated with texture-type B) sounds in the background. In the second development, the homophonic voices dissociate more and more toward the stratified polyphonies in section XVII (A_7) and in the synthesis (section XIX – A_8). The first step in the melodic clarification (A_2 – section III) is realized through an added solo oboe, turning over at the end of the section to the solo flute, with which the whole piece will end.

---

35   See Bruno Maderna, *Aura,* for orchestra, score (Milan: Ricordi, © 1972, repr. 1983, 131960).

	Exposition		First Development							
	Presentations			Interruption				Interruption	Intermediate Conclusion	
Section	I	II	III	IV	V	VI	VII	VIII	IX	X
Bars	1–68	69–88	89–106	106 bis	107–112	113–122	123–130	130 bis	131–139	140–160
Texture	A_1	B_1	A_2	I_1	B_2	B_3	A_3	I_2	A_4	B_4
	lines	points	lines	lines	points	points	lines	lines	lines	points
Instruments Timbre	strings +mel perc +harps	metal	strings +mel perc +harps +ob/fl	brass	wood (soft)	metal	strings +mel perc +harps	brass	strings +mel perc +harps	wood (sharp to soft) +strings
Register		very high		high	high to central	very high		high		high to low
Supplementary Features	polyphony	fast	melody + oboe	fast			figures melody	medium fast	fast iterative background	background chord
Supplementary Markers	a_1 a_2 a_3		a_2				a_1		a_3	
Timing	0	3'13"	3'30"	4'10"	4'20"	4'38"	4'54"	5'13"	5'30"	5'49"
Duration of sections	3'12"	17"	40"	10"	18"	16"	19"	17"	19"	32"

EX. 12   *Aura,* formal overview (Bruno Maderna, with Sinfonieorchester des Norddeutschen Rundfunks, live recording, Hamburg, 15 May 1973, *Bruno Maderna dirige Maderna,* Arkadia CDMAD 034.1, 1993).

Other characteristic elements within texture-type A are: a specific dynamic treatment consisting of accented departures after a longer decay and anticipating the further figural variants (a_1); unpitched percussion (a_2 – from bar 52 onward); and fast chordal structures in melodic percussion (a_3 – emerging at bar 64, only morphology in bars 67–68), the two latter assuming punctuating functions that will reoccur respectively in sections VII and IX.

Texture-type B is a foreground timbre associated with specific woodwind instruments as well as with given melodic percussion, and it is primarily varied through variable registral positions. The texture B_1 in section II presents a fast cloud of very high and metallic (or sharp wooden) sounds (piccolo, glockenspiel, and xylophone); texture B_2 in section V shows a modulation to a central register with dominating soft wood timbres (clarinets and marimba), while B_3 in section VI reiterates the initial features (with high metallic sounds). In B_4 (section X), the registral and timbral glissando is prolonged and the *staccato* cloud is progressively supported by a chord fermata in high strings, expressing (as a counterpart to section IX) the aforementioned function of intermediate conclusion before the oboe solo. In the last two occurrences, textures B_5 and B_6 follow one another (sections XV and XVI), remaining both in the low register. B_5 restates the fermata sustained from the preceding B texture, thus linking the two developments by a sonic signal. Furthermore, the clearly slower inner articulation of B_5, as compared to the preceding ones, prepares the long silences in B_6 that transform the statistical cloud into delimited figures.

The four brass interruptions share similar timbral, registral, and articulation strategies with texture-type A, the differences between the respective sections evoking tape-transposition where pitch and duration evolve in parallel: high *staccato* melodies in trumpets in section IV; a slight slowing down leading to more sustained melodies in

| | Suspension | | Second Development | | | | | | Coda |
Solo	Motive A	Interruption					Interruption	Synthesis	Final Improvisation
XI	XII	XIII	XIV	XV	XVI	XVII	XVIII	XIX	XX
160 bis	161–64	164 bis	165–72	173–203	204–08	209–22	222 bis	223–59	–
Solo	A_5	I_3	A_6	B_5	B_6	A_7	I_4	A_8	
	lines	extended tones	lines	points	points	lines	lines	lines	
Oboe	strings +mel perc +harps	brass	strings +mel perc +harps	wood (soft) +strings	wood (soft) +strings	strings +mel perc +harps +horns	brass	strings +mel perc +harps ww/brass	solo flute trumpets horns +strings
High		low		low	low		central		high
	homo-phony	very slow	homo-phony dis-sociation	slower +back-ground chord	figures +back-ground chord	stratified poly-phony	medium fast	stratified polyphony	fast +back-ground A_1
					a_1				
6'21"	7'04"	7'13"	7'45"	8'07"	8'42"	9'00"	9'43"	9'59"	11'55"
43"	9"	32"	22"	35"	18"	43"	16"	1'56"	2'29"

trumpets and one trombone in section VIII; a transposition "some octaves down" to the lowest trombones playing strongly extended tones in section XIII; and a return to trombones in high register, restating the melodic character of this stratum in section XVIII. The final improvisation begins with combinations of fast figures and sustained sounds in trumpets and horns (section XX) and can be considered the final arrival of the "re-acceleration" of the brass melodies.

A consideration of the timbral strategies attests an increasing fusion of the instrumental groups, at least with regard to the predominant timbres. Indeed, while in the exposition and the first development (sections I–X) the difference in timbres supports a formal articulation of successive, clearly delimited sections, in the second development and in the synthesis (sections XIV–XIX) brass and woodwinds join the melodic strings by participating in the expression of the structural function by multiplying the polyphonic sensation through a clearer stratification.

The selected examples considered in this contribution reveal Maderna's high consciousness of the role of spectromorphological relations in the musical material. Be it the way to create hierarchies within his precompositional material through filtering and repartition into sonically opposed categories, be it his use of selective reading of a dense and elaborated material, be it his strategies to explore the textural richness of Brown's score or of his own orchestral compositions to create dramaturgically intense formal developments that never "forget" the listener because of their re-invention of traditional categories of formal connections and assonances at different levels, Maderna always acted as a composer and performer very conscious of the range of variability of the available musical material and concerned to exploit this range with musical efficiency.

CREATING SOUND: THE MUSIC BEYOND/ WITHOUT THE STAGE

NICOLA SCALDAFERRI

"A Walk Through a Musical Garden"
Compositional Paths in Maderna's Late Works

> Thus, as Kretschmar says in Mann's *Doktor Faustus,*
> Beethoven's late works often communicate
> an impression of being unfinished...[1]

Three-Dimensional Music

Bruno Maderna's musical production is characterized by a continuous experimentation with compositional techniques that make him an exemplary case in the rich and articulated panorama of the late twentieth century. It moves on multiple levels that intersect each other: from research on a conceptual level to the choice of instrumental formations up to performative solutions. The famous expression *"selva foltissima"* (thick forest), proposed by Massimo Mila in the aftermath of the composer's premature death to define his catalogue as a whole,[2] reveals labyrinthine undertones if one goes so far as to consider both the close connections that exist between different works, and the specific compositional choices, which often present issues that call for particular theoretical reflection.

Within these processes, his precocious and varied familiarity with different technologies plays a very important role. He was equally at home with traditional composition on paper, electronic and mixed music, radio drama, and also audiovisual products. Even his rich production of functional music – such as radio and television background music and film soundtracks – always became a training ground of primary importance whose results had repercussions on the more specifically creative side. Just as fundamental was his intense activity as a conductor, which began at an early age and continued at a top level right up to the last days of his life; even though, at the time, his conducting was often

---

I wish to thank Angela Ida De Benedictis for her fundamental support throughout the research and the study of the materials at the Paul Sacher Foundation, Basel (hereinafter PSS), and for the numerous and fruitful suggestions she offered during the revision of the essay; Anne C. Shreffler, for the valuable information received and the guide to the Fromm Foundation documents held in the Houghton Library, Harvard University, Cambridge MA (hereinafter HL); Annamaria Macchi, Marco Mazzolini, Maria Pia Ferraris, and Simone Fuligno for being so helpful in the consultation of the materials stored in the Ricordi Archive; and Veniero Rizzardi and Giovanni Cestino for the help they gave me during the research and for the suggested improvements.

1 Edward W. Said, *On Late Style: Music and Literature Against the Grain* (New York: Pantheon Books, 2006), p. 10.

2 Massimo Mila, *Maderna musicista europeo,* ed. Ulrich Mosch (Turin: Einaudi, 1999), p. 7; first edn. 1976, p. 8.

perceived as a "distraction" from his work as a composer, it instead represented a factor capable of stimulating particular creative activity in certain stages of his full maturity.[3]

His remarkable mastery on a technical level was accompanied by strict control of the compositional phases. In the compositions of the 1950s, which marked the consolidation of his artistic personality, we find an abundance of preparatory materials that reveal extremely meticulous planning; these were gradually modified, sometimes decreasing in number, in the works of the following years (in what constitutes almost a second phase of his production), where procedures of controlled aleatoric music, personal collage techniques, and reuse of the same materials on several occasions were advanced. However, an exegesis based on a careful study of the sources has shown that what happened in the last period was anything but a renunciation of the principles of rigorous control, which Maderna never abandoned; instead, assuming that some techniques had been fully metabolized, it often tended toward the exploration of other paths, at times proposing unexpected solutions.[4] It suffices to consider, for example, the parameter of pitch, whose strict control mechanisms from a certain moment onwards seem to operate more spontaneously, following well-tested and deeply mastered paths that give his works a sort of harmonic color – almost an actual sound – with unmistakable features; at the same time, his experimentation moved more on the level of formal solutions and performative strategies.

In the last extremely intense years of his creative arc – cut short by his early death in November 1973 – one can grasp elements in his research that sometimes pose problems on both an exegetical and performative level, but at the same time stimulate specific reflections. The main points are as follows:

1) The work is understood, as Pousseur put it, as a "field of possibilities,"[5] within which it is possible to follow paths with multiple perspectives; the idea had already emerged during the 1960s (just think of works like *Hyperion*), but it now began to gain substance. This aims toward a reformulation of the concept of musical "text" itself, which often takes on a dynamic meaning, closely connected to the here and now of the performance, especially in cases when, alongside traditional instruments, recorded sound also comes into play.[6]

---

3   On Maderna's activity as a conductor and the different interpretations of the conflict with his compositional activity, see Angela Ida De Benedictis, "More than conducting, more than composing: Hermann Scherchen, Bruno Maderna, Luciano Berio," in *Komponieren & Dirigieren: Doppelbegabungen als Thema der Interpretationsgeschichte*, ed. Alexander Drčar and Wolfgang Gratzer (Freiburg im Breisgau et al.: Rombach, 2017), pp. 371–400: 380–90.

4   On the compositional processes in the last years of his composing phase, I refer in particular to two essays by Angela Ida De Benedictis: "Scrittura e supporti nel Novecento: alcune riflessioni e un esempio (*Ausstrahlung* di Bruno Maderna)," in *La scrittura come rappresentazione del pensiero musicale*, ed. Gianmario Borio (Pisa: ETS, 2004), pp. 237–92, and "'Qui forse una cadenza brillante': Viaggio nel *Venetian Journal* di Bruno Maderna," *Acta Musicologica* 72, no. 1 (2000), pp. 63–105.

5   Thus Henri Pousseur in *Scambi*, quoted in Umberto Eco, *The Open Work*, trans. Anna Cancogni (Cambridge: Harvard University Press, 1989), p. 1; first Italian edn.: 1962.

6   As Angela Ida De Benedictis points out in "Il suono oltre il segno: la carta, i limiti e gli inganni (cinque esempi)," in *AAA.TAC* 2 (2005), pp. 54–65: 60: "In the case of some mixed compositions (for instruments and tape) by Bruno Maderna, the presence of a score is even misleading [...], whereas the true text of the composition – the only one that gives us a complete and exhaustive image of the piece (and the only one that could help the scholar to create a truly performative edition) – is in this case to be seen in the author's recording" (original in Italian).

2) The performative dimension acquires greater centrality, which is often the moment of coagulation for what were originally free flowing trajectories. To all appearances, it might seem that Maderna is taking inspiration from aleatoric models and the happening movement that were so popular in that period; in actual fact, a more careful analysis reveals a search for new solutions for controlling the action of the performers, also building on his masterful experience as an orchestra conductor. Likewise, rather than winking at the hackneyed but equally lackluster rhetoric of the open work, he seems to aspire instead to an idea of work as "composing in performance."[7] This mainly happens where "traditional" performers are envisaged as singers and instrumentalists; however, even when electroacoustic and recording technologies are used – at the time still dependent on analogue techniques and the chronological rigidity dictated by magnetic tape – the envisaged solutions have such a futuristic feel that their concrete realization will only come about in later times with the digital means and techniques of live electronics.

3) Continuous reinvention of the relationship between traditional instruments and electroacoustic means. This path had been pioneered in the early 1950s as a dialectical relationship between "two dimensions"[8] and subjected over time to continuous reinterpretations, and now it is increasingly oriented toward the multimedia perspective of a dialectic between mediated and live performance.

4) Resorting to narrative solutions in which space and environment also take on an active, almost dramaturgical function. This concerns not only the classic themes of the diffusion and arrangement of sound sources, but also the perception, through sound, of the environment experienced by the audience, almost configuring what will soon take shape in the notion of soundscape.[9] This certainly happens in compositions fixed on magnetic tape, which, as well as being traces of mediated musical performances or synthetic sounds created from scratch, also become a sort of sound memory capable of preserving traces of experience. However, as we will see in the following pages, even in performances with traditional instrumental formations, these issues appear in often new and original forms.

This all came about within the concreteness of his compositional practice, almost always without the assumption of any explicit theoretical stance, but balanced by a remarkable number of interventions, often of an impromptu nature (as happens in

---

7   The idea of "composing in performance," to which we will return later, is borrowed here from the studies on epic traditions that refer to the formulaic theories of Milman Parry and Albert Lord. The extemporaneous combination of formulaic materials, memorized by the singers, are "composed" at the moment of performance in a text with a strict and recognizable consequentiality; see Albert B. Lord, *The Singer of Tales* (Cambridge: Harvard University Press, 1960), and John M. Foley, *The Singer of Tales in Performance* (Bloomington: Indiana University Press, 1995).

8   Already in 1952, with *Musica su due dimensioni* for flute, magnetic tape, and cymbal, Maderna had made a first attempt to relate traditional instruments and recorded sound, the first step in what turned out to be an event-filled journey; see Veniero Rizzardi and Nicola Scaldaferri, "*Musica su due dimensioni* (1952): Histoire, vicissitudes et importance d'une œuvre (presque) absente," in *à Bruno Maderna*, ed. Geneviève Mathon, Laurent Feneyrou, and Giordano Ferrari, vol. 2 (Paris: Basalte, 2009), pp. 423–48.

9   R. Murray Schafer, *The Tuning of the World* (New York: Knopf, 1977), is still a fundamental reference for this topic. For more on the use of space in a "dramaturgical" function (in a context of orchestral works), see the essay by Carlo Ciceri on pp. 87–113 of this volume.

interviews). Maderna often seemed to distance himself from the passionate discussions that animated many of his fellow composers. In fact, as Ulrich Mosch points out, he showed a certain reluctance to take part in the theoretical debate of the time – in which so many composers, from Boulez to Nono to Stockhausen, got caught up – and this led his contemporaries to consider his compositional activity as coming second to that of conducting, which seemed to absorb most of his time.[10]

This essay examines some experiences from Bruno Maderna's last creative phase. In particular, reference will be made to three works: *Tempo libero I* (1970–71), *Juilliard Serenade (Tempo libero II)* (1970–71), and *Giardino religioso* (1972). The first is a composition for magnetic tape created for an audio installation at the "Iᵃ Biennale Internazionale di Metodologia Globale della Progettazione 'Le forme dell'ambiente umano'" (First International Biennial of Global Design Methodology "Forms of the Human Environment"), held in Rimini in September 1970. The other two, for instrumental ensemble (with or without tape, as we will see in the case of *Juilliard Serenade*), were commissioned by two important American musical institutions: the Juilliard School of Music and the Fromm Foundation. This fact is further evidence of the fame he had gained overseas as a composer alongside that of conductor.[11] Written in a relatively short period of time, these compositions rank among the great works of Maderna's last creative period – the symphonic works *Quadrivium* and *Aura,* the radio plays *Ritratto di Erasmo* (Portrait of Erasmo) and *Ages,* a multifaceted experience like *Ausstrahlung* right up to the opera *Satyricon* are all noteworthy examples – and they enable us to tackle some critical issues in his compositional thought of that period. In fact, each work has its own unmistakable peculiarities and, at the same time, is in close correlation with the others. This is because not only do they share materials, a characteristic feature of those years (the tapes for *Tempo libero I,* for example, can also be combined ad libitum in the execution of *Juilliard Serenade,* whose materials then generate works like *Piece pour Ivry* for solo violin), but they are also linked at the deepest level of creative mechanisms. In fact, materials created for one piece may then also flow into the other, thus allowing a glimpse of a path of *opus continuum* that

---

10   See Ulrich Mosch, preface to the second edition of Mila, *Maderna musicista europeo* (see note 2), p. VIII. However, it is also true that even people very close to him, starting with his close friend Luciano Berio, fuelled this misunderstanding by upholding the idea of the "incompleteness" of certain works because they were written under pressure in a rush due to his commitments as a conductor; a position also reaffirmed by Boulez in 2009 in the afterword-interview "… Doué comme un diable …," in *à Maderna* (see note 8), vol. 2, pp. 557–61: 560. Even Maderna's reticence, when referring to his own works, could somehow lead one astray. For example, during one of the conversations put together on the television program *Un'ora con Bruno Maderna: Musica, specchio della società* (a documentary by Salvatore G. Biamonte and Giuseppe Sibilla, RAI, Milan-Venice 1969–70, broadcast on 11 October 1971), at 25'06" he can be heard to say: "I'm planning in the next few years, if some things go well enough for me, to largely give up conducting, to conduct less, […] and to dedicate myself much more to the work of composing […] then I'd greatly reduce my work as a conductor because I'd really like to try and see if I can write music, even a little better, to do my best […]" (original in Italian).

11   In the same period, Maderna carried out an intense activity as conductor in the U.S.A. For more on this see Maurizio Romito, "Da *Intolleranza 1960* a *Don Giovanni:* Bruno Maderna direttore d'orchestra negli Stati Uniti (II)," *Musica/Realtà,* no. 117 (November 2018), pp. 115–48 (Part I), and no. 118 (March 2019), pp. 117–224 (Part II); and the essays by Maurizio Romito and Anne C. Shreffler on pp. 277–97 and 299–327 of this volume.

grafts new suggestions on experiences and intuitions of previous years – a path where the dimensions that Maderna has put into play and mastered are often not just the two "classics" of instrumental and electroacoustic music. Indeed, a third dimension is added in all respects, namely that of the performative experience, which is just as rigorously controlled as the other two and assimilated in the process of creative action, thanks to specific forms of compositional writing.

Technologies and Paradoxes (*Tempo libero I*)

In 1970, in the Milan Studio di Fonologia, Maderna made the magnetic tapes for *Tempo libero I* that were later broadcast in the spaces of the "1ª Biennale Internazionale di Metodologia Globale della Progettazione 'Le forme dell'ambiente umano.'"[12] The event was promoted by the "Centro Internazionale Ricerche sulle Strutture Ambientali 'Pio Manzù'" and took place in Rimini from 20 to 30 September 1970.[13] In order to appreciate the uniqueness of this work, its compositional intentions, and the practical limits Maderna had to deal with, one needs to observe the context that stimulated its creation and hosted its presentation. Indeed, the rich program of the Rimini Biennale touched on issues ranging from the environment to design, from urban planning to organization; it unfolded between debates, meetings, demonstrations, and experiments that exploited the most advanced technology available at that time. The event focused on three themes: 1) "Organization and communication in the operational space"; 2) "Territorial planning as a balance of self-management in the human-environment ecological system"; and 3) "Leisure and environmental structures." An international team, put together on the occasion of a previous conference held in 1969, was at work on each theme.[14]

Maderna's presence fell within one of the events dedicated to leisure and environmental structures, one of the key themes of the Rimini Biennale, and one on which an international team coordinated by the German designer Herbert Ohl was at work. Ohl was responsible for inviting Maderna to take part in the project.[15] It is certainly worth underlining the strong convergence between some of the results achieved by the team and Maderna's

---

12   It should be noted that the form of the title used here (*Tempo libero I*) is the one widely documented for the Rimini premiere; as will be seen further on, other names will appear that also have to do with the story of the tape and its combination with *Juilliard Serenade*. As regards the date when the tape was made, see below, note 17.

13   The center was located in Verrucchio, today in the province of Rimini, but then in the province of Forlì. The Pio Manzù Foundation, which continues the tradition of the former center, is currently based in Bergamo.

14   See "Organigramma della ricerca," in *Iª Biennale Internazionale di Metodologia Globale della Progettazione: "Le forme dell'ambiente umano": 20–30 settembre 1970, Rimini: Guida Programmatica*, pubished as a special edition of *Strutture ambientali* 4–5 (August–September 1970), p. 68. Numerous interventions and transcripts of the debates from the Rimini event were also published in *Strutture ambientali* (founded within the "Centro internazionale ricerche sulle strutture ambientali 'Pio Manzù'") in May 1971 (triple issue, nos. 7–9).

15   See Maderna's own account when he took part in the "Tavola rotonda su *Tempo libero*," in *Strutture ambientali* (see note 14), now in Bruno Maderna, *Amore e curiosità: Scritti, frammenti e interviste sulla musica*, ed. Angela Ida De Benedictis, Michele Chiappini, and Benedetta Zucconi (Milan: il Saggiatore, 2020), pp. 278–91: 282; see also ibid., pp. 764–65.

compositional intentions, designed in fact to contribute to a crucial moment in the creation of an interactive computer experiment using the most advanced technologies of the time.[16]

Some references in Maderna's correspondence allow us to date the period of conception of the piece to September 1970, as well as to better define the context of the Rimini event in which it took place, and in particular the experiments carried out by Ohl's group.[17] The tape made by Maderna was released for a first hearing on 21 September via a sound installation; it was preceded by a round table on the theme of free time in which Abraham Moles (one of the pioneers of information and communication studies) also took part. In the Italian version of the Biennale program, the piece, presented as a "musical game," is referred to as *Tempo libero I,* translated into English as *Leisure I.* The catalogue provides a brief explanatory note:

> "Première" music on the theme "leisure I," composed for the Biennale, will be performed. The reception will take place through four groups of diffusors. Each group is independent of the others, like the elements of a piece of furniture, and may give rise to casual compositions through the provocation of the public.[18]

The "game" was then repeated several times a day until 24 September, as highlighted at the bottom of the program, where it appears listed among other experiments repeated more than once during the event. It is worth mentioning them in order to better understand the overall picture, in which a multifaceted figure like Maderna, one of the pioneers of musical and technological experimentation since the early 1950s and open to every kind of experimentation, fits perfectly:

---

16   Several parallel events deserve mention, such as Ohl's active presence in Milan in the late 1960s, or the presence of Ferrania 3m, a leading company in the production of photographic films, as one of the promoters of the Biennale, and for which Maderna made the soundtrack of the documentary *Lavoro a Ferrania* in 1962. The documentary can be acccessed on the YouTube channel of the Archivio Nazionale Cinema d'Impresa (www.youtube.com/watch?v=U_2Z3pNkgPI; last accessed on 15 June 2021). Even though Maderna's name appears in the title of the documentary as the composer of the electronic music, no other details regarding this collaboration have emerged to date. About *Lavoro a Ferrania* see also in this volume the essay by Leo Izzo, "Narrating with sounds," p. 181, note 21.

17   Reference is made here to the correspondence preserved in the composer's collection at PSS. In a letter to his adoptive mother Irma Manfredi, dated 31 July 1970, Maderna writes: "I will go to Milan to make a piece of electronic music at the RAI Milan Studio di Fonologia (the Studio that I and Berio set up many years ago), which will be used for the 'Ambiente dell'uomo' International Congress that will start in San Marino around 20 September [...]"; original in Italian in "Per un ritratto di Bruno Maderna: Estratti dalla corrispondenza," in Maderna, *Amore e curiosità* (see note 15), pp. 541–702: 628. Far more specific on the matter is the correspondence with Gerardo Filiberto Dasi, general secretary of the "Pio Manzù" Foundation, starting with a telegram dated 15 August 1970: "After meeting with Philips technicians, we kindly ask you to contact our Verucchio research center [Maderna adds "Forlì" by hand] [...] urgently to specify equipment for your *Tempo libero* experiment before the Rimini Biennale [...]." In a telegram dated 16 August 1970 Maderna replies "[...] 4 professional tape recorders are required, each independent with its own amplifier and loudspeaker or loudspeaker group stop each power 200 watts stop each tape speed 38 cm second stop total power 800 watts..." Again Dasi, in two identical letters dated 1 and 2 September 1970, refers to the payment provided for "the work and the provision of musical sound which, in accordance with the established agreements, you will prepare for the study on leisure carried out by arch. Ohl, at the I[st] International Biennale of Global Design Methodology Forms of the Human Environment" (original in Italian). My thanks to Angela Ida De Benedictis for kindly pointing out these letters (preserved in the PSS-BMC) to me.

18   In *Strutture ambientali,* nos. 4–5 (see note 14), n.p.

> Below are the experiments which will be carried out on 21, 22, 23, and 24 September outside the above program.
>
> From 10am to 11am and from 5pm to 7pm: Connection Rimini-Cleveland by satellite for the reception of miscellaneous programs (In Time Sharing the teletype terminal will be uninterruptedly connected with Mark I in Milan for the duration of the Biennale).
>
> From 11am to 12am and from 6pm to 7pm: Environment post-scoring by means of IBM computers.
>
> From 9am to 10am and from 4pm to 5pm: Listening to the musical game by Bruno Maderna *Leisure I.*
>
> Furthemore the Biennale is open to the public until 30 September.
>
> During the period from 25 to 30 September, experiments on the theme of leisure will be uninterruptedly carried out by means of a UNIVAC computer.
>
> Beside the projects and objects in the exhibition, the public is allowed to look at films, conferences, and debates (broadcast by television equipment).[19]

Some of the most significant of the more strictly musical events at the Biennale were the sound rehearsals with IBM computers, scheduled for the morning of 21 September, where the presence of computer music pioneer Pietro Grossi was envisaged.[20] Maderna does not seem to have had an active part in these demonstrations, although he does intervene in some public debates, where he never fails to express his perplexity regarding any kind of facile optimism about the musical use of machines, sometimes at odds with Grossi.[21]

Ohl's experiment, on the other hand, while not concerning musical themes, has strong correlations with the concept of Madernian free time. It was an interactive experiment carried out with the UNIVAC 1108 computer, physically located in Rome and remotely connected to a screen in Rimini, that employed a special program written in the Fortran V computer language.[22] It foresaw the active involvement of the public in a conversational process with the computer, conducted thanks to an "open" questionnaire with nine questions.[23] The public had to provide an answer (among those obviously entered and proposed by the programmer) to each question posed by the computer, thus making a choice that would direct the subsequent path of the questionnaire. Example 1 shows Question no. 2 ("What is the purpose of your free time?"), with the paths opened by the possible answers (→ **EX. 1**).

---

19 Ibid., p. 122.

20 "Monday 21 September, 9am: Round table on *The Computer and the Human Environment.* Participants: Renato Pennacchi, Renzo Marconi, and Giorgio Sommi. Conference by Pietro Grossi with projections. An experiment of environmental post-scoring by means of an IBM computer will follow"; ibid., p. 119.

21 The transcripts of the recorded debates were published in 1971 in *Strutture ambientali*, nos. 7–9 (see note 14). Maderna took part in the debate "La macchina, mediatrice tra uomo e ambiente," pp. 29–42, and in the "Tavola rotonda su *Tempo libero*," pp. 112–19, now in Maderna, *Amore e curiosità* (see note 15), pp. 265–77 and 278–91.

22 *Strutture ambientali*, nos. 4–5 (see note 14), p. 71.

23 These are the nine questions: 1) "What do you understand by free time?"; 2) "What is the purpose of your free time?"; 3) "How would you like to spend your free time?"; 4) "Where would you prefer to spend your free time?"; 5) "How would you pace your life during your free time?"; 6) "With what frame of mind would you face your free time?"; 7) "How would you dress during your free time?"; 8) "How would you solve the problem of meals during your free time?"; and 9) "Do you think you can put these ideas into action?"

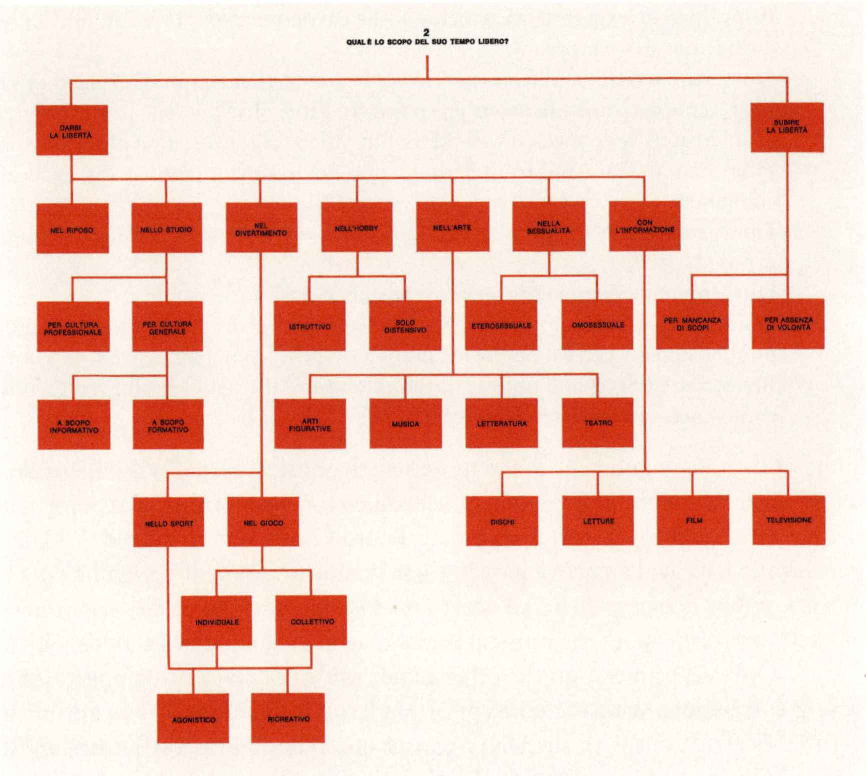

EX. 1   Interactive experiment with UNIVAC 1108 on leisure: scheme of the structure of the second question of the questionnaire, with the possible paths depending on the answers provided; taken from *Dialogo con un elaboratore Univac 1108 sul tempo libero* (Dialogue with a Univac 1108 computer about Leisure), in *1ª Biennale Internazionale di Metodologia Globale della Progettazione: "Le forme dell'ambiente umano,"* Rimini, 20–30 September 1970, n.p.

In this case there was an attempt at a dialogue between man and machine, at the end of which the computer would present a summary of the interview; all this always within the pathway established *a priori* by the programmer, who also wrote the conclusions provided by the machine as the outcome of the dialogue.[24]

---

24 A special brochure-catalogue is dedicated to this experiment (cited above in the caption for Ex. 1) in which it is explained in detail. It reads: "The experiment with a UNIVAC 1108 computer […] should be placed in the framework of the study on 'leisure' conducted by an international work group (coordinated by Herbert Ohl) […]. The experiment (the first with these characteristics), which consists in an exercise on a self-programming questionnaire on 'free time' carried out directly on the 'machine' by the public, basically has two objectives: a) as regards the object under investigation, the collection of data for an axiological definition of the notion of leisure […]; b) as regards the man-machine relationship, control of the behavior of the improvised operator engaged in operations that directly involve him, or rather the evaluation of the effects induced by the normalization of the largely mythicized relationship man-machine-information." *Dialogo con un elaboratore UNIVAC 1108* (see Ex. 1), n.p.

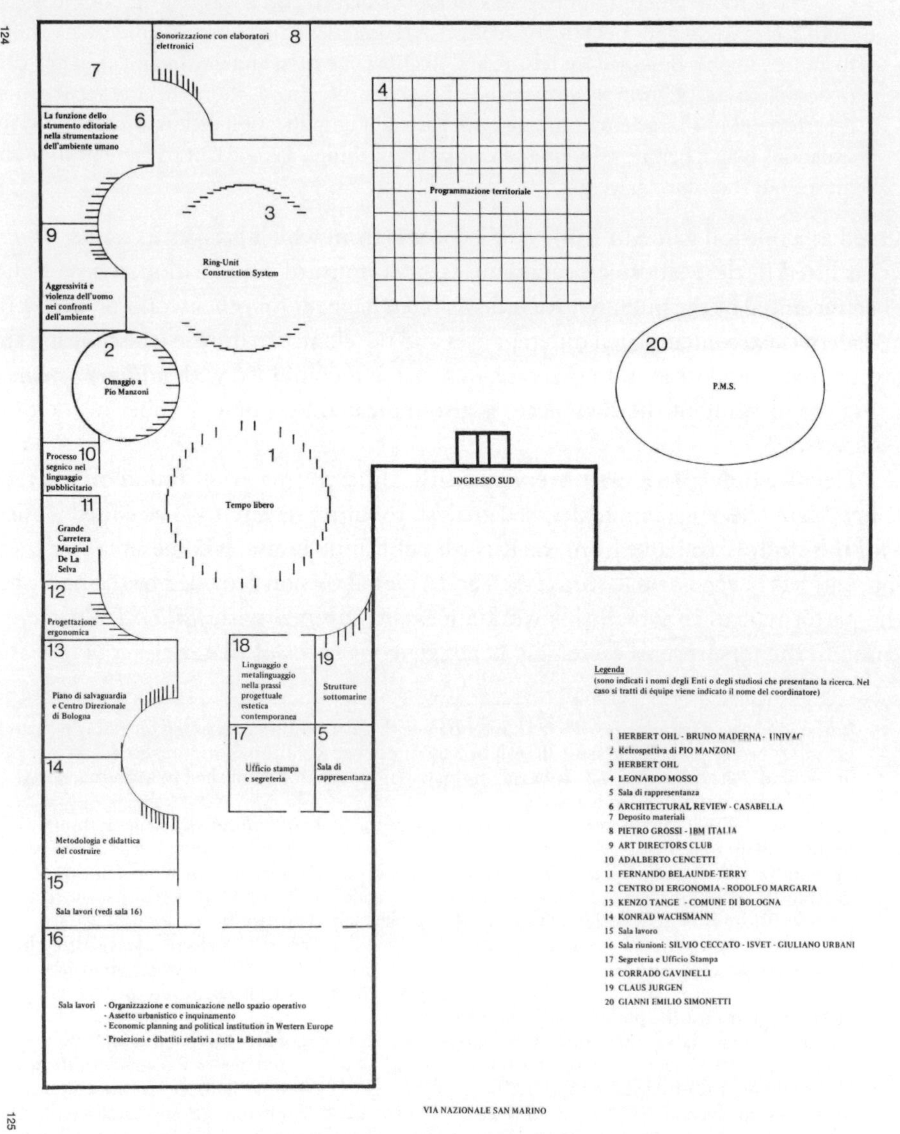

EX. 2 Map of the spaces planned for the Rimini Biennale on *Tempo libero* (Leisure) with indications of the spaces reserved for Ohl and Maderna; from *Strutture ambientali,* nos. 4–5 (1970), pp. 124–25.

The experiment with UNIVAC 1108 and the diffusion of Maderna's piece took place in the same environment (→ **EX. 2**) – the circular space number "1" – in which the video terminal is located. Three years later, in a radio conversation with Christof Bitter, Maderna recalled that space in the following terms:

[…] in the room where the piece was to be performed there was a group of architects from Stuttgart, including Ohl, an architect and designer who designed unique chairs and furniture, mainly designed for leisure and to allow one to sit and daydream, or in any case to be able to escape from the dimension of everyday life. In addition, this music, of course if performed in a large environment with the right amplification etc., is also designed for situations where people talk, sing, do all kinds of things. People can pay attention to the music, but they don't have to.[25]

Presented as a musical game in Rimini in a context from which it takes its name, *Tempo libero I* is listed in the Madernian catalogue as a real musical composition, whose rights have been acquired by the publisher Ricordi. As often happens for other works on magnetic tape, Maderna also contemplated different uses and the chance to diffuse it also within the context of other compositions. In this case, in which it is combined with *Juilliard Serenade* (1970–71), the merging of the two pieces is also indicated by a new number in the title: *Tempo libero II*.[26]

Here we only give a brief overview of the different materials found on the tape for *Tempo libero I*, leaving a more detailed analysis to future research.[27] The edited version used for this study is available from the Ricordi publishing house. It comes in a two-track version, entitled *Tempo libero*, lasting 23'32", and a digital version provided by the publisher for the performances in which this work appears combined with *Juilliard Serenade*.[28] Listening to the tape reveals extremely heteregeneous types of materials: concrete and

---

25   Bruno Maderna, *Gespräch über Freizeit*, interview with Christof Bitter recorded on 7 May 1973 and broadcast on the 24th of the same month by Saarländischer Rundfunk (original broadcast in German). The quotation here is based on the Italian translation published in Maderna, *Amore e curiosità* (see note 15), pp. 160–66: 162.

26   Such a possibility is also indicated on the title page of the score of *Juilliard Serenade*. It should be pointed out that the title presented in Rimini is *Tempo libero I* (and not just *Tempo libero*); thus the number was not added later at the time of the conception of *Tempo libero II*. In addition to the translation of the term as *Leisure I* in the Rimini catalogue, it should be noted that the term *Freizeit* also appears in the original title of the interview with Christof Bitter (see note 25); see Maderna, *Amore e curiosità* (see note 15), p. 741, as well as ibid., pp. 508–09, for the text written by Maderna in 1972 for *Juilliard Serenade* and the related "notes" on pp. 802–03, which show how the title often appears in the provisional form of *Tempo libero I* (see also below in the text, p. 160) in the programs for the premiere of *Juilliard Serenade*.

27   The archive materials at the Studio di Fonologia contain a total of four tapes, both four-track (catalogued with the letter "Q") and two-track ("Fon," which are actually stereo copies of the four tracks), dating back to 1970: "Q. 27," lasting 23'35", and the 23'30" copy "Fon. 161," indicated on the box as "first version"; "Q. 28," lasting 24'10", and the 24'05" "Fon. 162" reel, indicated on the box as "second version" in Marino Zuccheri's handwriting. See also *The Studio di Fonologia: A Musical Journey 1954–1983*, ed. Maria Maddalena Novati and John Dack (Milan: BMG Ricordi, 2012), pp. 234–35. In the Saarländischer Rundfunk archives (and in copy at PSS) there is a reel classified as *Freizeit I–III* that contains three different versions of *Tempo libero I*, of which the first seems to correspond to "Q. 27 / Fon. 161." From a note on this reel (broadcast by the German radio on 24 May 1973, together with the interview with Christof Bitter cited in note 25), it is clear that it is material recorded at the Milanese Studio on 19 April 1971. For all these data see Maderna, *Amore e curiosità* (see note 15), p. 742. By combining this information and listening to the tapes, we can hypothesize with a great degree of certainty that the version presented in Rimini coincides with the version of "Q. 27 / Fon. 161" (*Freizeit I* on the German reel). It should also be noted that the boxes of these tapes have diagrams relating to the duration and to a probable diffusion. All the data and tape checks were kindly provided by the editor of this volume, Angela Ida De Benedictis.

28   This is a copy of the tape "Fon. 161" (see previous note), digitized by Studio Agon in Milan during the 1990s. This tape is clearly audible in the recording of *Juilliard Serenade* (*Tempo libero II*), carried out live in Rome on 21 May 1971 and released on the BMG Ricordi CD CRMCD 358182 (1996).

electronic sounds; recordings of voices, sometimes taken from familiar contexts; ambient sounds; everyday noises and other occasional sound materials that partly come from Maderna's previous compositional activity (such as, for example, the manipulation of Cathy Berberian's voice already used for the piece *Dimensioni II* or some fragments of the elves' voices from *Don Perlimplin*); and even fragments "stolen" from the activity he was carrying out at that time at the Milan Studio, relating to the production of the soundtrack for radio plays or working sessions with Marino Zuccheri and Luigi Nono (whose voices are recognizable, together with Kadigia Bove's and Liliana Poli's).[29] Then there are situations or sound interventions that seem to have been designed and inserted ad hoc for the Rimini event (in particular single words or phrases, pronounced by Maderna or Zuccheri, such as "cybernetics," "helicopter," or "what do you think about the current weather situation?").[30]

Speaking in the debates that took place during the Rimini Biennale, Maderna dwelt on the contents of the tapes within the more general framework of the conception that led him to make certain choices:

> [...] it occurred to me that, at least musically, none of us is capable of having free time; many people walk the streets, [they] listen to the birds singing or the bells ringing, or the sound of the sea and the tide, and they don't realize and they don't notice them because they are used to not noticing them [...]. I then took the trouble to build magnetic tapes that had elements, let's say, concrete ones, that is, noises, words, phrases, some music too; and above all the series of these sound events was an unexpected series, precisely to stimulate the habit of listening to music. [...] My aim of course is not to be a teacher, but at least to attract interest in the sound devices, which are within everyone's reach, and which everyone can listen to or compose in their mind.[31]

Such a variety of sound situations almost seems to echo some of John Cage's sound experiments, particularly the experience of *Fontana Mix*, created at the Studio di Fonologia in 1958; however, Maderna's editing gives the piece a formal and musical feel that is his alone. The environmental component is also an important influence in the work, not so much as a descriptive or poignant situation (as often happens in the course of his radio plays, starting with his 1954 *Ritratto di città*), but rather to stimulate the perception of real-life situations that are offered for listening in a mediated form. They therefore become prompts for the listener's memory, who can "compose" them in his or her own mind, thus stimulating what Maderna himself elsewhere calls "*Zeitprojektionen*" (temporal projections).[32]

---

29   Among the tapes Luigi Nono elaborated in the Studio in the years immediately preceding *Tempo libero I*, we can mention those for the electronic compositions *Musica-Manifesto n. 1*, *Y entonces comprendió*, and *Contrappunto dialettico alla mente*. One can also make out snatches of the sound "jokes," prepared by Marino Zuccheri unbeknown to the composers during the work sessions, on the *Tempo libero* tape (currently kept in the NoMus archives in Milan, and in the Luciano Berio Collection at the PSS).

30   Original in Italian ("cibernetica," "elicottero," "cosa pensa lei della situazione del tempo?"). For more on this see the description of the work in *Bruno Maderna: Documenti*, ed. Mario Baroni and Rossana Dalmonte (Milan: Suvini Zerboni, 1985), p. 294.

31   *Strutture ambientali*, nos. 7–9 (see note 14), pp. 114–15; repr. in "Tavola rotonda su *Tempo libero*," in Maderna, *Amore e curiosità* (see note 15), pp. 282–83.

32   Maderna said this in 1957 during his lecture at the Darmstadt summer courses "Kompositorische Erfahrungen mit der elektronischen Musik," translated into English as "Compositional Experiences in Electronic Music," in Raymond Fearn, *Bruno Maderna* (Chur: Harwood, 1990), pp. 294–96: 295.

This emerges from Maderna's aforementioned radio conversation with Christof Bitter;[33] the conversation gives us great insight into the approach he adopted in conceiving his sound vision of leisure, also in keeping with the intentions stimulated by the event that frames it. At the same time, Maderna's account also reveals his desire to create an "open," "mobile," and "interactive" work (probably more on an intentional level than in terms of its actual production), very much in agreement with Ohl's experiments, if not directly inspired by them:

> I thought that the attitude of a person in their free time should ideally be different from the one he or she has in everyday life [...]. So I said to myself, what would happen if a person were enthusiastic about this whole experience – the noises, the voices, distances, the sound of the wind, or perhaps their thoughts on a music they had listened to the previous day or that they would like to listen to, and so on ... what if they then wanted to try to make a composition or a collage? [...] Basically [it's a collage] but without any surrealist connotations. Rather I'd say ... as you know, among the latest products of musical art and compositional technique there have already been several significant experiences within the so-called "open form." The open form is in fact like a piece of furniture for a sculptor. There are proportions that must be maintained, both spatial and temporal proportions. For example, I started with a few elements and I immediately envisaged the possibility of interpolating them, of psychologically opposing them. [...] And while I was working on this piece of furniture, I added new elements from time to time, even contrasting ones, which, however, should not disturb the harmonic balance of the whole. And so the piece grew by itself. Then when I felt the need not so much to set a limit, but to circumscribe an environment, then the piece has come to its conclusion, even though the piece itself can in theory last forever, because it is conceived for a space where people can themselves become tape players (a bit like they do with cassette tapes). Also, since it's a four-track tape, the scale can be variable ... And so the *piece of furniture* can last millions of years if you want! [...] Basically, the piece begins when you want to take some free time and ends when you don't need it anymore.[34]

The equipment required by Maderna for the diffusion of the piece (in particular the four tape recorders and the loudspeakers requested in the letter to Dasi cited in note 17) would seem to suggest a fairly conventional diffusion, one which perhaps played on repetitions and restarts of the tapes, and in which the interactive aspect could be the meeting and mixing of the sound events on the tapes with the extemporaneous noises of the environment. This effect is also explicitly mentioned by Maderna during the aforementioned conversation with Bitter, where he explains that sounds and chatter were mixed together and that people could or could not perceive the presence of the music.[35] A participating audience might also have been one of Maderna's requirements, in the light of the context in which the listening took place – especially the interactive experiment carried out with the UNIVAC 1108. Imagining a piece in which the sounds contained on the tapes are meant as a field of possibilities and can be freely enjoyed according to potentially infinite combinations –

---

33   See note 25. A copy is kept at PSS-BMC.
34   Maderna, *Gespräch über Freizeit* (see note 25); the translation here is based on the Italian version published in idem, *Amore e curiosità* (see note 15), pp. 160–61.
35   Ibid., p. 162.

Pousseur's *Scambi* is one of the earliest examples of this idea – was still wishful thinking for that era: fixation on tape, in fact, inevitably leads to choices which remain fixed in a rigid sonorous consequentiality. Even where there is a vast and heterogeneous stock of sounds, the writing on tape ends up by rigidly fixing what was intentionally conceived to leave room for a multiplicity of interpretive paths.

The desire to arrive at a narrative process not bound to rigorous consequential logics was nothing new for Maderna. It stemmed from his encounter with electroacoustic media, which, since the first experiments in the 1950s, had turned out to be the catalyst for the developments in his compositional practice compared to the practices of the time. In fact, Maderna's first encounters with technology are what brought him to a conception in which a work is seen as a sort of field of possibilities capable of making one aware of "numerous temporal projections which can no longer represented by a one-dimensional logic," whose influence will also be reflected in his compositional techniques and, by extension, in traditional musical composition on paper.[36] However, let us not forget that, whatever the wealth of ideas and solutions that can arise thanks to the presence of a "machine," Maderna always clearly underlined the centrality of human action in the crucial stages of the compositional process: "I am the machine's friend, and I think eveyone will agree with me […] if I say that the machine helps me to understand certain things better regarding how to compose. But I'm the one who composes […]."[37]

These are some of those ideas that constitute one of the leitmotifs in his creative arc. However, once again he is caught up in a sort of paradox: on the one hand, a technology pushes him to "reorganize my intellectual metabolism as a composer,"[38] imagining numerous temporal projections and even declaring "that one should hate coherence" and consequentiality;[39] on the other, it drives him back into the very strict discipline of magnetic tape, with a time measured in centimeters and a "putting back in sync."[40]

Perhaps it is no coincidence that Maderna's next step – almost in a sort of retaliation that tastes of liberation – was attempted with *Juilliard Serenade*, using the only "technology" which at that moment allowed him to create a field of possibilities that really left room to expand: traditional writing on paper, dialectically combined with procedures

---

36 The quotation comes from Maderna, "Kompositorische Erfahrungen" (see note 32), here in the translation proposed by Fearn in *Bruno Maderna* (see note 32), p. 295. This trend is already visible in Maderna's earliest electroacoustic experiments; see in this regard Rizzardi and Scaldaferri, *"Musica su due dimensioni"* (see note 8), pp. 423–48. More generally, on the effects of his work in the studio on traditional composition, see Nicola Scaldaferri, "Montage und Synchronisation: Eine neues musikalisches Denken in der Musik von Luciano Berio und Bruno Maderna," in *Elektroakustische Musik*, ed. Elena Ungeheuer (Laaber: Laaber-Verlag, 2002), pp. 66–82; and Angela Ida De Benedictis, "Riflessi del suono elettronico: sinergie e interazioni nell'orizzonte compositivo di Luciano Berio," in *Luciano Berio: Nuove prospettive / New Perspectives*, ed. Angela Ida De Benedictis (Florence: Olschki, 2012), pp. 293–336.

37 *Strutture ambientali*, nos. 7–9 (see note 14), p. 35; repr. in "Da un dibattito su 'La macchina, mediatrice tra uomo e ambiente,'" in Maderna, *Amore e curiosità* (see note 15), pp. 265–77: 72.

38 Maderna, "Compositional Experiences in Electronic Music" (see note 32), pp. 294–95.

39 As Maderna says in *Gespräch über Freizeit* (see note 25), translation here from Maderna, *Amore e curiosità* (see note 15), p. 163.

40 An expression that comes from the technical jargon used at the RAI Studio di Fonologia in Milan, indicating the realignment needed to correct the time delays created while the tapes were running.

suggested by his experience as a conductor. Thus, an open sound situation of an aleatoric nature, imagined starting from the tape, which in order to materialize has to actually switch toward a composition produced with certainly more traditional means, but which allow an interactive and combinatorial approach to be interpreted by the conductor. And this regardless of whether such freedom comes about not in real time, but is "delayed," thanks to the specific task carried out by the conductor in the preparatory stages of the performance.

Author and Composer (*Juilliard Serenade*)

Juilliard Serenade was commissioned by the Juilliard School of Music in New York and performed for the first time there, at Lincoln Center, under the direction of the composer on 31 January 1971. It is a chamber piece for an ensemble consisting of two flutes (second also piccolo), one oboe (also english horn), two clarinets (second also bass clarinet), bassoon, horn, trumpet, tenor trombone, xylophone, marimba, celesta, harp, two grand pianos, violin, viola, cello, and double bass (five strings). As specified in the score, different combinations of instruments can also be used for the performance (only flute, harp, and pianos, for example), backed *ad libitum* by "the 'collage' *Tempo libero I*."[41] The juxtaposition of the two pieces and the possibility of combining them is not just an accidental fact or the result of a chronological contiguity: instead, in *Juilliard Serenade* Maderna seems in some way to interpret the ideas and principles enunciated in the composition of the previous piece, with the difference that while the tapes of *Tempo libero I* contain heterogeneous materials fixed in a rigid form, the score of *Juilliard Serenade* constitutes in all respects a field of possibilities subject to multiple combinations, which lacks a performative path established *a priori* by the composer.

Juilliard Serenade is in fact made up of thirty-five sections, defined by Maderna as "sequences and structures"[42] and laid out in alphabetical order (the sections follow one another from the letter A_1 to W), which, it should be stressed, does not in any way indicate a predefined consequential order. These sections are divided into two types. Fourteen are, according to Maderna's own terminology, "at *maximum control*, to be played exactly as written"; they are strictly defined in terms of pitch, rhythm, and instrumental formation and are indicated with the letters "MC" (that is, the first letters of the original Italian indication "*massimo controllo*"). The remaining twenty-one sections, on the other hand, are "at *relative control*, to be played with a certain degree of freedom ('*a fantasia*' as in '*cadenze*' or '*soli*'),'' and are marked with the letters "CR" (the first letters of "*controllo relativo*").[43]

---

41 See the performance notes and the title page in Bruno Maderna, *Juilliard Serenade (Tempo libero II)*, score (Milan: Ricordi, © 1971, 131884). It should be noted that several copies of the score exist bearing the same plate number but relating to different editions, not always identical to each other. The differences only concern Maderna's introductory notes, which are sometimes missing, sometimes only in Italian (facsimile of the manuscript), and at others in printed letters and translated into English. All the English citations of the author's performance notes reported in the text are taken from this last edition.

42 Such terminology was dear to Maderna, who had already used *Sequenze e strutture* as the title of a piece for magnetic tape dating to late 1954.

43 All the citations in this paragraph, unless otherwise specified, are taken from Maderna's introductory text (original in Italian) published in the Ricordi score (see note 41), which provides detailed instructions for the performance of the piece.

Both types of sections vary greatly in length: for example, the strictly defined sections range from thirty-seven bars in the A_1+A_2 sections (followed by a further long bar 37bis) to two in the V_1 section. The instrumental combinations show just as much variety, ranging from solo instruments (as in the P_6, S, and T_1 sections, entrusted respectively to flute, violin, and oboe) to the rich timbral mixes of the F, L, or O_2 sections, to the percussive and pizzicato sounds of the N section, or just to the strings of the A double section. Furthermore, in all the sections, be they "at maximum control" or "at relative control," one can make instrumental substitutions, prescribed by Maderna in the score with the lettering "*ossia*": for example in section C, at relative control, for harp and two pianos, the cello can replace the harp; or again in section M (at maximum control), for horn, trumpet, trombone, celesta, and harp, the two pianos can replace the celesta. In total, four of the maximum control sections and fourteen of the relative control sections can be opened up to these possible substitutions. Finally, fifteen sections (all at relative control) can be repeated several times in the wake of the precise indications provided by the composer in his performance notes in the score.

In summary, the thirty-five sections offer an extraordinary variety of sound situations that lend themselves well to a kaleidoscopic combinatorial logic, guaranteeing ever-changing variety and sounds. Nor should it be forgotten that the same materials of *Juilliard Serenade* are also the source of a composition such as *Pièce pour Ivry*, for solo violin, likewise dating to 1971, which assembles fragments that the performer can combine at will.

The printed score of *Juilliard Serenade* reproduces the original manuscript, kept in the Ricordi Archive, and consists of nine large sheets of cardboard for a total of eighteen sides (one for the cover plus seventeen for the score). The cuttings of the autograph music sheets that make up the various sections are stuck with adhesive tape on each side of the cardboard sheets, with the subsequent addition of colored signs (unfortunately not visible in the printed score). The edition is completed by a two-page typewritten text of instructions (the original is kept at Ricordi and a copy at PSS), followed by three handwritten pages with a "List of instrumental combinations" (some *ossia*) and a "Table of the instrumental combinations." Maderna uses these pages to illustrate how the performance of the piece is to be carried out, which presupposes a preliminary editing by the conductor; in fact, the thirty-five sections are only the basic material on which the conductor has to intervene, both in terms of their chronological order and their vertical combination:

> The conductor may choose the order of succession of the sections and at the same time decide whether they should appear superimposed or singly [...]. The sections indicated as CR (relative control) can appear together with those indicated as MC (maximum control); obviously the CR sections will be played freely, while the MC sections will always be "conducted". The conductor may also vary the way in which MC and CR are superimposed, placing the sections in order that they may start and end together, alternatively spacing them differently. It is recommended to superimpose CR sections fairly frequently. [...][44]

---

44 These quotations and the following are taken from the performance notes in Maderna, *Juilliard Serenade (Tempo libero II)*, Ricordi score, latest edition with the author's notes translated into English (see note 41). Parts of the original introductory text were reworked in 1972 by Maderna for a concert program for a performance of *Juilliard Serenade* presented in Mannheim as a "new version"; text reproduced in Maderna, *Amore e curiosità* (see note 15), pp. 508–09; see also ibid., pp. 802–03.

Even for the sections to be repeated several times, Maderna clearly indicates the principles to be followed, providing instructions which in this case are intended for the musicians:

> [...] the first time, each instrument will play its part following as closely as possible the written indications [...]; the second time, each player must "find" a different interpretation by changing – but only slightly – dynamics, pauses, intensity of tone; from the third time onward each player will be free to "isolate" himself from the others [...], alternatively playing in "contrast" [...], or integrating and, at times, "imitating."
> [...] Consequently, this *Serenade* is not simply performed but virtually "recomposed" by the conductor, who, during rehearsals, should "feel" the want and structural necessity to link, superimpose, and develop the material at his disposal.

The score is therefore a repertoire of musical moments from which the conductor must draw by establishing a path based on the given indications. The conductor's role can therefore be assimilated to that of a "composer" – in the literal sense of the term – as he carries out an operation of selection and montage prior to the performance. Even Maderna himself did not shirk from doing this for each and every performance, in his role as interpreter of his own work. In fact, the materials relating to *Juilliard Serenade* in the composer's estate, which can be consulted at the PSS, contain a score Maderna used for one of his performances (presumably the world premiere): it includes seven large cardboard sheets on which cut-out photocopies of the various sections are glued, in an order that presents some differences with respect to the antigraph for the printed score kept in the Ricordi archives. In addition, rather significantly, the materials for the piece also include a set of photocopy clippings reproducing part of the sections, collected by the composer inside an envelope bearing the handwritten inscription *"Juilliard Serenade* | Framm disiecti da P_5 a W" (disjointed fragments from P_5 to W); these fragments had presumably been prepared for use in a possible future montage.[45]

In *Tempo libero I*, the conductor can achieve what was beyond the limits of the technology of the time, bound as it was to magnetic tape (where montage and mixing in any case force the piece to be "closed" in an order that does not allow changes), since he can choose the sections and assemble the piece for each performance. However, entrusting the conductor with the possibility of choosing his own performative path does not mean abandoning any of the rigorous strict principles, nor does it have anything to do with the speed at which Maderna worked. In fact, on the one hand, the thirty-five sections are extremely elaborate objects, finely chiselled and carefully prepared for a combinatorial game. On the other, the instructions provided by the composer are the result of careful

---

45 It would certainly be of great interest, but beyond the scope of these pages, to carry out a study of the various "re-compositions / performances" of *Juilliard Serenade*, including the one directed by Pierre Boulez on 29 January 1975 at the Juilliard School in New York (in combination with *Tempo libero I*), and, of course, the "authorial" interpretations by Maderna himself. Apart from the New York premiere, other performances are documented, such as the Italian premiere in Rome on 21 May 1971, and the *"Neufassung"* realized in Mannheim on 22 April 1972, also documented by the text written for the concert program (reprinted in Maderna, *Amore e curiosità* (see note 15), pp. 508–09) and by a schema of the performance kept at PSS (as the eighth and last page of a booklet whose previous pages contain a precise reproduction of the introductory notes to the score), on which Maderna affixes the handwritten label: "special version for concert on 22.4.72 at Mannheim, soloist A. Kontarsky, orchestra of the Süddeutscher Rundfunk-Stuttgart" (original in Italian).

preliminary reflections that already take into account the possibilities of development. This attitude is typical of early contrapuntal procedures – of which Maderna was a profound connoisseur – in which the final result is already guaranteed by the materials established at the outset; at the same time, it also leads back to the same Ohl experiment on "leisure," where the programmer had already entered all the elements and possible paths of the dialogue between man and machine in the UNIVAC, foreseeing the outcomes that could be obtained and also writing the "conclusions" provided by the machine at the end of the dialogue (Ex. 1).

Procedures of this kind are anything but approximate, just as Maderna's choice to delegate the definition of a path to a later date and/or to a third person is certainly neither a shortcoming nor carried out for the sake of mere convenience. On the contrary, the creative process also ends up incorporating within it the figure of the conductor-composer, as well as that of the individual musicians-performers, who in turn are required to make choices according to instructions that orient them in a binding way. It is significant to note how Maderna, in the introductory notes to the score, used the word "Author" (written with a capital letter in the original manuscript) and not "composer," as if to further mark the autonomy and distance between the composer understood as "author of the pages entrusted to the interpreters/performers" and someone who literally "reassembles" those fragments into a unique and coherent sound event.

Even where he seems to leave the field free, Maderna actually keeps tight hold of the reins of the possible paths, guaranteeing the final results *a priori*, without surrendering authorship. This is not only thanks to his role as a "programmer," but also thanks to tonal and parametric aspects which he always keeps under tight control, namely the pitches and the alchemy of the instrumental combinations. The unifying principle that glues the piece together ultimately becomes a characteristic sound, the result of the combination of a rigorous harmonic structure with that of timbre. It confers coherence and ends up becoming the stylistically characterising trait.

The notion of "composing in performance" was mentioned earlier, introduced to denote certain compositional practices in which the definition of rigorous and complex textual conformations is reached through the extemporaneousness of a part of the processes. In the classic cases, observed by Albert Lord and related to epic singing, each performer at the moment of the performance assembles the bricks that are the formulas fixed in his memory, based on a given plot that constitutes the backbone of the narrative, thus creating a text that is always consistent and recognizable.[46]

This process, despite all the differences of the case, certainly presents similarities with the procedure implemented by Maderna. Although the timing and authorial aspects are indeed very different (in the cases examined by Lord the choices are made in real time starting from materials encoded by tradition and memorized; in the case of Maderna's music they mostly come about during rehearsals starting from materials specifically provided in writing by an "Author"), the type of practices employed is quite similar and substantially ascribable to the following points:

---

46 See Lord, *The Singer of Tales* (see note 7).

• the presence of a field of elements that provide the material for the combinatorial game, which in Maderna's case is made up of the various precomposed sections;

• the existence of a common thread that confers a stylistic hallmark, mainly given by the harmonic color and timbral combinations; and

• the possibility of choice offered to the performer, who moves by combining the precomposed elements within the coherence framework established by the "Author" as a guiding thread.

Moving within the path traced by the first two components, the performer, with his or her choices, succeeds in creating a perfectly defined text as such, according to a procedure that is far removed from convenient vagaries, being traceable to an authorial logic capable of incorporating the figure of the performer in a functional way.

These kinds of processes, which in *Juilliard Serenade* are in place at the base of the whole piece, making it probably one of the most emblematic cases, are a common trait throughout Maderna's last creative phase.[47] The interview that Maderna gave during the rehearsals of his Concerto for violin and orchestra (1969–70), viewable on the television program *Un'ora con Bruno Maderna,* provides us with significant proof of this. For the occasion, the composer illustrates how the rehearsals represent the final phase of the compositional process and also explicitly clarifies that the feasible choices are in fact limited, therefore evidently already evaluated *a priori* together with the results that can be achieved:

> I finish the work of composition with the rehearsals. After this first performance [of the Concerto for violin and orchestra] there will be a fixed path, which will be entirely composed. There will be variations in the orchestral accompaniment, in the violin part, which will be three or four different ones; paths that can be established each time. However, not all the paths are possible: there will be three or four… formally useful ones.[48]

And likewise, he insists on complete respect for the notes to be played, explicitly declaring the importance of the connective tissue that is the harmonic component, the scaffolding that supports the entire composition:

> […] the notes cannot be changed, but everything else can be changed, staccati, phrasing, forte, piano […]. You have to observe the notes with the greatest precision, because it is the only pattern that holds all this stuff up […].[49]

Replying to a specific question, Maderna also admits that the possibility of new paths for each new performance involves the overcoming of a traditional view of the score as a "text," which however is always considered valid from a historical perspective:

---

47 As Angela Ida De Benedictis neatly points out, Maderna's creative arc moves between "(latent) rigour and (apparent) chaos […]. The archiving / reuse of 'partial materials' to be changed 'infinitely' seems to condition all the instrumental and electroacoustic production made by Maderna from about 1959–60 until 1973, the year of his death"; in "Scrittura e supporti nel Novecento" (see note 4), pp. 263–65.

48 Interview starting at 9'36" of the television documentary (see note 10), anthologized under "'Musica: un fatto necessario': Estratti da *Un'ora con Bruno Maderna* (IV)," in Maderna, *Amore e curiosità* (see note 15), pp. 358–60: 358.

49 Statements that can be heard at 5'40" and 6'20" in the same television documentary.

Do you no longer believe in the written score, that it should be strictly observed as it was in the past?

No, at least not nowadays. Of course, I always believe in the "famous" scores, as a historical-musical fact. But I don't think that today it is possible to reestablish a [musical] theatre again in that same way.[50]

Tempo libero II, or Tape and Memory Extensions

With *Tempo libero II,* which Maderna placed in brackets after the main title on the title page of *Juilliard Serenade,* the composer indicated two possible ways of performing the latter. In fact, it can be combined with the tapes of *Tempo libero I,* meaning that the field of possibilities made available to the conductor-composer also incorporate the sound events fixed on the tapes, and reuniting in a sort of ideal combination the diptych consisting of the two works. Maderna explained how the tapes should be used in the two pages of instructions introducing the score of *Juilliard Serenade:*

> The *Serenade* can also be played together with the "collage" TEMPO LIBERO I – recorded on magnetic tape.
>
> The loudspeakers can be arranged either in a frontal position, on the same level as the instruments, or in a circle; in the latter case, the loudspeakers should be put at the four corners of the hall and in contrast with the acoustic level of the instrumental group.
>
> The conductor will thus be in command of an enormous quantity of phonic and heterophonic situations which he will be able to arrange into divertissements, contrasts, integrations, imitations, etc.
>
> In agreement with the sound engineers, he will be able to introduce the tape at the points of his choice and select the desired volume of sound. The [Author][51] recommends the maximum accuracy in measuring and balancing the sound volume of the tape and instrumental group. Prominence should preferably be given to the instrumental group which should always be present and lead the game in TEMPO LIBERO II.[52]

This combination certainly continues what he had set out to do about twenty years earlier, when the game of two dimensions had sanctioned Maderna's entry into the world of electroacoustic composition. This time, however, it is not the sound generated by the machine (a sound that the listener cannot relate to a real experience) that is fixed on tape, but sounds captured from the real world (and not just from musical performances), with their more or less explicit references to people, the environment, and emotions. They are therefore not *objets trouvés* in the Schaefferian sense, but mediated sound events that maintain the atmosphere of their origin.

---

50   The excerpt can be heard at 9'50", anthologized in Maderna, *Amore e curiosità* (see notes 15 and 48), p. 358.

51   Here we have reintroduced the original "Author," with a capital A as it was in the original, translated by Ricordi as "Composer" (but see above in the text).

52   In the original version of this text, later reworked for the Mannheim theater program (see notes 43 and 45), it is interesting to note how Maderna defines *Tempo libero I* as a "counterpart" of *Juillard Serenade,* adding: "it goes without saying that this dramatically increases the combination possibilities for the conductor"; in Maderna, *Amore e curiosità* (see note 15), p. 509.

The conductor-composer is thus offered two types of sound events from which to draw to create their kaleidoscopic game: those performed live and those fixed on a medium, which largely come from real life events – mainly in the sense of "leisure sounds." Since the fixed events are a reflection of mediatized real situations, loaded with memories and evocative capabilities, they make real life emerge in the musical performance (in the artifact). If, in the first attempts at mixed music, it was above all the novelty of electronic sound that counterbalanced the instrumental one, the axis now seems to shift toward the dynamics between mediated sound and live sound. However, there is a difference in the use of the two kinds of materials: the score allows the conductor to actually recombine the elements at will, while the tape runs in a fixed way with a precise directionality, representing rather a kind of playback with the function of provoking and soliciting live instrumental interventions. The tape thus becomes a sort of memory of the past whose flow restates immutable sound situations opposed to the vitality and unpredictability of the performance.

Since the mediated sound, with its aura of individual sound objects offered at different levels of understanding and regardless of its recognizability, comes into contact with what is played live, it ends up comparing two different forms of communication. Maderna's own words also allow us to glean the deepest meaning of the concept of "dimension" for the composer, which primarily involves the component of musical communication:

> By "dimensions" I mean forms of musical communication: first of all through traditional means, that is, through performers who play or sing in the presence of an audience; and secondly with the proper means of electroacoustic sound – sound recording and reproduction – in which exclusively electronic procedures or even instrumental sounds can be used […] or in which electronic or instrumental sound procedures are fixed on magnetic tape and reproduced through loudspeakers.[53]

The dialectical game that is created between memory (tape) and what is performed by live musicians was captured by the critics who wrote about it in the reviews of the first performance of *Juilliard Serenade (Tempo libero II)* on 31 January 1971 in New York, under the direction of Maderna himself. For example, this is what Byron Belt wrote about the premiere the next day, on 1 February 1971:

> *Juilliard Serenade*, sub-titled *Free Time I* [sic], is a complex score that augments the traditional orchestral instruments with taped noise and voices. The tape provides the sort of aural scrim through which he hears everything in this era of constant noise, and the "musical writing" offers a kind of sonic *Last Year at Marienbad*, in which the memory is constantly tricked and titillated, but never really satisfied.[54]

Theodore Strongin, in *The New York Times*, is even more explicit. Not only does he underline the almost "autobiographical" data of the contents of the tape (drawing inspiration

---

53 As Bruno Maderna said in 1959 while presenting a concert dedicated to electroacoustic works in Darmstadt (typed text, original in German, at PSS-BMC; translated into Italian as "'*Musica su due dimensioni:*' Introduzione al *Kranichsteiner Kompositionsstudio III*" (1959), in Maderna, *Amore e curiosità* (see note 15), pp. 236–39: 236.

54 Byron Belt, "Outstanding Concerts," *Long Island Press* (1 February 1971). The reference is to Alan Resnais' 1961 drama film, *Last Year at Marienbad*, with its wealth of flashbacks intertwining past and present that make it a sort of journey into the memory of the protagonists.

from the program notes) and its stimulating function in soliciting live instrumental responses, he also seems to capture the third dimension of the conductor-composer who acts as a *trait d'union* between the two:

> *Juilliard Serenade* [...] is described in the program notes [...] as being like a biography. Assuming that music can somehow perform such a function in an abstract way, Mr. Maderna's music is so much his own and so unlike anyone else's that *Free Time I* [sic] becomes more of an autobiography than a biography. [...] It is scored for tapes, orchestra and taped sounds. The latter are mostly distant spoken voices, cavernous and distorted. They give the sense of events and emotions remembered from long ago. [...] The taped sounds are the starting point for the live ones, which, at first closely related, gradually develop their own personalities. If the taped sounds are memories, the live sounds are the responses of now to then. They are reflective in quality, and poetic. [...] Mr. Maderna ties everything together![55]

Fields and Provocations (*Giardino religioso*)

8 August 1972 saw the performance of the orchestral piece *Giardino religioso* in Tanglewood, under the direction of Maderna; its score was published by Ricordi in 1974, after the composer's death. The piece was commissioned by the Paul Fromm Foundation, together with Gunther Schuller's *Tre Invenzioni*, for the concert celebrating its twentieth anniversary, during which they premiered together with the revival of two previous commissions: Berio's *Circles* from 1960, and Elliott Carter's 1961 *Double Concerto for Harpsichord and Piano with Two Chamber Orchestras*.[56]

The letters between Maderna, Paul Fromm, and Sylvio Samana, the composer's impresario, written between the summers of 1971 and 1972, bear witness to the fact that the idea of this composition was crafted gradually.[57] The correspondence deals with aspects like the instrumentation, which initially also included the magnetic tape, but also the title. In fact, Maderna had originally intended to make an explicit reference to Paul Fromm in the title, calling it "*Paul Fromm's Garden* for Chamber Ensemble and

---

55 Theodore Strongin, "Gentleness Infuses Maderna's *Juilliard Serenade*," *The New York Times* (1 February 1971). In the theater program for the world premiere, Dennis Russell Davies writes: "For Maderna *Free Time* is like the biography of an individual, for the present moment is not only the summation of his previous existence, but also a part of what he will become" (*Notes on the Program*, Lincoln Center for the Performing Arts, second concert, 31 January 1971).

56 See the concert program ("Tanglewood Music Center Yearbook 1972," also available online; see https://archive.org/details/tanglewoodmusicc1972bost, last accessed on 4 October 2021). See also Paul Fromm's letter of 18 January 1972 to Bruno Maderna, preserved in the archives of HL (Paul Fromm Manuscripts, b 90M-52; MS Storage 290; Box 3, Folder Maderna), where we read: "Our special Tanglewood Anniversary Concert will be on Tuesday, August 8th. On the program will be the premieres of the Maderna and Schuller anniversary commissions together with Berio's *Circles* and Carter's *Double Concerto*. I am preparing an anniversary brochure which will be inserted in the programs during the week of the Tanglewood Festival and simultaneously be widely distributed in the United States and abroad." The same material also contains a note about the work by Bruno Maderna (cited below in the text), sent in June 1972 and published in the theater programs for the world premiere (where it is mistakenly attributed to Gunther Schuller; see in this regard Maderna, *Amore e curiosità* (see note 15), pp. 805–06) and subsequent reprints.

57 The letters are kept at PSS and HL. The Appendix to this essay contains some key excerpts.

Tapes,"[58] but the tribute was then eliminated in the final version of the title, now in Italian, as requested by Fromm himself (see also letter No. 3 in the Appendix, p. 169).

Even though only a few months had passed since the *Juilliard Serenade* experience, Maderna had meanwhile achieved compositional milestones, in which we find principles and techniques similar to those described on the previous pages. Among the works premiered in this period were *Venetian Journal* (New York, 12 March 1972), the orchestral scores of *Aura* (Chicago, 23 March 1972) and *Biogramma* (Rochester, 16 April 1972), and above all the multifaceted experience of *Ausstrahlung* (Persepolis, 4 September 1971).[59]

With *Giardino religioso* Maderna, however, almost seems to continue the thread of a discourse, taking it up again from where he had left off with the experience of *Juilliard Serenade (Tempo libero II)*. The connection is already suggested by the type of ensemble – a rather large chamber orchestra resembling the other ensembles used in those years (two horns, two trumpets, two percussionists struggling with timpani, marimbas, congas, rattles, triangles, plates, tam-tam, and celesta, two pianos, two harps, six violins, two violas, one cello, and one double bass) – and also by the initial intention to use magnetic tape, which according to a first idea should have accompanied the instruments live. But it is above all in the conception and structure of the piece that we can grasp the contiguity between the two works, especially if we consider certain situations of "opening" that seem to clash with the drafting of a score understood in the traditional sense. It is no coincidence that, after the premiere in August 1972, Maderna took quite a while to send Fromm the score he had requested several times in order to prepare the materials for the repeat performance of the piece, scheduled in Chicago in April 1973. Fromm himself was most annoyed by Maderna's delay in posting a score, which seemed to take longer to send than to compose.[60] However, the way in which the openings and the active role of the conductor in this piece are to be understood is precisely what allows us to see that Maderna, driven toward other forms of experimentation, has exceeded his previous achievements.

Giardino religioso is divided into ten sections, indicated by the letters of the alphabet from A to J. Here, too, there are sections rigorously composed and measured (such as the long section E, 48 bars) and free sections, for which the conductor must choose a personal interpretive path. There is, however, a preestablished order in the sequence of the ten sections, which is indicated in the score. The captions with the instructions for the conductor, unlike the score of *Juilliard Serenade*, are not given on separate pages, but

---

58   Letter dated January 1972 (HL). It should be noted that the idea of the "garden" is present from the very beginning.

59   The latter, in particular, is a fundamental work for the topics covered here; as Angela Ida De Benedictis in fact points out: *Ausstrahlung* "can be considered a sum of different experiences inherent in writing and textual ambiguity, as well as a sort of 'anthology' of the possible micro- and macroformal conformations of a mobile (or 'moving') composition"; from "Scrittura e supporti nel Novecento" (see note 4), p. 267. For more details on the montage, see pp. 280ff. of her essay.

60   The Appendix on p. 169 contains two excerpts from Fromm's letters (Nos. 5 and 6), written after the Tanglewood premiere, in which he asks Maderna's wife and Robert Holton to send him the score so that he can plan the next performances. For the Chicago repeat performance see below, note 62.

integrated within the musical text; they appear within the individual pages of the printed edition, which once again reproduces the original manuscript preserved in the Ricordi archives.

This time the conductor is offered a field of possibilities subject to strict constraints; it is no longer a question of carrying out an *ex novo* recomposition of the performance of the piece, but of following a path within a context whose boundaries appear rigorously traced. Compared to the open field of *Juilliard Serenade, Giardino religioso* constitutes a sort of *hortus conclusus.* This can be clearly seen by observing, in the graphic rendering of the two compositions, the different way of proceeding as regards the assembly of the precomposed elements. In the first case, as we have seen, it is left entirely to the conductor-performer, who manages to "compose" the work following the instructions of the author-programmer; in the second case, however, it is created and already fixed in the score by Maderna. The thirty-five sections of *Juilliard Serenade* are autonomous elements to be assembled in view of the performance, where each of the ten sections of *Giardino religioso* is already the result of an assembly of various elements.

Let us look at a concrete example. Examples 3 and 4 reproduce some sections of *Juilliard Serenade:* sections B and C (relative control, → **EX. 3**) and K2 (maximum control, → **EX. 4**); they are set out in the score as independent sections, and the conductor can select and assemble them freely. Example 5 instead reproduces section B of *Giardino religioso;* this page already constitutes a sort of mixing, carried out on three levels (as if it were three different magnetic tapes), in which three types of events are assembled, each with precise performance indications (→ **EX. 5**). More specifically, at the top we find the group of strings, which play a measured part to be repeated three times in *rallentando;* at the center, the free interventions of the two harps, "called" by the conductor in an extemporaneous way; at the bottom, the measured part of the two trumpets, which subsequently intervene in complete autonomy.[61] In fact, in this section Maderna has carried out a part of those operations in the score which, in *Juilliard Serenade,* were delegated to the conductor, namely those of combination and montage, while all the performers continue to be allowed margins of choice, such as repetitions and impromptu interventions, but always framed within controlled forms.

However, this does not mean taking a step back from *Juilliard Serenade,* nor does it return the conductor to a more traditional role. On the contrary, this *hortus conclusus* option allows for other forms of experimentation. In fact, if, on the one hand, Maderna relieves the conductor of the task of recomposing the text by offering the solution to this phase directly in the score, on the other he is given functions that broaden and enrich his usual one. The path that the conductor must follow is in fact not only a metaphorical one, in the "garden" of the text, but it is also associated with a real action: he must physically

---

61 These are the exact instructions that appear in the score: "The string section is played three times. The conductor only alludes to the tempo in the first bar, then leaving each performer to interpret the rall[entando] and dim[inuendo]. After a certain time the conductor will make the harps attack, indicating each single fragment (which must always be interpolated by asymmetrical pauses) and establishing, with gestures, a dynamic that is different every time, of his choosing. The trumpets will come in later, autonomously" (original in Italian).

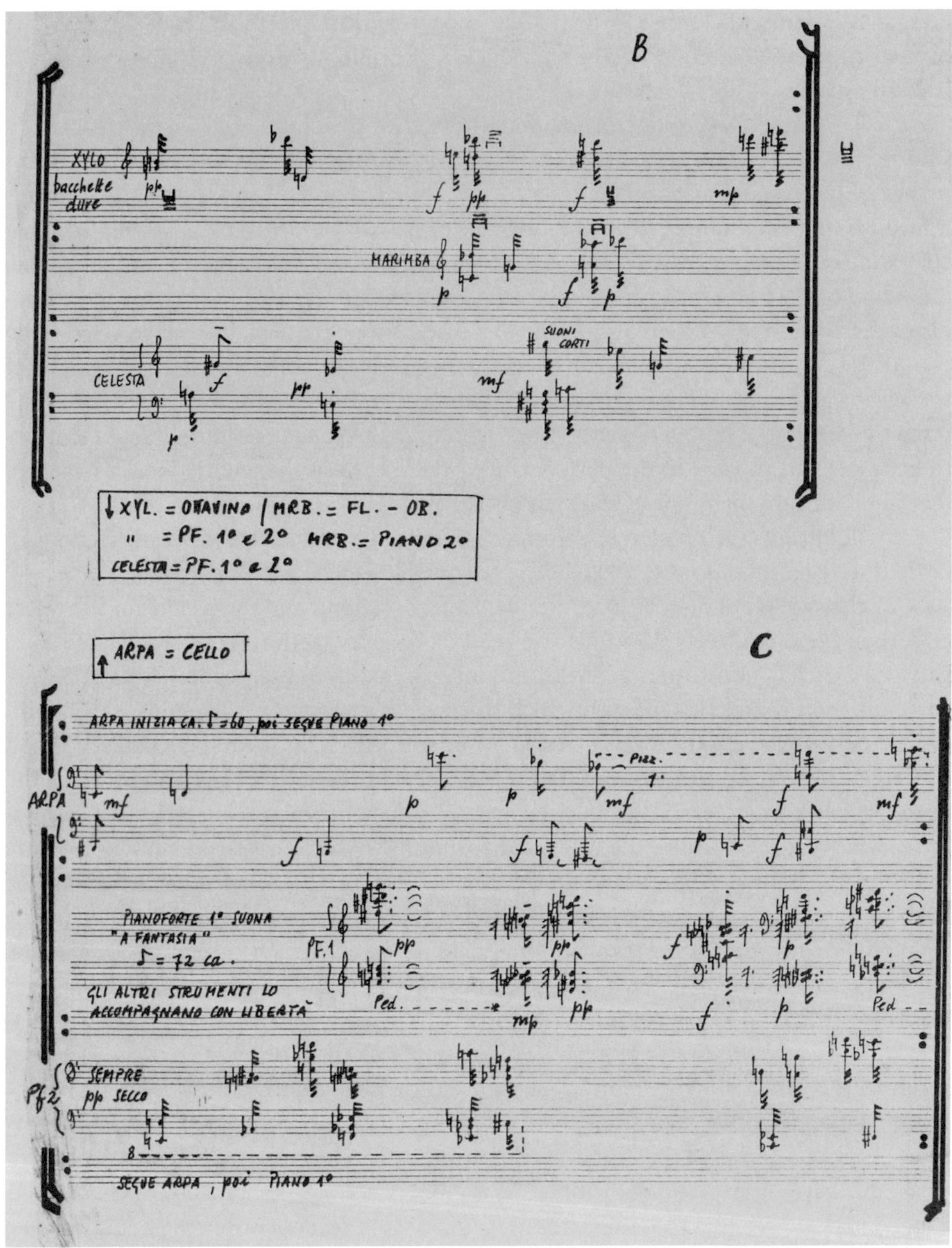

EX. 3   Bruno Maderna, *Juilliard Serenade (Tempo libero II),* score (Milan: Ricordi, © 1971, 131884), p. 3 (detail), sections B and C, at "relative control."

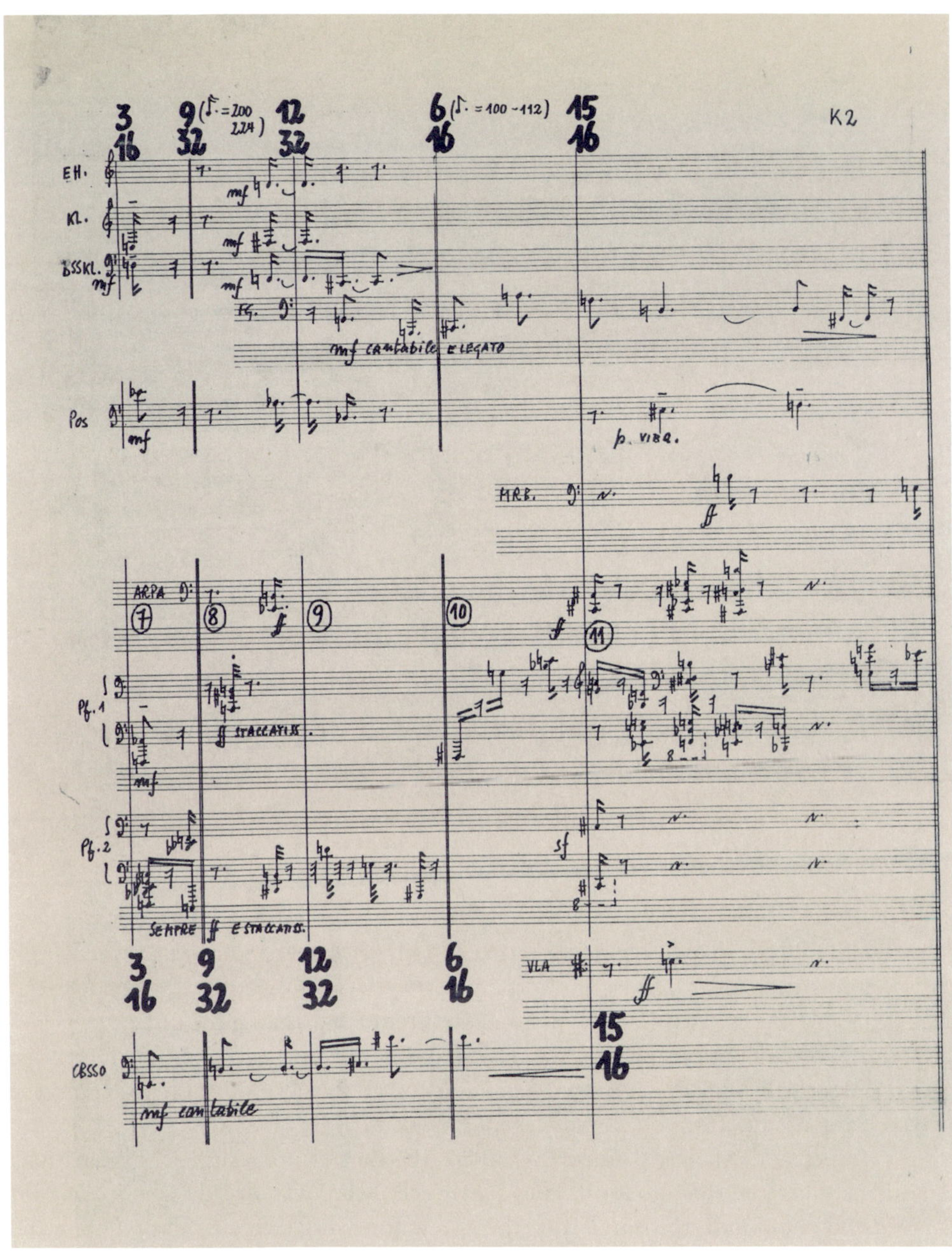

EX. 4   Bruno Maderna, *Juilliard Serenade (Tempo libero II)*, score (Milan: Ricordi, © 1971, 131884), p. 8 (detail), section K2, at "maximum control."

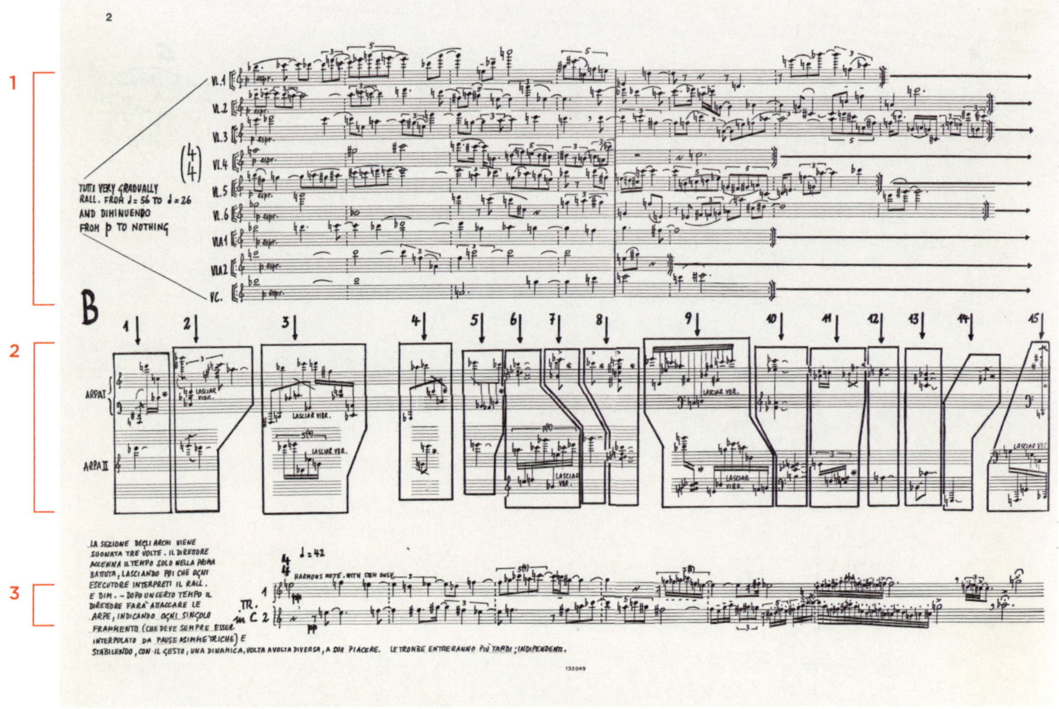

EX. 5   Bruno Maderna, *Giardino religioso,* score (Milan: Ricordi,
© 1973, 132049), p. 2, section B; montage of three elements,
corresponding to different instrumental groups with
different locations in the space: 1) strings in a semicircle,
2) harps in front of the conductor, and 3) trumpets at the
sides behind the strings.

move within the group of instruments, acting as both performer and *agent provocateur* for
the other instrumentalists. In fact, in certain sections (C, D, G, and H), the conductor is
required to play an active role as an instrumentalist, moving among the instruments and
performing specific actions; see e.g. the instruction in Example 6: "[…] in the meantime
the conductor will come down from the podium and go to play (only with his hands) the
two congas placed in front of his music stand." **(→ EX. 6)**

In the note Maderna himself wrote for the theater program, clear indications
appear that illustrate this situation. They partly echo what was already seen in *Juilliard
Serenade* but, above all, they underline these new functions, which end up giving the
conductor an almost ritual role:

> The title of the work has several connotations. It refers to certain "action" aspects of the com-
> position (for example the conductor performing on various instruments and in different
> stage locations) almost in the sense of a walk through a musical garden. But these musical-
> performing "acts" or "actions" also have a deeper meaning in that each such action is seen
> by the composer as an irrevocable commitment, an act of belief, as it were, very much in
> the manner of a religious belief or a liturgical act. *Giardino religioso* alternates between

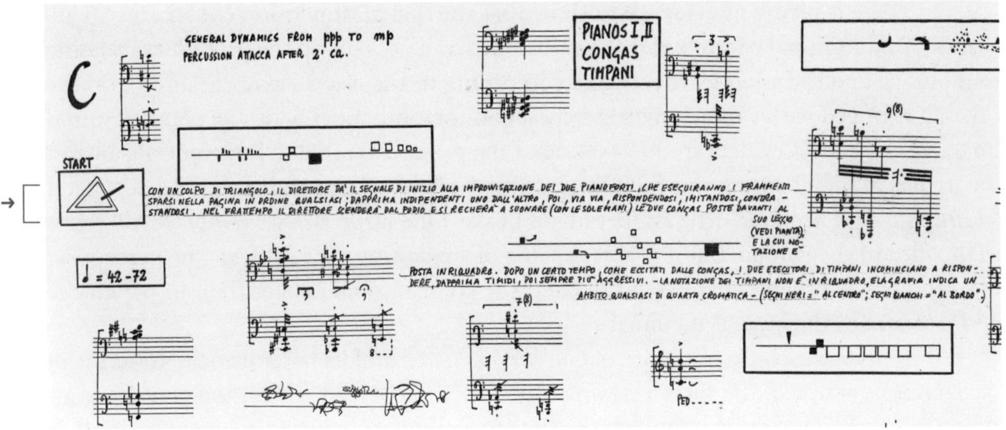

EX. 6   Example 6: Bruno Maderna, *Giardino religioso,* score (Milan: Ricordi, © 1973, 132049) p. 3 (detail), section C.

through-composed, completely specified sections and those in which the materials are given by the composer, but their precise articulation is "instigated" or "stimulated" freely by the conductor. The work is thus also a kind of dialogue of "closed" and "open" form.[62]

Apart from offering Maderna the opportunity to experiment with performative aspects, *Giardino religioso* also has implications in terms of space. This is evident from the placement of the instruments, arranged on three levels depending on their type (percussion, pianos, and harps are at the center, the strings around them, and the four winds on the outside) in relation to the conductor, who is at the center and moves in the central area.

The arrangement of the blocks of instruments on three levels naturally finds a precise reflection also in the layout of the sound events in the score, almost as if it were the transposition on paper of the contents of three magnetic tapes. For example, the B section observed previously (Ex. 5) is the mix of three different elements, each of which corresponds to a precise timbral block and a specific spatial location: the strings, with their measured sections, in the second row; the harps, with their extemporaneous interventions at the conductor's request, directly in front of him or her; and the trumpets (with their measured but autonomous interventions) at the sides. The long, measured section E is instead entrusted only to the instruments of the block located in the middle in front of the conductor (two pianos, two harps, and two marimbas), as if it were the track on the master tape.

The spatial arangement of the instruments seems to be established in relation to the presence of the conductor and the role he or she is required to fill: this time no longer as a "re-composer," but rather as a *provocateur*" and "conductor" in the strict sense of the term, since the conductor is called upon to contrast the different instrumental blocks and to make them interact, also interacting with them himself.

---

62 Note by Bruno Maderna, published in the theater programs for the world premiere (Tanglewood, 8 August 1972) and for the repeat performance in Chicago (13 April 1973); see also above, note 56.

There is plenty of evidence to show that the spatial dimension constitutes an authentic compositional parameter.[63] If, on the one hand, it takes up the procedures relating to montage and diffusion learned while composing in the electroacoustic studio, on the other, it is tinged with a more environmental connotation, moving on the plane of sound imagination. This is evident in the opening of the piece, entrusted to interventions by just the strings in high register, in which the caption explicitly suggests that they must suggest *"il risveglio degli uccellini"* (the awakening of birds). Of course, this certainly clearly refers to the idea of the garden, but it is also capable of suggesting, as a subtext, the perception of sound environments that extend beyond the conventional concert hall in which the performance of the piece is confined.

Despite the complex nature of *Giardino religioso* and its heterogeneity in terms of the solutions adopted, the piece certainly does not seem to fall within the context of an attempt at experimentation or an exercise in compositional virtuosity as an end in itself. It finds its outlet in a convincing and captivating sound result, which, as always in Maderna, is capable of connecting with the listener from the first moment. It is a "sound empathy" that knows no geographical boundaries and even winks at the American listener, if one gives credit to what emerges from the review by the critic Michael Steinberg, who refers to the premiere of *Giardino religioso* as "a curious and touching dream about what if Ives had been Italian, a work that is soft and lyrical and sometimes funny, and with a lovely atmosphere to it."[64]

---

63 This aspect was also pointed out in the essays by Carlo Ciceri and Pascal Decroupet in this book (see pp. 87–113 and 115–37).

64 Michael Steinberg, "Contemporary Music's Turn: Tanglewood's Festival Within a Festival," *The Boston Globe* (11 August 1972). My thanks to Anne C. Shreffler for pointing this out to me.

Appendix

Excerpts from the correspondence between Paul Fromm, Bruno Maderna, and Sylvio Samama[65]

1. Fromm to Maderna, 20 August 1971 (PSS and HL):
"I am happy that you accept the invitation to write a work for chamber ensemble to be premiered at the 20th Anniversary Concert of the Foundation during the 1972 Festival of Contemporary Music at Tanglewood. A copy of my letter to Mr. Samama is enclosed. I am especially pleased and encouraged that you will return to Tanglewood next year. We need the imprint and impact of your creativity, professionalism and broad musical horizon."

2. Fromm to Samana, 28 February 1972 (PSS):
"Dear Mr. Samama: will you help me in a sensitive matter? The enclosed is a copy of the form which Bruno sent me. Much as I am touched by the name of the work, I believe that the name would be considered corny and cause embarrassment to both Bruno and me. Perhaps you can suggest to him that dedicating the work to me would satisfy his good intentions just as well. We will print the brochure soon, and I therefore will appreciate having the new name of the work as soon as possible."

3. Fromm to Samama, 24 April 1972 (HL):
"*Religious Garden* sounds fine, but I wonder whether Bruno meant 'Sacred Garden?' Perhaps the title would be even more impressive if Bruno would translate it back from English into Italian to arrive at something like 'Jardino…' I will appreciate your contacting Bruno and letting me know the final title very soon. The printer's presses will be held until I hear from you."

4. Fromm to Samana, 9 October 1972 (HL):
"*Religious Garden* was favorably reviewed by the most influential critics […]. I myself found it a substantial work, and I intend to put it on the program of our Chicago concert this coming April."[66]

5. Fromm to Beate Christine Koepnick Maderna, 22 November 1972 (HL):
"Dear Christina [*sic*]: For months we have been trying to get the score of *Giardino Religioso* […]. I am planning on performances in Chicago and New York, but I cannot make any arrangements with the performing groups until I have the score."

6. Fromm to Robert Holton, 8 January 1973 (HL):
"Dear Mr. Holton: on November 22nd you wrote that I would receive the Maderna score and performance material by the middle of December. I am still waiting as we wish to perform […]. Why should it take longer to send the score than for Maderna to compose it? Frankly, my patience is wearing thin."

---

65 The archive housing the documents is noted with the acronyms PSS and HL (Houghton Library at Harvard University).

66 The concert took place on 13 April 1973 at Mendel Hall in Chicago; see Maderna, *Amore e curiosità* (see note 15), p. 805. Note however that the English title continued to circulate in letters and elsewhere.

LEO IZZO

Narrating with Sounds
Bruno Maderna's Music for Radio and Film

Introduction

The numerous occasions in Bruno Maderna's artistic life when he composed so-called *musica funzionale*[1] for film and radio are spread over many years, parallel to his activity as an art music composer. Although this music was initially little appreciated and scarcely known, seminal essays and articles on certain aspects, or indeed on single works,[2] have gradually brought his production of music for film and radio to light.[3] It goes without saying that a fundamental difficulty underlies any discussion of this topic, since radio and cinema have different linguistic specificities, require particular analytical perspectives, and, whatever their interconnections, boast their very own traditions, genres, and production processes. Added to this, we also have the noticeable fact that Maderna only worked intermittently on music for radio and cinema productions. Nevertheless, a number of constant features can be identified, and the proper degree of historical distance allows us to recognize the value and peculiarity of some of his most successful collaborations, in which the sound and/or musical component becomes crucial for the narration. In these cases, the composer's contribution goes beyond the routine of consolidated narrative genres and manages to introduce novel elements, albeit within the boundaries of well-defined linguistic codes.

---

1   In the late fifties, during their time at the RAI's Studio di Fonologia in Milan, Maderna and Berio used the adjective *"funzionale"* to indicate music intended for radio broadcasts. This expression is usually translated as "incidental music," and finds a counterpart in the German *"Gebrauchsmusik,"* as compared to absolute music (*absolute Musik*). Hence the choice to use the more neutral "music for film and radio" here.

2   The rediscovery and reevaluation of Maderna's radio and film production is based on a remarkable bibliography. On his music for radio and cinema and, more generally, on the work he carried out at Milan's Studio di Fonologia, see among others Angela Ida De Benedictis, *Radiodramma e arte radiofonica: Storia e funzioni della musica per radio in Italia* (Turin: De Sono, EDT, 2004); Maurizio Romito, "I commenti musicali di Bruno Maderna: radio, televisione, teatro," *Nuova Rivista Musicale Italiana* 34 (2000), no. 2, pp. 233–68, and ibid. 36 (2002), no. 1, pp. 79–98; Nicola Scaldaferri, "Montage und Syncronisation: Ein neues musikalisches Denken in der Musik von Luciano Berio und Bruno Maderna," in *Elektroakustische Musik: Handbuch der Musik im 20. Jahrhundert*, ed. Elena Ungeheuer (Laaber: Laaber Verlag, 2002), pp. 66–82; idem, *Musica nel laboratorio elettroacustico: Lo Studio di Fonologia di Milano e la ricerca musicale negli anni Cinquanta* (Lucca: LIM, 1997); and *New Music on the Radio: Experiences at the Studio di Fonologia of the RAI, Milan 1954–1959*, ed. Veniero Rizzardi and Angela Ida De Benedictis (Rome: RAI-ERI, 2000). On the jazz origins of many of Maderna's film scores, see my "'Espressioni jazzistiche in un clima d'arte': la sintesi di Bruno Maderna," in *Maderna e l'Italia musicale degli anni '40*, ed. Gabriele Bonomo and Fabio Zannoni (Milan: Suvini Zerboni, 2012), pp. 97–114; and "Da New Orleans a Vienna: strategie compositive in *Il mio cuore è nel Sud* di Bruno Maderna," *Mitteilungen der Paul Sacher Stiftung* 25 (2012), pp. 24–30.

3   Space limitations have prevented any in-depth analysis of his certainly important works composed for television.

The wealth of music for film and radio composed by Maderna might seem rather unusual for a post-war avant-garde composer. Moreover, from the perspective of now-outdated categorization, all this music enshrines the limits of a system of values that continues to favor a distinction between "high" and "low" cultural products, between intellectual elite and the general public.[4] However, Maderna's vast and varied work in these fields deserves instead to be approached with an open mind, in which the shared social and cultural divide between art music and popular music is envisaged as a sort of polarized *continuum*, within which intermediate positions and various forms of mediation coexist. This proves to be an essential concept for radio and/or audiovisual media, where the work is the result of the synergistic action of different forms of expression and professionalism.

One can easily get an idea of just how many variables come into play in this field of production by considering Maderna's very first radio and film collaborations in the immediate post-war period. In a very short time, the composer moved on from composing anonymous background music for insignificant, regionally distributed, penny-dreadful films like Max Calandri's *Sangue a Ca' Foscari* (1946) and *Il fabbro del convento* (1947) – just because he needed the money[5] – to the music he created for Giuseppe Patroni Griffi's radio play *Il mio cuore è nel Sud* (1949), a masterpiece of Italian radio for which Maderna wrote a complex score for chamber orchestra based on a personal reinterpretation of the twelve-tone technique. The unbridgeable gap between these different kinds of works from the immediate post-war period marks the two extreme and indeed distant points of a path that moves between art and musical craftsmanship without necessarily proceeding in a straight line from start to finish.

The aim of this article is not to explore works where Maderna was the sole or principal author (as was the case, for example, with his most famous radio plays, such as *Don Perlimplin* or *Ages*). On the contrary, the analysis will focus on works he created in collaboration with, or thanks to, other authors. In other words, we shall concentrate on cases in which Maderna was part of a preexisting narrative/dramaturgical/artistic project, and where he was thus obliged to mediate his own poetic needs with constraints linked to other authorial intent and to the project's final destination. The article will address three distinct stages in his relationship with radio and cinema that shed light on the inter-

---

4   For a discussion of these cultural dynamics in the American context, see the contribution by Lawrence W. Levine, *Highbrow/Lowbrow: The Emergence of Cultural Hierarchy in America* (Cambridge, MA: Harvard University Press, 1994). See also De Benedictis, *Radiodramma e arte radiofonica* (see note 2), pp. xv–xvi.

5   As Luigi Nono recalled in 1987, "Bruno's life at that time was very difficult. In practical terms he was just about making ends meet by writing soundtracks for fourth-rate films"; see "An Autobiography of the Author Recounted by Enzo Restagno," in *Nostalgia for the Future: Luigi Nono's Selected Writings and Interviews*, ed. Angela Ida De Benedictis and Veniero Rizzardi (Oakland: University of California Press, 2018), p. 39. Despite the poor quality of such films, it should be emphasized that their historical setting allowed Maderna to perfect the art of composing "in style" and the orchestration of preexisting pieces. This served to nurture that fruitful relationship with the music of the past, which characterizes Maderna's artistic biography (see the essay by Michele Chiappini on pp. 193–225 of this volume). Although the opening credits of these two films attribute the music to the composer Umberto Mancini, their true authorship is attested by the scores (signed by Maderna) filed at the archives of the Italian Society of Authors and Publishers (SIAE).

connections between Maderna the avant-garde composer and Maderna the background music writer, as well as on the association between music conceived for aesthetic enjoyment and music that is an integral part of a product for the general public.

1949–51: The Utopia of a New Mass Media: *Il mio cuore è nel Sud* and *Le due verità*

In February 1949, Alessandro Piovesan, a farsighted senior executive at the Italian broadcasting company (RAI), invited Maderna to take part in an ambitious project "to create a radio genre, call it 'radio-drama,' in which music played a lively role."[6] The work was to be based on a text by the young dramatist Giuseppe Patroni Griffi: "a banal, commonplace story about a place of misery" set in "any of the towns in the South."[7] Such a project was unheard of in Italy and called for a type of radio narrative in which the text acted in close synergy with the musical part. In fact, Maderna received an explicit request to use a style consistent with "jazzish expressions in an artistic spirit."[8] This was the initial idea behind the creation of *Il mio cuore è nel Sud,* a one-act radio play that Patroni Griffi himself described as a "*ballata*" [ballad], recalling an old tradition of narrative folksongs. The score for orchestra, soprano, narrators, and reciting voices was composed in the first half of 1949, when it also participated unsuccessfully in the pre-selection of the works for the first edition of the Prix Italia. *Il mio cuore è nel Sud,* lasting about thirty minutes, was finally broadcast from the RAI's headquarters in Rome on 11 March 1950.[9]

Il mio cuore è nel Sud reflected the cultural needs and forces that were at work in the Italy of this time. Italian musical life was going through a particularly effervescent moment, furthered by the autonomous exploration of musical areas that were either extra-national and foreign or banned by fascist ideology. For different reasons, American jazz and the gradually developing twelve-tone technique represented the two poles of this phenomenon.

---

6   Letter from Alessandro Piovesan to Bruno Maderna, dated 15 February 1949, in De Benedictis, *Radiodramma e arte radiofonica* (see note 2), pp. 15 and 217. All the correspondence regarding *Il mio cuore è nel Sud* is published in the same volume on pp. 217–23 (along with the previously cited letter from Piovesan, there are also eight letters from Giuseppe Patroni Griffi to Bruno Maderna; the original letters are at the Paul Sacher Foundation in Basel). For a detailed analysis of radio drama from the point of view of the compositional process and the relationship between music and drama, see Leo Izzo, *Il ruolo del jazz nelle musiche composte da Bruno Maderna per la radio e per il cinema* (PhD diss., University of Bologna, 2007), at http://amsdottorato.cib.unibo.it/228/1/Leo_Izzo_Tesi_dottorale.pdf; last accessed on 5 October 2021. On the relationship between jazz and the twelve-tone technique in Maderna's work, see also Christoph Neidhöfer, "'Blues' Through the Serial Lens: Transformational Process in a Fragment by Bruno Maderna," *Mitteilungen der Paul Sacher Stiftung* 18 (2005), pp. 14–20.

7   Letter from Alessandro Piovesan to Bruno Maderna, dated 15 February 1949, in De Benedictis, *Radiodramma e arte radiofonica* (see note 2), pp. 217–18: 218.

8   Ibid., p. 217.

9   For all this information see ibid., p. 218n. No recording of the radio drama exists in the RAI archives; according to the information provided by the radio broadcasting authorities, the RAI's Rome Symphony Orchestra was conducted by Maderna himself. On the other hand, a German version made in 1957 for Baden-Baden's Südwestfunk does exist (audio copy at the Paul Sacher Foundation). For this and further information, see ibid., p. 15, n. 47. A reproduction of Maderna's autograph score of *Il mio cuore è nel Sud* was published by Edizioni Suvini Zerboni in 1995 (S. 10987 Z.).

Moreover, the American films that flooded post-war Italy certainly had an influential role. From the forties onwards, Hollywood started to use jazz for the extradiegetic music of short scenes, instead of the essentially imitative formulas of late Romantic symphonic music. In fact, this stylistic innovation became a characteristic feature particularly of film noirs set in alienated, nocturnal, and degraded urban contexts,[10] and these ideas were merged in the creation of *Il mio cuore è nel Sud,* a play of visionary writing in which neorealist concerns and metropolitan anguish converge. Patroni Griffi's text develops on two parallel and independent layers. A first layer focuses on the representation of the urban environment, with the narrator's voice offering a vivid fresco of the poorer and more peripheral aspects of the town. At the same time, a second narrative layer tells the personal story of a marriage breakdown and the resulting madness. The score of *Il mio cuore è nel Sud* is almost entirely composed with the twelve-tone technique, and goes back to a phase of exploration of compositional techniques, that Maderna had inaugurated the previous year with the *Tre liriche greche* and the *Composizione n. 1* for orchestra. At the request of both Piovesan and the playwright, Maderna composed music that was characterized by continuous references to jazz, and achieved a synthesis between a style (jazz) and a technique (dodecaphony) that had rarely been accomplished in the history of music.[11] In Maderna's hands, this novel amalgam became a powerful dramaturgical means for staging the conflict between the town that was teeming with stories (portrayed with jazz-influenced orchestral music) and the obsessive, erratic, and delusional thoughts of the protagonist Dolores (depicted with dodecaphonic passages that are closer to Berg's methods than those of Webern and Schoenberg).

Analysis of one of the key scenes in the radio drama helps us to appreciate the fact that radio was opening up new narrative possibilities. It also highlights how Maderna behaved as if he were the playwright, taking over Patroni Griffi's role. From bar 45 onwards, after describing the bustling city life, the Narrator draws the listener's attention to a repetitive whistle:

> There's someone who whistles at a certain time in the evening / they always whistle, every evening / always the same… maybe it's a signal… maybe a lover's signal?[12]

This is a pivotal moment in the story, a sort of radio "change of scene" where the description of the town comes to an end and Dolores's personal story begins. Dolores is a young mother whose oppressive family life has driven her to exasperation and the search for

---

10   Different expressions, like film score, background music, off-stage music, or music off, are often used to indicate extra-diegetic music (whose sound source is external to the story). For more information on cultural motivations related to the concept of extra-diegetic music, see Claudia Gorbman, *Unheard Melodies: Narrative Film Music* (Bloomington and Indianapolis: Indiana University Press, 1987). On the narrative function of jazz music in films, see my "Il jazz nella musica per il cinema: 1927–1951," *AAA – TAC Acoustical Arts and Artifacts / Techonology, Aesthetics, Communication* 8 (2011), pp. 119–44.

11   Two of the very few exceptions that can be mentioned are Alban Berg's "Ragtime" in the first act of *Lulu,* already present in the 1937 version, and the short "Blues" featuring in Luigi Dallapiccola's *Volo di notte* of 1940. However, these cases are both culturally and temporally distant from Maderna and also underline a radical change in the object in question: the type of jazz that was well-known in Italy in 1949 was in fact quite different from the foxtrot and swing popular in the twenties and thirties.

12   Maderna, *Il mio cuore è nel Sud* (1949), score (see note 9), pp. 12–13, quote at bb. 46–49.

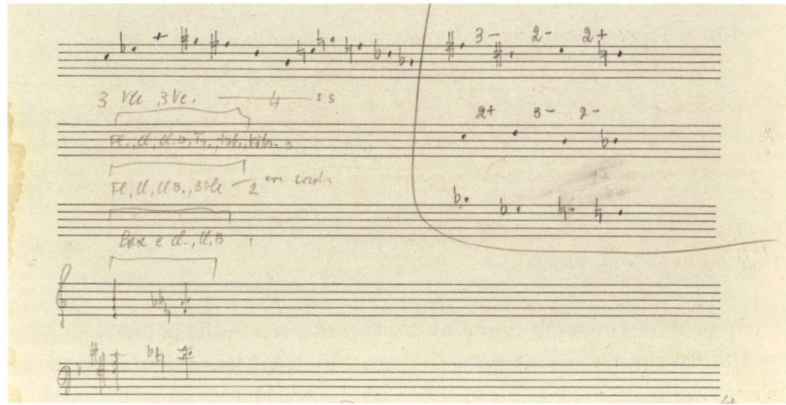

EX. 1   Sketch for *Il mio cuore è nel Sud* (detail); PSS-BMC.

EX. 2   *Il mio cuore è nel Sud:* Source chords, pitch distribution.

an imaginary escape route. She is convinced that the whistle of an anonymous prisoner coming from behind the bars of the nearby prison every night is a desperate signal of desire (and escape) addressed to her alone. This fantasy gradually grows into a hallucinatory obsession which chips away at the domestic life and the relationship with her husband, eventually leading to the story's tragic ending. The prisoner is the only character in the drama who is faceless and never speaks, and thus the sudden change of scene is entrusted to his appearance "on stage," represented by just the sound of the whistle (rendered with a descending semitone, B-B flat in the radio drama). This acoustic signal is both a perturbing element and a driving force in the tragedy, and its appearance therefore coincides with a crucial moment in the story. In fact, this mirrors Maderna's musical interpretation, since the entire score is created from this very descending semitone. Example 1 reproduces a copy of a manuscript that bears witness to the very first phases of the compositional work. On two staves, beneath some orchestration annotations, two chords cover the whole chromatic scale and harmonize the descending B-B flat semitone (→ **EX. 1**). This chord sequence stands out as a genuine harmonic motif associated with the convict's signal.

The pitch distribution of the two source chords (→ **EX. 2**) can be interpreted as the superimposition of two pairs of distinct triads.[13]

---

13   As this chord sequence develops, it sometimes gives rise to pseudo-tonal effects that become a sort of recurring element in the score, which could be interpreted as "the signal's motif."

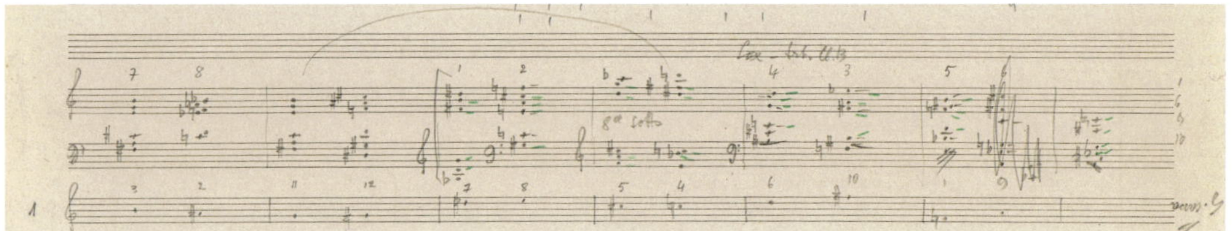

EX. 3   Autograph manuscript with the harmonic plan for
Il mio cuore è nel Sud (detail); PSS-BMC.

Analysis of the preparatory manuscripts preserved in the composer's legacy clearly shows that this was the generating nucleus from which Maderna then derived several concatenations of chords that he used to develop pitches and twelve-tone material. Example 3 reproduces the harmonic plan used by the composer as a starting point for writing the score in bars 33–63 (→ **EX. 3**).

The harmonic motif shown in Example 2 plays an important role in the scene in which the whistle is first heard. In the absence of any visual scenographic references, the music has to mark the action and guide the listener in the correct interpretation of facts and contexts, as well as helping to make sense of the dialogues. In the scene between bars 38 and 53 of the score, the Narrator first alludes to the whistle as if it were a secondary detail of the surrounding soundscape ("There is someone whistling…"). At the same time, however, the listener's attention is actually drawn to this same element ("he always whistles, every evening…"), with a shift of focus that resembles a cinematographic zoom. Maderna captures the idea of transition implied in the text and expands its temporal dimensions (developing it over sixteen bars), thereby giving even greater fluidity to the connection between the various settings, including the emotional ones. A change in style and orchestration musically underlines the change of scene: the whole initial part (dedicated to the description of the town) is characterized by jazz influences and by wind instruments, but from bar 45 onwards the strings take over, and every reference to jazz disappears. This transition is briefly described in Example 4: the vocal and instrumental parts are shown beneath the bar numbers, together with the repetition of two significant elements: a) the staged whistle (B-A sharp / B flat), as an internal element of the narrative setting (° symbol); and b) the harmonic motif of the "signal" (*) – also shown as a chord in the lower part of the diagram – taken up by flute, clarinet, english horn, three alto and one tenor saxophones, three violas, three cellos, and a vibraphone (→ **EX. 4**).

The last part of the initial long episode dedicated to the town corresponds to a *fermata* and a *decrescendo* of the winds, whose sound dissolves in the initial attack of the strings, with a gradual transition that is similar to a "crossfading" mix (bar 39). After a few bars of pause, the Narrator notices the presence of a sound ("There is someone who whistles at a certain time in the evening"; bar 46). Not long after, in bars 50–51, with no orchestral accompaniment, the sound of the whistle is repeated three times and the Narrator remains silent, almost as if he were a spectator listening for the drama to begin. Dolores's voice then comes "on stage" (bar 52) with her "Stop it, stop it, stop it …" in reply to the whistle. Her voice reveals her feelings of fear and fascination, but also manages to

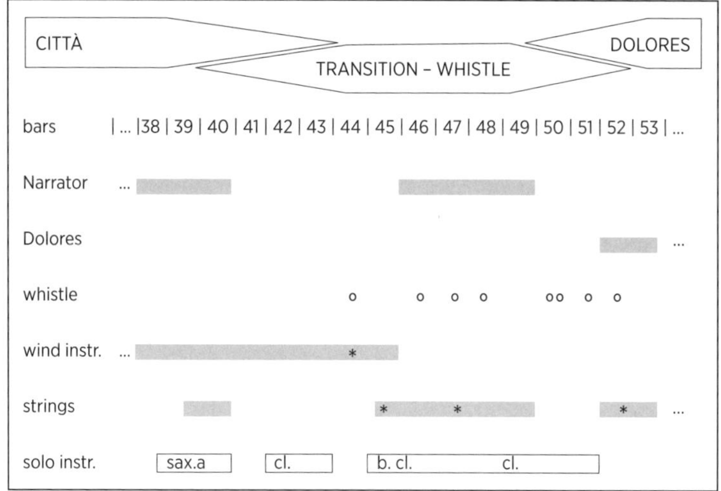

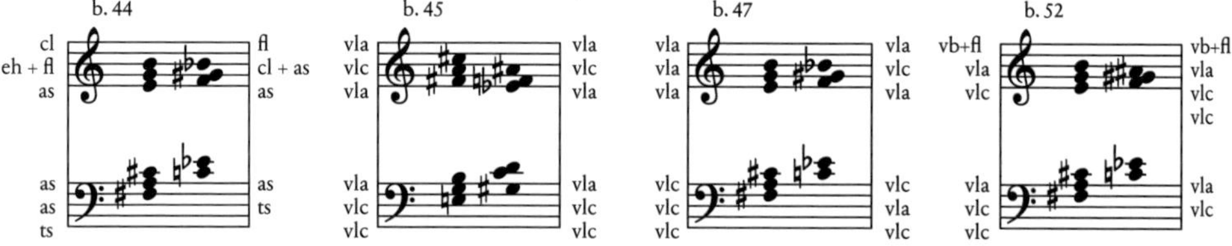

EX. 4   *Il mio cuore è nel Sud:* Diagram of how the musical dramaturgy evolves, bars 38–53.

give an emotional and symbolic interpretation to the "signal" that has just been heard. The music accompanies and comments on Dolores's mood, helping to shift the focus of the story from the external Narrator to a character within the drama. While the whistle is a "neutral" sound object for the Narrator, it evokes deep emotions in Dolores's mind, proving itself to be a powerful disturbing element. Maderna makes Dolores's interpretive (and empathic) act visible (or, better, audible) mainly through the orchestra's treatment of the clearly recognizable semitonal *harmonization* of the whistle, which is repeated several times in an iridescent sequence of chords.

The analysis of this brief episode clearly shows that the music in this work is much more than mere background music just there to accompany the action, since, at times, it even manages to shape and direct the flow of events. Maderna's score meets the demands of the text in an original way, contributing to weaving the story and sometimes suggesting significant associations that are only potentially expressed in the script. In other words, the music exploits the potential of the radio medium to create a "sound" dramaturgy that would not otherwise be possible.[14]

---

14   For an in-depth study of the compositional procedures, see Izzo, *Il ruolo del jazz* (see note 6), pp. 61–146. For further discussion of the role of the music's "emotional counterpoint" or "descriptive amplification" in *Il mio cuore è nel Sud* see also De Benedictis, *Radiodramma e arte radiofonica* (see note 2), pp. 118–22.

Encouraged by the recognition he had received for *Il mio cuore è nel Sud*, when Maderna next collaborated with the director Antonio Leonviola on the film *Le due verità* (1951), he also tried to replicate this union of jazz and dodecaphony in the field of cinema. Despite having proven itself a winning choice in the still developing genre of Italian radio drama, it turned out to be rather bold and less convincing for the film medium with its far more binding stylistic codes. The decision to use twelve-tone music for *Le due verità* was probably originally based on the suggestions outlined in the screenplay by Maurizio Corgnati. The film begins and ends in a courtroom, where a trial is underway for the death of a young girl called Marialuce, whose boyfriend is the only defendant. The fictional film makes use of a series of flashbacks to tell the same story twice: first, we see the public prosecution's reconstruction of the events, followed by the defense's account, in which the relationship between perpetrator and victim is completely turned upside down. A nocturnal and troubled Milan is the setting for what is thus a legal noir with psychological ramifications that summon forth major ethical issues of truth and interpretation, central themes also in Akira Kurosawa's contemporary (and better-known) *Rashomon* (1951).[15] Maderna put a great deal of effort into writing the first draft.[16] The music he composed involved a large chamber orchestra plus several quite unusual instruments for the time, such as electric guitar and Hammond organ. He devised original solutions of alternating solos (a rare occurrence in film music of the time) and ensembles, formulating new possibilities for mixing twelve-tone procedures with jazz influences. However, on hearing this dense and innovative music, Leonviola turned it down flat, considering it too distant from the film's expressive horizon. A profound and problematic disagreement ensued between composer and director, as shown by the draft of a non-autograph letter (with no named recipient or date, though certainly 1951) conserved among Maderna's papers:

> by asking me to compose the music for the film *Le due verità*, you have clearly shown your trust and your respect for me as a composer. [...] On hearing the themes that I had composed for the film [...] the director expressed his firm and very clear opinion, that the kind of music I had written was not at all suitable for his film. I quote two of the things he said: "This music is sad, just as the film is sad: I'm looking for happy music instead. Marialuce's character must be expressed by a light and bouncy musical theme, by a simple tune of the kind that usually accompanies Totò films."
>
> Now, I really don't want to disagree with the director's opinion: I don't even want to discuss whether it can be called an opinion. Quite simply, I can't do Totò's music, in the first place because my interpretation of the film is completely different; secondly because I can't afford to screw up in just one shot, with something ridiculous and foolish, the position that I have struggled so hard to achieve in contemporary music.
>
> I thus consider myself relieved of my obligation [...].[17]

---

15   Although the influence of Akira Kurosawa's masterpiece on the subject of *Le due verità* is still uncertain, it should be noted that *Rashomon* won the Golden Lion at the Venice Film Festival in 1951.

16   The SIAE Archives, Rome, hold about one hundred handwritten pages composed by Maderna for the first draft of the soundtrack of *Le due verità* (photocopies at the Centro Studi Bruno Maderna in Bologna). For a detailed compendium, see Izzo, *Il ruolo del jazz* (see note 6), pp. 220–27.

17   Draft of a letter housed in PSS-BMC in the folder "Aufzeichnungen, Vorträge, Notizen." A copy of the same letter is kept at the Studio di Fonologia Archives (correspondence, *ad vocem* "Leonviola, Antonio"). I am grateful to Angela Ida De Benedictis for having told me about their existence and also about the following documents mentioned in note 18.

The letter, most probably written in the heat of the moment after a head-to-head clash between composer and director, demonstrates a basic lack of communication, starting from Leonviola's use of the word "sad" to define something that for Maderna was probably of a far greater psychological complexity. Moreover, Maderna affirms his own independence not only as the composer of the music, but also as a playwright. In fact, the reasons behind this extreme gesture of handing in his resignation (which, in the end, never actually happened) are in fact not just because he wished to avoid writing "something ridiculous and foolish," but also because, on purely poetic-narrative grounds, his "interpretation of the film [was] quite different" to Leonviola's.

In the end, motivated by the chance of professional growth and financial needs, Maderna reluctantly composed completely new background music, hastily reworking a preexisting popular melody in a somewhat mundane manner.[18]

Beyond the questionable outcomes of this work and the existence of an innovative but never achieved musical project, the story of the composition of the music for *Le due verità* is an indication of the difficulty Maderna was experiencing in finding his place within the well-defined sectors of the film industry. On the one hand, he wanted to safeguard "the position" he had slowly but certainly not easily achieved in the panorama of contemporary music; on the other, he was well aware of the professional and contractual duties related to his role as a film composer. Thus, his decidedly utopian attempt to create an unprecedented synergy between forms of narration intended for the general public and music with an expressive authenticity came to an abrupt end with the first draft of the music for *Le due verità*.[19]

1954–59: The Skilled Craftsman:
Opinione pubblica and *Il cavallo di Troia*

After the difficult experience of *Le due verità*, Maderna's relationship with radio and cinema seemed to take a turn for the better: his collaborations on films and radio productions were characterized by greater concreteness and an acquired awareness of the specific production processes. At this stage, he seemed to set aside the idealistic momentum that marked his first steps in radio plays and films, a momentum that also stemmed from an attempt to remain faithful to his own compositional principles. And yet, even though all the scores conceived in this period for radio and cinema were on the whole more conventional, he still managed on many occasions to carve out his own inventive space to experiment and revisit some narrative clichés in a creative way.

---

18 Maderna's correspondence contains several letters about a copyright dispute over a folk-like theme written by the dancer and singer Lena Samara, who was working in the Parisian cabaret "Le Carroll's" in 1950 (see letters from the SIAE dated 3 October 1952, 17 December 1952, and 17 July 1953; PSS-BMC).

19 The original musical manuscripts of *Le due verità* are not housed in the composer's fonds at the PSS. Maderna registered various materials at the SIAE in Rome for copyright protection (photocopies of documents held at the Centro Studi Bruno Maderna; see n. 16). Further copies are present in the Luciano Berio Collection at PSS. For a detailed compendium of the preparatory materials for *Le due verità*, see Izzo, *Il ruolo del jazz* (see note 6), pp. 220–27.

The two main films that Maderna collaborated on in these years are *Noi cannibali* (1953), again by Leonviola, and *Opinione pubblica* (1954) by Maurizio Corgnati.[20] Despite their great diversity, both films are clear evidence of the composer's new approach.

Maderna assumed an apparently marginal role in *Noi cannibali,* a drama set in the post-war industrialized port of Civitavecchia. In accordance with the realistic gaze of the story, the soundtrack does not use extra-diegetic music: the few musical contributions come from within the scene and, as such, reflect the low and popular nature of the narrative. In the absence of extra-diegetic background music, Maderna concentrated on creating ambient sounds, which at certain moments actually become tangible sound materials with their own strong expressive potential and not simply a way to increase the realism of the scenes.

The soundtrack of *Opinione pubblica* perfectly complements the previous example. The film contains a great amount of extra-diegetic music which, almost in the style of classic Hollywood cinema, accompanies the entire dramatic action in the most emotionally charged scenes. Legal drama, sentimental tragedy, historical reflection, and social criticism are just some of the many themes the film tackles in an original way. The background to the story is the death of a woman in a small Tuscan town. Her husband Egisto, an unemployed worker, is first accused of her murder, but then acquitted. A young journalist named Jaiet conducts an unscrupulous press campaign that transforms the unwitting Egisto into a martyr, the victim of a judicial error, who garners the sympathy of national public opinion. The story turns into a tragedy when Jaiet decides to make a film of Egisto's life, in which the worker himself plays the leading role. The worldly and flamboyant world of cinema thus definitively corrupts the provincial life of the town, as the unfortunate Egisto navigates the increasingly fine line between film fiction and biographical facts that eventually culminates in the final tragic epilogue of the senseless and liberating killing of Jaiet.

Given his somewhat less-than-idyllic experiences in the film world, and after the experiment *"à la musique concrète"* of *Noi cannibali,* it could be said that *Opinione pubblica* was Maderna's first (and perhaps only) cinematographic collaboration in which his contribution falls within the great Hollywood tradition of background music. In creating the music for this film, Maderna worked as a skilled craftsman who puts his art at the service of narrative cinema. Music plays a decisive role in moments when it accompanies the psychological development of the protagonist. As the story unwinds, Egisto is constantly searching for an interpretive key to understand his past, and the film is full of introspective moments. Indeed, one of the key episodes in the film is built around one such moment, which is complemented by a virtuosic use of background music. During the filming of the scene portraying his wife's death, Egisto, in a trance-like state, relives on set the moments preceding her disappearance, under the gaze of Jaiet, the crew, and the director. In an intense monologue, he goes in search of a truth (his wife's betrayal), which, at that point, is still unbeknownst to him, experiencing mixed feelings that alternate between affection, confusion, fear, anguish, and anger. The music divides up Egisto's story and takes the audience with him on his emotional roller coaster with a rapid succession

---

20 Corgnati was the co-screenwriter for *Le due verità.* Charles Spaak and Carlo Fruttero contributed to the writing of the dialogues for *Opinione pubblica.*

of lugubrious ostinatos for timpani and brass, rhapsodic contributions of jazz piano solos, static and dissonant chord clusters, and emotionally intense passages for percussion alone.

The film received little attention from critics and public alike, and Maderna then abandoned this kind of project until 1968, when he started work on Giulio Questi's *La morte ha fatto l'uovo*, the last feature film he was ever to collaborate on.[21] Until the turn of the fifties, Maderna had worked more for radio than for the cinema, thanks to his and Berio's special relationship with the RAI following the establishment of the Studio di Fonologia.[22] *Il cavallo di Troia* (a two-act musical comedy by Gastone Da Venezia and Ugo Liberatore, directed by Mario Ferrero, 1959) is an exemplary piece of music-based entertainment, just one of the numerous radio productions on which Maderna collaborated in this period. The text is taken from a book by Christopher Morley, translated by Cesare Pavese in 1940 and published by the Bompiani publishing house in 1942.[23] Morley reinterprets the Trojan War in a modern key, generating a surreal dimension where classicism and modernity are continually confused: "the battlefield is like a football field; the warriors have a shower and chat with their coach every evening; the taxis chug to the nightclub where the 'Myrmidon Boys' are playing."[24] In the tradition of American musical theater, the dialogues are interspersed with musical pieces that allow the characters' thoughts and mood to emerge.[25] Musically speaking, the chosen style for the whole comedy is jazz, which amplifies the effects of the "temporal displacement" already present in the text, particularly when the nightclub music is heard as part of the ambient sound together with the chattering of the clientele.

21 During this long period, Maderna collaborated on composing the wholly electronic background music for Piero Portaluppi's *Lavoro a Ferrania* (1962), an industrial documentary of about thirty minutes on the manufacture of film at the Ferrania factory. The film, recently rediscovered by Cecilia Palandri, is kept at Ivrea's Archivio Nazionale Cinema d'Impresa. *Lavoro a Ferrania* is a traditional Italian industrial documentary, a specific sub-genre whose promotional intent went hand in hand with experimentation with media languages, and in which the directors often used the music of contemporary composers. For more on this, see Alessandro Cecchi, "Il film industriale italiano degli anni Sessanta tra sperimentazione audiovisiva, avanguardia musicale e definizione di genere," in *Suono/Immagine/Genere*, ed. Ilario Meandri and Andrea Valle (Turin: Kaplan, 2011), pp. 139–61.

22 For an exhaustive list of the radio drama productions with music by Berio and Maderna produced at the RAI in Milan and at the Studio di Fonologia in the fifties and sixties, see De Benedictis, *Radiodramma e arte radiofonica* (see note 2), pp. 56–60.

23 Einaudi acquired the edition in 1991 (all subsequent citations refer to this edition).

24 "Nota del traduttore," in Cristopher Morley, *Il cavallo di Troia*, It. trans. by Cesare Pavese (Turin: Einaudi, 1991), p. 121. See also De Benedictis, *Radiodramma e arte radiofonica* (see note 2), pp. 243 and 281–303. It is most likely that the director or screenwriters chose this text in the wake of the success of Warner Bros. *Helen of Troy* (1956), directed by Robert Wise. John Cage mentions Maderna's radio comedy in a letter to David Tudor, dated January 1959. At the time, Cage was a guest at the Studio di Fonologia working on *Fontana Mix*, and in his letter he uses the name of the epic Hollywood film when referring to Maderna's work: "The studio is very busy Bruno Luciano + Migliar[d]i (pop music) not doing their own work but radio requirement *Helen of Troy*"; see *John Cage and David Tudor: Correspondence on Interpretation and Performance*, ed. Martin Iddon (Cambridge: Cambridge University Press, 2015), p. 103.

25 A fine example of the playful dimension that emerges in this score is given by the passage entitled *Canzone di Cassandra*. In this modern transposition of Morley, the visionary becomes a die-hard pacifist demonstrator who is marginalized and ridiculed by everyone for her nefarious predictions. The original manuscript of this piece (in which tango, ragtime, and rhumba alternate) is reproduced in full in De Benedictis, *Radiodramma e arte radiofonica* (see note 2), pp. 289–303. See also Izzo, *Il ruolo del jazz* (see note 6), pp. 186–87 and 235–38.

EX. 5   Bruno Maderna, "Ouverture" from *Il cavallo di Troia* (bars 1–8): rhythmic modules superimposed in the exposition of the theme. Transcription of the autograph manuscript held at Edizioni Suvini Zerboni, Milan, reproduced with kind permission.

Whenever music is not linked to the often rather satirical representation of the characters, Maderna manipulates jazz stylistic models in an extremely original and innovative way. This is exactly what happens at the beginning of the *Overture* (→ **EX. 5**).[26] The melody performed by the three trombones refers to one of the songs from the radio drama, entitled "Cherchez la femme," but the melodic reference is immediately lost in a dense polyphony. A variant of the initial four-note motif is echoed by saxophones and trumpets in a rapid intertwining of sounds. In this case, Maderna adopted the language typical of the most advanced kind of orchestral jazz (Stan Kenton's progressive arrangements of the fifties), without however overshadowing the tonality of E-flat.[27]

---

26 The original score (kept in the archives of Milan's Edizioni Suvini Zerboni) is written for transposing instruments; the transcription in Example 5 is instead written at concert pitch.

27 The arranger in the field of jazz closest to this contrapuntal conception is Bill Holman, who worked for the Stan Kenton Orchestra for a while. *The Opener,* included on Stan Kenton and his orchestra's LP, *Kenton Showcase: The Music of Bill Russo, The Music of Bill Holman* (Capitol Records W524, 1955), is an example in which the different orchestra sections continually state the short motif of the main theme within a dense polyphonic texture. It is worth noting that Kenton and his orchestra performed quite regularly in Italy from the first half of the fifties onwards and had won critical acclaim. The most influential Italian jazz critic of those years recalled that "the formation [Kenton] brought to Italy in 1953 was the best he'd ever had, and also the jazziest." Arrigo Polillo, *Stasera jazz*, http://centrostudi.sienajazz.it/libroSJCap12.asp?lang=ita (consulted 16 June 2021).

The result is the superimposition of different and simultaneous metric groupings: the trombone motif (in binary form) is joined by a *pizzicato* double bass line, in a cyclical pattern of nine quarter notes (indicated with the letter "a" in Ex. 5), and the saxophone and trumpet lines, which initiate an imitative process based on a three-quarter motif ("b"). Maderna manipulated the rhythmic groupings in a complex way that was unusual for jazz and thus moved in a direction that was complementary to the reinterpretation of the jazz performed in his early works (think, for example, of the *Blues* episode that opens *Il mio cuore è nel Sud*),[28] where instead the unusual element was the pitch distribution.

1968: "Disconnected pieces [...] that can be composed and recomposed at will": *La morte ha fatto l'uovo*

Fourteen years after *Opinione pubblica,* and now a well-known conductor, composer, and promoter of new music, Maderna undertook his last and most significant cinematic collaboration on Giulio Questi's very particular film, *La morte ha fatto l'uovo* (1968). The film takes an irreverent look at the theme of man's alienation in consumer society, embracing but deforming the codes of film genres, like thrillers and erotic films, by freely re-composing materials from the cultural industry. The resulting poetics is one that Questi himself often compared to pop art.[29]

The film tells the story of the neurotic existence of the owner of a cutting-edge poultry farm. His life is torn between the contradictory experiences of the empty rituals of the modern bourgeoisie, the cynical marketing world, and his burnt-out marriage, as compared to the malevolent sadistic sexual fantasies he lives out in a hotel paid for by the hour and his aversion to the monstrous genetic experiments carried out on his farm. Questi adopted extremely innovative expressive techniques for the cinema of that time, mainly thanks to Franco "Kim" Arcalli's experimental editing work, which was manifestly inspired by the stylistic codes of advertising.[30]

The whole film is pervaded by the creative use of editing and a recombination of heterogeneous materials, with explicit references to the techniques of collage and pop art. In line with the film's themes and creative styles, Maderna's music also makes use of material of diverse origins and seems to pursue a poetics of pastiche and disorientation. In the soundtrack we can recognize elements deriving from avant-garde music juxtaposed

---

28　The reference is specifically to the first forty-five bars of the 1949 radio drama; see Maderna, *Il mio cuore è nel Sud*, score (see note 9), pp. 1–12. For reasons of space, mention is only made here of the use of jazz formulas in *Don Perlimplin, ovvero Il trionfo dell'amore e dell'immaginazione* (1961), a single-act radio drama based on the homonymous "love ballad" by Federico García Lorca, for which Maderna was the author of both the radio adaptation and music. This radio masterpiece itself could fill the pages of a single essay. See in this regard Giordano Ferrari, "This story of Don Perlimplin was…," in *The Prix Italia and Radiophonic Experimentation*, ed. Angela Ida De Benedictis and Maria Maddalena Novati (Milan: die Schachtel; Rome: RAI Trade, 2012), pp. 217–26, a volume that also contains the CD of the original radio recording of Maderna's radio drama.

29　See Giulio Questi, *Se non ricordo male: Frammenti autobiografici raccolti da Domenico Monetti e Luca Pallanch* (Soveria Mannelli: Rubbettino, 2014), p. 91.

30　Ibid.

with passages of popular music, such as sambas and bossa novas, which in the sixties were becoming *topoi* that represented the young bourgeoisie.[31] Giulio Questi told of his almost accidental meeting with the composer: "A series of circumstances brought me to meet Bruno Maderna, and I couldn't resist the temptation of taking advantage of his experimental skills and combining them with the experimentation of my film."[32] Despite the aura of fortuity that Questi assigned to their meeting, if one frames the film's music within the wider context of Maderna's experiences and the poetic choices he was making at this time, the composer's participation in *La morte ha fatto l'uovo* seems to be more of a deliberate and coherent decision based on the lucky encounter between two artistic personalities who were moving in converging directions.

A clear idea of the close relationship between director and composer emerges if we just take a look at the ways in which *Widmung*,[33] a piece for solo violin composed in 1967, is reutilized in the soundtrack. Manipulated fragments of the work appear in nine scenes in *La morte ha fatto l'uovo*, generally associated with the protagonist's feelings of loneliness, incommunicability, and alienation.[34] After the opening credits, the film actually begins with a short edited version of this piece,[35] marking one of the film's most intense

---

31 In his essay "Un Voyage via Barquinho: Global Circulation, Musical Hybridization, and Adult Modernity" (1961–69), in *Migrating Music*, ed. Jason Toynbee and Byron Dueck (London and New York: Routledge, 2011), pp. 112–26, Keir Keightley traces the development of the use of jazz-samba to offer a sugar-coated representation of the hedonistic and consumerist lifestyle of the young bourgeoisie, starting from Claude Lelouch's film *Un homme et une femme* (1966). As well as Francis Lai's well-known theme music *Un homme et une femme*, the film contains a suggestive flashback sequence in which Pierre Barouh sings Baden Powell's and Vinícius de Moraes's *Samba (Saravah)* in a new French version, which explicitly pays tribute to the Brazilian authors of the melody. In this scene, the enveloping sound of the bossa nova accompanies a sequence of pleasant memories of affluent tourism; and, in fact, the combination of music and images soon became a *topos* of the language of advertising. In *La morte ha fatto l'uovo*, the jazz-samba is provocatively associated with the commodification of the chickens, which produces a satirical effect that subverts mainstream values. Both Lelouch's and Questi's films also share the same protagonist: Jean-Louis Trintignant.

32 Questi, *Se non ricordo male* (see note 30), p. 94. Franco "Kim" Arcalli was the go-between for their meeting. He had got to know Maderna at the time of the antifascist resistance in Veneto.

33 *Widmung* (Dedication) was written for the violinist Theo Olof, who performed its world premiere on 27 October 1967 at the inaugural exhibition of Ottomar and Greta Domnick's private collection of abstract art in Nürtingen, Germany. By a curious coincidence, Nürtingen is also the hometown of Friedrich Hölderlin, the poet who was Maderna's inspiration for the *Hyperion* cycle. After using the piece in Giulio Questi's film, Maderna re-used *Widmung* as the second solo cadenza in Concerto for violin and orchestra (1969–70).

34 The use of *Widmung* is not reported in the existing documents on *La morte ha fatto l'uovo*. Moreover, at first sight, some of these documents may be a source of misunderstanding. Shortly after the film came out, for example, a record of Maderna's music was released (see Cinevox Record 1968, digitally remastered in 2007, CD Fin de Siècle Media, FDS 28). The track containing *Widmung* is titled *Speaking of Silence* on the record, the same title found on the non-autograph score filed at the SIAE in Rome. The latter document (of which a copy is kept at the University of Bologna) is not a reliable source for studying the genesis of the piece. A careful comparison between the original version of *Widmung* and the scores filed at the SIAE reveals that the latter were written out by a transcriber who listened to the tapes used for the soundtrack. These were therefore documents that had obviously been drawn up exclusively for administrative purposes to be filed for copyright registration. In some cases, probably due to minor variations in the tape drive speed during the transcription process, the pitches in these scores are one semitone higher than the original.

35 The passage refers to what can be seen from pp. 6ff. in the *Widmung* score (Milan: Suvini Zerboni, © 1976, S. 6999 Z.).

sequences. The fact that the technique of audio and film editing has risen to the ranks of a "genuine [creative] method"[36] can be inferred from the key elements on which the entire story is based, starting from the very title of the film. The genetic experiments carried out on the poultry farm spawn monstrous chickens whose bodies are "reassembled" to meet commercial needs, or better, animals who are just meat with no useless parts. The obsession with dismemberment and recombination also infiltrates the minds of the characters. In a key dialogue between Anna (Gina Lollobrigida) and her husband Marco (Jean-Louis Trintignant), her description of the firm's young assistant (Ewa Aulin) is torn between fascination and profound unease: "her naked body," she says, "seemed to be made up of lots of separate pieces [...] which can be put together and reassembled at will." In the film, the guitar solo that accompanies this conversation (called "Anna's Scene") is unique to this part of the soundtrack and seemingly nothing out of the ordinary, simply providing background music to the dialogue.[37] No trace of this episode of non-tonal music exists among the composer's manuscripts.[38] However, an in-depth analysis of this guitar solo, and particularly of its elaboration, demonstrates that it is in perfect musical correspondence with Anna's words. In fact, the instrumental part was obtained by assembling scattered fragments taken from the *Widmung* score. The process of transforming the original material involved different parameters: the instrument's tone, the order and arrangement of the segments, and even the guitarist's interpretation.[39] In fact, the guitarist performed his own free interpretation of, for example, the agogics and duration values indicated in the original score, also adapting some performing instruction originally written for the violin. The assemblage was probably carried out while the guitar performance was in preparation (through the identification and selection of certain passages from the score)

---

36 Questi, *Se non ricordo male* (see note 29), p. 91.

37 This brief musical episode is not included on the vinyl version of the soundtrack, released in 1968, nor on the 2007 remastered CD (see note 34), which also has several additional pieces as bonus tracks. However, there is a magnetic tape (listed as TS 10) in the audio archives of PSS-BMC on which this guitar part is easily heard.

38 PSS-BMC holds the manuscripts of just a few of the tonal episodes composed for *La morte ha fatto l'uovo*. On the vinyl version, these pieces correspond to the tracks for guitar and violin titled *Guaiaba, Musical Line, Conversation*, and *Sex Revolution in the Campus*. By contrast, no autograph material has been identified for the informal and atonal interludes (of which many exist for piano); in all probability, Maderna improvised these passages himself and manipulated them electronically before the final editing.

39 The guitarist is Julian Coco, originally from the Netherlands Antilles, who moved to the Netherlands in the early fifties to study music (he was the first student at Amsterdam Conservatory to graduate in guitar). Coco met Maderna in the second half of the sixties, when he regularly played double bass in the Utrecht Symphony Orchestra. In an interview in 1985 (Rob Zwetsloot, "Julian Coco terecht gelauwerd," *De waarheid*, 10 June 1985, p. 7), Coco recalls the deep friendship that bound him to Maderna even outside the music sphere, and also remembers all the times he collaborated with Maderna on experimental projects such as the TV production *From A to Z* and the theatrical production of *Poppetgom* (both from 1969). In 1968, Coco enjoyed his golden moment as a bossa nova guitarist on the Dutch scene, recording the album *Julian B. Coco* (Polydor Special 236 235, 1968) and receiving rave reviews for his "instrumental skill and versatility" (Paul Klare, "Julian Coco maat solo-plaat," *De tijd: dagblad voor Nederland*, 2 November 1968, p. 21, my translation). These qualities can be fully appreciated in the music of *La morte ha fatto l'uovo*, in which Coco not only performs the aforementioned more avant-garde episodes, but also carries out enchanting vocalizations with a Caribbean flavor and bossa nova and samba guitar rhythms.

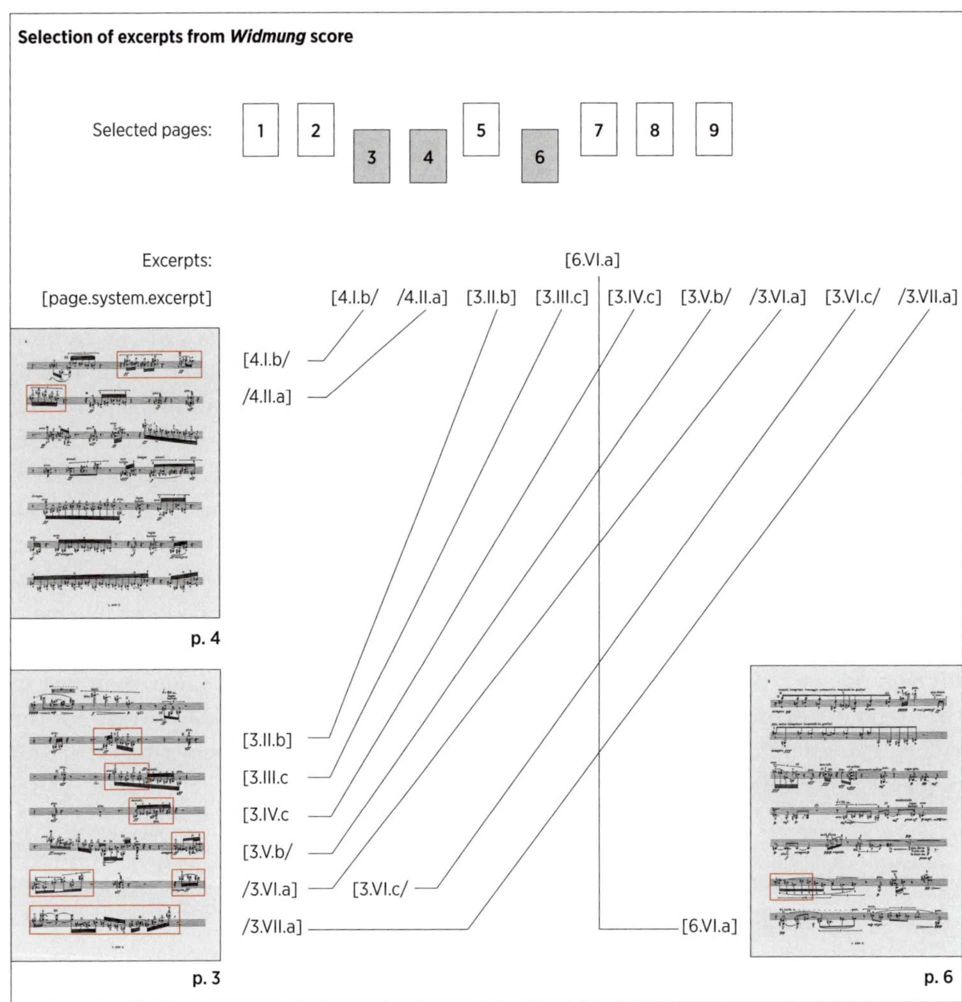

EX. 6   Diagram of the derivation of the fragments originating from *Widmung* in "Anna's Scene" in *La morte ha fatto l'uovo.*

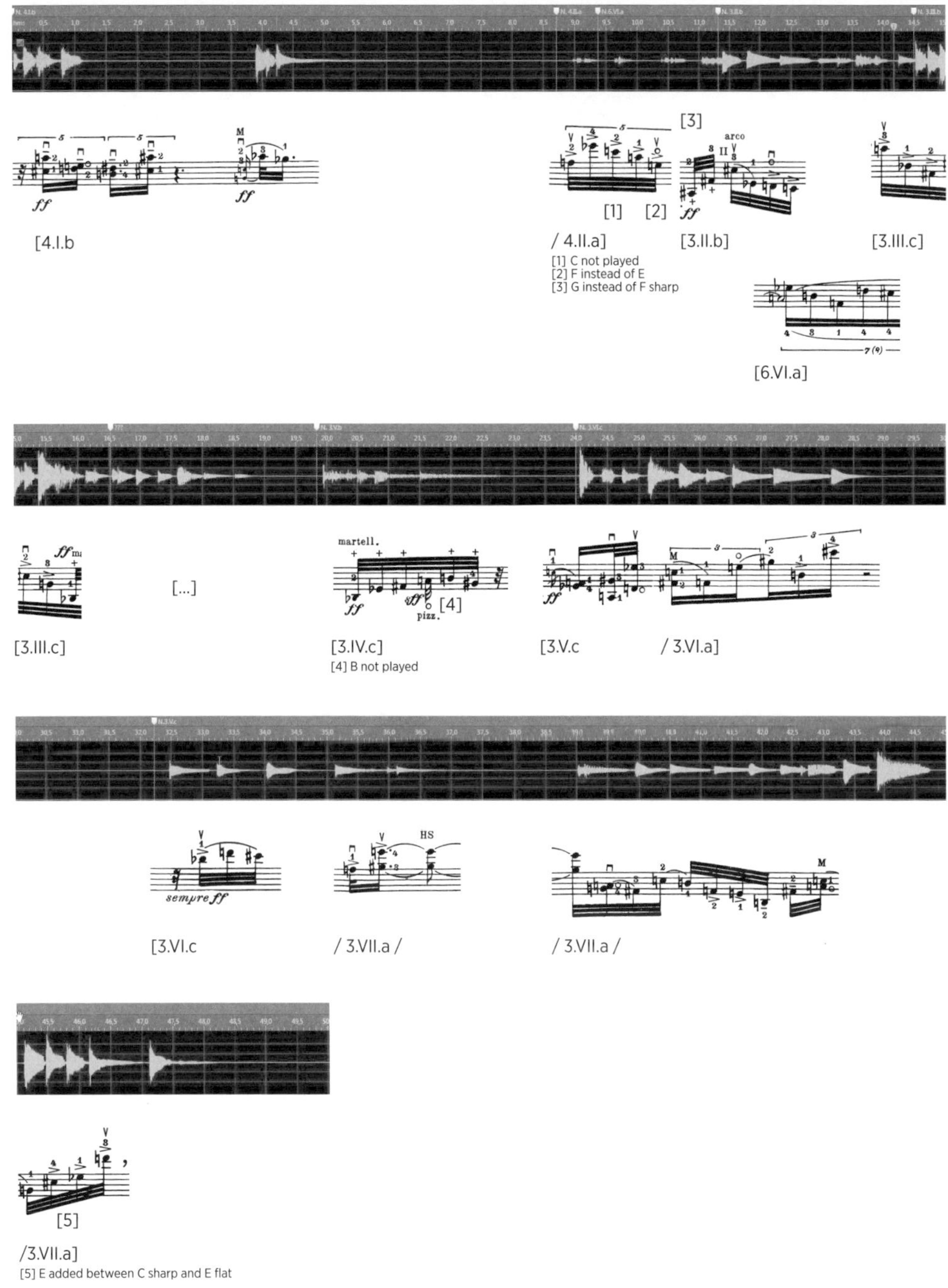

EX. 7 Reconstruction of the fragments from *Widmung* on the sound recording (tape "TS 10," PSS-BMC) for "Anna's Scene" in *La morte ha fatto l'uovo.*

and also during the actual tape editing phase. The result is a guitar episode that vaguely resembles the expressive resonance of *Widmung,* but whose origins can only be clearly revealed by means of analysis. Example 6 illustrates the different interpolations and the ways in which the elements of the original piece (mainly from pages 3 and 4 of the *Widmung* score) are distributed in the guitar recording (→ **EX. 6**).[40]

As can be seen in this Example, the fragments that can be heard on the recording are taken in blocks from three pages of the score that are not necessarily in order (p. 4 is before p. 3), whereas on each page the individual fragments follow each other in their original sequence.[41] On the contrary, in Example 7, the individual fragments taken from *Widmung* are arranged in order and aligned with the graphic representation of the relative spectrogram of the music accompanying "Anna's Scene." The result of this analysis is a sort of listening score, based on the assemblage fixed on the magnetic tape (→ **EX. 7**). Thus, the director Giulio Questi's founding principle of editing and re-composition is reflected not only in the process of composition of the music for this film, but also in the network of references that Maderna created with other preexisting compositions. Moreover, such an approach manifests a sort of "compositional method" that gained ground particularly at the turn of the sixties, and which came to be a characteristic feature of the Maderna of later years.

Conclusions

Two complementary and often intersecting trajectories emerge if we consider some of Maderna's most interesting works in the field of radio and film. In putting himself at the service of a radio or audiovisual work, Maderna managed to add innovative elements to the audio background which, in different ways and measures for each particular context, reworked and expanded the linguistic codes of the narrative frame within which he was working. This happens for example in his use of dodecaphony in *Il mio cuore è nel Sud* and in *Le due verità;* in the complex rhythmic pattern that characterizes the "Ouverture" in *Il cavallo di Troia;* or in the assemblage that mixes and alternates "art" and "popular" music or electroacoustic sounds and samba in *La morte ha fatto l'uovo.* At the same time, as an

---

40 *Widmung*'s score (see note 35) has no metric markings and is not divided into beats, making it difficult to accurately indicate a specific reference section within the piece. To improve the readability of Example 6, a form of encryption has been adopted which refers to the distribution of the musical elements as indicated in the Suvini Zerboni edition. Each segment of music clearly circumscribed between two pauses is indicated by an abbreviation that contains an alphanumeric sequence indicating the page number (arabic numeral), the number of musical staves on the page (roman numerals), and, finally, the order of appearance of segments in the same line (in lower case). A slash (/) is used to indicate segments that continue from one system to the next without a break, as in the case of "4.I.b/" and "/4.II.a." Some of the passages for which the analysis of the recording (see the following Ex. 7) failed to identify any correspondence between the performed part and the *Widmung* score are indicated with an ellipsis ([…]).

41 If we listen to a short passage at 12' from the beginning (see Ex. 7), we can recognize the simultaneous overlapping of two different guitar tracks. Even though it is much harder to identify these fragments and a certain margin of uncertainty does exist, fragment "6.VI.a" can be identified and is, in fact, the only element missing from pp. 3 and 4.

avant-garde composer, Maderna profited from the experience he had acquired in the world of radio and film and went on to experiment quite freely with technical and linguistic solutions also within the context of his instrumental and vocal music. Some techniques for the multiplication of the twelve-tone series that can be recognized in the drafts for *Il mio cuore è nel Sud* are the early signs of how he would handle and further develop the aspect of duration in the following years, whereas his exploration of the language of jazz in *Il cavallo di Troia* slightly preceded his use of the same styles in the more famous *Don Perlimplin.*

This almost symbiotic relationship between his activity as a composer of music for film and radio plays, and as a leading figure in the more experimental avant-garde, seemed to gain momentum and reach full maturity at the end of the sixties. In this period, he consolidated his artistic ties in the Netherlands and witnessed at first hand the radical transformation process young artists were going through. Indeed, he often became personally involved in some of the experiences and the most significant moments. In this new cultural context, strongly influenced by the Fluxus and Situationist movements, the gap between "high" and "low" culture, between art and everyday experience, narrowed immensely. Such a revolutionary attitude is also directly reflected in Maderna's work, which after all had always been impervious to any sharp distinction between art music and *Gebrauchsmusik. Widmung* is a prime example of this breaking of every kind of barrier: in just a few years, his composition for solo violin migrated from its first performance in an art gallery to the soundtrack for an elite and surreal film, to the second cadenza of the Concerto for violin and orchestra. The idea of de-composition and re-composition of his own material guided this entire process. The assemblage technique gradually pervaded every moment of the compositional process: from the reinterpretation and new assemblage of graphic and notational elements fixed in writing, to the collage of different texts/papers; and from the performer's own reconfiguration of certain elements, thanks to a certain freedom of choice granted by the composer, to editing carried out with electronic studio instruments, to the extrapolation and reuse of pieces and material from his earlier compositions or from his biographical past, which emerged in ever-new forms, regardless of the original purpose for which they were created. Even though the examples are few and far between, Maderna's work especially in the field of music for film and radio proves beyond a shadow of a doubt that his catalogue of works and his artistic biography should be considered as a whole, with no *a priori* preclusions. And notwithstanding the great number of important contributions available today, any interpretation of Maderna's work is still in progress.

REINVENTING SOUNDS: DIALOGUES WITH MUSIC OF EVERY EPOCH AND STYLE

MICHELE CHIAPPINI

The Writing of the Interpretation
Notes on Bruno Maderna's Arrangements

Writing and *interpretation*: the way these two terms are used in the single syntagma of the title may almost seem oxymoronic, since they traditionally refer to the compositional act and interpretive activity as if they were two disjointed and autonomous contexts. That is to say, on the one hand, the fixation of a musical text on a support, to be consigned to posterity, and, on the other, its subsequent concretization into a sound artifact to be listened to. It could be said that these human products are set apart at the two extreme poles of this dialectic, since it is at these very extremes that their differences are best perceived and their basic distinction is easily grasped.

However, equidistant from these two poles lies an internal border region where the division is not so clear-cut, a place of interference and overlapping. We can think of cases where the definition of a musical text is more connected with the aural and oral experience than with the traditional process of writing; or other examples in which a virtuous circle of recursive logic is generated and strengthened between the dimensions of the event – the rehearsals, the concert performance, the studio recording – and those of the written production. This happens, for example, during rehearsals, when a conductor shapes the score in a series of progressive layers, as he or she comes into contact with the visual and auditory dimension of its interpretive realization. This annotated score can in turn become a new normative text, and thus liable to a new and particular interpretation. This essay aims to observe this creative process from a critical and dynamic point of view, that is to say, in the synthesis of the interference between the dialectic's two terrains as it comes into being.

It is never easy to use a critical approach to document this process. At times one feels that the writing itself is a container of a residual gap, which bears witness to traces of what is a far more complex and articulated conception. The truth is that not all musical parameters are so easily discretized by writing systems; just think of dynamics, agogics (and therefore temporal oscillations), and, above all, timbre. Timbre is, of course, the most essential element at the moment of interpretive realization, since it involves every other musical parameter – first and foremost, pitch and duration. Ethnomusicologists, who have long debated such matters, are well aware that transcription is basically nothing more than a limited "representation of the musical or sonic event,"[1] or, to put it bluntly, a selective "visual documentation of sound."[2] In fact, this sonority as a multiparametric construction plays an exclusive role in the crucial passage that seals the transformation of

---

1   Jason Stanyek, "Forum on Transcription," *Twentieth-Century Music* 11 (2014), pp. 101–61: 103.
2   Nicholas M. England, "Introduction," in "Symposium on Transcription and Analysis," *Ethnomusicology* 8, no. 3 (September 1964), pp. 223–33: 223.

a given text into its interpretation, or, quite simply, into music, which is what reception theory considers the concretization and actualization of the essence of a (musical) work.

We have thus chosen to adopt this hermeneutic approach in examining the problems of musical transcription, which is immediately recognized as an area of osmosis and interference between the compositional and interpretive acts.

The following pages will attempt to cross a small portion of this territory, as we try to define Bruno Maderna's conception of interpretation and, in so doing, offer a few examples of what can rightly be called the "writing of the interpretation." Such examples do not follow any chronological order, but are deliberately arranged in a *crescendo* that reflects an attempt to address the crux of the matter in a gradual manner. These musical texts in themselves all have quite different origins and functions; however, here we have chosen to highlight what unites each text to another, focusing our attention on the aesthetic discourse. These different textual realizations are therefore considered as resulting from the varied choices made either freely or out of necessity by the transcriber-interpreter, which determine a certain amount of diffraction in the transcribed work as compared to the original hypotext.

This essay is purposely not a monographic compendium of Bruno Maderna's arrangements or orchestrations.[3] Instead, the analysis of some of his arrangements serves the basic idea that visualizes a close connection between Maderna's interpretive conception and poetic vision. Indeed, it is precisely in these pages that the writing-interpretation relationship actually seems to manifest itself at the extremes of the aforementioned dialectic: on the one hand, the interpretive dimension becomes an integrated element that is no longer something separate from, or the last step in, music composing; on the other, the compositional activity – which of course proceeds according to its own constructive rules (and which, as a speculative artifice, can also be materialized in a way that has nothing to do with the performance) – is achieved by a gradual focusing on those indeterminate elements in a given text which, at every step and editorial phase of the compositional process, keep on turning up as fuzzy parts of the work.

The "Revolution in Continuity"

An analysis of the great amount of evidence and written documents Bruno Maderna produced in the course of his life – albeit in fits and starts – allows us to understand how the debate on the interpretation of music and, more generally, on the relationship between the music of the past and that of the present was of vital importance for the composer. In fact, this pivotal point is almost symbolically linked to his first printed article: a programmatic

---

3   See in this regard the wealth of existing literature on the subject, with particular reference to an important essay by Claudia Vincis ("'Avec l'autorisation du maître': Bruno Maderna et la musique ancienne: entre 'reconstruction' et 'recréation,'" in *à Bruno Maderna*, ed. Geneviève Mathon, Laurent Feneyrou, and Giordano Ferrari, vol. 2 (Paris: Basalte, 2009), pp. 489–522), which offers the reader an excellent introduction to all of Maderna's arrangements. Also see Maurizio Romito, "Trascrizioni," in *Bruno Maderna: Documenti*, ed. Mario Baroni and Rossana Dalmonte (Milan: Suvini Zerboni, 1985), pp. 320–26.

"confession," prepared for the 1946 International Festival of Contemporary Music in Venice and designed to clarify the "purposes" of his new work, the *Serenata* for eleven instruments, performed for the first and only time at this event.

Maderna's "confession" expresses his point of view in a surprising and original reference to the impersonal dimension of the creative act. He denounces the self-referentiality and "the excessive particularism of the individualistic stance which is fashionable among the majority of contemporary musicians and musicologists":[4]

> There has been and still is much talk about what is perhaps "beleaguered" research, about personality in research, about sensitivity, morality. [...] There is a need for investigation rather than construction, and, all too often, inventories, statistics. [...] I lack any scientific convictions, but as far as music is concerned, I believe that it is not a matter of discovering but of creating. Picasso's famous "I do not seek, I find" is incomplete if you do not attribute the meaning of "I create" to that "I find."

The erudite reference is to the several statements Picasso made in the early 1920s, summarized in his controversial "Letter on Art" (1926).[5] These remarks seem to be in tune with Maderna's reasoning in criticizing the idea of "research" and "evolution," which removes the hypothesis of a teleological intentionality from the dominion of creation and definitively abandons a Romantic notion of the concept of "invention." The young composer's "confession" goes on:

> Now that we no longer have schools, beliefs, or poetics in common, and now that the artist no longer has external control over the excellence of his work, we still submit ourselves to subjective criticism, to a subjective idea of "beauty" [...]. On the other hand, the sage Montaigne confessed that he felt "similar to the bees that also plunder the flowers here and there, but afterward they make of them honey, which is all theirs." Of course, one can certainly not talk of a return *ab imis* as a remedy to the excessive particularism of the individualistic stance which is fashionable among the majority of contemporary musicians and musicologists; but there is no doubt that a serious obstacle will be removed when we approach music with the same modesty and with the same desire for simplicity, commonness, and perhaps even anonymity.[6]

---

4   This and all the other quotations from the text by Maderna come from *IX. Festival Internazionale di Musica Contemporanea – La Biennale di Venezia*, 15–22 September 1946 (Venice: Teatro La Fenice, 1946), pp. 61–62. The text appeared together with four other "Confessioni" (as indicated in the book's index) by Riccardo Malipiero, Valentino Bucchi, Guido Turchi, and Camillo Togni. Reproduced as "Dalle *Confessioni* [Una pagina di Bruno Maderna]" (1946), in Bruno Maderna, *Amore e curiosità: Scritti, frammenti e interviste sulla musica*, ed. Angela Ida De Benedictis, Michele Chiappini, and Benedetta Zucconi (Milan: il Saggiatore, 2020), pp. 89–91.

5   In 1923 Picasso had already stated: "In my opinion to search means nothing in painting. To find, is the thing"; see *Picasso: Forty Years of his Art*, ed. Alfred H. Barr Jr. (New York: Museum of Modern Art, 1939), p. 9. The "Letter on Art" was originally sent to the periodical *Ogoniok*, no. 20 (Moscow, 16 May 1926), but in 1939 it was Picasso himself who said that the letter was spurious. Maderna could have read the text in its first Italian translation ("Lettera sull'arte," *Belvedere: giornale d'arte* 2 (March 1930)), or in other contemporary translations in English or German (see list of editions published between 1930 and 1936 in *Picasso: Forty Years of his Art*, op. cit., p. 200). Now also in [Pablo] Picasso, *Collected Writings*, ed. Marie-Laure Bernadac and Christine Piot, preface by Michel Leiris (New York: Abbeville Press, 1989).

6   *IX. Festival Internazionale di Musica Contemporanea* (see note 4); original in Italian.

Maderna's second quote comes from Montaigne's essay "De l'Institution des Enfants" from the collection of *Essais* (Book I, no. 26).[7] The image of the bees speaks volumes: it refers to an act of looting of the signs and elements of the music of the past, which produces a personal work and does not admit either individualism or the self-referential satisfaction of originality or "invention." This is perhaps the first time we find a reference to a variegated set of signs and evidence from *history* to "find/create" – Maderna affirms via Picasso – and not invent out of nothing, according to a "subjective idea of beauty."

In short, Maderna's "confession" as a whole seems to represent a founding, albeit embryonic, stage in the composer's thought. Here we have the first sign of that humanistic sensitivity that would allow him to perceive the presence of history as a continuity and spiral recurrence, according to a cyclical view of the course of events. Hence, his precocious but wholehearted rejection of the idea of evolution and progress in a technicalistic and positivistic sense.

In the years to come, this thought was confirmed and strengthened in a sort of philosophy of history that can be summarized in the concept of "revolution in continuity." The wording follows the title of one of his writings from 1965 that probably most typifies the composer himself.[8] However, such a line of thought can also be perceived in the early stages of Maderna's maturity, for example, around 1954.

Let us now consider an untitled, typewritten text, written partly in German and partly in Italian, which was drawn up for a lesson on Schoenberg, Webern, and the subsequent developments in serial technique.[9] The lesson seems to have taken place in Darmstadt in the summer of 1954, during the first edition of the "Internationale Arbeitsgemeinschaft junger Komponisten": six free seminars on musical composition and interpretation given by Giselher Klebe and Maderna, both of whom had never taught in these *Ferienkurse* before.[10]

In the first part of the text, Maderna's attention is focused on two examples, taken from works by Arnold Schoenberg (op. 19, no. 6) and Anton Webern (op. 9). First of all, he skips over any analysis of the compositional technique:

> I have deliberately abstained from a technical analysis of the two works presented as an example, especially because a technical analysis would have distracted us from the historical

---

7 Michel de Montaigne, "Of the Education of the Children" (1579–80), in *The Complete Essays of Montaigne*, trans. Donald M. Frame (Stanford: Stanford University Press, 1965), pp. 106–31: 111 (hence the English quotation in Maderna's Italian text).

8 Maderna's "La révolution dans la continuité" was written in response to a study on serial music promoted by André Boucourechliev in *Preuves* 15, no. 177 (December 1965), pp. 28–29; also in *Bruno Maderna/Heinz Holliger: Festival d'Automne à Paris 1991* (Paris: Contrechamps, 1991), pp. 35–36.

9 Now published as "Conferenza sulla dodecafonia e gli sviluppi della tecnica seriale in Italia" (1954), in Maderna, *Amore e curiosità* (see note 4), pp. 169–78. The original typewritten text, with autograph and unidentified corrections, is held at PSS. The document consists of 10 pp., partly written in Italian (7 pp., numbered from 2 to 8 by the author) and partly in German (3 pp., only the first is numbered p. 1). For an in-depth analysis and greater contextualization of the document see Angela Ida De Benedictis, "Bruno Maderna: Vortrag über Arnold Schönberg," in *"On revient toujours": Dokumente zur Schönberg-Rezeption aus der Paul Sacher Stiftung* (Mainz: Schott, 2016), pp. 99–101.

10 See *Im Zenit der Moderne: Die Internationalen Ferienkurse für neue Musik Darmstadt 1946–1966*, ed. Gianmario Borio and Hermann Danuser (Freiburg im Breisgau: Rombach, 1997), vol. 1, pp. 111–16, and vol. 2, pp. 43–45.

analysis of their value as manifestations of a new mentality in composing, which arises as a consequence of a new need of being.[11]

Maderna chooses to concentrate instead on the aesthetic discourse, criticizing all those definitions that in music refer to a "return to," or all those terms that bear the suffix "neo-" before the noun. He wishes to unite all the musical phenomena from the modern age based on the idea of a continuity between the past and the present. Conversely, his thought is rooted in the belief that history must only be perceived in (or relegated to) technical and stylistic innovations of every era, which, as such, are contingent and transitory. At the same time, rifts or caesuras are not distinguished (or recognized) in any way on the preeminent plane of aesthetics. The human question, already discussed in his "confession" of 1946,[12] turns up again in this perspective of a perennial "revolution in continuity." That "new need of being," that "new mentality in composing," is no longer interpreted as the product of an individualistic stance, but as an impersonal need of becoming historical, which may tend to present itself in a recursive and intermittent manner. This is the search for, or rather the discovery of ("I don't search, I find," Maderna had written in 1946), a happy compromise between the means of expression and the needs of the society that expresses them, whence the call "for a logical and human position on reality, if we wish to approach the interpretation of artistic expression as the lyrical presence of our being":[13]

> Music is in continuous movement, like man. And furthermore, it is above all a "becoming" that comes about in a linear way, but which, nevertheless, cannot be transported or linked to a circumscribed historical period.
>
> If one takes *a close look* at the history of music, it becomes clear that principles persist longer than the personality of the composers. And by principles I am thinking of the actual use of the means, while by personality I have in mind the character of a historical period.
>
> It is obvious that a composer is more important as the creator of a synthesis between means and application, than an expression of his contemporary period.
>
> What I cherish most about Schoenberg is precisely this understanding of the importance of the objective means compared to the personality who expresses them.[14]

And he goes on:

> On the contrary, today we are more convinced than ever that *natura non facit saltus*, and that every revolution of human thought and feeling happens through slow and profound changes, where what preceded is subsumed with what follows *in the osmosis of* extension and, in most cases, as a rethinking, as an intensification of understanding and judgment.[15]

---

11 Maderna, "Conferenza sulla dodecafonia" (see note 9), p. 172.

12 Just think of his opening words at the Darmstadt lecture: "Schoenberg is not only the inventor of a new compositional technique; he is above all a man who needs intense expression in musical life, just as he needs it in his life today through rigorous and unedited experiences." Ibid., p. 169.

13 Bruno Maderna, "Un aspetto della musica nel dopoguerra," *Biennale di Venezia: arte, cinema, musica, teatro: notiziario di cultura contemporanea* 1, no. 5 (August 1951), p. 40, repr. in Maderna, *Amore e curiosità* (see note 4), pp. 229–31.

14 Maderna, "Conferenza sulla dodecafonia" (see note 9), pp. 169–70. Also in De Benedictis, "Vortrag über Arnold Schönberg" (see note 9), p. 101.

15 Maderna, "Conferenza sulla dodecafonia" (see note 9), p. 171.

"Osmosis" and "synthesis" are two concepts that refer to the problem of man's creative activity – already defined as the "lyrical presence of our being" – in the revolution of continuity. The composer does not speak of the New, or of "a return to" or any kind of "neo-"; instead, he talks of "extension," of "rethinking," of an "intensification" of thought, of the "conglomeration" of what comes before and what comes after.

Now, it is reasonable to believe that this creative paradigm in Maderna's poetics is associated with a corresponding interpretive type of model, where the understanding of the meaning of a work is linked to the "synthesis" and to the "osmosis" of countless references and stimuli that are also elaborated unconsciously in a moment of "intuition." It is the idea of a catalyzing synthesis of elements: a "catalysis," to use Maderna's refined language (see below), which, even in this context, is opposed to the idea of statistical and formalistic analysis, which, though certainly an objectifying procedure, is neither indispensable nor practical for the performative dimension. Maderna discusses this in an article written around 1956[16] as an introduction to the analysis of Luciano Berio's *Nones*, and conceived by Berio as a potential contribution to the fledgling journal *Incontri Musicali* (1956–60). Although the article remained a draft and was never published, Maderna's text was later edited by Luciano Berio himself and published posthumously in 1978, in the *Nuova Rivista Musicale Italiana*.[17] In his outline of the two "basic ways" in which one can analyze a work – that is, either by adopting a "statistical approach" or by liberating the "interpretive" dimension – Maderna moreover states:

> It is interesting to notice that the interpretive fact for almost all or at least a great number of particularly gifted interpreters is already a synthesis. They do not always need the analytical moment; very often they arrive directly at a concrete realization, "feeling" the musical fact in a moment of "lyrical" intuition. Pretty much skipping over that first fundamental mode of analysis we were talking about before [the statistical one]. Given that we live, if we really want to live in an organic way, it is impossible to think of these interpreters in the same way as a matter of "pure" intuition. After all, psychologists have amply demonstrated how we come to call "intuitions" some cognitive structures, called "contents," that are self-processing and develop surreptitiously in the subconscious.[18]

In his essay, Maderna describes the possible fulfillment of an interpretive, actualizing, and innovative perfection, as the ability to "live" the work, so to speak, "at any moment, feeling it grow in our understanding and being able to see it from every angle, always recognizing it as a whole."[19]

---

16   Many thanks to Angela Ida De Benedictis for the more precise dating of this text. Her research on the relative archival materials allowed her to date it to 1956, and not 1954, as was commonly thought.

17   See "Un inedito di Bruno Maderna," *Nuova Rivista Musicale Italiana* 12, no. 4 (1978), pp. 517–20, and particularly the passage on pp. 517–18. Now also with the new title "'Analizzare una opera': intorno a *Nones* di Luciano Berio," in Maderna, *Amore e curiosità* (see note 4), pp. 179–82. Maderna's original manuscript (5 sheets, original in Italian) is housed in the Luciano Berio Collection at PSS.

18   Ibid., pp. 179–80 (original in Italian). This passage is directly linked to the passage quoted by Benedetta Zucconi in this volume, "Analysis and Synthesis in Bruno Maderna's Creative Process: *Don Giovanni* and other Mozart Scores," p. 229.

19   Maderna, "Analizzare una opera" (see note 17), p. 180.

Another noteworthy feature is the return of the concept of "intuition," now linked to the emergence of an irrational component, the "subconscious," which is recognized as having an essential function in interpretive activity, as a place of an irrational catalyzation of content. In this regard, an excerpt from one of Maderna's autograph manuscripts is most telling.[20] One of the several textual variants clearly shows the editor's deletions eliminating a long passage that ends as follows:

> And indeed, it is precisely in this condition of osmosis that the ideal interpreter is to be found. He is not only a mediator between the public and the work written and conceived by the composer. He is more. He is a clear transformation, a catalysis, between the written work, fixed graphically by means of symbols, and the graphic realization of the same in terms of acoustic communication.[21]

"Our music is our acoustic body" is another pertinent, quasi succinct expression apparently coined by the composer in the presence of a young Konrad Boehmer in Cologne, in the early 1960s, as can be read in Boehmer's memoirs of Maderna.[22]

From this point of view, the position of the "ideal interpreter" becomes that of the composer-conductor, a category rooted in the compositional praxis of past centuries – says Maderna – since in the past "what was extrinsic in graphic symbols was directly communicated to the listener by the composer himself, who was almost always an excellent performer."[23]

It is significant that the examples Maderna chooses are precisely those "modal and tonal periods, [when] composer and interpreter were one and the same."[24] During a 1970 radio interview, he states that "the very art of conducting starts with the works of composers like Mozart [or] Wagner," going on to conclude that he feels that the activity of conducting must be carried out by an active composer.[25] Even more remarkable is the fact that Maderna feels part of that tradition: "in actual fact I only write *Kappellmeister-music*,"[26] he once said to Boehmer, considering his work as a musician as a whole, and referring to a concrete historical image of the composer-conductor. However, Maderna feels that this tradition is gradually being lost in a contemporary age, driven by what he calls

---

20 Bruno Maderna, ["Analizzare una opera…"], manuscript with autograph corrections, 5 sheets (see note 17).

21 Passage reproduced in "Analizzare una opera" (see note 17), p. 182, footnote 3.

22 Konrad Boehmer, "In Köln hab ich es donnern gehört…" (1985), in idem, *Das böse Ohr: Texte zur Musik 1961–1991*, ed. Burkhardt Söll (Cologne: DuMont, 1993), pp. 11–23: 19 ("Unsere Musik ist unser akustischer Körper"). According to Boehmer, Maderna said this as a means of encouraging him to overcome "his refusal to accept ancient music," explaining that one could learn to compose thanks to the music of all ages, from the Middle Ages to the modern day.

23 "Analizzare una opera" (see note 17), p. 181. For more about this see also Angela Ida De Benedictis, "More than conducting, more than composing: Hermann Scherchen, Bruno Maderna, Luciano Berio," in *Komponieren & Dirigieren: Doppelbegabungen als Thema der Interpretationsgeschichte*, ed. Alexander Drčar and Wolfgang Gratzer (Freiburg im Breisgau et al.: Rombach, 2017), pp. 371–400.

24 "Analizzare una opera" (see note 17), p. 181.

25 "A conversation with Bruno Maderna by George Stone and Alan Stout: WEFM, Chicago, 23.1.1970," in *Bruno Maderna: The Last Concert*, CD STR 10071 (Milan: Stradivarius, 1993). The quoted extract begins at 3'57". An Italian translation of the whole radio interview ("Conversazione con George Stone e Alan Stout") is in Maderna, *Amore e curiosità* (see note 4), pp. 55–85 (quote on p. 58).

26 Konrad Boehmer, "Retour à Maderna," in *à Bruno Maderna* (see note 3), vol. 1, pp. 341–53: 348.

"differentiation" and "specialization" (even though, in fairness, this historical tradition includes not only Maderna himself, but also Boulez and many of the protagonists of the Darmstadt courses of the 1950s, for example Fortner, Leibowitz, Stockhausen, Pousseur, Kagel, and Berio).[27]

In Maderna's case, this interpretive ideal was most probably strengthened by the practice of electronic music and the work he carried out at the RAI's Studio di Fonologia in Milan (where he started working unofficially in late 1954 until its official opening the following June).[28]

The experience gained in the in-studio composition of his first electronic songs, *Notturno* and *Syntaxis* – which Maderna presented in Darmstadt in July 1956 and the following summer 1957, respectively[29] – proves to the composer that with the new means "we develop and complete the communication needs we feel and try to realize, on a totally different level, in instrumental music," and that "musician and technician in this case are really one. A man conscious of his wish to communicate ever more clearly and simply to whoever wants to listen to him, whoever loves music."[30]

Thus we have another reference to the unity of the musical experience, to the "synthesis" of the compositional and interpretive fact, to the "catalysis" of a heterogeneity of signs, elements, and "sound structures" that reemerge, in a reappraisal of the paradigm of the "ideal interpretation": "there arise in the mind a number of temporal projections which can no longer be represented by a one-dimensional logic," explains Maderna in Darmstadt in 1957;[31] projections that are thus obliged to delegate the need for interpretation – an action that takes place alongside and at the same time as the very act of their conception and production – to an ideal "single person," that is, to the technician-composer.

A lengthy conversation between Maderna and the writer Aldo Maranca in 1964 provides unequivocal evidence of the definitive endorsement of this thought. Returning to one of the topics that had already featured in Darmstadt in 1956, namely a similarity

---

27 On this matter, see *Im Zenit der Moderne* (see note 10), vol. 2, pp. 164–68 ("Der Komponist als Interpret"); and Martyn Brabbins, "The composer-conductor and modern music," in *The Cambridge Companion to Conducting*, ed. José Antonio Bowen (Cambridge: Cambridge University Press, 2003), pp. 262–73, esp. 262–64.

28 See, among others, *New Music on the Radio: Experiences at the Studio di Fonologia of the RAI, Milan 1954–1959*, ed. Veniero Rizzardi and Angela Ida De Benedictis (Rome: RAI-ERI, 2000).

29 As regards the 1956 lecture, see "Kompositorische Möglichkeiten der elektronischen Musik (1956): Eine Diskussion," in *Musik-Konzepte: Sonderband Darmstadt-Dokumente I* (Munich: Text+Kritik, January 1999), pp. 80–105, esp. 93–94. The 1957 lecture, held on July 26, is translated into Italian as "Esperienze compositive con la musica elettronica," in Maderna, *Amore e curiosità* (see note 4), pp. 232–35. It must be noted that the English translation of the 1957 lecture published in Raymond Fearn, *Bruno Maderna* (Chur: Harwood, 1990), pp. 294–96, comes from a further Italian translation published in *Documenti* (see note 3), pp. 83–85.

30 ["A Note by Bruno Maderna"], in *New Music on the Radio* (see note 28), p. 270. As stated in ibid., pp. 286–88 (n. 6), this is a handwritten manuscript by Maderna dating to 1956 (which contains some autograph corrections by Berio), housed in the Archives of the RAI's Studio di Fonologia in Milan along with other documents from 1956. The contents of this "Note" form the basis for the report Maderna gave at Darmstadt in 1956; see "Kompositorische Möglichkeiten der elektronischen Musik" (see note 29), p. 94.

31 The original is in German; quote taken from the reading in Fearn, *Bruno Maderna* (see note 29), p. 295.

between electronic music and the visual arts in the relationship between a composer and his work, Maranca focuses on the immediacy of the relationship between the moment of conception and realization of an electronic piece. Maderna points out:

> there is a first stage in the actual realization of the contents and the material, then there is an organization of the material, a form that is given to this material, of which a percentage could almost be ascribed to the act of interpretation of that form. That is, it seems that at a certain moment in the work, the composer, the poet, or the painter switches to, and this will be the final form, an interpretation, to an interpretive representation of one's own thought. [...] This last phase is almost interpretive of themselves.[32]

There is finally a more general element that describes Maderna's far-reaching activity as a composer-conductor, and motivates the pressing need for so many of his interpretations and arrangements: in this case, the indefatigable and irrepressible pioneering spirit that impels his musical activity. In his portrait of Bruno Maderna, Massimo Mila tells us that "the constant presence of the past within the unprejudiced exploration of the future can certainly be assumed as one of the fundamental traits of Maderna's art."[33] The musicologist Giovanni Morelli makes an even shrewder observation on Maderna's boundless interest "for *revision*, and in that revision, for the *discovery* of 'other' dimensions of music, different from the traditional ones perpetrated in common didactics."[34] Thus, in Maderna's thought, pioneering work assumes a universal dimension and is evoked as a symbol of the "revolution in continuity," through an eternal and continuous rethinking of the history of *all* music, with no restrictions or specialized fields; it is therefore indissolubly connected with the deepest roots of his poetics. This brings to mind a *wanderer* who moves through the infinite "dimensions of music," continually referring to signs of a history that is there to be "found" – true to the motto "I do not seek, I find," cited in 1946 – and there to be "revived":

> I would like to revive the music of our ancients possibly in its spiritual quality, more than in its philological quality, just to show that it really isn't so old at all, and indeed that it is only as old as that truism [which says] that making New is actually nothing more than making Old; though better.[35]

Once again, the metaphor of revivification reappears in Maderna's language in reference to interpretive activity and its pioneering implications. In the preface to his arrangement

---

32 "Colloquio con Aldo Maranca" (1964), in Maderna, *Amore e curiosità* (see note 4), pp. 101–12 (quote on pp. 101–02).

33 Massimo Mila, "Per un ritratto di Bruno Maderna," in *Maderna musicista europeo*, ed. Ulrich Mosch (Turin: Einaudi 1999), p. 103; first edn. 1976.

34 Giovanni Morelli, "La carica dei Quodlibet: note sulle tipologie di una 'nuova scuola veneziana' all'uso degli incroci di lettura delle opere di Maderna, Nono e Malipiero," in *La carica dei Quodlibet: Carte diverse e alcune musiche inedite del Maestro Malipiero*, ed. Giovanni Morelli (Florence: Olschki, 2005), pp. 111–39: 112.

35 *Un'ora con Bruno Maderna: Musica, specchio della società*, a documentary by Salvatore G. Biamonte and Giuseppe Sibilla, RAI, Milan-Venice 1969–70, broadcast on 11 October 1971, Channel 2 (see *Radiocorriere* 48, no. 41, 10–16 October 1971, p. 72). A digital copy and a VHS version of this documentary are housed at PSS. The quoted extract (that starts at around 29'00") is published as "In dialogo con Maderna tra Milano e Venezia. Estratti da *Un'ora con Bruno Maderna (II)*," in Maderna, *Amore e curiosità* (see note 4), p. 201.

of *Orfeo* (1966–67), published by Suvini Zerboni in 1967, Maderna resumes and broadens the scope of the issue, unraveling the apparent contradiction between the objectivism of the proposed philological edition and the subjectivism of the musician's will:

> There are many editions of *Orfeo*, old and new, philological and practical. So many that it is natural to wonder why I felt so inclined to make a new one. It is most probable that I did it out of love; I had been waiting for the opportunity to "interpret" *Orfeo* for years.
>
> [...] With this in mind and much more, I set about realizing this great score with the aim of respecting the text as far as possible, but at the same time giving back, in a critical revision for us contemporaries, the emotions and the "feelings" that made *Orfeo* one of the greatest successes of the past.[36]

Maderna's deliberate use of the verb "interpret," which he even puts in quotation marks, instead of verbs like "perform," "conduct," or even "arrange," is most striking. This is because he is talking about what is above all an almost hermeneutical kind of interpretive act that gives back Monteverdi's *Orfeo* "in a critical revision for us contemporaries." For Maderna, although the text tries "as far as possible" to be close to and "critical" of its tradition, it is however necessarily destined to be read, interpreted, and "revivified," thereby continuing to develop that infinite and inexhaustible potential of its very essence as a work.

The Historical Position of Maderna the Interpreter

The distinctiveness of Maderna's position, as outlined in the previous section, immediately stands out when we try to place it within the historical context of the interpretation theories of the post-World War II period (especially in the decade beginning in 1945, and with particular reference to the Darmstadt experience). Several features distinguish his thought from what was certainly a generalized aesthetic tendency (albeit with many internal differences) characterized by a movement toward objectivity and by a concomitant tension toward reducing the presence of the figure of the interpreter.[37] Let us briefly consider the matter here.

---

36 See Bruno Maderna, "Premessa," in *L'Orfeo*, pastoral fable in two parts by Alessandro Striggio Jr., new realization and elaboration by Bruno Maderna (Milan: Suvini Zerboni, 1967) (original in Italian). Now also in Maderna, *Amore e curiosità* (see note 4), pp. 525–28. For an in-depth discussion about Maderna's arrangements of Monteverdi's works, see Michele Chiappini, "Scritture dell'interpretazione: Orfeo e Poppea nelle «realizzazioni» di Bruno Maderna nel centenario monteverdiano (1967)," in *Rivisitazioni e innovazioni. La ricezione di Monteverdi nei compositori italiani dalla seconda metà del XX secolo*, ed. Gianmario Borio and Angela Carone (Venice: Fondazione Giorgio Cini, 2022, pp. 55–89; online edition).

37 See *inter alia* Siegfried Mauser, "Tendenzen nach 1945," in *Musikalische Interpretation*, ed. Hermann Danuser, Neues Handbuch der Musikwissenschaft 11 (Laaber: Laaber, 1997), pp. 415–23, esp. 415; *Im Zenit der Moderne* (see note 10), vol. 2, pp. 149–65 ("Interpretationsästhetischer Paradigmenwechsel"); and *Neue Musik und Interpretation*, five congress papers, ed. Hermann Danuser and Siegfried Mauser, Veröffentlichungen des Instituts für Neue Musik und Musikerziehung Darmstadt 35 (Mainz: Schott, 1994).

First of all, it is worth pointing out that at Darmstadt, such an assumption never coincided, in either theory[38] or in practice,[39] with the utopian idea of suppressing or eliminating the figure of the interpreter. Instead, focus is placed on the representation of a varied intertwining of relationships with the musical text,[40] which was just as functional in this current period as it had been in previous eras. At the beginning of the 1950s, if anything tends to be rationalized, then it is the internal organization of the work. This is defined in the compositional process and "objectified" as the sum (or the removal) of fields of possibility and latent virtualities, which are always viable and retraceable through rational logic processes.[41]

At the level of musical notation, this process nevertheless corresponds to an increase in or an intensification of textual discretization, that is to say, one can now codify parameters other than pitch and duration, such as dynamics, the types of sound attack, or the agogic oscillations within the work. But, more generally, it is the musical timbre – the sonority as a multiparametric concretization – that makes itself more objectifiable at the moment of the interpretive realization, inasmuch as any of the other musical parameters involved therein become more discretizable.

On the other hand, the organization and codification of the work are in contrast with human activity, the home of that coefficient of irrationality and unpredictability – the "surprise,"[42] as Boulez puts it – that distinguishes both the activity of composition and that of interpretation. Such operations are always based on subjective choices.

The problem of objectivity *in itself* is therefore something that seems extraneous to the very concept of interpretation. However, we cannot overlook the fact that terms like "objective" and "objectivity" have undergone a recognized evolution and lexical variability within the history of interpretation theories;[43] nor can we underestimate the importance of the ideological and self-referential component underlying this type of representation.

---

38 For more on this subject, see for example Boulez's essays written in 1954, 1957, and 1963–80, published respectively as Pierre Boulez, "…Near and Far," in idem, *Stocktakings from an Apprenticeship*, ed. Paule Thévenin, trans. Stephen Walshe (Oxford: Clarendon Press, 1991), pp. 141–57: 157; "Alea," in ibid., pp. 26–38: 29–32; "Time, Notation and Coding," in idem, *Orientations: Collected Writings*, ed. Jean-Jacques Nattiez (Boston: Faber and Faber, 1986), pp. 84–89: 89. On similar topics, among many others, see (at least) Luciano Berio, "La 'nuova musicalità'" (1956) and "Aspetti di artigianato formale" (1956) in *Luciano Berio: Scritti sulla musica*, ed. Angela Ida De Benedictis (Turin: Einaudi, 2013), pp. 7–13 and 237–53; and Henri Pousseur, "La nuova sensibilità musicale," *Incontri musicali*, no. 2 (1958), pp. 3–37: 28–37.

39 See the analysis of the performance of the integral cycles of Stockhausen's *Klavierstücke* by David Tudor (1959), Aloys Kontarsky (1965), and Herbert Henck (1985), in Ulrich Mosch, "Bindung und Freiheit: Zum Verhältnis von Neuer Musik und Interpretation," in *Neue Musik und Interpretation* (see note 37), pp. 8–15; or the analysis of Schoenberg's *Phantasy*, op. 47, carried out by Rudolf Kolisch and Eduard Steuermann (Darmstadt 1954), discussed by Gianmario Borio, "Analisi ed esecuzione: note sulla teoria dell'interpretazione musicale di Theodor W. Adorno e Rudolf Kolisch," *Philomusica on-line*, vol. 2, no. 1 (2003), http://riviste.paviauniversitypress.it/index.php/phi/article/view/02-01-SG01/1 (consulted 7 June 2021).

40 See Mosch, "Bindung und Freiheit" (see note 39), p. 14.

41 In fact, in 1954 Boulez talked about the musical work "which is no longer architected, but *braided*"; see Boulez, "…Near and Far" (see note 38), p. 155.

42 Idem, "Alea" (see note 38), p. 29.

43 See Hermann Danuser, "Vortragslehre und Interpretationstheorie," in *Musikalische Interpretation* (see note 37), pp. 271–320, esp. 272–85 ("Etappen der Geschichte").

Long before the Darmstadt years, the *mythopoiesis* of objectivity can be identified as a characteristic feature of a precise epoch. It belongs above all to the composers and performers of the first generation of musical modernity – from Stravinsky to Hindemith, from Schoenberg to Malipiero himself – as a rational and voluntary distancing from the aesthetics of Romantic subjectivity. For example, Malipiero, Maderna's maestro, defined the performer as "a more or less perfect transmitting device that has to surrender his personality to fulfill the mission entrusted to him," noting however that "unfortunately many performers refuse to do this, deforming the works they interpret, deluding themselves that they are creating."[44]

This premise regarding the problem of objectivity in interpretation leads us into the examination of Maderna's position against the historical backdrop of the post-World War II period and, in particular, the Darmstadt years.

As far as the theory of interpretation is concerned, the Darmstadtian experience, at least in the 1945–55 decade, continues to follow the lines of Schoenbergian thought. The 1954 seminar *Neue Musik und Interpretation*, held by Theodor W. Adorno, Rudolf Kolisch, and Eduard Steuermann as part of the *Ferienkurse*, is a vivid example of one of its key moments.[45] The elements of continuity between Schoenberg's thought and that of his pupils are significant and based on a shared aesthetic conception of the musical work. The latter appears as the representation of the composer's musical thought – therefore of his will – which is made explicit and acquires meaning through the formulation of logical, rational, and retraceable links between hierarchical levels of internal structuring and multiple formal functions.[46] The whole content of the work, including its so-called human content, coincides formalistically with the representation of musical thought itself, and therefore with the logical and mental operations necessary for its realization. In this sense, Schoenberg and his pupils consider the structure and content of a composition to be "objective" elements, whereas analysis, aimed at recognizing the logical links on which the work is based, is the decisive prerequisite for its correct and valid execution.

Maderna's position does seem rather inconsistent with the interpretive paradigms of these years (1945–55), although his is certainly not an isolated way of thinking,[47] nor is it in open contrast with the theories briefly summarized here. Despite the fact that he also recognizes the problematic dialectic between objectivity and subjectivity, his conception of interpretation contains a number of significant differences as compared to the genealogy of Viennese-Darmstadtian thought. And this is probably where the most vital characteristic of Maderna as a musician achieves the greatest prominence: the fact that, along with Boulez, he was the best-known composer-conductor of his generation.

---

44 Gian Francesco Malipiero, *La pietra del bando* (Venice: Ateneo, 1945), p. 108 (original in Italian).

45 See Borio, "Analisi ed esecuzione" (see note 39), p. 3/14. As we learn here, Kolisch's and Steurmann's seminar lasted five days and, despite the title, was mainly addressed to theoretical considerations and to the examination of some problems regarding Beethoven's op. 59, no. 2, and Berg's op. 3.

46 See Rudolf Stephan, "Der musikalische Gedanke bei Schönberg," in idem, *Vom musikalischen Denken: Gesammelte Vorträge*, ed. Rainer Damm and Andreas Traub (Mainz: Schott, 1985), pp. 129–37.

47 See note 41. Note also the similarity between Maderna's thought on this subject and that e.g. of a composer like Luigi Nono; see Angela Ida De Benedictis, "Luigi Nono: Analyse des Themas der Variationen für Orchester op. 31 (1956)," in *"On revient toujours"* (see note 9), pp. 113–16.

We shall now go on to focus on the most significant aspects of Maderna's conception of interpretation between 1946 and the late 1950s by listing some of the previously identified and described elements and comparing and contrasting them with the dominant thought of Viennese-Darmstadtian descent.

The Conception and the Writing of the Interpretation

1. The first element is the emancipation of the interpretive fact from being subaltern and functional to compositional activity. As a result, the structural connection between interpretation and analysis is disengaged; the latter now takes on a formative function (for example as a teaching tool for a comparative research method),[48] but can no longer be implemented in the performance: "I purposely abstained from a technical analysis of the two works presented as an example, especially because a technical analysis would have distracted us from the historical analysis of their value," Maderna declares in the aforementioned lesson in Darmstadt in 1954, dedicated to Arnold Schoenberg;[49] and about two years later, in his introductory text to the analysis of *Nones,* he writes that for many particularly gifted musicians "the interpretive fact is already a synthesis," which does not need to go through the "analytical moment."

It therefore follows that musical writing for Maderna is a functional means of interpretation (similar to the Boulezian conception of "Time, Notation and Coding," as indicated above), that is, it is primarily aimed at performative execution. This vision is of course in direct contrast with the principle closest to the genealogy of Schoenbergian-Darmstadtian thought: that of an interpretation aimed at explaining the notational datum as the logical and genetically final output of the development of musical thought.

If we examine the arrangements Maderna made in the period between 1946 and 1952, we can find dozens of examples to support this thesis. If we consider the musical arrangement as a finished product – and therefore not as a work in progress (more about this in point 2) – we can identify several pieces in which the constructive dimension linked to the orchestration is immediately noticeable. Such pieces are where Maderna's writing clearly exhibits a *continuum* of interpretive choices linked to the concept of construction.

---

48   On the consistency of the Madernian comparative method, let us recall the wealth of documents left by Luigi Nono regarding the analysis activities carried out with his friend-maestro Maderna during the years of his training. See at least Luigi Nono, "Remembering Two Musicians" (1973), in *Nostalgia for the Future: Nono's Selected Writings,* ed. Angela Ida De Benedictis and Veniero Rizzardi (Oakland: University of California Press, 2018), pp. 325–27; idem, "Bartók the Composer" (1981), in ibid., pp. 338–44; "An Autobiography recounted by Enzo Restagno" (1987), in ibid., pp. 27–122; and "Interview with Renato Garavaglia" (ca. 1979-80), in ibid., pp. 247–62. The same subject is also dealt with in Susanna Pasticci, "Memorie di Petrucci a Venezia," in *Venice 1501: Petrucci, Music, Print and Publishing,* ed. Giulio Cattin and Patricia Dalla Vecchia (Venice: Levi, 2005), pp. 683–738, esp. 696–99; and Erika Schaller, "L'insegnamento di Bruno Maderna attraverso le fonti conservate all'Archivio Luigi Nono," in *Bruno Maderna: Studi e testimonianze,* ed. Rossana Dalmonte and Marco Russo (Lucca: LIM, 2004), pp. 107–16.

49   See note 9. For the following reference to the introductory text to the analysis of *Nones,* see "Analizzare una opera" (note 17); the passage cited here is on p. 179.

At first glance, this "constructive" orchestration makes use of the concept of broken lines and the proliferation of melodic fragments. In other words, motivic fragments from different parts, extrapolated from the hypotext, can be settled and strengthened on the same instrumental part, thereby producing a multiplicity of new contrapuntal lines (which are thus generated as new combinations of partial forms). This image is well expressed through the metaphor of a kaleidoscope, whose variegated and iridescent images are continually reflected within the tube, thanks to the different combinations of the identically colored pebbles.

It is certainly tempting to waste no time in asserting that Maderna's constructive orchestration is based on the concept of an analytical interpretation of the polyphonic-contrapuntal texture,[50] but let us start by looking at some musical texts.

Proof of this orchestral sonority in perhaps its purest essence is offered in his arrangement of Compère's *Nous sommes de l'ordre du Saint Babuyn* from the first suite of *Odhecaton* (1948–50),[51] just one of the many works that best represent this general tendency.[52] We now need to find a clear and systematic way to identify the presence of the Petruccian hypotext used by Maderna in the score,[53] by using different colors to identify the broken parts of the *frottola*'s four original voices (*cantus* = red, *altus* = yellow, *tenor* = green, *bassus* = blue) (→ **EX. 1**).

Let us now turn to the question of "analytical orchestration," or rather to a definition of the Madernian "constructive" type, which can also be defined by means of negation of the model of a well-known work like the six-voice "Ricercar" from Bach's *Musical Offering*, arranged for orchestra by Anton Webern in 1933.

Of course, we cannot go so far as to say that Webern's orchestration was actually outside of Maderna's poetic horizon.[54] Indeed, both Maderna and Webern share, for example, a greater interest in the horizontal over the vertical dimension, whence a substantial balance in the importance of the voices, which, in Maderna's arrangement, can

---

50 See Carl Dahlhaus, "Analytical Instrumentation: Bach's Six-Part Ricercar as Orchestrated by Anton Webern" (1969), in *Schoenberg and the New Music: Essays by Carl Dahlhaus*, trans. Derrick Puffett and Alfred Clayton (Cambridge: Cambridge University Press, 1987), pp. 181–91.

51 Ottaviano dei Petrucci, *"Odhecaton" (1501): Werke von Josquin, Compère, Okeghem und anderen Meistern des 15. Jahrhunderts, für kleines Orchester, von Bruno Maderna* (Milan: Suvini Zerboni, 1977; first edn. Zurich: Ars Viva, 1951), pp. 1–7.

52 This constructive orchestration could be said to include pieces like *Lo ferais dire, La plus de plus* (for some aspects), *Bergerette savoyere* from the first suite of *Odhecaton*, then *Nostre cambriere si malade estois* and *James, James, James* from the second suite with the same name, or again Legrenzi's *Basadonna*, particularly the final *Allegro*, where the original parts are "split" between strings and horns with greater frequency (more about this in point 2). The same also holds true for Frescobaldi's *Ricercare* and *Bergamasca*, even though it does not apply to the beginning of the pieces, but rather to the way in which they are gradually established, "revealed," and finally come to an end. Last but not least, the *Venexiana* and the *Romana* among the dances by Viadana, and a large part of Monteverdi's *Sonata sopra Sancta Maria* (all the pieces mentioned here are published by Edizioni Suvini Zerboni, except for the last unpublished arrangement).

53 As stated in Pasticci, "Memorie di Petrucci a Venezia" (see note 48), p. 699, Maderna's source was the anastatic facsimile of the choral book *Harmonices Musices Odhecaton* (Milan: Bollettino Bibliografico Musicale, 1932).

54 Maderna certainly knew of this work before he first conducted it in the early 1960s. He had studied it during his apprenticeship with Hermann Scherchen (whose repertoire contained since 1938 Webern's arrangement, which was the subject of a lengthy exchange of letters with the composer himself). See "From the Correspondence," *die Reihe* 2 (*Anton Webern*, ed. Herbert Eimert; 1958), pp. 13–22: 19–20.

sometimes produce changes in a chord from its root position to its inversions, due to a doubling in the low register of a part that is different from the original bass.[55] Moreover, the image of the "kaleidoscopically proliferating" fragments applies to both Webern and Maderna, and there is no doubt that the latter uses orchestration to arrive at a general clarification of the motivic structure of the interpreted passages. Indeed, we can listen to passages in *Nous sommes de l'ordre*, for example, at bars 43–47 and 69–78 (Ex. 1 E–G), which are impregnated with a Webernian allure, and where the motivic fragmentation is reduced to a single *tactus* that enhances the instrumental alchemy, accompanying and implementing what could be called the work's "timbric rhythm" (a sort of *Klangfarbenmelodie*).

Instead, we can give four main reasons for assuming that Maderna's "constructive" orchestration deviates from the Webernian example without denying or openly opposing it:

a. In Maderna, motivic fragmentation is conceptualized as extended melodic lines entrusted to a single instrument, which can even last between five and ten bars; the melody is thus not reduced to mere intervals or to the "points" that compose it (whereas in Webern's arrangement of Bach's six-voice "Ricercar," the eight-bar exposition of the subject of the fugue is settled into seven timbrically differentiated fragments). In Maderna's arrangement, the unit of measurement is not the interval but the fragment of the motive in its linear unfolding; and, in the end, what is preserved is not the idea of summing intervals, but the idea of melody. Proof of this is the great care Maderna takes in following the imitative cues of the counterpoint, whenever they occur, without ever interrupting the linearity of the instrumental parts.

b. Similarly, motivic fragmentation is not based on the concept of pitch classes, which gives rise to the free manipulation of registers, but on the concept of a real note, as demonstrated by the strict observance of the original registers of the sources. In other words, despite the fact that the contrapuntal lines of the hypotexts are fragmented between varied and different instrumental attacks, they run from top to bottom in Maderna's text and are settled in their original register. And that is not all: unlike Webern, Maderna always orchestrates *all* the parts that go to make up a piece. In the case of chamber music in particular (that is, in all his arrangements except for Frescobaldi's *Bergamasca* and Monteverdi's *Sonata*, which are for medium-sized orchestras), the link between the original register and the new instrumentation determines an economy of means that favors pairings and homogeneous and recurring doublings, often at the higher or lower octave.

c. Maderna often resorts to the doubling of original parts even in the most fragmented sections. Webern, on the other hand, considers doubling an exceptional option to be used only occasionally, and hence something best avoided. However, let us not forget that Madernian doubling is far more like organ registration than a rehabilitation of the Romantic concept of an instrumental mixture. One could describe it as a sort of "instrumental additive synthesis" based on the enrichment of a preexisting sound line by the overlapping of partial harmonics, which must remain perceptible and discernible.

---

55 This happens for example in the arrangement of *Ricercare super La-Fa-Sol-La-Re* in Girolamo Frescobaldi, *Tre pezzi, per orchestra da camera, trascrizione di B. Maderna* (Milan: Suvini Zerboni, 1991; first edn. Zurich: Ars Viva-Verlag Hermann Scherchen, 1954), p. 11 (bb. 81–85).

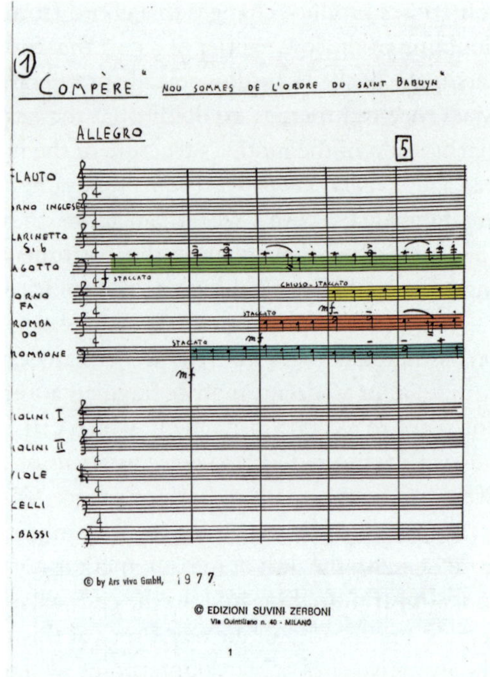

EX. 1A–G

Compère, *Nous sommes de l'ordre du Saint Babuyn,* in Ottaviano dei Petrucci, *Odhecaton, für kleines Orchester, von Bruno Maderna* (Zurich: Ars Viva, 1951; Milan: Suvini Zerboni, 1977), pp. 1–7. Copyist: Luigi Nono. (© Courtesy of SugarMusic S.p.A., Milan.) Here the four original parts of the hypotext have been highlighted.

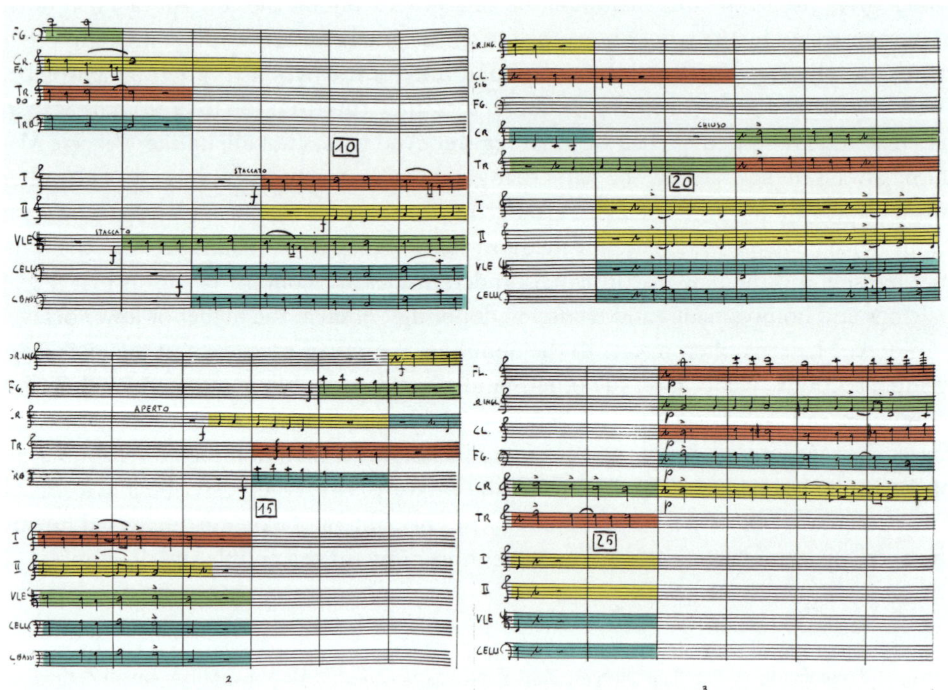

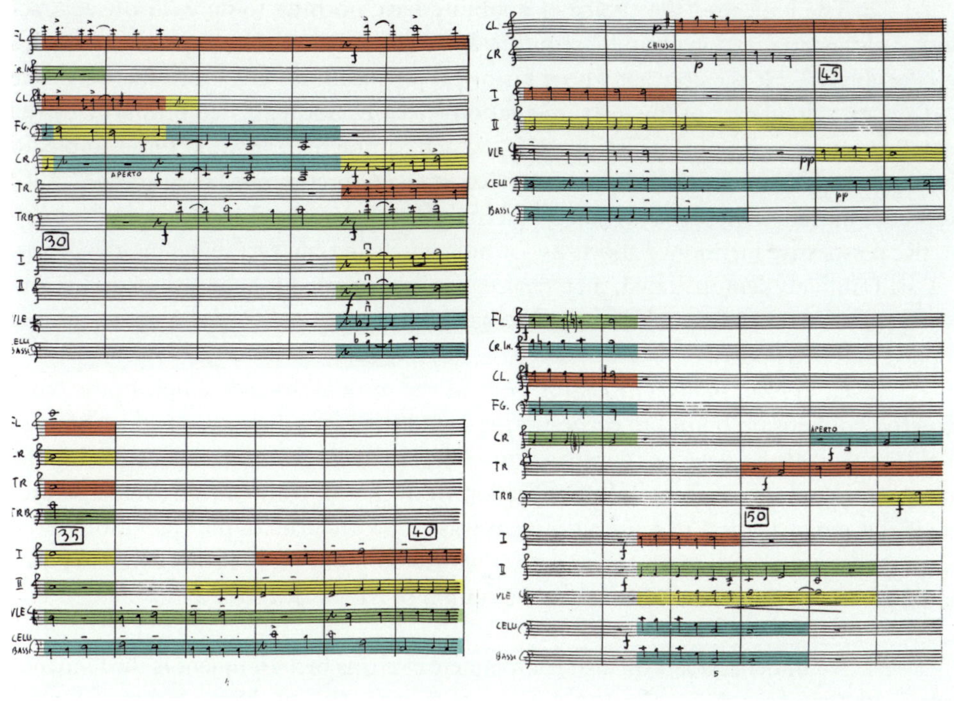

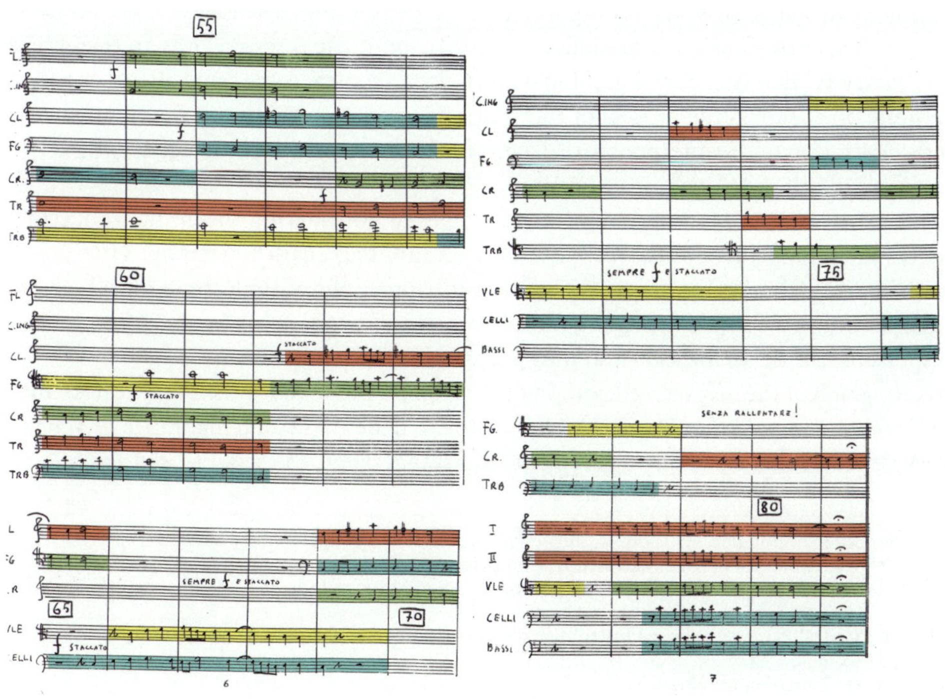

d. The logic and the choice of doubling have nothing to do with the abstract notion of the serialization of timbres, outlined so effectively in the same period by Boulez in "Possibly…"[56] It is a concept whose historical justification stems from that recursive and abstract circularity of the instrumentation – that is, not regulated primarily by the so-called idiomaticity of the instruments – which can be seen at work, for example, in the eleven expositions of the subject of the "Ricercar a 6" orchestrated by Webern.[57] With respect to the latter, Maderna's arrangement must therefore be read according to the interpretive perspective mentioned above: no formula or schema can ever represent it (whereas, as Carl Dahlhaus demonstrated, such devices can be obtained for the "Ricercar"),[58] and it is continuously changing due to the inexhaustible richness of the interpretive process applied to the hypotext.

Even in *Nous sommes de l'ordre,* perhaps the most clear-cut example of the "constructive" dimension bound to orchestration – and therefore the most "visible" of cases that lean toward the aspect of construction – there are still grounds for recognizing the unharnessing of the concept of interpretation from that of composition. Maderna proposes this emancipation in quite a different way to the theories of interpretation of the Viennese-Darmstadtian mainstream and, as we saw in points a–d, also as compared to a paradigmatic work such as Webern's orchestration of Bach's "Ricercar a 6."

2. An understandably natural consequence of this first argument is the tendency to reunite the compositional act with the interpretive act – acting as a sort of *Kapellmeister,* he tells Boehmer[59] – which foresees a greater amount of fine-tuning of the work on the event side than in its writing intended in the traditional sense.

This brings us back to Maderna's words about the interpreter as an operator of the "catalysis" that transforms graphic symbols into acoustic data,[60] and allows us to concentrate on the dynamic process of transcription, seen as a diachronic development of a written fixation of the interpretive realization (which, in turn, can interact over time with various and different levels of authorship).

Let us now examine a concrete example by considering the events concerning Maderna's arrangement of *Basadonna* from Giovanni Legrenzi's Sonatas op. 8 (1663), published by Ars Viva Verlag in 1953.[61] The various happenings well illustrate the whole process, outlining a complex picture of interference and overlapping between the subjects responsible for the realization and interpretation of the work.

An antigraph of the 1953 printed edition of *Basadonna,* preserved at the Historical Archives of Contemporary Arts in Venice (Archivio Storico delle Arti Contemporanee di Venezia, ASAC), shows that in order to carry out his arrangement, the score Maderna used as a

---

56   See Pierre Boulez, "Possibly…," in *Stocktakings* (see note 38), pp. 111–40.

57   See Loretta Jean Wood McNulty, "A Comparative Study of the Bach Transcriptions of Schoenberg, Webern, and Stravinsky" (Master's thesis, School of Music of Indiana University, Bloomington, May 1974), pp. 34–45, esp. 44.

58   See Dahlhaus, "Analytical Instrumentation" (see note 50), pp. 189–90.

59   See note 26.

60   See quotation in note 21.

61   Giovanni Legrenzi, *La Basadonna,* ed. Bruno Maderna (Zurich: Ars Viva, 1953).

hypotext had in turn already been elaborated and defined in all its details. The score in question is a handwritten edition of this sonata made a short time before by Malipiero with the help of an anonymous copyist.[62] This is the text on which Maderna fixes his own arrangement, literally "inscribing" it over the original readings present therein, in a single productive surge that seems to act in a transverse way with respect to the traditional conception of interpretive activity and composing (→ **EXX. 2-3**).[63]

The presence of two hands writing in black ink is evident from the very beginning (Ex. 2b), with one correcting the other: here we can see the penstrokes of both the anonymous copyist and Malipiero, as editor,[64] intent on preparing the text of their edition. This system of signs, in black ink, is certainly complete and executable, and was probably conducted as such by Maderna as part of a RAI radio program *Inediti musicali del passato,* featuring so-called ancient music, and broadcast on Channel Three ("Terzo Programma") from January 1951 onwards.[65]

The numerous pencil marks and alterations in red and blue pencil and blue pen on the ASAC manuscript were evidently added after Malipiero had edited the text, and are all certainly the work of Maderna. The fact that many of these marks have been rubbed out (although they are still legible), and the many other pencil deletions (on pages not reproduced here), bear witness to the various afterthoughts Maderna had while the work was still in progress. These intervene directly in Malipiero's text, using it as a palimpsest, and grafting onto it a section of wind instruments including brass and double reeds: two oboes, a bassoon, a horn, a trumpet, and a trombone. Maderna also adds an additional double bass to the string section, which maintains Malipiero's original divisions. To assign the parts to the new instruments, Maderna simply uses either the extended or abbreviated form of their names (see Exx. 2b and 3), in the manner of a change of instrument. This simple device is used not only to alternate between parts played by just the wind instruments, strings, or an orchestral *tutti,* but also to organize the different attacks of each instrument. At the

---

62 See Giovanni Legrenzi, *A Basadonna, per 6 istrumenti (e Basso), a cura di Gian Francesco Malipiero,* allographic manuscript score, with annotations and corrections by Malipiero, additions and signs of orchestration by Maderna and annotations by Luigi Nono, [1950–52], 22 pp. (filed as "ASAC/M O* LEGR"). See also Examples 2 and 3.

63 Many thanks to Angela Ida De Benedictis for her great help in the deciphering of the complex and multi-layered system of signs found on these pages. The reproductions are also available online at http://asac.labiennale.org/multimedia/a_basadonna_partitura/1_parte.pdf (consulted 7 June 2021).

64 Malipiero cancels the bass line in the fugue expositions of the various subjects (see Ex. 2b, p. 1, bb. 1–4, but also later bb. 4–8 on p. 2, from pp. 16 to 17, and from pp. 18 to 20), then writes its only right-hand realization for the rest of the piece, transposing the two parts of the violas into alto clef (transcribed instead by the copyist in treble clef) and interpolating indications for its execution; see always p. 1 (Ex. 2b), of the type *"mai legato, né staccato"* (neither *legato* nor *staccato*). He also specifies the name of the composer of the piece, "Giovanni."

65 Hence the "RAI – Sede di Venezia" stamp on the score (see Ex. 2a) and on the respective instrumental parts (always held at the ASAC), extracted from Malipiero's handwritten edition of this score. The additions made by the composer, for example the already mentioned *"mai legato, né staccato"* (Ex. 2b), correspond to what can be read on the loose viola parts. The orchestral material was, however, probably prepared at two different times, as demonstrated by the instrumentation described on the frontispiece of the score ("1 partitura, 3 I violini, 3 II violini, 2 viole [1 vla I e 1 vla II], 2 celli, 1 basso"), which is different from the greater number of parts of the sonata preserved to date. (Note that the main group indicated on the score only corresponds to the instrumental parts with the "RAI – Sede di Venezia" stamp.)

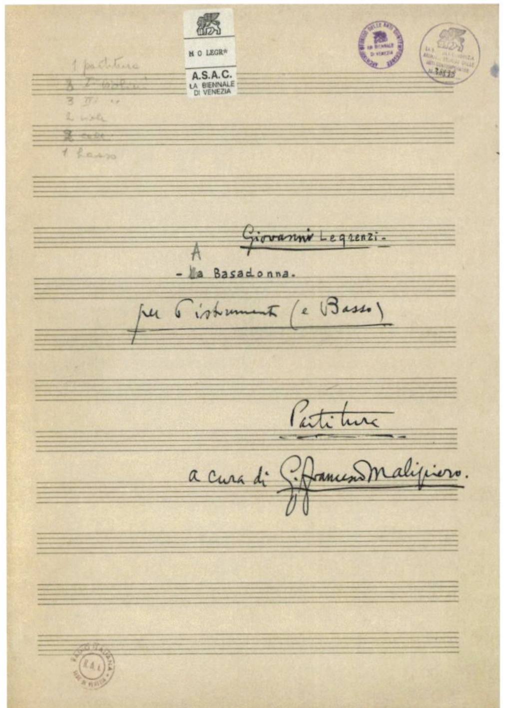
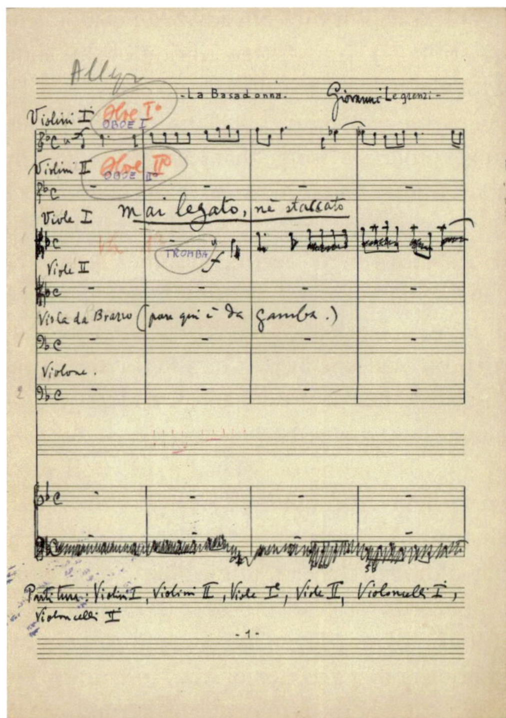

EX. 2A–B Giovanni Legrenzi, *A Basadonna,* sonata a 6, ed. Gian Francesco
Malipiero, with autograph notations by Bruno Maderna and Luigi Nono,
frontispiece and p. 1 (courtesy of ASAC, Venice).

same time, in terms of musical shape, this expedient manages to fragment the original
instrumental parts, creating new ones based on more circumscribed motivic cadences that
are adapted to the new orchestration, and sometimes doubled in the score.[66]

These few elements of "over-writing" make it easy to identify the text of Maderna's
arrangement, which is already in its final version in the manuscript kept at the ASAC. In
actual fact, many of its main details – the assignment of the new instrumental parts, the
unusual order of the staves in the score, the integration of elements in the agogics and
dynamics, the articulation and phrasing of the stringed instruments – coincide with the
fair copy that Luigi Nono, as copyist, made in 1953 for the printed edition published by
Scherchen's publishing house, Ars Viva Verlag (**→ EX. 4**).[67]

---

66 Technically speaking, and from a synchronic perspective, this characteristic of Madernian orchestration was already outlined in the previous point; as far as the *Basadonna* example is concerned,
we can say that it is most noticeable in the last section of the piece, the *Allegro* and the *Maestoso*
finale, bb. 64–83.

67 The order of the wind instruments in the score (see Ex. 4a) exactly confirms that the Ars Viva edition
written by Nono is a direct descendant of the manuscript score kept at the ASAC. In the printed
edition, starting from the top, we find the following unusual instrumental order: oboe I, oboe II,
trumpet, horn, trombone, bassoon. This matches the order given in Maderna's antigraph (Ex. 3),
where the exposition of oboe I (ex violin I) is followed by the trumpet attack (ex viola I in Malipiero), and then horn (ex viola II), trombone (ex cello I), bassoon (ex cello II), and oboe II (ex violino II).

EX. 3A–B Giovanni Legrenzi, *A Basadonna*, sonata a 6, ed. Gian Francesco Malipiero, with autograph notations by Bruno Maderna and Luigi Nono, pp. 16 and 21 (courtesy of ASAC, Venice).

All the same, the text of the ASAC score – as it was fixed in its final form by Maderna – sounds exactly the same as the one he conducted on 17 September 1952 in Munich, as part of a Bayerischer Rundfunk (BR) production dedicated to the music of seventeenth- and eighteenth-century Italy.[68] We may thus conclude by saying that Maderna's propensity to reunite the compositional act with the interpretive act can be grasped in a dynamic process of the "writing of the interpretation," completely oriented toward the performative realization. The annotated score fixes a new system of signs above a determined text and modifies it in compliance with particular poetic needs (let us not forget what Maderna said about the "graphic realization of the same [work] in terms of acoustic communication").[69] Later on, a series of voluntary and contingent causes turn it into a new fixed and normative text, which can be reproduced in an autonomous way and which, therefore, is attributable to a new and primary authorship.

---

68 A recording of the concert of 17 September 1952 (lasting 7'35") is conserved in the archives of the Bayerischer Rundfunk (BR) and includes the *Basadonna* and the *Marinona* by Giovanni Legrenzi; the same archives also hold a "Konzert für Streichorchester A-Dur" by Alessandro Scarlatti, dated 15 July 1954 (lasting 7'40"). See also Maderna's correspondence with the BR (also in the person of Werner Götze), and more specifically the letters of 15 February 1952, 17 June 1952, and 2 July 1952 (PSS-BMC), as well as the letter from Maderna to Luigi Nono, dated 13 September 1952 (ALN).

69 See note 21.

EX. 4A–B Giovanni Legrenzi, *La Basadonna,* ed. Bruno Maderna;
copyist: Luigi Nono (Zurich: Ars Viva, 1953),
pp. 1 and 9 (© courtesy of SugarMusic S.p.A., Milan).

3. If the writing of the interpretation can thus be defined more, and above all, in relation to the event (the concert, the performance, the rehearsal) than to a compositional process in the traditional sense, then there are certainly grounds for paying more attention to a corresponding sort of inclusive listening. Such a kind of listening is suitable for identifying precise associations, echoes, and references between historical events, and signs and effects, in the name of a "revolution in continuity" (once again, this recalls Luigi Nono's thought, especially regarding his poetics of the 1980s).[70] Maderna's scrupulous care and commitment in elaborating the programs of his concerts, in choosing the order and possible combinations of the pieces, can thus be explained in the light of this fundamental aspect of his interpretive conception. As can be seen from many of his work letters, diaries, program drafts, and lists of works that are often found among his manuscript material,[71] he comes to consider the design of the concert program to be a substantial and sometimes logical

---

70 See at least Luigi Nono, "Other Possibilities for Listening" (1985), in *Nostalgia for the Future* (see note 48), pp. 370–84.

71 Numerous examples of his manuscripts and notepads can be consulted in the legacy held at PSS, where we also find catalogued his "Agenden," "Besetzungslisten," "Musikerlisten," "Probenpläne," "Programmvorschläge," "Terminkalender," and "Werklisten."

end of the whole compositional-interpretive process. One could even say that it becomes an aesthetic artifact in all respects. To get an inkling of the wealth of this activity (as well as the vastness of the repertoire mastered by Maderna), see the manuscript notes reproduced in the Appendix, where, among the many examples contained in the Bruno Maderna Collection at PSS, there are several rough drafts of concert programs drawn up here and there in the 1950s (Apps. 1 and 2), in the 1960s (Apps. 3 and 4), and in a notebook of the 1970s (Apps. 5a and 5b).

The portrait that emerges from these programs is one of an extremely original anthology of the history of music as a whole, from Pérotin to Monteverdi and Frescobaldi to Earle Brown and Peter Schat. And this was generated by an almost insatiable curiosity and utopian tendency to embrace the whole multiplicity of the musical fact, without placing barriers between the so-called great repertoire, contemporary music, and early music.[72]

In a radio interview conducted with Georges Caraël, head of Radio Télévision Belge Francophone's (RTBF) Channel 3, and broadcast probably on the same channel on 25 June 1968, Maderna explains the fundamental principle he followed in creating his programs. He recognizes that the public also has an essential formative function in this (in a manner that is entirely consistent with that comparative approach to analysis, so well documented especially by Nono, as mentioned in point 1):

> As a conductor, I always try to propose mixed programs. We must not forget that in the last twenty or thirty years the public has not been brought up to date with contemporary music. [...] It seems clear to me that if one does not know the basics of the historical evolution of music, it is difficult for an audience to express their opinion on the music after Beethoven or, let's say, after Wagner and Verdi; and be able to evaluate the music of Pierre Boulez. I'd always do it this way: let the public listen to works taken from lesser-known repertoires, which already contain the seeds of contemporary music and all the contemporary ideas – that's the basis of contemporary music. [...] We've seen that it is much better to present this music to the public little by little, work after work, along with other works of the past, or of the more recent past, which enlighten it and explain it.[73]

Lastly, a significant rehabilitation of a certain irrational component and the category of "intuition" may also emerge within this Madernian poetics of juxtaposing repertoires: to quote the composer himself, the understanding of the meaning of a work is bound to the "osmosis" and the "catalysis" of multiple stimuli and references, elaborated "in a moment of 'lyrical intuition.'" And he goes on: "After all, psychologists have amply demonstrated

---

72 On this aspect see also Maderna's letter of 4 February 1972 to Francesco Siciliani, the then director of programming of the RAI Orchestra, Milan. Maderna proposes a program that "should include 50% music by Monteverdi (or earlier) to Mahler (not included), 30% from Mahler to Webern, and the remaining 20% from the late post-war period to the present day"; published in Maurizio Romito, "Lettere e scritti," in *Studi su Bruno Maderna*, ed. Mario Baroni and Rossana Dalmonte (Milan: Suvini Zerboni, 1989), p. 72; now also in Maderna, *Amore e curiosità* (see note 4), pp. 632–33. See also De Benedictis, "More than conducting" (see note 23), pp. 386–87.

73 Transcribed from the original tape (ca. 27'30"), filed as "Interview de Bruno Maderna par Georges Caraël" at the RTBF-SONUMA Archives, Brussels (Collection Title: Archives programmes). The passage in question is at ca. 16'15" of the recording. Original in French. An Italian translation ("Intervista con Georges Caraël") is in Maderna, *Amore e curiosità* (see note 4), pp. 344–57, quote on pp. 350–51.

how we give the name 'intuitions' to some cognitive structures, called 'contents,' that are self-processing and develop surreptitiously in the subconscious";[74] the conception, which is close to the coeval theory of the Boulezian "*surpris*" mentioned above, was then theorized, with almost disciplinary rigor, in Luigi Nono's lecture on "error as a necessity" (presented in the spirit of Wittgenstein's thought).[75]

4. In closing, let us once again consider the way Maderna overcomes the "classic" dialectic between the idea of "objectivity" (text, structure, organization, method) and "subjectivity" (the author's will/choices, the more limited will and more limited choices of the interpreter) as set out along the lines of Viennese-Darmstadtian thought.

Greater contextualization of such thought emerges in some manuscript notes Maderna probably wrote during his first year of teaching at Dartington, in Southwest England, in the summer of 1960.[76] This is a long fragment of text written in French, which was compiled from the French translation of an article by Herbert Weinstock on the problem of meaning in music.[77] His transcript contains numerous meticulous entries and comments in the margin, as well as significant additions to and omissions from the original hypotext. In fact, Maderna's interest in the latter is focused on the problem of listening and "perception." By transcribing and integrating Weinstock's words, the composer arrives at a definition of the typical receptive activity of this "*écoute de la musique*" that is perfectly in tune with his creative-interpretive paradigm. There is now talk of a "symbiosis" between "matter," made up of objectifiable and schematizable sound relationships, and the "desire" of those who intentionally trigger the work's aesthetic meaning through the establishment of new aesthetic qualities, formal developments, and energetic concentrations ("*l'énergie affective et [l]es significations évoquées*," mentioned at the end of the notes), always within the limits deriving from the same objective relationships.

The following short extract shows the original layout with the central body of the text and Maderna's marginalia:

> 1
> because, and we'll see this later, these are objective structures
>
> Unless we are ready to deny that music is meaningful at all, in any sense beyond that of aural titillation, we shall have to temporarily accept some hypothesis of what it may mean. We learn from listening to music that it conveys two significances: one is objective, present in its structure,[1] the other subjective, outside this, but which is the very structure of the composer's personality as a man, artisan, interpreter.

---

74   "Analizzare una opera" (see note 17), p. 180.

75   See Luigi Nono, "Error as a Necessity" (1983), in *Nostalgia for the Future* (see note 48), pp. 367–69.

76   See Bruno Maderna, "Dartington – 31 luglio 1960," manuscript text (original in French) containing several analytical diagrams found in an exercise book with "DARTINGTON" written on the cover by the composer himself (16 pp., PSS-BMC, "Textmanuskripte"). The following extracts are taken from pp. 1, 4, 5, and 6 of this text. For an Italian translation and an in-depth contextualization of the document see "Maderna didatta: 'Dartington – 31 luglio 1960,'" in Maderna, *Amore e curiosità* (see note 4), pp. 643–50.

77   See Herbert Weinstock, "La signification de la musique," trans. Claude Saimant, in *Profils: Art, Lettres, Musique des Etats-Unis* 3 (April 1953), pp. 41–53 (also in "Le retour au classique: Interrogation – Perspective," *La Revue Musicale,* double edn., nos. 308–09 (1978), pp. 63–74 ; orig. text: "Introduction: The meaning of music," in idem, *Music as an Art* (New York: Harcourt Brace, 1953), pp. 3–14; this source was used to model the English translation proposed here. See also "Maderna didatta" (note 76), pp. 644–45. The recognition of Weinstock as the basis of Maderna's text is due to Paolo Dal Molin.

[…] We must also consider the problem of perception, which is the fundamental principle of all communication with sound objects.

There can be no doubt that parts of both music's content and its effect are physical, the action on the human ear and mind of pure sound as such. It is easy to recognize, however, that this is not a salient, or even a very important part of the meaning of music as an art, in which what is all-important is the perception of a weave of sound relationships. It is nonetheless sensible to notice that many supposed effects of music are in truth effects of mere sound as such:[2] art's raw material.

But before starting to consider "sound" and "sound objects" as music's raw materials, we need to remember that music cannot just be "desire" or "matter," but that it is, undoubtedly, a symbiosis of "desire" and "matter."[3] Music, in short, consists (wishing to attempt a definition, however coarse it may seem) in the expectation of desires (under ideal conditions, in all their potential and meaningfulness) and their complete satisfaction.[4] […] It's better to judge the cogency with which the composer has organized whatever subject matter he was driven to employ. It is a measure of the ways in which he has articulated, organized, and disposed both his basic emotional energy and the meanings that he has evoked in the process of articulation and organization.[78]

2
Signal →
Signal perception

3
quote Monteverdi

4
satisfaction =
realization

As we can see, even when hypothesizing a listening theory, Maderna places more importance on the actual event, and therefore on the level of realization of that "weave of sound relationships" ("satisfaction = realization," he peremptorily notes in the margin), as something objective that gives rise to the possibility of meaningful and aesthetically acceptable concretizations. If, theoretically speaking, there are an infinite number of possibilities, the multiplicity of the single concretizations is actually limited by intrinsic principles of coherence. Maderna sheds light on this principle in an interview in the summer of 1969, at the Venice Biennale, during a pause in the rehearsals for his Concerto for violin and orchestra. He affirms that even in an aleatoric score like that of his new work, not all "paths" are possible; instead, they are restricted to quite a small number:

My compositional activity comes to an end with the rehearsals. After this first performance [of the Concerto for violin and orchestra] there will be a fixed path, composed as a whole. There will be possible variations in the orchestral accompaniment, or in the violin part, three or four different ones, and there will be paths that can be established from time to time. But that doesn't mean that all paths are possible in this: there will be perhaps three or four possible, formally useful paths.[79]

Going back to the Dartington notes, and to the question of overcoming the quintessential subject/object dichotomy, one is immediately struck by several similarities between the Madernian conception and several elements of a theory regarding the interpretation and reception of events that was also taking shape in the 1960s, particularly in the German-speaking countries. This ontology of the work of art, the so-called *Rezeptionsästhetik*, was formalized on the basis of some instances of hermeneutics and phenomenology.

---

78 See ibid., pp. 647–49, and a facsimile of the original in French on p. 646.
79 *Un'ora con Bruno Maderna* (see note 35), at ca. 9'00". Original in Italian.

According to this theory, as the reading of the contributions by Roman Ingarden and Wolfgang Iser in particular makes clear,[80] the meaning of a work of art that emerges in the process of interpretation is neither totally objective or schematizable, nor is it subjective, but rather it stems from the interaction of these two planes. As we have seen above, this was where Maderna talked about "a symbiosis of 'desire' and 'matter'" (*"une symbiose de "désir" et "matière"*) when he was transcribing and integrating Weinstock. Thus, different layers of stratification are set up and generated by this dynamic process, where "the productive impulse" inherent in the entire hermeneutical operation is mainly driven by some "twists" and "turns" of indeterminacy (*Unbestimmtheitsstellen*)[81] in the schema or score – "the 'unwritten' part of a text,"[82] according to Iser, or the unexpressed implications of the text that "picture things"[83] – which, however, are never completely eliminable. The interpreter's (or the reader's) task is thus to fill these "elements of indeterminacy" through the realization of the performance – the *"Konkretisation,"* to use Ingarden's jargon.[84]

In his poetics, however, Maderna never explicitly refers to the theory of "elements of indeterminacy," even though he had already addressed the issue when he started writing compositions of an aleatoric type (from the late 1950s onwards). His approach at that time began with a reflection on the openness of the musical work and its interpretation *in general,* and then went on to consider the fields of possibility of the various technical issues that this discourse involves – first and foremost, the question of form. As regards the demands of productivity/poetics implicit in the idea of indeterminacy – or, recalling Iser, in the unexpressed implications that "picture things" – the starting point for Maderna's whole argument in the aforementioned interview with Georges Caraël is precisely the observation that "aleatoric music has always existed," and he defines this as "the stimulating side of music."[85]

In light of this reflection, one might be tempted to reconsider the aforementioned examples and figures of *A Basadonna* and *Odhecaton* in terms of the productive dimension inherent in the concept of indeterminacy – all the more so because of the large and tangible diffraction between the hypotexts of these works and the definitive Madernian text. Instead, my last example relates to the category of the so-called orchestral "retouches," in which the diffraction rate between hypotext and transcription is actually far lower. Such a choice was determined by the fact that this very concept may find a more relevant definition in the middle ground between the compositional and the interpretive fact, a place filled with osmosis and interference, and where the Madernian "writing of the interpretation" resides.

---

80 See *inter alia* Wolfgang Iser, "The Reading Process: A Phenomenological Approach," *New Literary History* 3 (1971–72), pp. 279–99; and Roman Ingarden, *Untersuchungen zur Ontologie der Kunst: Musikwerk, Bild, Architektur, Film* (Tübingen: Niemeyer, 1962), esp. pp. 115–36 ("Das Problem der Identität des musikalischen Werkes").

81 Ingarden, ibid., p. 126.

82 Iser, "The Reading Process" (see note 80), p. 280.

83 Ibid., p. 285: "the written part of the text gives us the knowledge, but it is the unwritten part that gives us the opportunity to picture things; indeed, without the elements of indeterminacy, the gaps in the text, we should not be able to use our imagination."

84 Ingarden, *Untersuchungen zur Ontologie der Kunst* (see note 80), p. 12 and passim.

85 Maderna says this at ca. 7'00" in the interview (see note 73). See also "Intervista con Georges Caraël" (note 73), p. 347.

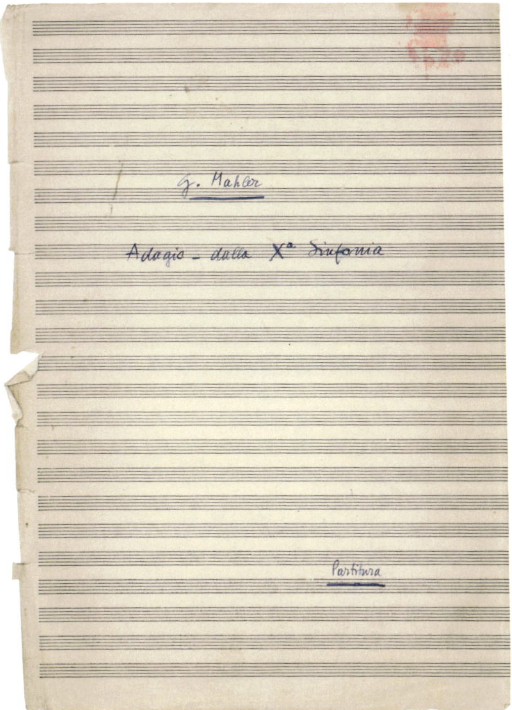

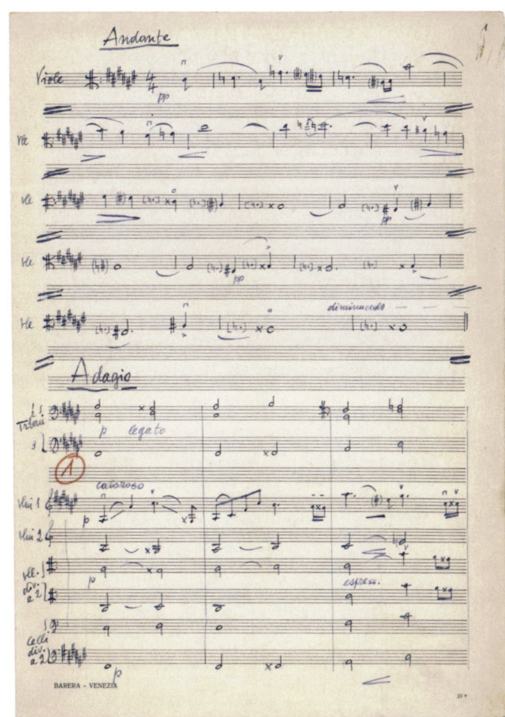

EX. 5A–B Gustav Mahler, "Adagio" from Symphony No. 10, autograph manuscript score by Bruno Maderna, frontispiece and p. 1, PSS-BMC.

The example in question is an autograph manuscript score by Maderna of the "Adagio" from Gustav Mahler's Symphony No. 10, preserved in the composer's legacy. It is a fair copy (→ **EXX. 5–7**), almost complete in all its parts, both in the details and in bar extension.[86]

This particular text seems to be a reproduction of the first printed edition of Mahler's Tenth, published in 1951 in New York, with some slight modifications.[87] In fact, many of the annotations Maderna made on his manuscript score are evidence of how,

---

86   Maderna conducted Mahler's "Adagio" from the Tenth for the first time on the evening of 15 May 1951 at Venice's Teatro La Fenice in a demanding concert program that, apart from the "Adagio", also saw the performance of Legrenzi's *Tre sonate per stromenti* (including *A Basadonna*) and works by Bach, Malipiero, and Debussy. The archive sources available to date do not document whether, on this particular evening, Maderna used the text of his score for the "Adagio" (even though an analysis of the paper documents can fully confirm this dating). Moreover, this particular concert repeated Mahler's Tenth in Venice three years after its Italian premiere there in 1948, when Hermann Scherchen conducted it at the International Festival of Contemporary Music.

87   See Gustav Mahler, *Symphony No. 10 (posthumous)* (New York: Associated Music Publishers, 1951). This score reproduces the "Adagio" and "Purgatorio" movements from a 1924 manuscript edition, edited by Ernst Krenek, with subsequent annotations by Franz Schalk, Alexander Zemlinsky, and Otto Jokl, which never earned Krenek's approval. This is why the editor's name is missing from the 1951 edition; see Susan M. Filler, "Manuscript and Performing Versions of Mahler's Tenth Symphony," in *Fragment or Completion? Proceedings of the Mahler X Symposium*, Utrecht 1986, ed. Paul Op de Coul (The Hague: Universitaire Pers Rotterdam, 1991), pp. 36–50: 47.

 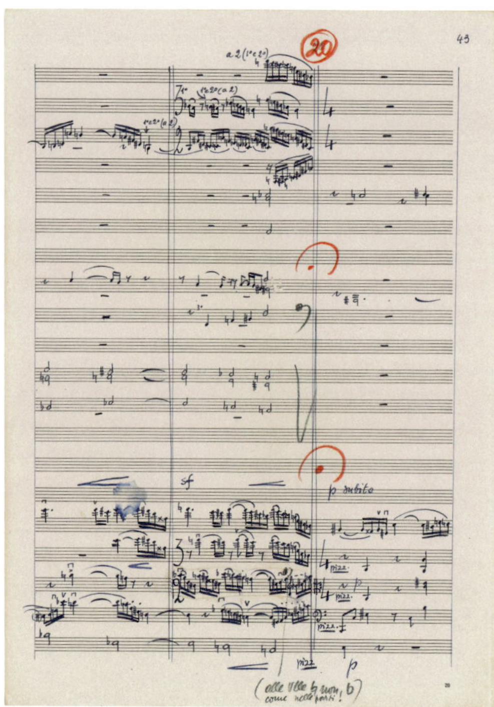

EX. 6A–B Gustav Mahler, "Adagio" from Symphony No. 10, autograph manuscript score by Bruno Maderna, pp. 27 and 43, PSS-BMC.

in some places in the text, he preferred and managed to reestablish Mahler's original reading, deeming some variants in the American edition to be incorrect. It should be remembered that Alma Mahler had set about publishing a facsimile of Mahler's autograph in 1924,[88] and it is safe to assume that this was the very source Maderna consulted either directly or indirectly (very probably through the teachings of Hermann Scherchen).[89]

As can be seen in the first bar of Example 6a (violins II *divisi*), Maderna, animated by an almost philological *vis*, adds a kind of footnote: "Forse La ♮? anche nell'autografo Sol" (Perhaps A [natural]? also G in the autograph), while in Example 6b, near the violas, we read "(alle viole ♮ e non ♭ come nelle parti!)" ([natural] for the violas and not [flat] as in the parts!). This confirms the fact that Maderna had the choice of reestablishing the original reading of Mahler's manuscript, and that he also had access to the loose parts of another edition (probably the same ones published in 1951), which were different from the autograph.

---

88   See Gustav Mahler, *Zehnte Symphonie* (Berlin et al.: Paul Zsolnay, 1924).
89   See Rudolf Stephan, "Zur Geschichte der Zehnten Symphonie Gustav Mahlers: Die Partituren von Franz Schalk, Willem Mengelberg und Hermann Scherchen," in *Fragment or Completion?* (see note 87), pp. 126–42: 133–36.

EX. 7   Gustav Mahler, "Adagio" from Symphony No. 10, autograph
manuscript score by Bruno Maderna, p. 11, PSS-BMC.

Now, as regards our final argument of the overcoming of the subjectivist and objectivist dichotomy in the interpretive action, see, among the various additional modifications, the one reproduced in Example 7, referring to bars 58ff. of the "Adagio" score.

In an actual footnote (no. "1"), Maderna writes: "Nelle parti il Fl[auto] 2° e 3° sono anch'essi all'8ª superiore. Io propongo così" (In the parts the 2nd and 3rd Fl[utes] are also at the higher 8th. I suggest this). This solution, however, does not appear either in the Mahler manuscript – where, ambiguously, we only find the flute I part without any mention of flutes II and III – or in the text of the 1951 edition, which has flute I's part performed "à 3."[90] Instead, Maderna inserts a doubling for flute I that is an octave lower, with flutes II and III playing in unison – a feature that, in all respects, is the fruit of his interpretation, and for which he claims full responsibility ("I suggest this"). And it is something that is certainly understandable from a musical point of view in light of the sudden dynamic deviation (*ff*), the orchestral *tutti*, and the greater thickening of the sound texture, which are emphasized in bar 58 itself.

---

90 Erwin Ratz opted for the same solution in 1964, in his edition of the Tenth for the Internationale Gustav Mahler Gesellschaft; but, as compared to the 1951 edition, he had the foresight to insert that "by 3 [à 3]" in brackets, almost as if it were an editorial addition. See Gustav Mahler, *Adagio aus der Symphonie Nr. 10, für grosses Orchester, Erstausgabe der Originalfassung*, Sämtliche Werke: Kritische Gesamtausgabe 11a (Vienna: Universal Edition, 1964), p. 6.

Thus, even in a work such as Mahler's Tenth Symphony, the interpreter's active role is not defined as an arbitrary action, but as a genuine interpretive act. The composer-conductor's freedom tends to act and develop more around the "elements of indeterminacy" of whatever hypotext is being considered (even when, as can be seen, it is a rigorously prescribed and detailed hypotext like a Mahler Symphony).

As a rule, the Madernian transcription is therefore determined and justified by the intrinsic qualities of the writing of a certain work, or rather, it is explained by how the latter was represented through writing, with notational parameters that are more or less complete or more or less determined by one (or more) hypotexts from different periods and places. The more or less evident process of diffraction is set off by the intrinsic qualities and elements of the source or textual sources the composer considers interpretable, which are then "filled" with new meaning in the realization of the performance, in that Madernian "satisfaction = realization." This process gives rise to the aforementioned dialectic between the "expectation of desires (under ideal conditions, in all their potential and meaningfulness)" and "their complete satisfaction."[91] In other words, the composer's poetics comes to fruition when it takes place in those very places in the hypotext that are considered open to implementation.

---

91   Iser was talking about "an active interweaving" or "a process of anticipation and retrospection"; see Iser, "The Reading Process" (see note 80), pp. 287ff.

Appendix

Appendix 1

A list of compositions drawn up by Bruno Maderna on the verso of a letter from Ladislao Sugar, dated 18 March 1952 (PSS-BMC). This is most probably an initial selection of pieces for the concert in Munich on 17 September (as cited above in the text, p. 213, and note 68), for which Maderna had agreed to conduct a varied program of Italian music. The list includes several titles of arrangements he made at the time of works by Vivaldi, Viadana, Legrenzi, and Monteverdi, as well as other authors (Bertoni, Scarlatti), performed by Maderna on the aforementioned RAI radio program *Inediti musicali del passato* (see p. 211).

Appendix 2

List of possible pieces to be conducted, drawn up by Maderna on the *verso* of a letter from Herbert Hübner, dated 24 September 1952 (PSS-BMC). The compositions listed here refer to a concert repertoire performed by Maderna in various locations (Rome, Barcelona, Oldenburg, and Darmstadt) between the end of 1952 and the beginning of 1953. Among the various titles there is a reference to the arrangement of Frescobaldi's *Tre Pezzi*, performed on Swiss-German Radio (SRG) in Zurich on 7 October 1952, as well as at the "Palestrina-Konzert" attributed to "Pergolesi" (but actually a reworking of Unico Wilhelm van Wassenaer), performed in its Italian premiere in Rome on 11 October 1952. Note that the "Danze Elisabettiane" (Elizabethan Dances) listed here are not an early reference to *Music of Gaity* (1967), but an arrangement by Hermann Scherchen of 1950, which Maderna performed quite regularly at the time; cf. Anonymous [ca. 1600], *Altenglische Violentänze, für Streichorchester bearbeitet von Hermann Scherchen* (Zurich: Ars Viva, 1950).

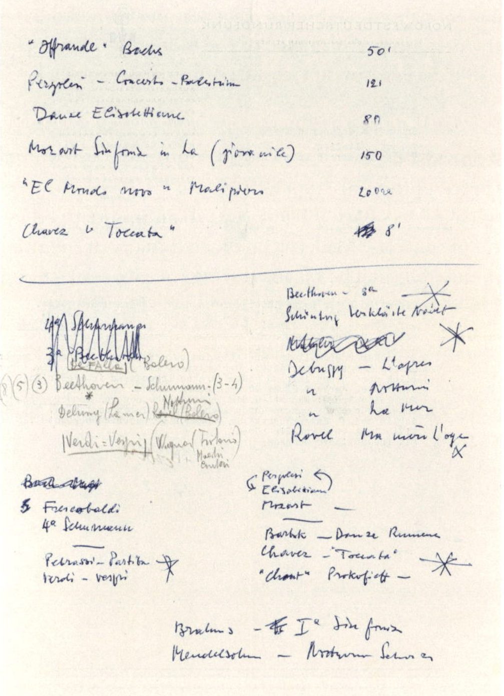

Appendix 3

Draft of a concert program: manuscript notes ("Programmvorschläge," PSS-BMC). This program, the third in a series of four devised by Maderna, probably refers to a series of concerts performed in Argentina in the summer of 1964. This particular concert, in its final form, was performed by Maderna on 17 August of that year, at the helm of the Buenos Aires Symphony Orchestra. It included: 1) Maderna's arrangement of Monteverdi's *Sonata sopra Sancta Maria;* 2) Maderna's Concerto for 2 pianos; 3) Ravel's *Ma mère l'Oye;* 4) *Available Forms I* by Earle Brown; and 5) Luigi Nono's *Canti di vita e d'amore* (cited in the note as "Hiroshima" from the title of the first part of the triptych). See *Orquesta Filarmonica de Buenos Aires, Undécimo concierto del abono a 12 Nocturnos,* concert program, Temporada Oficial, 17 August 1964 (preserved at PSS). The pieces by Pérotin and Gabrieli refer to two arrangements made by Maderna in the early 1960s (respectively: *Alle Psallite Alleluja/Haec dies* and *Ricercare del settimo tono,* materials at PSS-BMC); the former was performed in The Hague on 31 January 1963, the latter in Berlin on 12–13 February 1963. On the Argentina tour, Gabrieli's piece was performed during the evening performance of the following 24 August, while the Pérotin diptych was definitively excluded.

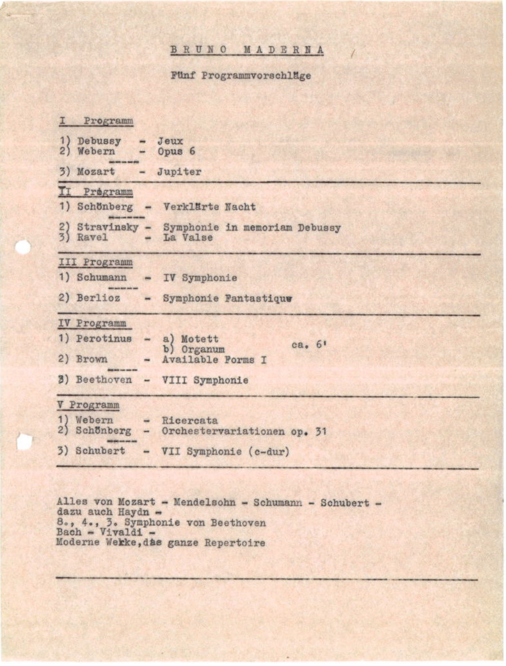

Appendix 4

Concert proposals; typewritten notes ("Programmvorschläge," PSS-BMC). These refer to an unidentified cycle of concerts. Maderna conducted many of the titles in question in The Hague during the two-year period 1964–66, at the helm of the Residentie Het Orkest.

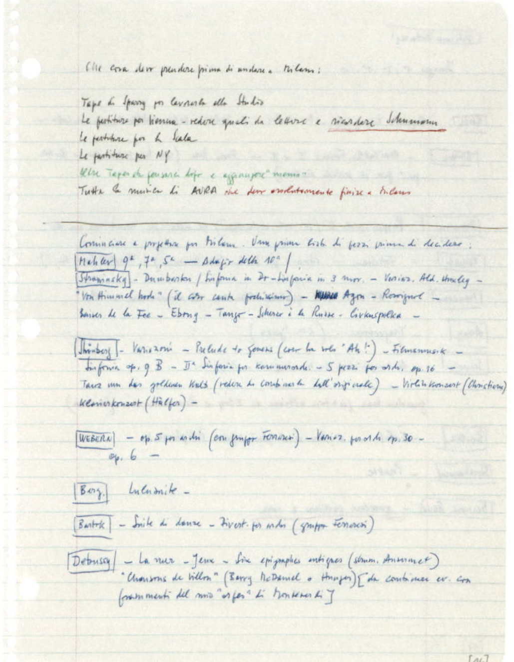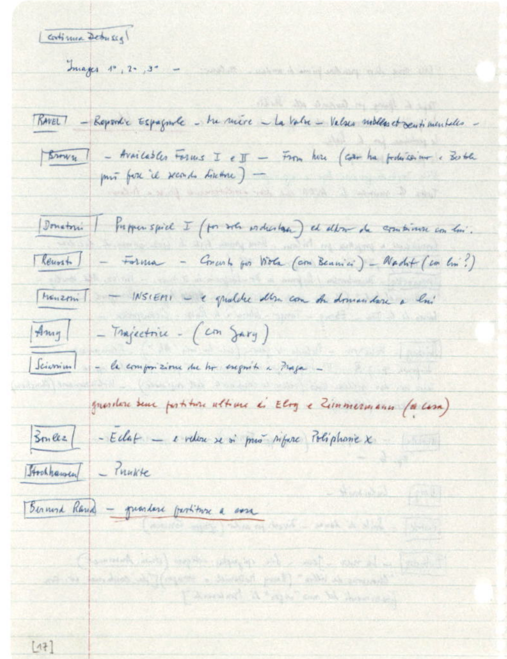

Appendix 5A–B

Manuscript notes written in a notebook dating back to the early 1970s ("Skizzenbuch" no. 6, pp. [16–17], PSS-BMC). The reference to "Milan" in 5A relates to his time as the artistic and musical director of the RAI's Orchestra of Milan in the 1972–73 seasons and planned for 1973–74.

BENEDETTA ZUCCONI

Analysis and Synthesis in Bruno Maderna's Creative Process
Don Giovanni and Other Mozart Scores

> Il *Don Giovanni* di Mozart è un'opera contemporanea.
> Volesse il cielo che tutte le musiche di oggi
> fossero avanguardistiche quanto il *Don Giovanni*.
> (Bruno Maderna, 1967)[1]

Bruno Maderna's artistic personality was repeatedly the victim of an old prejudice: his intense and all-encompassing activity as an orchestra conductor was considered to have somehow damaged his compositional flair, preventing him from dedicating the necessary time and space to exercising his talent. Thus, from this perspective, notwithstanding his apparently bright and promising future as a composer, much of his creativity would have remained largely unexpressed, or at the very least hampered and in some way debased, by his activity as a composer.

This commonplace is a regular *topos* in Madernian exegesis and reappears also in Michela Garda's 1989 in-depth study of the themes recurrent in the musical criticism directed at Maderna during his life and in the decade after his death.[2] The idea spread and took root particularly in the late sixties and early seventies, further endorsed by his frenetic life as a conductor without a permanent position who regularly appeared as a guest conductor in concert halls all over the world. Moreover, doubts about the reasons behind some of his compositional choices added further fuel to the fire. First of all, it was not clear as to whether his predilection for so-called "open form" composition was dictated more by practical necessity than by a poetic kind of urgency. Or again, whether this was a mere expedient to bungle up pieces he had conceived and composed in his free time away from conducting. The power of this prejudice was still recognized more than twenty years later by Ulrich Mosch (who edited the re-publication of Massimo Mila's *Maderna musicista europeo*, a collection of radio broadcasts transmitted between 1974 and 1975, shortly after the composer's death), although he does not go so far as to suggest that this was the only reason for the belated musicological interest in Maderna.[3]

---

1   "Mozart's *Don Giovanni* is a contemporary work. May heaven grant that all of today's music were as avantgarde as *Don Giovanni*"; Bruno Maderna in an interview with Giorgio Calcagno published posthumously on *La Stampa* (15 November 1973), p. 7. Now in Bruno Maderna, *Amore e curiosità: Scritti, frammenti e interviste sulla musica*, ed. Angela Ida De Benedictis, Michele Chiappini, and Benedetta Zucconi (Milan: il Saggiatore, 2020), pp. 197–99: 197.

2   See Michela Garda, "Rilevamenti sulla ricezione della musica maderniana," in *Studi su Bruno Maderna*, ed. Mario Baroni and Rossana Dalmonte (Milan: Suvini Zerboni, 1989), pp. 74–94.

3   See "Premessa del curatore," in Massimo Mila, *Maderna musicista europeo*, ed. Ulrich Mosch (Turin: Einaudi, 1999), pp. vii–xiv; first edn. 1976.

Mila once said: "When he was alive, we were used to considering him as potentially a great composer and – shaking our heads – we would sententiously observe: shame, he seems to waste his talent on conducting."[4] He would then use this premise as grounds for being the first to overturn this cliché, which even then was already beginning to present some critical aspects:

> Today, one year later, as we look at his work to remember him, we must first of all revise that opinion. His work as a composer is immense and above all complete. We used to think of Maderna as a conductor who could have been a great composer. A hundred years from now, we'll talk about Maderna as a great composer who was also a conductor, who deserves credit for the diffusion of modern music, and who placed his baton at the service of all his friends and colleagues from each and every country. But history will always focus on the composer.[5]

The conductor-composer dichotomy cannot however be simply dismissed out of hand. Indeed, it makes perfect sense if we choose to consider the figure of Maderna in terms of his reception, or rather, if we decide to adopt an approach that investigates the reaction he received both during his life and after his death from critics as well as public and academic journalism. In this case, the conductor-composer dualism achieves respectability as a perceived phenomenon, as a vulgate rooted in the thought of his contemporaries, which therefore has the power to condition their opinions.

However, as long as we try to analyze Maderna's work from a more general hermeneutical perspective, then all the contradictions and falsehoods contained in this dualism will always come to the fore. And this is not really, or not just (following in Massimo Mila's footsteps), to do justice to Maderna the composer rather than Maderna the conductor, but because both aspects were indeed two inseparable and consubstantial parts of one and the same artistic personality.[6] Conducting and composing were anything but two separate activities, and both contributed in equal measure to Maderna's artistic personality and his general approach to the musical object.

Such a reading finds ample confirmation in Maderna's very own statements when, during interviews, talks, lectures, and in his writings, he repeatedly pointed out the complementarity of his two main artistic activities. At the first performance of the Concerto for violin and orchestra in 1970, he and the violinist Theo Olof were interviewed by Christof Bitter. When Bitter asked whether his activity as a contemporary and classical music director could perhaps interfere with his work as a composer, Maderna replied:

> Perhaps... I couldn't say... For me, these two activities go together in the most harmonic way; at times it is tiring, since while composing one has to withdraw into oneself, whereas while conducting it is necessary to be as outgoing as possible, to project energy outside.

---

4   Ibid., p. 3.
5   Ibid., pp. 3–4.
6   Further support for this hypothesis and more on this subject in Angela Ida De Benedictis, "More than conducting, more than composing: Hermann Scherchen, Bruno Maderna, Luciano Berio," in *Komponieren & Dirigieren: Doppelbegabungen als Thema der Interpretationsgeschichte*, ed. Alexander Drčar and Wolfgang Gratzer (Freiburg im Breisgau et al.: Rombach, 2017), pp. 371–400: 380–90.

Nonetheless I believe that this union is ideal, as it creates a continuous contact with music not just as thought, as a formulation, but also as performing practice, as living sound material.[7]

Several years earlier, in 1956, Maderna had already been given the chance to further explore these concepts in an article commissioned by Luciano Berio for *Incontri Musicali* – although the work was never to appear in this journal. His essay arrived at the conclusion that these two activities were co-existent in a composer's artistic life, a practice that was modeled on previous centuries:

It has long been forgotten that during the modal and tonal periods composer and conductor were one and the same. What was expressed in graphic symbols was directly communicated to the listener by the composer himself, who was almost always a good performer. True to say that, nowadays, differentiation and specialization have become ever-more demanding, but it is equally true that composing is, and necessarily always will be, an activity of synthesis, not one of analysis. The performance, and I speak as a conductor, must always fall to those who, once they have understood it, are able to impose meaning on a work. And in order to impose meaning on it, there will be an increasing need for them to be internally convinced.[8]

Maderna does not consider the Cartesian analysis/synthesis dichotomy merely in terms of contraposition, but as complementarity and mutual interpenetration. We might thus wonder exactly how this mingling of composing and conducting came about, and whether it is possible to trace any tangible manifestations of this way of thinking, so as to confirm whether Maderna's words were more than a mere declaration of intent.

Some of the analyses Maderna carried out on Mozart's score for *Don Giovanni* have proved enlightening in helping to answer such questions. The documents are part of the composer's legacy and consultable at the Paul Sacher Foundation in Basel. Through the study of these documents we shall try to demonstrate that his analytical activity is actually the cornerstone that unites the poetics of Maderna the composer with the aesthetics of Maderna the conductor, especially as far as the musical canon is concerned. The rather unusual nature of these materials, and his notes on two other opera scores by Mozart – *La Clemenza di Tito* and *Così fan tutte* – make them precious sources among the little-documented evidence of Maderna's musical and dramaturgical studies on composers of the past.[9]

---

7   "Interview: Maderna-Olof-Bitter" (Saarbrücken, 28 May 1970), Saarländischer Rundfunk, Saarbrücken, in RS Archives, vol. no. MV 3639/0. The format here follows the interview Maderna originally gave in German (see De Benedictis, "More than conducting" (see note 6), p. 384), and is thus somewhat different from the one found in Raymond Fearn, *Bruno Maderna* (Chur: Harwood, 1990), pp. 308–11: 309. For a complete Italian translation see Maderna, *Amore e curiosità* (see note 1), pp. 153–59: 153.

8   "'Analizzare una opera': intorno a *Nones* di Luciano Berio," in Maderna, *Amore e curiosità* (see note 1), pp. 179–82: 181–82. On the origin of this text see also Michele Chiappini's essay in this volume, p. 198 and note 17.

9   Maderna's numerous transcriptions of early music are a case apart. Here, however, we are inclined to consider such materials as being more relevant to the compositional sphere, and that they have little to do with the exegetical intent or the conductor's voice expressed in his Mozart studies. For more about the role of interpretation in Maderna's transcripts, see Michele Chiappini's essay in this volume, pp. 193–225.

Maderna had always shown an almost exclusive interest in Mozart. This is already visible in the concert programs dating back to his days as a child-prodigy conductor: the music of the Viennese composer always featured in his performances, with a marked preference for programs combining contemporary works with masterpieces drawn from tradition.[10] At times this self-declared close and special affinity with Mozart's work even led him to question (at least on a personal level) Beethoven's role. In an interview in 1966, when asked about his favorite composers, he replied:

> Mozart and Schubert perhaps. Bach less. Mozart's art lies in his lack of contrivance. Think of the "Jupiter" symphony, which is so complex that you don't notice it at all. I have great difficulty with Beethoven. I like the Quartet op. 132 and the *Eroica*, especially the first movement. Beethoven's handicap is that Mozart and Schubert existed.[11]

His special love for Mozart was combined with an attention toward performance practice that was quite unusual for the period in question. According to Maderna, if the performance of a work is not historically informed – in the sense attributed to this term in recent decades – then ideally it should at least be in line with the creative thinking of its composer and with the aesthetics of its time. As far as performing Mozart was concerned, Maderna was able to say:

> It would be better to avoid conducting Mozart at all, but if you do it, you have to know him *perfectly*: I mean the historical period, what was going on in Germany, in France, the context of the time… Only then can you approach Mozart. We now also have the beautiful Bärenreiter edition,[12] in which all material by Mozart has been compared. Generally [in the scores in circulation] one finds many more embellishments than were used in Mozart's time, but they were added later. Only by knowing all this one can try to conduct Mozart properly. And then you get terrible critics…! Because people are refractory to novelty, they are afraid when someone comes along and dismantles the idea they have of Mozart, Kant, Leibniz, showing them that reality is different![13]

The documents on Mozart's *Don Giovanni* housed at PSS confirm these statements and bears witness to the in-depth analysis Maderna carried out before he brought the opera to the stage. The four different diagrams are drawn up on different sized, loose sheets of what is mainly graph paper and are not dated (→ **EXX. 1-4**). However, they probably date back to the period around the turn of the seventies, when Maderna was given the opportunity to conduct works by Mozart and Da Ponte in various theaters in Europe and abroad. In fact, September 1965 saw him conduct *Don Giovanni* at Kiel's opera house; the following

---

10   Regarding this, see De Benedictis, "More than conducting" (see note 6), pp. 385–86.

11   "Bruno Maderna: 'We kunnen nog niet zonder het vaandel': De dirigent van *Labyrint* over muziek en happening," *Vrij Nederland* (25 June 1966), p. 3 (original in Dutch).

12   The reference is to *Neue Ausgabe sämtlicher Werke*, ed. Internationale Stiftung Mozarteum Salzburg, from 1955 onwards.

13   "A conversation with Bruno Maderna by George Stone and Alan Stout: WEFM, Chicago, 23.1.1970," original recording available on the CD *Bruno Maderna: The Last Concert*, CD STR 10071 (Milan: Stradivarius, 1993). Maderna's English, very uncertain, has been slightly retouched here in some places. For an Italian translation of the entire conversation see Maderna, *Amore e curiosità* (see note 1), pp. 57–85 (passage quoted on p. 74).

year, in October, Maderna presented it at the Paris Opera; and then, several years later, in September 1972, he conducted *Don Giovanni* yet again at the New York City Opera.[14] It is reasonable to suppose that these diagrams came into being around the time of one of these performances. Given Maderna's action-packed artistic life, it is quite hard to imagine that he had enough time to dedicate himself to such a detailed form of analytic activity, without having its actual performance in mind.

Just as the precise dating of these documents can only be hypothesized, the chronological order of the four diagrams is equally uncertain. However, a *logical* order can be reconstructed, and this is the one followed here.

The first diagram (Ex. 1) is made up of a collection of sheets of graph paper, whose content is aimed at examining the timbral density and quality of the individual scenes in the opera. The horizontal lines correspond to each piece, and the numbers on the right-hand side of the diagram indicate the relevant pages in the score, with specific reference to the Eulenburg edition preserved in the composer's fonds.[15] Instead, each class of instruments, the singers, the chorus, and the diegetic interventions of the stage orchestra ("Büh[nen]Musik") at the end of Act I – thus also considered a character – are indicated in vertical columns. This gives us a total of twenty columns from left to right: strings, flutes, oboes, clarinets, horns, trumpets, trombones, timpani, and mandolin; followed by Don Giovanni, Leporello, Commendatore, Don Ottavio, Masetto, Zerlina, Donna Anna, Donna Elvira, the chorus, and the diegetic music. The intersections between an instrument and a voice and the scenes from the opera are marked with black rectangles covering two squares, sometimes reduced to a single square when only one of the two wind instruments is used – whereas three squares are used for the trombones (in fact, there are three performers) and the diegetic music.

---

14   On the American revival of *Don Giovanni* also see Maurizio Romito's essay in this volume, pp. 277–97, esp. pp. 295–96. The notes in Maderna's diaries (PSS-BMC, "Textmanusktipte, Agenden") also give February 1964 as the dates for a staging of *Don Giovanni* at the Stadttheater in Bern. The same date can also be deduced from two messages from the director Walter Oberer (a telegram dated 25 March 1963 and a letter dated the 29th of the same month), which mention a vague sort of readiness on Maderna's part following Oberer's request that he conduct the work. This collaboration is finally mentioned in a letter from Sylvio Samama – Maderna's agent at the time – to Christine Maderna on 16 August 1963. Among the documents related to the activities of the Stadttheater housed at Bern's Theatersammlung, there is nothing to confirm that Maderna conducted any such performance of *Don Giovanni*. However, the work was staged on these dates under the direction of Gabor Ötvös. In another of Maderna's notebooks referring to "Stagione [Season] 1972–73 / 1973–74" (as can be read on the cover), on the sheet relating to "November 1972" (fol. 3) we find "Eventuale esecuzione *Don Giovanni* con N.Y. City Opera a Los Angeles il 15" (Possible performance *Don Giovanni* with N.Y. City Opera in Los Angeles on the 15th), with the later addition of the word "CANCELLATO" (canceled). The same note ("*Don Giovanni* – City Opera / Los Angeles") also appears in a diary for 1972 compiled by Maderna's manager Sheldon Soffer.

15   Namely, Wolfgang Amadeus Mozart, *Il dissoluto punito, Ossia il Don Giovanni* (K. 527), edited from the autograph by Alfred Einstein (London et al.: Ernst Eulenburg, n. d., No. 918), with manuscript annotations by Bruno Maderna and an autograph dedication from Maderna's wife, Beate Christine Koepnick (PSS-BMC, score "BM PM 26"). The other diagrams described here also refer to page numbers and other elements from this score. Some catalogues have attributed the undated edition to ca. 1969, which – if it were to be established – would allow a *terminus post quem* for these diagrams.

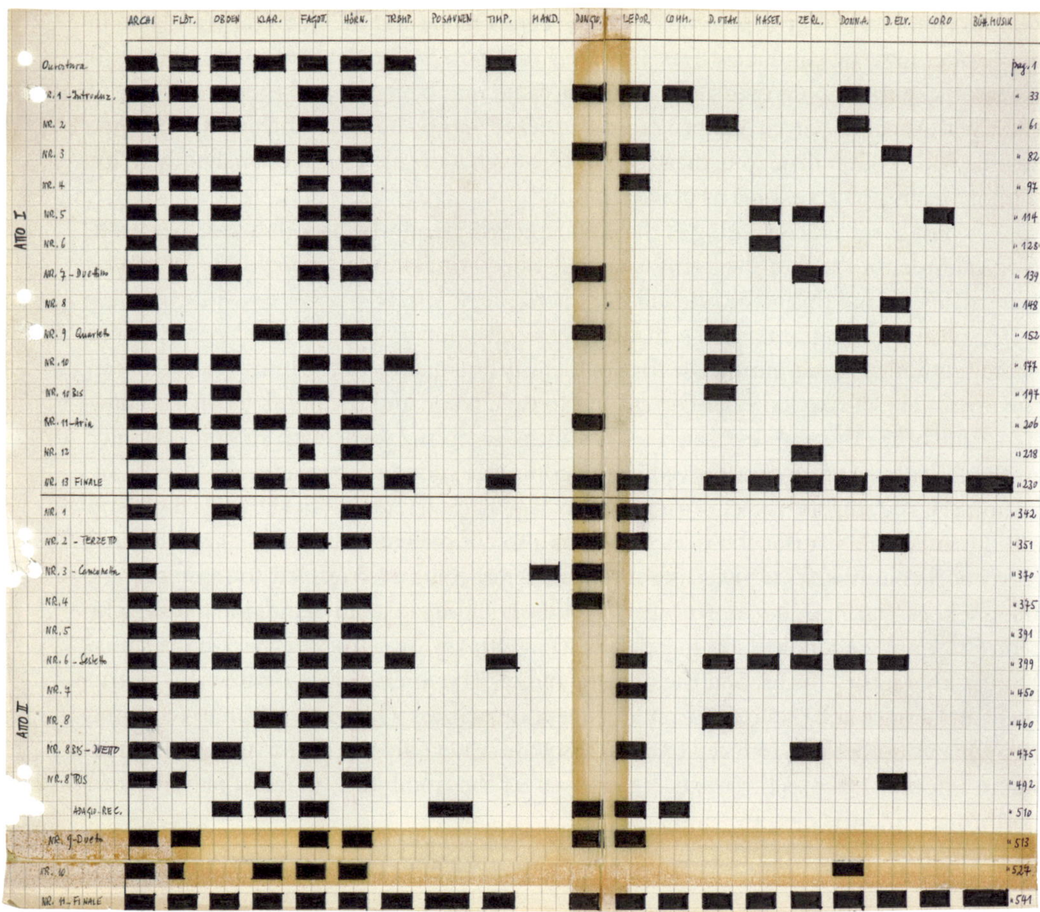

EX. 1   Bruno Maderna: Diagram 1 from Mozart's *Don Giovanni;* PSS-BMC.

The second diagram (Ex. 2) is also a study on timbre, and once again, as shown by the page numbers in the right-hand margin, the reference score is the aforementioned Eulenburg edition. This time, however, the analysis only considers instrumental timbres and leaves out the vocal parts. From time to time, black rectangles are used to mark the orchestral instruments in the columns. Unlike the previous schema, in this case the series of numbers (that is to say, the vertical sequence of lines) does not respect the linear development of the work, but the pieces are arranged in an order that reflects the *crescendo* of the timbral density. In fact, No. 8 from the first act, corresponding to Donna Elvira's aria "Ah fuggi il traditor" accompanied by strings only, appears at the top of the diagram, while at the bottom we find the finale of Act II, the moment of the maximum deployment of orchestral sound in all its various timbral declinations. Maderna orders the instruments in the diagram to underscore the centrality of some orchestral voices, arranging them (from mandolin to trombone) to give a visual image of a sort of "mirror" of timbral density. It

Atto						tonality	page
Atto	I	nr.	8		8	B - dur	pag. 148
"	II	"	3		19	D - dur	" 370
"	II	"	1		17	G - dur	" 342
"	I	"	6		6	F - dur	" 128
"	II	"	7		23	G - dur	" 450
"	II	"	9		25	E - dur	" 513
"	I	"	3		3	Es - dur	" 82
"	II	"	8		24	B - dur	" 460
"	II	Adagio Rec.				Amoll / Gdur	" 510
"	I	nr.	12		15	F - dur	" 218
"	II	"	8	tria	10	Es - dur	" 492
"	I	"	9		11	B - dur	" 152
"	I	"	10	bis	13	G - dur	" 197
"	I	"	7		7	A - dur	" 139
"	II	"	10		26	F - dur	" 527
"	I	"	1		1	F - dur	" 33
"	I	"	2		2	D - moll	" 61
"	I	"	4		4	D - dur	" 97
"	I	"	5		5	G - dur	" 114
"	II	"	4		20	F - dur	" 375
"	II	"	8	bis	9	C - dur	" 475
"	II	"	2		18	E - dur	" 351
"	II	"	5		21	C - dur	" 391
"	I	"	10		12	D - dur	" 177
"	I	"	11		14	B - dur	" 206
"	I	Ouvertura				F - dur	" 1
"	I	nr.	13		16	C - dur	" 230
"	II	"	6		22	Es - dur	" 399
"	II	"	11		27	D - dur	" 541

EX. 2   Bruno Maderna: Diagram 2 for Mozart's *Don Giovanni*; PSS-BMC.

should also be noted that next to the page numbers indicated in the right-hand margin, he also labels each number with its own tonality, while red numbers in the left-hand margin are used to show the order in which the various parts of the opera actually occur in the score.[16]

The third schema (Ex. 3) focuses on the roles of the characters (including the chorus). Once again these are divided into columns, while the opera scenes are neatly ordered along the vertical axis. Just like the previous diagram, the characters here too are "mirrored," arranged in an ascending/descending order, and placed on the right or left depending on their social status and dramaturgical specificity, that is to say, nobles

---

16   Maderna wrongly classifies numbers 8b and 8c from Act II ("8 bis / 8 tria" in the diagram), which he lists in red as "9" and "10" after scene 8 (first line of the diagram). However, despite this oversight, the final result of "27" is still right, since it is the sum of the fourteen numbers from Act I and the thirteen from Act 2.

NR.	COMMEND.	DON OTTAVIO	DONNA ANNA	DONNA ELVIRA	DON GIOVANNI	ZERLINA	MASETTO	LEPORELLO	CORO
1	1		1		1			1	
2		2*	2*						
3				3	3			3	
4								4	
5						5	5		5
6							6		
7					7*	7*			
8				8					
9		9*	9*	9*	9*				
10			10						
11					11				
12						12			
13	13	13*	13*	13*	13*	13*	13*	13*	13
14 (1)					14*			14*	
15 (2)				15*	15*			15*	
16 (3)					16				
17 (4)					17				
18 (5)						18			
19 (6)		19*	19*	19*		19*	19*	19*	
20 (7)								20	
21 (8)		21							
22 (9)					22*			22*	
23 (10)			23						
24 (11)	24	24*	24*	24*	24*	24*	24*	24*	24
NR. INTERVEN.	2	6	8	7	12	7	5	10	3

EX. 3   Bruno Maderna: Diagram 3 for Mozart's *Don Giovanni;* PSS-BMC.

vs. commoners, serious characters vs. comic ones, so that their presence on stage is underlined. Don Giovanni is at the center, and his role as a dramatic pivot (and as a *trait d'union* between the two social classes) is further highlighted by the use of a thicker border around his column. This time the diagram is not just a timbral analysis, but also offers a quantitative study on the vocal interventions of each character, indicated by the number of the scene that is being interpreted, written once again in pencil in the reference boxes. Maderna adds an asterisk when the voices perform ensemble pieces, probably to show that in these pieces each character's vocal part does not have full autonomy. Finally, the last line of the diagram reads "nr. interven." (number of interventions), that is, the sum total of the number of scenes in which each character appears.

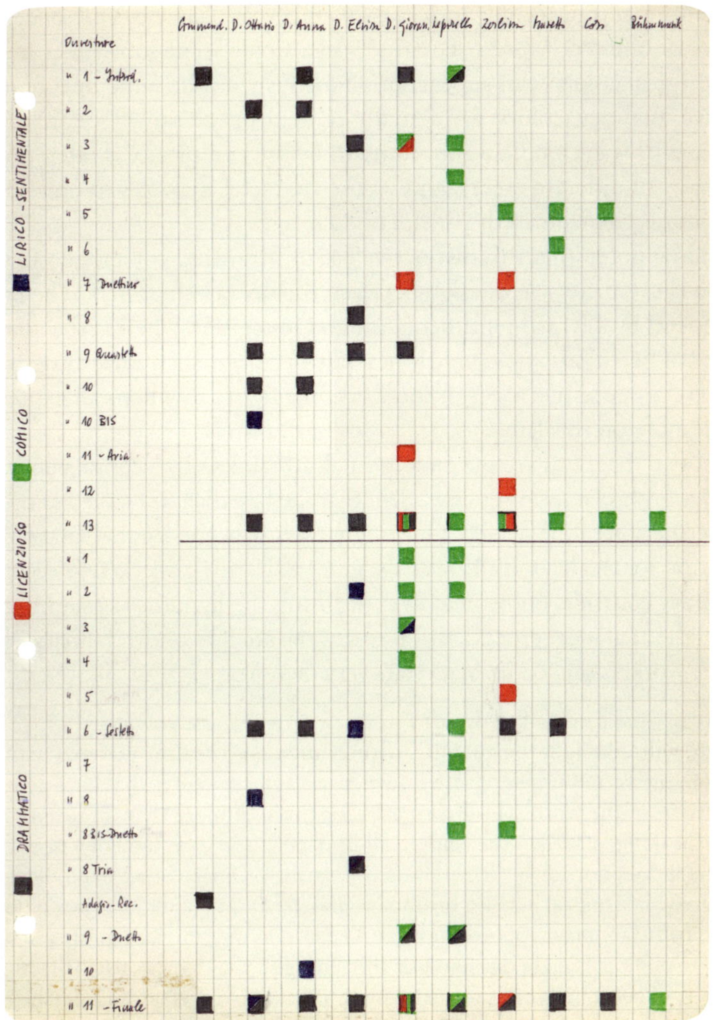

EX. 4   Bruno Maderna: Diagram 4 for Mozart's *Don Giovanni;* PSS-BMC.

The last diagram (Ex. 4) deals with the dramaturgy of the opera. The *dramatis personae* are arranged in an order that follows a similar logic to the one used for Diagram 3. Don Giovanni is still at the center, as the point of contact between the two worlds and also the reason why their destinies collide; but now both the diegetic music (*Bühnenmusik*) and the chorus have been added. Once again, the numbers from the first and second act are listed in order on the vertical axis, although sometimes a formal indication ("Duettino," "Quartetto," "Introd." "Aria," etc.) also appears. Maderna adds a vertical legend to the left of the diagram: four differently colored squares symbolize different dramatic-expressive registers: black = "drammatico" (dramatic), red = "licenzioso" (licentious), green = "comico" (comic), blue = "lirico-sentimentale" (lyrical-sentimental). Thus, a square with the appropriate "dramaturgical color" marks each and every character's presence on stage. The concurrence of different expressive registers in a single scene sometimes means that several "dramaturgical colors" can appear simultaneously on the same line, or even that several expressive qualities (colors) are actually present in the same "square": the most striking example of this is Don Giovanni himself, whose complexity is often underlined by the simultaneity of different colors, and whose character manages to unite dramatic, comic, and licentious elements in the finales of each act.

It should be noted that this distinctive use of "dramatic colors" allows us to observe a sort of musical-expressive division between the opera's characters. The nobles are always characterized by a lyrical-sentimental/dramatic register, whereas the commoners mostly make use of licentious and comic tones. Furthermore, such a use also reveals that Don Giovanni is the expressive focus of the work, the figure in whom all expressive elements converge (more on this later).

The first two diagrams are the ones most clearly linked by a consequential and interdependent relationship: it seems quite evident that the first diagram served as the starting point for the preparation of the second. One might even hypothesize that Diagram 1 was a preliminary version for the later drafting of Diagram 2. In this case, therefore, logical and chronological order coincide. Some help in confirming the hypothesis that Diagram 4 is the final piece in the analytical process, that is to say, the analysis of the dramatic characters that make up the work, is offered by Maderna's very own words:

> There are two basic ways of analyzing a work: the first of these, conducted with a statistical approach, will highlight the quantity, nature, and density of the material used, then go on to note the various types of series, sequences, and structures that have generated the various parts of the work. This first method is nothing more than an inventory which, broadly speaking, describes the work in all its details, and even though it does explain its structure, it does not convey its emotion, its warmth. On the other hand, however, how can we arrive at a logical but also instinctive understanding of music if we do not tackle it with this necessary means of investigation? The second way, instead, consists in setting the "interpretive" dimension of our soul free and letting the work speak to us directly, through the powers of persuasion of its formal symmetry and asymmetry – in a nutshell: through its own means of communication. It is true to say that this second method comes later and as a consequence of the first, but it is equally true that without this second and different investigation, the work would remain nothing more for us than an empty congeries of unnecessarily complicated and meaningless mechanisms.[17]

If we compare the diagrams from *Don Giovanni* with Maderna's words, we can easily see that the first three diagrams mostly belong to the first of these two analytical categories. These schemas are more descriptive, an essential starting point for the second exegetical stage, which instead is aimed at understanding the work from a logical point of view, through what has now become a qualitative rather than a quantitative description of the constituent elements. Thus, if one postulates that in our case Diagram 1 was a preparatory draft for Diagram 2, it then follows that the latter has a logical contiguity with Diagram 3, while Diagram 4 belongs to a later stage of his analytical research.

---

17   "Analizzare una opera" (see note 8), p. 179.

It is most likely that when Maderna talks about this – to use his definition – "statistical" work, he is referring to the twentieth-century repertoire. The explicit reference to "series, sequences, and structures" seems to confirm this, along with the fact that his observations were originally destined to appear on the pages of a periodical like *Incontri Musicali.* Moreover, the reference to the "density of sound material" is a clear indication of that interest in sound mixtures and timbral combinations common to composers from the late nineteenth century onwards. This might thus lead us to wonder whether Maderna's words – probably referring to a coeval repertory – can be correctly applied to the analytical documents he drew up for *Don Giovanni.*

In truth, the operation of using analytical tools from post-World War II music to analyze earlier repertoires was quite common among composers of the time. Modern criteria were often employed in the rereading of the early twentieth-century repertoire, particularly that of the Second Viennese School.[18] This is what Massimiliano Locanto has to say on the subject:

> The growing propensity for theoretical reflection led the composers of the second postwar period to reread the works of the first half of the century using their own methodological approach, often adopting a point of view that was more formalized than the original concept. This attitude then reverberated on analytical-musical methodologies in general, and not just on those analyses which aimed more or less deliberately to justify the compositional methods of the present through an "appropriating" reinterpretation of the past.[19]

However, Maderna's analysis of *Don Giovanni* seems to overcome the chronological limits of such an assumption. In fact, we get the impression that he projects his experience as a serial composer well beyond the boundaries of the twentieth century, to apply them to the repertoire of the classical tradition. And his analysis certainly does not attempt to find any kind of justification or ennoblement through – to use Locanto's words – an "appropriating reinterpretation" of the canonical repertoire. Instead, Maderna seems to observe the music of the past under the lens of twentieth-century experience, that is to say, based on his personal experience as a composer and contemporary musician. His analysis of *Don Giovanni* seems to investigate a piece starting from the greatest maximum common denominator that unites past and present but which is – inevitably – contemporary. Thus, Maderna seems to be the perfect embodiment of a composer who, according to Gianmario Borio, "unconsciously uses, or intentionally thematizes, a conceptual apparatus he has developed, defined, and transformed with regard to his own material."[20]

Let us now try to extrapolate and clarify three elements of modernity that can be found in Maderna's analytical diagrams. For reasons of comprehensibility, I have adopted a schematic subdivision here, but it goes without saying that there is no rigid separation between elements that are never independent but overlap and interpenetrate each other.

---

18   For more on this, see Gianmario Borio, "L'Analyse musicale comme processus d'appropriation historique: Webern à Darmstadt," *Circuit: Musiques Contemporaines* 15, no. 3 (2005), pp. 87–122.

19   Massimiliano Locanto, "Composizione musicale e pensiero matematico: un percorso dal primo Novecento alla serialità integrale," in *La matematica,* ed. Claudio Bartocci and Piergiorgio Odifreddi, vol. 3: *Suoni, forme, parole* (Turin: Einaudi, 2011), pp. 73–116: 75.

20   Borio, "L'Analyse musicale" (see note 18), p. 88.

1) The first element of modernity in Maderna's analysis of *Don Giovanni* is above all the graphical form of the analytical diagrams. The tendency to organize the analysis in Cartesian grids is reflected in all the diagrams he prepared, albeit with different criteria and functions. It recalls the practice, developed in the fifties, of arranging precompositional material in so-called "magic squares," that is, the matrices of figures and symbols that were such a characteristic feature in the music of the Second Viennese School and, later, in that of integral serialism.

2) A second revealing glimpse of modernity can be seen in the attention Maderna pays to the timbral parameter, the focus of the first two diagrams (Exx. 1 and 2), which thus becomes a possible key to understanding the score. After having highlighted the orchestration of each single piece in the first diagram, he then goes on to group the numbers in timbral "classes," whose order follows a gradual increase in the orchestral blend and, moreover, gathers together the pieces belonging to the same timbral connotation. His obvious interest in timbre leads one to think that he considered it a special key to analyzing the work, or that it was, at the very least, just as valid as other more conventional ones.

The idea of adopting the timbre and instrument parameter as an analytical criterion had first been expressed in 1985 by Carl Dahlhaus, also for compositions from the classical period.[21] However, the structural character Maderna seems to attribute to the timbral element in his diagrams appears to be the hallmark of a twentieth-century musical heritage, or indeed to confirm his belonging to a historical moment in the emancipation of the sound parameter that was completely alien to Mozart's time.

3) Point 2 mentions the structural character Maderna assigns to timbre. And it is precisely this fundamentally structuralist approach that represents the third element of modernity in his analysis of Mozart's work. The first two diagrams in particular clearly show how Maderna not only subdivides the work into its different scenes but – more importantly – breaks down the sound material into single units of meaning. He then goes on to create formal architectures based on these previously identified sound parameters, so as to observe how they are structured in meaningful constructs.[22] His mainly constructivist orientation emerges from these diagrams, reminiscent of the principles of "semiological-structuralist" thought, which, after all, were also shared by integral serialism.[23]

---

21   See Carl Dahlhaus, "Zur Theorie der Instrumentation," *Die Musikforschung* 38, no. 3 (1985), pp. 161–69. The importance of timbre and orchestration in the classical era has been the subject of recent research also in Emily Dolan, *The Orchestral Revolution: Haydn and the Technologies of Timbre* (Cambridge: Cambridge University Press, 2013).

22   For more about these analytical procedures, see Nicholas Cook, *A Guide to Musical Analysis* (Oxford: Oxford University Press, 1994).

23   As Kaletha and Kohl state, "The formal conceptions of post-World War II serial music were influenced by phenomenology, in general conveyed rather indirectly via their reception in structural linguistics." See Holger Kaletha and Jerome Kohl, "Decomposition of the Sound Continuum: Serialism and Development from a Genetic Phenomenological Perspective," *Perspectives of New Music* 42, no. 1 (2004), pp. 84–128: 100. See also Philippe Albèra, "Modernità: il materiale sonoro," in *Enciclopedia della Musica*, ed. Jean-Jacques Nattiez, vol. 1: *Il Novecento* (Turin: Einaudi, 2001), pp. 119–37. In his "Il pensiero musicale della modernità nel triangolo di estetica, poetica e tecnica compositiva," Gianmario Borio has instead considered the relationship between structuralism and seriality, also giving an account of the historical debates on this theme: see *L'orizzonte filosofico del comporre nel ventesimo secolo*, ed. Gianmario Borio (Bologna: Il Mulino, 2003), pp. 1–47.

2 Fl.	2 Ob.	2 Cl.	2 Fg.	2 Hr	2 Tr.	Timp.	Archi	– Ouv. / 4 / 12 / 26
2 Fl.	2 Ob		2 Fg	2 Hr	2 Tr	Timp	Archi	– 24
2 Fl.	2 Ob		2 Fg.	2 Hr.			Archi	– 10 / 20
2 Fl.		2 Cl.	2 Fg.	2 Hr.			Archi	– 5 / 15 / 18
2 Fl.			2 Fg.	2 Hr.			Archi	– 2 / 6
	2 Ob		2 Fg.	2 Hr.			Archi	– 8 / 11 / 14 / 17
		2 Cl.	2 Fg.	2 Hr.			Archi	– 3
1 Fl.	2 Ob		2 Fg.	2 Hr.			Archi	– 1 / 19
1 Fl.	2 Ob	1 Cl.	2 Fg.	2 Hr.			Archi	– 23
	2 Ob	1 Cl.	2 Fg.	2 Hr.			Archi	– 9
1 Fl.	1 Ob		1 Fg.	2 Hr.			Archi	– 21
	2 Ob			2 Hr.			Archi	– 16
1 Fl.	2 Ob		2 Fg.				Archi	– 7
							Archi	– 13 /
							Archi	– 22 /
							Archi	– 25 /

EX. 5 Bruno Maderna, analytical diagram for Mozart's *La Clemenza di Tito;* PSS-BMC.

As mentioned previously, Maderna also applied some of these analytical procedures to other works by Mozart. The Maderna legacy contains two analytical diagrams for *Così fan tutte,* which was staged at Bologna's Teatro Comunale between 22 and 27 April 1970.[24] The first analysis is made up of three sheets of squared paper, where Maderna has subdivided the work into a total of thirty-one different scenes, indicating the characters and tonality for each one. The second diagram is written on a bifolio with staves and adds the vocal ranges of every single character to the information given in the previous schema.

Much more material and a greater number of analyses exist for *La Clemenza di Tito,* which Maderna conducted at the Juilliard American Opera Center in New York between 21 and 23 January 1971.[25] Among these documents, four present the same analytical models as the ones used for the two operas based on Da Ponte's librettos. Just as for *Così fan tutte,* a diagram divides the opera into scenes showing the relevant characters, instrumentation, tonality, page numbers in the score,[26] and – in this case – agogic indications. In contrast, the remaining three diagrams are similar to the ones prepared for *Don Giovanni,* although the analyses are somewhat less graphical in style and more like alphanumeric

---

24 Bruno Maderna's legacy also contains an annotated vocal score of *Così fan tutte* (Wiesbaden: Breitkopf & Härtel, n.d., publisher's No. 1666).

25 There are around seventy sheets that also contain Maderna's complete transcription of the libretto; PSS-BMC, "Textmanuskripte."

26 A total of six sheets of squared paper. Unlike the other two works by Mozart, no score for *La Clemenza di Tito* could be found in Maderna's legacy; nevertheless, in the top left-hand corner of the first sheet, Maderna does note that these are "Pag. della partitura NMA – Bärenr[eiter] V" (Pages from the New Mozart Edition score).

grids. Thus, his analysis of *La Clemenza di Tito* again contains a diagram that shows the instrumentation of each scene in the order in which the instruments appear in the work. The second document instead uses an additive principle to group the same scenes in a sort of upside-down pyramid, at whose base lie the pieces with the least timbral density, whereas the moments of maximum deployment of the orchestral forces are at the top (→ **EX. 5**). And exactly like the third diagram for *Don Giovanni,* the last grid shows the pieces sung by each character.

This rapid excursus through materials dedicated to other opera scores by Mozart further confirms our observations for *Don Giovanni.* The presence of these other diagrams means that the analytical process examined in Examples 1–4 can be cast as something that goes beyond a sporadic occurrence, dispelling any doubts of it being an exceptional case within Maderna's *modus operandi.* On the contrary, at least as far as the repertoire analyzed here is concerned, not only are the diagrams for *Così fan tutte* and *La Clemenza di Tito* proof of Maderna's analytical practice, but they also testify to that very twentieth-century interest in timbral parameters, as well as that fondness for formal and graphic architectures typical of the constructivist mentality of the time. This supports the hypothesis that similar analytical procedures are not therefore a direct consequence of the nature of the musical material in question, but rather evidence of a "self-reflective" approach that characterized Maderna's artistic personality.

However, what makes *Don Giovanni* such an interesting case is the extra analytical grid as compared to *Così fan tutte* and *La Clemenza di Tito.* The last diagram (Ex. 4) is the only one that adds a dramaturgical-expressive aspect to the analysis of the work. If we reconsider his remarks about musical interpretation,[27] we can see that the analyses of *Così fan tutte* and *La Clemenza di Tito* can be counted among those quantitative/statistical surveys he indicated as the first necessary, but not sufficient, stage in the understanding of a piece of music. In fact, these diagrams are essentially descriptive analyses, whereas only Diagram 4 for *Don Giovanni* offers an interpretive approach that pays more attention to dramaturgy.

The presence of this Diagram 4 becomes all the more interesting because it allows contemporary exegetes to make progress in investigating the Madernian analytical process, as it evolves from a descriptive method to a much stricter interpretive procedure. What is more, Diagram 4 gives us an extraordinary insight into the impact the twentieth century had on Maderna's analysis, demonstrating how much it owes to contemporary critical literature, the source of many of the main themes he takes up when carrying out his analysis of Mozart's works and *Don Giovanni* in particular. Maderna's analytical diagrams for this work manifest a formal architecture in which, as we have already seen, the graphic and spatial aspect plays a major role. Let us recall how the characters were arranged in Diagrams 3 and 4: first, the central position occupied by Don Giovanni indicates the particular importance of this eponymous character in the work and his role as the fulcrum of the action, an aspect that had already been pointed out in the fifties by the Austrian philosopher and sociologist Alfred Schutz:

---

27   See above, quote related with note 17.

> All the other characters in the opera receive their force from Don Giovanni. His life is the efficient principle for the life of all the others, his passion makes all the others move. It is echoed by the earnestness of the Commendatore, the ire of Elvira, the hatred of Anna, the gravity of Octavio, the anxiety of Zerlina, the confusion of Leporello.[28]

But the main character's central position is also symbolic of how he becomes the meeting point, or better the keystone, for that mixture of comedy and tragedy in *Don Giovanni*. It is no mere coincidence that both diagrams place the nobles from *opera seria* (the Commendatore, Don Ottavio, Donna Anna, and Donna Elvira) to the left of Don Giovanni, while the common and comic characters – Leporello, Zerlina, and Masetto – are positioned in the right-hand columns. Such a division could even suggest a possible "political-social" reading of the work by Maderna, similar to what Frits Noske published in the same years about Mozart's *Le nozze di Figaro*.[29] Nonetheless, such a division between high-ranking and humble characters could actually reflect and underline the form and quality of their dramatic-musical roles rather than their social status – let us not forget that the vocally demanding arias, the closest elements to *opera seria* features, are sung by the "noble" characters, while the folk motifs and dance rhythms of *opera buffa* are generally left to those of humbler origins.

This mixture of social aspects and vocal-dramatic characteristics was already noted by Christopher Ballantine:

> [Anna's and Elvira's] music is in *seria* style: they are noble ladies who speak in the accents of a dying aristocratic world. Giovanni sings of course from within a more *buffo* tradition; as such, his musical style itself enacts the social dimensions of the assaults to which his behavior bears concrete witness, since his language – just as much as his profligacy – is both a product and a symbol of the Enlightenment, and of the Revolution to which it was giving birth.[30]

Thus, dramatic and lyrical-sentimental characters are typically placed on the left in Diagram 4 while the characters on the right share a comic and licentious style. Don Giovanni, placed at the center of the diagram, also graphically represents the traits of a transitional role between the two genres, and he is the only character to embody them in their entirety (sometimes managing, as happens for example in the two final acts, to be comic, dramatic, and licentious all at the same time). Within the age-old debate on the exact genre of Mozart's *dramma giocoso*, Maderna – and also Massimo Mila, who will write down his interpretation in 1988, in his book on *Don Giovanni* – adopted a position that stood midway between the Anglo-Saxon reading of the work, which tended only to recognize its funny elements, and its – mainly German – Romantic elevation to the drama of the Rake Punished.[31] By shedding light on the different characters attributed to each group, Diagram 4 allows us to take a deeper look at the perfect, almost symmetrical, formal balance

---

28   Alfred Schutz, "Mozart and the Philosophers," *Social Research* 23, no. 2 (1956), pp. 219–42: 230.
29   See Frits Noske, "Social Tensions in *Le nozze di Figaro*," *Music and Letters* 50, no. 1 (1969), pp. 45–62.
30   Christopher Ballantine, "Social and Philosophical Outlook in Mozart's Operas," *The Musical Quarterly* 67, no. 4 (1981), pp. 507–26: 516.
31   For a general overview see Massimo Mila, *Lettura del Don Giovanni di Mozart* (Turin: Einaudi, 1988), which is still a valid research tool.

highlighted in Diagram 3, created by the combination and alternation of the individual interventions by both the serious and funny characters.

However, Diagram 4 also prompts us to take a further step forward in observing Maderna's analytical thinking. It seems quite reasonable to ask whether one can demonstrate any kind of relationship between the quantitative studies on timbre and the specific importance of each character (Exx. 1–3) and the dramatic interpretation given in the last analytical grid (Ex. 4). If this were possible, then one could hypothesize, in particular, that Maderna may have exploited the timbral parameter to bring to light remote allusions hidden within the score, and to show unexpected connections between distant scenes and unforeseen links between the characters.

It is difficult to ascertain whether any eventual investigation based on orchestral colors could really produce concrete results in unveiling the dramaturgy. If we limit our study to the mere observation of the connections that emerge in Maderna's Diagram 2, it is still not that easy to identify connections between scenes like – to give just one example – the trio "Ah taci, ingiusto core" (II/2) and Zerlina's aria "Vedrai carino" (II/5). Such pieces are profoundly distant in terms of dramatic importance and formal structure, but, at the same time, they are the only ones to be characterized by an accompaniment of strings, flutes, clarinets, bassoons, and horns. Notwithstanding this, Maderna's analytical endeavor does not appear to be an isolated case, since support for this kind of analysis came from a long exegetical tradition that had arisen within pro-Wagnerian musicology in the period between the two wars, to then assert itself in the course of the twentieth century.[32] In fact, Mozart's use of tonality to characterize his works and build real dramaturgical architectures had been the subject of lengthy discussion. The opening words of Joseph Kerman's chapter on Mozart in his celebrated volume *Opera as Drama* already underline the fact that "The late eighteenth-century solution to the problem of action and the musical continuity found its consummation in the operas of Mozart."[33] In the following decades, David Rosen, in his *The Classical Style*, also talked about a "total conception of the opera in which everything is related to a central tonality, which itself has, not only a symbolic reference, but an individual sonority that it seems to evoke,"[34] referring in particular to the D-major tonality on which the entire work seems to be constructed. This argument was later taken up by Stefan Kunze, who would consider the aforementioned tonality as a sort of "tonic key" of the entire work and as dramaturgically related to the negative image of Don Giovanni.[35] And despite the frequent refutation of this analytical approach in recent decades, dismissed as a groundless attempt to apply a romantic, organismic, and evolutionary aesthetic to eighteenth-century music,[36] it cer-

---

32   See James Webster, "Mozart's Operas and the Myth of Musical Unity," *Cambridge Opera Journal* 2, no. 2 (1990), pp. 197–218.

33   Joseph Kerman, *Opera as Drama* (London: Oxford University Press, 1957), p. 99; new and revised edn. (Berkeley: University of California Press, 1988), p. 80.

34   David Rosen, *The Classical Style: Haydn, Mozart, Beethoven*, enlarged edn. (New York and London: W.W. Norton, 1997), p. 299 (1st edn. 1971).

35   See Stefan Kunze, *Mozarts Opern* (Stuttgart: Reclam, 1984, pp. 330ff.).

36   As well as the previously cited Webster (see note 32), see John Platoff, "Myths and Realities about Tonal Planning in Mozart's Operas," *Cambridge Opera Journal* 8, no. 1 (1996), pp. 3–15, and Carolyn Abbate and Roger Parker, "Dismembering Mozart," ibid. 2, no. 2 (1990), pp. 187–95.

tainly had an influence on the interpretation Maderna proposed for Don Giovanni. His Mozartian analyses thus show an analytical reading whose origins do not just stem from the purely twentieth-century approach of Maderna the composer, but also from Maderna the exegete, the product of the cultural breeding ground of his time.

By indicating the tone of every piece in the opera along the side of the diagram, Maderna seems to want to underline an integral part of the definition of each specific orchestral color. And although a comparison of sound mixtures and tonal structures does not produce any concrete results in revealing interconnections between the pieces of the work, this does not mean that Maderna did not at least try to establish some relations between the sound material that he had analyzed in a "statistical" form and the opera's dramaturgy. The lack of any sound recordings is most unfortunate because they could certainly play a key role in solving such dilemmas, allowing us to dispel any doubts regarding possible interpretive connections between pieces that are apparently distant in terms of their dramaturgical situation or sound dimension.

To narrow the field of conjectures, let us just limit ourselves to saying what Maderna's analytical schemes do impart, that is, the unmistakable homogeneity in the formal organization of the analytical schemes. As mentioned previously, the choice of Cartesian-style grids, the focus on the tonal parameter, and the general structuralist imprint that permeates all the analyses in question are all aspects that allow us to determine the solid twentieth-century roots of both Maderna's approach and his model for interpreting the dramaturgical perspective, further supported by approaches which were often suggested in contemporary analytical literature. Ultimately, his analysis of *Don Giovanni* could finally be reasonable proof of "the outcome of the encounter between the horizon of the compositional problems facing the interpreter and the set of questions posed and answered by the analyzed compositions."[37]

Massimo Mila's remarks on Maderna's constant commitment to the transmission and dissemination of musical compositions of every era immediately spring to mind, when he spoke of a "constant presence of the past within the most audacious exploration of the future."[38] And not only is this hypothesis quite acceptable, but – in the light of the documents discussed here – it deserves to be taken further, through a logical extension that works backwards: Maderna, who sets about analyzing Mozart scores with the typical instruments of the post-war composer, actually evokes the idea of a constant presence of the present within the exploration of the past – an exploration that, while perhaps eluding definition as "audacious," is nevertheless original in the way it is proposed. It clearly shows that not only do the present and the past complement each other and merge together within Maderna's artistic activity, but also that the role of composer and conductor – the former usually attributed to the here and now, the latter to a corpus that is established over time – are actually two complementary and inseparable parts. The analysis of *Don Giovanni* thus shows the manifestation of a process that synthesizes roles and temporal categories, and which, in the case of Maderna, seems to lead us right back to the etymology of the verb "compose," whose original meaning was *to put together* or *to unite* different elements.

---

37 Borio, "L'Analyse musicale" (see note 18), p. 90.
38 Mila, *Maderna musicista europeo* (see note 3), p. 6.

LEO IZZO

Bruno Maderna and His Arrangements

In the early 1960s, Maderna produced a large number of arrangements to be broadcast on radio and recorded on albums, indirectly becoming part of a cultural movement intent on renewing the Italian popular music scene. This important arranging experience evolved out of two occasions that had to do with the main media of popular music, that is, radio and records. In 1960 he took part in the launch of a radio musical program entitled *Arcidiapason*, and a few years later, in 1964, he recorded two LPs dedicated to Kurt Weill's songs, performed by Laura Betti.[1] Maderna's temporary foray into the world of popular music coincided with a period of fervent musical activity and multiple commitments and projects. These include the composition of *Don Perlimplin*, the writing of various pieces that were later merged into the *Hyperion* cycle, intense activity as a conductor, collaboration with several radio productions, the creation of a number of compositions for the theater, and his experiences in the field of electronic experimentation, conducted at the RAI's Studio di Fonologia in Milan.

It is not surprising to find that Maderna, one of the leading composers of the European musical avant-garde, was quite familiar with the world of song, or so-called "light" music. Entertainment music had been part of Maderna's biographical horizon since childhood. Jazz music (in its various forms), popular music, and hit songs were in fact the repertoires played by his father's band, "The Happy Grossato Company – Original Jazz Band." At the age of ten, Maderna had for a short time been the band's main performer as violinist and *enfant prodige*.[2] Throughout his working life as a composer – from the jazz style he used in his first radio drama *Il mio cuore è nel Sud* (1949) to the embedded quotes of *Satyricon* (1972–73) – the traces of this link with popular or jazz culture are easy to see. In several works one can even observe a genuine act of "mediation" between languages whose different origins and rules make them apparently irreconcilable.

The rich heritage of Maderna's song arrangements is still a well-kept secret. The arrangements based on popular songs, entertainment, or jazz written in the early 1960s to be broadcast on radio – as demonstrated by a number of recordings preserved in the RAI archives and by numerous manuscript scores, some of which have only just come to

Many thanks to Maria Maddalena Novati, curator of the RAI Studio di Fonologia Archives, Milan, for all her help and cooperation during the phases of this research. My heartfelt thanks also go to Angela Ida De Benedictis, who followed the different stages in the elaboration of this text, sharing valuable information and offering important food for thought.

1   *Kurt Weill 1900–1933: Cantato da Laura Betti, diretto da Bruno Maderna, presentato da Roberto Leydi, con la partecipazione di Vittorio De Sica* [1964], Ricordi SMRL 6031 (LP), and *Kurt Weill, 1933–1950: Cantato da Laura Betti, diretto da Bruno Maderna, presentato da Roberto Leydi* [1964], Ricordi SMRL 6032 (LP).

2   Regarding this, see my "'Espressioni jazzistiche in un clima d'arte': la sintesi di Bruno Maderna," in *Bruno Maderna e l'Italia musicale degli anni '40*, ed. Gabriele Bonomo and Fabio Zannoni (Milan: Suvini Zerboni, 2012), pp. 97–114. A photo of the "Happy Grossato Band" with a very young Maderna on the violin appears on p. 98.

light[3] – continue to be the domain of just a few specialized scholars. Even those very LPs dedicated to Kurt Weill's songs – which, on the contrary, did enjoy a wider circulation – have followed the same path toward an inevitable oblivion: never published in digital format, they are nowadays mostly considered cult objects for ardent collectors.

There are a number of reasons that make this albeit incomplete corpus of arrangements so important. The first of these belongs to a purely biographical sphere: all together, Maderna's arrangements amount to more than forty audio documents and manuscripts, thus representing a quite substantial part of his compositional work, concentrated in a short four-year period between 1960 and 1964. The second reason is linked instead to a qualitative observation: Maderna took the unusual task of arranging very seriously, paying great attention to detail. His arrangements share little of the routine nature of a great deal of popular music and stand out for their innovation and originality. They include several authentic masterpieces of this genre that deserve a diffusion beyond musicologists or Maderna scholars. A third reason is instead specifically related to Italian cultural history. The rapid changes in social fabric that came about in the early 1960s also affected the cultural products conveyed by the mass media, and the majority of Italian musicologists and music critics viewed popular music with suspicion. Criticism of "light" or "consumer" music came from two opposing fronts.[4] On the one hand, the first reception of Adorno's writings on music, which were just starting to appear in Italian translation, stoked the condemnation of popular music as standardized and alienating music.[5] On the other, the militant folk revival movement, associated with the rediscovery of oral music and protest songs, criticized popular music, known as *canzonette* or "escapist songs," because such music was misleading, detached from reality, and subject to mass standardization by the entertainment industry. Nonetheless, and in spite of the widespread aversion to popular music on the part of intellectuals (and not only them), there were a few publications on popular music that distanced themselves from militant ideologisms or the dogmatism of Adorno's reception. It is no coincidence that these contributions came from composers or musicologists who were very close to Maderna, such as Massimo Mila, whose articles appeared in the weekly magazine *L'Espresso* in the 1950s; Roberto Leydi, with his book on American song; and Luciano Berio, with his 1967 watershed article, "Commenti al rock."[6]

---

3   See the list of sources indicated in the Appendix to this essay (pp. 271–74).

4   For a brief but well-documented account of the positions of intellectuals with regard to popular music in the 1950s and 1960s see Roberto Agostini, "Alla ricerca della 'voce del popolo,'" in *Popular music e musica popolare: Riflessioni ed esperienze a confronto*, ed. Nicola Scaldaferri and Alessandro Rigolli (Venice: Marsilio; Parma: Casa della Musica, 2010), pp. 31–55. A similar perspective is also found in the chapter "Gli intellettuali e la canzone" in Jacopo Tomatis, *Storia culturale della canzone italiana* (Milan: il Saggiatore, 2019), pp. 211–82.

5   Three major translations of Theodor W. Adorno's essays were published in the space of just a few years: "Moda senza tempo: sul jazz," *Questioni* 6, nos. 5–6 (1958), orig. "Zeitlose Mode: Zum Jazz" (1953); *Filosofia della musica moderna*, with an introductory essay by Luigi Rognoni, trans. Giacomo Manzoni (Turin: Einaudi, 1959), orig. *Philosophie der neuen Musik* (1949); and *Dissonanze*, ed. Giacomo Manzoni (Milan: Feltrinelli, 1959) orig. *Dissonanzen* (1956).

6   See respectively Massimo Mila, "Le canzoni di Sanremo e quelle di Modugno," *L'Espresso* (18 March 1956), and "Per la bonifica della canzone," ibid. (23 March 1958), repr. in idem, *Cronache musicali 1955–1959* (Turin: Einaudi, 1959), pp. 502–05 and 506–08; Roberto Leydi, *Eroi e fuorilegge della ballata popolare americana* (Milan: Ricordi, 1958); and Luciano Berio, "Commenti al rock," *Nuova rivista musicale italiana* 1, no. 1 (1967), pp. 125–35, repr. in idem, *Scritti sulla musica*, ed. Angela Ida De Benedictis (Turin: Einaudi, 2013), pp. 108–20.

As someone who had been around different musical languages since he was a child, this variegated cultural context afforded Maderna a privileged and unbiased position from which to consider the world of song. His arrangements for radio, television, and his two LPs move with ease between different genres, from light opera to Weill, from popular and vernacular song to Broadway, continually crossing in both directions the assumed border that separates "high" and "low" culture, "art" and "popular" production, or even songwriters' artifacts and light music. Listening to these rediscovered arrangements today allows us to appreciate the farsightedness of the mediation between different musical and cultural worlds that Maderna carried out at a time when these spheres were still having difficulty in communicating with each other.

Arrangements for Radio

On 10 January 1960, *Radiocorriere*, the weekly information magazine of Italian radio and television (RAI), announced a new music program called *Arcidiapason*. The program, writes Salvatore Biamonte, intended to bring "a degree of great formal dignity to light music performances," offering "the greatest variety of repertoire" with musicians from different backgrounds being invited to collaborate each time.[7] The title of the broadcast was a direct reference to a successful music television program *Diapason*, which had aired in 1955 and which had offered viewers an overview of the latest musical trends with no genre boundaries, passing from Italian and French song (with Nilla Pizzi and Juliette Gréco) to jazz (with Claude Luter's orchestra) to electronic music (for example, the program presented excerpts of "short compositions of concrete and electronic music" presumably recorded in what would then officially become the RAI's Studio di Fonologia, Milan).[8]

Arcidiapason, however, promised to leave behind "the compromise of the so-called 'symphonic rhythms'" and to aim for "real concerts of light music."[9] Two of the arrangers involved in the program, Gino Marinuzzi Jr. and Mario Migliardi, were already known to the radio audience for their orchestral reinterpretations of hit songs. In their *Fantasia*

---

7   Salvatore Biamonte, "Arcidiapason," *Radiocorriere* 2 (1960), p. 15. All editions of *Radiocorriere* are now also available online at http://www.radiocorriere.teche.rai.it/.

8   See Alberto Tapparo, "Diapason," *Radiocorriere* 34 (1955), p. 14.

9   Biamonte, "Arcidiapason" (see note 7). The term "symphonic rhythm" in the quotation refers to a hybrid genre that enjoyed a certain popularity in the period between the 1940s and 1960s. Its repertoire included symphonic orchestrations of hit songs or compositions for large orchestra with jazz influences. The model for the rhythmic-symphonic genre was George Gershwin's *Rhapsody in Blue*, commissioned in 1924 by Paul Whiteman, a leading exponent of the so-called "symphonic jazz." In Italy "rhythmic-symphonic" music was mainly broadcast on radio (and later on television). The RAI had specialized orchestras ("rhythmic," "jazz," etc.) that mainly offered the general public refined orchestrations of well-known tunes. In the 1960s many intellectuals were highly critical of these operations with which pop music, albeit in a new orchestral guise, was associated with the sacredness of the symphonic concert. As Maurizio Corbella also points out on p. 120 of his "Il podio e lo schermo: La musica per film nella programmazione delle orchestre sinfoniche EIAR e RAI," in *La politica sinfonica della RAI: Storia delle orchestre radio-televisive italiane*, ed. Andrea Malvano (Alessandria: Edizioni dell'Orso, 2016), pp. 119–53, an example of this phenomenon is captured in the words of Umberto Eco, who, in defining the concept of "bad taste," refers precisely to the rhythmic-symphonic genre "for its desire to amalgamate the pleasures of dance music, the boldness of jazz, and the dignity of classical symphonism." See "La struttura del cattivo gusto," in Umberto Eco, *Apocalittici e integrati* (Milan: Bompiani, 1964), pp. 65–129: 127.

della domenica radio program, broadcast the previous year, they had presented "musical entertainment" based on a "wide assortment of pieces, from Neapolitan song to swing music from overseas, blended in a single score."[10]

Arcidiapason's real novelty lay in the presence of Bruno Maderna, described in Biamonte's article as "one of the most active 'serious' musicians of the contemporary school."[11] More specifically as regards his contribution to the radio broadcast, we are told that

> for *Arcidiapason* his attention is focused above all on the extremely rich heritage of our authentic folk songs. These motifs will be presented in an orchestral version that is harmoniously enriched, but which respects their original characteristics. As well as these performances for large orchestra, we will hear others by small, elegant ensembles and yet again others that will revisit the theme of Kurt Weill's famous "popular operas."[12]

In a later article by Alfredo Cucchiara, always on the pages of *Radiocorriere*, ample space is dedicated to the program, arriving at a sort of ambitious declaration of intent that merits being read in full.[13] The RAI, we read, aimed at improving the quality of interpretation: "As far as the field of light music is concerned, which is the one that interests us the most at the moment, the attempts to raise its standards, bringing its performances to a level of genuine artistic dignity, have to date almost always turned into a kind of super-decorativism." On the contrary, *Arcidiapason* stood out for its clear educational objectives, and Cucchiara tells us that one of the program's aims was to "educate the listener's ear to a more complex and modern musical language, which cannot be just a schematic melody with accompaniment, but which instead is made up of instrumental and harmonic subtleties, of rhythmic and timbral discoveries, of humorous and even parodic emphasis." In the journalist's opinion, the outcome was guaranteed by the encounter between musicians from different backgrounds: "It is a musical show, alternately entrusted to musicians of the light genre, of extremely modern instrumental sensitivity, and to young orchestral conductors who, brought up in the school of classical music, are now also testing themselves in this field, bringing with them the taste, the wisdom, and elegance of high composition." Finally, the article evoked the idea of musical "divertimento," of potpourri and "fantasy" music, "because one should talk of a modern form of musical fantasy for these concerts, which draw their lifeblood from the best Italian and foreign song, operetta, and jazz repertoires."

According to what we can read in *Radiocorriere*, it seems that Maderna participated in three hour-long broadcasts on 4 and 11 February and 17 March 1960, transmitted in prime time on the Second Program. The musical pieces were interspersed with some short texts by Mino Caudana (a popular journalist and television writer), read by the actor Stefano Sibaldi (who had dubbed Frank Sinatra). This information does not allow us in any way to determine the total number of popular music tracks Maderna arranged for radio. A substantial number of arrangements have nevertheless been preserved in the form

---

10   G. C., "Ore 13:25: appuntamento col 'Nazionale,'" *Radiocorriere* 3 (1959), p. 14.

11   Biamonte, "Arcidiapason" (see note 7).

12   Ibid.

13   For this and the following quotations see Alfredo Cucchiara, "Arcidiapason," *Radiocorriere* 13 (1960), p. 36.

of a sound document. The audio recordings, housed in the Archives of RAI's Studio di Fonologia in Milan, are contained on three different magnetic tapes (currently catalogued as "Fon. 091," "Fon. 098," and "Fon. 099"; see also the Appendix to this essay).[14] The second of these reels plays a particularly important role, since it is the only one to have an edited version of a complete episode of the *Arcidiapason* program. The musical episodes alternate with and overlap the speaker's voice on the tape. Instead, "Fon. 091" and "Fon. 099" only contain recordings of the musical pieces, without any spoken interventions. The reels are not accompanied by any recording sheets or documents detailing the contents, so it is impossible to know exactly how the tracks recorded on these last two tapes were used in this or other broadcasts. In fact, Maderna took part in two other similar radio programs after the *Arcidiapason* experience, but these recordings are missing: *Musica in frack* (aired on 30 September and 7 October 1962) and *Piccolo concerto* (aired on 7 March and 4 April 1964). It is most likely that some of the recordings made in 1960 for *Arcidiapason* may also have been reused for these (or other) subsequent transmissions.

These audio documents are accompanied by a number of autograph scores, some of which have long been housed in the composer's autograph collection at the Paul Sacher Foundation in Basel, while others have been identified relatively recently in the RAI's historical archives in Turin.[15] The chance to access both audio and paper documents "in Maderna's hand" (with Maderna conducting his own arrangements in the audio sources) has allowed us to stretch the interpretive boundaries of this research to the utmost.

An overview of the available audio and paper documents reveals a wide range of song forms and uses. Generally speaking, we can identify four different groups.

The first and most substantial group includes songs of international scope, with a predilection for American songs from the 1930s. They are mostly sentimental pieces, performed in slow or moderate tempo, originally made popular by a musical film or revue: *Mad About the Boy,* written by Noël Coward in 1932 for the London premiere of the musical revue *Words and Music; I Only Have Eyes For You* by Harry Warren with lyrics by Al Dubin, written for the 1934 film *Dames;* and *You Are My Lucky Star,* composed by Nacio Herb Brown with lyrics by Arthur Freed for the 1936 film *Broadway Melody.* We

---

14   A brief description of the content of these reels is in *The Studio di Fonologia: A Musical Journey 1954–1983: Update 2008–2012,* ed. Maria Maddalena Novati and John Dack (Milan: Ricordi, 2009), pp. 237–38. The first systematic work on these recordings was carried out by Maurizio Romito, "I commenti musicali di Bruno Maderna: radio, televisione, teatro," *Nuova Rivista Musicale Italiana* 34 (2000), pp. 233–68 (I), and 36 (2000), pp. 79–98 (II). At the time of his research, the scores of Maderna's arrangements had yet to be identified in the RAI archives, and in order to identify the titles of the songs arranged by Maderna, Romito carried out a patient and painstaking aural comparison between the recordings kept at the RAI and the knowledge of popular music tunes before 1960. My gratitude and recognition go to the author for having conducted a practically limitless research project, whose results are still indispensable today for any subsequent studies on these topics.

15   Andrea Malvano's book on the role of arrangers in the history of Italian radio contains a chapter dedicated to *Il fondo "Maderna,"* that is, to the handwritten scores of Maderna's radio arrangements housed in the RAI Archives, Turin. See Andrea Malvano, *L'arte di arrangiar(si): Trascrizioni e adattamenti storici dell'Archivio musicale Rai* (Lucca: LIM; Rome: RAI-ERI, 2015), pp. 228–39. On the correspondence between the audio sources and the autograph manuscripts preserved in the two archives cited in the text, see the Appendix at the end of this essay.

also find two Cole Porter classics: *In the Still of the Night,* composed in 1937 for the film *Rosalie,* and *Begin the Beguine* which was then used in the 1935 production of the Broadway show *Jubilee.* The latter song shares its Caribbean mood with the orchestral version of a Brazilian popular music classic, *Na baixa do sapateiro* (also known under the alternative title of *Bahia*) by Ary Barroso. On the edge of this close-knit group we find three songs whose origins have nothing to do with the American musical: a curious translation in Italian of *Ich küsse Ihre Hand, Madame,* a tango composed by Ralph Erwin with lyrics by Fritz Rotter, which had sprung to international fame through the 1929 film with the same title; *Paradise,* composed by Nacio Herb Brown, who co-authored the lyrics with Gordon Clifford for the 1932 film *A Woman Commands;* and again *Sweet and Lovely* by Gus Arnheim, Charles N. Daniels, and Harry Tobias (1931). In this group, the dance songs and ones with a steady rhythm are decidedly fewer and can be traced back to a previous period of American song. These include *Darktown Strutters' Ball,* composed by Shelton Brooks and made famous by the Original Dixieland Jass Band in 1917; and *Yes Sir! That's My Baby* by Walter Donaldson with lyrics by Gus Kahn (1925), whose title in the Italian version was *Lola,* translated by Angelo Ramiro Borella (a song which owes its popularity in the early 1950s to the version by the Duo Fasano).

The second group concerns Italian song, which, in its regional variations, inevitably had an important role in the program. Although Maderna's arrangements of Italian songs are not so many, the ones that appeared on the program trace a very clear historical arc. One of the arrangements is a dense potpourri dedicated to the heritage of songs in Romanesco, the dialect spoken in the city of Rome, which, starting from the revisitation of the tradition of *stornelli* folk songs of the 1920s, arrives at songs by modern-day singer-songwriters. Several pieces stand out in this orchestral "fantasy," for example, *Nannì ('Na gita a li Castelli)* by Franco Silvestri (1929); *Quanto sei bella Roma (canta se la vuoi cantà)* by Cesare Andrea Bixio (lyrics by Enzo Bonagura, 1943); *La Romanina* by Eldo Di Lazzaro (with lyrics by Giuseppe and Renato Micheli, 1937); and *Arrivederci Roma* by Renato Rascel (lyrics by Pietro Garinei and Sandro Giovannini, 1955). Maderna returns to the origins of the *canzone d'autore* (songwriter genre) with the orchestral version of the 1918 classic *Come pioveva!…* by Armando Gill (Michele Testa's *nom de plume*), which historically represents the moment when Neapolitan song was emancipated from the use of dialect. This excursus also includes an example of the reception of the syncopated rhythms of jazz (*Op! Op! Trotta cavallino,* composed in 1942 by Gorni Kramer with lyrics by Enrico Frati) and closes with a masterly touch in an exuberant orchestral version of the still legendary song, *Nel blu, dipinto di blu,* with which Domenico Modugno had won the Sanremo Italian Song Festival in 1958.

It is not hard to imagine that in the listening horizon of that era, such a heterogeneous mixture of songs, the quintessence of a light-hearted, tuneful and sentimental, picture-perfect Italianness, also carried other emotional values. For many radio listeners, and indeed for Maderna himself, feelings of nostalgia also connected these pieces with the recent past. Many of the older songs had enjoyed enormous radio success during the fascist regime and the war, becoming a symbol or a means of escape shared by the entire nation. And the very songs that came out after the war were enshrined in the wake of the (necessary) "light-hearted song" that accompanied the first decades of the post-war period.

The third group concerns the legacy of operetta, in particular Franz Lehár's *Die lustige Witwe*. Here too Maderna acted as a mediator between "high" and "low" culture, creating a well-structured orchestral potpourri in which some famous tunes (the romance "Wie eine Rosenknospe," the theme of the "Lippen schweigen" duet, and the dance scene from the third act) are interspersed with new inserts composed from scratch for the occasion.

Finally, the fourth group is a tribute to Kurt Weill, rendered through three excerpts from *Die Dreigroschenoper: Die Moritat von Mackie Messer, Die Ballade von der sexuellen Hörigkeit*, and *Die Zuhälterballade*. We can suppose that the insertion of these songs in a radio broadcast like *Arcidiapason* was close to Maderna's heart. In fact, it was a great chance to extend the reception of Kurt Weill's music from the small circle of the Italian intellectual elite to the far larger radio audience. A few years earlier, in 1956, Maderna had conducted the orchestra in the memorable Italian premiere of the *Dreigroschenoper* (translated as *Opera da tre soldi*), staged at Milan's Piccolo Teatro under the direction of Giorgio Strehler, a performance which had enthused Bertolt Brecht himself.[16] It marked the beginning of a fundamental phase in the renewal of Italian theater that followed a long period when, at the height of the Cold War, political reasons brought the Italian government to veto the work of the German playwright.[17] Furthermore, on 18 February 1958, Maderna conducted the Italian premiere of the musical *Knickerbocker Holiday* for the national radio program, an event that was widely covered on the pages of *Radiocorriere*.[18]

Three other pieces that do not draw directly upon the field of popular music are found among the available manuscript materials and should be included in this overview of song typologies: *Arianna*, music by Mario Migliardi with an arrangement by Maderna; the song *Aspettare*, composed by Maderna himself in 1959 for the radio comedy *Aspetto*

---

16 Contemporary criticism immediately recognized the importance of this Italian production, and a book was published a few years later with some reports and documents about the staging of the opera. See *L'Opera da tre soldi di Bertolt Brecht e Kurt Weill: Uno spettacolo del Piccolo teatro di Milano*, ed. Giorgio Guazzotti (Bologna: Cappelli, 1961). More information about the reception of Weill and Brecht's opera can be found in Stephen Hinton, "The Première and after," in *Kurt Weill: The Threepenny Opera*, ed. Stephen Hinton (Cambridge: Cambridge University Press, 1990), pp. 50–77.

17 For the Milan production, the composers Vittorio Fellegara and Gino Negri prepared a revisitation of the orchestration. In an article published a few years after the staging at the Piccolo Teatro, Luigi Pestalozza recalls that Fellegara and Negri considerably reduced the number of instruments envisaged in the score published by Universal Edition, using a total of nine orchestral elements better suited to the reduced spaces of the Piccolo Teatro (see Luigi Pestalozza, "La realizzazione," in *L'Opera da tre soldi* (see note 16), pp. 149–55: 151). The different backgrounds of the musicians who formed the Piccolo Teatro ensemble was in itself a factor of great novelty in the cultural panorama of the time. Jazz musicians, such as trombonist Athos Ceroni, guitarist Filippo Daccò, trumpeter Fermo Lini, and saxophonist Fausto Papetti, shared the orchestra pit with classical musicians, such as trumpeter Anania Battagliola, cellist Ferruccio Arcaini, and composer Giacomo Manzoni, here as pianist (replaced by Aldo Clementi in the 1958 revival; see ibid., pp. 125–28). The rather unusual conditions in which the musicians were prepared for the Milanese orchestration, with some of them playing more than one instrument bent, actually inadvertently resembled the conditions of the first staging of the opera, for which Weill had asked only seven musicians to play the parts of more than twenty; see Stephen Hinton, "*Die Dreigroschenoper*: The 1928 Full Score," in Kurt Weill and Bertolt Brecht, *Die Dreigroschenoper: A Facsimile of the Holograph Full Score*, ed. Edward Harsh (New York: Kurt Weill Foundation for Music; Valley Forge: European American Music Corporation, 1996), pp. 5–8.

18 See Remo Giazotto, "*Knickerbocker Holiday*," *Radiocorriere* (22 February 1958), pp. 3–4 and 12–13.

Matilde by Enzo Maurri;[19] and *Ora mi alzo,* the first of the two songs composed by Berio for *Allez-hop,* a mimed tale based on a work by Italo Calvino, performed on 21 September 1959 at the Teatro La Fenice in Venice.[20]

On the whole, the choice of pieces seems to have been inspired by an idea of great diversity, designed to offer an overview of the variety of forms that popular songs have assumed throughout history and in the most diverse cultural contexts. This principle is also reflected in the style of the arrangements, i.e. in the way in which Maderna handles the starting materials. The scores abound in moments of stylistic grafting with unexpected outcomes that disorientate the listener, as happens, for example, in *Come pioveva!...,* where, in the space of just a few bars, a Neapolitan melody turns into a song with expressionist hues, or when a motif of a Romanesco song is transformed into orchestral excerpts with a Stravinsky flavor.

By virtue of this tendency toward a plurality of styles, the "sound scenarios" of some arrangements present a series of rapid and continuous changes, their original melodies seeming to succumb to the centripetal force of a polystylistic divertissement: one example is the carousel of jazz-influenced variations in *Die Moritat von Mackie Messer.* Sometimes Maderna deliberately oversteps the normal role of an arranger,[21] since he does not limit himself to making orchestral revisitations that strictly adhere to the original idea of a piece, or which are slavishly anchored to maintaining the melodic and harmonic structures and mood. Quite often, he constructs unrestrained "divertissements" that follow divergent and unpredictable trajectories with respect to the musical starting material. In these cases, Maderna's contribution is more a rewriting than an arrangement in the real sense of the word, and the score suddenly moves away from the initial musical idea, venturing into newly composed lengthy contrapuntal sections that have little in common with the original matrix. These moments of digression are some of the most innovative aspects of these radio scores: listening to some excerpts from the aforementioned sound sources, one gets the impression that Maderna handled the original themes by assimilating and incorporating them in his own expressive sphere; in this way he has given his own indelible signature style to some arrangements, managing to reinterpret the arranger's role beyond any conventional clichés. And this tendency becomes even more evident in purely instrumental pieces or excerpts, especially those in *tempo moderato.*

An emblematic case in this regard is the instrumental arrangement of *Come pioveva!...* In the first exposition the motif stands out clearly: the melody of the verse is assigned to a mincing violin, while the vaguely caricatural tones of a tuba become apparent in the refrain (→ **EX. 1**).

---

19   See Angela Ida De Benedictis, *Radiodramma e arte radiofonica: Storia e funzioni della musica per radio in Italia* (Turin: De Sono, EDT, 2004), pp. 128–29 and 245–46. The songs *Aspettare* and *Arianna* almost certainly featured on *Arcidiapason* because they are part of the edited montage for the program contained on reel "Fon. 098" (see also the Appendix).

20   Recorded in 1960 by Maderna on Philips P 08509 L (Luciano Berio, *Allez-hop;* Orchestra Sinfonica degli Incontri Musicali, soloist: Cathy Berberian). The use of *Ora mi alzo* for *Arcidiapason* is pure conjecture.

21   A role that in the field of radio even came to be "codified" in specific manuals; see Pippo Barzizza, *L'orchestrazione moderna nella musica leggera: L'ABC dell'arrangiatore* (Milan: Curci, 1952; repr. 2017).

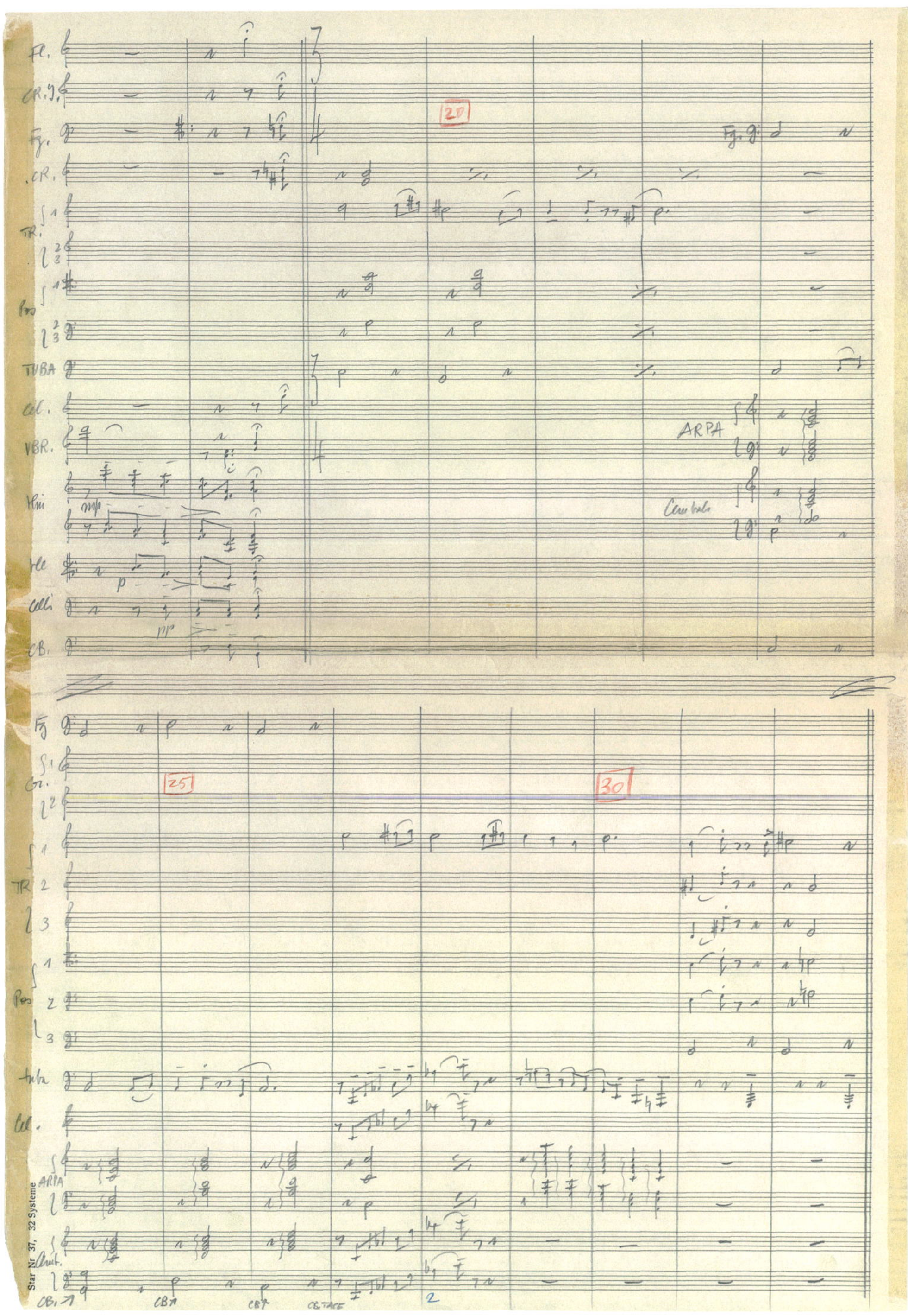

EX. 1   Armando Gill, *Come pioveva!...,* arrangement by Bruno Maderna, autograph score, p. 2 (courtesy of RAI Archives, Turin).

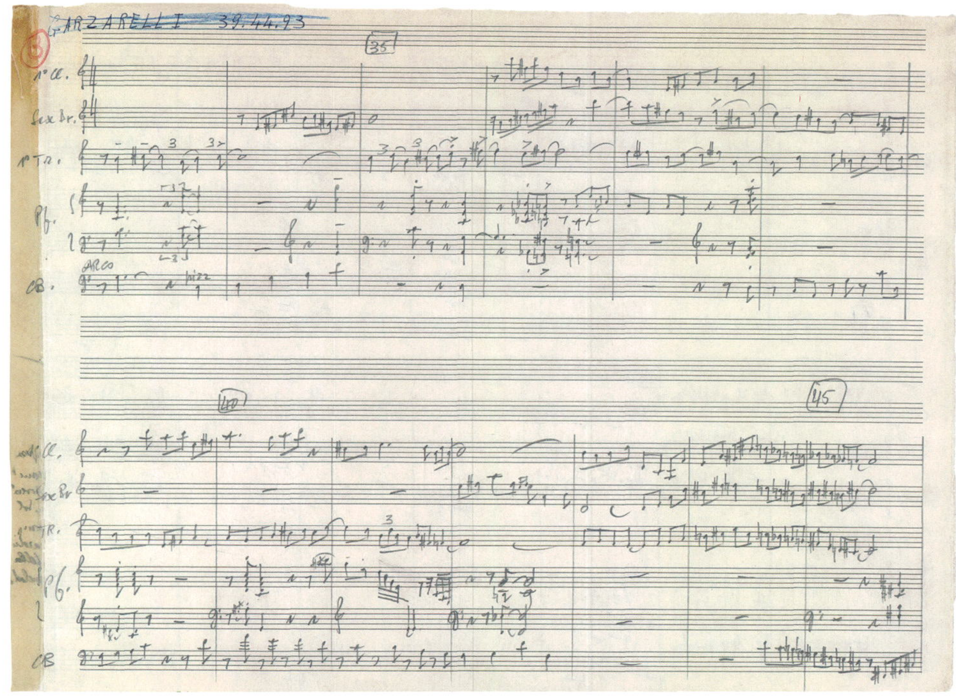

EX. 2   Armando Gill, *Come pioveva!...,* arrangement by Bruno Maderna,
autograph score, p. 3 (courtesy of RAI Archives, Turin).

Shortly before the exposition of the theme comes to an end, the piece quickly
deviates toward an extended counterpoint episode for a small set of instruments similar
to those of a jazz band: clarinet, trumpet, baritone sax, piano, and plucked double bass.
In bar 34 of the arrangement (→ **EX. 2**) the intertwining of the parts quickly abandons the
C major key to venture into a long atonal passage.

This intermezzo has a decidedly distancing effect because, stylistically speaking,
it stands diametrically opposed to the first utterance of the theme. What is more, at the
end of this disorientating digression, Maderna does not guide the material back to a real
refrain: the listener barely has time to recognize a fleeting allusion to the melody of the
refrain, hinted at by the strings, before the piece suddenly comes to an end.

In "re-reading" the recent and lively *Nel blu dipinto di blu,*[22] the newly composed
sections are interwoven several times in the melodic and harmonic progression, which
engages the listener in a continuous game of camouflage and deviation from the original

---

22   The score of this piece has yet to be found; only a few separate parts for some instruments were
found in the RAI Turin Archives. However, during the attempt to reconstruct the score starting
from these instrumental parts, it became clear that some of the documents listed under *Nel blu
dipinto di blu* actually belong to other works: of course, the process of identification and ordering
of this corpus of manuscripts is still incomplete (see Appendix). The starting point for the following observations is the listening to and analysis of the content of the tapes housed in the RAI
Studio di Fonologia Archives, Milan.

piece. Maderna's version does not begin with the melody of the verse, which never appears in the arrangement, but with a newly composed calm introduction by the brass section in *tempo rubato*. The chorus section, corresponding to the famous line "Volare, oh oh," is continually postponed and disregarded. Some way into the song, the trumpet finally seems to strike up the melody, but then immediately deviates toward a variation on the theme:[23] the phrasing simulates an improvised moment, with the accompaniment of a lively walking bass in swing time. When the chorus melody returns and is finally exposed in its entirety, two minutes have gone by since the beginning of the arrangement (which lasts just under 4'). However, very little time is spent in this haven of a familiar sound horizon: Maderna uses a new deviation to bring a small group of instruments, led by the clarinet, to literally "take flight," moving away from any immediately recognizable melodic or harmonic path and digressing toward counterpoint routes that seem inspired by the sophisticated cool chamber jazz of Jimmy Giuffre.

In some of the songs whose lyrics are far closer to poetry, Maderna apparently wants to use such divertissement devices to establish a subtle dialogue with the original text. This is particularly relevant in the case of Weill's instrumental version of *Die Ballade von der sexuellen Hörigkeit*. In the absence of the vocal part, Maderna abandons the strophic form of the original piece and settles for a single exposition of the theme, mainly entrusted to the violin. This is followed by a sophisticated jazz-style variation for trumpet, alto saxophone, piano, and double bass. In this second part, even though there is no sung text, the orchestra establishes a form of renewed madrigalism: the original musical path remains suspended, implied, or completely removed in favor of contrapuntal inserts, with extremely "dotted" rhythms, which seem to be commenting on the words of the original song. In the sung version conceived by Weill and Brecht, the second stanza begins with the scornful words "So mancher Mann sah manchen Mann verrecken" (Thus many a man watched many a man go to the dogs). In a purely instrumental elaboration, with no spoken words, one would expect the orchestra to take up the initial theme, perhaps with a different orchestration. Instead, this is exactly where Maderna's first "variation" takes place: he sets off an imitative process that seems to spring from the same recursiveness contained in those words. It is a sort of canon between trumpet and saxophone that initially takes up the thematic incipit of the piece, from which it then gradually moves away.[24] From this point on, until the end of the score, the arrangement diverges continually from the strophic form through a repeated "coming and going" of the melody, with frequent variations in tempo, stylistic scope, and changes in orchestration. In describing this procedure, Andrea Malvano spoke of "a technique of arrangement in progress, which never selects just one skin to cover the skeleton of the composition." Maderna, according to Malvano, "divides

---

23 It should be noted that the piece is labelled "Variazioni su *Nel blu dipinto di blu*" in the RAI files (see Appendix), an indication that does not however appear on the surviving pages of Maderna's autograph parts.

24 To date, the scores of the three arrangements taken from *Die Dreigroschenoper* (*Die Moritat von Mackie Messer*, *Die Ballade von der sexuellen Hörigkeit*, and *Die Zuhälterballade*), which can be heard on reel "Fon. 091" (see above and note 14), have yet to come to light. Only the separate parts are catalogued at the RAI Archives, Turin, but were unavailable for examination in the course of this study (see Appendix).

the piece into various segments, and gives each of them a different color," subjecting "the text to a cycle of variations, which however continually undergo transformations in style, language, and orchestration."[25] These changes of direction are not only effective expedients to astound the listener, but also reveal a deep knowledge of and links with the original songs. In *Die Ballade von der sexuellen Hörigkeit* there is a clear relationship between these deviations from the original and the words of Bertolt Brecht's song. The theme of the piece is man's incoherence, the contradiction between man's moral force in the light of day and the weakness that overcomes him at night, when faced with the lure of desire.[26] In fact, the frequent and unexpected deviations of the orchestral texture allow Maderna to effectively underline this condition of unstable unpredictability and the protagonist's incessant stream of second thoughts.

The implementation of an arrangement "in progress" in the instrumental version of *Moritat* expands a structural idea already implicitly present in the original song.[27] In *Dreigroschenoper*, this number is sung by a storyteller who lists Mackie Messer's numerous misdemeanors as if he were leafing through the crime news in a newspaper. Each new stanza introduces a different victim and is set in a different part of London: the beach, the pier, Soho. Similarly, with each repetition of the melody, Maderna transports the theme to a new stylistic setting and soundscape, with changes in tempo, instruments, and tonality. From the initial effect of a "mechanical accordion" achieved with muted trumpets, there is a sudden shift each time to a jazz trumpet solo, to a powerful big band from the swing era, and to a decadent waltz one might hear at a funfair, ending with a solitary and meditative clarinet. The principle of stylistic discontinuity in this arrangement paradoxically becomes the element that gives the piece unity and coherence. It is interesting to note a number of abrupt changes in direction and tempo that are sometimes inserted in the middle of a musical phrase. When one listens to these unexpected and apparently "anti-musical" combinations, so unusual in the tradition of popular music arrangements, they seem to relate back to an aesthetic that was typical of magnetic tape editing, rendered in this case by strictly orchestral means.

At the beginning of *Mad About the Boy*, a sentimental song with a lighter theme compared to the songs by Weill and Brecht,[28] the arrangement choices are more traditional, but nevertheless they still reveal a strong link with the meaning of the words and the mood of the song. In Coward's song, written as we said before for the musical *Words and Music* (1932), a group of girls who are in love with a film star uneasily describe how their infatuation and obsession with their idol has in fact made them "mad." In lines like "this dream that pains me and enchains me," unattainable love is described as a state of

---

25 Malvano, *L'arte di arrangiar(si)* (see note 15), p. 231.

26 In Brecht's verse: "Er soll den Tag nicht vor dem Abend loben / Denn bevor es Nacht wird, liegt er wieder droben." As we will see later, Maderna handles the same song in a very different way in his arrangement (with voice) for the recording of the first of the two LPs dedicated to Kurt Weill (see note 1).

27 As has already been pointed out, the score for this arrangement, which appears on the same reel as the previous one (see Appendix), has yet to come to light. Instead, the piano part for the version sung by Laura Betti for Ricordi records is housed at PSS-BMC (see Appendix).

28 A recording of this arrangement is in the reel "Fon. 098" (see note 14); the manuscript is housed at the RAI Archives, Turin (see Appendix).

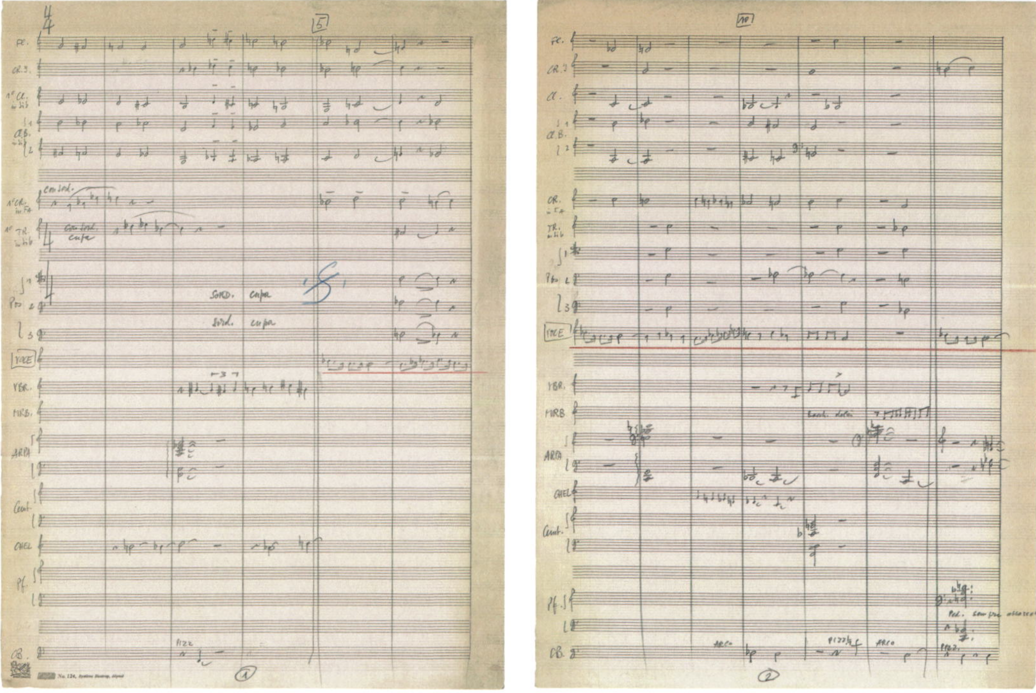

EX. 3   Noël Coward, *Mad About the Boy,* arrangement by Bruno Maderna, autograph score, pp. 1–2 (courtesy of RAI Archives, Turin).

EX. 4   Noël Coward, *Mad About the Boy,* transcription of bars 5–8 in Bruno Maderna's arrangement.

clouded reasoning and confusion. Maderna accentuates this psychological dimension, invoking a sorrowful atmosphere, characterized by a strongly chromatic harmonization. See, for example, the orchestra's role for the words of the incipit "Mad about the boy," which Cathy Berberian interprets with languid resignation and ironic detachment in a particularly low register. In the original harmonic structure, the ii–V cadence, Gm(♭5)7 C7, so typical of jazz music, is repeated twice in the first four bars of the chorus, creating an effect of sorrowful suspension that delays the arrival of the minor tonic (Fm). In Maderna's arrangement, this emotional climate is even more intense and gloomy. The new harmonization adds powerful chromatic tensions that once again follow a principle of counterpoint. If, starting from the manuscript, we try to translate the chordal verticality of each of the instruments utilizing the usual chord names used in jazz, it is easy to see how Maderna's harmonic progression moves away from the more usual harmonic paths, while adapting itself to the linearity of the theme (→ EXX. 3-4). [29]

After the first sung chorus, Maderna inserts a digression entrusted mainly to the clarinet accompanied by the orchestra (bars 35–53 of the autograph manuscript). As in the cases mentioned previously, this instrumental intermezzo again does not follow the harmonic structure of the piece, but proceeds without a definite tonal landing place, amplifying the sense of disorientation described in the words.

These few cases seem to show that at times the composer's inventiveness prevails over the pragmatic dimension of arranger. Moreover, in some of these arrangements, Maderna's poetic horizon is all too clear. One example is the unique introduction of *I Only Have Eyes For You*, as can be heard on the RAI "Fon. 098" reel. In the recording, Warren's song is preceded by a brief spoken part, accompanied by a single flute (the initial twelve bars of the manuscript (→ EX. 5). While the speaker's voice in a discursive and fictitiously autobiographical way introduces the radio listeners to the sentimental subject of the song, the flute performs some rapid volutes anticipating the key of the piece (E flat major), to then leave room for an instrumental group in which the sax predominates (Ex. 5, bars 13ff.). In this sort of "dialogue" with the speaker, the solo flute almost becomes a character in itself, a feature that recalls one of Maderna's most successful ploys adopted in *Don Perlimplin*, a radio opera he created two years later, in which the protagonist's "voice" is entrusted to Severino Gazzelloni's flute alone.[30]

---

29 In Example 1 the vocal part is transcribed as it appears in the score, whereas the verticality expressed in chord symbols is my interpretation. It should be noted that the rhythmic interpretation performed by Cathy Berberian in this passage is quite different from what can be read in the score: Berberian perfectly interprets the role of jazz singer, making significant modifications to the rhythmic course of the theme, expanding and contracting the melody.

30 The original radio recording can be heard on the CD included with *Imagination at the Play: The Prix Italia and Radiophonic Experimentation*, ed. Angela Ida De Benedictis and Maria Maddalena Novati (Rome: RAI-Trade; Milan: Die Schachtel, 2012). After all, as Angela Ida De Benedictis showed in her study on radio drama in Italy, Maderna was one of the first to use spoken opening credits in an "artistic" way, transforming them from a functional need to a constitutive element of the work. In the early years of his radio activity, Maderna also experimented with the possibility of making a character "speak" through sound, such as the sound of a whistle (as in *Il mio cuore è nel Sud*, radio ballad by Giuseppe Patroni Griffi, 1949) or a flute (as in *L'Augellino belverde*, Carlo Gozzi's philosophical fairy tale, radio adaptation by Vittorio Sermonti, 1958). See De Benedictis, *Radiodramma e arte radiofonica* (see note 19), passim (esp. p. 86).

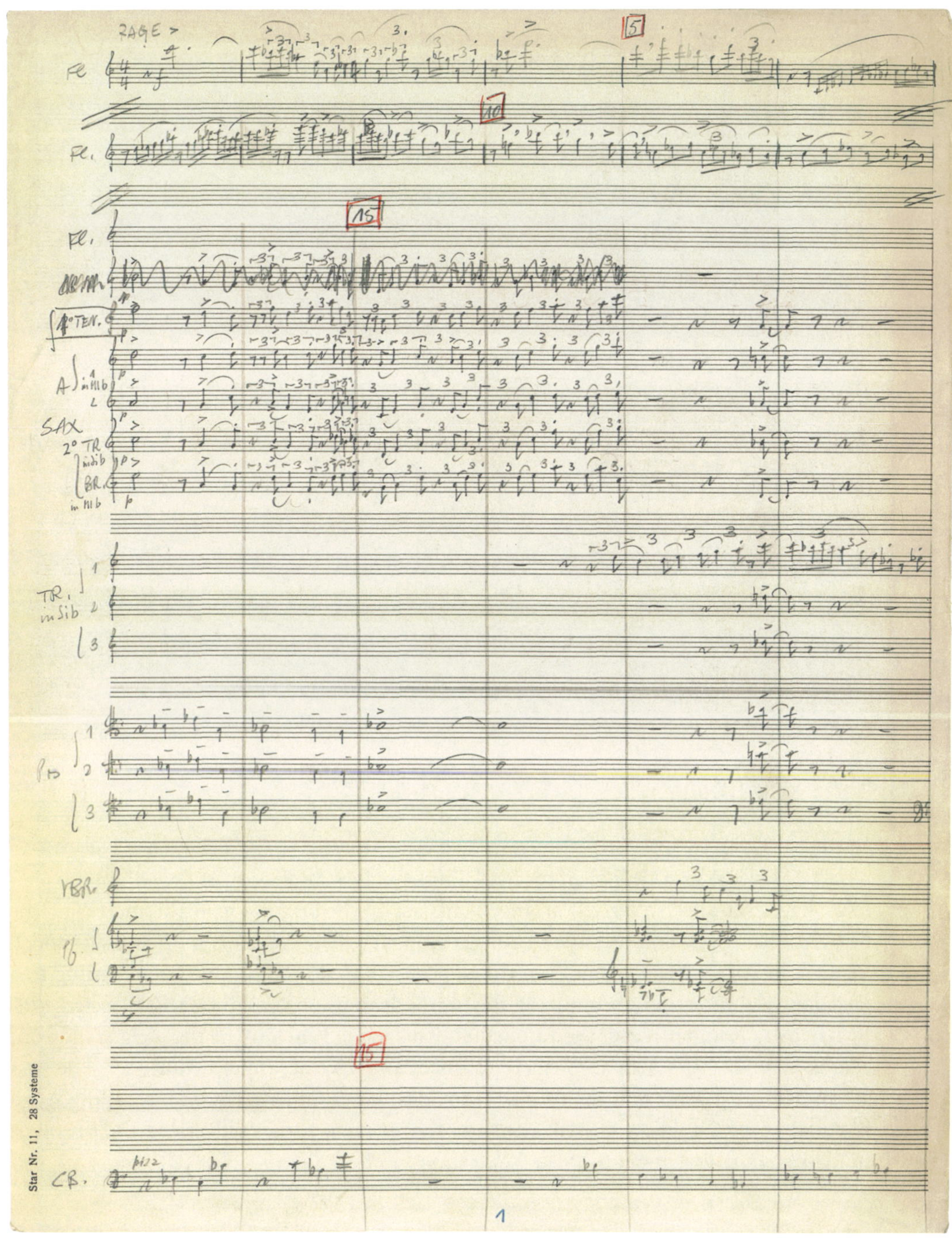

EX. 5 Harry Warren, *I Only Have Eyes For You,* arrangement by Bruno Maderna, autograph score, p. 1 (courtesy of RAI Archives, Turin).

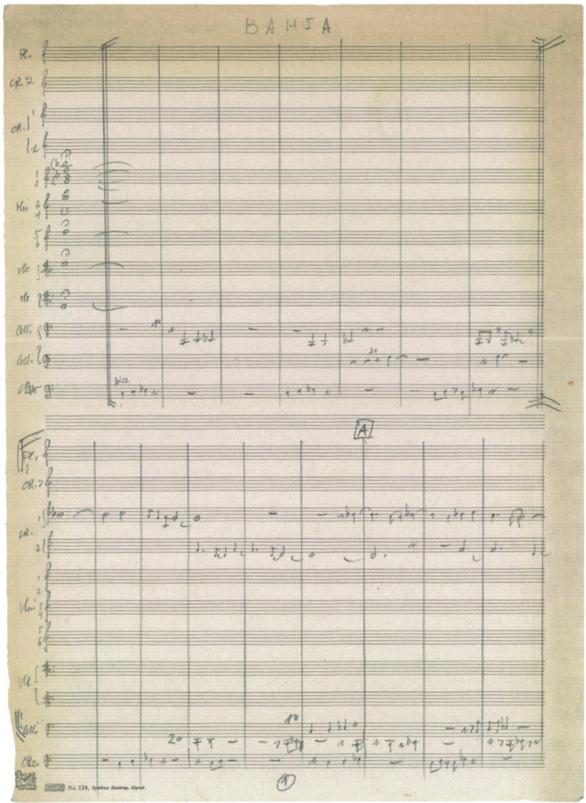

EX. 6   Ary Barroso, *Bahia [Na baixa do sapateiro]*, arrangement by
Bruno Maderna, autograph score, p. 1 (courtesy of RAI Archives, Turin).

Maderna also clearly left his mark on the orchestral version of *Bahia*.[31] In the pieces we have examined so far, the arrangements act on the original material, increasing the degree of harmonic complexity or adding completely new elements to the initial model. Instead, in *Bahia,* Maderna goes in the opposite direction and operates according to a principle of subtraction, minimizing the harmonic tensions and the variety of elements. In Barroso's original piece, the rarefied and suspended melody of the song stands out against a modal bass ostinato, which produces an effect of languid stillness.[32] The bass accompaniment, which in the original provides the propulsive rhythm, recalling Afro-Brazilian musical folklore and the rhythm of the partido alto, is pulverized and dissolved in Maderna's arrangement **(→ EX. 6)**.

---

31   The audio recording appears on reel "Fon. 098" (see note 14) and on the autograph manuscript housed at the RAI Archives, Turin (see Appendix).

32   Barroso's original song, sung by Carmen Miranda in 1938, describes scenes of loving despair and poverty. In the English version, released internationally thanks to the Disney short animated film *Three Caballeros* (1944), the song completely changed its mood, becoming imbued with nostalgia for exotic traits and focused on the contemplation of local Brazilian color.

The rhythmic figure emerges in fits and starts, distributed in the interventions of the double bass and cello, blending with the high pedal tone held by the strings. Maderna's arrangement expands the idea of continuity and cyclicity that also characterizes the original piece, but abandons any link with folk dance. The result is a music that is timeless, suspended, and iridescent. The evanescent opening and the gradual fading of the piece is reminiscent of a work like *Composizione n. 1* (1948–49). Indeed, overall, this arrangement of *Bahia* seems to confirm Massimo Mila's words, for whom "each of Maderna's musical pieces is an organism that is born, that is to say, it comes out of nothing, from silence, it develops and dies."[33]

The Two Ricordi Albums Dedicated to Kurt Weill's Songs

After *Arcidiapason* was broadcast, both radio and television gradually started to pay more attention to the music of Kurt Weill.[34] A few months later, in December 1960, Roberto Leydi's educational program *Ritratto di Kurt Weill* aired in three episodes on the radio's Third Program.[35] The first and last episodes, entitled respectively *Da Mahagonny a Der Silbersee* and *L'esperienza Americana*, dealt with Weill's music through events in the composer's life.[36] The central episode was entirely devoted to the broadcasting of *Il protagonista* (rhythmic Italian version by Marcello Cortis) and *Lo zar si fa fotografare* (rhythmic Italian version by Boris Porena), with both operas featuring Maderna conducting the Orchestra and Chorus of RAI-Rome.[37] In 1963 the initiative was repeated on TV in the *Parole e musica* program:

---

33 Massimo Mila, *Maderna musicista europeo*, ed. Ulrich Mosch (Turin: Einaudi, 1999), p. 31; first edn. 1976.

34 Generally speaking, Brecht's and Weill's production in these years represented an important benchmark for musicians and left-wing intellectuals who aimed to reestablish the very idea of song. Their poetics represented an alternative to both the revisitation of orally transmitted music and the mass production of musical entertainment. Two cases are prime examples of this phenomenon: in 1957, Sergio Liberovici's discovery of songs to texts by Brecht, during a trip to Germany with Luigi Pestalozza and Giacomo Manzoni, which coincided with his decision to found the work group "Cantacronache"; not long after, Weill and Brecht's song *Seeräuber-Jenny* – in German, with the title *Jenny delle spelonche* – appeared on the record *Le canzoni della malavita* (Ricordi, 1958) by Ornella Vanoni, who had already sung the song at Giorgio Strehler's suggestion. For more on this see Tomatis, *Storia culturale della canzone italiana* (see note 4), pp. 240–60.

35 The ethnomusicologist Roberto Leydi, a key figure in the post-war Italian cultural scene, started working in the 1950s as a journalist for the RAI and the *Avanti!* and *Europeo* magazines. His extensive knowledge of twentieth-century music, jazz, and music of oral tradition was fundamental for composers like Berio and Maderna, with whom, in 1954, he collaborated in writing the text for *Ritratto di città*, the first work produced at the nascent Studio di Fonologia. For more on the figure of Roberto Leydi see Nico Staiti, "Ricordo di Roberto Leydi," *Il Saggiatore Musicale* 12, no. 2 (2005), pp. 435–39; and Domenico Ferraro, "Roberto Leydi e il 'Sentite buona gente,'" *Musiche e cultura nel secondo dopoguerra* (Rome: Squilibri, 2015). See also Angela Ida De Benedictis, "Opera Prima: *Ritratto di città* and the Beginning of Electroacoustic Music in Italy," in *New Music on the Radio: Experiences at the Studio di Fonologia of the Rai, Milan 1954–1959*, ed. Veniero Rizzardi and Angela Ida De Benedictis (Rome: RAI-ERI, 2000), pp. 26–54.

36 The three episodes of are announced in the radio listings published in *Radiocorriere* 50 (1960), p. 23 (*Da Mahagonny a Der Silbersee*, broadcast on 12 December 1960); no. 51 (1960), p. 21 (the program dedicated to *Il protagonista* and *Lo zar si fa fotografare*, on 18 December); and no. 52 (1960), p. 21, for *L'esperienza americana* (broadcast on 25 December).

37 Unfortunately, to date, the recording of the program has not been found among the RAI Archives.

EX. 7   Cover of *Kurt Weill 1900-1933* (LP, Ricordi SMRL 6031; 1964).

the opening episode, titled *Ritratto di Kurt Weill* once more, was again edited by Roberto Leydi, with the collaboration of Bruno Nicolai, and included some songs entrusted to three emerging voices: Milly (the stage name of Carla Mignone, who had played Jenny in the historic Milanese production of *Opera da tre soldi* in 1956), Giulia Lazzarini, and Lilian Terry.[38]

The year 1964 also saw Maderna record two albums for Ricordi, *Kurt Weill 1900–1933* and *Kurt Weill 1933–1950*,[39] which seem to represent a sort of natural point of arrival for previous radio and television experiences, now channeled into a broader editorial project. The venture could basically boast four strong points: 1) the presence of a protagonist of the musical avant-garde like Maderna, whose innovative and adventurous approach to arrangement, already experimented with in *Arcidiapason* and other experiences, was promising in terms of the re-actualization and rethinking of the original pieces; 2) the chance to supplement the albums with a rich biographical, critical, and iconographic apparatus edited by Leydi himself;[40] 3) the translation into Italian of most of the texts, which would keep the expressive power of the theatrical performance alive and allow it wider circulation in Italy; and 4) the presence of an exceptional performer like Laura Betti (→ **EXX. 7-9**). Laura Betti had been in the spotlight in Italy for quite some time as a sensitive interpreter of *canzone d'autore* (songs by songwriters) and as an unconventional character on the Italian entertainment scene. According to Betti herself, her friendship with Maderna had started a few years before, when "in Milan, [...] I used to visit him at the radio from time to time."[41] Her contribution to the success of the two albums dedicated to Kurt Weill should

---

38   The program was broadcast on the National TV Program on 15 September 1963; see *Radiocorriere* 38 (1963), p. 10. This article is the source of the information given here.

39   See note 1.

40   The album cover was in the form of a book and contained a fourteen-page and a twelve-page booklet. The first record also has a text by Massimo Mila, "Berlino, una grande città," which reuses an article that had previously appeared as "Scoperta la vera voce di Kurt Weill," in *L'Espresso* 9, no. 2 (1964). See also below and note 47.

41   Roberto Chiesi, "'Bisogna nuotare nel forse:' Intervista a Laura Betti," *Cineforum* 437 (August–September 2004), pp. 56–63: 61.

EXX. 8–9 Bruno Maderna and Laura Betti during the recording of
Kurt Weill 1900–1933 (the flutist Severino Gazzelloni is shown
from behind; archival photo, courtesy of Cineteca di Bologna).

not be underestimated. As Fedele d'Amico notes in the catalogue of the 1960 XXIII Venice
International Festival of Contemporary Music, in his review of her recital *Giro a vuoto n. 2*
that featured songs by composers, poets, and musicians with different degrees of fame,[42]
"her performer's tools" were of exceptional quality, just as her tendency to transform every
vocal interpretation into a dramatic action was outstanding:

> infallible diction, a voice that lends itself to every situation, a musicality that can function
> in the finest detail. [...] In Laura Betti every medium has its own jaunty self-sufficiency:
> voice, words, musical inflection and gesture, lights and shadows, rigidity and slurs can play
> against each other, they enlighten and contradict each other, commenting and making
> fun of one other, with absolute control over the final result. [...]
> Betti invests the stage action with a non-veristic but detached and allusive tone, sprinkling
> it with insightful omissions; and she counterpoints it to the rest with acrobatic lightness.
> She is never over-emphatic: and when she hovers on the edge of rhetoric she knows how
> to stop suddenly, like the matador half a meter from the bull.[43]

Maderna had been able to explore this type of vocal style during the Milan performance
of *Opera da tre soldi* in 1956. Together with the director Giorgio Strehler, he had mainly
worked with non-singing actors (with the exception of Milly) and, as Luigi Pestalozza
writes, was successful in the "not-insignificant enterprise of technically preparing the

---

42   The show was staged on 3 and 4 October 1960 within the Biennale Music Festival and was hailed
by critics and public as an original combination of theater and music that presented a new,
courageous, and irreverent female character. The director was Filippo Crivelli; the list of authors
who wrote the lyrics of the songs included Alberto Arbasino, Camilla Cederna, Ennio Flaiano,
Franco Fortini, Alberto Moravia, and Pier Paolo Pasolini; the list of music composers included
Fiorenzo Carpi, Luciano Chailly, Gino Marinuzzi Jr., and Mario Peragallo. The texts were published in a booklet *Giro a vuoto*, ed. Laura Betti (Milan: Scheiwiller – All'insegna del pesce d'oro,
1960). On Laura Betti see at least Goffredo Fofi, "Una giaguara nella dolce vita: La cantante," in
Laura Betti illuminata di nero: Cineteca speciale (October 2005), pp. 8–11: 8.

43   Fedele d'Amico, "Laura Betti," in *La Biennale di Venezia: XXIII Festival Internazionale di Musica
Contemporanea* (Venice: La Biennale, 1960), pp. 88–89.

actors," which he did with "such firmness and expertise for which [...] we have witnessed astounding rehearsals."[44] Weill's music, the critic also notes, demanded that the vocal performer become "a detached expositor, continually set 'against the music,' with a tendency for a voluntary self-distancing from the emotions of the event, of such far-reaching epic relevance."[45]

For her part, Betti had studied Weill's music when she had taken part in Brecht and Weill's ballet *The Seven Deadly Sins*, staged at the Teatro Eliseo in Rome on 14 May 1961 in Fedele d'Amico's Italian rhythmic version (*I sette peccati capitali*, directed by Luigi Squarzina, choreographed by Jacques Lecoq, and conducted by Daniele Paris), where she shared the stage with the famous Italian dancer Carla Fracci. In the following years, Betti inserted numerous Weill songs in her own shows, and her 1962 song recital opened with an *Omaggio a Kurt Weill* which contained, in Italian translation, most of the songs that would later end up on the two LPs conducted by Maderna.[46]

According to the critics, the essential quality of Betti singing Weill was her close attention to the text, a feature that must have deeply impressed Maderna. According to Massimo Mila, her performances stood out for their

> respect for words, their taste for words. Sensible and expressive acting. And this quality is the not-at-all secret, but exceptionally sharp and efficient weapon with which Laura Betti manages to pull it off in her courageous and moving commitment to Kurt Weill. [...] It is an authentic philological talent that allows her to put the words in the foreground, not only in the physical sense of allowing them to be perceived, but to bring forth the drama that is at the core of every song through the sung word. [...] Kurt Weill's song lives in the field of play no less than in the field of art. If the words lose their meaning, then it is like a wasp without a sting. It is this sense of words, this root cause of anger, that Laura Betti knows how to exalt.[47]

Betti herself tells us that the recordings were carried out in a climate of great enthusiasm. She remembers that the composer

> only worked at night. [...] Bruno had a great influence on the musicians, they loved him, they all respected him, and we always and only worked at night, nobody argued. The crazy thing was that these scores had to be copied quickly and distributed and so I had to dash around to hand them out. It was madness. The musicians, the best in the business, received them at the last minute.[48]

---

44 Luigi Pestalozza, "I 'songs' di Weill," *Avanti!* (17 February 1956); also accessible online in Milan's Piccolo Teatro archives at: http://archivio.piccoloteatro.org/include/pdf.php?ID=4946 (last accessed on 10 December 2021). Another review by the same author appears in "La realizzazione musicale," in *L'Opera da tre soldi* (see note 16), pp. 149–55.

45 Pestalozza, "I 'songs' di Weill" (see note 44).

46 The Laura Betti fonds at the Cineteca di Bologna houses the informative brochure that was published for the show at the Teatro Gerolamo in Milan, in November 1962: *Laura Betti presenta Omaggio a Kurt Weill e Giro a vuoto n. 3*. The performance of the show at Rome's Teatro delle Arti was also announced in the newspaper *l'Unità* on 1 March 1963, p. 7. According to some sources, it appears that Laura Betti also staged her *Omaggio a Weill* at the twenty-seventh Maggio Musicale Fiorentino in 1964; however, the festival catalogue does not confirm this.

47 Massimo Mila, liner notes for the album *Kurt Weill 1900–1933* (see note 1), taken from idem, "Scoperta la vera voce di Kurt Weill," *L'Espresso 9* (see note 40).

48 Laura Betti in "Bisogna nuotare nel forse" (see note 41), p. 61.

The orchestra was made up of a variety of instruments that always changed with each song. Unfortunately, the liner notes included with the two albums do not tell us the names of the musicians who were given the difficult task of juggling between jazz and high-art traditions.[49] And the latter aspect is actually one of the strong points of the two LPs, which – even though they have almost faded into obscurity – represent one of the most successful moments of the meeting between high-art and popular music in Italy.

The two albums generally maintain the educational perspective of the radio broadcasts of the previous years, and, except for a few cases, the tracks are usually organized in chronological order. The first volume is dedicated to the songs composed between 1930 and 1933 and features the following songs sung by Betti – with the "extraordinary"[50] participation of Vittorio De Sica – mostly in Italian translation (songs in the original language are shown in bold here):

> from *Die Dreigroschenoper* (1928): *Barbara song, Ballata della schiavitù sessuale, Tango Ballade, Jenny dei pirati, Moritat, Salomon song, Ballata dell'agiatezza;*
> from *Happy End* (1929): *Surabaya Johnny;*
> from *Das Berliner Requiem* (1929): *La ragazza annegata;*
> from *Mahagonny* (1927–1930): **Moon of Alabama,** *Wie man sich bettet.*

Instead, the second volume, which covers the years 1933–50, contains songs from the following period, sometimes intermixed with each other, many of which are interpreted in the original language (English or French):

> from *Maria Galante* (1934): **Le grand lustucru, J'attends un navire;**
> from *Der Silbersee* (1934): *Lied der Fennimore;*
> from *I sette peccati capitali* (1933): *Songs from the ballet;*
> from *One Touch of Venus* (1943): **Speak Low, That's Him;**
> from *Knickerbocker Holiday* (1938): **How Can You Tell an American, September Song;**
> from *Street Scene* (1947): **Lonely House.**

In the absence of a monograph in Italian dedicated to Weill, Leydi prepared an unusually extensive and in-depth critical apparatus to be published with the record. The detailed cover notes, published in small booklets supplied with each LP, were the first attempt to

---

49 A summary list of the participants was drawn up on the basis of the interview I held with the saxophonist Gianni Basso in 2004. In addition to the flutist Severino Gazzelloni, Basso remembers the presence of numerous high-level Italian jazz musicians; these included Sergio Valenti (saxophone), Attilio Donadio (saxophone and clarinet), Oscar Valdambrini and Sergio Fanni (trumpet), and Gil Cuppini (drums). Mario Midana and Mario Pezzotta (trombones) were also probably present at the sessions along with a small string and woodwind section from the RAI Symphony Orchestra, Milan. Basso met Maderna in the early 1960s, when he regularly performed with Oscar Valdambrini at the Taverna Messicana in Milan. He told me that those evenings were an opportunity for Maderna to discover "new" jazz (probably cool and bebop). Basso states that, after these encounters, Maderna "got excited and wanted to test us with those arrangements" of Kurt Weill's songs. The challenging dialogue between jazz practice and classical training was a constant during the recordings: "apart from me" – recalls Basso – "all the other musicians had a diploma and were therefore well able to cope when faced with a difficult part." The recordings seem to have been made at the Zanibelli Studio in Via Ludovico il Moro in Milan.

50 As stated on p. 11 of the liner notes. For editorial details see note 1. The titles of Weill's songs and works are reported here as they appear on the LP.

offer a historiographical reflection on Weill in Italy. In each text, Leydi retraced the crucial moments of Weill's life,[51] proposed an interpretation of his political position in his association with Brecht, and made an in-depth analysis of the novelty of Weill's statements regarding the multiple cultural influences in the Berlin of the 1930s, such as easy listening, cabaret, operetta, expressionism, and avant-garde theater.

The presence of a singer like Laura Betti; the translation of German lyrics into Italian;[52] the general layout of the work, intended as an extraordinary educational means with which to approach Weill's music and the composer himself: all had obvious consequences on the way in which Maderna reworked the original pieces.

Unlike the versions of *Moritat von Mackie Messer* and *Die Ballade von der sexuellen Hörigkeit* for orchestra that had been aired on the *Arcidiapason* radio program, these new arrangements are, apart from some daring exceptions, decidedly closer to Weill's choices in terms of harmony, accompaniment formulae, and overall form. In arranging the songs, Maderna adopts a far more discreet role. The focal point of the pieces remains on the sung words and thus reduces the number of newly composed inserts or passages characterized by strong stylistic deviations.[53] The moments when the arrangement moves away from the original are carefully apportioned and mostly limited to choices in instrumentation or momentary contrapuntal parts that affect the overall color of the orchestration. A prime example of this type of intervention is given by the extremely delicate alto flute part that Maderna adds to the score of *Wie man sich bettet*, shortly before the end, to accompany the voice (→ **EX. 10**). In such cases, Maderna reinterprets and employs contrapuntal means to comment on the idea behind the orchestration present in Weill's piece.[54]

Occasionally the parts added in counterpoint to the song seem to comment on the words and have an "epic" effect on the interpretation of the piece, producing an alienating effect. In *Barbara Song*, for example, the two whirling contrapuntal lines of flute and mandolin that accompany the voice seem to want to reveal the irrepressible passions of Polly, the character who performs the song in the *Die Dreigroschenoper*, and

---

51   In the first LP: *Kurt Weill, una biografia: 1900–1933*, followed by the text by Massimo Mila quoted above in note 40. In the second LP: *Sulla via dell'esilio, La nuova patria americana, Il successo: una conclusione.*

52   As can be seen from the tracks marked in bold in the list reported above, only the German songs were translated. Although the liner notes fail to mention who edited the translations, this information can be partially gleaned from the aforementioned program printed for the 1962 recital *Laura Betti presenta Omaggio a Kurt Weill e Giro a vuoto n. 3* (see note 46; document consulted at the Pier Paolo Pasolini Collection, Laura Betti bequest, Cineteca di Bologna). In this booklet (without numbered pages) we can read: "The translations of the original texts and the recorded captions for the first part of the show *Omaggio a Kurt Weill* were edited by Fedele d'Amico, Ettore Gaipa, Roberto Leydi, Giorgio Strehler" (original in Italian). The translations of the songs from the *Opera da tre soldi* are taken, with very few adaptations, from the performance staged in Milan in 1956.

53   The collection also contains pieces where Maderna seems to reproduce Weill's original choices with hardly any modifications; for example, this is the case of the *Ballata dell'agiatezza* ("Ballade vom angenehmen Leben") and the *Tango Ballade* ("Zuhälterballade"), both from *Die Dreigroschenoper*. The latter number saw Vittorio De Sica sing a duet with Betti and is almost exactly the same as the instrumental version recorded for radio.

54   In these cases, the creative process could be explained by the concept of "writing of the interpretation," introduced by Michele Chiappini to describe the transcriptions of early music (see his essay in this volume, pp. 193–225).

EX. 10   Kurt Weill, *Wie man sich bettet* (from *Mahagonny*); arrangement by Bruno Maderna (note the part for flute in G added under the guidelines for the song); autograph score, pp. 15–16, PSS-BMC.

contradict her personal declaration of self-control.[55] In the second refrain, where Polly expresses the need to restrain one's impulses and desires ("Yes, it's always better to be cold at heart / and you must not let your feelings show. / Such a lot of things can happen / your only answer must always be: NO!"),[56] the dancing lines of mandolin and flute worm their way into the song and seem to comment on these words, generating an effect of emotional dissonance. With a movement of unstoppable acceleration, in an intoxicating sensual climax, the music contradicts the character's words and reveals her hidden desires, which are promptly manifested in the next stanza.

Not surprisingly, the songs where Maderna strays most from the profile of the original are especially those which had already become part of the jazz repertoire, established favorites that were no longer connected to the stage show for which they had originally been composed: *Moritat, Speak Low, September Song.*

---

55 The piece has not be found among Bruno Maderna's autograph scores.
56 The original lyrics are "Ja, da kann man sich doch nicht nur hinlegen, / Ja, da muß man kalt und herzlos sein. / Ja, da könnte so viel geschehen, / ach da gibt's überhaupt nur: Nein." The Italian translation sung by Betti reads "Sì, è meglio esser fredda e senza cuor / e lasciarsi andare non si può. / Non si sa quel che può accadere / bisogna sempre dire: NO!"

The arrangement of *Moritat* still has something of the phantasmagorical instrumental version made three years earlier for radio. This still missing score is also based on the idea of a continuous variation of styles and sound images, with an evident taste for the grotesque.[57] After the song by Betti, the theme is entrusted to bizarre and unpredictable instruments, such as the vibrato and caricatural sound of a musical saw (whose effect is vaguely similar to a Theremin) and the equally parodistic one of the baritone sax. As the piece draws to a close, Maderna ironically inserts a false ending: just when the piece seems to end on a sumptuous and bombastic chord played by the whole orchestra, the theme is suddenly taken up again, reappearing unexpectedly, murmured by Betti in the calming tempo of a waltz, melancholically fading into silence, like a merry-go-round spinning round and round.

Of the three songs mentioned, the arrangement of *Speak Low* certainly stands out as a pearl of creativity and taste, notable for the subtle balance between the creative contribution of the arranger and respect for the original text. Unlike the cases above, the central idea of this reworking has less to do with a particular stylistic or harmonic deviation, but more with the way Maderna handles the orchestral color in the incipit of the motif.[58] The faint sound of a flute emerges from the initial silence (Severino Gazzelloni on the recording); other wind instruments are gradually added with a canon-like effect (→ **EX. 11A**), always in pianissimo, little by little creating a musical texture that is both evanescent and vibrant at the same time. The progressive overlapping of the parts generates an evocative spatial effect: an iridescent polyrhythm arises from the polyphonic intertwining, obtained through the oscillation of rhythmic modes based on dotted quarter notes, enriched by the continuous rhythmic phase shift of the attacks of the wind instruments.[59] This all generates an impression of vagueness that persists throughout the entire first exposition of the theme.

In this way Maderna expands the idea of harmonic and rhythmic immobility that characterizes the beginning of the melody and uses the orchestration to interpret the very nature of the song by Weill and Ogden Nash. Indeed, the sense of uncertainty and slowing down created by the rhythmic stratification reflects the central topic of the text. Furthermore, Laura Betti's interpretation helps to perfectly convey the general feeling of suspension: the words ("Our moment is swift [...] We're late, darling, we're late [...]"), pronounced in a whisper, float in an echoing and magical space. But this evanescent dimension is suddenly shattered by the thunderous entrance of a solo trumpet (bar 72) and the start of the walking bass, which evoke the improvisational context of a jazz quintet. Not long after, the arrangement continues with an idea of contrapuntal jazz that is pure Maderna: first the alto and tenor saxophones enter (from bar 77), then two trumpets begin to chase each other in imitative figures (→ **EX. 11B**). The continuous tonal changes and the overlapping interventions of the instrumental lines momentarily obscure the tonal center and the squaring of the phrase, thus preparing the dramatic effect of the returning motif.

---

57 The part for piano, written by a copyist, is the only remaining musical manuscript for this arrangement. See also the Appendix to this chapter.

58 Maderna's autograph score is preserved in PSS-BMC.

59 A similar rhythmic complexity can be found in some orchestral jazz pieces by the Stan Kenton orchestra, which used extremely talented composers and arrangers, such as Bill Holman, Pete Rugolo, and Bob Graettinger. Listen, for example, to the beginning of *Egdon Heath* by Bill Russo (on the album *Kenton Showcase: The Music of Bill Holman and Bill Russo*, Capitol Records – H525, 1954).

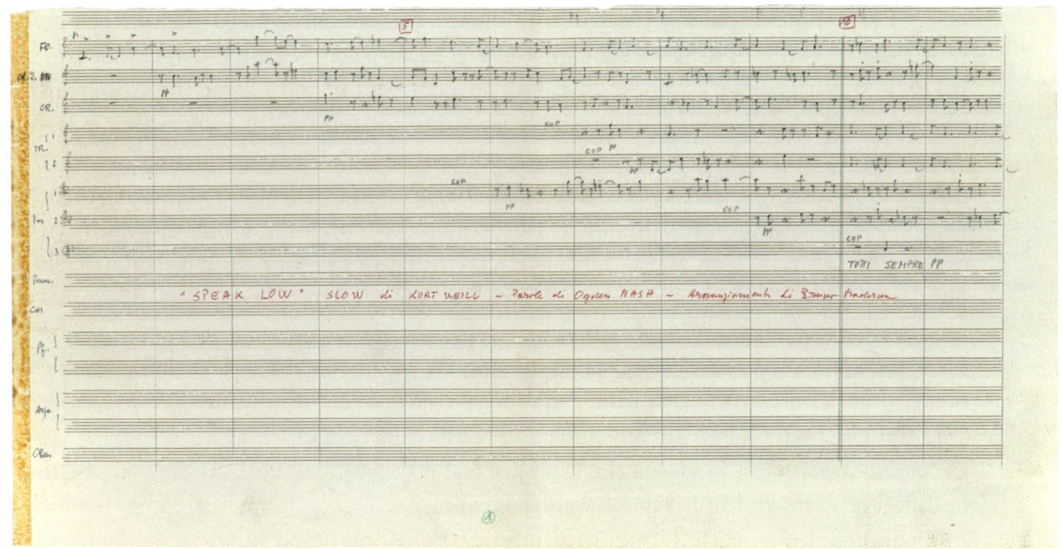

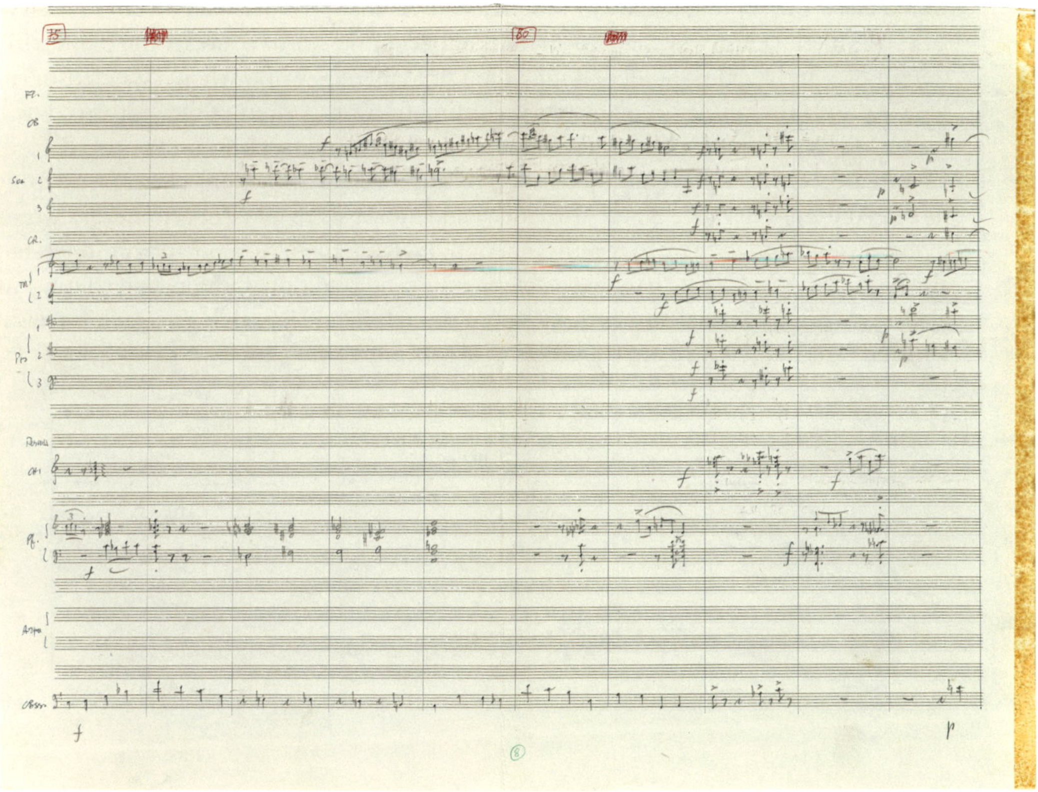

EX. 11A–B Kurt Weill, *Speak Low* (from *One Touch of Venus*), arrangement
by Bruno Maderna, autograph score, pp. 1 and 8; PSS-BMC.

Just as the sound was created from silence, the end of the piece mirrors the beginning as it fades away in a manner shared not only by the arrangement of *Bahia*, but also by many of Maderna's own compositions. This idea of opening and closing the arrangement in a gradual and delicate way is so closely linked to the sense of the words that it seems like a madrigalism that musically expresses both the initial words "Speak low" (hence the title), and also the line that leads to the end of the piece: "The curtain descends, ev'rything ends too soon." All these features make this score more than just a simple arrangement of *Speak Low*, but rather, an authentic creative rewriting of the song, in which the original piece is rethought and changed into a "new" Weill/Maderna composition.

More than fifty years later, listeners can still appreciate the freshness of Maderna's arrangements, which have lost none of their masterful ability to communicate. The principle of "multiplicity," which had already appeared in the selection of songs for radio, becomes the *modus operandi* of Maderna the arranger and is clearly seen both in the combination of different styles and in his dense and rich expressive palette (which stretches from the irony and the light-hearted tones of a potpourri of Romanesco songs to the lucidity of the reinterpretations of Weill). The very idea of creating bridges and opportunities that would allow the coming together of musical worlds that prejudice had divided – such as jazz, twentieth-century avant-garde, and popular music – today reveals the pioneering importance and lucid groundbreaking vision of Maderna's work, whose "syncretism" in 1960–64 was a forerunner of many of the cultural transformations of the years to come.

From this point of view, the arrangements that one can hear on the two Ricordi albums are steeped in the cultural heritage of Kurt Weill and the topicality of Maderna's music. And this relevance is still alive today and allows us to cite Roberto Leydi's words in his introduction to the two records, not only applying them to Weill and his songs, but also to arrangements that "have been able to transcend tradition, fashion, and contingent evidence with substantial authenticity – even though they themselves are tradition, fashion, and evidence – to live on, regardless of events, right up to our own time" ...[60]

---

60 Roberto Leydi, introductory notes to the LP *Kurt Weill 1900–1933* (see note 1). A slightly modified version of the text was reutilized in the second volume, *Kurt Weill 1933–1950*.

Appendix

The Sources of Bruno Maderna's Arrangements for Radio:
Recordings and Relevant Manuscripts

Only the sound and handwritten sources of popular music arrangements made by Bruno Maderna for radio are cited here (see Section "Arrangement for Radio" of this text). The consideration of the manuscript sources calls for a fundamental methodological premise that concerns all the paper sources of works created for radio programs. These scores were intended to be recorded on tape for broadcasting, and, even when they are defined in every aspect, should be considered evidence of a pre-final stage in the arrangement work. Precisely because they were conducted (and often edited on tape) by the composer himself, the final stage of these reworkings is documented instead by the audio recordings (when available), which often present variations with respect to the written source decided during their execution and/or recording. [61]

Based on this premise, the recordings are considered here to be primary sources. Therefore, the tracks are listed here following the order in which they appear on the three reels housed in the Archives of the RAI Studio di Fonologia, Milan (catalogued "Fon. 091," "Fon. 098," and "Fon. 099"),[62] and indicating, for each piece recorded on tape, the corresponding manuscripts (where they exist).

Some titles refer to a well-structured potpourri or collage of different pieces. In only one case (*Fantasia su Roma*) is the entire potpourri set out in a single score. In other cases, such as *Aspettare*, *Arianna*, and *Lehar*, the sequence of sections that have been assembled on the tape does not correspond to the written sources. For this type of piece, the comparison between the recordings and the existing manuscripts is fundamental for the reconstruction of the formal structure of the arrangement.

Most of Maderna's handwritten scores bear traces of an identification number: a figure in black ink or red pencil. Details of any existing data, which might have served to catalogue the tracks or their sequence during recording, are given in the description that follows. The list gives the title of each arrangement as it appears on the title page of the scores; the original title (if different) follows in square brackets. In the absence of a reference title in the score, an identifier is suggested in curly brackets.

Maderna inserted sections of his own compositions in many arrangements to serve as an introduction, interlude, variation, or as a connection between preexisting songs. Where these newly invented parts were drafted on separate manuscripts, a note indicates the internal division of the individual parts with reference to the corresponding paper sources.

The manuscripts of Maderna's radio arrangements are housed in two different archives: a large part is deposited in the RAI's Archives in Turin (RAI-Tu in the list);[63] instead, other sources are preserved in the Bruno Maderna Collection at the Paul Sacher Foundation in Basel (PSS-BMC).

---

61   For more detailed information on these methodological premises, see Angela Ida De Benedictis, "Le nuove testualità musicali," in Maria Caraci Vela, *La filologia musicale: Istituzioni, storia, strumenti critici*, vol. 2 (Lucca: LIM, 2009), pp. 71–116 (in collaboration with Nicola Scaldaferri), and idem, "Il suono oltre il segno: la carta, i limiti e gli inganni (cinque esempi)," *AAA – TAC: Acoustical Arts and Artifacts / Technology, Aesthetics, Communication* 2 (2005), pp. 53–65.

62   See above in this essay and note 14. It should be noted that along with the scores listed here, the historical RAI Archives, Turin, contain three other scores of arrangements by Bruno Maderna, but the recordings of these pieces have yet to come to light. The songs are *Begin the Beguine* by Cole Porter, *Sweet and Lovely* by Gus Arnheim, Charles N. Daniels, Harry Tobias, and Donald Novis, and *The Darktown Strutters' Ball* by Shelton Brooks.

63   For an archival description of the scores housed at the RAI, Turin, see the *Catalogo delle partiture* on the site of the RAI Archives (www.osn.teche.rai.it).

Reel "Fon. 091"[64]

1	***Tango Ballade [Zuhälterballade]*** Music by Kurt Weill, lyrics by Bertolt Brecht, from *Die Dreigroschenoper* (1928). • Arrangement for orchestra. • Maderna also re-used the same arrangement for the *Ballata del magnaccia* included on the *Kurt Weill 1930–1933* album (Ricordi SMRL 6031). • Separate parts (partially handwritten) at RAI-Tu. The manuscript score has not been located.
2	***Ballade von der sexuellen Hörigkeit*** Music by Kurt Weill, lyrics by Bertolt Brecht, from *Die Dreigroschenoper* (1928). • Arrangement for orchestra. • Interspersed with long newly-composed parts. Different from the arrangement made for the *Ballata della schiavitù sessuale* included on the Ricordi album *Kurt Weill 1930–1933*. • Separate parts at RAI-Tu. The manuscript score has not been located.
3	***Moritat [Die Moritat von Mackie Messer]*** Music by Kurt Weill, lyrics/words by Bertolt Brecht, from *Die Dreigroschenoper* (1928). • Arrangement for orchestra. • Different from the arrangement made for *Moritat* included on the Ricordi album *Kurt Weill 1930–1933*.[65] • Separate parts at RAI-Tu. The manuscript score has not come to light.

4	***Ora mi alzo***
	Music by Luciano Berio, words by Italo Calvino, from the "mimed tale" (*racconto mimico*)
	Allez-hop (1959).
	• Version for orchestra and voice; soloist: Cathy Berberian.[66]
	• The RAI-Tu archives contain only one fragment of an autograph score (for voice, trumpet,
	   tenor saxophone, electric guitar, harpsichord, piano, and drums) written on the *verso* of fol. 2
	   of the *Bahia* score (see below, reel "Fon. 098"). At the top of the page, we can see the name
	   of the author and the title of the piece, first written in pencil and then rubbed out.

5	***Nel blu, dipinto di blu*** (RAI card title: "Variazioni su *Nel blu dipinto di blu*") Music and lyrics by Franco Migliacci and Domenico Modugno. • Arrangement for orchestra. • Separate sheets for some instruments at RAI-Tu, with handwritten notes. The manuscript score has not been located.
6	***In the Still of the Night*** by Cole Porter • Arrangement for orchestra and voice; soloist: Cathy Berberian. • Separate autograph sheets at RAI-Tu. The manuscript score has not been located.

7	***{Fantasia su Roma}***
	Potpourri for orchestra taken from:
	   Nannì ('Na gita a li Castelli) by Franco Silvestri;
	   Quanto sei bella Roma (canta se la vuoi cantà), by Cesare Andrea Bixio and Enzo Bonagura;
	   La Romanina by Eldo Di Lazzaro and Giuseppe Micheli;
	   Arrivederci Roma by Renato Rascel, Pietro Garinei, and Sandro Giovannini.
	• Autograph score for orchestra and individual parts at RAI-Tu
	   (the front page has the autograph title "Roma Bbona" [*sic;* Beautiful Rome], cancelled out).

---

64 The seven songs on the reel were presumably used for the program *Arcidiapason* (1960).

65 Autograph parts of this version housed at PSS-BMC.

66 Slightly different version from the one recorded by Luciano Berio, *Allez-hop*, Philips, P 08509 L, 1960; cond. Bruno Maderna. There is no indication, however, of who wrote the arrangement (note that in the score of the mimic tale by Berio-Calvino, published by Suvini Zerboni in 1971, the song in question only has a piano accompaniment).

Reel "Fon. 098"

1	*I Only Have Eyes For You* Music by Harry Warren, lyrics by Al Dubin. • Arrangement for orchestra. • Autograph score for orchestra and separate individual parts at RAI-Tu (the front page has a circled number "8").
2	*Bahia [Na baixa do sapateiro]* by Ary Barroso. • Arrangement for orchestra. • Autograph score for orchestra and separate individual parts at RAI-Tu (p. 5 has a circled number "11"). • On the verso of some sheets we find musical compilations that refer to different pieces.[67]

3	*Aspettare*
	by Bruno Maderna, from *Aspetto Matilde,* musical radio comedy by Enzo Maurri (1959).[68]
	• Arrangement for small jazz band, big jazz band, and voice.
	The recording is an edited version of two different pieces:
	   1) *Aspettare,* small jazz band and voice (soloist: Cathy Berberian):
	• Autograph score and separate individual parts for small jazz band and voice at RAI-Tu
	(note that there are substantial differences between the music in the score and on the recording).
	   2) a piece for big jazz band that acts as an instrumental interlude.
	• Autograph score at PSS-BMC.[69]

4	*Mad About the Boy* by Noël Coward. • Arrangement for orchestra and voice (soloist: Cathy Berberian). • Autograph score for orchestra and separate individual parts at RAI-Tu (the front page has a circled number "10").

5	*Arianna*
	Potpourri of pieces for orchestra by Bruno Maderna and Mario Migliardi.
	On the tape the speaker presents *Arianna* as a piece by Migliardi conducted by Maderna.
	In actual fact, it is a collage of three different pieces:
	   1) *Arianna* by Mario Migliardi, arrangement for orchestra by Maderna:
	• Autograph score for orchestra and separate individual parts at RAI-Tu
	(the front page has a circled number "12");
	   2) a *Swing,* presumably composed by Maderna, for small jazz orchestra:
	• Autograph score drawn up on the *verso* of some sheets of the score for *Bahia*
	(see above, no. 2);
	   3) a piece for solo piano, presumably composed by Maderna
	(the manuscript has not been found).

6	*Lehar* Potpourri from *Die lustige Witwe* by Franz Lehár [70] • Arrangement for orchestra. • The recording is a collage of three pieces from Franz Lehár's operetta interspersed with two orchestral interludes (*Blues-tempo*), composed by Maderna. • Autograph score for orchestra and separate individual parts at RAI-Tu.[71]

---

67   This is the breakdown of the contents appearing on the different pages of the manuscript: fol. 1r: *Bahia* p. 1; fol. 1v: untitled piece [but: *Swing,* mm. 12–15; see below in this essay, no. 5, *Arianna* potpourri]; fol. 2r: *Bahia* p. 2; fol. 2v: Luciano Berio, *Ora mi alzo,* fragment (see above, cf. reel "Fon. 091," no. 4); fol. 3r: *Bahia* p. 3; fol. 3v: *Swing* [see below in this essay, no. 5, *Arianna* potpourri] mm. 1–11; fol. 4r: *Bahia* p. 4; fol. 5r: *Bahia* p. 5; fol. 5v: *Bahia* p. 6.

68   See De Benedictis, *Radiodramma e arte radiofonica* (see note 19), pp. 245–46 and passim.

69   The piece, preserved among the materials of the *Aspetto Matilde* radio drama, is listed with the title *Intermezzo.* It should be noted that in the Luciano Berio Collection at PSS there is an (incomplete) photocopy of the manuscript of the song *Aspettare.*

70   Contrary to Malvano's claims, the recording of this potpourri is not lost. The tape is indispensable for understanding the formal organization of the potpourri and the sequence of the parts.

71   The layout of the score is as follows: Part 1: arrangement of the romance *Wie eine Rosenknospe,* Act II (4 fols.; the final bars of the recording are not noted in the score; Part 2 (4 fols.), which in turn is divided into *Hesitation,* numbered 1 in red pencil (arrangement of the duet *Lippen schweigen,* Act III), *Blues-tempo,* numbered 2 in red pencil, *Blues-tempo,* numbered 3 in red pencil; Part 3: *Cake-walk,* arrangement of the dance scene, Act III (2 fols.). The parts appear in this order on the recording: *Hesitation* [0:00]; *Blues tempo – 2* [0:52]; repetition of *Hesitation* [1:50]; *Blues tempo – 3* [2:32]; arrangement of *Wie eine Rosenknospe* [3:43]; *Cake-walk* [5:17].

Reel "Fon. 099"

1	*Lola [Yes Sir! That's My Baby]* Music by Walter Donaldson, lyrics by Gustav Gerson Kahn (Italian adaptation by Angelo Ramiro Borella). • Arrangement for orchestra and voice. Soloist unknown. • Autograph score for orchestra and separate individual parts at RAI-Tu (the front page has the circled number "3").
2	*Op! op! Trotta cavallino* Music by Gorni Kramer, lyrics by Enrico Frati. • Arrangement for orchestra and voice. Soloist unknown. • Autograph score for orchestra and separate individual parts at RAI-Tu (the front page has a circled number "4").
3	*Come pioveva!...* by Armando Gill (Michele Testa's *nom de plume*). • Arrangement for orchestra. • Autograph score for orchestra and separate individual parts at RAI-Tu (the front page has two circled numbers "5" and "7"). • The score has three sections, indicated with the letters "A" (sections of verses and refrain), "B" (contrapuntal jazz interlude), and "C" (short resumption of the refrain). It ends with the indication "Attacca tango," which refers to piece no. 4, *Ich küsse ihre Hand, Madame* (*Signora mia gentil*), which immediately follows on the recording with no interruption.
4	*Ich küsse ihre Hand, Madame* Music by Ralph Erwin, lyrics by Fritz Rotter. • Arrangement for orchestra and voice (in the Italian version). Soloist unknown. • Autograph score for orchestra and separate individual parts at RAI-Tu (the front page has a circled number "6"). • The sections are labeled with the letter "D," continuing on from the previous score.
5	*You Are My Lucky Star* Music by Nacio Herb Brown, lyrics by Arthur Freed. • Autograph score for orchestra and separate individual parts at RAI-Tu (the front page has two circled numbers "8" and "1"). • The piece is immediately followed on the recording by *Paradise* (no. 6) with no interruption.
6	*Paradise* by Nacio Herb Brown.[72] • Autograph score for orchestra and separate individual parts at RAI-Tu (circled numbers "4" and "7"). • The bars are numbered following on from the preceding number.

---

[72] In Maurizio Romito, "I commenti musicali" (see note 14), p. 113, the arrangement of *Paradise*
is wrongly indicated as *It's a Sin to Tell a Lie* by Billy Mayhew. It should nevertheless be
remembered that when he wrote this essay, he did not have access to the manuscript sources
(unavailable at the time) and the songs were identified only by ear.

ACROSS BORDERS: THE CONDUCTOR AND THE INTERPRETER

MAURIZIO ROMITO

"This Bruno Looks Like Fiorello"
Maderna in the U.S.A. (1965–72)

Maderna made his debut on the American music scene on 21 February 1965 with the performance of Luigi Nono's *Intolleranza 1960* in Boston, four years after its memorable opening in Venice. Prior to this, Maderna's fame as a conductor in the United States was mainly limited to communications from European contemporary music festivals, radio broadcasts, or the few available recordings. Who could remember the reviews in several American newspapers in 1932–33 that talked about a child prodigy, a certain Brunetto Grossato, who was causing quite a stir on the other side of the Atlantic? The child was director of the Diano Marina town band and the seventy-eight-member orchestra at Venice's Teatro La Fenice, often compared to Willy Ferrero and acclaimed as "the coming Toscanini."[1] And much the same could be said about Maderna the composer. Even in the early 1960s, the chances to hear his works live were few and far between, limited to some electronic music auditions and to the few chamber music pieces performed on tour by European musicians and only rarely by local artists. The fate of some of his important works is, however, bound up with events in America; for example, an early *Requiem* (1946), presumed lost, which Virgil Thomson speaks of in glowing terms,[2] in an unsuccessful attempt to promote its performance in the United States; or his *Tre liriche greche* (1948), whose first known performance seems to have taken place in Kansas City on 27 February 1959, conducted by Harold Decker, who then released it on record.[3]

The staging of *Intolleranza 1960* at the Opera Company in Boston under the direction of Sarah Caldwell may have been beset by numerous technical difficulties and political protests, but it was, as the set designer Josef Svoboda recalls, a "sensational" production.[4] Maderna's conducting played a crucial role in this. Joseph Silverstein, the

---

The present text summarizes a more extensive study published in its entirety, with a timeline of concerts and oriented reviews, as "Da *Intolleranza 1960* a *Don Giovanni:* Bruno Maderna direttore d'orchestra negli Stati Uniti," *Musica/Realtà,* part 1, no. 117 (November 2018), pp. 115–48, and part 2, no. 118 (March 2019), pp. 177–224; Appendix, part 1, no. 122 (July 2020), pp. 199–225, and part 2, no. 123 (November 2020), pp. 197–233.

1   See among others *The New York Times* (11 September 1932), *The Pantagraph* (4 November 1932), *The Journal News* (14 November 1932), and *The Evening Times* (28 November 1932). In these reviews, as in the Italian programs and reviews of 1932–33, Maderna's age (twelve in 1932) was lowered to nine.

2   See Virgil Thomson, "Venice and Its Musical Life," *The New York Herald Tribune* (10 August 1946). The discovery was made by Veniero Rizzardi, who also edited the 2011 edition for Suvini Zerboni in Milan. See also Rizzardi's essay in this volume, pp. 331–56.

3   Record released by the University of Illinois School of Music, Custom Recording Series, CRS 7.

4   Josef Svoboda, *I segreti dello spazio teatrale* (Milan: Ubulibri, 1997), pp. 70 and 77. Luigi Nono remembers the event quite differently; see *Nostalgia for the Future: Luigi Nono's Writings and Interviews,* ed. Angela Ida De Benedictis and Veniero Rizzardi (Oakland: University of California Press, 2018), pp. 321–24: 323.

concertmaster of the Boston Symphony Orchestra from 1962, remembers that "he was highly respected by the Boston Symphony musicians who worked with him."[5] A few days after the performance, Nono himself waxed lyrical about Maderna in an open letter he sent from the USA to the Italian magazine *Rinascita:*

> Bruno has been magnificent once again: he imposed everything with his experience and assurance; the orchestra good (not more), quick in reading, but technically not perfect [...]. Then, with Bruno's assurance, everything went all right: Bruno has held up the stage and all the rest with his bull-like musical and human power. Without him it would have been impossible!!![6]

Nono's words, which were after all harshly critical of the entire production, incited one of the performers[7] and the critic Michael Steinberg to express their outrage on the pages of *The Boston Globe.* Steinberg's reply reports some of the off-the-record comments Maderna and Nono had made about the musical outcome of the production:

> About the quality of the actual performance, Bruno Maderna, who had conducted all previous productions of Nono's opera, stated to this reporter that the Boston *Intolleranza* was "musically the best." Nono, while he had reservations about certain of the singers, also stated both to Leon Kirchner and to this writer that the musical side of the performance was more satisfactory here than in previous productions.[8]

A unique document that has only recently attracted scholars' attention is TV footage of the performances in Boston. The program, which combines the two performances, was produced by WGBH-TV, Channel 2, in cooperation with National Educational Television (NET), and broadcast on 11 March 1966.[9]

The American experience of 1965, however, remained an isolated incident, and several years had to pass before Maderna embarked on a real conducting career in the United States. In October 1967, two important New York management agencies, owned by David Schiffman and Sheldon Soffer, expressed their interest in representing Maderna in the United States. Their first letters to the impresario Sylvio Samama reveal just how little-known Maderna was on the other side of the Atlantic at the time in question. On 16 October 1967, Schiffman wrote to Samama that Maderna "is all but unknown in the

---

5   Personal communication, 18 November 2015.

6   Luigi Nono, "A Letter from Los Angeles" (1965), repr. in *Nostalgia for the Future* (see note 4), p. 187.

7   See Beverly Sills, "Not So, Nono," *The Boston Globe* (29 May 1965); see also idem, *Bubbles: A Self Portrait* (Indianapolis and New York: Bobbs-Merrill, 1976), pp. 99–101.

8   Michael Steinberg, "Nono's Letter: Dishonest, Vain, Silly, But What Is the Real Issue?" *The Boston Globe* (30 May 1965).

9   The film is "in fact a combination of the two live performances, with the addition of the necessary close-ups of performers shot in the studio"; firsthand account shared by Keit Luf, WGBH Archives Manager, personal communication, 11 September 2007. Among the various other studies see Barbora Příhodová, "The Power of Images in Performance: Josef Svoboda's Scenography for *Intolleranza 1960* at Boston Opera Company," in *Activating the Inanimate: Visual Vocabularies of Performance Practice,* ed. Celia Morgan and Filipa Malva (Oxford: Inter-Disciplinary Press, 2013 [eBook]), pp. 31–40, and Claudia Vincis, "'To Nono: a No:' Luigi Nono and His *Intolleranza 1965* in the U.S.," in *Crosscurrents: American and European Music in Interaction, 1900–2000,* ed. Felix Meyer et al. (Woodbridge: Boydell, 2014), pp. 320–34.

United States. All that is known of him is that he is a great conductor of modern music; very few know that he conducts music of all styles and periods."[10] His words are echoed by Soffer in another letter to the same impresario on 15 January 1968:

> Let me first explain that the name of Bruno Maderna in America is still relatively unknown. [...] I have written and called every major orchestra this season about Maestro Maderna and did not get a very enthusiastic response. However, I believe that there is a future in America for this distinguished musician.

Sheldon Soffer was thus appointed Maderna's representative in the USA. He first tried to program Maderna's debut for January 1969 with the Chicago Symphony Orchestra, but this was then postponed to the following year. As a matter of fact, Maderna's new enterprise in America did get underway in 1969, but in October, and with William Steinberg's Pittsburgh Symphony Orchestra, in what turned out to be a most strategic choice.[11]

Maderna and Soffer met for the first time when the composer arrived in Pittsburgh. The impresario was immediately impressed by Maderna, and on 13 October 1969 described him to Samama as an "absolutely charming, disarming, and a beautiful person. I am so happy to have made his personal acquaintance at long last, and hope that our relationship will be a long one." A few days later, a first interview with Maderna appeared in the local press. When questioned about the differences between European and American orchestras and conductors, Maderna starts by saying: "If one wants to hear the world's finest symphony orchestras, stay in the United States. However, if it's opera you are after, there is only one place to hear it – in Europe."[12]

The reviews immediately remark on some of his characteristics that will then constantly recur in the American critique of Maderna: his excellent mastery of conducting technique, his profound sensibility as a musician, and the stimulating breath of fresh air he had brought to programming.

Maderna returned to the United States again in January 1970 to conduct the Chicago Symphony Orchestra. He presented two demanding orchestral works in the first concert – his recent *Quadrivium* of 1969, and Luciano Berio's *Epifanie* – preceded by his own transcriptions of Schubert, which, unlike the rest, did not fully convince the press. The concert came to a close with two brilliant pieces by Stravinsky, *Scherzo à la russe* and *Circus Polka*, the perfect complement to the opening transcriptions thanks to their dancelike nature and the quotation from Schubert's *Marche Militaire*, op. 51, no. 1, in the finale of *Circus Polka*. Some of the critics saw Maderna as "a plump gentleman with a jovial nature quite at variance with the traditional maestro-stereotypes," "with a precise

---

10   Unless otherwise specified, all the correspondence cited here and elsewhere in the text is unpublished and held in PSS-BMC and/or the private archives of Sylvio Samama. I am extremely grateful to Maderna's, Leo Samama's, and Sheldon Soffer's heirs for kindly granting permission to quote the excerpts from letters.

11   "It is of the utmost importance that the Pittsburgh concerts go well, since Steinberg is also Musical Director of the Boston Symphony for another three years and I am hoping that we can include Boston on the itinerary for 1970–71"; Soffer to Samama, 17 June 1969.

12   Martin Schneider, "Bruno Maderna Here to Lead Concert Pair," *The Daily News* (McKeesport, 16 October 1969).

beat that Fritz Reiner would have viewed with approval";[13] for others, the program was a beautifully constructed "gem," and they discern a slight physical resemblance to Fiorello La Guardia, the mayor of New York between 1933 and 1945.[14]

However, it is the second program in particular that reveals the real extent of Maderna's conducting skills. Once again, he mixes early, classical, and modern in an original way. At its core is Giovanni Gabrieli's polychoral motet *In ecclesiis*, transcribed by Maderna himself. Its spatial distribution is reflected in the organization of the two contemporary works that precede and follow it: Earle Brown's *From Here*, for chorus and instruments, conducted by Brown and Maderna together, and Jan van Vlijmen's *Serenata II* for flute and four instrumental groups. The program opens and closes with Mozart's Symphony No. 31 (K. 297) and Schoenberg's *Variations for Orchestra* op. 31, whose masterful interpretation inspired the following comment:

> the many listeners who stood their ground Thursday and applauded at the close of the concert seemed not merely to be hailing his performance of the Schoenberg *Variations for Orchestra* but giving their vote of approval to this total contribution to the season.[15]

Maderna now became an overnight sensation. An interview held immediately after the first concert provides the first lively description of the composer and a glimpse into his personality:

> [Talking with him] was like riding a merry-go-round that never stopped. Arm gestures, waves of laughter, and a mixture of smiles and frowns punctuated each rapid swing from topic to topic. With words popping from Italian to English. I was lucky to understand half of what he said. But what I understood made sense.
> Underneath this outgoing warmth, friendliness, and vibrancy exists a professional deeply dedicated to his profession, secure enough to poke fun at it, and knowledgeable enough to look at modern music with directness and understanding.[16]

In the same interview, Maderna mentions early, classical, and contemporary composers (including Machaut, Peri, Monteverdi, Mozart, Beethoven, Stockhausen, Boulez, Berio, and Cage), but the conversation revolves around the expressivity and communication of modern-day music:

> We still can't write as beautiful as Monteverdi. What's missing is soul. Too many composers are afraid to feel or express emotion. They are cold and impersonal. They must speak with the heart. [...] Even if the most exciting things are happening on stage they mean nothing if they don't reach the audience.

Further evidence of the fact that Maderna was now firmly in the public eye is the lengthy radio conversation he held with George Stone and Alan Stout, recorded on 23 January

---

13   Robert C. Marsh, "Symphony's 'new music' night – at least it's a beginning," *Chicago Sun-Times* (16 January 1970).

14   See Thomas Willis, "Maderna's modern!" *Chicago Tribune* (16 January 1970). The comparison with La Guardia will become a recurring *topos* in the New York press (see also note 21).

15   Robert C. Marsh, "Maderna: We'll miss him," *Chicago Sun-Times* (23 January 1970).

16   Kenneth Sanson, "Maderna: 'Music must be felt,'" *Chicago Today* (18 January 1970), also for the next quote.

1970 at WEFM in Chicago,[17] and especially the commission he received shortly after he left America to compose an orchestral piece of around "30–35 minutes."[18] He will call this work *Aura* (1972).

A few months later, on 15 May 1970, Maderna debuted in New York, conducting Saverio Mercadante's *Il Giuramento* at the Juilliard School. The production marked the centenary of the composer's death, and was then brought to Italy the following month (conducted by Thomas Schippers) to open the thirteenth edition of the Festival dei Due Mondi in Spoleto. On the morning of the premiere, Soffer wrote to Samama:

> The last rehearsal went marvelously last night. He whipped the orchestra into a real frenzy of genius. It was the first full orchestra rehearsal (with all the musicians present) that he had. The students have been horrible (orchestra, not singers). It is the time we are in, not Bruno. It is a miracle that Bruno has stayed calm and cool always. But that is part of his genius.

The reviews are unanimous in praising the brilliant performance, its sense of rhythm, and colorful interpretation. On 18 May, as the performances came to an end, Soffer immediately wrote to Samama to inform him about the possible dates scheduled for the next season:

> I am certain Bruno will have called you to tell you of his <u>triumph in New York</u>. [...] He really performed a <u>miracle.</u> The students and audience adored him in all respects, so much so that he has been asked back for next January 1971 to conduct <u>The Juilliard Ensemble in Alice Tully Hall (Lincoln Center)</u> on January <u>31, 1971.</u> Then Peter Mennin (President of Juilliard) would like him to conduct the first student orchestra in his own <u>QUADRIVIUM, Mozart and Debussy.</u> Then, if and when the opera department gets straightened out, of course, <u>on January 14 and 15, Mozart's *LA CLEMENZA DI TITO.*</u> [...] Bruno made such a success with the kids that everyone adored him and wanted him back.

And he remained true to his word. Maderna's desire to compose something for the Juilliard Ensemble turned into the commission for *Juilliard Serenade*,[19] and in early 1971 Maderna returned to New York. On 8 January, just after his arrival, Soffer wrote to Samama:

> Bruno arrived last Sunday in fabulous physical and spiritual shape. He looks twenty years younger and is as ebullient as ever. Much has happened since his arrival. He has been rehearsing like mad at Juilliard and composing a great deal. The *SERENADE* will be ready by Monday morning.[20]

During the rehearsals for *La Clemenza di Tito*, Maderna was interviewed by Raymond Ericson.[21] He mainly talked about his planned works: *Music of Gaity*, described as "a little suite based on old English tunes in the Fitzwilliam Virginal Book. I chose the title because it was the function of music in the sixteenth century to provide gaiety in the form of serenades, dances, and chansons. I like the music, it is so beautiful"; *Quadrivium*, said to be

---

17 The conversation was broadcast by WEFM on 28 June 1970; an audio excerpt is published on the CD *Bruno Maderna: The Last Concert* (Milan: Stradivarius, 1993; STR 10071).
18 Samama to John S. Edwards, 17 March 1970.
19 Letter from Samama to Peter Mennin, 9 October 1970.
20 In fact, the score for *Juilliard Serenade* indicates the place and date of completion: "New York 1971."
21 See "This Bruno Looks Like Fiorello," *The New York Times* (24 January 1971).

"a joke," "something very brilliant. It is a concerto for percussionists with the orchestra divided into four groups"; and *Juilliard Serenade,* a piece that is "not superficial. It reflects the psychological problem of free time, which will be a very important problem in the future, if all goes well."[22]

Soffer was a keen observer of all the intense preparations for the New York concerts, and on 19 January he wrote to Samama:

> BRUNO has been working very hard, and I thought you would like to know that he is looked after like the best prima donna in the world. [...]
> There is much excitement here in New York... Lincoln Center told me that for the concert on the 31st he has already sold more tickets than the Pousseur concert when it was over.[23] [...]
> More reflections... going to all Bruno's rehearsals at Juilliard strongly confirms that he is a GREAT CONDUCTOR. One with great soul, understanding, and incredible musicianship. I am truly amazed at what he is making with the kids at Juilliard.

La Clemenza di Tito was quite successful. Maderna added two arias to the work (not indicated in the program but acknowledged by the critics): one for Servilia, "Vado, ma dove" K. 583 (after her duet with Annio, I:5), and the other for Vitellia, "Vorrei spiegarvi, oh Dio!" K. 418 (beginning of Act II). But the warmest reception was reserved for the two contemporary music programs performed in the next few days. For some, he managed to achieve an equilibrium in the relationship between words and music in his interpretation of *Pierrot lunaire* that outdoes even Schoenberg's own recording.[24] For others, the musical qualities of *Juilliard Serenade* reflect the salient aspects of his skill as a conductor: "His conducting was like his composing: gracious, easy-going, warm – and absolutely sure."[25]

As Soffer explained to Beate Christine Koepnick Maderna on 1 February, just a few days after the concert:

> Such reviews for modern music in New York City are indeed rare, as the press firstly is not kind toward modern music in New York and secondly they are primarily ignorant of fine modern music. However, from these reviews, they must have studied a few hours to learn and appreciate Bruno's great talent.

He also wrote to Samama that same day:

> As you can see from the reviews, BRUNO HAS HAD TWO TRIUMPHS: one with *QUADRIVIUM* and the other with his *SERENADE.* Just read those reviews: they are truly spectacular. He had many many problems, but stayed calm and cool most of the time. [...]
> On Friday, he started the rehearsals at 8 a.m. as the strings did not show up in full force on Wednesday. They started at 8 and rehearsed the whole program until 2. From 2–5 he rehearsed the *SERENADE* and the Sunday program and then the concert that evening.

---

22 On 29 January 1971 Robert Breuer conducted another interview with Maderna ("Gespräch mit Bruno Maderna in New York," *Aufbau*) about electronic music and his stage work *Hyperion.*
23 Henri Pousseur had been the first guest composer-conductor in the "New and Newer Music" concert series at Alice Tully Hall.
24 The reference is to the 1940 recording with Erika Stiedry-Wagner (Columbia M461).
25 Theodore Strongin, "Gentleness Infuses Maderna's *Juilliard Serenade," The New York Times* (1 February 1971).

> That is enough to have a heart attack. […]
> He is not only a great conductor and a marvelous composer, but also a FANTASTIC
> HUMAN… We all adore him.

In the summer of 1971, two interviews seem to have paved the way for Maderna's return to the United States. The first extensive conversation outlines his life story for the first time ever on American soil, providing numerous unpublished details about his childhood, his studies, and his first compositions (including the 1946 *Requiem,* "a curious cocktail of Stravinsky and Bartók," and the Concerto for two pianos and instruments of 1948).[26] Maderna remembers when he was starting out on his conducting career, from the courses with Scherchen (1948) to the concert at the ISCM Festival in Palermo-Taormina (1949), right up to his debut in America with Nono's *Intolleranza 1960.* "If the Philharmonic is brave enough to invite Bruno Maderna," concludes the journalist, "why not the Metropolitan or the New York City Opera?"

Not long after, in another interview, the Italian composer states some fundamental ideas about electronic music and reveals the "secret" to his composing:

> Electronic music is not a substitute for instrumental music. With a studio full of electronic equipment, we can't reproduce the feeling one human being can produce with a single instrument. […] The secret is to make the sound, the composition like a mobile in which you can always find something new.[27]

Thus, in the summer of 1971, Maderna returned to the United States for a two-month stay during which he held concerts with the Chicago Symphony Orchestra, the Boston Symphony Orchestra, and seminars in composition at Tanglewood.

The critic of the *Chicago Daily News* gave Maderna an enthusiastic reception – "one of the most talented, exciting and generally musical conductors now before the public" – and defined the execution of Stravinsky's *A Card Game* as "simply the best performance I have ever heard."[28] Although the reviews are not entirely unanimous in declaring Maderna's transcription of Gabrieli's *In ecclesiis* a success, almost all bemoan the absence of any kind of contemporary music (even Maderna's own works) from the program, which would have allowed him to showcase his expertise. "So all in all," writes Soffer to Samama (1 July 1971), "Bruno's appearance under the worst possible circumstances – heat, lack of rehearsals – was a high success."

On the contrary, the two concerts marking his debut at Tanglewood enjoyed a resounding success. Roy C. Hammerich recalls the immediate positive impact Maderna made on the members of the Boston Symphony Orchestra during rehearsals:

> They liked him for his thorough knowledge of the music he was conducting, for the strongly decisive attitude he had about it, for his clearly-understood means of communicating his ideas and for his friendly, but no-nonsense and unpretentious manner.

---

26 See Dorle J. Soria, "Artist Life," *High Fidelity and Musical America* 21, no. 6 (June 1971), pp. MA–4–6.

27 Lynda McDonnell, "Maderna a Maker of Modern Music," *The Stars and Stripes* 30, no. 79 (6 July 1971), p. 11.

28 Bernard Jacobson, "No challenge at Ravinia," *Chicago Daily News* (30 June 1971).

> [...] The players had no difficulty in understanding what he wished them to do, a factor which increased their respect.
> Such appreciation of guest conductors by orchestra members is uncommon [...].[29]

The multitude of lengthy reviews bear witness to an almost total convergence of critical opinion. Right from the opening bars of Schubert's Symphony No. 2 it was obvious to many that "a real master was in control of the orchestra and music," and that "he can mold a phrase to perfection." His clear, straightforward, expressive gestures received the highest praise: "his lack of self-conscious mannerism was a very rare sight on the conductor's podium." Schubert was performed with brio, vivacity, and an almost Rossinian exuberance in the sections with a fast tempo, but with just as much precision and mastery in the details and delicacy of phrasing in the *Andante*. The density of the writing of Schoenberg's Chamber Symphony op. 9 resulted in "an impressive job of clarifying line and form" capable of clearly expressing the passionate intensity of the piece.[30] In Chopin's Concerto No. 2 Maderna accompanied the soloist Earl Wild (another artist managed by Soffer), following his tempos in a brilliant way. Years later, in the 1990s, Wild will still be heard to say: "the best accompaniment he received in Chopin's F minor Concerto was from Bruno Maderna, who actually cried during the slow movement"; and again: "it was unforgettable when I played it with him."[31]

In the second concert, Maderna – who replaced William Steinberg – conducted Bruckner's Symphony No. 7 for the first time. Gunther Schuller was absolutely thrilled by the performance of his *Five Bagatelles*. Mozart's Symphony No. 38 (K. 504) was interpreted "with a decided emphasis on the lyrical nature of the work, and the result was truly fascinating" (while other critics were not convinced by the too regular, almost mechanical and metronomic rhythm of the first two movements). His interpretation of Bruckner's Symphony – much faster than those of Steinberg and Erich Leinsdorf – was praised as "superb," "with a depth of perception one hasn't been subjected to since Charles Munch." Despite its extraordinary flexibility and unrestricted exploration of tempo, the performance was solid and coherent as a whole: Maderna sculpted Bruckner's Symphony "as a grandiloquent work of Wagnerian breadth and epic dimensions," and in the intense and solemn "Adagio" "one heard the glory of the Boston orchestra at its finest." It all ended with "an unprecedented outburst of applause and vocal acclaim from [a] wildly tumultuous audience [that] must be recorded as the greatest given any conductor this season, even Bernstein," "one of the biggest ovations of the summer."[32]

---

29   Richard (Roy) C. Hammerich, "Defying the Arts," *The Springfield Republican* (8 August 1971). The Hammerich's article is reproduced as Appendix 2 on p. 327 in this volume.

30   As to the four quotes in the text, see respectively Martha deB. Beaver, "Boston Symphony At Tanglewood," *Daily Hampshire Gazette* (16 July 1971); Edward French, "2 New Conductors in Fine Debut," *The Knickerbocker News* (12 July 1971); Richard (Roy) C. Hammerich, "Maderna Elicits Extra Measure Of Responsiveness," *The Springfield Union* (12 July 1971); and Michael Steinberg, "Fleisher, former pianist, conducts Boston Symphony," *The Boston Globe* (12 July 1971).

31   The quotes come from Jed Distler, "An American Success Story: The Pianist Earl Wild," in *Earl Wild: The Complete RCA Album Collection*, Sony Classical (5 CDs), booklet, p. 8; and idem, "In conversation: Earl Wild, the pianist-transcriber at 80," *Classical Pulse!* no. 14 (February 1996), p. 18.

32   The quotes in the text are from Franklin G. Coleman, "Tanglewood Weekend," *The Lakeville Journal* (12 August 1971); Martha deB. Beaver, "Boston Symphony Orchestra At The Berkshire Festival," *Daily Hampshire Gazette* (13 August 1971); Raymond Morin, "Two Guest Conductors Score at Tanglewood," *Worcester Telegram* (9 August 1971); and Jay C. Rosenfeld, "All-Mozart at Tanglewood," *The Berkshire Eagle* (9 August 1971).

In 1971, the Contemporary Music Activities at Tanglewood were under the guidance of Gunther Schuller, with Lukas Foss, Bruno Maderna, and Charles Wuorinen as guest teachers. Gunther Schuller explained how the courses were organized in a letter sent to Maderna on 14 June 1971:

> you will have a certain number of private composition students, perhaps 6 to 8 whom you would teach one hour a week in private lessons. [...]
> Next, you would do at some point in your stay at Tanglewood, two or three consecutive weeks of seminars, i.e. three two-hour seminars per week. These will be with all the composition students present at Tanglewood and can range all the way from discussions of the students' works to lectures or discussions on subjects which you would like to talk about or subjects of interest to the students.[33]

The students assigned to Maderna for individual lessons were Michael Bayer, Rocco Di Pietro, Clare Franco, Gerald Levinson, Lucas Vis, Emory Waters, and Claude White (as an auditor). Charles Israels, Louis Karchin, Oliver Knussen, and Conrad Pope also attended his seminars in composition, which were open to Gunther Schuller's pupils. This time Maderna stayed in Seranak, the historic summer home of Serge and Natalie Koussevitzky. The serene and harmonious atmosphere that reigned at Tanglewood is aptly described in a letter from Soffer to Samama, dated 2 July 1971:

> Bruno is entrenched at Tanglewood and he is in "Paradise." His house is wonderful, and his studio even more beautiful. He meets with his students in his studio and is very excited about the countryside... the scenery... the marvelous view from the studio... the quietude of the country and the house. He has only 5 students plus Lucas [Vis], which is indeed an easy load. The conducting workshops will be worked out this afternoon with Michael [Tilson Thomas] and Gunther [Schuller]. But it seems that Bruno is considered by all THE MASTER, composer as well as conductor. He met with two of his students today and three tomorrow privately, then he will put them all together. As for the Musical Theatre, that will be worked out in a few days. All in all, I have never seen Bruno to be such a <u>young</u> person... he is like a child... he sings, etc.

28 July and 18 August witnessed the organization of two "Composers Forums" under the supervision of Maderna and Schuller, with music by the students in the course. A year before, Maderna had already announced his intention of creating a collective composition with his pupils.[34] Tanglewood was the perfect opportunity to make this project happen, thanks to the Music Theater Project, inaugurated in 1971 under the guidance of Ian Strasfogel.[35]

The new collective work is based on Trimalchio's Feast from the *Satyricon* by Petronius Arbiter. Ample details of the performance scheduled for 8 August are given in *The Springfield Republican*.[36] As Ian Strasfogel recalled: "a few things can be stated with certainty. The piece was absolutely NOT by Maderna, it was a collective improvisation, led

---

33 The letter is held in the Boston Symphony Orchestra Archives. I am grateful to Ellen Highstein, Director of the Tanglewood Music Center, for kindly granting permission to publish. The document is reproduced on pp. 325–26 in this volume.

34 "imagine... a composer sharing the music with the students, like Leonardo da Vinci and his assistants"; letter from Soffer to Harry Kraut, 5 November 1970.

35 See also the previously cited letter of 14 June 1971 from Schuller to Maderna (see note 33).

36 Hammerich, "Defying the Arts" (see note 29).

by me, based on a brief text which I devised from the Petronius Arbiter original. There was no orchestra, only a piano. It lasted at most fifteen minutes."[37] The performance featured baritone Lenus Carlson in the role of Trimalchio and Rocco Di Pietro on the piano. Nonetheless, accounts are anything but unanimous. Emory Waters recalled:

> the idea met with a great deal of resistance from the members of the Composition Seminar (we were all young and anxious to establish our own voices as composers, and weren't interested in any sort of collective undertaking). Eventually there was a meeting facilitated by Mr. Schuller in which the project was dropped.[38]

The fact that the project was dropped is also confirmed by some of the other participants in the course, such as Louis Karchin, Lucas Vis, Gerald Levinson, and Oliver Knussen, who all seem to recall that such a collective project did not get very far.[39]

Instead, Rocco Di Pietro, recalls the improvised nature of a performance that was still in an embryonic stage at the time and would only later become the work performed at Scheveningen in 1973:

> I worked also as his assistant on *Satyricon,* at Tanglewood, I improvised with him during rehearsals and he had me arrange Webern's *Kinderstück* for celesta for Trimalchio's Banquet scene.
> Maderna used this workshop approach as his "Renaissance studio" and later wrote some of it down in a rather free manner on loose sheets [… The] seminar was a birthing process, an embryo for Maderna, who ended up being the composer after all, since we were playing his sketches.[40]

As part of the Music Theater Project, Maderna conducted the first performance in the United States of Harrison Birtwistle's "dramatic pastoral" *Down by the Greenwood Side* and, for his last concert at the Festival of Contemporary Music, Gunther Schuller's *Double Quintet.* Just before his almost two-month stay in Tanglewood came to an end, Paul Fromm invited him to write a new composition (the future *Giardino religioso*) for the Twentieth Anniversary Concert of his Foundation. He also sang Maderna's praises for the great contribution he had made to the season's musical events: "I am especially pleased and encouraged that you will return to Tanglewood next year. We need the imprint and impact of your creativity, professionalism and broad musical horizon" (letter dated 20 August 1971, PSS-BMC).

In November 1971, Maderna returned to the United States to conduct the Philadelphia Orchestra and the Greater Miami Philharmonic. He took the podium in Philadelphia to conduct Mozart's Piano Concerto No. 20, K. 466 (with Vladimir Ashkenazy), and, for the first time, Mahler's Symphony No. 5 (it is interesting to note that his teacher, Hermann Scherchen, had made his American debut in October 1964 with exactly the same

---

37 Personal communication, 18 November 2015. For further details on the creation of *Satyricon,* see the contribution by Angela Ida De Benedictis in this volume (pp. 19–57); see also the contribution by Anne C. Shreffler (pp. 299–327) for a fuller account on the "Trimalchio" project.
38 Personal communication, 29 October 2015.
39 Personal communications of 30 October 2015 (Karchin), 19 January 2016 (Vis), 31 October 2015 (Levinson), and 11 November 2015 (Knussen).
40 Personal communications, 6 May 2014 and 2 December 2015.

Symphony and with the Philadelphia Orchestra). Although the "Adagio" of Symphony No. 10 has been in the repertoire since 1951, it is only from the mid-1960s onwards that Mahler started to become a more constant and meaningful presence in Maderna's programs. With great plasticity and warmth, Maderna's execution in Philadelphia progressively acquired intensity, through a kaleidoscopic multiplicity of expressive behavior: "Outwardly implacable" during the first two movements (*Scherzo* included), Maderna "stressed the cries and sorrows of the voices of single instruments with strong effect." But it is above all in the *Adagietto* that Maderna "finally came to grips and entered a passionate yet controlled wrestling with the orchestra for more shading, for highlights, shadows, growing intensity," showing, at the end of the performance, "a flair for the score and a gift with orchestral sound."[41] Soffer enthused about this success in a letter to Samama on 9 November 1971, amazed "especially since he had never conducted the Mahler 5th. He really is a genius."

Maderna then conducted a "Viennese Promenade Concert" in Miami, with the participation of the soprano Kate Hurney, in which, along with the waltzes of Johann Strauss Jr. and Richard Strauss, he presented his own transcriptions of Schubert. His concert with the pianist Malcolm Frager stood out with a "first-rate impressionistic reading" of Debussy's *Jeux*.[42]

In the interview Maderna gave between the two concerts, he used the second program from 21 November (with music by Schoenberg, Mozart, Wagner, and Debussy) as the starting point for illustrating the "formula" with which he created his programs:

> Forty per cent traditional, 30 per cent from the period of Mahler to Stravinsky, 30 per cent good modern music. I have found that formula works. People don't get mad when I use it, they even get excited. It makes for a concert with peaks and valleys.[43]

In January 1972, Maderna returned to the United States for his first appearance with the New York Philharmonic Orchestra, whose newly appointed Music Director was Pierre Boulez. In the lengthy interview before the concerts, he began by distinguishing between conductor-musicians, like Arturo Toscanini (who "was a marvelous conductor, but he was only a cellist"), and conductor-composers like Pierre Boulez, who in his opinion carried out a conducting activity "steeped in musical culture":

> Toscanini… each time he conducted music from another time except the one in which he lived, it was plain he couldn't understand it. His Mozart was marvelous as conducting, but it wasn't Mozart. In Verdi, Wagner, Dukas, he was incredible. But he was not cultivated enough. In music you must be a humanist, not merely a specialist. With Toscanini, I find specialization only.[44]

---

41 Quotes from James Felton, "Milan Maestro Takes On Mahler"/"New Conductor Takes On Mahler," *The Evening Bulletin* (5 November 1971); and Daniel Webster, "Maderna, in Debut, Shows Flair For Mahler and Mozart Scores," *The Philadelphia Inquirer* (5 November 1971).

42 See Evelyn Spitalny, "Music: Frager Charms Philharmonic Audience With Mozart," *The Daily Sun Reporter* (23 November 1971).

43 Doris Reno, "Making a Music Formula Work," *The Miami Herald* (14 November 1971).

44 See Donal Henahan, "Is Toscanini or Boulez The Better Conductor?" *The New York Times* (9 January 1972). The interview sparked a lively discussion; see "Was Toscanini Maligned?" *The New York Times* (27 February 1972), and "Toscanini defended," *Music Journal* 30 (November 1972), p. 38.

Instead, for Maderna, a conductor has to be "a musician of the widest technical and philosophical grasp," just like the pre-World War II conductors Mitropoulos, Scherchen, Rodziński, Walter, Klemperer, and Kleiber, whose vast and profound knowledge he was hard-pressed to find in those around him, with the exception of Bernstein, Boulez, and Solti. The focal point of the interview sees him take a firm and decisive stance against the figure of the "star" conductor, against his power, his politics, and his self-aggrandizement ("the era of the star conductor is finished, *must* be finished"). It is hard not to notice the reference to Herbert von Karajan, whom Maderna had already openly criticized in some interviews appearing a few years earlier in the Dutch press, one of which was unequivocally entitled, "We don't need demigods like Karajan."[45]

Nevertheless, he did have a few differences of opinion even with Boulez. In fact, the latter's program for the New York Philharmonic in 1971–72 included a retrospective of the complete works of Alban Berg and compositions by Franz Liszt that were still little-known to the public of New York. Maderna, however, had just stated in the interview with Donal Henahan that "personally, I do not understand a Liszt revival at this moment." A misunderstanding that Samama also communicated to Soffer on 30 October 1970 in his account of the programming of the New York concerts:

> BERG: No problems, whatever they like
> LISZT: NO NO NO! (Not Luigi and not Liszt!)
> If you want to have Bruno killed, try a more efficient way! The Avant-Garde is not yet that decadent
> *DER WEIN + WESENDONCK LIEDER:* with greatest pleasure.
> Bruno prefers Wagner to Strauss (If Johann … Strauss, if Richard … Wagner!)

Michael Wiener's review of the first concert still contains echoes of the overwhelming execution of Bruckner in Tanglewood the previous summer; other critics emphasize the warm, almost "mediterranean" interpretation of the Austrian and German composers on the program. Harold C. Schonberg appreciates the ingeniously constructed program, with Wagner's *Wesendonck Lieder* providing an interesting counterpoint to Berg's concert aria *Der Wein;* despite the rather rapid execution of Mendelssohn's symphony, the critic finds Maderna "especially impressive in the slow movement, where he managed to get the most singing of lines without the least trace of sentimentality" and recognizes in general "a first-class orchestral technician."[46] In the wake of Maderna's comments about Toscanini, Winthrop Sargeant is more critical and expresses an extremely harsh judgment of Maderna's interpretation; however, he does recognize that his conducting has a number of interesting aspects, including his choice of a certain elasticity of tempo ("there were rubatos in his performances that have not been heard here since the time of Mengelberg. […] It represents a return to the great nineteenth- and early-twentieth-century tradition of interpretation").[47]

---

45 See "Bruno Maderna: Halfgoden als Karajan hebben we niet nodig," *Algemeen Dagblad* (8 February 1967).

46 "Music: A Counterpoint," *The New York Times* (15 January 1972).

47 "Musical Events," *The New Yorker* (22 January 1972), pp. 80–81.

His second program presented a juxtaposition that initiates reflection on the concept of "concert": Vivaldi's baroque double Concerto for two mandolins, Stravinsky's *Dumbarton Oaks* Concerto (which, in turn, is modeled on Bach's *Brandenburg Concertos*), and in the middle his own Concerto for violin and orchestra (1969–70). The reviews praise Maderna's work and the intense performance given by the soloist, Paul Zukofsky. On the other hand, the interpretation of Mozart's Symphony No. 38 (K. 504) was not entirely convincing, considered rather impersonal and devoid of the expected finesse. Only Harold C. Schonberg has something more positive to say, affirming that "his ideas about Mozart were very much in the modern style." However, he notes a certain lack of balance in the contrapuntal episodes and concludes, caustically: "Toscanini would not have liked this."[48]

Finally, Maderna took part in the third concert in the "Prospective Encounters" series with works by Earle Brown (*Event: Synergy II*, conducted together with the composer) and by R. Murray Schafer (*Requiems for the Party-Girl*). These innovative concerts in Greenwich Village were Boulez's idea and included debates between performers, composers, and audience. The evening – moderated by the critic Alan Rich – aroused a lot of interest, and each song was performed twice, before and after the composers spoke.

In March 1972, before going to Chicago, Maderna presented the premiere of his *Venetian Journal* for tenor, orchestra, and magnetic tape as part of a concert conducted by Dennis Russell Davies in New York. The work had been commissioned by Paul Sperry and marked Maderna's first collaboration with the American artist.[49] A year later, Maderna chose Sperry to interpret Habinnas in the first performance of his *Satyricon* and, as soloist, in a concert at the RAI in Milan with arias by Mozart. Sperry then commissioned Maderna to write two other works, "one aria for tenor and orchestra and one cycle of Italian lieder with piano and accompaniment,"[50] although neither was ever actually written.

"Whenever Bruno Maderna conducts the Chicago Symphony," wrote Bernard Jacobson when the conductor returned to the United States, "a fresh and stimulating breeze seems to blow through normally traditionalistic Orchestra Hall."[51] On the program were works by Debussy, Mozart, Stravinsky, and Schoenberg. The Schoenberg works were *Verklärte Nacht*, criticized for the choice of tempo, and the Concerto for violin and orchestra, op. 36 (performed by Esther Glazer). The interpretation of Debussy's *Jeux* lent itself to a quite vivid comparison with the performance heard a few months earlier under the direction of Pierre Boulez.[52] "Maderna's conception of the piece," wrote the same Bernard

---

48   "Music: Solo Mandolins and Maderna," *The New York Times* (22 January 1972). Winthrop Sargeant also remarks on this imbalance in "Musical Events," *The New Yorker* (29 January 1972), p. 86.

49   For more information about Sperry and the premiere of *Venetian Journal*, see Angela Ida De Benedictis, "'Qui forse una cadenza brillante': Viaggio nel *Venetian Journal* di Bruno Maderna," *Acta Musicologica* 72, no. 1 (2000), pp. 63–105; and Anne C. Shreffler, "Maderna Goes to Tanglewood," in this volume, pp. 302–05.

50   Samama to Paul Sperry, 22 March 1973. A few days before, on March 13, Soffer had written to Samama that "BOSWELL'S VENITIAN JOURNAL [sic] went well … even though we never thought that we would ever have a decent run through (which we never had) … but typically like Maderna the last days are hectic as hell."

51   "Maderna opens the *Windows*," *Chicago Daily News* (17 March 1972). Also for the next quote in the text.

52   Boulez had conducted *Jeux* in Chicago with the Cleveland Orchestra on 10 and 12 December 1971.

Jacobson, "is much more physical than Boulez' highly abstract reading"; and if at the beginning he seems "to be breaking up the line of the music with little pauses that made it sound misleadingly sectional," as the work progressed "Maderna's long-term planning took effect in a culmination of vivid dramatic strength."

However, what really distinguished this final appearance with the Chicago Orchestra was the presence of three important compositions in their premiere performances: *Aura* ("the more striking of the new pieces"), commissioned by the Chicago Symphony Orchestra for their eightieth anniversary celebrations;[53] Jacob Druckman's *Windows*, awarded the prestigious Pulitzer Prize a few months later on 1 May 1972; and *Trialogus* by Marvin David Levy. Maderna had conducted Druckman's *Incenters* a year before in New York, defining it as "one of the pieces that I liked most in the last years."[54] In *Windows* he found a close affinity with the composer's style, much appreciating his taste in sound material, the richness of timbre, the instrumental expressivity in both the "structural" and "melodic" sense, and above all the persistence of musical memories (in particular, Debussy, performed not surprisingly at the same concert), which, in an extremely filtered form, seep through the "windows" that open onto the dense orchestral fabric. His fondness for Druckman's composition led him to perform it again at Tanglewood the following summer, and he also tried to put it on the programs of his last concerts at the RAI in Milan and at the BBC in London. Instead, Levy's *Trialogus* contains a singular tribute to the composers and the works on the program, with quotations from Schoenberg's *Verklärte Nacht*, Stravinsky's Concerto for piano and wind instruments, and from *Aura* itself (the string harmonics, bars 69–78).

April 1972 thus found Maderna in Rochester, where together with Debussy and Schumann, he conducted his own new orchestral piece, *Biogramma*, commissioned for the Eastman School of Music's Fiftieth Anniversary Festival. This is the third work – in just under a month – to premiere in the United States. Maderna gave a masterful and extremely original interpretation of the piece:[55] rather than executing the score in a linear fashion, from the first to the last page, he began with Section B (pp. 13–14, bars 29–98), completely reinventing the writing for about four minutes. Although the passages are rigorously "closed" and the published score leaves almost no permutations to the conductor's discretion, in this performance the instruments are called in an unordered sequence in which the deep timbre of the horns stands out, alternating with the high tones of the piccolo and violin. An orchestral fabric is thus created which is made up of sweeping "aulodias," gradually layered into "dialodias" or more dense polyphonies, in which the full orchestral sound is only hinted at for a brief moment. The execution continues with Section A, then with Section C (performed in a sequence of small episodes), and finally with the magical and seductive beauty of Section B (bars 1–28), followed by a new interpretation (almost

---

53   Bernard Jacobson, "More musical novelties from Maderna," *Chicago Daily News* (24 March 1972).
54   Conversation between Maderna and Druckman (24 January 1972), housed at the New York Public Library. An Italian translation is in Bruno Maderna, *Amore e curiosità: Scritti, frammenti e interviste sulla musica*, ed. Angela Ida De Benedictis, Michele Chiappini, and Benedetta Zucconi (Milan: il Saggiatore, 2020), pp. 448–54.
55   The complete recording of the concert is kept at the Eastman School of Music.

four minutes long) of pages 13–14, which seem to become the expressive nucleus on which Maderna's interpretation is concentrated. The instruments enter randomly once again; the combination of timbric layers, the instrumental density, and the dynamic weave are ever-changing, searching this time for a more complete orchestral sound. In the end, the atmosphere goes back to being rarefied, endowed with a limpid and poignant lyricism, which leaves room for "gestures" dear to the composer, such as the mysterious conclusive appearance of the english horn (just as happens in Concerto No. 3 for oboe and orchestra) or the stopping on the tense and vibrant sounds of the solo violin. In this surprising performance, the protagonist is no longer just the conductor-sculptor who creatively shapes aleatoric passages, but the composer himself, who writes directly on the sound, producing a different reading of his material and giving us an unpublished and absolutely fascinating image of the score.

Echoes of that vibrant performance can be found in the Eastman School of Music's Fiftieth Anniversary Yearbook:

> Maderna was here. That was one of the really bright spots of the year. Inside this one man there is more vitality, excitement, and love of music and life than there has been around Eastman for a long, long time. He stood Philharmonia on its ear for the entire time he was here. Musicmaking with passion: a good lesson for all of us.[56]

In the summer of 1972, Maderna returned to Tanglewood to teach composition, and in the absence of Gunther Schuller (who left the artistic direction to Seiji Ozawa), he also became "Acting Head" of Contemporary Music Activities.[57] Just like the year before, he supervised the organization of two "Composers' Forums" in the Theater-Concert Hall (22 July and 15 August) with performances of music written by the pupils in his course.

The first of the two concerts he performed with the Boston Symphony Orchestra is remarkable for its eclectic program. The concert was originally supposed to open with Andrea Gabrieli's *La battaglia* (1587), one of the works Maderna had intended to explain in the composition course.[58] It was therefore replaced by another of his transcriptions, a *Ricercare* (as indicated in the program) by Giovanni Gabrieli, which, in actual fact, turns out to be the arrangement of the motet *Exsultavit cor meum* from the second book of the *Symphoniae sacrae* (1615).[59] In the Boston Symphony's not so flawless execution, Maderna tried to recreate the antiphonal "double choir" of St. Mark's Basilica by distancing the two wind quartets about ten meters from each other. The program continued with Earle

---

56 *Eastman School of Music 50th Anniversary Year, 1971–1972* (Rochester: Eastman School of Music, [ca. 1975]), p. 103.

57 The pupils assigned to Maderna for individual composition lessons were Curtis Curtis-Smith, Louis Karchin, and Max Lifchitz. See also photo reproduced as Example 4 in the next chapter (p. 324).

58 A notebook housed at PSS contains Maderna's notes for "*La Battaglia* di Andrea Gabrielli, parti e strumentazione da fare sul posto, dimostrazione corso" (*La Battaglia* by Andrea Gabrielli, parts and instrumentation to be done on the spot, course demonstration). He had previously made a transcription of the piece, performed with the Rotterdams Philharmonisch Orkest in 1968.

59 In the program notes, Andrew Raeburn writes that "Bruno Maderna transcribed this work of Gabrieli in 1960 for two trumpets, two trombones, two horns and two bassoons," but no document has been found confirming the fact. The same work had already been transcribed by Maderna for four trumpets and four trombones and performed several times in the 1960s; yet another arrangement of it had also been used in the radio drama *Ritratto di Erasmo* (1969).

Brown's *Available Forms I*, which received "the evening's longest and loudest ovation (with a few boos mixed in)" and proved to have "much more life and humor" than the recording Maderna made for RCA in 1964.[60] The first part of the program came to a close with a group of works by Charles Ives, the most impressive being *Scherzo (Over the Pavements)* and *The Unanswered Question;* Maderna conducted the latter with the concertmaster and assistant conductor Joseph Silverstein, and the critics expressed their appreciation of the meaningful choice to perform the first part of the piece with ever-increasing intensity. The second part of the program, featuring Mozart's Symphony No. 41 (K. 551), left them divided. Some speak of "a magnificent reading" and "a model of precision and mobility,"[61] but most talk about a quite dull, rather ordinary execution, and the choice of tempo (too fast) comes in for much criticism. In an interview with the *Worcester Sunday Telegram*, Maderna tried to answer his critics:

> The other day, when I rehearsed the Boston Symphony in Mozart's "Jupiter" Symphony, I saw disapproval among some of the players over my tempos. They gradually accepted my thoughts.
> I have a large collection of books about Mozart and his music. From study I have learned that what Mozart sometimes called a minuet – because he was expected to – was more in the character of a folia. If it's played as a stately minuet, Mozart's intention is missed. […] My study also proves that an "andante" in Mozart can mean anywhere from 66 to 72 on a metronome […]. So there should be no set tempo, as used by some eminent conductors of the past.[62]

The second concert also opened with a transcription from Giovanni Gabrieli. Announced as *Canzona a 12,* it is a new arrangement and a free formal interpretation of *Canzon XVI* from the *Canzoni et Sonate* (1615), which Maderna had already used in *Ritratto di Erasmo* (1969), and which was later published under the title *Canzone a tre cori.* The critics seem to think that the arrangement of this *Canzona* worked better than the previous *Ricercare.* Even though the rendition of Stravinsky – with Earl Wild at the piano – had a few problems in intonation and coordination with the soloist, the interpretation turned out to be "impressive" and the audience "enthusiastic." The execution of Brahms's Symphony No. 1 was considered "far less ponderous than is usual" and once again attacked for its too flexible tempos; comments range from a "giddy show of originality at any price" to "an unusual interpretation because we don't recall it being given such a forceful, intense, dramatic reading before."[63]

---

60 Franklin G. Coleman, "Tanglewood," *The Lakeville Journal* (13 July 1972). The previous quote is from Michael Steinberg, "Bruno Maderna conducts; BSO offers 4 Ives works," *The Boston Globe* (10 July 1972).

61 See respectively Edward French, "Mozart Magic Felt at Tanglewood," *The Knickerbocker News* (10 July 1972), and Richard Vincent, "Mozart, Modern Masters Make Tanglewood a Marvel," *Times Union* (10 July 1972).

62 Raymond Morin, "Maderna, an Innovator in Music," *Worcester Sunday Telegram* (30 July 1972).

63 For the quotes see [Richard Vincent], "Symphony Gored, Critic Bored At Tanglewood," *Times Union* (24 July 1972); Richard Conway, "Tanglewood Artists Offer Varied Works, Quality," *Springfield Daily News* (22 July 1972); John Hinners, "Tanglewood," *The Lakeville Journal* (27 July 1972); and Michael Steinberg, "Bernstein at Tanglewood," *The Boston Globe* (24 July 1972).

The concert on 5 August 1972 marked Maderna's debut with the Cleveland Orchestra at the Blossom Music Center, the orchestra's summer home. The first part of the program was dedicated to the pianist Earl Wild, with compositions by Liszt and Stravinsky, of which Maderna conducted the Concerto for piano and wind instruments (for the third time with the same soloist). The second part of the program featured Schumann's Symphony No. 2, one of his favorite works in the 1970s, together with the Concerto for violin and orchestra by the same composer. This time he was welcomed as "a refreshing nonconformist" who stood out with "his unorthodox programming and individual interpretations."[64]

Three days later, at a concert for the twentieth anniversary of the Fromm Music Foundation on 8 August 1972, Maderna presented *Giardino religioso* at Tanglewood's Festival of Contemporary Music. Paul Fromm had commissioned the work the year before. As an acknowledgment of his American patron's wonderful garden, Maderna had initially thought of naming the piece *"Paul Fromm's Garden" for Chamber Ensemble and Tapes*, but Fromm himself had objected, feeling that the name would be considered corny and cause embarrassment.[65] Maderna paid heed to his client's wishes and changed the title to *Religious Garden*, with a wordplay that translates the German word "fromm" (pious, devout, religious). But it is Fromm himself – in a letter to Samama on 24 April 1972 – who steered the composer toward the Italian title:

> *Religious Garden* sounds fine, but I wonder whether Bruno meant "Sacred Garden"? Perhaps the title would be even more impressive if Bruno would translate it back from English into Italian to arrive at something like "Jardino…"

Samama's reply on 8 May 1972 announced the final title as *Giardino religioso*, which was eventually produced without the use of magnetic tape.

As the reviews clearly show, Maderna's execution followed the conducting indications in the score, signaling by hitting a triangle, playing the congas (p. 3, section C), or improvising inside the piano or on the celesta (p. 13, sections G and H). The applause lasted for about five minutes: *Giardino religioso* was acclaimed as "a genial work," "a fascinating piece of music," and "something bordering on the mystical."[66] And in the insistent signals of the trumpets, which overlap the *continuum* of strings in the closing section, the American critics perceived the same mood as in the final part of Ives's *The Unanswered Question*.

In the last concert of the Festival of Contemporary Music (10 August 1972), the missing performance of the premiere of Alfred (Fred) Lerdahl's *Chromorhythmos* forced Maderna to make a sudden change of program.[67] He announced from the stage that the two pieces by Druckman and Webern would be repeated in reverse order in the second part of the concert, entrusting Bruce Hangen, a student in the composition course, with

---

64 Wilma Salisbury, "Italian Conductor Impressive at Debut," *The Plain Dealer* (7 August 1972).

65 See letter from Fromm to Samama, 28 February 1972. See also, in this volume, the essay by Nicola Scaldaferri, pp. 161–68, and the documents 2–3 reproduced in the Appendix on p. 169.

66 See respectively Jay C. Rosenfeld, "Schuller's *Tre Invenzione* [sic] debut," *The Berkshire Eagle* (9 August 1972); Raymond Morin, "2 Original Works Premier at Tanglewood Concert," *Worcester Telegram* (10 August 1972); and Richard Conway, "Tanglewood Continues Festival of Contemporary Music," *Springfield Daily News* (9 August 1972).

67 About this program change see also the following essay of Anne C. Shreffler in this volume, p. 323.

the role of second conductor for the *Variations*, op. 30. The student's execution was "more hard-edged and sharply defined in rhythm than Maderna's more fluid, lyric one,"[68] and the interpretation of *Windows* with the Berkshire Music Center Orchestra, while not equaling the orchestral sounds and timbre of the Chicago Symphony, "sounded first-class."

The day after the concert, on 11 August 1972, Paul Fromm wrote to Maderna:

> Dear Bruno:
> You contributed immeasurably to our week at Tanglewood.
> First, and most of all, you wrote a beautiful new work, but you also gave freely of your admirable professionalism as the conductor of unusually fine performances.

At the time of writing, Maderna had yet to undertake his last engagement with Tanglewood: a new staging of Claudio Monteverdi's *The Coronation of Poppea*, in English, presented during the second season of the Music Theater Project, under the direction of Ian Strasfogel, just like the year before. The latter had announced to the press that the "production will be set not in imperial Rome, but in some timeless totalitarian society,"[69] and that this new version

> focuses exclusively on the social and political realities of the regime of the demented Emperor Nero and his decadent court. [...] I've set my *Poppea* in futurist times as a kind of operatic "Clockwork Orange," emphasizing the grotesqueness of Imperial Rome.[70]

Although the work was presented in a drastically reduced version – for some by a third, for others by as much as a half – the production acquired particular importance from Maderna's orchestration, which was not indicated on the program but openly acknowledged by the press.[71] A reconstruction by Alan Curtis was used in Tanglewood, which, as Leighton Kerner writes, was taken as a basic version "expanded instrumentally from a chamber-music accompaniment into an orchestra of two dozen by Bruno Maderna."[72] What is more, Ottavia's two scenes – "Disprezzata regina" (I:5) and "Addio Roma!" (III:7) – were also transcribed and reorchestrated specifically for the mezzo-soprano Joyce Castle.

The critics enthused about Maderna's dazzling direction and his firm control over the orchestra: "the principal hero, aside from Monteverdi himself, [...] who conducted so sensitively all evening long, especially in that overpoweringly beautiful love duet that ends the opera."[73]

---

68 Michael Steinberg, "Druckman's Pulitzer Prize *Windows*," *The Boston Globe* (12 August 1972). Leighton Kerner was also of the same opinion; see "Poppea of the Space Age," *The Village Voice* 17, no. 35 (31 August 1972), p. 36. He felt that Maderna's interpretation "emphasized Webern's demands for a special shimmering lyricism." For the next quotation see Donal Henahan, "Music: A Tanglewood Replacement," *The New York Times* (12 August 1972).

69 *Tanglewood News Release* (8 August 1972). The work was performed on 13, 14, and 16 August.

70 Donal Henahan, "What! Never Seduced by *Poppea* Even Once?" *The New York Times* (13 August 1972).

71 See also Herbert Kupferberg, *Tanglewood* (New York: McGraw-Hill, 1976), p. 219. The transcription was kept by Bruce Hangen, Maderna's assistant and the conductor of the third recital, who donated the materials to PSS in 2019.

72 Kerner, "Poppea of the Space Age" (see note 68).

73 Ibid. Strasfogel himself recalls Maderna's conducting of the final duet as "a marvel of concentration and fire" (personal communication, 9 May 1989).

Only three days after *The Coronation of Poppea*, Maderna directed the Detroit Symphony Orchestra in two concerts at the Meadow Brook Music Festival. His own *Biogramma* originally featured on the program, but due to the lack of preparation time it was unfortunately canceled, also because the author himself considered it a work "of such delicacy it would not come off in an open air pavilion."[74] In the first concert – with the bass Jerome Hines, who sang pieces by Mozart and Verdi and three arias dedicated to the character of Mephistopheles (by Berlioz, Gounod, and Boito) – Maderna revealed his careful and expert conducting skills. But it was above all in the second part of the program – Schubert's "Great" C-major Symphony – that Maderna "demonstrated his genius," showing himself to be "a great conductor instead of a merely good one." The second concert also established him "as a great man with the baton" with the execution of Paderewski's Piano Concerto, op. 17, which, in his autobiography, the soloist Earl Wild would remember as a "fabulous performance."[75]

On 22 August 1972, Maderna accepted a commission from the Koussevitzky Music Foundation to compose a new work for orchestra, awarded "in recognition of your valuable contributions to the music of our time."[76] Unfortunately, the composition was never to see the light of day.

In September 1972, Maderna led the National Symphony Orchestra in Washington in a program entirely dedicated to music of the twentieth century. Alongside works by Bartók and Stravinsky, Ives's Symphony No. 4 was particularly memorable. Not only did the critics appreciate Maderna's communicative dimension, but they also praised his conducting skills when faced with the rhythmic complexities of the Ives score. "His rhythmic and metric sense is uncanny," wrote Thomas Willis, observing how he manages to keep time "with a left hand chopping motion and the other with conventional baton technique – and still manage page turns without losing his place."[77] Some of the distinctive features of Maderna's execution that deserve mention are the repetition of the first movement – performed the first time with the optional chorus singing the anthem *Watchman, Tell Us of the Night*, the second time without – and "a little unnecessary sentimentality in the fugue." The reviews talk of a moment of silence and of "cheers and a standing ovation" at the end of the symphony.[78]

September 1972 also saw Maderna conduct a controversial edition of Mozart's *Don Giovanni* for the New York City Opera, remembered many years later by the then director Julius Rudel as "a gigantic fiasco."[79] The dual production, in Italian and English,

---

74 Collins George, "2 Artists Bring Vigor, Fun to Concert," *Detroit Free Press* (19 August 1972).
75 Earl Wild, *A Walk on the Wild Side* (Palm Springs: Ivory Classics Foundation, 2011), p. 746. For the preceding quotes in the text see Don Newman, "Conductor Displays Vigor in Meadow Brook Debut," *The Oakland Press* (18 August 1972); George, "2 Artists Bring Vigor, Fun to Concert" (see note 74); and Collins George, "Prodigy and the Paderewski Star in the Symphony Finales," *Detroit Free Press* (22 August 1972).
76 The letter of commission and Maderna's reply are kept at the Library of Congress in New York. My thanks to the Koussevitzky Foundation for having kindly granted permission to publish.
77 "Modernism by Maderna at J.F.K. Center," *Chicago Tribune* (9 September 1972).
78 For the quotes see Robert Evett, "Glorious Symphony," *The Evening Star and Daily News* (7 September 1972); and Willis, "Modernism by Maderna at J.F.K. Center" (see note 77).
79 Peter G. Davis, "Rudel Reflects on the City Opera," *The New York Times* (25 March 1979).

was directed by Frank Corsaro, who conceived it as "a charade, a black comedy, a Neapolitan Hogarth, extraordinarily realistic, a dirty show with *two* villains – the Don and Leporello."[80] At the end of the first performance, Harold C. Schonberg wrote that "Mr. Corsaro's treatment [...] approached vandalism," and when the curtain dropped, director and conductor "got as lusty a collections of boos as has enlivened the New York State Theater since it was opened. They deserved every bit of it"; Maderna, he goes on,

> conducted as though his baton were tied to the tip of a metronome. Mozart's supple rhythms took on a sort of rigid paralysis. [...] But the big moments of the score – those overwhelming D minor scales, the end of the banquet scene – had all the power and grandeur of a lost firefly on a foggy night.[81]

These harsh words are echoed by those of Alan Rich, who judged the production "a disaster [...] an act of perversity and vandalism [...] under Bruno Maderna's stiff, timid beat."[82] Reigniting the controversy that had just been put to rest, Earl Bennett recalls that "he insulted Toscanini," and yet, he goes on, "his conducting debut lacked sensitivity, flexibility and drama. Tempos were rigid and communication with singers was almost non-existent. He deserved the boos he got at curtain call."[83] Apart from the only positive review by Sam Norkin, for whom Maderna "led a beautifully integrated *Giovanni*, full of verve," all the other critics were united in their harsh and disparaging reviews of its interpretation.[84]

Maderna's execution may also have been affected by his health, which forced him to cancel five of the originally planned ten performances, as well as the opening of the Los Angeles Opera season, scheduled for November 15 (he was replaced by Charles Wilson). The news of his precarious health was also leaked to the press at the end of October, where we read that Maderna "was said to be ill"[85] and that in the New York performance, he "seems to have fallen victim himself, however, to some incapacitating malady since the opening."[86]

This disappointing *Don Giovanni* by Mozart – his favorite composer[87] – was also one of the most criticized of all his interpretations, and it brought Maderna's career in America to an end. It was a short but intense period during which he achieved considerable

---

80 Ralph Zachary, "Corsaro," *Opera News* 37, no. 2 (August 1972), pp. 16–17; see also Frank Corsaro, *Maverick: A Director's Personal Experience in Opera and Theater* (New York: Vanguard, 1978), pp. 89–97.

81 Harold C. Schonberg, "City Opera Lifts the Curtain on Its New *Don Giovanni*," *The New York Times* (17 September 1972).

82 "The House Is, at Last, a Home," *New York* 5, no. 40 (2 October 1972), p. 67.

83 "N.Y. State Theatre," *Music Journal* 30 (November 1972), p. 59.

84 See Sam Norkin, "City Center's *Giovanni* Is Full of Verve," *Sunday News* (17 September 1972). The second performance seems to have gone a little better, during which Maderna "showed a bit more élan but nothing startling"; Speight Jenkins, "City Opera *Don* a total cropper," *Dallas Times Herald* (1 October 1972). In the subsequent English version (which did away with the less successful elements) it is also noted that he "added little vigor" (Bob Micklin, "A Rose by Another Name Loses Something," *Newsday*, 1 October 1972), and that his conducting "has improved" (Peter Wynne, "A better *Don Giovanni*," *The Record*, 21 September 1972).

85 Donal Henahan, "City Opera: *Don Giovanni* Given With 4 New Faces," *The New York Times* (28 October 1972).

86 Martin Bernheimer, "*Don Giovanni* Opens Opera Season," *Los Angeles Times* (17 November 1972).

87 See *Una polifonia di suoni e immagini*, volume attached to the Luciano Berio boxset *C'è musica & musica*, ed. Angela Ida De Benedictis (Milan: Feltrinelli, 2013), p. 129. See also the essay by Benedetta Zucconi in this volume, pp. 227–43.

notoriety as a conductor, and which saw his own writing flourish in the same extraordinary manner. Without considering the theatrical experiment linked to *Trimalchio (Satyricon)*, five of his last works (*Juilliard Serenade, Venetian Journal, Aura, Biogramma,* and *Giardino religioso*), together with some new transcriptions of early music, all came to light precisely during this happy, albeit frenetic time in America.[88]

Maderna had hoped to find a permanent position in the "New World" that could finally have ensured him not only some peace of mind, but also the calm he needed to devote himself to composing. "It seems that I am a decent composer," he had written on 27 June 1971 to his adoptive mother, Irma Manfredi, aboard the jumbo jet bound for Chicago.[89] In another letter, dated 18 August 1972, and perhaps the last he wrote to her from the United States, he adds:

> My working life here moves at a dizzying speed. Concerts, compositions, projects for the future, commitments, teaching, interviews, trips. In short, there is no longer any time for a private life. But that's the way it is now. I hope to work like this for only two or three seasons more. Then I want to organize my life in a calmer way and spend more time writing music.[90]

Sad to say, his premature death robbed him of these ambitions…

---

88 We could also add the 1971 *Y después* for guitar to this list of works, performed for the first time by Narciso Yepes in New York on 1 December 1973, just a few days after Maderna's death.

89 See "Per un ritratto di Bruno Maderna: estratti dalla corrispondenza," in Maderna, *Amore e curiosità* (see note 54), pp. 542–638: 630 (original in Italian).

90 Ibid., p. 634 (original in Italian).

ANNE C. SHREFFLER

Maderna Goes to Tanglewood
The Role of American Networks in the Origins and Reception of *Venetian Journal* and *Satyricon*

Bruno Maderna's extensive connections with the U.S. music scene have received much less attention than the American careers of many other European composers, for example Luciano Berio and Pierre Boulez.[1] Yet Maderna spent a lot of time in the United States, where during the last few years of his life he gained increasing respect as a conductor and composer, working with top ensembles including the Chicago Symphony Orchestra, the Boston Symphony Orchestra, the Philadelphia Orchestra, and the New York Philharmonic.[2] As Maderna the conductor became better known in the U.S., Maderna the composer also received increasing recognition. Especially his late works, with their timbral richness and gestural expressivity, as well as their zany humor and high-energy theatricality, were eagerly received by many Americans as a welcome change from the increasingly academic new music culture in the U.S. At the same time, Maderna's use of controlled aleatoric techniques resonated with similar efforts by many American composers at the time, especially Earle Brown, with whom Maderna enjoyed a close friendship.[3]

I owe a tremendous debt to Angela Ida De Benedictis, Curator of the Bruno Maderna Collection at the Paul Sacher Foundation in Basel, for the impetus to take on this topic in the first place, for her skillful help in navigating the archive, and also for many stimulating conversations about Maderna and his music. I am grateful to Paul Sperry and Ian Strasfogel, who welcomed me into their homes in New York and generously shared their memories and Maderna materials. I also wish to thank the many people who recounted their experiences of Maderna for me: Joyce Castle, Anne Haenen, John Heiss, Barbara Hocher, Poppy Holden, Philip Morehead, William Neill, and Rocco Di Pietro. I would also like to thank Ian Strasfogel for helping me contact many of my interviewees, and Brent Wetters for putting me in touch with Rocco Di Pietro. Many thanks to Nadia Bacchiet of Casa Ricordi, Promotion Department, for providing me with performance records for *Venetian Journal*, Mary M. Manning, University Archivist and Curator of Performing and Visual Arts Collections, University of Houston Libraries, for looking into the Débria Brown file for me, and last but not least, Bridget Carr, Archivist, Boston Symphony Orchestra, for her generous help during my visits.

1   For Berio's U.S. activities, see Tiffany Kuo, "Composing American Individualism: Luciano Berio in the United States, 1960–1971" (Ph.D. dissertation, New York University, 2011). Robin Maconie discusses Boulez's New York years in *Avant Garde: An American Odyssey from Gertrude Stein to Pierre Boulez* (Lanham, MD: Scarecrow Press, 2012).

2   For a detailed discussion of Maderna's American conducting activities, see Maurizio Romito's article in this volume, pp. 277–97.

3   On Maderna's relationship with Brown, see Pascal Decroupet's article in this volume, pp.115–37: 127–34. See also Richard Toop, "Their Man in Europe, Our Man in America: Earle Brown and the European Avant-Garde," in *Beyond Notation: The Music of Earle Brown*, ed. Rebecca Kim (Ann Arbor: University of Michigan Press, 2017), pp. 142–58.

This essay will focus on the role of American patronage networks in the origins and reception of two works that Maderna composed within the last two years of his life. The monodrama *Venetian Journal* (1972), for solo tenor, instrumental ensemble, and tape, was commissioned and performed by the American tenor Paul Sperry, to a libretto by the American playwright Jonathan Levy. The opera *Satyricon* (1972–73), commissioned by the Netherlands Opera, was based on a multilingual libretto drawn in large part from an idiomatic American translation of the Latin text from the late first century by Petronius Arbiter, and staged by the young American director Ian Strasfogel, who had already worked with Berio in the U.S.[4] The opera was preceded by a workshop experiment on the subject of "Trimalchio's Feast," an episode in Petronius' *The Satyricon*, scheduled within Strasfogel's Music Theater Project at Tanglewood during the summer of 1971. Maderna's opera received its American premiere in the summer of 1973 at Tanglewood, again staged by Strasfogel.

The two works have much in common besides their chronological proximity, and in fact *Venetian Journal* can be seen as a kind of dry run for *Satyricon*, even though they do not share any musical material. Both of their multilingual texts prominently feature contemporary colloquial American English. Both have "mobile form" scores with modular interchangeable elements, abundant musical quotations, and over-the-top bawdy and scatological humor.[5] And both are theatrical: *Satyricon* is clearly an opera, and *Venetian Journal*, although not written explicitly for the stage, is a monodrama written in the first person.[6] In his performances, Sperry emphasized the work's theatricality by wearing a velvet coat.[7] Strasfogel observes that "These two pieces seem closest to [Maderna] as a person. They are funny, they are free, they are delightful, they are obsessed with music history. They are not textbook exercises of any sort, they are just expressive experiments."[8]

The origins of both works were bound up in networks made up of individuals and privately funded institutions, which is typical of American patronage structures. Lacking the state-run and state-financed arts institutions that are common in Europe, new music in the United States has generally depended upon a concatenation of smaller, private funding sources that augment their modest resources by connecting with other patrons and institutions, creating a mix of public funding (usually in the form of foundation grants), university support, and private patronage. In particular, the Juilliard School, the Chicago Symphony Orchestra (and its Ravinia Festival), and Tanglewood became focal points of Maderna's American activities. Individuals – agents, singers, patrons, stage directors, and administrators – also form crucial nodes of this network. At Tanglewood,

---

4   On 9–10 January 1967, Strasfogel staged *Passaggio* by Berio, along with the *Combattimento di Tancredi e Clorinda* by Monteverdi/Berio, at the "Evening of Musical Theater" of the Juilliard School of Music.

5   Raymond Fearn points out these and other elements shared by the two works: see his *Bruno Maderna* (Chur: Harwood, 1990), p. 227.

6   Angela Ida De Benedictis points out how the author of the text, Jonathan Levy, accentuated *"la dimensione 'scenica'"*; see her article "'Qui forse una cadenza brillante': Viaggio nel *Venetian Journal* di Bruno Maderna," *Acta Musicologica* 72, no. 1 (2000), p. 70.

7   Paul Sperry, personal communication (interview), 3 December 2015 in New York City.

8   Ian Strasfogel, personal communication (interview), 28 November 2015 in New York City.

the American composer and impresario Gunther Schuller and the German-American patron Paul Fromm formed the nexus of an extensive collaborative network for Maderna's composition, conducting, and teaching activities. During this time Maderna's American networks intersected with European institutions as well, as my investigation will show.

Using a combination of written and oral materials, I shall provide a fuller picture of how *Venetian Journal* and the first idea of what would become *Satyricon* came to be commissioned and developed, in the process shedding light on Maderna's impact on the new music scene on the American East Coast during the early 1970s. In addition, I will investigate how these works were received by American audiences, critics, and musicians, including other composers. Finally, I will suggest that the American context had some effect on the musical vocabulary and formal design that Maderna used in these two works.

I shall leave aside questions of the actual compositional process as preserved in sketches and drafts, and focus instead on the people, institutions, and circumstances behind the works' origins and reception. In my thinking about patronage networks, I follow Howard Becker's concept of "Art Worlds." Becker's theory of art shifts the focus from the creators and their intentions to specific actions by people and institutions, the division of labor, and the conditions under which art works were created. More than just "background," these actions and networks are of integral significance to the results of the finished artwork.[9]

For this account I draw on interviews with Ian Strasfogel, Paul Sperry, Rocco Di Pietro, Anne Haenen, Poppy Holden, William Neill, and others who were involved with *Venetian Journal* and *Satyricon,* as well as on archival material held in the Bruno Maderna Collection of the Paul Sacher Foundation (Basel) and in the Boston Symphony Orchestra/ Tanglewood archives. A word on oral history is in order. Memory can be notoriously fickle. Research shows that memories are not "archived" as with paper files, but rather are literally pieced together at the moment when they are recalled. This process involves multiple parts of the brain; therefore calling up a memory means literally to reconstruct it. Each time this is done, the memory may change in subtle ways. Therefore memory may become less reliable over time, as other memories and experiences are layered upon each other, and as one's attitudes and feelings about past events change.[10] This is why I also emphasize written sources, since they are more reliable for factual evidence than interviews conducted forty-five years after the fact. Yet oral accounts often give a richer and more subjectively tinged flavor of the experience than that preserved in written documents. I have tried whenever possible to corroborate the factual information given in interviews. When my interview subjects give contradictory information that cannot be corroborated, I will simply provide the different versions and let the reader appreciate the different memories that people had of the same event.

---

9 Howard Saul Becker, *Art Worlds* (Berkeley and London: University of California Press, 2008). See especially pp. 1–39.

10 See a summary of scholarly research on memory on the website, "The Human Memory": http://www.human-memory.net/processes_recall.html (consulted 18 June 2021).

Maderna in New York: Paul Sperry and *Venetian Journal*

In early 1971, Maderna was man of the hour in New York City. In January of that year, he led the world premiere of his first American commissioned work, *Juilliard Serenade*. He also conducted a staged production of Mozart's *La Clemenza di Tito* with the Juilliard Opera, as well as a concert with the Juilliard Orchestra that included two of his own works: *Quadrivium*, in its New York premiere, and *Music of Gaity*.[11]

It is therefore not surprising that the young tenor Paul Sperry got the idea to commission a new work from Maderna in early 1971.[12] Sperry, who had made his New York recital debut only two years earlier, saw in the Maderna commission an opportunity to help promote his career in Europe and the U.S.[13] After graduating from the Harvard Business School and working in various business enterprises, Sperry had come late to singing. "Of course, I was terribly lucky," Sperry told the *New York Times* in 1976; "My family left me very comfortably off, which meant that I did not have to enter competitions or seek patrons, simply to gather money."[14]

The linchpin of Maderna's American patronage network was his American agent, Sheldon Soffer.[15] After hearing Sperry's New York debut recital, Soffer had encouraged him to sing contemporary music. Commissioning Maderna had also been Soffer's idea, Sperry recalls, and he welcomed the suggestion. Soffer had been working tirelessly to build Maderna's American presence, so connecting him with a young performer who could bring his music before American audiences fit very well with these plans. The commission was also compatible with Sperry's artistic goals, as he had taken Soffer's advice and decided to devote himself to contemporary music and the song repertoire.[16]

The *Venetian Journal* commission, as Sperry remembers it, was linked to Maderna's plans for *Satyricon* from the beginning. When they met in New York in January 1971, Maderna told him that he "had a commission from the Netherlands Opera for an opera based on *Satyricon*." Maderna told Sperry he wanted the opera to be a collection of fragments, since the Petronius text was comprised of fragments. Maderna and Sperry agreed on the kind of piece they wanted: why not write a vocal piece that would let Maderna try out some ideas for his opera?

---

11   For more information on Maderna's conducting in New York, see M. Romito's essay in this volume, pp. 277–97.

12   De Benedictis, "Qui forse una cadenza brillante" (see note 6), p. 63.

13   See the review of Sperry's debut recital by Raymond Ericson: "Sperry's Recital Graced by Style," *The New York Times* (9 October 1969). Sperry's accompanist was a twenty-six-year-old assistant conductor of the Cleveland Orchestra named James Levine.

14   John Gruen, "The Tenor From the Harvard Business School," *The New York Times* (8 February 1976), p. D23. The $1500 commission he offered Maderna made sense from the economic as well as the artistic point of view, Sperry told me. The performances of the Maderna piece would help him to gain exposure, and at a bargain: putting on a recital in Alice Tully Hall would have cost $5000. Sperry, personal communication, 3 December 2015 in New York City.

15   Soffer was Maderna's agent for North America, while Sylvio Samama of the Concertdirectie Dr. G. de Koos in the Netherlands represented Maderna in Europe. The information and quotations in the next three paragraphs come from my interview with Sperry (see note 7).

16   Sperry explained: "There's no question that singing at the Met or at La Scala would make me much more saleable around the country [in the U.S.]. But I'd much rather sing songs. Songs are what I love best." Gruen, "The Tenor From the Harvard Business School" (see note 14).

In the meantime, Sperry had engaged his friend, the playwright Jonathan Levy, to write the text. When Levy presented two different concepts for the libretto, Sperry told me, "I jumped at the comedic one, because that's one of my strong suits." Sperry did not know at the time that comedy was also one of Maderna's strong suits. The choice of the young Boswell's first trip to Italy, the land of literature, ruins, and erotic adventures, proved to be extremely fortunate. Things moved quickly. By February 1971, Sperry was corresponding with Maderna's European agent, Sylvio Samama, about his vocal range, and about plans for the premiere.[17] On 4 March 1971, Jonathan Levy wrote to Maderna about his ideas for the text and included a substantial draft. (In her extended study of *Venetian Journal*, Angela Ida De Benedictis discusses the libretto and its source in detail, and includes a complete transcription of this letter.)[18]

Venetian Journal (known in the early years as *Boswell's Journal*) ended up being a comic monodrama. Like the classic "alt-operas" from the early twentieth century, Arnold Schoenberg's *Pierrot lunaire* and Igor Stravinsky's *Histoire du Soldat*, *Venetian Journal* does not need to be staged, but it occupies an imaginative and performative space that is intrinsically theatrical.

In fact, Maderna's theatrical instincts were fully deployed in the preparation of the work. Jonathan Levy and Sperry witnessed this when they went to Tanglewood in the summer of 1971 in order to work with Maderna on the piece. "We were a little worried about Bruno's setting of English," Sperry recalls. The first thing Maderna did was to take Sperry to a small recording studio at Tanglewood, where they recorded three versions of Sperry speaking the text.[19] After the first reading, Maderna urged Sperry to try to speak it in a different way. The second reading was considerably more dramatic, but it was still not what Maderna wanted. He then said to Sperry, "Read it as though it's twenty years later and you're remembering it." "And I read it differently," Sperry recalled. "That was a really interesting challenge." In fact, the third version strikes a different tone: that of a world-weary man recounting episodes from a misspent youth, for which he is clearly more than a bit nostalgic. Maderna used excerpts from Sperry's readings in the final tape he prepared at the Studio di Fonologia Musicale (RAI) in Milan to accompany *Venetian Journal*.

Part of the agent's job was to keep Maderna on track with his multiple projects. During the fall of 1971, Soffer nagged Maderna relentlessly to get to work on *Venetian Journal* and his other composition deadlines. "As the rehearsal schedule in Miami leaves you 6 days free, why don't you come to New York and work with him on the new piece and stay at his apartment," Soffer wrote.[20] Maderna may have worked with Sperry in

---

17 "Die 'Tessitura' von Paul Sperry ist von C bis a-moll und wenn es nicht zu viel Instrumente gibt am tiefsten A anstatt C." (The tessitura of Paul Sperry is from C [C^3] to a minor [sic, meaning A^4], and when there are not too many instruments, the low A [A^2] instead of C.) Letter from Sylvio Samama to Bruno Maderna, 19 February 1971 (PSS-BMC).

18 De Benedictis, "Qui forse una cadenza brillante" (see note 6), pp. 64–76 and 104–05.

19 These recordings are preserved in PSS-BMC (tape catalogued as "TS 1055").

20 Letter from Sheldon Soffer to Maderna, 12 October 1971, PSS-BMC. Sperry had offered Maderna the use of his old apartment in New York after Sperry had moved into a larger one.

November of that year, and indeed Rocco Di Pietro remembers taking composition lessons with Maderna in Sperry's apartment.[21] It is unclear whether Maderna began composing *Venetian Journal* at this time.[22]

Plans for a New York performance of *Venetian Journal* under the direction of the composer were already being discussed by 19 February 1971.[23] There were hopes that Boulez, who had been appointed music director of the New York Philharmonic starting in the 1971–72 season, would program the work in the orchestra's new music series, "Prospective Encounters," but this did not pan out.[24] The premiere was eventually scheduled to be part of the series "New and Newer Music" at Alice Tully Hall, where the work was premiered on 12 March 1972, with Paul Sperry and the Juilliard Ensemble conducted by Dennis Russell Davies.[25]

Sperry recalls being involved with his "offspring" at every stage of the process: he suggested the librettist, informed the composer about the particular qualities of his voice, suggested performance venues, and contributed vocal material to the tape. Independently of the composer, Sperry also altered the accompanying tape part for subsequent performances after the premiere, as De Benedictis describes.[26] During the short and chaotic rehearsal period, Sperry urged the composer to give more guidance to the musicians. He recalls that Maderna then added order numbers to the individual segments within each page in the score, which was published in this form.[27]

Commissioning *Venetian Journal* turned out to be a good strategy, from which both Sperry and Maderna (and presumably also Soffer) benefited. After the successful premiere, Sperry went on to perform *Venetian Journal* multiple times on both continents, at prestigious venues including the Royan Festival (France), the Aspen Festival, the Cleveland Institute, the Cabrillo Festival, the Los Angeles Philharmonic New Music Group, the San Francisco Symphony Orchestra, the Saarländischer Rundfunk, Speculum Musicae in New York, and many others.[28] Sperry got a real career boost, as well as a foothold in the European new music scene – not to mention a role in *Satyricon*. Maderna got more

---

21   Rocco Di Pietro, personal communication (phone), 11 July 2016.

22   De Benedictis concludes that he might have worked between the last months of 1971 and early 1972, and given the number of sketches of both *Venetian Journal* and *Satyricon* outlined together, most likely only in the first months of 1972. See "Qui forse una cadenza brillante" (see note 6), pp. 76–77.

23   Letter from Sylvio Samama to Maderna, 19 February 1971, PSS-BMC.

24   Letter from Sheldon Soffer to Paul Sperry, 21 April 1971, PSS-BMC: "Enclosed please find the reply I got from Pierre Boulez in reference to the new MADERNA PIECE. I do not feel too badly about it as Bruno will once again be asked to conduct and be at the NEW AND NEWER MUSIC series at Alice Tully next January, most likely on a Sunday in the middle of the month while he is here for the New York Philharmonic. Don't fret. This will be better, more of a showcase. But, who knows, Boulez might want to perform it in other cities, like he is doing the *JUILLIARD SERENADE* for BBC in 1972."

25   According to De Benedictis, a formal contract for the work, signed on 11 August 1971, indicated the date and place of the premiere. See "Qui forse una cadenza brillante" (see note 6), p. 63.

26   Ibid., pp. 86–87 (note 60).

27   Paul Sperry, personal communication, 3 December 2015 in New York City. Sperry's account is confirmed in the materials for *Venetian Journal* in PSS-BMC. These include photocopies of score pages (from transparencies), showing the same handwritten score as that published in the Ricordi edition, but without the internal order numbers within each page.

28   The records at Ricordi indicate eight U.S. performances between 1972 and 1984.

American exposure, and more importantly, he got to try out some of the structural ideas of a modular collage score (a technique he had also explored in other works), as well as dramatic techniques of humor, satire, and parody that he would explore further in *Satyricon*. *Venetian Journal* also played directly into Sperry's desire to avoid recitals that were "deadly serious"; in a 1976 interview with the *New York Times*, Sperry said, "[F]or a performer to refuse to be entertaining is to deny half of his responsibility."[29]

From Tanglewood to Amsterdam: *Satyricon*

In 1971, during Maderna's first summer at Tanglewood, he was engaged for the entire eight-week season to teach private lessons in composition and conducting, give composition seminars, and to collaborate with the Music Theater Project.[30] This initiative was brand new in 1971, and it added a welcome infusion of opera to the Tanglewood mix.[31] The Music Theater Project was Strasfogel's brainchild, and was fully supported by Schuller, who with Seiji Ozawa was one of two co-directors of the Tanglewood festival that summer. In his opening remarks for the festival, Schuller emphasized the innovative new project: "With limited forces of small casts and orchestras and slight scenic demands, these pieces use the elements of opera in strikingly fresh, exciting ways which must influence the opera composer and performer of tomorrow."[32] This ambitious project, funded by the National Opera Institute and the Martha Baird Rockefeller Foundation, was fully in keeping with Schuller's emphasis on contemporary music at Tanglewood.[33]

In addition to co-directing Tanglewood, Schuller was also the director of the annual Festival of Contemporary Music. This "festival within a festival," jointly produced by the Berkshire Music Center and the Fromm Music Foundation, has long been acknowledged as one of the most significant events for contemporary music on the East Coast, and it continues today. For many years, Fromm provided crucial support for this festival, which regularly featured two composers in residence, one American and one European. During the summer of 1971, Schuller and Maderna were the principal composition teachers, and students could also study with Lukas Foss and Charles Wuorinen. Later that summer, Fromm would commission Maderna for a new piece to be performed at Tanglewood to

---

29   Sperry, quoted in Gruen, "The Tenor From the Harvard Business School" (see note 14).

30   Maderna had been invited in July 1970 for the following summer. See letter from Soffer to Samama, 23 July 1970, PSS-BMC. See also letter from Gunther Schuller to Maderna, 14 June 1971 (App. 1, pp. 325–26). The official contract letter from Tanglewood administrator Harry Kraut to Maderna and his agent Sheldon Soffer is dated 15 June 1971 (both of the latter in Box TMC 26: Faculty/ Guest Lectures. Personal files J–T Box 2, Boston Symphony Orchestra Archives; hereinafter, BSO Archives).

31   Ian Strasfogel, "The Music Theatre Project – 1971," p. 2 (photocopy of draft typescript on New England Conservatory stationery). Ian Strasfogel, personal archive (a second copy is in held in PSS).

32   Gunther Schuller, quoted in press release of 17 Jun. 1971. Tanglewood Music Center Yearbook, 1971, p. 412; https://archive.org/search.php?query=tanglewood%20music%20center%20yearbook%201971 (consulted 18 June 2021).

33   Program book, 11–17 August, Festival of Contemporary Music, Tanglewood 1971, p. 4. All the program books for the Boston Symphony Orchestra and Tanglewood are available online in the database HENRY; http://cdm15982.contentdm.oclc.org/cdm/landingpage/collection/PROG (consulted 18 June 2021).

EX. 1   Bruno Maderna with (from right to left): Paul Fromm, Gunther Schuller, and Elliott Carter; Tanglewood, 1972; © Whitestone Photo; PSS-BMC.

celebrate the twentieth anniversary of the Fromm Foundation in 1972 (→ **EX. 1**): this would become *Giardino religioso,* whose title elegantly disguises the nod to the patron in Maderna's original title, *Frommer Garten.*[34]

"Maderna Proves Committee Can Create Musical Work of Art"

Plans for the opera *Satyricon* had long been in the works when Maderna signed an official agreement with the Netherlands Opera in July 1972 to conduct the work.[35] Dutch impresario Hans de Roo, the director of the Netherlands Opera, had long been friendly with Maderna; moreover, the composer had been a key player in the Dutch musical avant-garde since the 1960s.[36] Maderna had spoken of his opera plans to Sperry already in January 1971, as we have seen.

---

34 See letter from Paul Fromm to Sylvio Samama, 28 February 1972, Paul Fromm Manuscripts b 90M-52, Box 3, Folder Maderna. Houghton Library, Harvard University. See also the essays by Maurizio Romito (p. 293) and Nicola Scaldaferri (p. 169) in this volume.

35 The agreement between Maderna and the Nederlandse Operastichting for conducting *Satyricon* as well as the other work on the program, Ligeti's *Aventures et Nouvelles Aventures,* is dated 7 July 1972 (PSS-BMC). See also Angela Ida De Benedictis' essay in this volume, pp. 36 and 41.

36 Hans de Roo was the intendant of the Nederlandse Operastichting (Netherlands Opera Foundation, later known as the Dutch National Opera). On Maderna in the Netherlands, see Robert Adlington, *Composing Dissent: Avant-Garde Music in 1960s Amsterdam* (Oxford and New York: Oxford University Press, 2013), pp. 60–75.

A key moment in the opera's origins was Maderna's involvement in a short theatrical improvisation on the subject of "Trimalchio's Feast," a ribald episode from Petronius' *Satyricon*, scheduled at Tanglewood that summer as part of the inaugural season of Ian Strasfogel's Music Theater Project. The possibility that the opera *Satyricon* could have originated in an improvisation is tantalizing, given its modular score (in which the order of sections is free), the large number of quotations from other works, and its playful, unbuttoned tone. Although it seems clear that this theatrical experiment was in some way a precursor to the final version of the opera, specific connections are hard to identify. Many participants remember taking part in the event, but no scores, parts, or librettos have survived.

In what follows, I draw on archival sources and oral history to reconstruct the chronology as well as many previously unknown details about the event itself. Although it is not possible to reconstruct the event completely, a number of new details have emerged.

In November 1970, eight months before the 1971 Tanglewood summer season, Soffer wrote to Maderna that "Tanglewood has accepted your plan about the composition project."[37] The details of Maderna's plan, which had probably been discussed orally, are not spelled out – this could refer to the theatrical experiment, or to some other plans unknown today. The first written description of the project comes six months later, preserved in a letter from Strasfogel to Maderna dated 31 May 1971.[38] Strasfogel had met Maderna through de Roo during the run of *La Clemenza di Tito* at Juilliard in January 1971 (as Strasfogel explains in the letter). He writes to Maderna that Tanglewood is starting a new Music Theater Project under his direction. (He uses the common shorthand "Tanglewood" for the Berkshire Music Center, the music school component of the summer festival.) This initiative will feature staged productions of Weill's *Mahagonny Songspiel*, Satie's *Socrate*, Offenbach's *Croquefer*, Ligeti's *Aventures et Nouvelles Aventures*, and Birtwistle's *Down By the Greenwood Side*, in the intimate space of Tanglewood's "West Barn."

Strasfogel outlines his vision for the experimental work: "As Gunther [Schuller] has already mentioned to you in New York, we wish to schedule as our sixth piece an original work constructed by the Music Theater Project and your most interested and gifted composition students[,]" which would be "evolved under our joint and most strict supervision, during the week of August 9th on the bill with the Ligeti and Birtwistle." He describes the singers who would be available for the project: "1 coloratura, 1 lyric soprano, 1 mezzo, 2 tenors, 1 lyric baritone, 1 dramatic baritone and 1 bass. These people are not involved in the Birtwistle and Ligeti and so would have the group piece as their only commitment." Strasfogel suggests that they have a preliminary meeting in Boston, New York, or Tanglewood to work out the details. He emphasizes the substantial time commitment involved: "I myself plan to spend about two hours a day for meetings with you and the composers, rehearsals, improvisation sessions, forums, critiques – in other words, all the activities that would make this an ideal laboratory situation for the artists concerned."

---

37 Letter from Sheldon Soffer to Maderna, 24 November 1970 (PSS-BMC).
38 Letter from Ian Strasfogel to Maderna, 31 May 1971 (PSS-BMC). All quotations in this and the next paragraph come from this letter.

On 14 June, Schuller wrote to Maderna describing what his duties would be that summer, including "the collaborative composing project we talked about in New York" (→ **APP. 1, PP. 325–26**).[39] Evidently, Maderna had already discussed his ideas about the experiment with Strasfogel, Schuller, and de Roo in New York earlier that year. These conversations must have occurred in late January 1971 when Maderna was in New York.[40]

Whereas Strasfogel had emphasized the collaborative nature of the project, Schuller writes to Maderna that

> we would like you to take charge of a music-theater piece which would be composed by, let us say, four or five of the best composition students at Tanglewood under your supervision and in which you could, of course, also participate actively. To the extent that this piece needed to be conducted in performance, you would be the conductor. You would be able to use a small complement of instrumentalists, plus some of the singers, actors and mimes we will have at Tanglewood. I know you are very interested in this kind of collective composing process, and Ian and I feel very strongly that it must be included as a very important part of our Music-Theater Project.[41]

There appear to have been two different visions of the project from the outset. While Schuller emphasizes the process of group composition, which would be carried out by the students under Maderna's supervision (he invites Maderna to "take charge"), Strasfogel envisages the work as a collaboration between the two of them, stage director and composition teacher, furthermore involving the singers' input as well as the composers'. Strasfogel mentions "improvisation sessions," and was very interested in having singers contribute to these.[42] Schuller does not use the word improvisation at all, but rather refers to a "collective composing process." These two conceptions are not mutually exclusive, but they do reflect different emphases, as well as different origins: the first was probably Maderna's idea, and the second, Strasfogel's. There is still no mention of "Trimalchio's Feast" or *Satyricon*.[43]

The work's subject is explicitly named for the first time in print in a Tanglewood program listing events for 21–29 July 1971 (→ **EX. 2**). This announcement describes "a new work written collaboratively by composition fellows at Tanglewood this summer under the supervision of Bruno Maderna. The new collaborative work is based on the

---

39   Letter (also copied to Soffer) from Gunther Schuller to Bruno Maderna, 14 June 1971 (photocopy of carbon copy in the BSO Archives).

40   The *Clemenza* performances at Juilliard ran from 21–23 January, and the premiere of *Juilliard Serenade* took place on 31 January 1971 (see also the "Chronology" in this volume, p. 447).

41   See Appendix 1, p. 326, letter from Schuller to Maderna, 14 June 1971.

42   In a memorandum about the Music Theater Project (prepared shortly after the 1971 Tanglewood season had ended), Strasfogel again describes the aim "to involve the composers at Tanglewood with the Music Theater Project," and adds that the piece would "evolve through improvisational sessions." In the same document, Strasfogel describes how he began the staging rehearsals for Offenbach's *Croquefer* with group improvisations with the cast, led by the two actors who served as narrators (cf. "The Music Theatre Project – 1971" (see note 31), p. 2, Ian Strasfogel, personal archive; a copy is held in PSS).

43   Internal (undated) Tanglewood announcements to the Friends (sponsors) and participants of the Berkshire Music Center list "A New Work by Composition Fellows" scheduled to take place on 11–12 August. Tanglewood Music Center Yearbook, 1971, p. 406; https://archive.org/search.php ?query=tanglewood%20music%20center%20yearbook%201971 (consulted 18 June 2021).

THE MUSIC THEATER PROJECT AT TANGLEWOOD

The Music Theater Project, made possible in part by grants from the National Opera Institute, Martha Baird Rockefeller Foundation and the Fromm Music Foundation, has been inaugurated this year to provide practical experience in the music theater repertory, for both advanced students and professional singers of exceptional ability.

The present performances are to be followed by performances in the Festival of Contemporary Music on August 8, 9, 11 and 12. The planned repertoire for the next program includes Adventures by Ligeti, Socrates by Satie, Down by the Greenwood Side by Birtwistle, and a new work written collaboratively by composition fellows at Tanglewood this summer under the supervision of Bruno Maderna. The new collaborative work is based on the Trimalchio's banquet sequence of the Satyricon by Petronius Arbiter.

Staff
Artistic Director of Tanglewood – Gunther Schuller
Head – Ian Strasfogel
Chief of Musical Preparation – Martin Smith
Coaching Staff: Bruce Cohen
                  Henry Mollicone
                  Philip Morehead
Technical Director – Richard Lee (Tom Field Associates)
Assistant to Mr. Schmidt – Carole Lee Carroll
Assistants to Mr. Strasfogel – Gordon Davis
                                David Hammond
House Manager – Andy Friendly
Technical Fellows: Neil Burlingame
                    Linda Chipparoni
                    James Freeman
                    David O'Farrell
                    Clio Taub

EX. 2   Program book, "The Music Theater Project at Tanglewood," announcement of "Trimalchio's banquet sequence of the *Satyricon*" (Tanglewood Yearbook 1971).

Trimalchio's banquet sequence of the *Satyricon* by Petronius Arbiter."[44] Maderna's supervision is mentioned, but not Strasfogel's. Again, as in Schuller's letter quoted above, the word improvisation is not used, and in fact the new work is said to be "written."

A Tanglewood news release of 3 August 1971 that lists upcoming productions of the Music Theater Project does not mention the collaborative composition.[45] Yet the project was the subject of a lengthy article in the local newspaper published on 8 August (more about this below). Therefore, some time between mid-July (when the Trimalchio piece was announced in the *Mahagonny* program) and 3 August, the plans to perform the piece were dropped. There is no program for it in the Tanglewood Yearbook for 1971. In an internal memo for the New England Conservatory (where Strasfogel was head of the Opera Department), drafted shortly after the end of the Tanglewood season that year, Strasfogel wrote:

---

44 This announcement appears in the program for performances of the Music Theater Project's productions of *Mahagonny Songspiel* and *Croquefer*. Tanglewood Music Center Yearbook, 1971, p. 418: https://archive.org/stream/tanglewoodmusicc1971bost#page/n417/mode/2up (consulted 18 June 2021).

45 Tanglewood Music Center Yearbook 1971, p. 420; https://archive.org/stream /tanglewoodmusicc1971bost#page/n419/mode/2up (consulted 18 June 2021).

> It soon became apparent … that both singers and composers were far too busy with other activities in Tanglewood to devote enough time to the evolution of such a work. We abandoned the project with such regret, since certain efforts of the performers had been so exciting and suggestive of new possibilities in music theatre. Certainly, such work must be done – but as part of a year-round activity.[46]

It is not clear when the subject of "Trimalchio's Feast" was decided upon for the subject of the Tanglewood experiment, or who first suggested it. Strasfogel had written to Maderna on 31 May 1971: "I have thought a great deal about possible subject matter and am eager to have your ideas." Therefore, it appears that Maderna did not mention the subject either to Strasfogel or to Schuller when they were discussing the Tanglewood experiment earlier that year. Perhaps Maderna already knew that he wanted to use this subject, and simply had not communicated this yet (Maderna was a notoriously bad correspondent). It is also possible that the opera project was not yet linked to the Tanglewood experiment; Maderna knew he wanted to write an opera on the *Satyricon* material, but had not yet decided upon the subject of the theatrical improvisation.

Strasfogel suggests that the collaborative composition inspired Maderna to use the subject of "Trimalchio's Feast" for his opera, and offers this reconstruction long after the fact:

> My assumption is that Hans de Roo had wanted to commission Bruno for a long time, and perhaps he had already discussed an opera with him, when Hans saw the work that I did with Bruno, he got enthusiastic and wanted to invite me to stage it, and Bruno, by then, I guess, got the idea to do the piece, based on the fact that Trimalchio would always be something he would like, because it was so excessive, and full of humor, and full of energy and vitality.[47]

Maderna, like many educated Europeans, had known the *Satyricon* text since he was young.[48] So the question is not when Maderna became acquainted with the text, but rather when he decided to use it as the subject for an opera, and for the Tanglewood experiment. In an interview with Piet Hein van de Poel of Dutch Radio shortly after the opera's premiere in March 1973, Maderna said, "for me the text was the main thing – just the text, which, by the way, I had loved for a long time. […] A society is portrayed and described in it, which could not better represent today's society, with all its ugliness."[49] Maderna and de Roo were both eager to give each other credit for the idea. In a TV documentary made ten years later (after Maderna's death), the composer is shown in a prerecorded interview, saying: "I wrote *Satyricon* because de Roo asked me to, and he did it with such conviction that I *could* do it, it had the effect on me of a stimulus. Since I had known the piece for a long time, I had wanted to do it for a long time." De Roo, in the same documentary (speaking in 1983), says, "The idea for *Satyricon* came from him himself."[50] Rocco Di Pietro

---

46 Strasfogel, "The Music Theatre Project" (see note 31), p. 4; Ian Strasfogel, personal archive, copy in PSS. Also quoted in De Benedictis' essay in this volume, on p. 35.

47 Strasfogel, personal communication (interview), 28 November 2015 in New York City.

48 See De Benedictis's contribution to this volume, p. 22.

49 Interview broadcast on 16 March 1973 on the occasion of the world premiere of *Satyricon* (NOS archive, copy in PSS-BMC); in the broadcast Maderna spoke in German (translation mine).

50 *Terug naar Maderna*, TV documentary by Hans Heg and René van Gijn produced by NOS in 1983 (German version: *Zurück zu Maderna*, 1987). The remarks were made in German (translation mine).

likewise recalls that Maderna chose the theme, which had interested him for a long time, for the Tanglewood project, adding that he "had an uncanny ability to turn commissions into something he was already doing."[51]

Whether it was Maderna himself, de Roo, Strasfogel, or another collaborator who suggested the subject, the *Satyricon* material was "in the air." Fellini's popular film had been released in the U.S. in March 1970, and according to Di Pietro was still playing in movie theaters during the summer of 1971.[52] A widely-available Penguin edition had just come out in a revised edition in 1969.[53] Given the inherently collaborative nature of music theater, who first had the idea for *Satyricon* as the subject for an opera is perhaps not so important. The main point is that the theme was perfect for Maderna's operatic experiment, and the workshop atmosphere at Tanglewood was an ideal place to try out ideas.

"Trimalchio's Feast" at Tanglewood

Many details about the planned performance of an improvisatory theater piece on "Trimalchio's Feast" are recorded in an article by Roy C. Hammerich in a local newspaper, the *Springfield Republican*, published on 8 August 1971 (→ **APP. 2, P. 327**). The work was announced with the eye-catching headline "Defying the Arts: Maderna Proves Committee Can Create Musical Work of Art." According to the article, the first public performance will take place "tonight" (that is, Sunday, 8 August), "tomorrow" (Monday, 9 August), "Wednesday and Thursday" (11 and 12 August), "along with three other, existing, short music dramas."[54] Strasfogel is named as director of the Music Theater Project, and Maderna as its musical advisor. The piece "will be 20 to 30 minutes long, will have 10 to 15 in the cast, and will be evolved from Trimalchio's banquet sequence from the *Satyricon* by Petronius Arbiter."

---

51 Rocco Di Pietro, personal communication (phone), 11 July 2016: "It was Maderna's idea. He wanted to use the *Satyricon*. He really liked the subject. Fellini's film was still playing in the theaters. Maderna spoke of the opera he was going to write."

52 Another film based on *Satyricon*, directed by Gian Luigi Polidoro, was released in Italy in 1969, the same year as (but about six months ahead of) Fellini's more famous version (see also Susanna Pasticci, "La presenza del *Satyricon* sulla scena culturale degli anni Settanta, da Maderna a Pasolini," *Musica/Realtà*, 91 (2010), pp. 77–126). The Polidoro film was never released in the U.S. Maderna emphasized that the Fellini film had no impact on his work; see the aforementioned interview with Piet Hein van de Poel for Dutch Radio (see note 49). Strasfogel confirms, "But for certain it had no effect. I was responding more to the translation than to the film. We were both responding to the original material." If the film and the opera have anything in common, "it was just the raucousness of the late sixties early seventies: sexual directness and freedom, and wildness"; Strasfogel, personal communication (interview), 28 November 2015 in New York City.

53 Petronius, *The Satyricon* and *The Fragments*, translated and with an introduction by John P. Sullivan (Penguin Books, 1965). Reprinted with revisions in 1969, reprinted 1971. Among his multilingual sources, Maderna would use a different English translation for the opera (see the contribution of Benedetta Zucconi, in this volume, p. 61, note 10).

54 Printed programs document performances of Birtwistle's *Down By the Greenwood Side*, Satie's *Socrate*, and Ligeti's *Aventures et Nouvelles Aventures* on Wednesday and Thursday, 11–12 August, but there are no programs for Music Theater Project performances on Sunday and Monday. See also references to the Tanglewood Music Center Yearbook 1971 (see note 45).

Hammerich describes the working process:

> For two weeks the members of the group have been creating a music drama, collectively and separately, by composing passages of melody and words on the basis of suggestions made during group sessions and changing them during subsequent group sessions.
> […] Bits from Petronius' writing (sights, dialogue, movement) are discussed with a view toward reproduction in music and action.
> Short sequences, having been chosen by the group, are taken to semi-isolation by sub-groups of three or four singers, actors and composers where the sequence is reproduced in music and action.
> This reproduction is displayed before the whole group for acceptance, rejection or modification. Thus, gradually, the whole music drama is "composed" by the whole group.
> "They learn: they discover," said Maderna. "All the problems are seen with many eyes."

It is not clear whether Hammerich observed this process himself or was simply told about it. But some of these details are confirmed by the memories of Strasfogel and Rocco Di Pietro.[55] The latter described how the composers worked separately from the singers[56] (Hammerich wrote that they had worked "collectively and separately"). This was necessitated by the scheduling at Tanglewood, in which the composition seminars overlapped with the meetings of the Music Theater Project, but also had to do with the two different visions of the project.

According to Di Pietro, there were "six or so" composition students involved in the group composition project.[57] Maderna gave the students assignments in their individual lessons. In the seminars, "we would discuss, play, and exchange the fragments we had written and arranged." Maderna encouraged the use of preexisting music. "At his request," Di Pietro recalls, "I arranged a version of Webern's *Kinderstück* for celesta." He also recalled how

> at one composition seminar, he asked us to improvise from notes on the blackboard. He asked me to do this on the vibraphone, which I don't play. But since I was a pianist, I could figure it out. I took the mallets and played with him and Christiane Edinger, a violinist. You were allowed to play the notes forwards, backwards, transposed, etc., but they were to be the basis.

Evidently, Maderna's musical preparation with the composers took place separately from Strasfogel's work with the singers. Strasfogel recalled in November 2015 how he had aimed that summer to foster a kind of improvisation ensemble, as is common in spoken theater.[58] Unlike actors, singers usually have little experience with vocal improvisation, and that summer they found it challenging, he recalls. Nonetheless "we did a workshop

---

55 Di Pietro was a composition fellow that summer and served as Maderna's assistant in the project. Lucas Vis was Maderna's designated assistant (see letter from Sheldon Soffer to Bruno Maderna, 24 November 1970, PSS-BMC.) Programs from that summer list Vis as a composition fellow.

56 Personal communication (phone), 11 July 2016.

57 The quotations in this and the following paragraph are from Rocco Di Pietro, personal communication (phone), 11 July 2016. There were in fact six students, including Vis: see Romito, "'This Bruno looks like Fiorello,'" in this volume, p. 285.

58 Ian Strasfogel, personal communication (interview), 28 November 2015 in New York City (all quotations in this paragraph).

improvisation with a pianist, … with a baritone named Lenus Carlson… as Trimalchio, … and we played around with the kind of vulgarity and the sprawling drunken abandon of it all." There were three or four other singers as well.[59] Whereas Maderna worked regularly with the composers, he was not present during most of the rehearsals with the singers: Strasfogel remembers that "he came by once or twice and said 'Very nice, very nice,' and went off."

The composition workshop also worked with the *Satyricon* text when singers were not present. Di Pietro told me

> we all had paperback copies of the Penguin translation of *The Satyricon*.[60] We would read various passages out loud, and eventually I ended up as the main reader. I wasn't an actor, but I guess I was able to voice the different characters in appropriate ways.[61]

All the participants I spoke with confirmed that the piece was not performed publicly as part of the Music Theater Project's regular season, but that some kind of private performance or run-through of a collective composition/improvisation based on "Trimalchio's Feast" did take place. Strasfogel recalls that "we performed it for an invited audience, consisting mainly of the other singers in the group and other singers at Tanglewood… with maybe four people from Lenox. Not a large audience at all. Surely in the West Barn – 100–125 people."[62] Di Pietro confirms that there was a "run-through and people went to it," and that it took place in the Barn.[63] He remembers that there were six to ten people on stage (the *Springfield Republican* had mentioned ten to fifteen), and that the audience consisted of conducting students and possibly others, including Schuller. Di Pietro also relates how the participants brought sheets of written music with them. Some of this consisted of excerpts from preexisting music (such as di Pietro's arrangement of the Webern *Kinderstück*), and some of it was music that had been worked out in group composition exercises during the seminars. According to Di Pietro, Maderna did not conduct per se, but he was definitely in charge, "barking out commands and cues constantly during the performance. He would shout, for example, 'forte!' 'now you!' 'softer!' The fragments were numbered, and he would call out the numbers. Like in an Earle Brown piece." Di Pietro does not remember much about the singers, but he does recall that he himself read one of the characters as a speaking role.

Therefore there were two sets of preparations going on for the Trimalchio piece: one with the singers of the Music Theater Project, and one in the composition seminars. At some point they came together and gave an informal performance or "run-through." Even though both groups practiced improvisation, the participants in the run-through did use written parts and probably also written texts (Strasfogel's jottings for Carlson, or perhaps the Penguin volumes that Di Pietro remembers reading from). The fact that

---

59 Strasfogel has recently contacted Carlson in the meantime, and relates that "he remembered less than I did. He remembers just that I sat down at a table and wrote some text for him."
60 Maderna would use the Arrowsmith translation for his final version (see note 53).
61 Rocco Di Pietro, personal communication (phone), 11 July 2016.
62 Ian Strasfogel, personal communication (interview), 28 November 2015 in New York City.
63 Rocco Di Pietro, personal communication (phone), 11 July 2016 (all quotations in this paragraph).

Maderna encouraged the use of preexisting music is also interesting, given the prominent use of quotations in the final version of *Satyricon.*

"And at the end, Bruno was delighted," Strasfogel recalls. He remembers that de Roo was at Tanglewood that summer and saw the private performance of the Trimalchio piece, whereupon he asked Maderna to write an opera for his company on that subject, and both composer and impresario asked Strasfogel to stage it.[64] It seems clear that Maderna and de Roo had already discussed plans for a *Satyricon* opera before that summer, but the Trimalchio piece could well have put new wind into the project's sails.

"Improvisation was in the air"

The Strasfogel-Maderna experiment should be understood in the context of widespread experimentation with indeterminacy, aleatory, open forms, improvisation, and new forms of music theater during the 1960s and early 1970s in Europe and the United States. Indeed, Maderna's other works from this time, including *Quadrivium* (1969), *Ausstrahlung* (1971), *Aura* (1972), and *Giardino religioso* (1972), also employ modular elements and graphic notation mixed with conventional notation.

Earlier that summer at Tanglewood, an open-form indeterminate piece by Lukas Foss, also on the composition faculty, was performed by a quartet of distinguished musicians, including percussionist Jan Williams and violinist Paul Zukofsky. The 7 July performance in the tent of *Map: A Musical Game* was a high-status private event reserved for donors, the "Friends of Music at Tanglewood."[65] The piece was constructed as a theatrical game. There were "winners" and "losers," complete with mock humiliation rituals to be carried out by the losers (such as crawling around on hands and knees and beating the floor with a superball mallet). Di Pietro recalls that Maderna did not like Foss's *Map.* It is easy to understand why. Whereas Foss created group improvisations where the individual players had a great deal of freedom, and *Map* created a light-hearted, convivial atmosphere, Maderna viewed improvisation as a part of a strictly musical process. Rather than constructing verbal scores that give the performers a great deal of leeway, he preferred to have performers improvise on a set of specific pitches, Di Pietro recalls.[66] But in spite of the differences between Foss's and Maderna's approaches to open form, the composition students had already been doing improvisation exercises with Foss for weeks, so when Maderna arrived and began work on the collective composition, they were not fazed in the least.

Whereas Maderna may have objected to Foss's more open improvisation, he was very sympathetic to the works of Earle Brown, in which players are directed by the conductor through a modular score using a variety of notational forms. Maderna conducted *Available Forms I* with the Boston Symphony Orchestra at Tanglewood during the summer

---

64 Strasfogel, personal communication (interview), 28 November 2015 in New York City.

65 Tanglewood Music Center Yearbook, 1971, pp. 398 and 400: https://archive.org/search.php?query= tanglewood%20music%20center%20yearbook%201971 (consulted 18 June 2021).

66 Rocco Di Pietro, personal communication (phone), 11 July 2016. For Foss's views on improvisation and open forms, see Lukas Foss, "Improvisation versus Composition," *The Musical Times* 103, no. 1436 (October 1962), p. 684.

of 1972, a work he had repeatedly advocated since he had led the world premiere in 1961 at Darmstadt.[67] Brown's technique of using hand signals to guide the ensemble through the numbered modular units of the score proved to be highly influential, and indeed Maderna adopted his own version of the technique in some of his compositions,[68] and he even used it with much earlier music. As William Neill recalls, when Maderna conducted Monteverdi's *L'Incoronazione di Poppea* at Tanglewood in 1972, he prepared pages of ornamentation for the singers. Neill, who sang the role of Nerone, recalls that the cast had to memorize the numbers corresponding to particular ornaments so that Maderna could indicate spontaneously during the performance, using hand signals, which ones he wanted the singers to use. These were never the same from rehearsal to rehearsal, or even in the performances. It was important to Maderna to be able to vary the ornamentation depending on the "emotional mood of the moment," according to Neill. Neill's description of Maderna's hand signals in *L'Incoronazione di Poppea* in 1972 is strikingly similar to Di Pietro's account of Maderna's hand signals in the Trimalchio improvisation the previous summer.[69]

Common to both Brown's and Maderna's approach to open form is the notion of a completed work, which is designed and notated in such a way that it can be performed in different, equally valid realizations. Both composers often used the analogy of Calder's mobiles. Unlike Cage's indeterminate works of this period, there remains in Maderna's scores an interactive connection between the notation and the sound, and the order of events is flexible within the given limits. (In *Venetian Journal*, modularity applies within the page, but the order of pages is fixed. In *Satyricon*, the "set pieces" are interchangeable, but the order of events within each piece is more or less fixed.) As De Benedictis has pointed out, the scores of *Ausstrahlung, Venetian Journal, Satyricon*, and similar works from this period are not incomplete, as they are often described, but rather consist of modular, precisely notated texts that are designed to allow multiple (infinite) paths through the labyrinth.[70]

Satyricon: From Improvisation to Finished Work

While it seems clear that the Tanglewood improvisation anticipated many elements of Maderna's *Satyricon*, no direct musical connections can be found between the 1971 event and the version of the opera premiered in the Netherlands nineteen months later. But

---

67   See Romito's essay in this volume, pp. 291–92. Richard Toop analyzes Maderna's performance decisions in his recording of *Available Forms I* with the Rome Symphony Orchestra (released 1967); see Toop, "Their Man in Europe, Our Man in America (see note 3), pp. 153–56. See also the contribution of Pascal Decroupet in this volume, pp. 127–34.

68   See for example how Maderna employed similar hand signals while rehearsing his violin Concerto in the Italian TV-documentary *Un'ora con Bruno Maderna: Musica, specchio della società*, by Salvatore G. Biamonte and Giuseppe Sibilla, RAI, Milan-Venice 1969–70, broadcast on 11 October 1971. A digital copy and a VHS version of this documentary are held at PSS. A brief excerpt from this program is available on YouTube: https://www.youtube.com/watch?v=6VOSVVelpHo (consulted 18 June 2021).

69   William Neill, personal communication (phone), 26 September 2016. Two different scores of Maderna's *L'Incoronazione di Poppea*, performed in Tanglewood, have been held in PSS since 2019.

70   Angela Ida De Benedictis, "Scrittura e supporti nel novecento: Alcune riflessioni e un esempio (*Ausstrahlung* di Bruno Maderna)," in *La scrittura come rappresentazione del pensiero musicale*, ed. Gianmario Borio (Pisa: ETS, 2004), pp. 237–91: 282–83.

there was a great deal of continuity in the theatrical conception of the two projects, due to their common subject and to the involvement of Strasfogel, who prepared the group improvisation at Tanglewood and served as stage director in the opera's first two productions. The Tanglewood experiment left its traces above all in the improvisatory spirit, humor, and open form of *Satyricon*.[71] Therefore even if (as is likely) no specific musical material from that improvisation made its way into the completed opera, many of the most fundamental aspects of *Satyricon* were already in place in the summer of 1971. Indeed the idea of structural choices, the use of musical quotations, and the idea of a mix-and-match theater had long been crucial elements in Maderna's compositional aesthetic.

Just as important for *Satyricon* as the Trimalchio experiment was Maderna's work with individual singers at Tanglewood. Maderna, an experienced opera conductor, enjoyed writing for specific singers and developing his musical and dramatic ideas based on their personalities and abilities. Two of the singers at the Dutch premiere of *Satyricon* – Paul Sperry (Habinnas) and Poppy Holden (Scintilla) – had been at Tanglewood during the summer of 1971, although they had not been involved with the Trimalchio piece. Sperry recalls that Maderna created the role of Habinnas for him after working with him that summer on *Venetian Journal*. Poppy Holden relates, "Maderna had heard me sing a top B flat above the Queen of the Night's F in Tanglewood, showing off in the Ligeti [*Aventures et Nouvelles Aventures*], so I had only myself to blame."[72] Maderna also met the tenor William Neill (Trimalchio) at Tanglewood, who sang Nerone in the Music Theatre Project's production of Monteverdi's *L'Incoronazione di Poppea* in 1972, as noted above.[73] Just as Maderna had created *Venetian Journal* with Sperry's voice and personality in mind, he tailored the roles in *Satyricon* to fit specific singers whose voices he knew well.

Satyricon: Rehearsals and Premiere

Satyricon was premiered with an international cast in the Circustheater in Scheveningen on 16 March 1973.[74] When rehearsals started in February in Amsterdam, the work was still very much in flux. Strasfogel recalls that he arrived in Holland not having seen "a note of the music, a word of text"; he had been working with the designing team in America without any input at all from Maderna.[75]

---

71 Fearn, in *Bruno Maderna* (see note 5), p. 271, likewise sees the Tanglewood experiment as the immediate impetus for the "'mobile' nature of *Satyricon*."

72 Poppy Holden, personal communication (e-mail), 8 August 2016.

73 Maderna was so taken with Joyce Castle's portrayal of Ottavia in that production that he richly orchestrated her two main arias, not caring that this created "islands of Respighi-like sound" among the otherwise spare and minimal accompaniment. Personal communications from Strasfogel, Joyce Castle (phone, 26 September), and William Neill.

74 More details about the premiere and the work itself are provided in Angela Ida De Benedictis' contribution to this volume, pp. 19–57.

75 Poppy Holden, who sang in *Aventures et Nouvelles Aventures* as well as the role of Scintilla in *Satyricon,* said (of the Maderna) that she also had not received any music before arriving in Amsterdam. William Neill recalls having received only a portion of the score, perhaps ten to fifteen minutes of music, a week before the rehearsals began, and the rest after he arrived in Holland (personal communications from Holden, e-mail, 8 August 2016, and Neill, phone, 26 September 2016).

Because of his previous collaboration with Maderna, Strasfogel had been under the impression that he would be writing the libretto for the work that became *Satyricon*. He wrote to de Roo in April 1972:

> Maderna and I had a lengthy meeting in New York on April 19 to discuss *TRIMALCHIO* in some detail. Among other things, we agreed that I would lay out the scenario quasi libretto between now and the beginning of July when we begin our collaboration in Tanglewood.[76]

As late as December 1972 (a little over three months before the premiere), Maderna's publisher Salabert even inquired of Samama, Maderna's European agent, about Strasfogel's role in drafting the scenario and adapting the Petronius text.[77] But Maderna ended up writing the entire libretto himself, drawing from the Arrowsmith and other translations of *The Satyricon*.

The night before the first rehearsal, Strasfogel realized that he had not only to stage-direct the opera, but also to order the scenes. Upon receiving the score, a stack of unbound pages, he asked, "'But what's the order, Bruno?' and he said, 'Do what you like!'" Strasfogel said, "ooookaay, but how do you go from one [scene to the other], what's the connection? He pointed to a box of reel-to-reel tapes." This box contained six to eight hours of tape materials that Maderna had made at the Studio di Fonologia in Milan. Strasfogel, who was then in his early thirties, almost panicked:

> I was directing an opera, it was my European debut, and we had four weeks to go before the premiere, I had never seen the music, never heard it, and I had to make a piece of some sort out of it. I had to create the order, and I also had to make the selection of tapes that I would use. … I was rehearsing six hours a day, then I would come home and work for another six hours on these tapes.[78]

The work's flexible modular structure, as well as the fact that the singers had received the material only a short time before, made the rehearsals into a high-wire act. Maderna made changes to the music constantly, adding high notes for Poppy Holden and giving a solo scene on the text of *Love's Ecstasy* to Anne Haenen, who sang the role of Chrysis, only two days before the premiere.[79] For Débria Brown (Fortunata), an African-American mezzo-

---

76 Letter from Strasfogel to de Roo, 24 April 1972, Ian Strasfogel, personal archive. (A second copy is held in PSS.) Fearn attributes Strasfogel as a librettist (along with Maderna) for *Satyricon*, but this is incorrect; Raymond Fearn, *"Satyricon," The New Grove Dictionary of Opera: Grove Music Online: Oxford Music Online* (Oxford University Press), accessed 18 June 2021, http://www.oxfordmusiconline.com.ezp-prod1.hul.harvard.edu/subscriber/article/grove/music/O904644. See also De Benedictis' essay in this volume, pp. 36–37.

77 Letter from Constant Minescaut (general director of Edition Salabert, Paris) to Samama, 8 December 1972 (PSS-BMC).

78 Strasfogel, personal communication (interview), 28 November 2015 in New York City.

79 In the score (published posthumously in 1974 by Salabert) there are two scenes on this text for solo voice and one instrument (english horn and flute, respectively), entitled *Criside I* and *Criside II*. Another scene, entitled *Love's Ecstasy,* is scored for four voices and three instruments. Haenen recalls her nervousness upon learning that she would have to start the opera with this solo scene, which she received only two days before the premiere; Anne Haenen, personal communications by e-mail (31 July 2016) and on videocall (8 August 2016). Her account is confirmed by the fact that the printed program from the premiere does not list this scene, although it does appear in various sketches for the work, as well as in Strasfogel's general plan, dated 9 March 1973 (published in this volume on p. 52).

SATYRICON
First American Performance

Music by Bruno Maderna

Libretto by Bruno Maderna
(based on Petronius Arbiter's *Satyricon* translated into English by
William Arrowsmith)

Scenario and Production by Ian Strasfogel

Associate Director, Gustavo Motta

Conducted by Gunther Schuller

Scenery and Lighting by John Wright Stevens

Costumes by Jeanne Button
(Courtesy Netherlands Opera)

Musical Preparation by Dixie Ross Neill

Carder Vaughn, Stage Manager   Chris J. Dorsey, Technical Manager
Janet Warren, Costume Coordinator and Make-up
Wanda Whalen, Assistant to Mr. Stevens
K. Vinton Taylor, Assistant to Ms. Warren
Karen Reynes Dorsey, Production Assistant
Dennis Dorn, Master Electrician
Laura Crow, Wardrobe Supervisor

CAST

Trimalchio .... William Neill
Fortunata .... Sandra Walker
Habinnas .... John Aler
Scintilla .... Janet Kenney
Eumolpus .... C. Evans Clough
Criside .... Emelia Simone
Niceros .... Ronald Corrado
A Slave .... Ad Rijsdijk

EX. 3   Program book, Festival of Contemporary Music, Tanglewood 1973,
5 August 1973, p. 10 (Oliver Knussen Collection, PSS).

soprano who made her career primarily in Germany and was a renowned interpreter of Carmen, he wrote a sultry "Habanera"-like song (*Fortunata e Eumolpus*).[80]

Maderna conceived of *Satyricon*, indeed of all operas, as integral multimedia dramas in which the visual and musical elements were indissolubly united. Therefore he did not hesitate to make directorial suggestions. Haenen relates, "I do remember Maderna's rasping voice, interrupting rehearsals all the time with 'Ian, Ian, I got an idea…'"[81]

Some time during the rehearsals for *Satyricon*, Maderna was diagnosed with terminal lung cancer. He returned home to Darmstadt to see his doctor, and came back to Holland only to conduct the premiere on 16 March 1973. Lucas Vis took over the rest of the run. Whereas Strasfogel and Holden remember that Vis also had taken over the rehearsals after the first week, Haenen and Neill remember that Maderna was there for the entire rehearsal period: according to Haenen, "there were no stage rehearsals and no music rehearsals without Bruno." Haenen adds that Maderna looked unhealthy (his skin was gray), but that he appeared to be sober and was completely focused on the rehearsals.

---

80   The *Carmen* references in this number have been pointed out by Benedetta Zucconi, *"Satyricon" di Bruno Maderna (1973)* (Università degli Studi di Pavia, 2010–11; copy in PSS), pp. 40, 83–84, and 132. Brown, who made her New York City Opera debut as Carmen in 1958, was one of the first wave of African-American opera singers invited to sing at major opera houses in the U.S. She was a member of the city theaters in Aachen, Stuttgart, and Karlsruhe, and ended her career as Professor of Voice and Artist in Residence at the University of Houston.

81   Anne Haenen, personal communications by e-mail (31 July 2016) and on videochat (8 August 2016). Donal Henahan similarly describes Maderna's contributions to the staging of *Don Giovanni* at the New York City Opera; see Henahan, "When the Stage Director Takes On the Opera," *The New York Times* (12 November 1972). See also Romito's essay in this volume, p. 296.

Strasfogel staged *Satyricon* anew at Tanglewood on 5 and 6 August 1973, in the second part of the program, after *Triptych* by Bo Lawergren. Strasfogel used a different order of numbers than in the Dutch premiere performances, and, except for Neill in the main role, a new cast, with Schuller conducting (→ **EX. 3**).[82] (The Festival of Contemporary Music was overseen by Schuller and funded by Paul Fromm's Foundation, in the meantime newly incorporated as the Fromm Music Foundation at Harvard.) Maderna was not able to be at Tanglewood that summer, as his illness was already quite advanced. Strasfogel was quite happy with the results. With adequate rehearsal time, a new staging concept, and Schuller's conducting, the work's American premiere presented the work in the best possible light, in his view.

Reception of Maderna's Later Music in the U.S.

Maderna's own music had been performed in the U.S. since at least 1959.[83] While American critics did not warm to the Concerto for violin and orchestra, Maderna's other works were for the most part very well received.[84] Critics praised his music as "expressive of emotional content,"[85] noting its "luxuriance of sound and the flexible sense of rhythmic landscape"[86] and its "careful workmanship and a concern with breaking out of familiar patterns."[87] His music "should be better known here than it is," a *New York Times* critic wrote in 1971, and lauded Maderna's "marvelous ear for sonorities combining delicate colors in exquisitely tinted tonal pastels."[88]

Venetian Journal generally shared the positive reception accorded to Maderna's music in the U.S. The *New York Times* noted of the premiere on 12 March 1972 that "The *Journal* has a fair amount of wit, instrumental flair and perhaps the first-ever electronic simulation of a copulating couple."[89] Ten years later, Daniel Cariaga of the *Los Angeles Times*, in a sympa-

---

82   See the program of the Festival of Contemporary Music, Tanglewood 1973, pp. 9–11 (http://collections.bso.org/digital/collection/PROG/id/545172/rec/1, consulted 18 June 2021). The date of 4 August, given for the American premiere of *Satyricon* in *Bruno Maderna: Documenti*, ed. Mario Baroni and Rossana Dalmonte (Milan: Suvini Zerboni, 1985), p. 316, and adopted by Geneviève Mathon, "À propos du *Satyricon*," in *à Bruno Maderna*, ed. Geneviève Mathon, Laurent Feneyrou, and Giordano Ferrari (Paris: Basalte, 2009), vol. 1, pp. 69–86: 70 and elsewhere, is incorrect. The material for Strasfogel's staging of *Satyricon* at Tanglewood are held in PSS.

83   For details on performances of Maderna's music in the U.S., see Romito's essay in this volume, pp. 277–97.

84   On the violin Concerto, which had been performed by Paul Zukofsky and the New York Philharmonic (with Maderna conducting) on 20 January 1972, see Harold C. Schonberg, "Music: Solo Mandolins and Maderna," *The New York Times* (22 January 1972), p. 36.

85   Louis Snyder, "Jeers and Premieres at a Musical Milestone," *The Christian Science Monitor* (14 August 1972), p. 4, about the world premiere performance of *Giardino religioso* at Tanglewood. Snyder summarizes: "If there was any special favorite, it would seem to have been Mr. Maderna who received continuing plaudits both from the listeners and the performers whom he had just taken for 'a walk through his musical garden.'"

86   Eric Salzman, "Modern Works Given by Chamber Group," *The New York Times* (6 March 1961), p. 30, about *Serenata n. 2*.

87   Donal Henahan, "A Festival in Search of Itself: At Tanglewood," *The New York Times* (20 August 1972), p. D11, about *Giardino religioso*.

88   Allen Hughes, "2 of Maderna's Musical Works Unfold Rich Shadings at Tully," *The New York Times* (31 January 1971), p. 64, on *Quadrivium*, performed by the Juilliard Orchestra.

89   Peter G. Davis, "Tongue-in-Cheek Cantata Has World Premiere," *The New York Times* (13 March 1972), p. 41.

thetic and perceptive review, praised Maderna's mordant wit: "[*Venetian Journal*] comments, by not commenting, on the follies of one man – and thus, humankind; [...] it traverses a simple narrative, but one which can be read for complexities apparent and inherent."[90]

The Tanglewood production of *Satyricon* in the summer of 1973, on the other hand, got a decidedly mixed reception. Although an in-house BSO account trumpeted the work's success, calling it "the world's first X-rated opera," and mentioning that Julius Rudel of the New York City Opera "has ventured to the Berkshires just for this performance," the critics were divided.[91] Michael Steinberg of the *Boston Globe* dismissed the work as "lazy claptrap."[92] Ten days later, in summarizing the Festival of Contemporary Music, his opinion had not changed:

> Worse [than *Triptych* by Bo Lawergren], because longer, was Bruno Maderna's *Satyricon*. During the telling of the tale of the widow of Ephesus, a muted trumpet plays Chopin's Funeral March with wrong notes. That fairly gives you the measure of the composer's wit and invention.[93]

If that was the *Boston Globe,* one could only expect worse from the more conservative *New York Times.* Donal Henahan, true to form, wrote that *Satyricon,*

> a thesaurus of recently fashionable ideas, [...] trafficked heavily in the put-on, the parody, the mock-sensual and the tongue-in-chic [*sic*] degeneracy of Petronius Arbiter. It had [...] a lot of humor of the sort that used to be called sophomoric but is now offered everywhere on stages as evidence that artists are not sophisticated snobs.[94]

> Amusing? Yes, much of the time. [... T]he serious question remains: how Petronius, the classicist of camp, can be trumped in this respect. The struggle to parodize a parody soon becomes tiresome.[95]

The alternative New York paper *The Village Voice,* on the other hand, offered a generous and favorable review that saluted the opera world's first "intentionally funny orgy," and appreciated the work's humor and "riotous feast of musical styles and quotations." *The Village Voice* also praised Maderna's compositional abilities:

> [S]ince Maderna is still one of the more talented composers around, [the score] drew some vocal lines of genuine, fresh, modern-sounding lyricism and orchestral music having some of the kind of delicacy found in the best of Berg.[96]

But in general, mainstream East Coast critics were not very receptive to Maderna's un-buttoned approach to music theater. Perhaps this was because "director's theater" was still quite new in American opera at that time, and perhaps also because of a general

---

90 Daniel Cariaga, "Sperry, La Barbara Solo With New Music Group," *Los Angeles Times* (9 February 1983), p. G1.

91 Kenneth R. Miller, "Some Impressions of the Berkshire Music Center – 1973," program book of the BSO, week of 19 October 1973, pp. 155 and 157.

92 Michael Steinberg, "The Good, the Bad, and the Out-of-Tune," *The Boston Globe* (9 August 1973), p. 37.

93 Michael Steinberg, "The Festival of Contemporary Music," *The Boston Globe* (19 August 1973). Steinberg was much more taken with Donald Martino's *Notturno* on the same program.

94 Donal Henahan, "The Avant-Garde Looks Backward," *The New York Times* (19 August 1973), p. 119.

95 Donal Henahan, "Music: New *Satyricon* at Tanglewood," *The New York Times* (7 August 1973), p. 29.

96 *The Village Voice* (16 August 1973). In the copy I consulted (courtesy of William Neill) the author's name was cut off. It could have been Tom Johnson, the chief music critic of *The Village Voice* during these years (he signed the previous review on the same page).

prudishness on the part of the American classical music establishment. *Satyricon* furthermore was miles away stylistically and aesthetically from the prevailing twelve-tone idiom practiced (albeit in different ways) by Donald Martino, Gunther Schuller, Milton Babbitt, Roger Sessions, and other leading American composers.

But whereas certain critics may have been "uptight" (to use an early seventies expression), young musicians admired Maderna tremendously. Strasfogel recalls:

> He was like the Pied Piper with some of the younger generation. With some of the older players in the orchestra, it was maybe touch and go, but with the younger generation, we totally got it; we felt that he was really one of us, and that was a fascinating experience.[97]

Maderna's work, in their eyes, fit perfectly with "the raucousness of the late sixties and early seventies: sexual directness and freedom, and wildness. This was something that was new for us all, and great fun, very much a part of that era, the flower power era."

Most of all, they respected Maderna's phenomenal musicality: he could sightread the most complex scores and get the best out of any orchestra. Di Pietro recalls that he and other composition students were attracted to Maderna precisely because he did not hold to any aesthetic orthodoxy, "Darmstadt" or any other kind. They admired the combination of sensuousness and intellectual content in Maderna's music, so distant from the world of American academic serialism. "Consistency is deadly" was the message they gratefully received from Maderna.[98] "It's very hard to find any composer anywhere who has that kind of humor and freedom," Strasfogel relates. "He brought something very special to the world of serious, composed, classical music. Everyone loved him, even those who didn't get along with each other."[99]

Even if certain critics had difficulty accepting Maderna's music theater works, Maderna himself was viewed as a very sympathetic figure. Composer John Heiss, who was at Tanglewood during the summer of 1971, recalls that Maderna was "a singular presence" and that he related extremely well to people.[100] In January 1972, the *New York Times* featured Maderna in an extensive interview, recounting some of his jokes (which he made "on the average of once a minute"), and relating details about the composer's difficult childhood, his wartime experience, and his many musical adventures.[101] New York journalists could not resist commenting upon Maderna's resemblance to their beloved former mayor, Fiorello La Guardia. They also had no qualms about describing Maderna's accent, his weight, his height, his hair, and his "ebullient" and "voluble" personality, casually indulging in Italian stereotypes that are quite cringe-worthy today.[102]

---

97   Ian Strasfogel, personal communication (interview), 28 November 2015 in New York City (also the quotation from Strasfogel in the following paragraphs).
98   Di Pietro, personal communication (phone), 11 July 2016.
99   Strasfogel, personal communication (interview), 28 November 2015 in New York City.
100 John Heiss, personal communication (phone), 13 July 2016.
101 Donal Henahan, "Is Toscanini or Boulez the Better Conductor?" *The New York Times* (9 January 1972), p. D15.
102 "About two years and seventy pounds ago, he looked a lot more like Fiorello La Guardia than he does now, but still the resemblance is strong." Henahan, ibid. La Guardia, a first-generation American of Italian and Jewish descent, was mayor of New York City from 1934 to 1945. Because of his first name and his short stature, he was affectionately known as "the Little Flower." See also Raymond Ericson, "This Bruno looks like Fiorello," *The New York Times* (24 January 1971), p. D15.

Conclusion: Maderna and American Music Networks

Maderna's American activities were supported by patronage networks made up of performers, patrons, conductors, administrators, theater directors, music festivals, professional orchestras, conservatories, and many others who interacted with him about matters both profound and mundane. The professional and personal ties that linked these individuals and institutions amplified the effectiveness of their efforts. Strasfogel's interest in theatrical improvisation proved fruitful for the development of Maderna's thoughts about "Trimalchio's Feast," and, in accordance with the collaborative nature (and structural openness) of the work, it was again Strasfogel who shaped the order, material (taped and live), and dramatic structure of *Satyricon* in its first two realizations. Schuller, as co-director of the Tanglewood Festival (and a highly influential figure in the East Coast new music scene at that time), brought Maderna to Tanglewood. Fromm provided funding and support for Tanglewood's Festival of Contemporary Music and commissioned Maderna for *Giardino religioso.* Sperry played multiple roles; having instigated and commissioned *Venetian Journal,* he went on to perform the work multiple times and to appear in *Satyricon.*

Sheldon Soffer, Maderna's manager for the U.S., was the most crucial catalyst. Soffer's voluminous correspondence shows his great affection for the composer as well as his tireless efforts on his behalf. Soffer spared no effort to get Maderna established in the U.S. and seemed to know everybody. Maderna's American network expanded rapidly, with Tanglewood, Juilliard, the New York Philharmonic, and many other institutions and people all drawn together into Soffer's epistolary web.[103]

It may seem strange that in an article about two theatrical works, the one institution absent from the networks described is the American opera house. To my knowledge, *Satyricon* has, as of 2021, never been performed in the U.S. by a professional opera company. (The American premiere was performed by the Berkshire Music Center Fellows, who were advanced students.) Opera companies in the U.S. depend on private – individual and corporate – sponsorship for support; therefore they typically avoid new works that do not have broad public appeal. Even the landmark works of European opera are very rarely performed, and when they are, it is usually at festivals rather than as part of an opera company's regular season.[104]

As Maderna's presence and influence in the U.S. grew, he began to conduct American music regularly, including Ives's *The Unanswered Question* and Ives's rarely performed and metrically complex Fourth Symphony.[105] Di Pietro recalls having long talks with Maderna about Ives during the summer of 1971 at Tanglewood, and accompanying him to

---

103 In late November 1972, on the advice of his European agent Sylvio Samama, Maderna left Soffer's firm and switched his U.S. management to Harold Shaw (letter from Sheldon Soffer to Maderna, 21 November 1972, PSS-BMC). The first contacts with Soffer date back to 1967–68 (see the essay by Romito in this volume, pp. 278–79).

104 The ambitious premieres staged by Sarah Caldwell and the long-defunct Opera Company of Boston, including the American premiere of Nono's *Intolleranza 1960* in 1965, the occasion of Maderna's American conducting debut, are unfortunately a distant memory.

105 See Romito's essay in this volume, pp. 292–93.

the Housatonic River at Stockbridge, one of the *Three Places in New England*.[106] We have already witnessed Maderna's longtime advocacy of Earle Brown; Richard Toop believes that Maderna's death may have even contributed to the drying up of Brown's European career after 1973.[107] About another American work that Maderna had conducted at Tanglewood in 1972, Soffer wrote, "Congratulations: Druckman won the Pulitzer Award for *WINDOWS* … thanks to you … You really are marvelous in everything."[108] (Maderna had his likes and dislikes; that same summer, he refused to conduct Fred Lerdahl's *Chromorhythmos*, to the composer's considerable irritation.)[109]

The sounds and rhythms of American music left audible traces in Maderna's newer works of the 1970s. *Satyricon* and *Venetian Journal* both have a distinctly American flavor. Their texts are largely in idiomatic American English, an aspect that is brought out when their performers are American. In the *Carriera di Trimalchio* of *Satyricon*, for example, the Trimalchio delivers the colloquial lines (following the Arrowsmith translation), "Was I licked? Hell, no!" In this number, Maderna's music turns Trimalchio into a parody of a boorish, rich American. As Donal Henahan noted, "Trimalchio indulges in an orgy of boasting to the strains of the 'Stars and Stripes Forever,' looking and sounding exactly like any self-made, oil-depleting tycoon."[110] In *Trimalchio e il monumento*, "the whole ensemble revel[s] in an Ivesian stew of march tunes," similar to the second movement of *Three Places in New England*, as Leighton Kerner pointed out in his review.[111] *The Village Voice* critic noted that the score "splashed a Charles Ives stew of Sousa all over the stage."[112] Even Maderna's Boswell, of course nominally a Scotsman, sounds American in Levy's colloquial text for *Venetian Journal*. The American English libretto and Paul Sperry's idiomatic performance go a long way toward making his adventures seem like those of a green young American tourist.

One reason why Maderna is still remembered with such affection in the U.S. is that he did not present himself with the nimbus of a "great composer" or a "famous conductor." Rather, he rolled up his sleeves and got to work, which was much appreciated, even by those who found his somewhat haphazard approach to rehearsal annoying. Whether he was conducting major American orchestras, working with advanced pre-professional music students at Juilliard and Tanglewood, directing the Festival of Contemporary Music at Tanglewood, teaching composition (→ **EX. 4**), or coaching singers in productions of Mozart and Monteverdi operas, Maderna made an impact as a musician, thinker, and man of the theater. With his strong personality, formidable musical skills,

---

106 Rocco Di Pietro, personal communication (phone), 11 July 2016.
107 See Toop, "Their Man in Europe, Our Man in America" (see note 3), p. 146.
108 Letter from Soffer to Maderna, 2 May 1972 (PSS-BMC). About Druckman's *Windows* see also Romito's essay in this volume, p. 290.
109 "No, I won't tell you what I think about Bruno," Lerdahl told in 1973; see Michael Steinberg, "Works by Lerdahl, Kim to premiere," *The Boston Globe* (13 May 1973), p. 62.
110 Donal Henahan, "Music: New *Satyricon* at Tanglewood," *The New York Times* (7 August 1973), p. 29. This famous Sousa march is a staple of American orchestras and bands everywhere, and it is played every summer at Tanglewood, accompanied by a fireworks display.
111 Leighton Kerner, [untitled review of the Tanglewood *Satyricon*], *Opera News* (September 1973), p. 49.
112 *The Village Voice*, 16 August 1973.

EX. 4   Bruno Maderna teaching at Tanglewood, 1972 (Hawthorne Cottage); © Whitestone Photo; PSS-BMC. From right to left: Ira Taxin, Louis Karchin, Robert Xavier Rodríguez, Sheila Silver, Stephen Drury, unidentified women.

original theatrical ideas, and uncanny ability to get professional orchestras to plumb the expressive depths of modern works, Maderna was on the cusp of a major presence in American musical scene by the early 1970s. One can only imagine how his legacy in American music would have been even more pronounced had his life not been cut short.

Appendix

June 14, 1971

Mr. Bruno Maderna
149 Martinstrasse
Darmstadt, Germany

Dear Bruno:

I've been meaning to write to you for weeks about Tanglewood, but so
many problems at the Conservatory have kept me from doing so. Anyway,
I figured that you were pretty busy too, and a letter now would probably
arrive just at the right time for you to think seriously about Tanglewood.

As I see your duties there, you will have a certain number of private
composition students, perhaps 6 to 8 whom you would teach one hour
a week in private lessons. If you wanted to and if the students found it
acceptable, you could teach them collectively pr in small groups of 2 or
3. Traditionally, however, our composition students have received private
lessons.

Next, you would do at some point in your stay at Tanglewood,two or three
consecutive weeks of seminars, i. e. three two-hour seminars per week.
These will be with all the composition students present at Tanglewood and
can range all the way from discussions of the students' works to lectures
or discussions on subjects which you would like to talk about or subjects of
interest to the students. In general, my experience is that these seminars
have to be structured to some extent, otherwise they become uncontrolled
talk-fests with the composers who have the greatest egos talking the most
and the others being bored.   You can, of course, include some aspects of
performance of contemporary music in your seminars. Also, I would
appreciate having some idea of what topics you might deal with in the seminars, since we will be having two other guest teachers, Lucas Foss and
Charles Wuorinen, and naturally I would like to coordinate the topics with
yours and avoid duplication.

The third general area in which you will be working is with the conducting
students. Since I don't want to kill you off in one summer, I want to divide
the teaching of the conductors among a variety of people including Michael
Thomas, Ozawa, myself and perhaps Bernstein. I think it is best to wait

APP. 1   Letter (also copied to Soffer) from Gunther Schuller
to Bruno Maderna, 14 June 1971, 2 pages; Boston Symphony
Orchestra Archives (with kind permission).

Mr. Bruno Maderna   page 2   June 14, 1971

for the final decision on that question until we get to Tanglewood and
discuss the conducting program together with Michael Thomas who will
be the main organizer of the program.

The last item for your consideration is the collaborative composing project
we talked about in New York. Ian Strasfogel and I are heading a Music-
Theater Project in which we will be performing works ranging from Ligeti
and Birtwhistle to Offenbach and Satie, all in staged performances. We
are putting on two programs, and in the second of these we would like you
to take charge of a music-theater piece which would be composed by, let
us say, four or five of the best composition students at Tanglewood under
your supervision and in which you could, of course, also participate actively.
To the extent that this piece needed to be conducted in performance, you
would be the conductor. You would be able to use a small complement of
instrumentalists, plus some of the singers, actors and mimes we will have
at Tanglewood. I know you are very interested in this kind of collective
composing process, and Ian and I feel very strongly that it must be included
as a very important part of our Music-Theater Project.

There are, of course, many other activities in which you might wish to
become involved, but just the things I have enumerated above will keep you
very busy. I think you will find it very rewarding because the level of talent
at Tanglewood is very high.

I am so happy that you are coming to Tanglewood and that we will be working
together again after so many years. I am sure that we will spend many happy
hours over a glass of vino.

Ciao a presto,

Gunther Schuller

P.S. You can write me at the New England Conservatory until June 25.
After that I will be at Tanglewood.

cc: c/o Mr. Sheldon Soffer, New York City

bcc: HJK, DRG, GS
GSwr   (Dictated by Mr. Schuller and signed in his absence.)

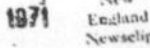

DEFYING THE ARTS

Maderna Proves Committee Can Create Musical Work of Art

By R. C. HAMMERICH

Republican Staff

LENOX — There is a small group of creators at Tanglewood who are defying one of the most deeply established beliefs in the arts. . .that a work of art cannot be created by committee.

Advising the group of 10 or 15 young composers and performers is Bruno Maderna, a musician of high international stature.

For two weeks the members of the group have been creating a music drama, collectively and separately, by composing passages of melody and words on the basis of suggestions made during group sessions and changing them during subsequent group sessions.

It will have its first public performance at Tanglewood tonight and continues tomorrow, Wednesday and Thursday along with three other, existing, short music dramas.

They are doing it for educational purposes, namely, mainly, to stretch their compositional muscles as part of the reestablished opera department in the Berkshire Music Center, the summer academy of the Boston Symphony Orchestra.

The rejuvenated department is called the Music Theater Project and is supported by grants from several foundations. Involved are a dozen singers and two actors plus any of the center's composing or conducting fellows or members of the center orchestra as needed.

Its director is Ian Strasfogel of the New England Conservatory of Music. Maderna, who is not exactly typical of the world's leading contemporary musicians, is its musical advisor.

But he exhibits several of the typical attributes, i.e., popular conductor, avant garde composer, busy lecturer and teacher, amiable associate.

Early in his visit at Tanglewood this summer he won the enthusiastic support of the members

See DEFYING
Page LT 2

of Boston's orchestra while rehearsing them for his appearance July 11 as guest conductor. They liked him for his thorough knowledge of the music he was conducting, for the strongly decisive attitude he had about it, for his clearly - understood means of communicating his ideas and for his friendly, but no-nonsense and unpretentious manner.

On the podium during rehearsals it was obvious that he knew exactly how he wanted each phrase and passage to sound, which is not always the case with conductors.

His decisions about interpretation of the score were strongly held, and, in spite of some difficulty with the English language, he showed no lack of understanding of the orchestral language. The players had no difficulty in understanding what he wished them to do, a factor which increased their respect.

Such appreciation of guest conductors by orchestra members is uncommon; and it included those members who don't care for the kind of music Maderna composes.

At 51 he is not a radical youth, but he is one of the founders of the Fonologia Musicale in Milan, one of the early important studios for electronic music, and an advocate of atonalism.

His compositions show a strong influence from the work of the Viennese school (Schoenberg, Berg) which broke away from the traditional, tonal structure of music, and his name is sometimes coupled with the contemporary, atonal Italian composers, Luciano Berio and Luigi Nono. To the casual listener, their music may sound discordant and chaotic.

Maderna is a smiling, voluble, ebullient, energetic, jovial Italian with the sort of gregarious personality that can make him an effective teacher, especially in the atmosphere surrounding the group - creation of the little music - drama that will have its birth tonight.

It will be 20 to 30 minutes long, will have 10 to 15 in the cast and will be evolved from Trimalchio's banquet sequence from the "Satyricon" by Petronius Arbiter.

The "Satyricon" is a satire on the vulgar and dissolute life of the citizens of Rome, written at the time of the reign of Nero and the decline of the Empire. Trimalchio was a very wealthy citizen.

Ordinarily a composer or librettist, in splendid isolation, puts down on paper, one by one, the notes and words he thinks will enable his reader to reproduce his musical or literary ideas. The performer then, as best he can, recreates what he thinks the composer's "true meaning" is.

In this case at Tanglewood the method of composition is cumbersome. Bits from Petronius' writing (sights, dialogue, movement) are discussed with a view toward reproduction in music and action.

Short sequences, having been chosen by the group, are taken to semi-isolation by sub-groups of three or four singers, actors and composers where the sequence is reproduced in music and action.

This reproduction is displayed before the whole group for acceptance, rejection or modification. Thus, gradually, the whole music drama is "composed" by the whole group.

"They learn; they discover," said Maderna. "All the problems are seen with many eyes."

APP. 2   Roy C. Hammerich, "Defying the Arts: Maderna Proves Committee Can Create Musical Work of Art," *Springfield Republican* (8 August 1971).

SEARCHING FOR ROOTS:
THE DEVELOPMENT OF A STYLE

VENIERO RIZZARDI

Venice to Europe
Bruno Maderna Before and After 1948

For apparently fortuitous reasons, it was only well into the 2000s that Maderna's production prior to his adoption of dodecaphony could be assessed in all its consistency. The late discovery of the most important scores belonging to that phase, namely, the Concerto for piano and orchestra of 1942 and the *Requiem* of 1946, which came to light between 2006 and 2009,[1] allowed us to complete a "portrait of the artist as a young man" which till then was still only a rough outline. And then it also showed us that Maderna in his twenties was anything but an immature artist, albeit part of a musical world that was completely different from the one with which he had always naturally been associated. Beyond a well-defined divide marked by a date – as we shall see in a moment – his mature production begins: a relatively brief period of less than twenty-five years cut short by his untimely death in 1973, a year at the center of an era when avant-garde poetics and the related narratives were still in full force. The composer, who more than any of his colleagues was, both literally and metaphorically speaking, a "citizen of Darmstadt," produced his main body of work in the 1950s and 1960s, the period which encompasses almost all the happenings of the post-dodecaphonic European avant-garde. It thus goes without saying that Maderna could not have partaken in the crises and afterthoughts that his generation would already experience at the end of the 1970s. Nor can we say whether the surprising eclecticism shown by Maderna in his later years, that of *Venetian Journal* (1972) and *Satyricon* (1972–73), heralded a new and not a sporadic poetic orientation. Nor should it be read as an unlikely postmodern premonition: the novelty of that polystylism coexisted with another different orientation, which was instead in coherent evolution with his previous production. Despite all their "openness" and formal mobility, his purely instrumental works, such as *Aura, Biogramma* (both from 1972), and the Concerto No. 3 for oboe and orchestra (1973), are completely lacking in parody and pseudo-citations from music of the past.

This creative trajectory was mainly a continuous one, and its beginning can be seen in the late 1940s. It was Maderna himself who provided a date: "[…] I am certainly on the edge of a world. We need to go much further, but first I need to do a job that only the two of us can do: calmly review all the results and all the unfinished research from '48

My heartfelt thanks to Angela Ida De Benedictis, Benedetta Zucconi, and Michele Chiappini for their advice and suggestions – offered individually, and together as the team of curators of *Amore e curiosità*, the ultimate collection (in Italian) of Maderna's writings and interviews, regularly cited in this article.

1   Both published by Suvini Zerboni, Milan (see below, notes 19 and 25).

onwards."[2] This is what Maderna wrote to Luigi Nono in mid-1952, in a letter dedicated to new compositional problems: not long after having completely rethought his technique, he was taking on electroacoustic creation for the first time. In fact, anyone who knows the genesis of the first *Musica su due dimensioni,* for flute and magnetic tape,[3] will understand that the "world" that was opening up before his eyes was not just that of the sound expansion offered by precisely this new technical-musical dimension, but that of a new order of thought which was thereby coming into force.[4] It was not until the inauguration of RAI's Studio di Fonologia in Milan a few years later that Maderna would fully immerse himself in an experimental practice that will make him reconsider the relationship between writing and sound. However, in that first attempt to combine instrumental material with a new and unheard-of resource, Maderna was studying how to employ a selection criterion that would make it possible to handle both materials on the same level of constructive abstraction: linked to the permutation game with the series and, in any case, always to the tool of writing. Although Maderna had only been using the twelve-tone composition method for less than four years, he was already applying it with creative formulas: only a short time previously he had used it to derive his own generative systems capable of expanding the series of pitches toward an enlarged and orderly repertoire of actual sound objects.[5] In 1952, as soon as he had devised such a method, Maderna already imagined that it could be employed to multiply and transform these objects and even guide them to the new world of synthesized sound.

Leaving aside for a moment the nature and detail of these procedures, and the problems encountered in the need to put them into practice, let us instead consider the emphasis on the "edge," on the need to "go much further," and to develop and tackle "research" from a slightly earlier phase, in which Maderna involved, on an equal footing, a slightly younger composer. Luigi Nono had met Maderna in 1946 and in fact had been

---

2   Maderna to Luigi Nono, letter of 30 May 1952 (Archivio Luigi Nono, Venice, henceforth ALN). Unless otherwise specified, all the letters quoted from now on are translated from the Italian.

3   On the theoretical assumptions and the genesis of this composition see Veniero Rizzardi and Nicola Scaldaferri, "*Musica su due dimensioni* (1952): Histoire, vicissitudes et importance d'une œuvre (presque) absente," in *à Bruno Maderna,* ed. Geneviève Mathon, Laurent Feneyrou, and Giordano Ferrari, vol. 2 (Paris: Basalte, 2009), pp. 423ff.

4   See what Maderna has to say about this in the lecture he gave on electronic music ("Kompositorische Erfahrungen mit der elektronischen Musik") in Darmstadt on 26 July 1957; Italian translation as "Esperienze compositive con la musica elettronica," in Bruno Maderna, *Amore e curiosità: Scritti, frammenti e interviste sulla musica,* ed. Angela Ida De Benedictis, Michele Chiappini, and Benedetta Zucconi (Milan: il Saggiatore, 2020), pp. 232–35. An English translation ("Compositional Experiences in Electronic Music") based on a previous Italian edition can be found in Raymond Fearn, *Bruno Maderna* (Chur: Harwood, 1990), pp. 194–96.

5   On the music and serial techniques devised by Maderna from 1950 onwards, see Veniero Rizzardi, "The Tone Row, Squared: Bruno Maderna and the Birth of Serial Music in Italy," in *Rewriting Recent Music History: The Development of Early Serialism 1947–1957,* ed. Mark Delaere (Leuven and Walpole, MA: Peeters, 2011), pp. 45–66. Also see the essays by Carlo Ciceri, Pascal Decroupet, and Christoph Neidhöfer in this volume. Further developments of Maderna's serial procedures are explained in Christoph Neidhöfer, "Vers un principe commun: Intégration de la hauteur et du rythme dans le *Quartetto per archi in due tempi* (1955)," in *à Bruno Maderna,* vol. 2 (see note 3), pp. 323–58, and in Gianmario Borio and Veniero Rizzardi, "Die musikalische Einheit von Bruno Madernas *Hyperion,*" in *Quellenstudien II: Zwölf Komponisten des 20. Jahrhunderts,* ed. Felix Meyer (Winterthur: Amadeus, 1993), pp. 117–48.

promoted from pupil to colleague after just a couple of years of intense apprenticeship, ending precisely in 1948, a date which must have long been fixed in both their minds as "year zero" of a new musical life, and more.[6]

The steps that transformed the language of European music in a handful of years were rapid, the work of a generation of young artists driven by a strong sense of historical responsibility. In the post-war period, such an attitude was subjectively motivated and sanctioned by the need to activate a collective process of spiritual and civil reconstruction. In Italy, in particular, this subjectivity also assumed a political character: the cases of Maderna and Nono, both individually and as a partnership, are exemplary in this sense. Maderna was born in 1920 and had been enrolled in the army, but then, following the armistice and the events that in 1943 had split the nation in a civil war, he had turned to militant anti-fascism and joined the Resistance: apart from what can be gleaned from official documents, it has never been possible to clarify his exact role, but he must certainly have been actively involved, although never in actual fighting. Nono, who was four years younger, had joined the Venetian anti-fascist circles, carrying out just a few supporting tasks. The two met for the first time in 1946: despite their different educational and social backgrounds, and above all their levels of experience, from this moment on and for quite some time their studies, research, creative principles, ideals, and political orientations developed in a common process. In retrospect, Nono gave a decidedly political interpretation to this beginning:

> In postwar Italy a kind of research and musical creativity is developing that clearly differentiates it from others.
> Linked to the urgency of a new kind of ideal subject matter, caused by the Resistance is the search for adequate technical means, for new possibilities, including those of electronics. The ideological commitment is accompanied by a commitment to language. Bruno Maderna, a pivotal figure on the new Italian musical scene, pointed the way. In 1951 he composed a chamber cantata, *Quattro lettere* [Four Letters][…]. In this composition, there is a reciprocal interaction between an idealistic subject matter that is new and complex and a musical conception and invention that aims to project itself in a new way.[7]

The year 1948 was pivotal for the whole of Italian society: a controversial election saw the end to the precarious compromise between the various political forces (Catholic, Liberal, Social-Communist) that had called the shots in the resistance to fascism. The year marked the beginning of a democratic regime that would confine the forces of the left to the opposition for a long time. The following years were marked by hard social conflict and a bitter debate between the Catholic party (Christian Democracy) governments and the opposition of the socialist and communist parties, this last one the strongest by popular

---

6   Nono gave a lengthy account of the fundamental meeting with Maderna in a long interview in 1987; see "An Autobiography of the Author Recounted by Enzo Restagno," in *Nostalgia for the Future: Luigi Nono's Selected Writings and Interviews*, ed. Angela Ida De Benedictis and Veniero Rizzardi (Oakland: University of California Press, 2018), pp. 27–122: 27–29.

7   Luigi Nono, "Music and Resistance," in ibid., pp. 273–76: 274. The reference is to *Quattro lettere* (*Kranichsteiner Kammerkantate*), which was actually composed in 1953. The work is also known as *Vier Briefe*, for soprano, bass, and chamber orchestra, on the texts of four letters (from Franz Kafka to Milena Jesenská; from Antonio Gramsci to Julia Schucht; from the partisan Bruno Frittaion to his family; and one anonymous letter written by "an industrialist").

consensus in Western Europe. This phase, which internationally coincided with the onset of the Cold War, also left its mark on the field of cultural production by the formation of opposing fronts. On the one hand, we have the resumption of the unrestricted, free international circulation of culture, which had been severely limited during fascism, especially from the mid-1930s onwards. In the field of music, various experiences had only finally emerged from the semi-clandestine condition of a few years before: apart from jazz, the music of the Schoenberg school, suppressed or exiled together with its exponents in Nazi Germany, had in the meantime taken on the merit of the musical language of exile, anti-authoritarian resistance, and democracy.

However, at the same time, the "formalistic" nature of these languages made them unpopular with cultural policies that encouraged the push toward a direct politicization of symbolic languages: in fact, since the 1930s, the political-cultural trend in the USSR had been one of social realism. In this sense, the Second International Congress of Composers and Music Critics, organized in 1948 in Prague by the Syndicate of Czech Composers, served to spread and impart the dictates of realism also to Western political organizations and militants, with an influence that persisted even beyond the "de-Stalinization" that started after the Twentieth Congress of the Communist Party of the Soviet Union in 1956. In Italy, the communist leaders urged artists and intellectuals "to get in touch with real life as it unfolds in a society that is renewing itself."[8] But the latter, despite their relative indifference to music – similar to the ingrained detachment of many Italian intellectuals of the time – had soon found themselves facing internal dissent precisely in the field of music. One telling example is the controversy which, in 1948–49, saw a young but authoritative music critic from the communist newspaper *l'Unità*, Massimo Mila, oppose none other than Palmiro Togliatti, the national secretary of the party, regarding the quality of the music produced at that time by Prokofiev and Shostakovich.[9]

Thus the climate in which Maderna had the "year zero" of his artistic, civil, and everyday life, and which, retrospective hyperbole aside, translated into a substantial number of decisive events and encounters. It is worth noting that 1952, the year when he wrote to his friend Nono about wanting to "take stock" of the new phase that had started four years earlier, was the very same year when they enrolled in the Italian Communist Party – a choice that is not unrelated to their musical activity, but which, for the aforementioned reasons, did nothing to favor it. This new phase acquires further meaning from his life story, which is just as interesting and revealing. In fact, Maderna's artistic biography contains all-Italian, even local, peculiarities that mark the formation of his personality, also in relation to the parallel creation in the following period of an international network that would revolve around him, as composer, conductor, organizer, and driving force.

---

8   Roderigo di Castiglia [Palmiro Togliatti], "Direzione ideologica," *Rinascita* 6, no. 5 (May 1949), p. 241.
9   See Roderigo di Castiglia [Palmiro Togliatti], "Orientamento dell'arte," in *Rinascita* 6, no. 10 (October 1949), pp. 453–44, and Massimo Mila, "Disorientamento dell'arte," in *Rinascita* 6, no. 11 (November 1949), pp. 500–01. Mila, who was more of a liberal socialist, had not only negatively judged music bent to suit the criteria of realism, but above all rejected the claim that a politician could make competent and dispassionate judgments in the field of art. At the time, in the communist camp, this had been a sensational case of violation of the rules, meaning that the militant intellectual could not step outside the canon established by the party.

Malipiero and his modern "Venitian school"

A strong body of historical narrative includes Maderna in the generation of those composers born in the 1920s who found their true musical selves by adhering to dodecaphony and, subsequently, to a canon derived from the latter. Maderna was born in 1920, and thus a relatively short chronological gap distances him from Nono (1924), Berio (1925), Boulez (1925), Stockhausen (1928), and Pousseur (1929). Yet at that time a few years meant a lot: Maderna not only got his training, but reached artistic maturity in a musical Italy and Europe that were nothing like the ones in which, a few years later, he would find himself playing a central role.

The extreme precociousness with which, as an *enfant prodige*, he had already made his debut on the podium around 1930, objectively affected his career path, since quite a few people, and not always selflessly, had seen the development of "Brunetto's" talent as a good investment, even in the literal sense. The boy, as is well known, had lost his mother and been taken away from his father, who had never officially acknowledged him, and entrusted to a protection consortium. He was eventually mentored by a wealthy lady from Verona, Irma Manfredi, who became in all respects his adoptive mother and a fundamental point of reference for his whole life. It is clear that the choice of teachers and the school where he would be trained was the subject of much discussion among the circle of people who followed the development of the young musician. After an initial study period with Arrigo Pedrollo, a composer from Vicenza of a certain prestige (and also a former *enfant prodige*) suggested by the authoritative voice of Ildebrando Pizzetti in 1934, it was not until 1937 that Maderna encountered the rigorous discipline of Alessandro Bustini's lessons at the Accademia di Santa Cecilia in Rome.[10]

A year after gaining his diploma in June 1940, Maderna was not only well aware of his talent and driven by a healthy curiosity, but he was above all extremely intent on shaping an up-to-date composer personality, in the uncertainty and in the obvious conflict with a teacher who was typically wary of modern styles.[11] The lyrical piece *Alba*, for contralto and strings, written in 1939 as an exercise, had been barely tolerated by Bustini, who had accused the student of the shortcomings of "lyrical enthusiasm" and "tormented chromaticism."[12] This is how the eighteen-year-old composer summed up his situation: "I am too anachronical [sic]. The best part is that I don't know if I'm avant-garde or conservative. My music comes and goes, like this, like a swing: now morbid, now babbling."[13] Toward the end of that year things had already changed, and his longstanding attraction for Debussy seemed to

---

10 For biographical details see Geneviève Mathon's concise chronological narrative, "Chronologie," in *à Bruno Maderna* (see note 3), vol. 1, pp. 519–40.

11 See Raffaele Pozzi, "Classicismo Romano: Maderna allievo di Bustini," in *Maderna e l'Italia musicale degli anni '40*, ed. Gabriele Bonomo and Fabio Zannoni (Milan: Suvini Zerboni, 2012), pp. 45–82.

12 Quotations from Maderna's letters to Irma Manfredi, dated 7 May and 9 November 1939 (PSS-BMC), partly published in "Per un ritratto di Bruno Maderna: estratti dalla corrispondenza," in Maderna, *Amore e curiosità* (see note 4), p. 560. On *Alba* see also the essay by Paolo Dal Molin in this volume, pp. 415–39: 420–25.

13 Maderna to Irma Manfredi, letter of 23 April 1939, in "Per un ritratto di Bruno Maderna" (see note 12), p. 558.

be heading toward other horizons. In a letter dated December 1939, Maderna had warned his adoptive mother that he had run up a "huge bill" to pay for the purchase of scores and records by Stravinsky (*Petrushka, Symphony of Psalms, Jeu de Cartes*) and Hindemith's *Unterweisung im Tonsatz*, published in 1937, "for which I have long been hankering," and which would immediately become a fundamental reference for him.[14] Another letter tells us that those months were a period of intense exchanges between colleagues – including Guido Turchi and Carlo Maria Giulini – on the issues of contemporary music, with meetings and collective listening.[15]

Maderna finished his studies in Rome as the war was beginning and returned to Verona, his adoptive mother's hometown. Despite the insistence of one of his mentors at the time, the composer and organiser Pino Donati, who believed that staying in Rome would have helped the young musician's career, Maderna took a different path, and who knows whether his meeting with Gian Francesco Malipiero, who had been following the young musician's development since at least 1937, played some role in this decision.[16] From 1940 onwards, he regularly attended and participated in that "Corso internazionale di perfezionamento per compositori" (International Masterclass for Composers), held by the old Maestro at the Venetian Conservatory of which he was director. At least until 1943, despite the war, Maderna took part in this seminar-like, unstructured course, during which it is hard to imagine that he received any educational guidance, however advanced the course might have been. But it is also true that this was precisely when his first mature attempts at composition came into being, and that they were affected by a change of perspective compared to the "Roman" compositions, which all in all were still orchestral works of a fairly demanding nature, such as *Introduzione e Passacaglia "Lauda Sion Salvatorem"* for orchestra (1942), based on the sequence of that name. The opportunity to conduct it for the first time only presented itself in 1947; given his rapid evolution in those years, it is more than likely that five years on he must have seen that composition as more than a simple classroom exercise. The neo-baroque form of the debut work should not surprise us, and is easily explained as originating from a previous composition for organ, a work that was likely left unfinished.[17]

His lessons in "advanced composition" at the Venetian Conservatory gave rise to at least one documented recital, a concert entitled *Dell'arte di comporre*, which on 22 June 1942 inaugurated a remarkable Concerto for piano and orchestra by Maderna. The poster shows that the evening was organized by the local section of the Fascist Union of Musicians and makes no direct reference to educational activities of any kind; however, all the listed composers – Gino Gorini, Ettore Gracis, Giulio Bertola, Mario Zafred, and Sante

---

14   Maderna to Irma Manfredi, letter of 19 December 1939, in ibid., p. 561.
15   Maderna to Irma Manfredi, letter of 22 January 1940, in ibid., p. 561.
16   This can be deduced from the contents of a letter from Guido Bianchini to Irma Manfredi, dated 23 July 1937 (PSS-BMC).
17   In 2006 a four-page manuscript fragment was unearthed, the beginning of an *Introduzione e Passacaglia* for organ signed "BM 1941," which stops at bar 66 of the *Passacaglia*. Up to this point it matches the orchestral work (manuscript currently held at the Centro Studi Bruno Maderna, University of Bologna). The composition probably stems from Maderna's friendship with the Venetian organist Sandro Dalla Libera, whom Maderna met during the courses at the Accademia Chigiana in Siena in 1941.

Zanon – were students in Malipiero's course. The orchestra is not indicated; the soloist was Gorini.[18] Four years later Maderna wrote a version for two pianos as a way of promoting his career, but the score soon disappeared and was only found many years later, in 2007.[19] Shortly after the first performance, Maderna was drafted into the army in August 1942, and in the following three years his activity slowed down considerably.

Maderna held a special place among that group of students in Malipiero's class. As we will see, it is likely that, in the early 1940s – uncertain years of war, suspended between an era that was obviously falling to pieces and an unfathomable future – Malipiero already recognized in this young man a possible continuity of learning, a sort of perfect inheritance. And, moreover, he must have had a profound influence on Maderna. Throughout his whole career, Maderna rarely put down in writing his thoughts about his own work of composition: one of the very few examples, a passage from a letter written at the beginning of 1943, seems to reveal some poetic and methodical fundamentals which, in their evolution, are related precisely to the influence of the two key figures of this phase: Hindemith and the same Malipiero. Maderna, in the midst of his military commitments, was working on a new composition, a string quartet only completed several years later. This is what he wrote to his adoptive mother:

> This morning I worked on the "adagio" for the quartet [...]. Thinking about relationships between the notes without the help of the piano produces a curious effect, there is almost a sense of liberation in all this, liberation from the bondage of the harmonic relationships to which, by nature, I have always been somewhat of a slave, partly because of Debussy and impressionist music, of which I was a fervent admirer during my adolescence, but above all because of the antiquated educational system still in vogue in our conservatories. With Malipiero I got rid of these restraints by transferring my keenest attention to the rules of counterpoint, but the greatest temptation for me has always been a vertical music, which allowed me to conceive a line not in its own right, but always in a relationship, rather, almost originating from a harmonic atmosphere. After all, this is the basis of Hindemith's *Unterweisung*, and it is, we can say, his Poetics. Only he achieved it through the observation of the harmonic effects in the encounters between two notes, so unique in his purely horizontal style. Instead, I am gradually finding it in a more mature analysis of the chord, almost as if harmonic technique were increasingly refined in a process that could be called the spiritualization of matter [...].[20]

Maderna's relationship with Malipiero, however, eludes the conventional characteristics of "education" and cannot be easily documented in terms of the importance it certainly had, also in the light – as we will see further on – of how it came to an end, rather than an interruption, in that fateful year 1948. But there is no doubt that in those years Malipiero's teaching produced at least one long-lasting consequence, that is, the rooting of the myth of the

---

18   See the poster reproduced in Angela Ida De Benedictis, "Destini incrociati: Sull'edizione del *Concerto per pianoforte e orchestra* (1942) di Bruno Maderna," in *Maderna e l'Italia musicale degli anni '40* (see note 11), p. 143.

19   See the "Introduzione" by the editor to the critical edition of Bruno Maderna, *Concerto per pianoforte e orchestra* (1942), ed. Angela Ida De Benedictis (Milan: Suvini Zerboni, 2011) pp. v–xx.

20   Maderna to Irma Manfredi, letter of 19 January 1943, from the barracks of the Alpini regiment based in Meran, reproduced in "Per un ritratto di Bruno Maderna" (see note 12), p. 572.

Venetian musical civilization as a premise for a possible new music, a factor that proved so important for the more advanced developments in the work of Maderna, and of Nono himself. It is well known that from the early 1920s Malipiero had been working all out on the recovery and rediscovery of "ancient" practices as a premise for a program of renewal of the national musical culture, charged as it was with the historical weight of opera. Malipiero enjoyed a unique position among the Italian composers of his generation in that he developed a pioneering interest in some historical repertoires, such as Franco-Flemish polyphony, the sixteenth-century music of St. Mark's Chapel, and the eighteenth-century Italian instrumental repertoire. The same cornerstones can be found in Maderna's musical genealogy, for among other things he had also worked as a transcriber and co-editor of the works of Monteverdi and Vivaldi, edited by Malipiero for Universal Edition and Ricordi, respectively.[21]

A *Requiem* for rebirth

The following year, at the end of the war, was an extremely busy moment for Maderna. Having settled in Venice, the young musician seemed determined to make a decisive change in his career. The completion of a majestic *Requiem* for soloists, chorus, and orchestra seems to have played a particularly important role in this sense. The first mention of this work is found in a letter to Malipiero, dated 31 August 1945, where it is already described as a work that had been "interrupted for many months" and first needed to be completed: "this work will truly be a milestone for me."[22] If in August the composition of the work had been interrupted "for many months," it may be that he had already started it in 1944, and that, albeit intermittently, it had occupied most of his spare time in the last two years of the war. The chronology of the works composed during the 1940s can now be traced with some certainty; and, in fact, there is a large gap following the works composed in 1942, before his enrollment, such as the aforementioned Piano Concerto, the *Introduzione e Passacaglia* for orchestra, or the String Quartet, started (and interrupted) in January 1943. We need to wait until 1946 for the next works, even though, in March of that year, the composition of the *Requiem* seems to have made progress. His letters show us that in this phase Maderna relied a lot on being constantly in touch with the Venetian Maestro and his advice:

> [...] Malipiero spoke to me with so much kindness. He gave me the marvelous presentation letter for Milan and told me of his intention to write an article in *Le Arti* about my *Requiem*. This would be of immense importance for me. It would pave the way for both the [Venice] Festival and for countless other occasions.[23]

And indeed, the article, which appeared a few months later, is evidence of a rare display of enthusiasm on the part of Malipiero:

---

21   On Maderna the transcriber, see the essay by Michele Chiappini in this volume on pp. 193–225.
22   Maderna to Gian Francesco Malipiero, letter of 31 August 1945, preserved in Archivio Gian Francesco Malipiero, Istituto per la Musica della Fondazione Giorgio Cini di Venezia (henceforth AGFM).
23   Maderna to Irma Manfredi, 23 March 1946, in "Per un ritratto di Bruno Maderna" (see note 12), p. 77. This is the Venetian magazine *Lettere ed Arti*, headed by Sergio Solmi and Roberto Nonveiller, not *Le Arti*, which had ceased publication in 1943 (see following note). The letter "for Milan" has to date not been found.

> B.M. has no problems with form or harmony and possesses a highly developed sense of polyphony [...] all this proof of musical vitality satisfies us, excites us, prevents us from having doubts. In any other country in the world, B.M.'s Requiem Mass would have been called a miracle, its praises would be sung in honor of a rising star; instead, since I was born in Venice, I am obliged not to give the name of the composer for the simple fact that he is my pupil.[24]

Maderna, whose current money problems were forcing him to waste energy on casual work (such as music for small film productions), therefore continued to receive exhortations, encouragement, and opportunities from Malipiero. It is clear that the long-awaited "milestone" of the *Requiem* had assumed the value of a powerful promotional tool for the young musician. In fact, up to this moment Maderna had been very active, but had yet to be presented with an opportunity for a debut that lived up to his ambitions: "I continue to work on the second part of my mass, and I hope to write the words 'the end' in a couple of weeks. Given the monumental dimension of the work it certainly isn't easy to keep up the pace I have maintained so far."[25] At the beginning of July Maderna received the official invitation to participate in the IX International Festival at the Biennale di Venezia:

> I will keep the letter in memory of my first official step as a composer. Malipiero is going to write an explanatory article about my *Requiem* for an American magazine. The article will be completed by musical examples. This is the second step. I can't wait to do the third, fourth, to even start running.[26]

Another letter, undated but probably also from July 1946, speaks of a planned trip by Malipiero to the United States that "will pave the way" for the performance of the *Requiem*.

But right at this moment, an unexpected, direct "American" connection turned up. In that summer, Virgil Thomson arrived in Europe. At fifty, he was a more than well-established figure on the music scene in his homeland: an extravagant composer with a taste for high living, perfectly at home in the community of cosmopolitan avant-gardes and in that of his wealthy patrons, he was a typical member of the elite, well connected with the powerful foundations that move on the international scene when political action must be conducted in a discreet, indirect, and transverse way. He had in fact recently established a close relationship with Nicolas Nabokov, who was actively collaborating with the State Department in the musical reorganization of Europe just after the war.[27] On his arrival in Italy, after a brief stop in Milan, Thomson was in Venice, the guest of one of the most prominent Russian émigré families, the Georgian Prince Chavchavadze. He was staying in one of the most beautiful sixteenth-century buildings in Venice, the

---

24 Gian Francesco Malipiero, "La leggenda del lebbroso," *Lettere ed Arti: Rassegna mensile* 2, no. 7 (July–August 1946), pp. 43–45: 45.

25 Maderna to Irma Manfredi, n.d., but later than 21 April 1946, in "Per un ritratto di Bruno Maderna" (see note 12), pp. 578–79; also in Bruno Maderna, *Requiem per soli, coro e orchestra*, ed. Veniero Rizzardi (Milan: Suvini Zerboni, 2006), pp. v–xii: viii.

26 Maderna to Irma Manfredi, 6 July 1946, in "Per un ritratto di Bruno Maderna" (see note 12), p. 580. The article in the "American magazine" never materialized. The musical examples mentioned in the letter were eventually not delivered to Malipiero: Maderna kept them, and they are reproduced here for the first time (see Ex. 2 on p. 342).

27 See Frances Stonor Saunders, *Who Paid the Piper? The CIA and the Cultural Cold War* (London: Granta, 1999), especially pp. 118 and 222.

Contarini-Polignac Palace, former residence of the famous patron Winnaretta Singer, better known as the Princess Edmond de Polignac.[28] Thomson visited a very affable and jovial Gian Francesco Malipiero. It was the first time the Venetian Maestro had met with a foreign musician since the end of the war.[29] At the Conservatory, Malipiero introduced him to Gorini and Maderna, as his best pupils: "Virgil Thomson met me and looked at my scores and wrote a beautiful article in the *New York Herald Tribune,* the Paris edition, and he said: 'a new Verdi,' like that!"[30] He recalled the episode in a letter dated 31 July:

> Two nights ago, I had one of the best American critics and musicians, Virgil Thomson, listen to my *Requiem.* In America, as Malipiero told me, he is the one who sets the agenda for music. The critic in question was literally thrilled and never stopped congratulating me. He took my address and […] said he wanted to be the one to take it, the Mass, to America.[31]

A couple of weeks later, indeed, on August 10, an article on musical life in Venice came out in Paris in *The New York Herald Tribune* (i.e. the European edition of *The New York Times*). The subheading reads "Concerts Are Found Excellent and Malipiero's Maturing Pupils Almost Constitute a Venetian School":

> It was a privilege to inspect the score of certain young Venetians and to hear them performed, if only under studio conditions. The most impressive of these in expressive content, as well as in technical complexity, is *Requiem* mass for double chorus, soloists, strings, three pianos and thirteen brasses, by Bruno Maderno [sic]. A short Concerto for Eleven Instruments, by the same author, scheduled for performance at the September Festival of Contemporary Music, is gay and ingenious, but, less handsomely planned than the *Requiem.* This last, for all its attachment to contrapuntal textures, achieves an intensity of expression that places its young author in the high company of Berlioz and Verdi. It is not every day that one encounters religious music at once so noble of tone and so striking in effect. One wonders if this boy of twenty-six might not perhaps be destined to make that curative contribution to the Italian Opera that his master has long essayed and never quite pulled off.[32]

---

28 Massimo Mila had spread the news from Beate Christine Koepnick Maderna that in 1927 the Princess of Polignac would have rented nothing less than Milan's Orchestra della Scala to allow the young boy Maderna to perform on the podium. However, this episode does not appear in any of Maderna's biographical documents, nor in the archives of the Milan theater. See Massimo Mila, *Maderna musicista europeo,* ed. Ulrich Mosch (Turin: Einaudi, 1999), p. 115; first edn. 1976, p. 111. See also "Notizie sulla vita di Bruno Maderna," in *Bruno Maderna: Documenti,* ed. Mario Baroni and Rossana Dalmonte (Milan: Suvini Zerboni, 1985), p. 13.

29 See Virgil Thomson, "Europe in '46," in *The State of Music and Other Writings,* ed. Tim Page (New York: The Library of America, 2016), p. 546.

30 Maderna's words in "A conversation with Bruno Maderna by George Stone and Alan Stout: WEFM, Chicago, 23.1.1970," partially published, in edited form, on the CD *Bruno Maderna: The Last Concert,* CD STR 10071 (Milan: Stradivarius, 1993). The transcript of the original interview is quoted here, in Maderna's not always perfect English. An Italian translation of the whole radio interview ("Conversazione con George Stone e Alan Stout") is in Maderna, *Amore e curiosità* (see note 4), pp. 55–85 (quote on p. 58).

31 Maderna to Irma Manfredi, n.d., postmarked 31 July 1946, in "Per un ritratto di Bruno Maderna" (see note 12), p. 581.

32 Virgil Thomson, "Venice and Its Musical Life," *New York Herald Tribune,* European edn. (Paris, 10 August 1946), p. 2. Slightly reworked and with a different date (25 August 1946) as "Venice Unvanquished," in *Music Chronicles: 1940–1954,* ed. Tim Page (New York: The Library of America, 2014), pp. 528–29. The 2014 edition tacitly amends any mistakes or typos in the original.

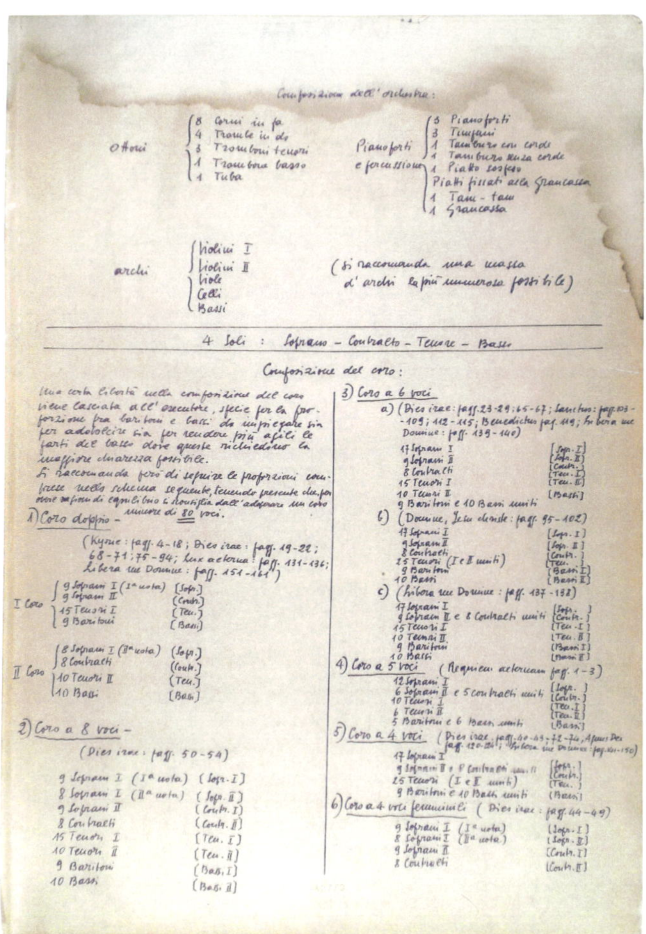

EX. 1   Bruno Maderna, *Requiem per soli, cori e orchestra:*
instruments of the orchestra and distribution of the chorus.
Heliographic copy of the autograph score, the only original
material surviving of the composition (courtesy of the
Purchase College Library, State University of New York).

Beyond the plausibility of his predictions, Thomson's opinion is revealing: he had recognized a dramaturgical approach in the "gesture" of the *Requiem,* if not in its style. Later Thomson would try to get the score performed in the USA, but the difficulties in putting together such a large number of musicians meant that the enterprise fell through; moreover, in the year and a half that had gone by in the meantime, Maderna rapidly moved away from that language and lost interest in the score (→ **EXX. 1–2).**

Due to its position in the collective and personal events of the time, the *Requiem* could be ascribed to the subgenre of "War Requiem," although there was no explicit intention in this sense. But this background comes to the fore in a couple of statements from two different parts of a 1970 radio interview – one of those rare moments when Maderna

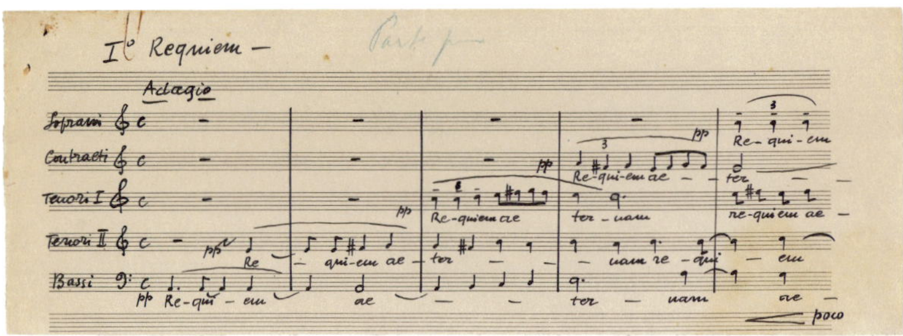

EX. 2   Bruno Maderna, *Requiem per soli, cori e orchestra:*
incipits of 1. "Requiem aeternam," 2. "Kyrie," and 3. "Dies irae,"
prepared by the author for Gian Francesco Malipiero. Annotations
in blue pencil likely by Malipiero himself. Autograph (PSS-BMC).

indulged publicly in retrospection: "I was finishing my studies in 1940, and after I was in the war like all people, and half one side, half on the other side, with the partisans […] and in the world I was nothing, with all Italians; zero, we were all zero […]. The only possible thing to do [was] to write a *Requiem* [for the dead]."[33] In 1987 Luigi Nono recalled: "He used to say that this *Requiem* was meant to be like a garland of flowers that floated along the river, and that the idea had come to him while reading Shakespeare's *Hamlet* at the point where Ophelia slowly disappears into the river."[34] An elegiac intent arising from personal interest seems to have descended on the format of monumental necessity. This is an atypical *Requiem;* it is also a result of a deliberate contradiction in its inspiration, which perhaps also dwells in the dimension of religious experience, of which any traces, particularly in his work, will soon disappear.

In the same radio interview, Maderna speaks of it as a "transitional" work ("a passage, a slow passage") and, in retrospect, "a naturally and relatively – how do I say? – naïve work." The point of view expressed by the composer can certainly be justified in 1970, when, as mentioned above, a canon of linguistic progress was in full force. In the historical distance, the "transition," at least in this case, should therefore not be understood as the moment in which the artistic production precedes the beginning of the completion of a further step, but rather as the coexistence of different possibilities, of multiple influences, of linguistic vectors that at the height of the 1940s prevented a well-read, curious, and already experienced young composer from dedicating himself to just one "school," unless it was precisely the anti-dogmatic and unprejudiced one of a Malipiero. But after all, Maderna always stood out for this independence even when, shortly thereafter, other guiding stars begin to shine.

Again in that interview of 1970, Maderna gave an ambiguous affirmative response when asked whether he had already started composing with the twelve-tone technique at the time of the *Requiem:*[35] the perfunctory backdating is perhaps explained by the fact that, for Maderna, dodecaphony was then still a distant, albeit visible, horizon. After all, in 1942 he had conducted Webern's op. 30, and one can easily imagine how many discussions he had with Malipiero on the subject. Yet this system, at the time of the *Requiem,* still seems to have been foreign to him, and at that moment he conceived the departure from the world of tonality in quite different terms. In this sense, the aforementioned letter of 1943 on the composition of the Quartet is most revealing, as is a fragment from a letter of similar tenor some years later, probably around 1948, which, in a very different context (alongside an exaltation of Schoenberg and dodecaphony as a fulfillment of modernity), testifies to the persistence of Hindemith as an important point of reference. Here, while commenting on the *Engelkonzert* from *Mathis der Maler,* Maderna indirectly defines the evolutionary position of his language:

---

33 "A Conversation with Bruno Maderna" (see note 30). Once again, Maderna's English is faithfully transcribed from the recording.

34 Nono, "An Autobiography of the Author" (see note 6), p. 28.

35 "[George Stone:] By this time had you started to write music in twelve-tone technique… [Maderna:] Yes, this *Requiem* was the passage; a slow passage… you know, we didn't know the music of Vienna so well before the war." In "A Conversation with Bruno Maderna" (see note 30).

The technique of attributing the function of oscillatory and dynamic elements to the chords formed by the pure ratios of the physical scale, as opposed to the static nature of the classic 3rd and 5th chords, is linked to the ancient polyphonists, but is integrated by the concepts of atonalism introduced by Hindemith in the *Unterweisung*, atonalism understood here as a suspension of romantic tonality.[36]

In the early 1940s the young composer, while mastering this theory, already knew in which direction to develop it: in fact, while Hindemith, working on interval tensions, would have developed a style that proceeds in horizontal lines in counterpoint, Maderna seems to naturally tend toward this thought by going in another direction, that is – as we read in the aforementioned letter of 1943 – that "of a vertical music, which [allows me] to conceive of a line not its own right, but always in a relationship, rather, almost originating from a harmonic atmosphere."[37] This is a far-reaching declaration, a precious key to understanding the grounds for, and the continuation of, an attitude that can be found even far beyond this youthful phase, even in the serial and post-serial periods to come, right up to his very last works: in Maderna, in fact, among the various "precompositional" steps, the generation of a harmonic field is almost always the fundamental phase of the implementation of a material; and in the works of his last years, it will even be the main structuring presence in the more "open" and informal if not improvised processes.[38]

The language of the *Requiem* – and, presumably, that of the *Serenata* of that same year – is one of a music that is no longer tonal, in which the harmonic dimension is precisely an "atmosphere" dominated by the use of quartal chords, and where the interval is considered per se, unrelated to preestablished functional connections. On the other hand, Maderna is as close to Hindemith as he is far from the trends of Italian music of the time, such as the recovery of modal procedures, which the sacred genre would have easily embraced. The knowledge of counterpoint that Maderna shows off in the *Requiem*, and which had so amazed the apprentice Luigi Nono, is certainly a product of excellent schooling; but Malipiero's hand cannot be seen in this, although it is instead present in a different dimension, that of a cultural specificity that has been reclaimed for

---

36 Manuscript sketch published with the title "[Intorno alla Sinfonia del *Mathis der Maler* di Paul Hindemith]" in Maderna, *Amore e curiosità* (see note 4), p. 94. In a previous elaboration of the same fragment we read: "especially if we pay attention to their function as an oscillatory element in the static nature of the 3rd and 5th chords. A technique used by the ancient madrigalists and taken up in our time by Malipiero." This text is reproduced and discussed in the critical notes "Note bibliografiche e commento ai testi" in ibid., p. 732.

37 Maderna to Irma Manfredi, letter of 19 January 1943 (see note 20).

38 Evidence of this practice comes from one of the rehearsals for the Concerto for violin and orchestra (1969–70), captured in the TV documentary *Un'ora con Bruno Maderna: Musica, specchio della società*, by Salvatore G. Biamonte and Giuseppe Sibilla, RAI, Milan-Venice 1969–70, broadcast on 11 October 1971. While instructing the orchestra to collectively improvise durations, dynamics, phrasing, and articulations at will, Maderna however refers to the rigorous respect for the pitches indicated for each part "because it is the only scheme that keeps all this stuff going … because there is a harmonic scheme, where there are two or three forms, chord positions, [and] the notes go inside those positions there, and not in others." About the existence of a harmonic matrix underlying several orchestral compositions of the 1960s (including the aforementioned Concerto for violin), see also Borio and Rizzardi, "Die musikalische Einheit von Bruno Madernas *Hyperion*" (see note 5).

the first time: the *Requiem* is in fact the first product, even an exemplary one, of a possible "neo-Venetian" repertoire, the prototype of successive remakes of the polychoral Renaissance repertoire at St. Mark's, of which he recreates almost every possible combination. Without, of course, prescribing a physical separation and distribution of the different groups (a typical practice of a later avant-garde), the score lets us imagine a music that does not involve listening with a frontal "staging," but virtually distributes the sound masses in a space that is far more richly articulated. If we compare the variety in the composition of the choral groups throughout the work with the treatment of the four soloists, we get an idea of Maderna's remoteness from the dramaturgical ideal of a great nineteenth-century mass: solos and duets function halfway as chamber numbers, and not even the finales fall to the temptation of employing all four soloists in a *concertato* style. It is not unthinkable that Nono's visionary *Prometeo* (1984) bears more than an echo of the *Requiem*.

Turning Points

Venice was a place of primary importance for the musical rebirth of the Italian post-war period. In the city where Maderna had recently settled after his study period in Rome and the events of the war, the Festival of Contemporary Music resumed in 1946, after its interruption four years earlier, with a program open to artists who had been silenced or exiled by fascism, and especially to new generations. As we have seen, Maderna was in all respects a leading figure: on 21 September 1946, he was entrusted with conducting a "Concert of the Young Italian School" at the Teatro La Fenice as part of the Festival, in which his new *Serenata per undici strumenti*[39] appeared alongside Riccardo Malipiero's (Gian Francesco's grandson) *Piccolo concerto*, Valentino Bucchi's *La dolce pena*, a trio for flute, clarinet, and viola by Guido Turchi, and Camillo Togni's *Variazioni* for piano and orchestra (→ **EXX. 3-4**). The five young composers, aged between twenty-four and thirty, are presented in the program by Gian Francesco Malipiero, in the form of a letter, and each of them is asked to make a "Confession." What Maderna puts in writing is not a real declaration of poetics, but rather an assertion of the value and dignity of artisanal creation:

> There is a need for investigation rather than construction, and, too often, for taking stock, for statistics.
> They tell us that scientific activity is aimed at discovering nature and God with more or less rational means, and that art is only a lyrical intuition of the absolute. I have no scientific convictions, but as far as music is concerned, I believe it is not about discovering but about creating.
> [...] there is no doubt that a very serious obstacle will be removed when we face the music with the same modesty and with the same desire to be simple, common, possibly

---

39 Maderna's letters in this period always refer to the composition with the title of *Concertino,* to be replaced by the definitive one on the occasion of the first performance.

EX. 3   Maderna conducting at the Ninth Contemporary Music Festival of the Venice Biennale, 21 September 1946 (courtesy of Teatro La Fenice, Venice).

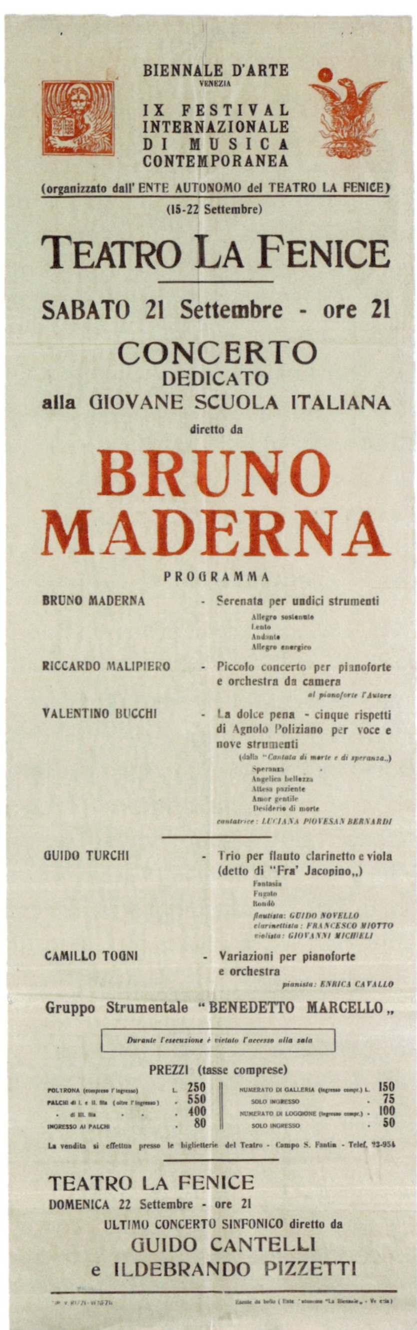

EX. 4   The "Young Italian School" concert of 21 September 1946 at the Ninth Contemporary Music Festival of the Venice Biennale (courtesy of Teatro La Fenice, Venice).

anonymous, which brought forth *tropes* and *antiphons* precisely from those monks who held fame in absolute contempt, and who wrote that music for the exclusive and greater glory of God.[40]

His cautious and allusive words do not seem to be directly related to the nature of the music he presented on that occasion, but appear to emphasize above all a distance from any kind of experimental leanings. The score of his *Serenata*, on the other hand – which is still missing to date – had been composed in parallel with the completion of the *Requiem*, and was probably not the work with the most innovative language on the evening's program, at least in comparison to the dodecaphonic experiments by Malipiero Jr. and Togni.

The concert of 1946, despite a rather negative reception from public and critics, represented an important sign of renewal for Italian music, but it was the 1948 Festival in particular that would be the most soundly representative of the new languages that were in the making. Maderna presented a new Concerto for two pianos and instruments, which he must have started composing little less than a year before. The vicissitudes of this concert accompanied an important transition for the composer, also encouraged by a number of significant encounters, partly linked to his growing success as a conductor. Luigi Dallapiccola enters the scene, so to speak. Maderna began to turn to him for an opinion of his work and, at an unspecified moment in late 1947, sent him the first movement of the Concerto. The answer came, "after a few months," on 11 December 1947 with a detailed analysis:

> As a positive observation, I will first of all note the seriousness and goodness of your *orientation;* something I consider fundamental. [...] I used the word "orientation" (a very generic word) because, if Busoni is to be believed, "personality" is the last of the artist's qualities to come to light, in order of time. And I say "orientation" also because it is by no means out of the question that other composers in a few years should feed you and give you new ideas. (I have no doubt that these composers will be "Maestros" and therefore your orientation will continue to be serious and good, until you write a completely personal work).

Dallapiccola adds that that first movement seems sufficient to him:

> In my opinion this is already a formally completed work, with a clearly visible articulation in four parts: Allegro – Meno ("quasi Adagio") – Vivace ("quasi Scherzo") – tempo presto ("quasi Finale") [...] I wonder, however, what can be found in the second and third parts of a "Concerto" that seems to me to have already been completed in the first. Might the formal scheme I proposed be somewhat affected by the influence of G.F. Malipiero? What of it? Malipiero is a "Maestro" in every sense of the term, and there is nothing wrong with a young composer being affected by his influence, which in the present case is beneficial.[41]

---

40 Bruno Maderna in *IX. Festival Internazionale di Musica Contemporanea – La Biennale di Venezia 1946, 15–22 September 1946* (Venice: Teatro La Fenice, 1946), pp. 61–62; now published with the title "Dalle *Confessioni* [Una pagina di Bruno Maderna]," in Maderna, *Amore e curiosità* (see note 4), pp. 89–91.

41 Luigi Dallapiccola to Maderna, 11 December 1947, in "Per un ritratto di Bruno Maderna" (see note 12), pp. 584–85; also in *Studi su Bruno Maderna*, ed. Mario Baroni and Rossana Dalmonte (Milan: Suvini Zerboni, 1989), pp. 56–57, and Paolo Cattelan, "Biografia di un concerto di Maderna: Il 'Concerto per due pianoforti e strumenti' (1947–49)," in *Malipiero Maderna*, ed. Paolo Cattelan (Florence: Olschki, 2000), pp. 299–333: 308–09.

Dallapiccola probably realized that Maderna needed the opinion of an authoritative voice other than that of Malipiero, and above all that the young artist had decided to turn to the leading Italian composer of dodecaphonic music, presenting him with a work that is, however, anything but dodecaphonic: this is perhaps the reason why he insists on the concept of *orientation*, foreshadowing, if not really suggesting, that it might change. Dallapiccola has probably sensed that the young composer is living through a critical but at the same time very promising moment. Five years later, but now in another era for new music, Maderna will present his Concerto in these terms: "This composition was decisive for my artistic growth, since I believe that this is where I found the way for the first time to express myself in a personal manner, after composing numerous pieces in a style similar to Bartók and Stravinsky."[42] The combinatory and permutative treatments of the material, the use of canonical forms, make the Concerto for two pianos the non-dodecaphonic forerunner of the proto-serial and serial compositions that immediately followed. Significantly, this was the only pre-dodecaphonic composition that Maderna continued to promote, after considerable revision, almost following Dallapiccola's first observations to the letter: the first movement, tactfully judged as not "completely personal," albeit a finished composition, was eliminated and replaced by a new introduction tailored to the next two movements, now merged and simplified.[43]

Even before its presentation at the Venice Festival in September 1948, the score had attracted the attention of other composers outside Italy: Karl Amadeus Hartmann had found out about it through Rolf Liebermann;[44] most impressed, he immediately asked Maderna to conduct it at the "Musica Viva" concerts he curated in Munich at the Bavarian State Opera. From this moment on, Hartmann became a key figure in determining the fortunes of Maderna (and subsequently also of Nono) in Germany.

At the same time as the concert was being presented, a collateral event at the Festival had decisive consequences: an International Course for Conductors, entrusted to Hermann Scherchen by the direction of the Biennale, was held between August and September of that year and jointly established a trend, a method, and a community. Both Maderna and Nono took part at Malipiero's suggestion.[45] The course immediately transcended its stated didactic purpose and became the decisive occasion for young Italians to get to know the European experiences of which the German conductor – a teacher, friend, and interpreter of Schoenberg and Webern – had been the protagonist. The studies proposed by Scherchen were quite distant from and opposed to the old-fashioned music

---

42   Typewritten note (1952) by Bruno Maderna for the Concerto for two pianos and instruments, written in German, original in PSS-BMC; published in part by Giordano Montecchi in *Dialogo con Maderna* (Milan: RAI, 1989), p. 117, and, in its entirety in Maderna, *Amore e curiosità* (see note 4), pp. 479–80, with extended commentary in ibid., pp. 480–85. Note the incorrect dating of the note to "1961" (found in various articles on Concerto for two pianos); see ibid., pp. 789–90.

43   A detailed reconstruction of the complex history of this composition can be found in Cattelan, "Biografia di un concerto di Maderna" (see note 41), followed by Stefano Bellon's analysis "Il 'Concerto per due pianoforti e strumenti' di Bruno Maderna verso Darmstadt: un'analisi della partitura," in *Malipiero Maderna* (see note 41), pp. 335–54.

44   See letter from Hartmann to Maderna, dated 16 July 1948 (PSS-BMC).

45   Nono, "An Autobiography of the Author" (see note 6), p. 28.

education, steeped in nationalism, in use at the Italian conservatories; and above all they encouraged the young participants to discover and get a quick update on the Vienna School. The lessons soon exceeded the designated timetable and were transformed into the life of a temporary community of artists.

This episode pushed Maderna to rapidly finish revisiting his technical-compositional coordinates, which quickly led to his "conversion" to dodecaphony. The process had probably started a year earlier, at the same time as his correspondence with Dallapiccola. A few months after submitting the Concerto for two pianos, Maderna had asked him for news particularly about his *Sex Carmina Alcaei*,[46] which, in just a few months, in fact provided him with the format and model for his three *Liriche greche* of winter 1948, the work that marks his turn to dodecaphony.

The Venetian circle that formed around Scherchen included young musicians from distant worlds: in fact, for the occasion the Maestro had called as his assistant Hans-Joachim Koellreutter, a German flutist and composer who had been his pupil shortly before emigrating to Brazil in 1937, where he soon formed a school based on the initiatives of the "Música Viva" movement. Koellreutter arrived in Venice with a large group of students who had already been acquainted with the dodecaphonic method for several years.[47] Among them was Eunice Catunda, who, encouraged by Scherchen, soon formed a friendship with Maderna and Nono, and who remained in Venice until the spring of 1949, carrying on a lively exchange of experiences with the two young composers. Born in 1915, Catunda, a pianist of absolute excellence, an expert and up-to-date composer, and an extremely well-read intellectual and communist militant, was given an opportunity to exercise an important influence on Nono and Maderna himself.[48] However, in encouraging them to a precocious reflection on the political nature of artistic work, she herself received important input from them in return: in the letters she wrote from Brazil in 1949–50, she defines herself as a pupil of Maderna, who, albeit from afar, continued to be her main point of reference.[49] After all, at that time, her teacher Maestro Koellreutter had to be considered a sort of apostle of the twelve tones: thanks to Scherchen's interest, he had in fact been commissioned by the new-born International Center for Contemporary Music *Il Diapason* to hold an intensive course on dodecaphonic technique in Milan in November and December of 1948. The course, entitled "New Fundamentals of Musical Composition," was attended by, among others, Catunda, Maderna, and Nono. The notebook containing Nono's notes from the course[50] clearly shows that Koellreutter based

---

46 Dallapiccola replied on 27 June 1948, as can be read in "Per un ritratto di Bruno Maderna" (see note 12), pp. 586–87.

47 The Brazilian group, according to an advertising card for the course issued by the Conservatory, was made up of Sônia Born, Eunice Catunda, Sula Jaffé, Gení Marcondes, Alfonso Penalva Santos, Miriam Sandbank, Ester Scliar, and Antônio "Totó" Sergi, and was, along with the Italian one, the most numerous. As regards the figure of Koellreutter and his activity in Brazil see Carlos Kater, *Música Viva e H J Koellreutter: Movimentos em Direção a Modernidade* (São Paulo: Musa, 2000).

48 In 1987 Luigi Nono would still remember the important role Catunda played in developing his own path; see Nono, "An Autobiography of the Author" (see note 6), pp. 53–55.

49 Various letters from Catunda to Nono, 1949–53 (ALN).

50 The book is housed in the Gastone Fabris Collection at the Conservatory of Ferrara library.

his teaching of twelve-tone technique on the principles of "natural" tonal relationships and affinities proposed by Hindemith. Nono's notes provide an important clue for understanding the origin of the techniques used by Maderna and Nono himself in their first dodecaphonic and proto-serial compositions, especially as regards the criteria used to select the material. One finds, for example, the use of the typical Hindemith rule of the evaluation of the interval according to its degree of "tension," and the consequent terminology of "melodic," "harmonic," and "compensated" tone rows. All these elements are found in the sketches of the works composed in that period by the two Venetians, such as Maderna's *Studi per "Il Processo" di Franz Kafka* and Nono's *Variazioni canoniche sulla serie dell'op. 41 di Arnold Schönberg*, both from 1950, and also in some later ones. It is certainly no shot in the dark to argue that this attention to the quality and expressive "weight" of the interval will endure as an implicit criterion of production and selection of materials in all of Maderna's subsequent music, and even more so in that of Nono.

At this point Maderna seems already to be accredited as a composer committed to new techniques: in fact, he is invited to present a paper at the First International Congress of Dodecaphonic Music, held in Milan from 4 to 7 May 1949, jointly organized by Riccardo Malipiero and Wladimir Vogel. A preliminary meeting of the organizing committee had been held the previous December in Orselina, in the Canton of Ticino, with Hartmann, Koellreutter, and Catunda, among others, taking part.[51] The Milanese meeting represented a first moment of collective reflection for composers on a trend in a technique that, in the post-war period, seemed to determine the line of musical progress. Although the Congress was a reserved meeting, it enjoyed considerable success in terms of international participants (it opened with a warm greeting from Schoenberg by telegram), and there were certainly more than a few interesting developments.[52]

The composition of the three *Liriche greche* was completed a few months before the Congress in Milan. Then there was also a complete symbolic constellation in the event, reported by Catunda in her Venetian journal: the triptych was offered, together with similar compositions by Nono and Catunda, as a collective tribute to Scherchen on the occasion of a concert he conducted in March 1949 in Florence, with music by Dallapiccola.[53] The relevance of Maderna's *Liriche greche* goes beyond the objective importance of being

---

51 Although she took part in this preliminary stage, Catunda did not participate in the Milan meeting. Due to the sudden onset of a health problem that later turned out to be non-existent, she was forced to return to Brazil at the end of April 1949, giving up various musical activities planned together with Scherchen, Maderna, and Nono.

52 See Carlo Piccardi, "Tra ragioni umane e ragioni estetiche: i dodecafonici a congresso," in *Norme con ironie: Scritti per i settanta anni di Ennio Morricone*, ed. Sergio Miceli (Milan: Suvini Zerboni, 1998), pp. 205–69. Also, especially for the happenings in Milan, Angela Ida De Benedictis, "Oltre il Primo Congresso di Dodecafonia: Da Locarno a Darmstadt," *Acta Musicologica* 85, no. 2 (2013), pp. 227–43.

53 See Eunice Catunda, "A minha viagem para Europa," in Carlos Kater, *Eunice Katunda, Musicista brasileira* (São Paulo: Annablume-Fapesp, 2001), p. 60. The only remaining manuscript of Nono's two lyrical works *Ai Dioscuri* (Alcaeus) and *La stella mattutina* (Ion of Chios) in fair copy has no dynamic and expressive indications, and is therefore to be considered unfinished. They were composed about a year before his first work, the *Variazioni canoniche sulla serie dell'op. 41 di Arnold Schönberg*, for orchestra.

the first example of his dodecaphonic music; in their reference to the model of analogous compositions by Dallapiccola,[54] with their archaizing melos grafted onto the new radical technique, a canon was born of an "Italian way" within the international experience of serialism – soon to become a formula that will have wide circulation. Besides, both Maderna and Nono immediately distanced themselves from Dallapiccola: their attachment to dodecaphony right away corresponds to the attempt to extend its fundamental principles, according to an attitude of decisive, personal appropriation. Both sets of *Liriche* in fact contain series that have been dismembered, permuted, and filtered by means of principles and operations that reveal an attitude of deliberate "heterodox" experimentation. In these first experiments, the series for Maderna (and Nono) still had a thematic aspect, but it soon changed its function, becoming instead the generator of more extensive and complex material.[55] It was not long before he invented the multi-parametric serial devices, when the techniques he had taught himself met up at the Darmstadt courses with what had been developed by young European colleagues. The productive fervor underway in the "year zero" of 1948 is demonstrated by a flowering of new and important works: the *Fantasia e Fuga* for two pianos in 1949 (presented at Darmstadt), the *Composizioni* nos. *1* and *2* for orchestra, the *Studi per "Il Processo" di Franz Kafka*, and the *Improvvisazione n. 1* for orchestra all came to life in the space of less than two years, between 1949 and the beginning of 1951.

With these compositions, Maderna experiments with models of generation and treatment of the material based on some basic principles: the use of the tone row as a structure that is in itself expressly characterized on the basis of Hindemith's criterion of interval tension; the proliferation and the practical disappearance of the tone row itself, chosen on the basis of various automatic devices for the permutation of the pitches; and the use of preexisting material, such as a folk tune or a dance rhythm, which is subjected to serial procedures and therefore concealed.[56]

In this phase of conscious transition, the composer's problems went hand in hand with his growing success as a conductor. Even before his public debut as a leading figure of the new dodecaphonic generation, and a few days before the dodecaphonic congress in Milan, Maderna had participated in the spring of 1949 at the International Society of Contemporary Music (ISCM) Festival in Taormina, conducting a new version of the Concerto for two pianos and instruments and gaining the general approval of his colleagues. In Palermo, Maderna received invitations from Roger Desormière and André Souris to conduct for Radio France, from Wladimir Vogel for Lugano, and again from Karl Amadeus

---

54 *Cinque frammenti di Saffo* (1942), *Sex Carmina Alcaei* (1943), and *Due Liriche di Anacreonte* (1945), all on Italian texts in the recent translation by Salvatore Quasimodo (Milan: Edizioni di Corrente, 1940), also used by Catunda, Maderna, and Nono. On the relationship between Dallapiccola, Maderna, and Nono, see Gianmario Borio, "L'influenza di Dallapiccola sui compositori italiani nel secondo dopoguerra," in *Dallapiccola: Letture e prospettive*, ed. Mila De Santis (Milan and Lucca: Ricordi-LIM, 1997), pp. 357–87.

55 Nono later mentioned this evolution in his fundamental 1957 article "The Development of Serial Technique," in *Nostalgia for the Future* (see note 6), p. 148.

56 See above, note 5. The techniques and devices devised by Maderna were also used by Nono in all his compositions until 1954.

Hartmann.[57] And it was precisely at Hartmann's request that just a few days later, on 9 April 1949, he received an invitation from Wolfgang Steinecke, director of the Kranich-stein Institute, to participate in the next summer courses in Darmstadt with one of his compositions. Maderna responded with four proposals: the 1948 Concerto for two pianos, the dodecaphonic *Fantasia e Fuga*, the *Tre liriche greche*, and the latest *Composizione* [no. 1] for orchestra.[58] For practical reasons, the choice fell on the piece for two pianos; Maderna, however, was not present in Darmstadt in 1949, being unable to afford the trip.[59]

It was a real joint coordinated action that launched Maderna's international career: on the one hand, Hartmann; on the other his friend and collaborator Scherchen, who had been teaching in Darmstadt since 1947, and who would also take up the baton for Nono, making his debut the following year with the *Variazioni canoniche*. Scherchen used his prestige to intensively promote his "Venetian school" in Germany, where, as is well known, the moment was particularly favorable for contemporary music, above all with the regional radio orchestras, whose artistic directors, such as Herbert Hübner with the "Das neue Werk" festival on Hamburg's Norddeutscher Rundfunk, were creating concerts and festivals entirely dedicated to young composers.

Inventing a new "Venitian school"

A late and enlightening episode can be added to the *Bildungsroman* of the young Maderna. In 1970, Malipiero wrote an article for Venice's main daily newspaper, *Il Gazzettino*, full of enthusiasm after listening to a radio broadcast of *Grande Aulodia*, conducted by Maderna at its premiere in Rome. When months later Maderna wrote to thank the old Maestro (in the meantime their relationship had cooled, also under the strain of some feelings of resentment and a few misunderstandings), he admitted the following:

> Many years ago, when I came to your composition course for the first time, you set me on the right path for Music and taught me, with few but sincere words, how to get rid of all the indecision and vices that I had inherited from an antiquated school. Thanks again for your work of "salvation" and "contamination."[60]

---

57 "[…] declared by Desormière, Souris, etc. an excellent conductor and invited to conduct a concert for next November on Radiodiffusion Paris, invited to Munich by Hartmann, Ascona and Lugano by Vogel. My piece […] was considered, alongside Vogel's *Thyl* [*Claes*], one of the best pieces of the Festival (how kind of them). In the end, everything went very well, and the result is better than expected. Now I have to finish several things in Milan with Souris, Searle, and Lutyens." Maderna to Luigi Nono, letter dated 2 April 1949, original in ALN, published in "Per un ritratto di Bruno Maderna" (see note 12), pp. 590–91.

58 Letters from Wolfgang Steinecke to Maderna, 9 and 13 April 1949 (PSS-BMC), and from Maderna to Steinecke, 11 May 1949 (Internationales Musikinstitut Darmstadt). Reproduced in Bruno Maderna and Wolfgang Steinecke, *Carteggio/Briefwechsel*, ed. Rossana Dalmonte (Lucca: LIM, 2001), pp. 23–26.

59 On 13 July 1949, in response to news received from Italy, Catunda wrote to Nono (ALN) from Rio de Janeiro: "[…] I got a bit angry! Mainly to learn that Bruno did not go to Darmstadt because he did not have enough money to get the necessary visa. There is too much injustice in this vast world." It was not until the following 19 August, while the courses were still in full swing, that Wolfgang Steinecke wrote to Maderna, after "a long stay in hospital," that he had only read the telegram announcing his withdrawal at a later date. See Maderna and Steinecke, ibid., pp. 36–37. Maderna's telegram has not survived.

60 Maderna to G.F. Malipiero, letter of 26 July 1970 from Überlingen on Lake Constance (AGFM).

On reading Malipiero's article, rather than an exchange of courtesies, we find a shared acknowledgment of non-generic nostalgia. The article almost literally returns to what he had written in *Lettere ed Arti* in 1946,[61] including a display of what now, after twenty-four years, seems to be extravagant modesty, for Malipiero never names the "he" who was obliged to leave, but who is still a "disciple" and therefore cannot be publicly praised:

> … He presented himself armed with a diploma, in actual fact it represented his expulsion from school, a kind of release. I suggested that he get a breath of fresh air, he obeyed me, and the progress he made in a few months was surprising. During the war, an unexpected guest, he appeared with a formidable "Mass," a miracle. In fact, he felt that he had now reached maturity, but this crucial feeling fatally distanced him from me. [...] I don't know if he has disowned or destroyed the famous "Mass." It may be that in the chaos he simply lost it, but he cannot erase it. [...] Five decades have passed since the day he joined forces with a very turbulent young man (whom I followed in the first steps of his musical studies), nevertheless he remained faithful to his talent, his sensitivity, and if he sometimes wanders and abandons the *rod* of power he walks proudly, the "Mass" has never left him, he confirmed this with his *Grande Aulodia per flauto, oboe e orchestra*, recently listened to on the radio… [62]

The process of "salvation" and "contamination" had therefore only lasted a "matter of months," after which the "miracle" had taken place: the composition of the *Requiem*, which in 1970 was now missing, buried for more than twenty years, a chapter that perhaps only Malipiero, along with its composer, could claim to be familiar with.[63] In Malipiero's article, understandably, this composition is not placed in a historical perspective, that is, as the culmination of a phase of rapid maturation by a talented young musician; instead (excluding the implicit irony in the actual non-existence, at the time, of the *Requiem* itself), it represents the culmination *tout court* of a career: "the 'Mass' has never left him," writes Malipiero, likening it to *Grande Aulodia*, two compositions in which, moreover, it is difficult to see objective similarities or analogies. And he supposed that it had been "disowned or destroyed," or perhaps, less romantically, lost and forgotten. In fact, the oblivion and dispersion of the most important scores and related sketches prior to 1948 are easily explained by biographical events; moreover, they are perfectly attuned to that change in poetic direction and that opening of an international horizon, already described here, which left behind an entire culture, and not just a musical one.

It is significant that just when Maderna was rebuilding his craftsmanship on the grounds of new assumptions, he gathered around him a group of young apprentice composers, among whom the name Nono stands out.[64] This educational initiative, which was

---

61 See above, note 24.

62 Gian Francesco Malipiero, "A un discepolo," *Il Gazzettino* (28 February 1970). Malipiero had a column in the newspaper entitled "L'antimusica." Maderna conducted the *Grande Aulodia* with the RAI Symphony Orchestra of Rome on 7 February, with soloists Severino Gazzelloni (flute) and Lothar Faber (oboe). The "very turbulent young man" mentioned by Malipiero is Luigi Nono.

63 And, of course, Virgil Thomson. Very few others, including Nono, had the chance to catch a glimpse of the score before it ended up forgotten among the papers of an American choir. For events relating to the composition of the work, its "loss," and its discovery (in 2006), see *Esumazione di un Requiem: Edizione anastatica della partitura e note informative sul ritrovamento del giovanile "Requiem" di Bruno Maderna*, ed. Veniero Rizzardi, Studi di musica veneta: Archivio G.F. Malipiero, Studi 3 (Florence: Olschki, 2007).

64 Leading members of the group were Renzo Dall'Oglio, Gastone Fabris, and Romolo Grano, whose subsequent musical careers, however, took place on the margins of composition.

not motivated by material interests (despite his precarious economic situation, Maderna received no money from the students),[65] was intended above all as a response to a need for sharing, for study and collective work, for a true workshop. In the last years of his life, Nono again underlined how important Maderna's anti-academic teaching had been to him, even considering the latter to be the last exponent of a musical knowledge in which "theory" and "practice" would "form a perfect union"[66] – an organic intertwining, even a communal one, of creation and thought, of speculation and craftsmanship, typical of remote eras of Western art music.

Retrospective emphasis apart, who better than Nono could evaluate, at a distance of time, the revolutionary scope of Maderna's program as it had developed in Venice in the 1940s: i.e. the attempt to reestablish a community for research and creation around the study of contemporary and Renaissance music; and together, to experiment with new compositional techniques derived from such a comparative study, with a deliberate over-shadowing of the classical-romantic legacy. This fact is known and often repeated in his biographies, although perhaps it appears more rarely where thought takes the concrete form of the musical process. If, for example, we examine a proto-serial work such as the 1951 *Improvvisazione n. 1* per orchestra, we find that throughout the composition the pitch and the rhythmic articulation are elaborated in a relationship that is completely analogous to the procedures used for isorhythmic motets;[67] similarly, in *Composizione in tre tempi* of 1954, three popular songs are used, each by analogy with the function of the "tenor," as generative material, hidden in the stratification of its transformations. The very same technique is also found in several compositions by Nono in those years, such as *Epitaffio per Federico García Lorca* No. 1 and *La victoire de Guernica*. Moreover, we also find at the start of this phase (1949–50) a parallel, impassioned, even collaborative transcription and orchestration of Renaissance texts, as in the case of Ottaviano Petrucci's *Odhecaton*.[68]

---

65   See Luigi Nono's account in "An Autobiography of the Author" (see note 6), p. 40.

66   See Luigi Nono, "Interview with Michelangelo Zurletti," in *Nostalgia for the Future* (see note 6), pp. 359–64: 360.

67   This and other similar generative processes are illustrated in detail in Rizzardi, "The Tone Row, Squared" (see note 5), and idem, "La 'Nuova scuola veneziana', 1948–51," in *Le musiche degli anni Cinquanta*, Archivio Luigi Nono, Studi 2 (Florence: Olschki, 2003), pp. 1–59.

68   As can be read in a letter from Maderna to Paul Collaer, dated 21 December 1949, *Odhecaton*, published on Maderna's behalf in the issues of Scherchen's Ars Viva (the printed copy reproduces a manuscript where one can recognize Nono's handwriting), should instead be considered a collective piece, a product of the workshop: "Everything is going well for *Odhecaton*. I have several students who are working on the preparation of the score. Each of them makes a thematic, historical, harmonic analysis etc. of the pieces from the Petrucci collection. They go in search of the songs of the troubadours from whom the piece derives, of all possible information on the author and on the era and the milieu where he was received, and then they also prepare an instrumentation of the pieces in line with their character and the instruments of our small orchestra. During the practical lessons they conduct [the passages] and can understand the mistakes they have made. We are all raving about the beauty of the music and the simplicity that hides, on the contrary, a wonderful formal complexity. My students on the solfège courses sing the same music in two or three voices and their interest, even that of the younger pupils, is extraordinary." Paul Collaer, *Correspondance avec des amis musiciens*, ed. Robert Wangermée (Sprimont: Mardaga, 1996), pp. 413–14 (original in French). See also Susanna Pasticci, "Memorie di Petrucci a Venezia, quattro secoli dopo," in *Venezia 1501: Petrucci e la stampa musicale*, ed. Giulio Cattin and Patrizia Dalla Vecchia (Venice: Fondazione Levi, 2005), pp. 683–737: 696–703. Pasticci's essay provides an ample discussion of the techniques used by Maderna and Nono in this phase.

Maderna's newly formed "school" also had another teacher, Hermann Scherchen, who in turn made the students carry out a parallel apprenticeship that included not only study but also editorial work and assistance in practical matters. This happened while Scherchen was admittedly beginning his "second life,"[69] and the young Venetian musicians certainly did not play a secondary role in this new start. Indeed, 1950 was a year of important changes for the German conductor, also in the private sphere: he left Zurich, where he had settled during the war, because of the ill feelings of the local community toward his communist sympathies; he settled in Italy, where he took up residence on the Ligurian Riviera; he laid the foundations for a complex initiative (concerts, seminars, a magazine), dedicated to electroacoustic music, that came to life in 1954 in Gravesano, in Italian-speaking Switzerland; and he set up a publishing house dedicated to new music that in many ways became a training ground for young composers. This is why Nono's first scores bear the "Ars Viva" imprint, and this is the publishing house where he also acted as copyist and secretary, often sharing the jobs with Maderna, and then moved on to become his delegate and alter ego. Between 1952 and 1953, Villa Robilant in Rapallo was the site of this very active workshop.

These years and these occasions allowed Maderna to perfect a modern figure of conductor-composer-animator, a role partly foreseen by Scherchen and later personified by Pierre Boulez: someone devoted to new music, one's own and that of others, but at the same time mindful of the repertoire, reinterpreted to function as a "progressive" vision of the same, and extended to include the reworking and diffusion of "early" music in direct relationship, as already mentioned, to its original production.[70] This is how Maderna achieved rapid success in the post-war scenario of European musical life and its productive network. Germany therefore became a natural pole of attraction; and the decision, taken in 1952, to settle in Darmstadt – in which private affairs certainly played their part – was the consequence of a direction that his activity had already taken. The development of his career was thus more and more virtually at odds with the eagerness with which he wanted to give his new school local roots, and also with the militant initiatives that he wished to start following his recent membership in the Communist Party. Maderna was increasingly physically apart from his "workshop," and at this point Nono acted as the Maestro's substitute in the role of tutor to the young Venetian group, which remained together until at least 1953. Maderna clarified his appointment halfway through 1952:

> Now I'm going away, old man, you are left with the task of keeping the show going in these months. In Venice there is already a small <u>music</u> center "in fieri" […] which must not be lost. You are my true friend, in these months you can stand in for me in all respects.

---

69 The biographical reference is inspired by the title of Hermann Scherchen's posthumous memoirs, *Mes deux vies: Récit autobiographique*, Préface de Paul Badura-Skoda et Rolf Liebermann (Clichy: Tahra, 1992). The separation between the two phases of his life is implicit in the title Scherchen himself gave to the autobiographical essay that summarized the 1891–1950 period: "Mein erstes Leben"; published in idem, *Werke und Briefe*, ed. Joachim Lucchesi, vol. 1 (Berlin et al.: Peter Lang, 1991).

70 See as regards this Angela Ida De Benedictis, "More than conducting, more than composing: Hermann Scherchen, Bruno Maderna, Luciano Berio," in *Komponieren & Dirigieren: Doppelbegabungen als Thema der Interpretationsgeschichte*, ed. Alexander Drčar and Wolfgang Gratzer (Freiburg im Breisgau et al.: Rombach, 2017), pp. 371–400.

> You must be the driving force: help the lazy, be patient with those who do not understand, express yourself, fill them with love for music, for real life. You can do it. You have all the skills to do it. You studied with Scherchen and with me. You <u>must do it</u>.[71]

In light of the subsequent events, the "school" in which Maderna, after 1948, found himself almost simultaneously as pupil and teacher, was the informal but solid foundation for the creation of a feeling of belonging to a new international dimension, also made up of concrete opportunities for activities, contacts, and prestigious performances initially guaranteed by figures like Hartmann and above all Scherchen. This school was in fact the origin of the fortunes of the two Venetians, of their role as the first Italian representatives of the generational *nouvelle vague* that around 1950 turned the page in the history of European music. But this belonging was also established – and always in an anti-nationalistic key – as a local core of "Venetianness" that was both real and imagined at the same time, in the sense that we have tried to describe so far: a collective practice of study and craftsmanship, and, operationally-speaking, of experimental grafting of archaic compositional techniques onto new language orders. Maderna and Nono therefore invested themselves with the title of "Nuova scuola veneziana" (New Venetian School), an expression that we find in their enthusiastic letters and that, for a short time, they even considered using as an anonymous "signature" on their compositions.[72]

It is more than likely that Gian Francesco Malipiero regretted not having been the architect of these or similar fortunes, seeing that he had been their initial inspiration and promoter. He had been deprived of a mediating role that also sought to take action, a role which, however, the historical and cultural coordinates of the post-war era had prevented him from maintaining.

In 1957, Malipiero composed a "concert pamphlet," *Magister Josephus*, that may have expressed this very position. This work portrays, in four voices with orchestra, the sixteenth-century master musician Gioseffo Zarlino as an old man, disappointed by the developments of his own school (which was in fact Venetian). A moderately dramatic representation of a *fait accompli* which, by analogy four hundred years later, led Malipiero's students away toward opportunities that the Maestro himself had encouraged but was himself unwilling to follow.[73] In Italy – in Venice – two competing constellations were operating in 1948, both dedicated to the development of new experiences with the language, but also to a kind of cultural updating. The faction that came out on top was the most radical, the one that was common to, more compatible with, and aligned on the different trends that, at that moment, were changing the face of Europe and its music.

---

71   Maderna to Luigi Nono, n.d., probably May 1952 (ALN).

72   The information comes from an account by Renzo Dall'Oglio collected by the writer in June 1994. For details of the common techniques developed by Maderna and Nono see Rizzardi, "La 'Nuova scuola veneziana'" (see note 67).

73   I owe this suggestion to Giovanni Morelli, "La carica dei quodlibet: Note sulla tipologia ideale di una 'nuova scuola veneziana' all'uso degli incroci di lettura delle opere di Maderna, Nono e Malipiero," in *La carica dei quodlibet: Carte diverse e alcune musiche inedite del Maestro Malipiero*, Archivio G.F. Malipiero, Studi 2, ed. Giovanni Morelli (Florence: Olschki, 2005), p. 123. For a discussion of *Magister Josephus* see John C. G. Waterhouse, *Gian Francesco Malipiero (1882–1973): The Life, Times and Music of a Wayward Genius* (London: Routledge, 2013), pp. 296–301.

CHRISTOPH NEIDHÖFER

"La révolution dans la continuité"
The Presence of the Past in Bruno Maderna's Creative Process (1948–55)

> ... it is easy to understand that a new mentality and its manifestation in a new technique do not necessarily entail negation of the distant or immediate past. On the contrary, today we are more than ever convinced that *natura non facit saltus* ...[1]

For Bruno Maderna, exploration of new musical territory went hand in hand with a rethinking of the past. For one, he was convinced that, whether or not a composer is willing to acknowledge as much, there is always something of the old that lives on in the new in one form or another. Furthermore, in his own work, Maderna actively drew on practices from the past to invent new compositional strategies. In so doing with seemingly limitless imagination, he pioneered a wide range of compositional procedures that had a profound impact on contemporary music in the 1950s and beyond, with many of his inventions and ideas being taken up by other composers as well who had studied or worked with him. This essay examines a number of Maderna's compositional techniques to illuminate how he took inspiration from music and music theories from the past for his own new compositional techniques. The following examples are taken from works written between 1948 and 1955, during which time he developed his own version of (integral) serialism. My focus will be on Maderna's poetics and its sources of influence. I will not go into the impact of Maderna's techniques on other composers.[2]

Like virtually every Italian composer of his generation – given the kind of training one would receive privately or in conservatories at the time – Maderna began writing in neoclassical styles. Following the works of his early maturity, he started to adopt

---

I wish to thank Angela Ida De Benedictis, Sabine Hänggi-Stampfli, and Carlos Chanfón for their kind support during my research for this essay at the Paul Sacher Foundation.

1   Bruno Maderna, ["Arnold Schoenberg"], typewritten text in Italian and German with corrections by Maderna and an unidentified hand, held at PSS-BMC (fol. 3, original in Italian). Now published as "Conferenza sulla dodecafonia e gli sviluppi della tecnica seriale in Italia" (1954), in Bruno Maderna, *Amore e curiosità: Scritti, frammenti e interviste sulla musica*, ed. Angela Ida De Benedictis, Michele Chiappini, and Benedetta Zucconi (Milan: il Saggiatore, 2020), pp. 169–78, quote on p. 171. All translations into English are mine. For the continuation of this quote see Michele Chiappini's essay in this volume, p. 197. For a description of the document see Angela Ida De Benedictis, "Bruno Maderna: Vortrag über Arnold Schönberg," in *"On revient toujours": Dokumente zur Schönberg-Rezeption aus der Paul Sacher Stiftung* (Mainz: Schott, 2016), pp. 99–101.

2   Maderna's commitment to tradition and innovation, which he often mentioned in his writings and interviews, has frequently been discussed in the literature on the composer, starting from Massimo Mila, *Maderna musicista europeo*, ed. Ulrich Mosch (Turin: Einaudi, 1999; first edn 1976).

twelve-tone techniques around 1948 within a musical language that remained largely neoclassical for another number of years, with stylistic influences notably from Bartók, Debussy, Hindemith, G.F. Malipiero, and Stravinsky. During these years, and with every work, Maderna rapidly expanded his compositional means, conceiving new techniques that were as much rooted in compositional principles known from the past as they broke new ground in thinking about musical material, within the aesthetic program of the avant-garde. As he stated in 1953–54, he rejected the kind of neoclassicism that represented a straightforward return to earlier styles. For him, music had to evolve continuously, as a metaphor for human life and development, which likewise know no return to an earlier stage untouched by the experiences of what had occurred in between:

> Because of the harshness of life today (I want to say since 1914 to today) the possibility of an aesthetic outside the pulse of life has become impossible for us. Hence it goes without saying that in our current reality there can be no return to Neoclassicism or Neoromanticism or other Neo-Neo possibilities.
> Why can there be no return? It is because every Neo shows a limited world. A world that has not yet grasped nature as a phenomenon. [...] Music is in continual motion like a human being.[3]

Concerning the impossibility of a complete break with the past, Maderna stated in 1965:

> There can be no breaks, no ruptures in a civilization: it is an ontological impossibility. Cultures are neither abstractions nor things: they are human facts. Revolutions are themselves rooted in continuity, and if they break the course of things, they at the same time confirm this continuity. The rupture that atonal music seems to have provoked, and that serial music seems to perpetuate and deepen, is only an appearance of rupture. We composers ourselves believed to have made a leap and to have opened a radically new era with serial music. Legitimate illusion![4]

As the following examples will show, Maderna considered historical materials from a number of perspectives to conceive new procedures, whereby links with the past remain clearly audible in certain cases, while at other times the connection is more remote. I propose to distinguish three broad areas in which this happens in Maderna's poetics:

1) conversion of historical compositional and music-theoretical concepts into modern compositional methods;

2) allusion to older musical *topoi* and genres through the lens of new compositional techniques; and

3) transformation, often beyond recognition, of historical musical source material – such as folksong melodies – using the newest permutational techniques.

Maderna frequently combines these approaches, reevaluating materials and ideas in refreshingly novel ways.

---

3   Maderna, ["Arnold Schoenberg"] (see note 1), fol. 1 (original in German). See also Maderna, *Amore e curiosità* (see note 1), p. 169.
4   Bruno Maderna, "La révolution dans la continuité," in André Boucourechliev, "La musique sérielle aujourd'hui," *Preuves* 15, no. 177 (1965), pp. 28–29: 28.

Pitch Gamuts Modeled on Ancient Modes

As soon as he had embraced twelve-tone techniques, Maderna sought to expand them. We shall begin with examples taken from two early dodecaphonic works for orchestra, *Composizione n. 1* (1948–49) and *Composizione n. 2* (1949–50), where he approached serial principles partly from a modal perspective. Example 1 reproduces a sketch for the concluding section of *Composizione n. 1* (→ **EX. 1**).[5] The final version of the corresponding passage is shown in Example 2, reproduced from the critical edition of the score (→ **EX. 2**).[6] In bars 401–05, above percussion rolls on snare drum, bass drum, and cymbal, and between segments of an eighth-note rhythm on woodblock, the vibraphone and piano articulate wide-leaping gestures that transliterate a dedicatory note to the conductor of the premiere: "A NINO SANZOGNO." Every letter of the name – including the preposition "A" (*to*) – is translated into a pitch: in Example 2, pitch A_2 (for "A") sounds twice, pitch A_4 (for "N") four times, pitch F_3 (for "I") once, pitch Bb_5 (for "O") three times, and the remaining ones (D_4 for "S," $F\#_4$ for "Z," and Eb_5 for "G") once each.[7] The *pitch-class* succession as a whole is more heavily weighted than the sequence of letters, with pitch class A (located in two different octaves, as A_4 and A_2 for "N" and "A" respectively) accounting for almost half of the pitch events, in a clear departure from twelve-tone chromaticism. The sketch in Example 1 shows how Maderna arrived at this progression through the construction of a pitch gamut inspired by modal theory. At the top, starting with A_2 (in black pencil), he writes out a scale that corresponds to the succession of the first seven letters of the alphabet, reading "B" as Bb following German terminology. This scale corresponds to Ptolemy's Dorian mode ("Dorico"), here transposed to start on A. Maderna shows the eighth note (A_3) in square brackets, presumably because it duplicates an earlier pitch class. He then continues to the following scale degree, shown as B_3, to obtain the next, new pitch class (different from the previous Bb). For reasons that will soon become clear, Maderna then chooses Db_4, rather than $C\#_4$, for the next scale degree, continuing from there diatonically within the ancient Phrygian mode ("Frigio"). Following its final (Cb_5), he proceeds to the ancient Lydian mode ("Lidio") on $C\#$, showing the lower representation of its final in square brackets.

The resulting larger gamut – Maderna adds one more pitch in purple at the bottom and at the top – consists of a total of twenty-six pitches in twenty-four unique spellings: each of the twelve pitch classes occurs in two different spellings (Ebb and D, Eb and $D\#$, E and Fb, etc.), with each spelling used once except for A and $C\#$, which appear in two locations each. As Maderna indicates with the two facing arrows at the top of the page (→←), the gamut is intervallically symmetrical around a central axis between Fb_4 and Gb_4, marked by a vertical arrow.[8]

---

5   For reasons that probably have to do with the modal nature of the material, this sketch is preserved among the manuscripts for *Composizione n. 2*. I wish to thank Angela Ida De Benedictis for drawing my attention to this sketch.

6   Bruno Maderna, *Composizione n. 1* for orchestra, ed. Angela Ida De Benedictis (Milan: Suvini Zerboni, 2007), p. 88.

7   C_4 designates middle C.

8   This idea of symmetry does not apply to the actual spellings of the pitches, however. In order not to duplicate any spellings (except for A and $C\#$, the duplicate locations of which he marks in square brackets), Maderna had to balance the major second A_3-B_3 with the doubly augmented prime Cb_5-$C\#b_5$, and to choose a doubly augmented prime at the bottom (Abb_2-A_2) as opposed to a diminished third at the top ($C\#_6$-Eb_6). Furthermore, in Maderna's spelling the inversionally symmetrical Phrygian mode in the middle begins with a diminished third (B_3-Db_4) but ends with a major second (Bbb_4-Cb_5).

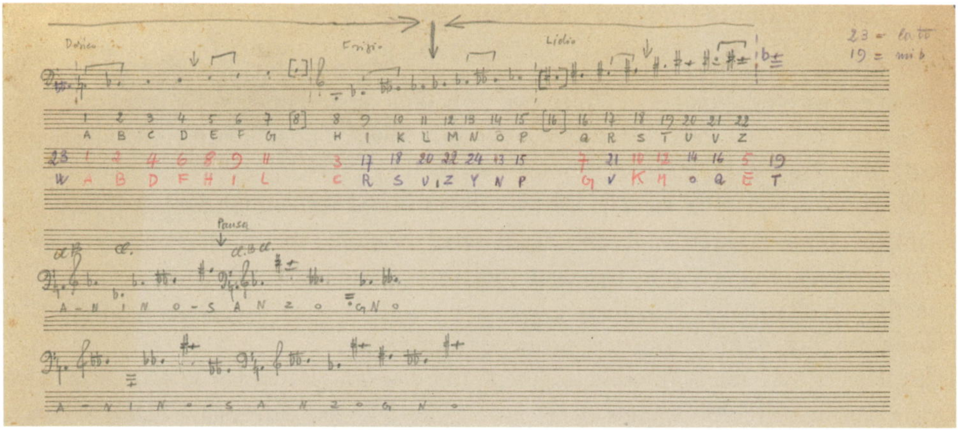

EX. 1   Bruno Maderna, sketch for *Composizione n. 1*, bb. 401–05; PSS-BMC.

Maderna numbers the scale degrees shown in black from 1 to 22, not counting those that duplicate a pitch class in its particular spelling (A_3 and $C\sharp_5$), and assigns to each number a letter from the Italian alphabet (plus K). Each letter thus represents a uniquely spelled pitch class.[9] In a second round, shown beneath in red and purple, Maderna relabels the gamut, this time including the lowest and highest members, in a reading that reflects the (abstract) distance of each uniquely spelled pitch class from the final A. The later a letter occurs in the alphabet, the more remote is the relationship between the corresponding uniquely spelled pitch class and this final, in a measurement that takes into account both the directed pitch-class interval from the final (i.e. the distance between pitch class A and the particular uniquely spelled pitch class, measured in an upward direction) and the specific spelling. Letters "A" and "B" represent pitches A_2 and $B\flat_2$ as before. Letter "C" is assigned to the next chromatic scale degree, in its spelling as B natural (B_3) rather than $C\flat$ because $C\flat$ is more remote from A on the spiral of perfect fifths ($C\flat$ lies *ten* perfect fifths below A, B *two* perfect fifths above A). Maderna then assigns letter "D" to C_3, the closest representative of the next chromatic scale degree up ($B\sharp$ would be more remote). For letter "E," for the next chromatic scale degree, Maderna chooses $C\sharp$ ($C\sharp_6$) rather than $D\flat$ because $D\flat$ would be more remote from A. And so forth until the last two pitches furthest removed from A in this kind of measurement, $A\flat\flat_2$ and $A\flat_4$, numbered 23 and 24 with letters W and Y.[10]

Further down in the sketch Maderna drafts two versions of the dedication. The first, intended for bass clarinet and clarinet, projects the dedicatory note onto the first gamut of letters above, the one where the pitches are labeled alphabetically and numerically from bottom to top. The melodic contour of this transliteration thus corresponds to the progression

---

9   I use the term "uniquely spelled pitch class" to mean the group of all pitches that are spelled the same way irrespective of the register in which they occur, in contradistinction to the term "pitch class," which classifies pitches under octave *and* enharmonic equivalence.

10   Since the latter two letters largely fall outside the Italian alphabet, they are ultimately not needed for the transliteration of the dedication anyway. One might wonder why $A\flat$ is classified here as further removed than $A\flat\flat$ from A. The reason is that $A\flat\flat$ lies below $A\flat$ on the chromatic scale and hence comes before it in an ascending reading of these two remaining uniquely spelled pitch classes.

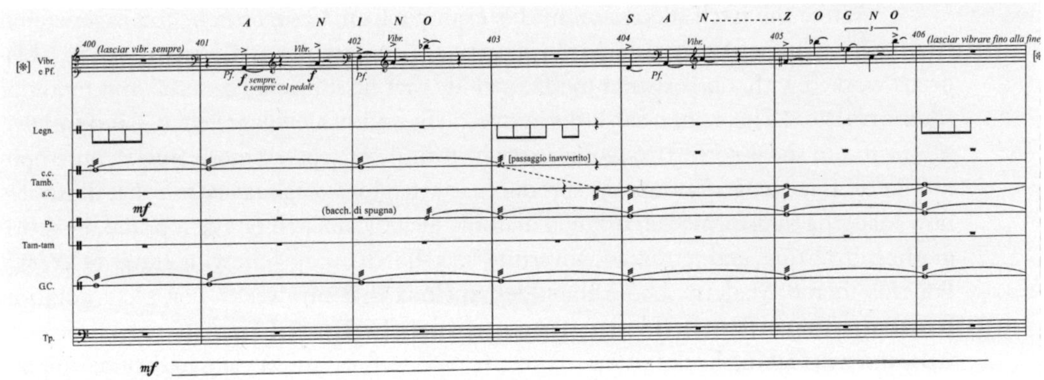

EX. 2   Bruno Maderna, *Composizione n. 1* for orchestra, bb. 400–06; detail from the score, p. 88 (Milan: Suvini Zerboni, 2007).

of the relative positions of the letters within the alphabet. (Letter A corresponds to the lowest note, Z to the highest.) In the second version, shown below, Maderna performs the dedicatory phrase on the second gamut of letters. Save for A_2, the pitches are all different in this reading, resulting in a different overall contour. This is the configuration used in the final version of the work (Ex. 2, vibraphone and piano). Presumably for practical reasons, Maderna respells the pitches in this final scoring, however, and in so doing masks the key to the transliteration. Whereas it would probably have been difficult to deduce the gamut behind the original spelling of the dedicatory note without access to the sketch anyway, Maderna's decision to disguise the generative process even further (by way of enharmonic respelling) is typical of his compositional practice in a broader sense, as we will see again later.[11]

---

11   In an undated sketch preserved at the Archivio Luigi Nono in Venice (catalogued as M01.02.01/08), Maderna drafts a different version of this pitch gamut, evidently modeling it on the same ancient modes but without mentioning them by name. In this sketch, the Dorian mode at the bottom, again starting on A2, is spelled the same way, but the following transposed Phrygian and Lydian modes are enharmonically respelled. Maderna labels the pitches with letter names (in the way he first did in Ex. 1), starting at the bottom with letter A for A_2, B for $B\flat_2$, C for C_3, etc., ascending through the gamut and assigning the same letter whenever a pitch class recurs in its actual spelling. (Maderna omits the lowest and highest pitch from Example 1.) The spelling of this version of the gamut reads as follows: pitch A_2 = letter A, pitch $B\flat_2$ = letter B, C_3 = C, D_3 = D, E_3 = E, F_3 = F, G_3 = G, A_3 = [A], B_3 = H, $C\sharp_4$ = I, D_4 = [D], E_4 = [E], $F\sharp_4$ = L, $G\sharp_4$ = M, A_4 = [A], B_4 = [H], $D\flat_5$ = N, $E\flat_5$ = O, F_5 = [F], $G\flat_5$ = P, $A\flat_5$ = Q, $B\flat_5$ = [B], C_6 = [C], $D\flat_6$ = [N]. Maderna would not have been able to encode the dedicatory note to Nino Sanzogno at the end of *Composizione n. 1* in this spelling of the gamut, however, because it does not contain letters S and Z. In the same sketch, Maderna also examines what would happen if he enharmonically respelled the Lydian mode at the top as in Example 1. This spelling would bring him again only to letter Q ($C\sharp_5$ = [I], $D\sharp_5$ = N, $E\sharp_5$ = O, $F\sharp_5$ = [L], $G\sharp_5$ = [M], $A\sharp_5$ = P, $B\sharp_5$ = Q, $C\sharp_6$ = [I]), which must in turn have been the reason why he spelled the Phrygian mode in Example 1 mostly with flats and double flats, to get beyond letter Q. That Maderna's sketch preserved at the Archivio Luigi Nono likely dates from around the time of *Composizione n. 1* (1948–49) is supported by other manuscripts in Maderna's hand held in the same file (M01.02.01), which include transcriptions of movements from the opera *Totila* by Giovanni Legrenzi. These movements ("Sinfonia, Ritornelli e Arie barbare e pietose dall'opera *Totila*") were performed in Venice on 25 September 1949. See Michele Chiappini, "La scrittura dell'interpretazione: Teoria e pratica della trascrizione musicale durante gli anni veneziani di Bruno Maderna (1946–1952)" (PhD diss., Alma Mater Studiorum, Università di Bologna, 2015), pp. 162 and 212. I wish to thank Nuria Schoenberg Nono for granting me access to the sources held at the Archivio Luigi Nono.

While the pitch succession in this example from *Composizione n. 1* is generated from the spelling of a text via a newly constructed supermode, in *Composizione n. 2* Maderna worked with a preexistent modal melody that he subjected to serial and modular transformation. There are clear links between the end of *Composizione n. 1* and *Composizione n. 2* in the way the two works carry historical concepts of mode into a contemporary musical language. Example 3 reproduces a sketch for *Composizione n. 2* that illustrates how Maderna transformed an original diatonic melody, notated on the top staff, by retrograding, inverting, and retrograde-inverting it as shown on the following staves (→ EX. 3).[12] For this theme, Maderna chose the oldest melody that survives in complete notation (i.e. comprising melody and lyrics), the ancient Seikilos Funeral Epitaph (second century AD), and by reaching back this far in documented musical history situates contemporary compositional practice in the longest music-historical context possible.[13] To the right of this melody at the top, Maderna analyzes the overall relative weighting of its pitches by tabulating the number of occurrences of each pitch class from the mode, here identified as (ancient) Phrygian. Presumably in order to expand the pitch-class material, Maderna projects the retrograde, on the second staff, onto a transposed (ancient) Lydian mode starting on E, with the same kind of statistical analysis given to the right (obviously showing the same relative distribution, under transposition). The inversion, on the third staff, is read into a Dorian mode transposed to start another step up, on F, with the statistical analysis to the right showing the same result as before, under inversion, except for one deviation for pitch class C. The latter occurs only five, not six times, because Maderna replaces the first note of the melody with a rest. For the retrograde-inversion he creates a special mode starting on C♯, i.e. one step *below* the original Phrygian mode. This new synthetic mode consists of the seven scale degrees shown in ascending order (C♯, D♯, E, F, G, G♯, A♯), to which Maderna adds the three pitch classes shown below (D, F♯, A). He calls this material "Dodecafonico," even though two pitch classes, B and C, are not present here.

The rationale behind Maderna's choice of the "dodecaphonic" mode is given in the number table in the lower right-hand corner of the sketch shown in Example 3, where he keeps track of the distribution of the twelve pitch classes in the four serial-modal versions of the melody ("Totale frequenza," i.e. total number of occurrences of the pitch classes) and records the overall statistics. As is evident from the sums shown at the very bottom, twelve for every pitch class, Maderna strives for an overall balance where each pitch class is used the same total number of times overall. This statistical balance – likely referred to in the title of the sketch ("Proporzione dodecafonica," dodecaphonic proportion) – in turn

---

12   This sketch was first analyzed in print by Joachim Noller, "Dimensioni musicali: Le composizioni di Bruno Maderna nel primo dopoguerra," in *Studi su Bruno Maderna*, ed. Mario Baroni and Rossana Dalmonte (Milan: Suvini Zerboni, 1989), pp. 95–108: 97. Susanna Pasticci – who edited the critical edition of the composition (Milan: Suvini Zerboni, 2006) – presents an exhaustive analysis of the score and compositional process of the entire work in "'Une musique d'écoute facile': Sur la *Composizione n. 2*," in *à Bruno Maderna*, ed. Geneviève Mathon, Laurent Feneyrou, and Giordano Ferrari, vol. 2 (Paris: Basalte, 2009), pp. 91–122 (sketch reproduced on p. 100). I am indebted to both articles in the following discussion.

13   See Mila, *Maderna musicista europeo* (see note 2), pp. 14–15, and new edn. (1999), pp. 12–13; Pasticci, "'Une musique d'écoute facile'" (see note 12), pp. 92–94. For a transcription of the Seikilos Epitaph and commentary see *Documents of Ancient Greek Music*, ed. Egert Pöhlmann and Martin L. West (Oxford: Clarendon Press, 2001), pp. 88–91.

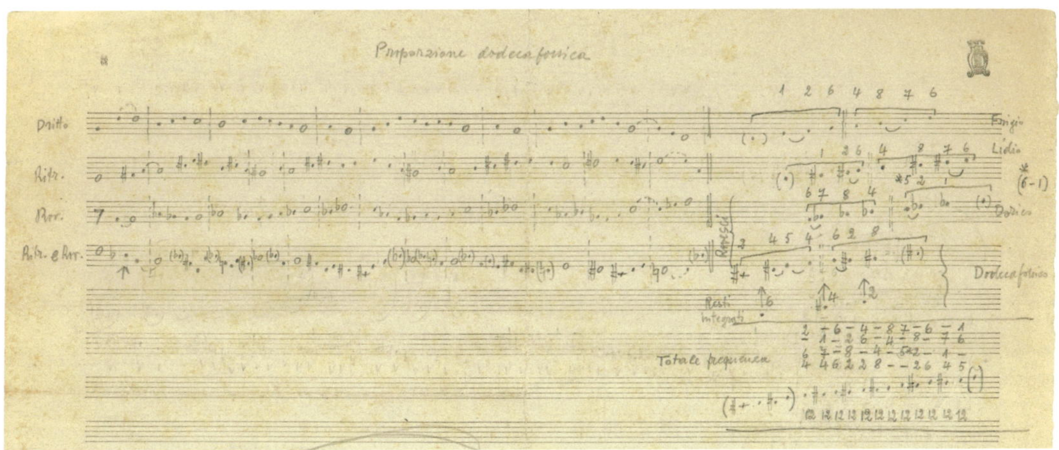

EX. 3   Bruno Maderna, sketch for *Composizione n. 2* (excerpt), PSS-BMC.

means that Maderna had to work with a default collection of pitch classes for the "retrograde-inversion," using what was "left over" from the other three forms to complete the overall super-aggregate of 12×12 elements. Pitch classes B and C already occurred a total of twelve times in the first three forms and hence were no longer available for the "retrograde-inversion" ("Ritr[oso] e Rov[escio]"). Maderna in fact had to eliminate one instance of pitch class C in order not to exceed the total of twelve occurrences allowed, which he did in the inversion by replacing the first note by a rest. Given that the pitch material for the "retrograde-inversion" is larger than that for any of the other forms – forty-four notes compared to thirty-four ("Dritto" and "Ritr.") or thirty-three ("Rov.") – Maderna created a primary structure of thirty-three notes, whose contour is derived from the original melody (under RI), into which he inserted the remaining eleven notes shown in parentheses.[14]

Composizione n. 2 opens with the Seikilos Epitaph melody in the english horn – a close modern relative of the ancient aulos[15] – over solo strings sustaining selected pitches from this theme, mostly in different octaves. Following this first statement, flute and oboe sound the melody backwards, in heterophony as shown in → **EX. 4** (bb. 8–15),[16] with sometimes the oboe, sometimes the flute leading and the solo strings (not shown in Ex. 4) continuing to expand their echoing pitch field. All of this unfolds in the (ancient) Phrygian mode, until starting in b. 14 Maderna introduces the other three modes from the sketch in Example 3. In b. 14 (Ex. 4), the english horn enters with a statement of the "retrograde-inversion" in the "dodecaphonic" mode and the clarinet with the retrograde of the inversion in the Dorian mode (compare clarinet line with third staff of the sketch in Ex. 3). One measure later the alto saxophone enters with the retrograde in the Lydian mode

---

14   The contour of the primary structure deviates in a number of places from the original melody (under RI), presumably due to unavailability of the necessary pitches. Maderna erroneously uses E six, not five, times in the "retrograde-inversion."

15   See Pasticci, "'Une musique d'écoute facile'" (see note 12), p. 102.

16   Henceforth, all references are to the published score, ed. Susanna Pasticci (Milan: Suvini Zerboni, 2006).

EX. 4   Bruno Maderna, *Composizione n. 2,* bb. 6–27,
strings and second horn part omitted;
from the score, pp. 2–6 (Milan: Suvini Zerboni, 2006).

EX. 5 Bruno Maderna, *Composizione n. 2,* bb. 266–70; score, pp. 45–46 (Milan: Suvini Zerboni, 2006).

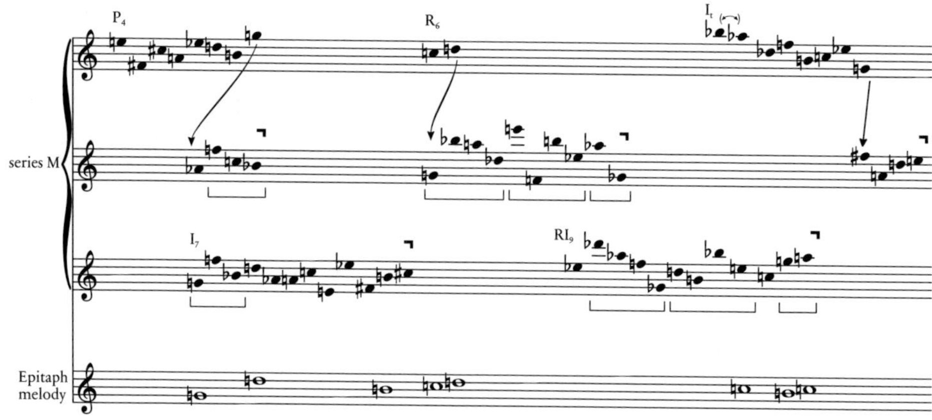

EX. 6   Serial layers and Epitaph melody in bb. 266–70
of *Composizione n. 2* summarized.

(second staff of the sketch in Ex. 3). Meanwhile the strings continue to expand the sustained pitch field accordingly (not shown here). Within only about one-hundred seconds of music, Maderna thus carries us from an envisioned ancient diatonic sound world to a contemporary chromatic idiom.[17] By b. 17 the pitch field in the strings (not shown) has acquired all twelve pitch classes. The rest of this opening section continues with various contrapuntal layerings of the Epitaph melody and its modal-serial derivatives, some of this material transposed, projected onto a slowly moving pitch canvas in the strings.

Following the echoes in this first section of a time long past, heard through a chromaticized lens, the second section of the work brings us closer to the present by referencing more recent styles and genres. As Susanna Pasticci has shown, the second and third sections are built from a complex of twelve-tone series generated via a continuous derivation procedure.[18] In the second section (bb. 68–198), a gradually expanding contrapuntal serial texture unfolds in the guise of an *English Waltz* (score, p. 15), which at its climax segues into a (serial) *Wiener Walzer* (score, p. 23, from b. 143 on).[19] The third and final section of the work (bb. 199–294, starting on p. 33 of the score) turns to another dance, featuring a *Rumba* built from serial counterpoint. During these dances the original Epitaph melody has completely vanished, only to reappear at the very end of the work. Example 5 shows the moment where the melody resurfaces in the english horn (in b. 267), surrounded by counterpoint built entirely from a twelve-tone series (labeled "series M" in Maderna's sketches)[20] and its transformations (→ EX. 5). As illustrated in → EX. 6, Maderna realizes certain parts of the series melodically while bending other segments vertically into chords, as I have indicated with brackets. Timpani and xylophone play melodic and/or rhythmic ostinato patterns on the first tetrachord of "series M."[21] Modeled on a *Rumba* accompaniment, syncopated rhythms are set against ostinato runs in the non-pitched percussion (Ex. 5).

---

17   See Pasticci, "'Une musique d'écoute facile'" (see note 12), p. 103.
18   Ibid., pp. 106ff.
19   An *English Waltz* will appear again later in *Grande Aulodia* and *Venetian Journal*. See the contribution by Carlo Ciceri in this volume, p. 105.
20   See Pasticci, "'Une musique d'écoute facile'" (see note 12), pp. 108–10.
21   This tetrachord, E-F♯-C♯-A, links series M with the retrograde in the Lydian mode of the original Epitaph melody, which starts with the same tetrachord in a slightly different ordering (Ex. 3, second staff).

From Twelve-Tone Thematicism to Serial Matrix

In the 1950s, Maderna pursued three objectives in particular. First, he explored ways to move beyond twelve-tone procedures of the Second Viennese School. Second, he continuously took inspiration from older music in pursuit of new compositional possibilities. And third, he put his new techniques in the service of immediately graspable musical expression and a deep-seated humanism. In his writings and interviews, Maderna spoke of these three aspects with considerable consistency over the years. Concerning what would have been considered then to be more standard twelve-tone technique, Maderna explained in the aforementioned text written in 1953–54:

> As far as I am concerned, what from the beginning interested me were the first attempts of Webern to manipulate a series in such a way as to allow an ever larger choice of sound material.
> What I did not like about twelve-tone theory is the principle by which, once a series is given, it has to reappear in its entirety, continuously, vertically and horizontally, for the sake of consistency in the musical discourse. This concept, which corresponds to the oldest concept of return, seemed too narrow to me. A return has to be able to happen under different conditions. The voyage of Ulysses is famous.
> It teaches us that there cannot be a return [and] that life in its eternal becoming changes continuously.
> Thus why should one not have a technique that resembles the technique of life in its becoming?
> Slowly but surely I proceeded to the study of serial permutation, until I succeeded in developing more and more complex and rigorous systems of permutation.[22]

Regarding the continuing importance of the study of older music for his work as a composer and conductor, Maderna still stated in 1965 that:

> Now, at forty-five, with twenty years of daily experience as composer [and] as performer of serial music, I feel more than ever entrenched in the continuity of my musical civilization – a civilization of one thousand years that I know very well (I do not stop studying, for my personal pleasure, for my concerts, and especially for the enrichment of my thinking as composer, the works of my true masters, the Flemish polyphonists).[23]

Renaissance polyphony (and presumably other historical compositional techniques as well) not only served as a source of inspiration, it also represented a benchmark against which Maderna would measure his own compositional integrity and skill as a serial composer: "And we handle it [the serial principle] with as much ease and freedom, and we live it as forcefully, as the Flemish masters lived their own principles of expression."[24]

Maderna's affection for Renaissance counterpoint is clearly evident in the two passages from *Composizione n. 2* we just saw (→ **EXX. 4–5**). In both excerpts, the series (Epitaph melody, "series M," and their transformations) unfold linearly. Additionally, in the second passage they are also bent into the vertical dimension to form chords. Maderna's

---

22 Maderna, ["Arnold Schoenberg"] (see note 1), fol. 6 (original in Italian). See also Maderna, *Amore e curiosità* (see note 1), p. 175. In the last sentence Maderna twice uses the term "*mutazioni*" (mutations), which, given the context here, I translate as "permutations."
23 Maderna, "La révolution dans la continuité" (see note 4), p. 28.
24 Ibid.

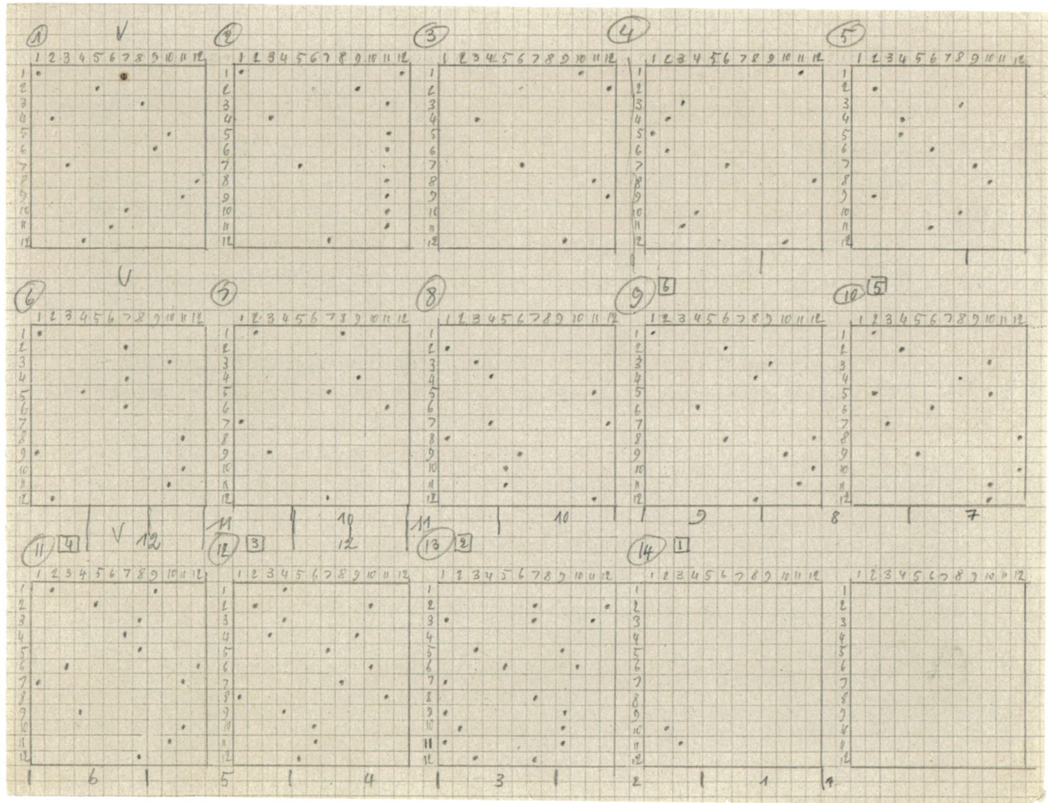

EX. 7   Sketch of pitch matrices for "Kommerzialbrief," second
movement of *Quattro lettere (Kranichsteiner Kammerkantate)*
by Bruno Maderna (1953); PSS-BMC.

ultimate goal at the time was to break away from such traditional procedures, however, as he explained in the text from 1953–54 quoted above. By 1951 he had invented a procedure that enabled him to generate constantly mutating serial materials by way of a matrix technique that transcended the conventional concepts of linear counterpoint and twelve-tone harmony based on verticalized row segments or multi-voiced chord progressions. As the next examples will demonstrate (→ **EXX. 7-14**), Maderna achieved this by driving counterpoint underground, so to speak, that is, not by rejecting an old practice, but by fundamentally transforming it.

Example 7 reproduces Maderna's sketch of the matrices through which he generated the pitch material for the "Kommerzialbrief" (business letter), the second movement of *Kranichsteiner Kammerkantate* (1953).[25] Each of the twelve ranks in the matrices represents one pitch class. On the y-axis, 1 stands for pitch class A at the top, 2 for B♭ immediately below, 3 for B, and so forth up to 12 for G♯ at the bottom. Maderna employed

---

25   The work is also known under the titles *Quattro lettere* and *Vier Briefe* (see "Chronology of Bruno Maderna's Works" on p. 445 in this volume).

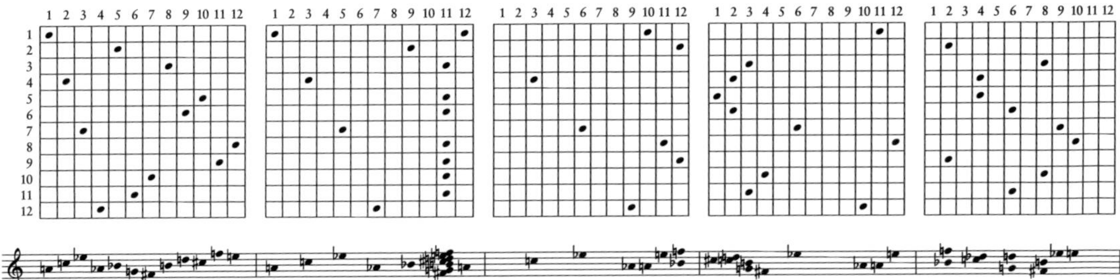

EX. 8   Pitch-class content of first five matrices illustrated.

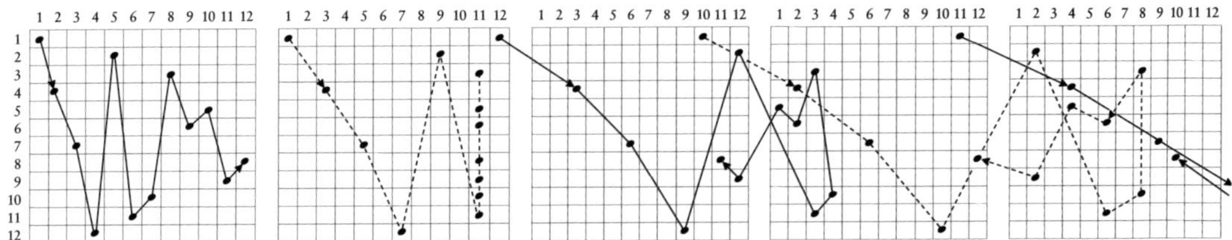

EX. 9   Contrapuntal stretching of twelve-tone series in first five matrices illustrated.

this labeling convention for pitch classes throughout his career; and by choosing A=1 as starting point (rather than C) – by way of reference to the first letter (with its meaning as pitch) from the alphabet as well as to traditional ensemble tuning – he again sustains a close link to traditional practice, as metaphorical as this link might be. The x-axis of the matrices represents time, abstractly measured in twelve increments (columns) per matrix. Each dot in the matrices symbolizes a particular occurrence of a pitch class in a particular temporal position, as I have illustrated in Example 8 for the first five matrices.

By reading the twelve dots in the first matrix from left to right, we recognize a twelve-tone series.[26] In the following matrices, the pitch classes appear in constantly changing constellations with the overall density increasing toward matrices 12 and 13 (Ex. 7). While with this procedure – which Maderna used time and again throughout the 1950s[27] – the identity of the original series gets quickly obliterated, in this example we can still recognize parts of the series in the second and third matrices, as I have illustrated in Example 9. Matrix 2 contains a stretched version of the first half of the series (compare the shape of the dotted line up to column 11 in matrix 2 with the shape of the first half of the series in matrix 1). The remaining pitch classes, on the other hand, are projected

---

26 What in Example 7 looks like a large dot in the middle of the first rank of the first matrix (position 7/1) is the imprint of a cigarette ash burn.

27 The procedure, which was explained in the sketches of Maderna and Luigi Nono by Gianmario Borio and Veniero Rizzardi, was first described by Gianmario Borio in "L'influenza di Dallapiccola sui compositori italiani nel secondo dopoguerra," in *Dallapiccola: Letture e prospettive – Una monografia a più voci a cura di Mila De Santis* (Milan: Ricordi, 1997), pp. 357–87: 382–83, and "Sull'interazione tra lo studio degli schizzi e l'analisi dell'opera," in *La nuova ricerca sull'opera di Luigi Nono*, ed. Gianmario Borio, Giovanni Morelli, and Veniero Rizzardi (Florence: Olschki, 1999), pp. 1–21: 15–17.

entirely into column 11 of matrix 2 as if the series had run into a wall. A third statement of the series starts in the last column of matrix 2. The series is stretched here even more by skipping over two columns each time, until from the seventh dot on (matrix 4, column 4) the series is "bent backwards," concluding in column 11 of matrix 3. And so forth for the following statements of the series.

This is the kind of procedure that Maderna had in mind when he spoke, in the text quoted above, of "more and more complex and rigorous systems of permutation" ("sistemi sempre più complessi e rigorosi di mutazioni") that he had developed in response to what he perceived as the shortcomings of more traditional twelve-tone technique.[28] For one, by way of this procedure the series itself is no longer recognizable on the surface beyond a certain point. Further, "harmonies" are generally not the result of verticalized row segments (the exception here is column 11 of matrix 2), but are generated via a more complex permutation principle. Moreover, rhythm in an abstract sense is generated as part of the same process, in that the matrices tabulate pitch constellations in temporal succession. Meanwhile, as we see in Example 9, links to traditional counterpoint remain, here in the allusion to proportion canon, where each successive statement of the series unfolds at a slower pace. Furthermore, in possible reference to retrograde canon, the later parts of most series are projected "backwards."

The key to Maderna's procedure appears in the sketch reproduced in Example 10 (used for *Quattro lettere* and for *Divertimento in due tempi* as well). The columns of this chart contain ascending and descending number sequences. The values in the first column, read from top to bottom, gradually increase from 11 to 16 and then decrease down to 10. The second column reads the first column upside down. Columns 3–4, 5–6, 7–8, and 9-10 form similar pairs, oscillating between different peak values. The last two columns, on the other hand, move within narrower, different ranges. Following his usual practice at the time,[29] Maderna reads this number chart to generate the pitch-class permutations in the matrices of Example 7 as follows: the values in the first row of Example 10 (11, 10, 9, 12, etc.) determine the distances between successive entries of the first pitch class A of the series, measured in numbers of columns *skipped* between entries. Thus, the second dot for pitch class A, at the beginning of the second matrix, occurs eleven positions after its original appearance in matrix 1. The third dot for A, in column 12 of matrix 2, appears ten positions after the second dot, and the fourth dot (in column 10 of matrix 3) another nine positions later, etc. The values in the second row of Example 10 are used for the shifts of the dots representing the second pitch class (C) of the series. Since initially these values are 1 higher compared to the ones immediately above in the first row, in the matrices of Example 7 the temporal distance between the first two pitch classes gradually increases with every new statement of the series (up to the eighth statement).

---

28 Although Maderna did not write out the analysis itself in the lecture text, it appears that he must in fact have illustrated the technique with the matrices from the third movement ("Kafka – Brief an Milena") of this work. The conjecture is in Nicola Verzina, *Bruno Maderna: Étude historique et critique* (Paris: Harmattan, 2003), p. 57.

29 Described by Gianmario Borio in "L'influenza di Dallapiccola" (see note 27), pp. 382–83, and "Sull'interazione" (see note 27), pp. 15–17.

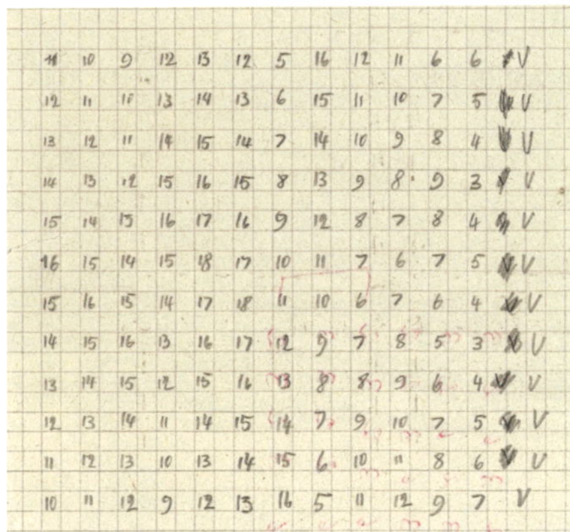

EX. 10   Sketch for "Kommerzialbrief," second movement of *Quattro lettere (Kranichsteiner Kammerkantate)* by Bruno Maderna (1953), showing the number table used for the serial permutation (excerpt), PSS-BMC.

EX. 11   Maderna's transcription of matrices 11–14 from Example 7, read backwards; excerpt from sketch, PSS-BMC.

The same principle applies to the next four pitch classes (with one small exception), which accounts for the augmentation canons formed by the first hexachords of series (i.e. the stretched contours visualized in Ex. 9). Since in the lower half of the first column in Example 10 the number values continuously decrease by 1 (from 16 down to 10), the second hexachord of the series in matrix 2 (Ex. 9) is projected vertically into the same column 11. Since the second column of Example 10 likewise features a decreasing number sequence in its lower half, the corresponding dots in the third statement of the series (Ex. 9, matrices 3 and 4) now form a retrograde. The turning point is in column 4 of matrix 4, from where the series runs backwards, ending in column 11 of matrix 3.

Example 11 shows the beginning of Maderna's transcription of the matrices into staff notation, in a retrograde reading that starts with matrix 14 – renumbered by Maderna in Example 7 as ⌐I⌐ – and that assigns to each column the duration of an eighth note or rest. Matrix 14 (⌐I⌐) is mostly empty, which accounts for the long rest before G and F♯

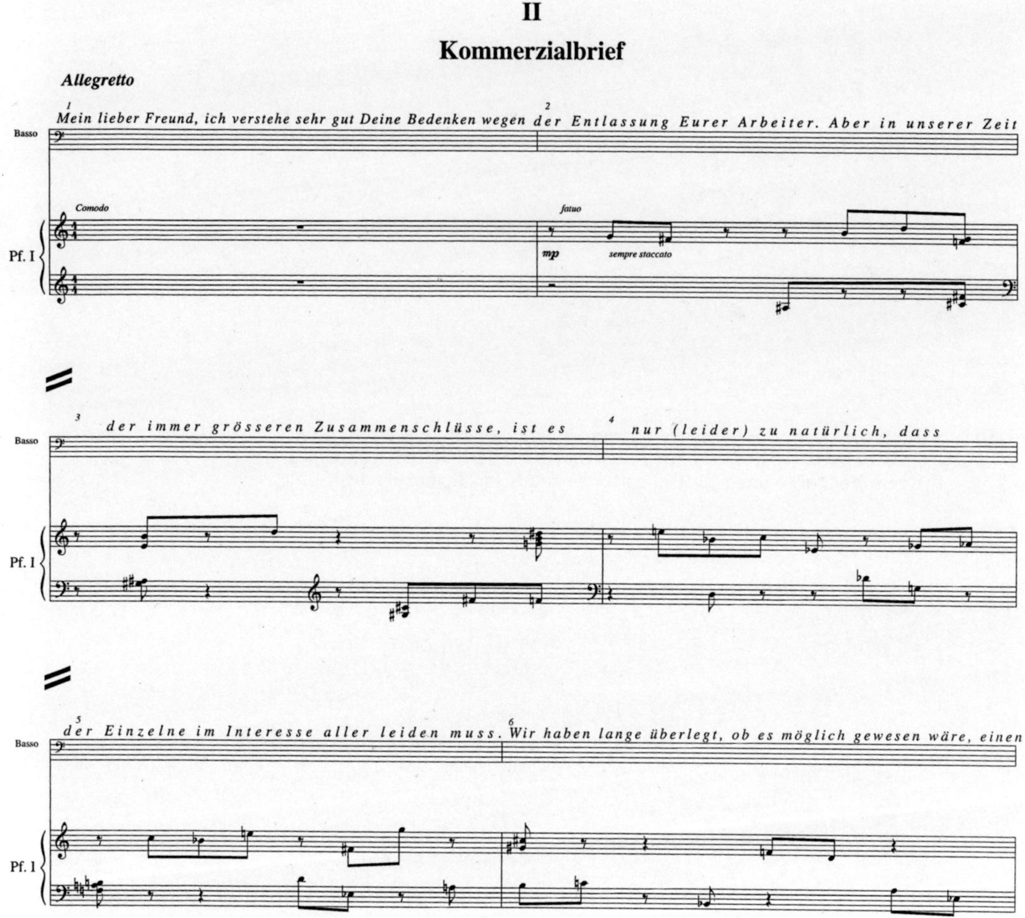

EX. 12   Bruno Maderna, *Quattro lettere (Kranichsteiner Kammerkantate)*, opening of "Kommerzialbrief," bb. 1-6; from the score, p. 10 (Milan: Suvini Zerboni, 2003).

enter in Example 11. In Example 7, starting with matrix 14 ([I]), Maderna marks below the matrices the lengths of the corresponding bars (with |) and their bar numbers (bb. 1, 2, 3, etc. backwards). The last nine columns in matrix 14 ([I]) are empty, which accounts for the complete silence in bar 1 and for the first eighth-note rest at the beginning of bar 2 in Example 11 before the entry of the first two pitches. The bar numbers shown beneath the matrices in Example 7 (reading backwards from matrix 14 to matrix 6) demarcate the content of the first twelve bars of the movement.[30] The draft of Example 11, now realizing the pitch-class material in specific registers, already corresponds to the final version, the

---

30 Bars 10–12, not shown in Example 11, each superimpose two different segments from the matrices (in Ex. 7 "10," "11," and "12" appear twice each below matrices 6–8).

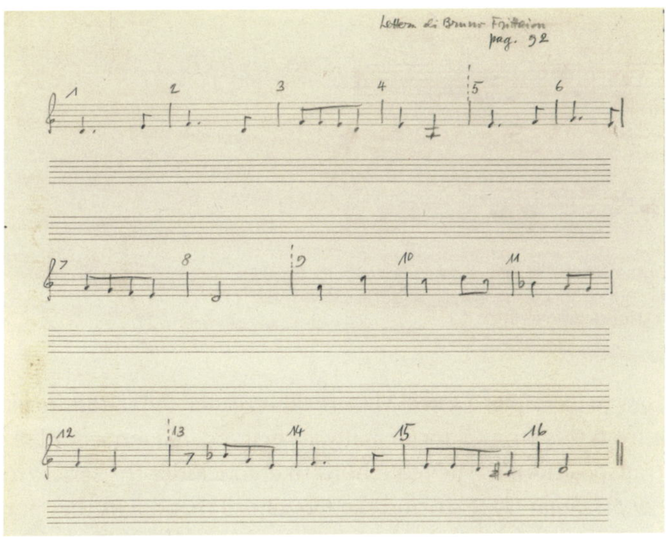

EX. 13　Melody of *Fischia il vento* in Maderna's transcription for *Quattro lettere (Kranichsteiner Kammerkantate)*; sketch, PSS-BMC.

beginning of which is shown in Example 12, reproduced from the critical edition.[31] The cold, mechanical character of the piano part reinforces the chilling atmosphere conveyed by the text from a ruthless business letter recited by the bass voice.[32]

The political engagement, with respect to text setting and musical structure, closely links this second movement with the other parts of *Kranichsteiner Kammerkantate.* As Nicola Verzina has shown in his excellent analysis of the work,[33] movements 1, 3, and 4 each use as a basic series one of the first three phrases from the partisan song *Fischia il vento* [The wind whistles], whose melody is reproduced in Example 13 as Maderna wrote it out in his sketches. (Maderna demarcates the four four-measure phrases with vertical dotted lines.) Movement 2, as Verzina correctly conjectured in the absence at the time of sketches that would corroborate this (our Exx. 7 and 10), makes use of the fourth phrase from the song (bb. 13–16 of Ex. 13). While the exact derivation is not documented, it can be inferred from a comparison of the melody with Maderna's twelve-tone series. Example 14a shows how the last phrase can be segmented into trichords of two different types, a diminished triad, marked by a solid bracket, and two trichords with prime form (013), marked by dotted brackets. Example 14b illustrates how Maderna may have built the first hexachord of his twelve-tone series from trichords of these two types, arranged so as to avoid pitch class

---

31　Bruno Maderna, *Kranichsteiner Kammerkantate,* score for soprano, bass, and chamber orchestra, ed. Nicola Verzina (Milan: Suvini Zerboni, 2003), here p. 10.

32　The origin of this business letter and of the letter from one business man's wife to another, recited later on in the movement, is not known. See ibid., p. xvi.

33　Verzina, *Bruno Maderna* (see note 28), pp. 87–111.

EX. 14   (a) Fourth phrase from *Fischia il vento* (bb. 13–16, Ex. 13)
with trichords marked; (b) Twelve-tone series (from Ex. 7)
with first two trichords marked.

duplication.[34] As we saw in Examples 7 and 8, Maderna then generated the entire pitch material of the movement from this series.[35] Incidentally, its first ordered tetrachord (A-C-E♭-A♭) is the same (under transposition) as the tetrachord that concludes the series from Luigi Dallapiccola's *Canti di prigionia* (1938–41) and the tetrachord that opens the "prayer row" from his opera *Il prigioniero* (1944–48), both politically engaged works that influenced composers of Maderna's generation.

In *Kranichsteiner Kammerkantate* the human-political engagement and its metaphors operate at deep levels of structure. Since the twelve-tone series of the second movement is derived from the phrase of a partisan melody, the entire pitch material of the movement – generated exclusively via permutations of that series – is charged with the political meaning of the song. Furthermore, by dropping the lyrics of *Fischia il vento* and replacing them with texts from cynical corporate letters, Maderna sharpens the political message, bringing it closer to the present.[36]

---

34   While the second half of the series contains another trichord with prime form (013) (motive B-D-C♯), it is impossible to segment the second hexachord (even if reordered) into discrete trichords of one or both of these types.

35   The sketch reproduced in Example 7 closely resembles the template of matrices that Maderna used in *Divertimento in due tempi* for flute and piano, written in the same year (1953), and for some time this sketch had hence been considered to be another (abandoned) version of the matrices for this work. The matrices used in *Divertimento in due tempi* employ a different twelve-tone series but subject it to exactly the same permutation, via the number table in Example 10, with the result that the number of dots per column (but not the pitch classes they represent) is exactly the same in the matrices for both works. The only difference (aside from the use of different series) is that in *Divertimento in due tempi* Maderna maps matrices 13 and 14 onto matrices 1 and 2. For an analysis of this work see Christoph Neidhöfer, "Bruno Madernas flexibler Materialbegriff: Eine Analyse des *Divertimento in due tempi* (1953)," *Musik & Ästhetik* 9, no. 33 (2005), pp. 30–47.

36   In the other three movements Maderna likewise omits the lyrics from *Fischia il vento*. He and Nono frequently used preexisting melodies and their rhythms in their works of this period (e.g. three traditional Venetian melodies in Maderna's *Composizione in tre tempi* (1954), *Bandiera rossa* in the second movement of Nono's *Epitaffio per Federico García Lorca I* (1951–52)), but never the original texts associated with these melodies. The first movement of Maderna's *Kranichsteiner Kammerkantate* sets a (slightly adjusted) letter of a resistance fighter condemned to death (Bruno Frittaion), the third movement features a letter by Franz Kafka to Milena Jesenská, and the fourth movement sets a prison letter by Antonio Gramsci. For a detailed description of these sources and translations see the pages devoted by the editor to "The Literary Texts" in Maderna, *Kranichsteiner Kammerkantate* (see note 31), pp. xv–xx. The sketch of Example 13 contains in the top right-hand corner Maderna's reference to the text used in the first movement ("Lettera di Bruno Frittaion / pag. 92"), taken from the original edition of *Lettere di condannati a morte della Resistenza italiana (8 settembre 1943 – 25 aprile 1945)*, ed. Piero Malvezzi and Giovanni Pirelli (Turin: Einaudi, 1952), p. 92 (new edn. 2003: pp. 124–25).

Integration of Parameters, Melody

That Maderna's engagement was of a broader humanist kind, grounded in a profound understanding of larger cultural and historical issues, is clearly evident from his letters, writings, interviews, and the works themselves (e.g. *Tre liriche greche*, 1948; *Ritratto di Erasmo*, 1969; *Ausstrahlung*, 1971). The following final example, from *Quartetto per archi in due tempi* (1955), dedicated to Luciano Berio, shows another instance where Maderna developed a musical material with a particular cultural meaning, as abstract as this meaning may be in this case. Example 15 illustrates how he constructed the twelve-tone series for the Quartet. As with *Composizione n. 2* and *Kranichsteiner Kammerkantate*, the series for this work – the sketch seems to suggest – is likewise rooted in a cultural object, this time not an ancient tune or more recent partisan song, but the historical ensemble of the string quartet itself in a fictional *scordatura* (i.e. without an actual retuning of the instruments). As shown on the top staff (→ **EX. 15**), Maderna imagines the four instruments tuned a semitone lower (cello, in bass clef), a semitone higher (first violin, after the second treble clef), a whole tone lower (second violin), and a whole tone higher (viola), respectively. He must have chosen this imagined *scordatura* so as to obtain a complete circle of fifths, which in turn yields all twelve pitch classes (reading from bottom to top the pitch classes in "cello" – "first violin" – "second violin" – "viola" produces a complete circle of fifths). At the bottom of the sketch, Maderna lists the pitches in ascending order with their corresponding pitch-class numbers (again with A=1, A♯=2, B=3, etc.). Through elimination of the three highest pitches, which duplicate pitch classes as marked by the brackets, Maderna obtains the twelve-tone series for the work.[37] This series ending on A♯, as a pitch-class series, is then subjected to order permutation by way of the matrix technique as shown in Example 16, which reproduces the first twelve of a total of sixty-five matrices.[38] The original series, labeled A (blue ink) in the first matrix (→ **EX. 16**), is transformed into series B through shifts whose values are taken from the succession of pitch-class numbers in the series itself (with two variations): the first dot of series A is shifted three positions to the right, the second dot ten positions, the third dot six positions, and so forth, following the number sequence 3-10-<u>6</u>-<u>5</u>-9-12-1-4-<u>8</u>-<u>7</u>-11-2 (the underlines mark the two variants compared to the original number sequence at the bottom of Ex. 15). The third series C is generated from the second via moves whose values follow a permutation of this number sequence.[39] And so forth.

---

37 For analyses of this work see Gianmario Borio, "Tempo e ritmo nelle composizioni seriali di Luigi Nono," *Schweizer Jahrbuch für Musikwissenschaft* 21 (2001), pp. 128–32; Markus Fein, *Die musikalische Poetik Bruno Madernas: Zum "seriellen" Komponieren zwischen 1951 und 1955* (Frankfurt am Main: Peter Lang, 2001), pp. 138–79; and Christoph Neidhöfer, "Vers un principe commun: Intégration de la hauteur et du rythme dans le *Quartetto per archi in due tempi* (1955)," in *à Bruno Maderna* (see note 12), vol. 2, pp. 323–58.

38 Pascal Decroupet analyzes the opening of the work with respect to the matrices and the assignment of durations in "1951–1955: Entwicklung und Verzweigung der Konzepte seriellen Komponierens," in *Im Zenit der Moderne: Die Internationalen Ferienkurse für Neue Musik Darmstadt 1946–1966*, ed. Gianmario Borio and Hermann Danuser (Freiburg im Breisgau: Rombach, 1997), vol. 1, pp. 344–47.

39 The number sequence is shifted by two positions to the left, followed by a partial retrograde reading: 10 (in place of 6) -5-9-12-1-4-8-7-11-2-2-[11 omitted]-7. These values are applied to the dots in series B, to obtain series C, in the order in which the corresponding pitch classes occurred in the original series. I discuss the larger principle behind the rotation of the number sequence and the substitutions in Neidhöfer, "Vers un principe commun" (see note 37).

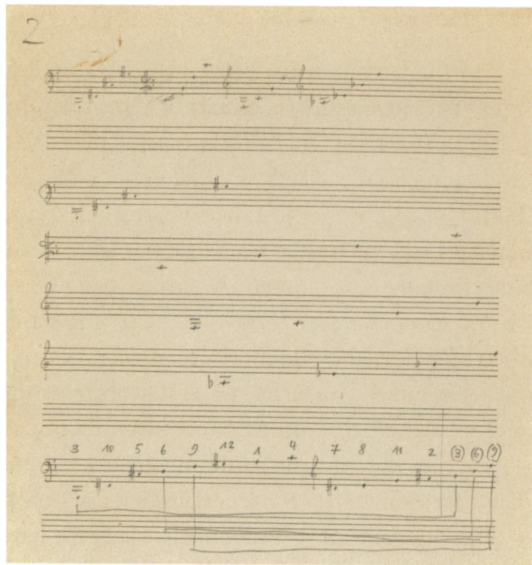

EX. 15   Bruno Maderna, sketch for the derivation of the twelve-tone series for *Quartetto per archi in due tempi*, PSS-BMC.

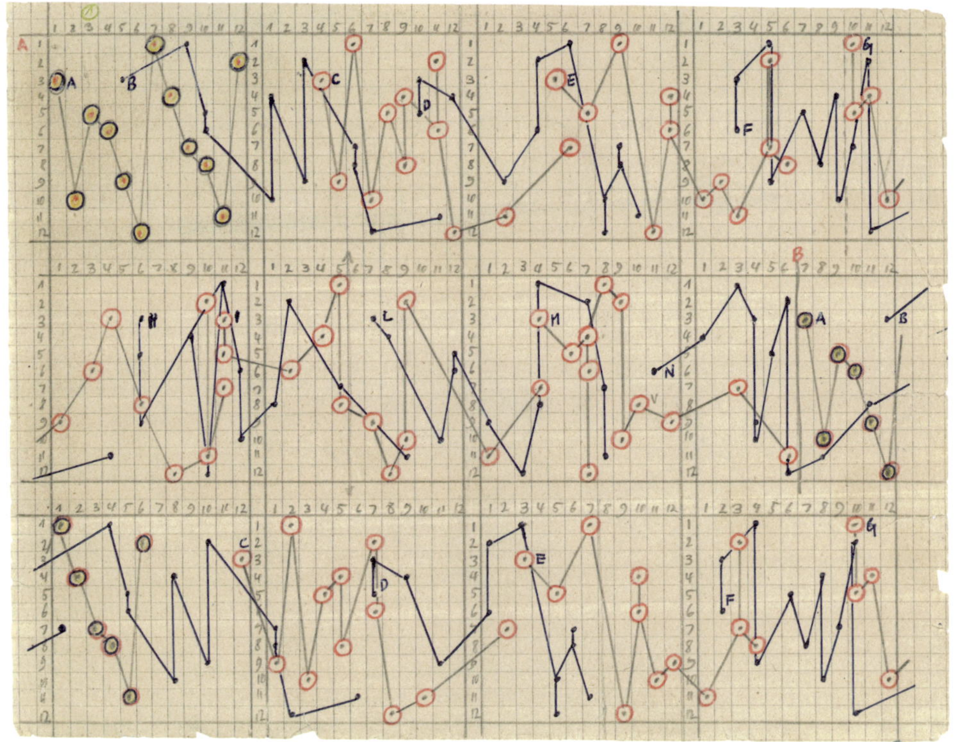

EX. 16   Bruno Maderna, sketch for *Quartetto per archi in due tempi*; PSS-BMC.

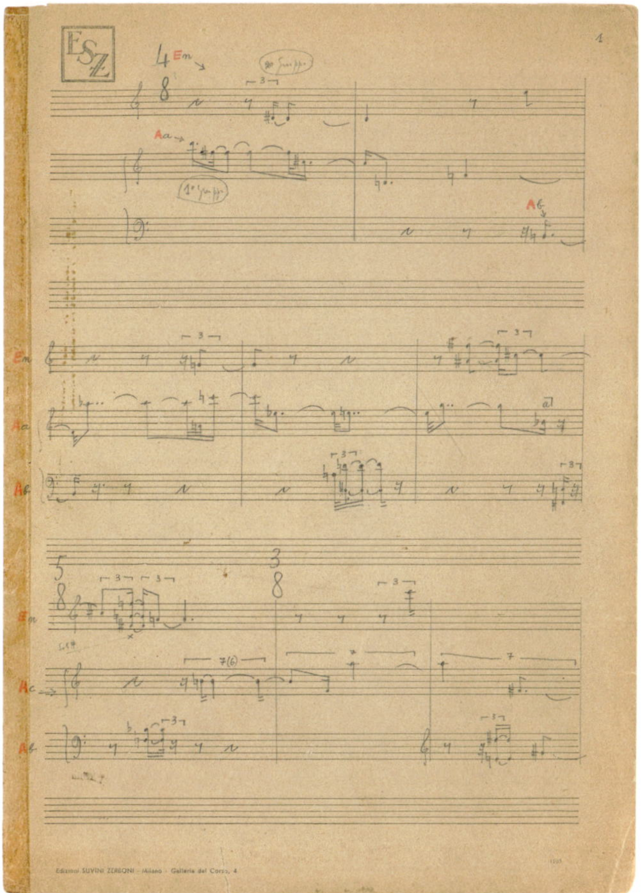

EX. 17   First page of continuity draft for *Quartetto per archi in due tempi,* in which Maderna identifies the serial layers; Luciano Berio Collection, PSS.

Example 17 reproduces the opening of Maderna's continuity draft in which he marks the serial layers (→ **EX. 17**).[40] In "group 1" we recognize the original series ("A$_a$") and the entries of the second and third ("A$_b$" and "A$_c$"). They are assigned durations based on the pitch-class number sequence, and permutations thereof, of the original series itself. The succession of durations in the melody of "A$_a$" follows the pattern (now counted as multiples of 32nds) 3-10-5-6-9-12-1-4-7-8-11-2, which corresponds to the pitch-class number sequence of this series (bottom staff of Ex. 15). Series "A$_b$," with its inserted rests resulting from the skipped columns in the matrices (Ex. 16), features durations that are multiples of triplet 32nds, according to the permuted number sequence 6-9[+]-1-8-11[+]-2-7-4-12[+]-5-10-3[+],

---

40 On the way to this draft, Maderna discarded a number of other possible realizations of the serial matrices. See Fein, *Die musikalische Poetik Bruno Madernas* (see note 37), pp. 147–58, and Neidhöfer, "Vers un principe commun" (see note 37), pp. 332–38.

EX. 18   Bruno Maderna, *Quartetto per archi in due tempi*,
first edition, I, bb. 1–10 (Milan: Suvini Zerboni, © 1956, S. 5182 Z.).

where the rests may be stretched, as I have indicated with [+], to ensure that series "A_a" and "A_b" remain aligned overall as per the matrices. This number sequence is again derived from the pitch-class order of the original series.[41] In this way, rhythm and pitch are fully integrated via a common principle, i.e. the pitch-class order, and permutations thereof, of the original twelve-tone series, which – as documented in Example 15 – originates from an arpeggiation of the open strings of the ensemble in a fictive artificial tuning.

In the final scoring of the opening of the Quartet (→ **EX. 18**), the line of series "A_a" is passed among different instruments (some pitches are transferred to different registers). By breaking up the line into shorter melodic gestures with highly charged expressive profiles through continuously changing timbres and dynamics, Maderna moves away from more traditional linear counterpoint while still appealing to the power of melody. Melody remains a hallmark feature of his music, both in the form of such shorter, highly expressive gestures of a post-Webernian kind and in the shape of longer, highly differentiated melodic lines, which Massimo Mila described in 1975, in a radio broadcast in which he discussed the oboe and violin concertos and many other works, as *"melodia assoluta."*[42] Melody is one of a large number of traits that Maderna carried over from earlier musical practices into his own, without returning to older musical styles, however.[43] His relationship with history is one of great responsibility: not only can the past not be ignored or altogether rejected, but what has come down to us – cultural, historical, and scientific knowledge, as well as human artifacts such as instruments and architectural spaces – must be engaged from, and brought into contact with, current perspectives, in a process of cross-fertilization between old and new ideas leading to the discovery of fresh musical territory. The *Quartetto per archi in due tempi*, with its new intricate serial counterpoint, timbral differentiations, and new rhythmic fluidity, represents a milestone in Maderna's compositional development, as he himself acknowledged in his letter of 15 April 1955 to Wolfgang Steinecke, the director of the Darmstadt Summer Courses:

> I think I have finally truly found myself with this work. – It is a case of healthy and positive "revolution in permanence." – Everything that I previously composed is old "kitsch"![44]

---

41 It is derived from the variant of the original number sequence (3-10-<u>6</u>-<u>5</u>-9-12-1-4-<u>8</u>-<u>7</u>-11-2) mostly via "skip-1" permutation, starting with 6 and reading from left to right and then from right to left. The principle behind this permutation is explained in Neidhöfer, "Vers un principe commun" (see note 37), p. 340.

42 Mila, *Maderna musicista europeo* (see note 2), pp. 36–43 (new edn. 1999: pp. 32–40).

43 The exceptions are works where Maderna purposely quotes or references older styles.

44 Bruno Maderna and Wolfgang Steinecke, *Carteggio/Briefwechsel*, ed. Rossana Dalmonte (Lucca: LIM, 2001), p. 90 (original in German).

STAGING AND PERFORMING TEXTS: A GLANCE THROUGH EARLY DRAMATURGICAL AND VOCAL WORKS

CLAUDIA VINCIS

The *Studi per "Il Processo" di Franz Kafka,* and Their Stage Sources

The *Studi*: the Chronology of their Genesis

The concert conducted by Hermann Scherchen on 13 September 1950 was the one fixed point among the dozens of variables and variations on the tortuous path to the finalization of the program for the "XIII Festival Internazionale di Musica Contemporanea della Biennale di Venezia," and in particular for the symphonic-choral series.[1] The event would have been remembered for having hosted the first Italian performance of *A Survivor from Warsaw* and, secondly, for the world premiere of *Studi per "Il Processo" di Franz Kafka* by the thirty-year-old Bruno Maderna, a work whose fortune would be more musicological (for its contribution to the development of serial techniques) than performative in nature. This is the program for the event:

> Darius Milhaud, *Suite* for two pianos and orchestra, op. 300
> Bruno Maderna, *Studi per "Il Processo" di Kafka*, for soprano, speaker, and orchestra[2]
> Wladimir Vogel, *Sette aspetti di una serie dodecafonica* [Seven aspects of a dodecaphonic series], for orchestra
> Arnold Schoenberg, *Il superstite di Varsavia* [A Survivor from Warsaw], for speaker, male chorus, and orchestra
> Rome RAI Symphony Orchestra and the Teatro La Fenice Chorus

Several modifications had been made to the program in the previous months, except for the name of the conductor, Darius Milhaud ("the best and most insatiable devotee of dodecaphonics that exists in the world of modern music"),[3] those of the two pianists Arthur Gold and Robert Fizdale, and that of Maderna. Even Arnold Schoenberg and his

---

Most of the sources consulted for this essay are housed at the Paul Sacher Foundation in Basel, in the Bruno Maderna Collection (PSS-BMC), and at the Archivio Storico delle Arti Contemporanee della Biennale di Venezia (ASAC). My heartfelt thanks go to my friends and colleagues who have shared the results and documents of their research with me, in particular Michele Chiappini, Paolo Dal Molin, and Angela Ida De Benedictis, the last two also being careful and benevolent readers.

1   ASAC, Fondo storico, serie Musica, envelope no. 3, "Festival Internazionale di Musica Contemporanea 1949–1950."

2   A performance of the work conducted by Scherchen is kept on tape "A. 034" at the RAI's Archivio dello Studio di Fonologia Musicale in Milan; see *The Studio di Fonologia: A Musical Journey 1954–1983, Update 2008–2012*, ed. Maria Maddalena Novati and John Dack (Milan: Ricordi, 2012), p. 234. The recording is unavailable for consultation, resulting as "damaged" on the fact sheet, but it is most likely that it is the premiere.

3   The definition is by Franco Abbiati, in his review of the "Musica contemporanea al XIII Festival di Venezia," in *Il Nuovo Corriere della Sera* (Milan, 14 September 1950).

"Der Tanz um das goldene Kalb" from *Moses und Aron* first appears and is then deleted from the surviving draft copies; it seems that originally the composer himself had intended to present it.[4] Documents relating to the Biennale, held at the end of March–April 1950, mention the Italian composer's *Musiche su Kafka*, but in the plans dated 14 May 1950 this has been replaced with the far vaguer *Musica per orchestra*:

Symphonic Concert conducted by H. Scherchen / Rome RAI Symphony Orchestra, (Teatro La Fenice, 21.30)

Milhaud	Concerto for two pianos and orchestra	1st perf.
Soloists:	Gold-Fizdale Duo	
Maderna	*Musica per orchestra*	1st perf.
D. Santa Cruz	Concerto for piano and orchestra	1st perf.
Soloist:	C. Arrau	
W. Vogel	*Sette aspetti di una serie*[5]	1st perf.

Moreover, in January of the same year, Maderna had seen the possible performance of his new work by Milan's Orchestra dei Pomeriggi Musical go up in smoke. The group's founder and artistic director was Ferdinando Ballo, who also happened to be the organizer of the Biennale Festival.[6] If this new work had been *Composizione n. 2* for orchestra and Maderna had thought of bringing it to Venice in the impossibility of performing it in Milan, it would have made its way to Darmstadt at the latest in late May,[7] thus excluding it from the Biennale, as per "regulations."[8]

---

4   A copy of Hermann Scherchen's letter to Ferdinando Ballo, dated 11 January 1950 (PSS-BMC), reveals in fact that "Arnold Schoenberg has just invited me to conduct the premiere of his great piece 'Der Tanz um das goldene Kalb' from the opera *Moses und Aron*. | Since this work will also be in the Ars Viva [catalogue], I in turn am offering you the world premiere for Venice. | As you know, there has been talk of this work for forty years among initiated musicians. Some American friends, who had the opportunity to see the finished version of this great piece by Schoenberg, wrote to me enthusiastically. Schoenberg himself informed me that a great ballet and a huge set are needed. This world premiere would be a truly sensational event for you and cause a stir for Venice, like never before | Kindly phone to let me know of your broad but also binding decision" (original in German).

5   ASAC, Fondo storico, serie Musica, envelope no. 3, "Festival Internazionale di Musica Contemporanea 1949–1950."

6   For the concert he would conduct in Milan on February 4, Scherchen had unsuccessfully proposed "drei Zwölftonwerke zur Uraufführung zu bringen" (three dodecaphonic works to be performed for the first time) to Ballo (see Scherchen's letter of 31 December 1949 to Luigi Nono, kept in the Luigi Nono Archive in Venice), including one by Maderna (see Maderna's letter of 29 January 1950 to Scherchen, kept at the Akademie der Künste in Berlin, in which he also claims to have received the news from Ballo himself).

7   See Bruno Maderna and Wolfgang Steinecke, *Carteggio/Briefwechsel*, ed. Rossana Dalmonte (Lucca: LIM, 2001), pp. 37–41, letters from Steinecke, dated 15 April and 24 May 1950.

8   By decision of the Commission for the Biennale Festival, in agreement with the objections raised by Ferrante Mecenati and Guido Pannain, works by Italian authors were admitted to the festival program only if they had never been performed before, not even on radio. Among all the documents attesting to this motion, see the "Progetto di una Memoria per la Presidenza della Biennale di Venezia relativa ai programmi per il Festival Internazionale di Musica Contemporanea" (Plan for a Memoir for the Presidencies of the Venice Biennale relating to the Programs for the International Festival of Contemporary Music), dated Milan, 15 January 1950, and kept at the ASAC, Fondo storico, serie Musica.

Nonetheless, Maderna's letters, particularly those he exchanged with Scherchen, seem to restore a more stable link, at least in his intentions, between the future *Studi* and the "XIII Festival Internazionale di Musica Contemporanea," even though the documentary discontinuity suggests that momentary second thoughts cannot be ruled out (indeed, *Musica per orchestra* might itself even be a draft).

A letter from the composer dating back to the end of February of that year leaves no room for misunderstandings about the desired destination or the state of the art of the project:

> for the next Venetian festival, I will write a special work for speaker and large orchestra based on a text by Kafka. I would be happy if you [Scherchen] agreed to conduct it, and later, if you wish, I promise to speak to Ballo.[9]

It thus seems that on that date the composer had only one aim in mind. On 5 April, Scherchen and Maderna talked about the publication of the work, and therefore about the priorities of the catalogue of Scherchen's Ars Viva music publishing house, with no suggestion of the existence of a score. A few more facts about the nature of the composition could in the meantime have emerged in talks or exchanges of letters that have yet to be accounted for, if Scherchen felt that radio was the perfect broadcasting medium:

> My dear friend Bruno, / […] Which do you think would be more important to publish first: Maderna – Kaffka [sic] or *Il Musica*?[10] We only have to choose one and I almost think that the Kafka would be even more important, since I also hope to use it for the radio.[11]

It seems that at the beginning of the following month Scherchen was still in the dark about how the work was progressing. The tone of his "Have you finished the score of the *'Processo'*?" on 8 May reveals a degree of concern.[12] Then four days later he replied to Maderna – evidently reassured by the promise of its imminent dispatch – saying, "So I look forward to […] the orchestral parts of your music. Writing your work on Kafka on staff paper in good black ink will suffice. (No scratchings out, please, since corrections must be pasted on this paper),"[13] suggesting that in mid-May the composition of the *Studi* was well under way, or at least this is what Maderna would have us believe.

And so, on 5 June, the program for the September concert was reformulated by Scherchen in a version that is still far from the final one and only partially attested – it seems – in the surviving documents of the Biennale: Schoenberg's name no longer appears, also temporarily deleted from the drafts of the program, but "Maderna – Kafka" and other new additions are clearly involved, presumably all with the backing of the same

---

9   Typewritten letter from Bruno Maderna to Hermann Scherchen, dated 22 February 1950 (Berlin, Akademie der Künste). Only a photocopy of the document remains in the archive. Original in German.

10   The reference is to the already mentioned *Composizione n. 2* for orchestra.

11   Letter from Scherchen to Maderna, dated 5 April 1950 (PSS-BMC; original in German). For more on this letter see also note 16.

12   Letter from Scherchen to Maderna, dated 8 May 1950 (PSS-BMC; original in German).

13   Letter from Scherchen to Maderna, dated 12 May 1950, in which he invites him to obtain the particular fourteen-staff manuscript paper from Sanzoni in Florence, from Mr. Mauksch's shop (PSS-BMC; original in German).

conductor-publisher: "I have just informed [Venice] – the Program will be: / Vogel / San Domingo [Domingo Santa Cruz] / Maderna – Kafka / Milhaud / Chavez."[14] Vogel's *Sette aspetti di una serie dodecafonica* would always feature on the program; Carlos Chávez' *La hija de Cólquide* would have wandered among the symphonic events, until it was omitted along with Santa Cruz' Concerto for piano and orchestra.

A letter from Ballo, dated 12 July, in favor of Maderna's proposal to "entrust the soprano part to Ginevra Vivante,"[15] clearly shows that the vocal component had been modified with respect to the "two speakers" of before. It also shows that the *Studi* had been on the official program of the Festival for quite some time, even though nothing was known about the title, length, or indeed the score, which was probably still incomplete:

> Dearest Bruno / I need to know titles-subtitles-length etc. of your piece pending receipt of the score. […] I am therefore eagerly awaiting the two scores, especially yours that really interests me.[16]

According to the date at the bottom of the autograph manuscript, the composition was completed on August 16, 1950, less than a month, that is, from its first performance. This is not surprising considering the serious difficulties that Maderna seems to have encountered

---

14   Postcard sent by Scherchen to Maderna from Prague on 5 June 1950 (PSS-BMC; original in German). As the Biennale documents indirectly confirm (see the prospectus transcribed above, note 5), the "mysterious San Domingo" (Rossana Dalmonte, "Premessa," in Bruno Maderna, *Studi per "Il Processo" di F. Kafka per soprano, voce recitante e orchestra* [1950], ed. Rossana Dalmonte (Milan: Suvini Zerboni, 2010), p. vii) is none other than the Chilean composer Domingo Santa Cruz (see *The Harvard Biographical Dictionary of Music*, ed. Don Michael Randel (Cambridge, MA: Harvard University Press, 1996), p. 784), whom Scherchen had met two years earlier during his tour of Chile and Argentina (17 April – 12 August 1948), when he had been awarded an honorary doctorate from the University of Santiago de Chile (April 1948), conferred on him by the then dean, Domingo Santa Cruz. See *Hermann Scherchen: Werke und Briefe*, ed. Joachim Lucchesi (Bern: Peter Lang, 1991), p. 287.

15   The Venetian soprano Ginevra Vivante (1906–96) was widely known for her early and contemporary chamber and oratorio repertoire (in particular by Dallapiccola, Malipiero, Zanon, Cortese, Stravinsky, and Vivaldi; see Franco Rossi, "Ginevra Vivante," *Venezia Arti* (1991), p. 157). Her first meeting with Maderna could date back to the "Ciclo di musiche vivaldiane: Concerto di musica sacra" on 3 October 1947, conducted by Nino Sanzogno, since she was one of the performers on the program, which also included Maderna's revision of the Concerto for violin and orchestra F. I n. 13. The following year Scherchen conducted her at Ca' Giustinian in the concluding concerts of the 1948 International Conducting Course, attended by the two young composers, Nono and Maderna. On 17 September 1949, Vivante appeared again in the "Concerto sinfonico vocale di musiche inedite di Antonio Vivaldi" at the Teatro La Fenice, during which the transcription of the *Beatus Vir* was performed, the hymn for soloists, double chorus, and double orchestra by Bruno Maderna, conducted by Angelo Ephrikian. On Maderna's transcriptional activity in the Venetian years (1946–52) see also, in this volume, the essay by Michele Chiappini, pp. 193–225.

16   Letter from Ferdinando Ballo to Bruno Maderna, dated 12 July 1950 (PSS-BMC, original in Italian). The second score mentioned is that of Maderna's transcription of the cantata *Il Sepolcro* (1705) by Marc'Antonio Ziani, performed, with Mario Rossi conductor, on 12 September, in the same series of symphonic-choral concerts at the Festival. In the aforementioned letter of 5 April (see note 11), Scherchen had already expressed his thanks "für die Cantate" (for the cantata). The passage introduced the doubt that "Cantate" could instead refer to the *Studi*, with all that follows for the chronology of their genesis (as Dalmonte maintains in the aforementioned "Premessa"; see note 14). In actual fact, no other source supports such a hypothesis, and shortly after in the same document we read: "was ist nun mit der Cantata sepolcra in Florenz?" (what's happened to the Cantata sepolcra in Florence?), which allays every doubt.

in the previous weeks. He had thus apologized to Wladimir Vogel in late June for having hitherto ignored his invitations to speak at the Second International Congress of Dodecaphony to be held in Locarno at the end of August:

> Maestro and dear friend,
> Please forgive my long delay in replying to your most gracious letters. Lateness due to my absence from Venice and mental exhaustion that in recent times has forced me to absolute rest. I can't tell you how difficult it is in these conditions to fulfil my commitments: to write a composition on Kafka's text for the Venetian festival, to conduct a concert at the Basilica of Maxentius in Rome on August 24, to prepare my lecture for the 2nd Locarno Congress [...] I don't feel like speaking about my own work regarding the harmonic and rational possibilities of the series, both because to date I haven't perfected the system, and because of the already mentioned exhaustion that has impaired my work opportunities to quite an extent.[17]

And the trouble persisted. It was Maderna's first wife, Raffaella Tartaglia, who wrote a short reply to Mario Corti, the artistic director of Accademia di Santa Cecilia concerts, on 6 August 1950, because her husband was "too busy to deal with correspondence."[18]

Thus, everything seems to have gone down to the wire, including the introductory notes to the *Studi* for the Festival's general program compiled by Emilia Zanetti, the event's chief press officer, who put together one of Maderna's writings from 1946 with excerpts from a fleeting conversation and some of his brief notes on his latest effort:

> Nowadays, when we have neither schools, convictions, nor poetics in common, and when the artist no longer has external control over the quality of his work, we often submit ourselves to subjective criticism, to a subjective idea of what is 'beautiful.' Even now we continue to see the results of both the disorientated and eclectic taste of the public, and also of the arrogant isolation of musicians: disjecta membra, a loss of the unity of intention and force which through successive generations animated great musicians toward the realization of an ideal of ordered beauty.
>
> Of course we cannot speak of a return ab imis as a cure for that excessive particularism of the so fashionable individualist stance ... but there is no doubt that a serious obstacle will be removed when we approach music with the same modesty and the same desire for simplicity, communality, even anonymity, which gave rise to the 'tropes' and 'antiphons' of those monks who completely disdained fame, and who wrote their music for the greater glory of God.[19]

---

17 Letter from Maderna to Vogel, dated 28 June 1950, published in Carlo Piccardi, "Tra ragioni umane e ragioni estetiche: i dodecafonici a congresso," in *Norme con ironie: Scritti per i settant'anni di Ennio Morricone*, ed. Sergio Miceli (Milan: Suvini Zerboni, 1998), pp. 205–69: 267–68 and no. 115.

18 Letter from Raffaella Tartaglia to Mario Corti, dated 6 August 1950, kept at the Accademia di Santa Cecilia in Rome, Historical Archives.

19 The two paragraphs come from Bruno Maderna's "Confessione," published in the program of the *IX Festival Internazionale di Musica Contemporanea – La Biennale di Venezia 1946*, 15–22 September 1946, Teatro la Fenice (Venice: Teatro La Fenice, 1946), pp. 61–62 (now in Bruno Maderna, *Amore e curiosità: Scritti, frammenti e interviste sulla musica*, ed. Angela Ida De Benedictis, Michele Chiappini, and Benedetta Zucconi (Milan: il Saggiatore, 2020), pp. 89–91). A different English translation of this text, entitled "From the 'Confessions' of Five Composers of the Giovane Scuola Italiana (IX International Festival of Contemporary Music, Venice 'Biennale' 1946)," is in Raymond Fearn, *Bruno Maderna* (Chur: Harwood, 1990), pp. 293–94.

This is what Maderna has to say about himself in 1946, to mark the occasion of the "premiere" of his *Serenata per undici strumenti* at that year's Venetian Festival. Are we to believe that his profound attachment to dodecaphony, already noticeable in the Concerto for two pianos, harps and drums (1948 Festival),[20] has been appeased by the rule, the need for that humility – read selflessness – that the young musician saw as a condition for creating?

Regardless of how this certainly significant turning point in the composer's artistic life took place, he is not fond of underlining its technical importance. And even less so for this very recent score, its ink barely dry, which will probably be realized in the broader version of a stage drama. Even the form, which is the alternation between a canon and a lied, is in expressive functions. It is, in fact, the relentlessness of the trial "which slowly turns into a sentence," in contrast to Leni's erotic motif, which seems to represent the longed-for escape, and which then leads back to the trial, almost always via the tortuous paths of the psychic complexes. But the author cautions against "presuming to solve the difficult problems contained in *Il processo* [*The Trial*] by transferring them to music's most passionate lyricism." The attempt to approach Kafka's great work is already sufficient ambition for him: [to approach] this apologue of modern-day man and his tragic blindness.[21]

Further changes were also made to the program of the concert conducted by Scherchen, announced on the bill released to the press in late August,[22] which still lists Chávez, whose name was then removed. However, almost beyond all expectations, at least on the part of the promoters and performers of the premiere of Maderna's *Kafka*, the score arrived in time to prepare for its performance, given that Scherchen was satisfied with both the sectional rehearsals carried out by the Rome RAI orchestra the week before the Venetian concert, and by the "excellent" speaker Ubaldo Lay.[23]

---

20 Published as a *Concerto per due pianoforti e strumenti*. The first performance took place at the Biennale Festival on 17 September 1948 (soloists: Gino Gorini and Sergio Lorenzi; conductor: Ettore Gracis).

21 E[milia] Z[anetti], [untitled], in *La Biennale di Venezia, XIII Festival Internazionale di Musica Contemporanea – IV Autunno Musicale Veneziano*, Teatro la Fenice 4–24 September 1950 [general program], pp. 62–63. Unless otherwise specified, all the reviews quoted from now on are translated from the Italian.

22 ASAC, Fondo storico, serie Musica, envelope no. 3, *Festival Internazionale di Musica Contemporanea 1949–1950*, plan with permission from the police station, dated 21 August.

23 In fact, on the postcard Scherchen sent from Rome to Bruno Maderna, Raffaella Tartaglia, and Luigi Nono on 7 September 1950, he writes: "we've already 'finished' Kafka with regular split rehearsals / I hope that Vivante will be quite ready when I start in Venice! / book me the room at the Monaco (a twin) / the Speaker is good – this afternoon we're already going to do his work with the speaking / […] I arrive on 12 IX at 5 (?) in the morning and please wait for me at the station" (PSS-BMC, original in less-than-perfect Italian). The misinterpretation of the place of sending (Prague in place of Rome) and the month the postcard was sent ("VI," June, instead of "IX," September), led Rossana Dalmonte to formulate conjectures that she cannot support, and to erroneously backdate the completion of the work to three months before it actually happened; see Dalmonte, "Premessa" (see note 14), p. vii. At the time, the Roman actor Ubaldo Lay (1917–84) was a permanent member of the Radio Roma (RAI) Prose Company and had worked with Maderna that same year, as the voice for the radio play *Il mio cuore è nel Sud* (1949), broadcast on the second Italian network (Rete Rossa) on 11 March 1950.

Reaction to the Premiere

The outcomes of the XIII Festival di Musica Contemporanea enjoyed a different reception in the national and foreign press. A number of Italian critics complained strongly about the absence of musical theater,[24] whereas the more positive foreign ones stressed the importance of the symphonic-choral concerts, in which they recognized "the appearance of an early Italian school." "This is really more than enough," explained Ballo, "to justify the symphonic part of the 1950 Festival. *With the exception of a piece by Maderna,* all the pieces enjoyed tremendous public success."[25]

A glance through the articles shows us that – emphasis on the successes apart – the organizer of the review was telling the truth: in fact, except for a "large group of listeners who applauded fiercely without knowing [...] about dodecaphony [...] and who were not at all familiar with the composer,"[26] most of the audience present were described – with disapproval, sarcasm, or a shared condescending attitude depending on the journalist – as bored, annoyed, or rowdy:[27]

> The *Studii* [*sic*] miraculously came to an end. There was an indulgent audience in the theater who, however, did not want to have anything to do with studying.[28]

> The audience that had applauded Milhaud largely disapproved of Maderna, even interrupting a hearing toward the end that, at least in the orchestral part, seemed to go on too long.[29]

> The concert conducted by Hermann Scherchen unleashed those noisy discussions that ruin calmness and transport listeners to another world, almost a world of sport. [...] The *Studi per "Il Processo" di Franz Kafka* (for soprano, speaker, and orchestra) by Bruno Maderna have transformed the Teatro La Fenice into a *bona fide* stadium, because protests, jokes, and the other run-of-the-mill reactions are unacceptable, they condemn the audience, not the composer [...].[30]

---

24 See in particular Giuseppe Pugliese, "Squallido senza l'opera il Festival della Musica," *Il Gazzettino di Venezia* (28 November 1950) (ASAC, Press Review, *Festival Internazionale di Musica Contemporanea 1950*), an article whose publication in the main regional newspaper had sparked the wrath of the organizers. Budget restrictions and regulatory limits (see note 8) led to investment in ballet rather than musical theater, to contain costs without reducing the target audience and at the same time to try and differentiate the Venetian event from similar European ones.

25 Ferdinando Ballo, *Relazione sul XIII Festival 1950. Realizzazione del programma*, p. 7 di 11 (ASAC, Fondo storico, serie Musica, envelope n. 3, *Festival Internazionale di Musica Contemporanea 1949–1950*). The following year, Maderna himself recalled the event in "Un aspetto della musica del dopoguerra," *La Biennale di Venezia* 5 (August 1951), p. 40: "From 1946 onwards, the interest of the public and of the musicians was always growing, until it reached an immediacy of assimilation, particularly for the compositions of Arnold Schoenberg: opus 46 *A Survivor from Warsaw* (1948) enjoyed such enthusiastic approval that the performances had to be repeated, just as happened with the concert conducted by Hermann Scherchen at the last Biennale Festival in Venice (1950)" (reprinted in Maderna, *Amore e curiosità* (see note 19), pp. 229–31: 230).

26 Emilia Zanetti, "Arcadia e inferno a Venezia," *La Fiera Letteraria* (Sunday, 1 October 1950), p. 7.

27 "Uproarious" is instead the adjective with which the performer Ginevra Vivante records the evening in her diary, also adding that "during the performance of Maderna's music. Whistles and screams (a waste of Vivante!). Cond. Scherchen; Ubaldo Lay speaker – at the Fenice." The photocopy of her diary, together with a photograph of this premiere, in which the soprano is pictured next to Maderna and Scherchen, is kept at the Fondazione Ugo e Olga Levi in Venice, Fondo Ginevra Vivante.

28 Abbiati, review (see note 3).

29 Beniamino Dal Fabbro, "Letture di Kafka con formulette dodecafoniche," *Milano sera* (14 September 1950).

30 Gian Francesco Malipiero, "Il XIII Festival Musicale Veneziano (II Parte)," p. 2, Venice, Fondazione Giorgio Cini, Archivio Gian Francesco Malipiero (typewritten document).

The usual detractors, like Guido Piamonte, served as a sounding board. Close to Malipiero and the musical institutions of the city, he described the *Studi* as a "joke in bad taste," one played both by Maderna on the listeners, but also by Ballo on his successors, taking delight in pointing out the serious precedent that had been created: "when faced with Maderna's piece, even the most detached and clueless amateur, the most ham-fisted dabbler in melodramas, the maker of provincial operas, has the full and unquestionable right to demand admittance to the Festival."[31] For his part, Guido Cardi perceived "a painful representation of dodecaphony, or rather, of phonophobia."[32] Emilio Radius, more at home with Verdi than with Schoenberg, could not see "any unity," "any atmosphere, in the *Due* [sic] *studi per 'Il Processo' di Franz Kafka*," but "only instrumental and vocal exasperation": "Listening to them– he wrote – you think of a poor devil who is about to drown and who needs to reach out at any cost."[33] However, since here, just as in Cardi's rather harsh criticism, the title of the work is reported in the "extra" version published in *Radiocorriere*,[34] rather than in that of the general program, it is conceivable that this audience was not sitting in the seats of the Teatro la Fenice, but in front of a transmitter. And such a doubt appears well-founded if one considers that a year and a half earlier, Maderna had accused Radius of having reviewed Palermo's XXIII Festival di Musica Contemporanea (22–30 April 1949) "without having listened to the music or at least without having understood it."[35]

On the opposite front, we have the unreserved admiration of the co-editor of the *Diapason* magazine, Luigi La Pegna, who was known to be close to the dodecaphonic world:

> Let us say that Maderna (Venice 1920) is the one who struck us most of all. A single listening is certainly not enough to judge such a complex and dynamic work, but it is impossible to have any doubts about it. In any case, after listening to his *Studi* we glimpsed some evident qualities in Maderna of which his previous works contained no suggestion.[36]

Or the comments by the German composer Brigitte Schiffer and by another Germanist:

---

31   Guido Piamonte, "Musica Contemporanea a Venezia: Modesto risultato del 13° Festival," *La Provincia* (Como, 4 October 1950); also published in *Il giornale di Vicenza* (11 October 1950).

32   Giulio Cardi, "Burrasca dodecafonica al Festival Musicale di Venezia," *L'Umbria* (Perugia, 6 October 1950).

33   Emilio Radius, "Qualcuno al festival musicale di Venezia ha avuto intanto il coraggio di non annoiare," *L'Europeo* (24 September 1950).

34   In the announcement of the live broadcast on RAI's "Rete Rossa" of the "Concerto Sinfonico," conducted by Scherchen from Venice's Teatro La Fenice, the piece was in fact mentioned as *Due studi per "Il Processo" di Franz Kafka*; see *Radiocorriere* 27, no. 37 (10–16 September 1950), p. 24.

35   This is what Maderna writes in a draft of a letter to the director of *L'Europeo*, Arrigo Benedetti (undated, and dictated to Raffaella Tartaglia), challenging some of Radius's statements regarding alleged performances by Schoenberg (that actually never happened) or trenchant criticism of pieces by young Italian composers performed in Palermo: "[…] And out of the goodness of your heart please ask your collaborator not to keep on thundering from above with such categorically slanderous headlines and to read the scores he speaks of far more carefully, because it is set down in black and white and I believe that it has never been and never will be pleasant for anyone to have to, I won't say, go back on but at least regret the judgments made, probably without having listened to the music or at least without having understood anything. / I don't know if you have read the aforementioned report, but I believe that out of journalistic correctness it would be appropriate to invite Mr. Radius to moderate his too offensive incompetence" (PSS-BMC).

36   La Pegna, "Les Jeunes Italiens a Venise," *Diapason* 1, no. 10 (October 1950), pp. 28–30: 30. Original in French.

There is nothing superficial in Bruno Maderna's *Studi per "Il Processo" di Kafka,* an obsessive, hallucinating work of a violence, a force, a vehemence dictated by his conviction, by his mastery of the subject; the revolt of the spirit against injustice, the voice of conscience, the terror of being swallowed up by the law machine, and all this not on a personal but on a general level: this is what this inexorable music expresses with its hard language, with its precise, clear, rich, varied, original instrumentation, with this sound that is as haunting and overwhelming as its theme.[37]

Impressive topics, in the hands of dodecaphonic musicians, are undoubtedly those passages from *Il processo* di Kafka that the young Bruno Maderna presented us, not without a great deal of ingenuity, in a suggestive soundtrack, which had an exquisite interpreter in Ginevra Vivante.[38]

The latter acclamation, from the poet and Germanist Giorgio Vigolo, however, was not entirely sincere, as, on the contrary, it was subject to an awkward compromise, to a paradoxical acknowledgment (similar to the one demanded by his review of Dallapiccola's *Prigioniero*).[39] Receiving such appraisal meant questioning technical choices and aesthetic orientations:

The search for impressive topics, even if they are frightfully distressful and depressing, denounces a deep-seated crisis of the system which feels strangled by its technical aridity and is trying to open violent ways of communication. This could demonstrate that even the dodecaphonic movement has not completely escaped a general neo-Romantic climate which seems to want to characterize the second half of the twentieth century, as the first half was characterized by Neoclassicism, which today has completely faded away.[40]

The reception of the *Studi per "Il Processo" di Franz Kafka* was undoubtedly further compromised by the incautious comparison appearing on 13 September 1950:

Victory belonged to Arnold Schoenberg, whose *A Survivor from Warsaw* was encored, amidst the enthusiastic applause of the large audience, guided through the demanding haven of Schoenberg's enthusiasm by Maestro Scherchen's magic baton, a formidable connoisseur of contemporary music and a great conductor.[41]

Of the "three dodecaphonic works written by three composers of different temperament and preparation who presented different aspects of the atonal system," *Studi per "Il Processo" di Kafka* did not even hold their own against Vogel's "scholastic" *Sette aspetti di una serie dodecafonica.* Some critics felt that the concert program – in contrast to the documentary evidence – had been created around the first Italian performance of the *Survivor.* And although it had finally given Maderna the chance to also appear at the Biennale Festival alongside mature and international composers, and particularly the father of dodecaphony, it had actually done him an immediate disservice. Emilia Zanetti sympathized, pointing out that

---

37 Brigitte Schiffer, "XIIIème Festival International de Musique Contemporaine: IVème automne musical vénitien," *Bourse Egyptienne* (Cairo, 4 December 1950). Original in French.
38 Giorgio Vigolo, "Clima neoromantico," *Il Mondo* (Rome, 30 September 1950), p. 15.
39 See Giorgio Vigolo, "Il prigioniero dodecafonico" (1949), in idem, *Mille e una sera all'opera e al concerto* (Florence: Sansoni, 1971), pp. 35–38: 37.
40 Vigolo, "Clima neoromantico" (see note 38).
41 Luigi Maria Guadagnino, "Panorama del Festival Internazionale di Venezia," *Portici* (Bologna, December 1950). Ibid. for the following quotations in the text.

Maderna himself had described "his latest product" as nothing more than "an attempt," giving it the name of *Studi*:

> Thus it must be assumed that coming together as one with an otherwise successful piece by Schoenberg, as most critics saw it, is the least the thirty-year-old composer could have hoped for. [...] From dodecaphonic orthodoxy, which he is increasingly exploring, to the means used in today's performance: the speaking voice (Ubaldo Lay) and soprano voice, that of the servant Leni (Ginevra Vivante), the materials may not appear dissimilar. Except that the difference in practice is already that which exists between a maestro and a willing epigone at the beginning of his path.[42]

As far as the intermediate positions are concerned, the above-cited words of Maderna's "Venetian" Maestro, which magnanimously play on the literal meaning of the work's title, then went on to justify so much blame for the audience by defending the student: "they are studies, that is, preparatory works; one can always hope that the experiment will be followed by a successful work."[43] Indeed, most of the commentators who saw the *Studi* as an unsuccessful attempt or as a composer's mistake felt that he had lost his way. "Accepting or rejecting," observed an authoritative dodecaphonist, "is sometimes too easy: it is better postponed, after due consideration, hoping that greater maturity leads to a greater possibility of full expression."[44] Instead, the considerate promoter of *Musique contemporaine*, the short-lived magazine published by the prestigious committee, conscientiously indicated "the need for a double effort: on the part of the audience, that of accepting innovation, and on the part of the composer, that of adapting his style, so that they both may be happy to meet each other in the future."[45]

Another cause for scandal was first of all the spoken part, then the composition of the orchestra. Too long and "rational," wrote Massimo Mila about the former, complaining more generally – the *Sprechgesang* of *A Survivor from Warsaw* being a contributing factor – about the intrusion of the spoken word in the concert.[46] This is what sparked the aforementioned Radius's superficial comparison with another *Sprecher* from the year before:

> another attempt at contemporary musical drama with speech and song. Maderna's model seems to be Ghedini. In fact, his two studies resemble the *Billy Budd* we saw last year; but we must add that, with their hastiness, they complicate the problem instead of solving it and compromise Ghedini's already difficult assumption.[47]

As regards the text, only Riccardo Malipiero found his intention to set *The Trial* deleterious, considering it a transition for a historically and aesthetically complete world (a view also endorsed by some literary critics). He thus differed from Vigolo and from those who, on the contrary, had seen in the *Studi* "an important step in evolving an individual attitude

---

42 Zanetti, "Arcadia e inferno a Venezia" (see note 26).

43 Malipiero, "Il XIII Festival Musicale Veneziano" (see note 30).

44 Riccardo Malipiero, "Il XIII Festival di musica a Venezia," *Il Popolo: Quotidiano del Mattino* 7, no. 218 (1950), p. 3.

45 Tsveta Maneva, "Festival de Venise," *Revue Musique Contemporaine* 1 (1951), pp. 66–67: 66. Original in French.

46 Massimo Mila, "Musica documentaria di Schoenberg: Il festival musicale a Venezia," *l'Unità* (14 September 1950), p. 13.

47 Radius, "Qualcuno al festival musicale di Venezia" (see note 33).

toward dodecaphonism," and more precisely a change "to the 'psychological,' 'romantic' aspects of the idiom."[48]

> Bruno Maderna, or the Maderna of unrest. This young Venetian musician is in fact one of the disconcerting young people of his generation: he carries out research on himself and on the cosmos of abstract music, he tends to express himself through all that the art of sounds can give, technique and spirit, tools and form. And his research matures in works that, like the one this evening, sometimes leave rather bloody traces: his arrangements tend to go beyond normal limits and in this one senses the effort of a mindful personality, of an aspiration, but who is sometimes troubled by research that goes beyond his own means. *In this particular case, the connection to Kafka's famous book evidently takes him into the field of expressionism. In other words, a field that we believe to be out of date, but one that he wishes to get right to the heart of:* it is therefore an experience and as such respectable and noble, which we consider completely personal, a preparation for something that will certainly come, and which will be something different to what is still being presented to us.[49]

The other critics, however, were dissatisfied with the passages that Maderna had selected from *The Trial*, considering them inadequate for the purpose. The day after the concert, Franco Abbiati in the *Corriere della Sera* and Beniamino Dal Fabbro in *Milano Sera* started pointing this out. The former disapproved of the predominance of the "narrative element" over the "novel's psychological one" and the management of the music, while lukewarmly applauding its "lyrical aims" and the "precise sound timbre."[50] The latter was even more unkind:

> This is summed up in a reading of passages from Kafka's novel, chosen from among the least significant in themselves, in which, from time to time, a singing voice acts as a character, while the orchestra indulges in a thoughtless mass of dodecaphonic formulations with sickly sweet timbres and arbitrarily disordered patterns.[51]

And it came to an end a few weeks later, with Luigi Maria Guadagnino's instructive comment in a more friendly periodical, which spares us any lengthy textual comparison:

> There was a performance of the young Bruno Maderna's *Studi per "Il Processo" di Kafka* for soprano, speaker, and orchestra. Maderna cautions against "presuming to solve the difficult problems contained in *The Trial* by transferring them to the music's most passionate lyricism." Perhaps this was why Maderna chose not to tackle the psychological issues of *The Trial* and remains entangled in the narrative that passed from the novel to the speaker, and the words that he speaks seemed overly long. This was an attempt by Maderna, and an attempt it has remained. We must praise the commitment and the assumption that shines through here and there to give a musical interpretation to psychological figures that in Kafka are veiled by symbols and allusions. Maderna's style is that of the dodecaphonists but evidently the material did not respond to his "artistic intentions." The work is cerebral and long-winded, and the scansion of the "spoken words" is annoying.[52]

---

48 [n.n.], "The Venice Festival," *Tempo*, new series, no. 17 (Autumn 1950), pp. 1–3.

49 Malipiero, "Il XIII Festival di musica a Venezia" (see note 44). My emphasis.

50 Abbiati, "Musica contemporanea al XIII Festival di Venezia" (see note 3).

51 Beniamino Dal Fabbro, "Letture di Kafka con formulette dodecafoniche," *Milano Sera* (14 September 1950).

52 Guadagnino, "Panorama del Festival Internazionale di Venezia" (see note 41). The alleged quotation from a declaration by Maderna is taken from the program for the world premiere, by Emilia Zanetti (see note 21).

In order to demolish the experiment – as often happens in situations of loss or discomfort – the press had played on the topics mentioned in the program notes, and in particular the quotes attributed to the composer himself. This is demonstrated by the way in which Abbiati takes up his pen to return to and bend the hypothesis or indiscretion about the fate of the *Studi* that could be read between the lines in Zanetti's review:

> They begin with a too ostentatious taste of mystery, a seance, where it is not the tables that dance but the most remote and scattered sounds, and the heart-breaking vocalizations and the pounding and amateur dramatic speeches. They stick to this murder mystery, with this report of court proceedings, for which, if anything, *the melodramatic stage would be more appropriate.*[53]

Before 1950: New Documents for a Stage Version of *"Il Processo"*

> No matter how this certainly significant turning point in the composer's artistic life took place, he is not fond of underlining the technical importance. And even less so on the occasion of this very recent score, its ink barely dry, which will probably be realized in the broader version of a stage drama.[54]

The existence of a project to adapt the novel for the stage is a fact that Maderna scholars have known about for several decades, at least since the late 1970s,[55] when they learned of the existence of "a squared notebook" with "a stage version of the first twenty-eight pages of the novel":

> It is a proper libretto (15 pages in all of fine and careful writing) complete with precise and exhaustive directions as well as a detailed plan of the stage layout, all scrupulously faithful to the Kafkaesque text.[56]

Five years later, before examining the score of the *Studi,* Gianmario Borio transcribed and commented on the three-act scheme present in the eleven loose sheets of notes that are in a second notebook dedicated to the project, located in the meantime at the Paul Sacher Foundation in Basel (→ **EX. 1**).[57]

---

53 Abbiati, "Musica contemporanea al XIII Festival di Venezia" (see note 3). My emphasis.

54 Z[anetti], General program of the Venice Biennale (see note 21), p. 62.

55 See Rossana Dalmonte, "Letture maderniane del *Processo* di Franz Kafka," in *Bruno Maderna: Studi e testimonianze,* ed. Rossana Dalmonte and Marco Russo (Lucca: LIM, 2004), pp. 9–40: 18ff.

56 Giordano Montecchi, *"Studi per 'Il Processo' di Franz Kafka,"* in *Bruno Maderna: Documenti,* ed. Mario Baroni and Rossana Dalmonte (Milan: Suvini Zerboni, 1985), pp. 200–01: 201. Montecchi seems to be referring to the notebook indicated henceforth as "notebook 2."

57 See Gianmario Borio, "La tecnica seriale in *Studi per 'Il Processo' di Franz Kafka* di Bruno Maderna," *Musica/Realtà,* no. 32 (1990), pp. 27–39, transcription on pp. 27–28. Borio did not investigate the handwriting on the sheets, clearly not Maderna's. The new documentary sources, discussed in detail below, allow us to now ascribe them to Antonio Tartaglia. The covers of the two squared notebooks (PSS-BMC), numbered "1" and "2" by Maderna, both have the handwritten header "Bruno Maderna / Riduzione del 'Processo' di Kafka" (Bruno Maderna / Adaptation of the "Trial" by Kafka), presumably written by Irma Manfredi. Both contain fifteen pages each (the page count takes into account the use of the notebook, in which the body of the transcription is on the *verso* of each page and any sporadic glosses or musical indications on the *recto* of the next page, the one on the right). The second notebook also contains eleven loose sheets, torn from other supports.

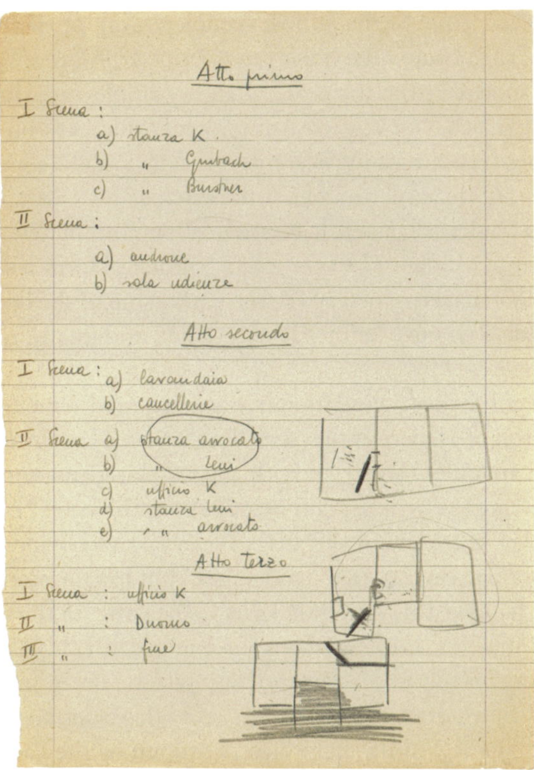

EX. 1   Project for the stage adaptation of Kafka's *Il Processo* [*The Trial*]
(ca. 1949); general outline of the work in three acts; Notebook 2,
loose sheet, manuscript by Antonio Tartaglia, PSS-BMC.

Rossana Dalmonte then took up the topic again, reflecting on the anteriority
(so far taken for granted) or the posteriority of the theatrical project with respect to the
accomplished *Studi,* and on the relationship of these documents to the occurrences of
Kafka to be found in the composer's letters:[58] first of all the well-known reply from Luigi
Dallapiccola to a lost letter from Maderna, which, while not backdating his compositional
debut with Kafka and the challenges raised by the transposition of his prose, is at least
proof of his lively interest two years prior to 1950:

> Text and music! The eternal problem. Why Alcaeus and not Kafka? You ask me. But some-
> body else might ask me: why Kafka and not Alcaeus; with just as much right. At the cost
> of making mistakes, I don't think verse should force music beyond the natural.[59]

And again Dalmonte, in the same volume, used the then known sources of the stage
adaptation to describe its features. Apart from the schema reproduced in Example 1, we
have notes and drawings for the second scene of the second act, and the left-hand pages

---

58 See Dalmonte, "Letture maderniane del *Processo*" (see note 55).
59 Letter from Dallapiccola to Maderna, dated 27 June 1948, PSS-BMC. On this topic see also the essay
by Paolo Dal Molin in this volume, pp. 415–39.

of the two notebooks contain a fair copy of the almost complete draft of the first act, based on the first two chapters of the novel in the Italian translation by Alberto Spaini.[60] In addition to the dialogues extrapolated from the prose, there are ample stage directions regarding the characters and their behavior and costumes, while there are only three annotations written close together regarding a musical intervention. Finally, we note the presence of a "loudspeaker in the auditorium" and one "on the stage."

Some recent additions to Maderna's papers have provided important new facts on what proves to have been an attempt to adapt *The Trial* into a "theatrical form with musical inserts."[61] The new information concerns, first of all, the authorship of the operation; then, its actual, by now irrefutable, existence before the 1950 *Studi;* and finally, the same dramaturgical destination.

In September 2014, the Paul Sacher Foundation in Basel acquired some materials from Franca Tartaglia, the grandson of Maderna's first wife, Raffaella.[62] These include two other squared notebooks, which are quite similar, in both their making and numbering ("1" and "2"), to the already known ones (see diagram below under the letter "B"). They too contain the first act of the play (complete in this case), but with two obvious formal differences: the text is only transcribed on the right-hand pages, thus mirroring the notebooks mentioned above, and the handwriting is not Maderna's. The writer of the two new supports is Antonio Tartaglia, Raffaella's brother, whom the composer had got to know while serving as an Alpino, "during his stay in the Merano hospital after developing osteomyelitis in his leg."[63] And (apart from a draft compiled together with Maderna), he is also responsible for the other documents regarding the project, acquired by the Paul Sacher Foundation in 2014, whose substance and contents are summarized below:[64]

---

60 Like the other translations in Europe, the first edition of the Italian translation – Franz Kafka, *Il processo*, trans. Alberto Spaini, European Library 6 (Turin: Frassinelli) – came out in 1933 to celebrate the fiftieth anniversary of his birth. In 1945, after the purge of Jewish authors from editorial catalogues on account of the war, Frassinelli published a new edition, followed in 1946 by a "third edition" and, in 1948, by a "IV reprint of the first edition." References to the pages from the translation found in Maderna's sources show that he did not use the first edition of 1933. An annotated photocopy (not by Maderna) of a post-war copy can be found among the materials pertaining to the *Studi per "Il Processo" di Franz Kafka* preserved in the Suvini Zerboni Archive in Milan (this is the first of the literary sources to be described, with some misunderstandings, by Rossana Dalmonte in her critical comment on Bruno Maderna, *Studi per "Il Processo" di F. Kafka*, score (Milan: Suvini Zerboni, 2010), p. xvi. This photocopy, which cannot be traced back to the creative phases of the work and/or to Maderna, might have served the publisher to locate the fragments of the novel Maderna had used in a German edition, to be then published in the score along with the Italian text.

61 Dalmonte, "Letture maderniane del *Processo*" (see note 55), p. 11.

62 The daughter of school inspector Gino Tartaglia and a cousin of the composer's adoptive mother (Irma Manfredi), Raffaella Tartaglia (1929–93, according to the Tartaglia family tree housed at PSS-BMC), had graduated in Foreign Languages and Literature from the University of Florence and was employed at Police Headquarters. She relates that her first meeting with Maderna took place in 1943. They were married on 10 November 1945 in Mozzecane, a small town a few kilometers from Verona, hiding the fact from his adoptive mother until February 1946. See Mario Baroni and Rossana Dalmonte, "Notizie sulla vita di Bruno Maderna," in *Documenti* (see note 56), pp. 56–57.

63 Ibid., p. 56 (from an account by Raffaella Tartaglia).

64 The abbreviations "AT" and "BM" on the list refer respectively to the initials of the two authors.

A) 12 sheets of lined foolscap paper, *r/v*, of which
    2 sheets *r/v* of schemas (AT; reproduced in Exx. 2–4 below);
    1 page of the draft of Scene I of Act I (AT);
    1 sheet with the *incipit* of a draft in four columns (AT; see below, Ex. 5);
    8 sheets numbered from 2 to 9 (the first is missing), with the draft of Act I,
    with Scene Ia (fols. 1–7r) drawn up in alternate blocks by AT and BM,
    and Scene IIa (fols. 7v–9) mostly in BM's hand.
B) Two squared notebooks (with 15 and 18 pages respectively, covers excluded)
    written entirely by AT on just the *recto* of each page and sometimes glossed on
    the opposite page, with few indications about the music; on the cover,
    the circled numbers ① and ② added by hand in the upper right-hand corner.
C) Various materials including:
    C1a = 3 sheets *r/v* containing an undated letter from AT to BM (3 pages, see Appendix 1),
        with the presentation of Act II and the attached draft of Act II, Scene I (3 pages).
    C1b = 1 bifolium *r/v* containing Maderna's reply, undated.
    C2 = 10 sheets *r/v* of a lined exercise book with the heading "Scene II of Act II"
        (compiled entirely by AT); 4 sheets of foolscap paper (pages numbered from 1 to 6)
        with draft of Scene I, Act II (AT).
    C3 = 6 numbered pages of lined sheets of paper, without a heading, with the
        adaptation of Chapter III + a loose sheet of paper with some information about
        systematic interventions (compiled entirely by AT).

All these documents clearly show that Antonio Tartaglia played a supporting role in the elaboration of the project, which at times might even have been more productive and proactive than that of his brother-in-law. We also learn that the two worked at the same time, confronting each other, sharing ideas on adaptation, scenarios, and drafts, and that only the composition of the music is left entirely to Maderna.

Until proven otherwise, Maderna's letter to his brother-in-law (C1b) allows the *terminus ante quem* for the start of their collaboration on the drafting of Act II to be fixed as April 1949, thus confirming the existence then of most of the documents for the project that have emerged to date. The letter is the composer's reply to Tartaglia's letter included in dossier (C1a), both of which are undated. On the fourth page of this letter, Raffaella Tartaglia adds a short message for her and Antonio's father, telling him about the young couple's financial circumstances. It is precisely this "third" familiar voice that allows us to establish a *terminus ante quem* for this letter (and the remaining materials): "[…] we have a savings account of Lit. 50,000, income from royalties. If it lasts until April, we'll need it in Palermo; otherwise we can kid ourselves that we are capitalists." The temporal reference (April) and the geographical one (Palermo) seem to allude to Bruno and Raffaella's trip to Sicily for the "XXIII Festival della Società Internazionale per la Musica Contemporanea" (ISCM), which was held in the Sicilian city between 22 and 30 April 1949, and at which Maderna was to conduct a concert on the last day.

As regards the elaboration of the adaptation, some papers gathered in A and the two just-mentioned letters, together with the various drafts present in C, clarify some aspects of the project before the drafting of Acts I and II, respectively.

The two sheets of diagrams (A) summarize aspects of the drama as well as the functions and manner of its components (→ **EXX. 2–4**).

EX. 2   Project for the stage adaptation of
Kafka's *Il Processo* [*The Trial*] (1949);
manuscript by Antonio Tartaglia, fol. 1*r*,
with the relevant translation; PSS-BMC.

Music
a) the drama is in the music
b) the drama is in the union of music + theater
c) the drama is in the theater + music
d) the drama is in the theater; the music accompanies and emphasizes
e) the drama is in the theater; functional sounds and rhythms
f) the drama is in the theater; expressive noises
g) the drama is in the theater; functional noises

Ways of acting

1) free recitation of drama theater { a) humble tone
b) dramatic tone

2) recitation of spoken theater with a fixed rhythm { a) quiet tone
b) dramaticv [tone]

3) recitation with a fixed rhythm and a firm tone { a)
b)

4) sung recitative { a)
b)

5) singing { a) lyric
b) dramatic

6) song

7) cry-scream moan etc.

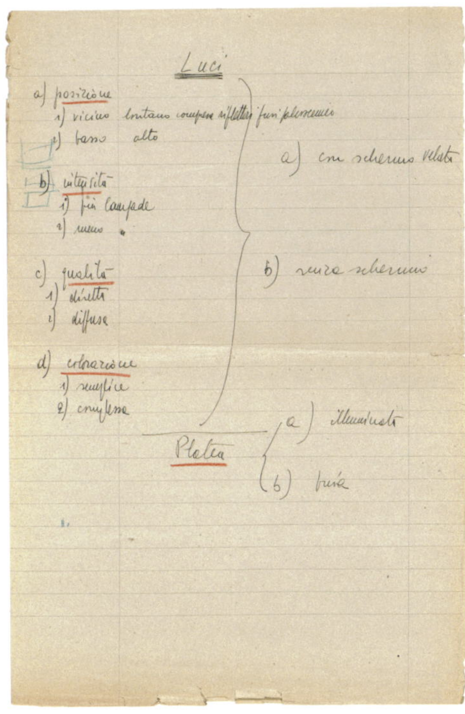

EX. 3   Project for the stage adaptation of Kafka's *Il Processo* [*The Trial*] (1949); manuscript by Antonio Tartaglia, fol. 2*r*, with the relevant translation; PSS-BMC.

EX. 4   Project for the stage adaptation of Kafka's *Il Processo* [*The Trial*] (1949); manuscript by Antonio Tartaglia, fol. 2*v*, with the relevant translation; PSS-BMC.

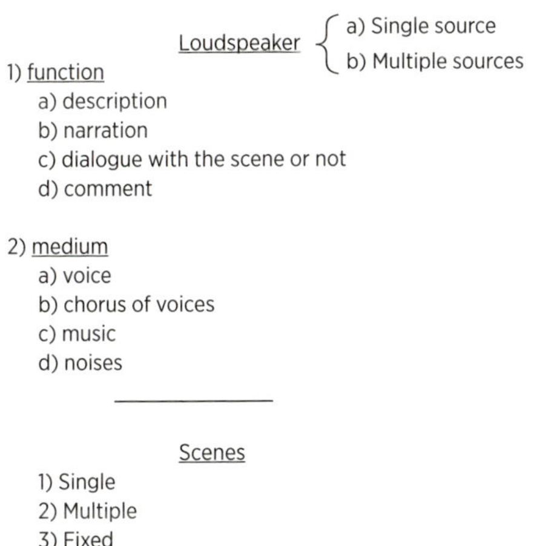

Loudspeaker { a) Single source / b) Multiple sources

1) function
    a) description
    b) narration
    c) dialogue with the scene or not
    d) comment

2) medium
    a) voice
    b) chorus of voices
    c) music
    d) noises

Scenes
1) Single
2) Multiple
3) Fixed
4) Mobile

Scenery and costumes
    a) from realism
    b) from abstractionism

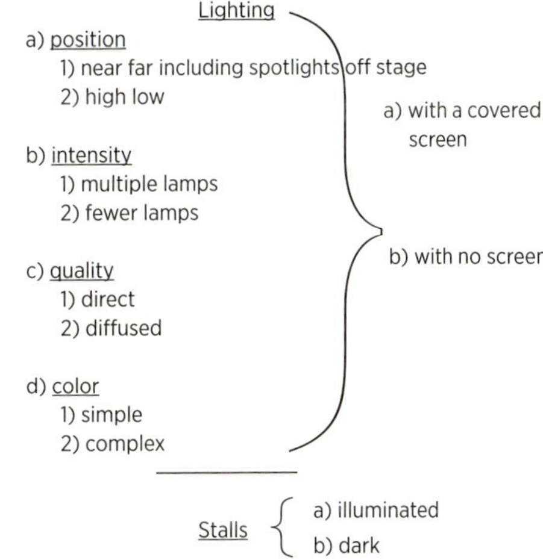

Lighting
a) position
    1) near far including spotlights off stage
    2) high low

b) intensity
    1) multiple lamps
    2) fewer lamps

c) quality
    1) direct
    2) diffused

d) color
    1) simple
    2) complex

a) with a covered screen

b) with no screen

Stalls { a) illuminated / b) dark

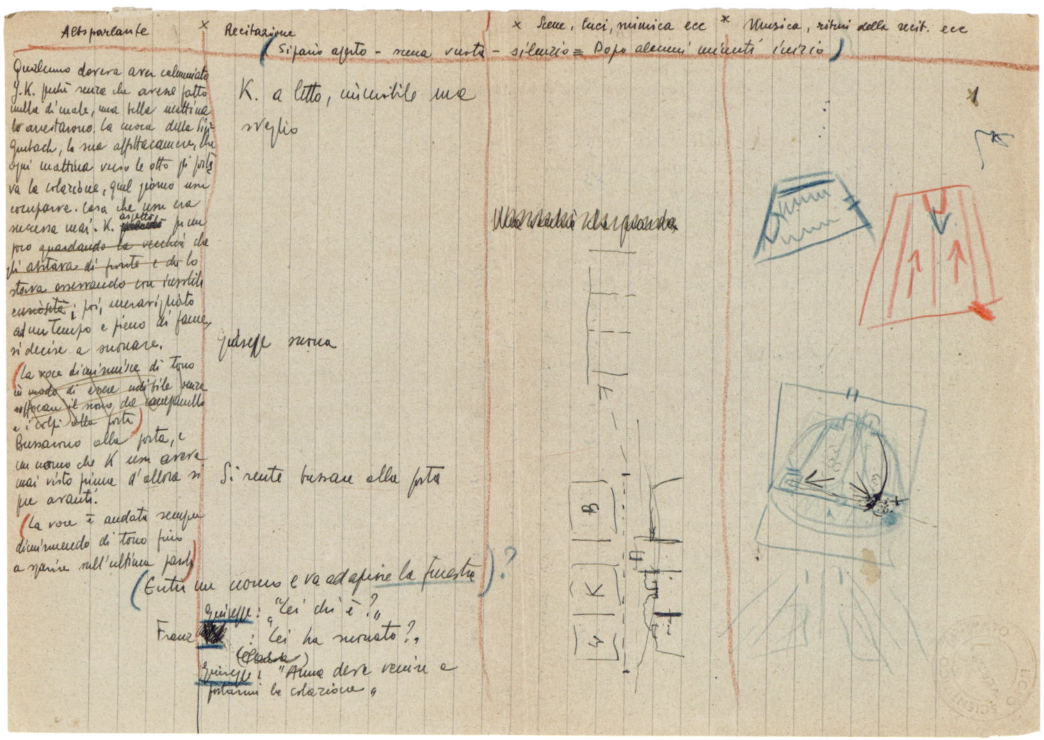

EX. 5   Project for the stage adaptation of Kafka's *Il Processo* [*The Trial*] (1949); first draft in four columns; manuscript by Antonio Tartaglia (column headings by Bruno Maderna); PSS-BMC.

Example 5 shows the draft mentioned in group A,[65] in which the beginning of the adaptation of the text – in an intermediate stage between the draft described in A and the one in the notebooks – is divided into four columns: the first for the "Loudspeaker" ("Altoparlante"), the second for the "Acting" ("Recitazione," with K.'s first lines – indicated with the respective Italian for Josef, "Giuseppe" – and Franz, plus some directions), the third for "Scenes, lights, gestures etc." ("Scene, luci, mimica ecc."), and the fourth for "Music, rhythm in act[ing] etc." ("Musica, ritmi della recit[azione] ecc.").

The different drafts of Act I – draft (A), Tartaglia's two notebooks (B), and those of Maderna (described above in section 2) – make some direct references to these lists. However, there are far fewer instances than we might have hoped for, and it is worth noting that they refer in particular to the "function" and "medium" of the "loudspeaker" (Ex. 3). This goes to explain the abbreviations Maderna used in his notebooks for the three interventions of the "loudspeaker in the auditorium" in Scene I. The first, as the curtains open, and the third, at the beginning of the episode with Miss Grubach, are similar in nature:[66]

---

65   As can be seen at the bottom right of Ex. 5, the lined foolscap sheet, written on the *recto/verso*, bears the stamp of the "Liceo Scientifico di Stato / Verona" (State Scientific High School, Verona).

66   The following quotations all come from Bruno Maderna's notebook "1" (PSS-BMC, *Studi per "Il Processo" di Franz Kafka*) on fols. 1–2*v* and 15*v* respectively.

> Loudspeaker in auditorium (2a–1b) (repeated three times while the Loudspeaker increases in volume from nothing to soft and slow but distinctly)
> Someone must have slandered K., because without doing anything wrong, one fine morning they arrested him. […] There was a knock on the door and a man K. had never seen before stepped forward. (The voice gradually decreases in tone until it disappears on the last word.)
> Loudspeaker in auditorium (1b–2a) That evening, the day had passed quickly, up to his eyes in hard work, K. went home immediately. […]

The second, just after the beginning of the same scene, shifts the narrator's voice into the first person, entrusting it first to "choruses of voices" when the questions come thick and fast, then to a single voice, namely that of K.'s conscience as he tries to reassure himself:

> Loudspeaker in auditorium (1c–2b) – Who I am? What are they talking about? What authority do they obey? Laws are in their heyday! Who dares to abuse me in my home? (Very short pause) (2a) Maybe it's a joke. But yes, it's a prank my bank colleagues have played on me for my thirtieth birthday.[67]

Another abbreviation – directly connected to the "acting methods" outlined in the sketch reproduced here in Example 2 – is found on the third page of draft A, in a stage direction that was deleted and therefore does not appear in the following drafts (→ **EX. 6**). It regards a moment in the intense dialogue between Josef ("Giuseppe"), Willem, and Franz:

> Gius.:   I'm not familiar with this law of yours
> W.:   Tough luck
> Giuseppe: Because it only exists only in your heads
> W.:   You'll see (1)

The first musical intervention is inserted on the last line, noted by Maderna, at the foot of the page, in the text:

> (1) ([side]drum w[ith] s[nares]

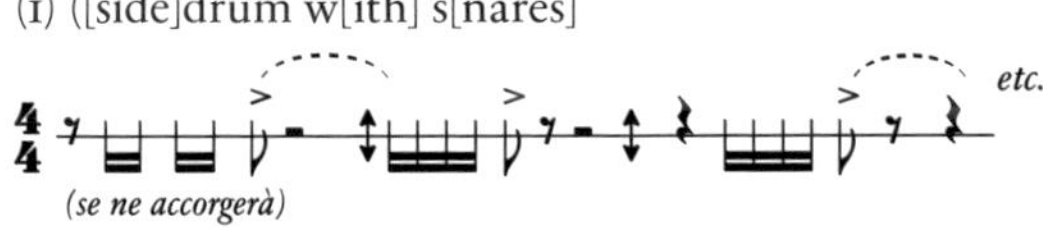

> cymbal slur played with a felt stick between the line "You'll see" ("se ne accorgerà") and the *pp* entrance of the drum

which was rewritten in the notebooks as:

> A cymbal hit with a felt stick ties the line to the entrance of the sidedrum with snare which repeats the rhythm of the phrase: [you'll see]

> etc. then a rhythmic polyphony develops echoing the s. drum always on the same rhythmic cell. The ligaments are now always made with a cymbal but hit with a foam drumstick (for now, the rhythms remain linear)[68]

---

67 Ibid., fol. 4*v*.
68 Ibid., fol. 8*r*.

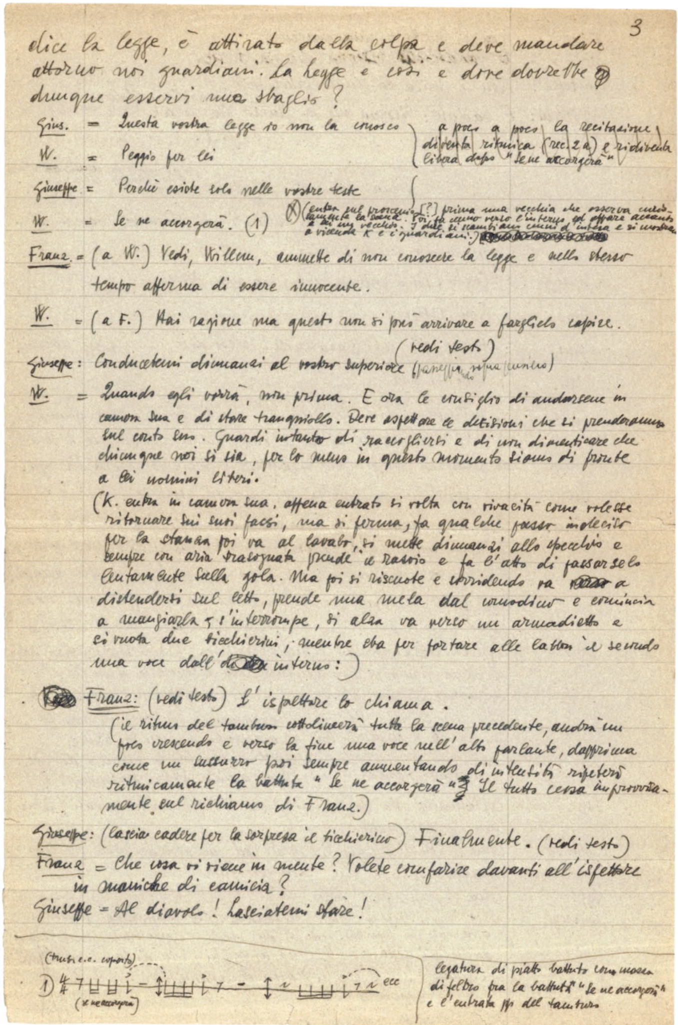

EX. 6   Project for the stage adaptation of Kafka's *Il Processo* [*The Trial*]
(1949); draft of Act I, Scene I; manuscript by Bruno Maderna; PSS-BMC.

A similar musical amplification of Willem's threat was prepared in the draft (Ex. 6) by modifying the recitation with a gradual passage to a "fixed rhythm," "soft tone" diction, indicated by means of the abbreviation "rec. 2a," an explicit reference to the typology of the "Ways of Acting" schema (Ex. 2):

> the recitation gradually becomes rhythmic (rec. 2a) and becomes random again after "You'll see."

In the two surviving letters mentioned previously, when Act II was already in the pipeline, Maderna and Tartaglia once again exchanged views on the sense of these kinds of internal changes **(→ APP. 1, PP. 412-14):**

Dear Bruno [...], I'd like to take this opportunity to send you the draft of Scene I, Act II, section (a) I suggest that the order of the Act II scenes should be as follows:
I scene: a) entrance hall A with washerwoman, K, student and usher.
b) reception room B transformed into a chancellery with K, usher, prisoners, clerks, and informer
Scene II: a) K - uncle - lawyer
b) K - Leni
c) K - whipster
d) K - Block and dismissal of lawyer
Let's talk about Scene I a) which is the one I am sending you. As you can see from reading the scenario and especially the attached draft, the scenery is easy to achieve. I kept the grand staircase because it is a remarkable example of that architectural nonsense that we already noticed in various points. Instead, I've introduced a small door without a frame and which therefore merges with the wall (and which can only be seen if open) (based on the type of one that leads to the hallway from your dining room) because Bertoldo's appearance and his escape is clearly visible from there. I imagine it without the frame so as to give the idea of secrecy and so to speak of the omnipresence of the law which, for suspicious packages watches over you and catches you off guard. Above this door I've introduced a tall, narrow window through which you can see some steps (as in the sketch). Bertoldo and the washerwoman on the run will reappear from this window for the last few lines.
These new elements (door and opening) can also appear in the dramatization of Scene II of Act I; but they could also only appear in this scene for obvious reasons. The dialogue, as you will easily see, has been somewhat modified with the intention, at least, of making it shorter and livelier, without altering its atmosphere.
Toward the end of the scene, on rereading the text more thoroughly, it seemed to me that the verbal action could have well been turned into first mime and then gradually into a ballet. I defer to your judgment as a musician who knows about these things and who will immediately see all the potential. For my part, I would add that music and ballet would be an important step in the right direction on the path of the gradual, veristic, and <u>precise</u> "bourgeois denaturalization" toward <u>pure meanings</u>.
In any case, if the ballet doesn't work, it is easy to end the scene "in the usual manner." We come now to section (b). The scenery could be the following.
The usual living room B without the loggia (but it could also be left empty). Around the outer walls and at a convenient distance, very high wooden gates rise up (you can remove the overhead and thus give the illusion of them going on forever) beyond which you can see the employees working on their books. Around the gate and at a distance that leaves a handy passageway corresponding to P2 of the benches on which the prisoners sit, opposite the gate.[69] The layout is more or less like this

Don't expect perspective, because it's too difficult. So, after Bertoldo and the Washerwoman have disappeared, the ballet has come to an end (the music could continue throughout the following scene), K goes back to the sofa. The Usher enters from P3 and invites him to the chancellery and brings in K (who does not understand the lay of the place) into the chancellery via P2. They walk down the passageway, saying what they have to say, to point I where the Informer

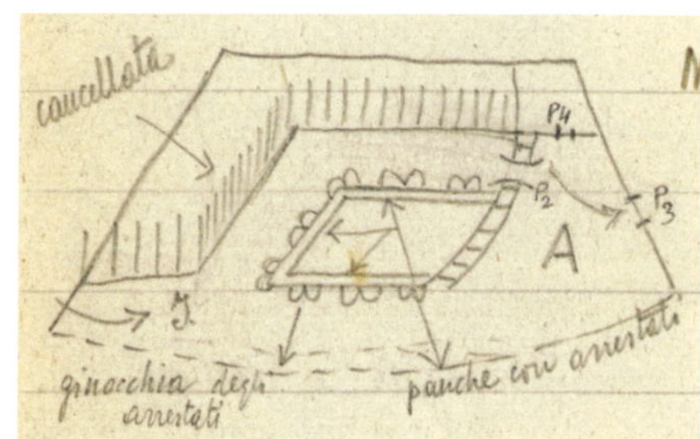

---

69 The abbreviations "P2" etc. refer to the diagrams reproduced on the bottom right.

appears with whom K returns. The famous scene takes place at P2 in the A part: K looks well and the Informer bad. The curtain falls and Scene I ends; but I'll open it immediately meaning that during section (a) of the scene, hall B must remain closed off by side curtains, and that K, miming that he feels good and is breathing better, comes running out from P3.

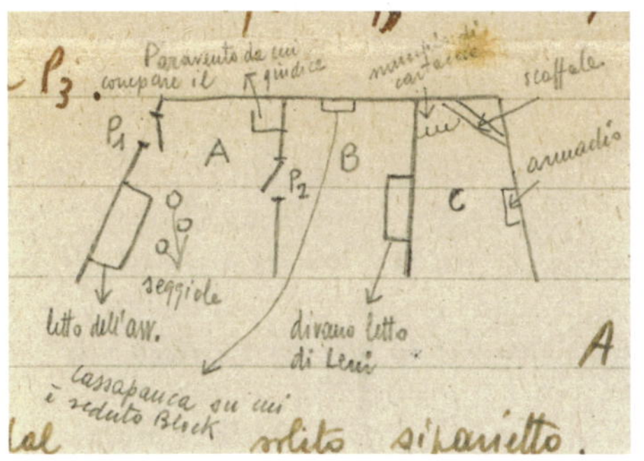

Scene II. Here's the layout [see drawing on the left]: it is divided into three parts: right [*recte* left] (A) lawyer's room entered through P1. In between Leni's room (B) entered through P2. On the right K's office (C), A and B are open. C is closed off by the usual side curtain.

Section (a) of Scene II: K and uncle enter A: conversation with the lawyer and arrival of the judge, until Leni, who in the meantime has retired to B, breaks the plate.

Section (b): K and Leni are talking and Leni is offering her help; after showing that the sofa bed on which they are sitting is her bed, she makes K stand up by telling him that you can go directly into his office through an opening in the wall (architectural oddity taken from the Tintorelli episode). In fact, just above Leni's bed a kind of large window opens, giving onto K's office at floor level. (The outline of the scene is this A | B [Leni's bed] C the big window is thus high up on the side

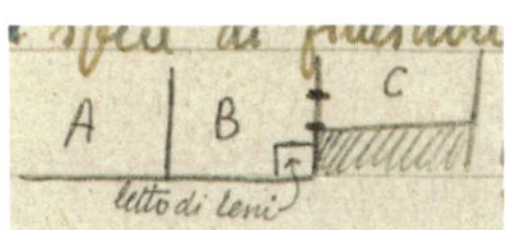

of B (K has to get on the bed) but it is at floor level in C.) In C we witness the whipping episode (section C of the scene). After pushing Franz, K returns to B with Leni (side curtain closes C), where the rolling on the ground episode takes place and Block enters with whom K – Leni exits – holds a conversation.

He then recoils from Block's picture of the situation and exasperated by his servility, he returns to A where the scene of the lawyer's dismissal and the last part of the act take place. Dear Bruno, I should now explain all the reasons why I've done what I've done, but I think that everything, even the detail of the big window, is quite evident. I've tried to be brief and clear, but these are things that don't always go hand in hand. Arm yourself with patience and study the sketches and explanations, and trust yourself where they are obscure. Of course, I had to leave out a lot of things, but I'm tired of writing. I would have liked to send you the complete and finished Second Act, but I think it's better that we come to a general agreement at the outset to avoid unnecessary work and any waste of time. Study everything quickly and <u>send me back</u> the full list of your suggestions as soon as possible. Until you answer, <u>I won't work</u>.

Say hello to your wife and give her lots of kisses. You are both always in my thoughts. Toni[70]

We shall not dwell here on Tartaglia and Maderna's attention to the "architectural nonsense" contained in *The Trial*. It should, however, be noted that contemporary critics had also highlighted this characteristic,[71] which the two collaborators render in the plan through a definition of the scene obtained by taking elements from the novel and inventing new ones for purposes of effectiveness. It is the second step that interests us most: not only because we learn, not surprisingly, that Tartaglia leaves the elaboration of the music entirely up to Maderna, but above all because it hypothesizes a contrast between two

---

70   Greetings from his wife, Leda Scodellari, follow in different handwriting and pen.
71   See for example Gérard Boden, "Aspects de l'œuvre de Franz Kafka (i)," *Revue de la Méditerranée* 4, no. 22 (November–December 1947), pp. 648–75: 665.

situations, which undergo a gradual transition in the adaptation: from the veristic and <u>precise</u> "bourgeois denaturalization" toward "<u>pure meanings</u>." If, to understand this phrase, one were to seek a foothold in the maze of Kafka criticism that had accumulated up to 1949, one would be faced with the themes of the abstraction of reality and their literary rendering, which were always so commonplace,[72] and with that equally thorny matter, especially after 1945, of the mirroring in Kafka of a bourgeois society now considered as being on the wane or, on the contrary, perceived as still alive ("the world that also belongs to its many modern-day and too naive readers").[73]

Since we cannot analyze the drafts here in this light, suffice it to observe that there was already an outline of a dichotomy between "verism" and "abstract art" in the aforementioned schemes (A) for the "scenery and costumes" (see Ex. 3), and that this contrast was however implicit in the development of the first six "Ways of Acting" (see Ex. 2). The formula used by Tartaglia may thus pertain to all the forms of dramatization of the novel and, consequently, to some aspects of *The Trial* to be highlighted in the play.

The draft of the first scene of Act II drawn up by Tartaglia, enclosed in his quoted letter to Maderna (C1a, App. 1), and the composer's reply would confirm this hypothesis. The dialogue between the Washerwoman and Josef (Chapter III of *The Trial*), from the moment she realizes that they are being watched by the student, gives rise "in gradual steps" to a mime and then to a ballet. Between the "Shut up, Bertoldo is watching us" and the court guard's entrance on stage, Tartaglia inserts a long description of the movements, the scenery, and some suggestions for the music:

> At this point, it is as if the Washerwoman has succumbed to the volition of others and against which she cannot put up a fight. The scene therefore can give rise to a mimed-ballet. The music (it will begin at the most opportune moment) is the real protagonist of the drama, of which the ballet will be the visual expression. The miming will start "naturally" and gradually become more and more "stylized" in ballet until the student disappears up the stairs.[74]

Just as significant in terms of the mimed part is the last page of the same scene, where Tartaglia is interested in bringing out the paradox that closes the episode in the chancellery, when a girl and the informer, after meeting in court (dressed "in tight trousers like the Castle messengers"), accompany an exhausted Josef to the exit of the building:

---

72 This was also the case in the first Italian reviews of the translation of the *The Trial* (see for example that of Mario Robertazzi in *Pan: Rassegna di lettere arte e musica* 2, no. 3 (1 March 1934), pp. 626–28) and – at the opposite chronological extreme – in the writings of Carlo Bo, Remo Cantoni, Franco Fortini, Luciano Anceschi, and others. Bo's reaction after reading *The Castle* leads him to write: "Kafka arrives at his positions through an exhausting and lively analysis of the common events of our life, but mind you, all events are interpreted according to a particular vocabulary for which it is legitimate to divert an identical amount of intention, an equal amount of respect from everything toward an absolute and abstract image." See Carlo Bo, "Intorno a Kafka," *Costume* 2, no. 1 (January–February 1946), pp. 29–38: 30.

73 Franco Fortini, "Gli uomini di Kafka e la critica delle cose," *La Rassegna d'Italia* 4, no. 2 (February 1949), pp. 148–54.

74 Letter from Antonio Tartaglia to Maderna (see above, C1a), fol. 5. This passage is followed by the phrase "The scene is roughly like this" and a precise sketch.

> It seemed to him that all his strength returned to him at once [...] "Thank you very much,"
> he repeated, shook their hands once more and did not let go until he thought he saw that
> they found it hard to bear the comparatively fresh air from the stairway after being so long
> used to the air in the offices. They were hardly able to reply, and the young woman might
> even have fallen over if K. had not shut the door extremely fast.[75]

Which Tartaglia transforms into:

> K.: (lifts his head and realizes that he is outside, breathing heavily and visibly feeling better
> and better as the other two begin to flag. When he turns to thank them) Thank you very
> much! Thank you very much! (and to shake their hands, the two of them are about to slide
> to the ground). K. holds them up and pushes them back in, immediately closing the door
> P2. Then with a gesture of relief, he crosses A jumping and running and exits through
> P3. | End of Scene I Act II.[76]

Finally, in Maderna's letter to his brother-in-law, along with the suggestion to go on with
the drafting of Act II separately, and a synopsis of Scene II,[77] we can read of his satisfaction
with "the mimed ending," indicating the need to "devise as many solutions as possible that
have the meaning, as you well say, of pure actions," and defining music as a "rather generic
but extremely effective medium" for these purposes, since it is able to evoke and express
meanings without words. Tartaglia's "pure meanings" and Maderna's "pure actions" refer, in
short, to the solution, with mime or dance, foreseen already in the first outline included in
A1 (see Ex. 2): "a) the drama is in the music | b) the drama is in the union of music + theater":

> Dear Toni. Well done. Now we must go on. I think that for the 2nd Act it is better for us
> each to continue on our own. Later on, we'll choose the best version.
> Here's my idea (I enclose a drawing of the multiple scene with its game of side curtains):
> [...] End of the Act.
> I confess that I haven't done any work yet. But I started again today. I've had a lot of things
> to do in the past few days. Getting back to our work, let me congratulate you on the
> mimed ending. We must devise as many solutions as possible that have the meaning, as
> you say, of pure actions. And we must not forget that we also have the music: a rather ge-
> neric but extremely effective medium. In short, it works. I'll refrain from commenting on
> my idea. I'll go on in the hope that you will understand everything and why. Meanwhile,
> get ready. In a week's time you could come here for three or four days and we could thus
> draw up the 2nd Act. Take care![78]

---

75 Translation from Franz Kafka, *The Trial*, Project Gutenberg, trans. David Wyllie (2003), chap. 3, p. 137.

76 Draft C3, p. 6. (Original in Italian: "Gli parve che d'un tratto tutte le forze gli fossero ritornate [...]
'Tante grazie' ripeté K. stringendo loro le mani, e li lasciò andare solo quando si accorse che,
abituati all'aria dell'ufficio, mal sopportavano quella relativamente fresca che veniva dalle scale,
per cui erano appena in grado di rispondere, e forse la ragazza sarebbe caduta se K. non avesse
chiusa la porta con estrema prontezza" (trans. Kafka); "K.: (alza la testa e s'accorge di essere
fuori respira forte e visibilmente si sente sempre meglio mentre i due cominciano ad afflosciarsi.
Quando si volta per ringraziarli) Tante grazie! Tante grazie! (e per stringer loro le mani, i due
stanno per scivolare a terra. K. li sostiene e li ricaccia dentro chiudendo subito la porta P2. Poi
con mimica di liberazione attraversa saltando e correndo A ed esce per P3. | Fine I scena II atto"
(Tartaglia's adaptation).

77 Similar to the one preserved among the eleven aforementioned sheets included with the second
of the notebooks kept at PSS-BMC (see above, note 55), and analyzed in Dalmonte, "Letture maderniane del *Processo*" (see note 55), pp. 20ff.

78 Maderna to Antonio Tartaglia, undated letter "C1b" (April 1949?), PSS-BMC.

From the Theater Project to the *Studi*

Old and new sources give us no information about how the collaboration between Tartaglia and Maderna started, nor as to which of the two was the first to think of coming to grips with the difficult task of adapting Kafka's *The Trial* for the stage. Carrying out such an undertaking in the early years of the second post-war period was, apparently, an "act of worship"[79] in a new phase of the national reception of the author, following that first privileged and secret one in which the followers of Kafka ("anonymous master of many well-known pupils")[80] seemed to have gained more fame in the national literary field than the master himself:

> Kafka's work was burned in Germany, and permission for publication in Italy could no longer be obtained. In the meantime, however, forbidden to the general public, Kafka penetrated into small circles of initiates through French and English translations, and perhaps also through the original texts, which became increasingly unavailable – and Italian translations were now nowhere to be found. Young authors eagerly took possession of his work.

As Fortini tells us, in France, in 1948, there was even talk of Kafka's "popularity." It was therefore necessary to limit that success "to just one part of the middle class who are readers" and to demonstrate its shortcomings:

> Kafka read outdoors, exploited in its most mechanical and external aspects, is exorcised, deprived of any healthy or deadly poison. They have made it theater, they will make it cinema.[81]

As regards the last remark ("they have made it theater"), we do not even know whether Maderna and Tartaglia were familiar with the adaptation of *The Trial* co-authored by André Gide and Jean-Louis Barrault, performed for the first time at the Théâtre Marigny in Paris on 10 October 1947 and published in that same year.[82] The Italian public had been presented with an Italian version (*Il processo: Due tempi*), edited by Cesare Vico Lodovici, on 3 February 1949, at the University of Rome's Teatro Ateneo, with Giulio Pacuvio directing and Sandro Ruffini in the role of Josef K. The performance received a lukewarm reception from the press as, for example, can be sensed in the remarks made by the screenwriter Ermanno Contini the following day:

> Such a subject [that of Kafka's novel] is made for the written page, which allows the reader's integrative imagination to flow freely: bringing it to the stage is a hopeless undertaking. Gide himself recognizes that he decided to try this venture only to offer his friend Barrault the pretext of a personal show in which the great qualities of the man of the theater and the actor were accompanied by the great qualities of mime. Taking up this adaptation to make it into a normal show was a serious mistake.[83]

---

79 Fortini, "Gli uomini di Kafka" (see note 73), p. 148.
80 Alberto Spaini, "Prefazione," in Franz Kafka, *America*, trans. Alberto Spaini (Turin: Giulio Einaudi, 1945), pp. vii–xii: vii, from which the following quotation also comes.
81 Fortini, "Gli uomini di Kafka" (see note 73), pp. 148–49.
82 André Gide and Jean-Louis Barrault, *Le Procès: Pièce tirée du roman de Kafka*, based on the translation by Alexandre Vialatte (Paris: Gallimard, 1947).
83 Ermanno Contini, "Le prime rappresentazioni: Ateneo: *Il processo* di Kafka," *Il messaggero* (Rome, 4 February 1949). See also, on the same day, the review by Silvio d'Amico, "*Il processo* di F. Kafka: Né la clarté, né il frammentismo si addicono all'autore del *Castello*: Novità all'Ateneo," preserved – with no indication of the newspaper of origin – like the previous one among the numerous documents on the Roman production at Genoa's Archivio Museo Biblioteca dell'Attore. My heartfelt thanks to the Archive, in the person of Gian Domenico Ricaldone, for his valuable help and for providing me with the documents mentioned.

The text of the two Frenchmen was, however, nothing like Maderna and Tartaglia's work in terms of both its structure (two parts with two and three scenes each) and intentions. Nor are the shared attention to dialogue, the use of the loudspeaker (but only for off-screen characters), the accurate graphic descriptions of the stage and those of behaviors and movements, or even the directions for the *"mimique"* exclusive elements that allow us to establish links.

But no matter what inspired them, Tartaglia and Maderna's plans ran aground. In the aforementioned long letter from the composer to his brother-in-law, there is a hint of the reasons that had hitherto prevented Maderna from concentrating on such a demanding project[84] and on which its ultimate incompleteness could also have depended. As a last stage, the sources offer a scenario from the second part of Act II drawn up by the composer and a draft of the same scene written by his collaborator. As Tartaglia had announced in the synopsis of the act contained in the letter to Maderna (C1a, App. 1), the adaptation would no longer follow the order of the hypotext, but would be assembled from fragments taken from chapters V–VIII, with inversions and transformations (for example, in Part I of Scene II Tartaglia assigns the words of the painter Tintorelli to other characters). These are the same chapters of the novel on which a large part of the 1950 *Studi per "Il Processo" di Franz Kafka* is based (chap. VI–VIII and two short fragments from IX). But, apart from the episode featuring Leni, already envisaged by Maderna in 1949, and which Tartaglia created using some of the lines spoken by the woman in the work presented in Venice, there do not seem to be any other intersections between the two texts.

We must therefore state that the *Studi* differ from the theater project not only in genre, but also in the text. If we consider the employment of the speaking voice in the *Studi,* one could suppose that it was born from the transformation of the idea of the speakers included in the first plan, even though in this case their intervention was more limited and quite different from the part entrusted to Ubaldo Lay. Then, Maderna's first note about the stage music (which saw the generation of a polyrhythmic fabric from Willem's "you'll see") has been put together with the first section of the *Studi,* with rhythmic cells derived from the words of the text.[85] The "skin" and "metal" instruments, on the other hand, are similar: the former calls for cymbal and side drum with snares, while the latter uses the same set of instruments, but more elaborate and differently employed (together with a triangle, bass drum, tambourine, side drum without snares, and tam-tam). However, in addition to the fact that the deduction of rhythmic motifs from words and their contrapuntal treatment were already common practice in Maderna (see for example *Tre liriche greche* and *Il mio cuore è nel Sud*), the two "chapters" are musically different in every respect:

---

84   In the first half of 1949 Maderna had been active on numerous fronts. For example, on February 17, he wrote to Nino Sanzogno that he had finished *Composizione n. 1* for orchestra; in March he had finished the *Tre liriche greche.* The list obviously does not end after his trip to Sicily for the "Festival della Società Internazionale per la Musica Contemporanea" (ISCM; see above): from 4–7 May he was invited to Milan to give a lecture on dodecaphony at the First Congress for Dodecaphonic Music (where, moreover, he heard Ernst Krenek's *5 Lieder op. 82 nach Worten von Franz Kafka* from 1937–38, performed by the contralto Margherita De Landi and her husband Edward Staempfli; and by June 28 he had already composed the music of the radio play *Il mio cuore è nel Sud.*

85   See Dalmonte, "Letture maderniane del *Processo*" (see note 55), p. 16.

the whole opening of the *Studi* is played at the lowest dynamic levels, while in the stage adaptation, the musical reiteration of the "you'll see," ⌐⌐⌐ ♪, reproduced by the speaker in the auditorium together with "Josef Kappa" (in a "reverse series," ♪ ⌐⌐⌐, would have had to increase "tension and force" up to the resounding, peremptory "Josef Kappa! (pause) The inspector is calling you," pronounced with a "metallic voice, in military tone" from the on-stage speaker.[86] The comparison should then also be extended to the "visionary finale" of the *Studi,* which ends fortissimo with "Jo-o-o-o-sef Kappa!"

Returning to the text of the two works, we can at least specify that the difference between Maderna and Tartaglia's project and the 1950 work does not consist – as one might have thought – in the disassembly and reassembly of the novel,[87] already envisaged in fact in the second act of the theater play.[88] The certainty of the latter's antecedence to the *Studi* may instead reinforce the idea that in 1950 Maderna was taking important steps toward "drama in music," which after all was also mentioned in the first schemes for the stage adaptation (see Ex. 2), although it rarely appears in his drafting; in short, this is confirmation of the distinctive features of what, almost thirty years ago, with fewer documents available, seemed to be a "change in perspective":

> The abandonment of the theater project coincides in the *Studi* with the transition to a dramatic concept that does away with the division into roles and the temporal continuity of the action. It could be said that this change in perspective already contains the concept of a "musical drama" in the broad sense of the term – of a drama that takes place primarily in music which more than a decade later will give rise to *Hyperion.*[89]

The erotic moment is excluded from the dialogue that occurs in the novel (and in Tartaglia's adaptation):[90] Leni no longer has an interlocutor. Her lines are even more self-referential and only echoed by the orchestral part. That "hybrid and deformed thing" – in which "the speaking voice never managed to coincide with that singer"[91] and the orchestra "was never been able to intervene effectively" – contained, with no offense to Gian Francesco Malipiero, seeds that Maderna would cultivate in radio plays and much more.

Maderna-Kafka After the Premiere of the *Studi*

On 30 September 1950, Scherchen peremptorily asked Maderna "ich muss ALLE Kritiken über den *Prozess* haben" (I must have ALL the reviews of the *Processo*) and questioned him about his intentions of publishing the work with Ars Viva.[92] Letters from the conductor-publisher followed for other performances with reminders to send materials

---

86   From the first of Maderna's notebooks "Riduzione del *Processo* di Kafka" (Adaptation of Kafka's *The Trial*), housed at PSS-BMC (see above, note 55).
87   According to Borio, "La tecnica seriale in *Studi per 'Il Processo'*" (see note 57), p. 28.
88   Dalmonte had noticed this in her observations on Maderna's setting for the second scene; see idem, "Letture maderniane del *Processo*" (see note 55), p. 20.
89   Borio, "La tecnica seriale in *Studi per 'Il Processo'*" (see note 57), p. 28.
90   See C2, pp. 4ff. (from Scene II, Act II).
91   Malipiero, "Il XIII Festival Musicale Veneziano" (see note 30).
92   Letter in the PSS-BMC.

for the press ("I look forward to receiving 'the Kafka'"),[93] although this only happened a few years later (the *Studi per "Il Processo" di Franz Kafka* were included in the Ars Viva Zurich catalogue, printed in November 1954, among the "Works for Speaker and Orchestra"). Steinecke's reply tells us that in May 1951 Maderna proposed the *Studi* for the concert programs of that year's Darmstadt *Ferienkurse,* in place of an unfinished *"Composizione n. 3."*[94] But his proposal was rejected because, apart from arriving late, it would have required a new financial commitment on the part of the organizers to engage voices and instruments not previously envisaged. A few months later it was Paul Collaer, Deputy Director of the Belgian Institut National de Radiodiffusion (INR), who expressed his intention to include the *Studi* in the program of a concert scheduled for 28 March 1952.[95]

In the documents regarding the same two-year period (1951–52), especially among Maderna's letters, new hypotheses emerge about Kafka, perhaps also inspired by the *Studi,* and there is, in any case, a certain focus on the work of the Prague artist. On 3 February 1951, the writer and director Giuseppe Patroni Griffi, who had co-authored with Maderna the radio play *Il mio cuore è nel Sud,* wrote to the latter: "I'm thinking of Kafka," promising to return to the subject in a future letter, unfortunately never found or perhaps never written.[96] In August of the same year, Anton Gronen Kubitzki, the speaker for the Venetian performance of *A Survivor from Warsaw,* tried to involve the composer in the elaboration of a "sort of screenplay" in the spirit of *Survivor* (which Maderna would have known how to "infuse with the great lyricism [...] which he had masterfully traced in the lyrical fragments of Kafka, for example in the beautiful moments of the sung voice"), yet offering him a libretto by the twenty-four-year-old Ferdinando Baldi.[97] Moreover, nothing seems to have come of Maderna's reply to Erwin Piscator on 5 June 1952, about collaborating on a theater-music project around *America:* "I am thinking, for example, of a theme from Kafka. I find great potential in his novel *America.* This is obviously just my personal

---

93   See letters from Hermann Scherchen to Bruno Maderna, dated 30 November 1950 and 25 February 1951 (orig.: "Den 'Kafka' erwarte ich ungeduldig"); PSS-BMC.

94   Maderna and Steinecke, *Carteggio/Briefwechsel* (see note 7), pp. 43–45 and p. 44, n. 49.

95   See letter from Paul Collaer to Bruno Maderna, dated 16 August 1951; PSS-BMC.

96   Letter published in Angela Ida De Benedictis, *Radiodramma e arte radiofonica: Storia e funzioni della musica per la radio in Italia* (Turin: De Sono, EDT, 2004), p. 376.

97   Letters from Anton Gronen Kubitzki to Bruno Maderna, dated 14 August and 30 August 1951 (PSS-BMC): "[...] I would be delighted to know if you would find it interesting to set the enclosed text by Ferdinando Baldi to music in the spirit of *Survivor.* | Scenically speaking I have imagined the execution of the work along with some other episodes of the genre, with the idea of creating a somewhat new form of stage performance. | To be in technical harmony with the other works, the orchestra should include a group of woodwinds, celesta, harp, piano and Hammond organ, percussion, and strings. | I would be really happy if the text, which I consider really good, could be of interest to you, because I am sure that you would then know how to infuse it with the great lyricism that is its own. Using the language that, although inspired by the theories of the late great man who gave us the *Survivor,* would benefit from the great lyricism that Berg derived so intensely from it, which you yourself masterfully traced in the lyrical fragments of Kafka, for example in the beautiful moments of the sung voice. The text of course handled in the same way as the *Ode to Napoleon* or *Survivor.* | Answer me immediately, immediately, please, so that I'll know whether I can count on the work for the next Autumn season, or rather November–December" (original in Italian). Gronen Kubitzki performed (and recorded) the *Survivor* with the RAI Orchestra of Turin, conducted by Maderna, on 20 October 1961.

suggestion."[98] What is more, the protagonist of Kafka's *The Trial* apparently continued to occupy Maderna's thoughts, since his friend Nono, in one of the letters of encouragement he sent him that same year, reproaches him for wanting to almost wallow in restlessness and discontent, urging him to react, metaphorically relegating the protagonist of Kafka's *The Trial* to the past ("You've got into the habit of wanting to feel miserable, without <u>Grund [reason]</u>! Live plain and simple, Joseph K. is truly in the past, and we live for today and tomorrow and we are of today and tomorrow").[99] Finally, the note that defines the planned *Composizione n. 3* as "perhaps the 2nd series Kafka *Studi*" probably also dates to the second half of February or the first days of March 1952.[100]

The rest is history: Maderna would return to the writer's works again in 1953 with *Quattro lettere (Kranichsteiner Kammerkantate)* choosing this time a letter from the *Briefe an Milena*, published posthumously only the year before: Kafka at his *most personal*.[101]

---

98 Typewritten draft from Bruno Maderna to Erwin Piscator, dated 5 June 1952 (PSS-BMC, original in German). The search for additional items of this correspondence among the German director's papers, kept at the Morris Library of Southern Illinois University, Carbondale, within the Manuscript Collections, failed to provide any results.

99 PSS-BMC (undated letter).

100 See Maderna and Steinecke, *Carteggio/Briefwechsel* (see note 7), p. 44, n. 49. The date was determined by Paolo Dal Molin.

101 The work, also known as *Vier Briefe*, for soprano, bass, and chamber orchestra, premiered at the *Internationale Ferienkurse für neue Musik* in Darmstadt on 30 July 1953. This was followed by just three performances, all after Maderna's death; see the editor's "Premessa" to Bruno Maderna, *Kranichsteiner Kammerkantate* (1953), ed. Nicola Verzina (Milan: Suvini Zerboni, 2003), pp. vii–ix; and Nicola Verzina, "Musica e impegno nella *Kranichsteiner Kammerkantate* (1953): il tema della libertà," in *Bruno Maderna: Studi e testimonianze* (see note 55), pp. 199–226, in particular p. 200, n. 1.

Appendix

Caro Bruno, dato che papà ti deve scrivere, ne approfitto per spedirti l'abbozzo
della I scena del II atto, sezione (a)
La distribuzione delle scene del II atto io la proporrei così:
I scena: a) androne A con lavandaia, K, studente e usciere
         b) salone B trasformato in cancelleria con K, usciere, arrestati, impiegati e informatore
II scena: a) K - zio - avvocato
         b) K - Leni
         c) K - frustatore
         d) K - Block e licenziamento avvocato
Parliamo della I scena a) che è quella che ti mando. Come puoi constatare dalla lettura
del canovaccio e soprattutto con lo schizzo annesso, la scenografia è facilmente realizzabile.
Ho mantenuto lo scalone perché è un notevole esempio di quell'assurdità architettonica
che abbiamo già notato in vari punti. Ho introdotto invece una porticina senza inquadratura e che perciò si confonde con la parete (e che si scorge solo se aperta) (nel tipo di quella
che a casa tua dalla sala da pranzo porta nel corridoio) perché di lì è ben visibile l'apparizi-
one di Bertoldo e la sua fuga. La porta senza inquadratura può dar l'idea della segreteria
e può così dire dell'onnipresenza della legge che in ignoti calli sorveglia e sorprende. Sopra tale
porta ho introdotto una finestra alta e stretta donde (come nello schizzo) si scorgono degli scalini.
Da tale finestra ricompariranno Bertoldo e Lavandaia in fuga per le ultimissime battute.
Questi nuovi elementi (porticina e feritoia) possono figurare anche nella sceneggiatura della
II scena del I atto; ma potrebbero comparire anche soltanto in questa scena per ovvie ragioni.
Il dialogato, come vedrai facilmente, è stato un po' modificato con l'intenzione, almeno,
di renderlo più breve e più vivace, senza alterarne l'atmosfera.
Verso la fine della scena, rileggendo bene il testo, mi è parso che l'azione dialogata
avrebbe potuto benissimo risolversi in mimato prima e balletto poi con gradualità di
passaggi. Il giudizio lo lascio a te musicista che di queste cose te ne intendi e che
vedrai subito tutte le possibilità. Per parte mia aggiungo che musica e balletto
segnerebbero un buon passo avanti nella via della progressiva "snaturalizza-
zione borghese" verista e precisa, verso significati puri.
Ad ogni modo se il balletto non andasse è facile terminare la scena "more solito"
Veniamo ora alla sezione (b). La scenografia potrebbe essere la seguente.

APP. 1   Undated letter from Antonio [Toni] Tartaglia
to Bruno Maderna, fols. 1–3; PSS-BMC.

Il solito salone B [ara] senza il lastricato (ma si potrebbe anche lasciarlo, vuoto). Intorno alle pareti perimetrali e a conveniente distanza si alzano delle cancellate di legno altissime (si può togliere il soffitto e darebbe così l'illusione di prolungarsi all'infinito) al di là delle quali si scorgono gli impiegati al lavoro sui loro libri. Intorno alla cancellata e a distanza tale da lasciare un comodo corridoio in corrispondenza alla P_2 delle panche su cui siedono, fronte alla cancellata, gli arrestati. La pianta è pressapoco questa

Non pretendere la prospettiva, perché è troppo difficile. Dunque, dopo che Bertoldo e lavandaia sono scomparsi, terminato il balletto, (la musica potrebbe continuare per tutta la scena seguente) K è internato al divano. Entra da P_3 l'Usciere che lo invita alle cancellerie e lo fa entrare K (che un ri capace della topografia dei luoghi) nelle cancellerie per P_2. Percorrono il corridoio, dicendo quel che han da dire, fino al punto I dove compare l'Informatore col quale [K] ritorna indietro. Alla P_2 dalla parte di A avviene la scena famosa: K sta bene e Informatore male. Cala la tela e fin I scena; ma la rialzo subito per dire che durante la sezione (a) della scena, il salone B deve restare chiuso dai siparietti, e che K, con la mimica di sentirsi bene e di respirar meglio esce correndo da P_3.

II scena. Ecco la pianta: ... è divisa in 3 parti: a destra (A) stanza dell'avvocato da cui si entra per P_1. In mezzo stanza (B) di leni in cui si entra per P_2 ... A destra ufficio di K (C) A e B sono affetti. C è chiuso dal solito siparietto.

Sezione (a) della II scena: K e zio entrano in A: colloquio con l'avvocato e comparsa del giudice fino alla rottura del piatto da parte di leni che vi è ritirata, nel pattempo in B.

Sezione (b): K e leni parlano e leni offre il suo aiuto; [xxx], dopo aver mostrato che il sommier su cui son seduti è il suo letto, vi fa salire in piedi K dicendogli che per un'apertura nella parete si va direttamente nel suo ufficio (stranezza architettonica presa dall'episodio Tintorelli). Infatti proprio sopra il letto di leni si apre una specie di finestrone che dà nell'ufficio di K a livello del pavimento [Il profilo della scena è questo [diagramma] quindi il finestrone è alto dalla parte di B (K deve salire sul letto) ma è a livello del pavimento in C] In C si assiste all'episodio del frustatore (sezione c della scena). Dopo la spinta a Franz, K ritorna in B con leni (siparietto richiude C) qui dove avviene l'episodio del rotolamento per terra e la comparsa di Block con cui K — uscita leni — si intrattiene. Si ribella poi al quadro dipinto da Block ed esasperato

continuazione della lettera

⊗ della sua servilità, ritorna in A dove avviene la scena del licenziamento
dell'avvocato e la fine dell'atto.

Caro Bruno, adesso dovrei spiegar tutte le ragioni per cui ho fatto quello che
ho fatto, ma credo che in tutto abbastanza evidente anche il particolare del
funzione. Ho cercato di essere breve e chiaro, ma non come che non una
vanno facilmente d'accordo. Armati di pazienza e studia schizzi e spiegazioni
e dove sono oscuro aiutati tu. Ho dovuto naturalmente tralasciare un mucchio
di cose, ma sono stufo di scrivere. Avrei voluto mandarti il secondo atto completo
e rifinito, ma penso che è meglio stabilire degli accordi generali in via preliminare
per evitare lavoro inutile e perdita di tempo. Studia bene il tutto alla svelta e
rimandami la mess completa dei tuoi suggerimenti al più presto. Finché
non rispondi non lavoro.

Salutami tua moglie e baciamela abbondantemente. Vi ricordo sempre
tom

Carissimi saluti e abbracci

Leda

PAOLO DAL MOLIN

Maderna and the Poets, 1938–48

Gabriele D'Annunzio (*La sera fiesolana*)

The diary entry for 8 March 1938 of a seventeen-year-old student at Rome's Santa Cecilia Academy reads:

> Gabriele D'Annunzio died suddenly on 3 [*sic*] March.
>
> It is undoubtable that with him Italy has lost a great poet. But for me he had already died at least fifteen years ago. Indeed, it is hard to think of his recent production without feeling a certain sense of pity.
>
> He had now become a total wreck. Apart from him being well into his dotage, deranged, and displaying such childish behavior, it must be said, and this had been going on for a long time, that he was now one of those characters who belonged to a world which, in our experience, in our evolution that took place straight after the war, could be said to have disappeared. A "fish out of water."
>
> However, there is always his work which, one must admit, bears witness to a great poet and, in my opinion, at least a third of this will remain, uncontaminated by the passing of time, uncontaminated in the admiration of posterity.
>
> In my opinion, he will still have the well-earned right to be the third alongside Carducci and Pascoli and to be represented with them, as indeed is consistent with facts, in the compendiums of literature, as the last wonderful bud and the last meaningful fruit of our glorious literature.[1]

Maderna was not alone in reacting in this way toward D'Annunzio and his myth, and shared this revulsion for the commemoration of the "poet-soldier" with other more direct

---

All the letters quoted here, but lacking archival references, are housed in the Bruno Maderna Collection at the Paul Sacher Foundation (PSS-BMC). Most of the cited excerpts have already been published in "Per un ritratto di Bruno Maderna: estratti dalla corrispondenza" (see note 7). Some of these – provided to Raffaele Pozzi by Angela Ida De Benedictis – served as the basis for the selection published by Pozzi in his "Classicismo Romano: Maderna allievo di Bustini" (see note 1). The present article uses these and new sources to approach the topics of Pozzi's paper and the essays by Rossana Dalmonte on Maderna's poetic choices from a different perspective ("Scelte poetiche e letterarie," see note 36; and "Prima della serie," see note 33). I am grateful to Angela Ida De Benedictis, Claudia Vincis, Duilio Caocci, Gabriele Bonomo, and Jonathan Pradella, without whose help I would never have been able to pass this test; thanks also to Carlos Chanfón and Nicola Verzina. Note that the critical literary essays are mostly cited from the first edition. Unless otherwise specified, all the passages quoted from printed books or unpublished documents are translated from the original Italian version.

1   PSS-BMC, "Diario – Annotazioni e pensieri" (1938–39), cols. 8–10. The annotation already appeared in *Bruno Maderna: Documenti*, ed. Mario Baroni and Rossana Dalmonte (Milan: Suvini Zerboni, 1985), pp. 76–77, and is used by Raffaele Pozzi, "Classicismo Romano: Maderna allievo di Bustini," in *Maderna e l'Italia musicale degli anni '40*, ed. Gabriele Bonomo and Fabio Zannoni (Milan: Suvini Zerboni, 2012), pp. 45–82: 66. The young composer confuses the day of D'Annunzio's state funeral (3 March) with 1 March, the actual day of his death. Maderna studied in Rome from October 1937 to June 1940.

and authoritative literary voices.[2] In stating that the poet had "already died at least fifteen years ago," Maderna was blue-pencilling the poet's entire period of exile in the Vittoriale degli Italiani (1921–38) and therefore implicitly also deleting the *Libro Segreto*, despite its abundance of literary gems and even premonitory visions.[3] Instead, he assigned "at least one third" of the literary work of "a great poet" to history, and such a verdict presumably originated from his studies and the environment he frequented. The concluding remarks, referring to Carducci, Pascoli, and D'Annunzio as the three crowns of Italian poetry, is indeed a superficial commonplace in line with national propaganda.

Maderna would certainly have learned before 1938 to make distinctions within D'Annunzio's lyrical works on the basis of consolidated schemes. This is attested by two comments on the pages of a notebook of "Temi di italiano" (Italian essays), where he also analyzed several poems, including ones by the aforementioned Carducci and Pascoli, probably as practice for the cultural knowledge tests in the composition course.[4] The first comment deals with D'Annunzio's *I Seminatori* (from *La Chimera*), deemed to be "too baroque and rhetorical." The second instead mulls over the earlier *Canto novo* (Libro IV, ii), examining its content, versification, sound figures, and inspiration:

> This poem can really be said to be a pure lyric.
> There is no search for precious expressions, that rhetorical tendency and those psychological subtleties which the poet will later have; instead what dominates is pure feeling, artistic emotion, and that sense of spontaneity that is found in the soul of the true artist.

Maderna had clearly become aware of and spotted the first safe haven in D'Annunzio, *Canto novo*, the vertex of "pure lyric," so different from the poet's later "deviations," which actually include that "amusing exercise" of *La Chimera*.[5] With an eye to the future, we might say that Maderna was on his way toward the second of the "three greatest periods" of D'Annunzio's "long-lasting art."[6]

In fact, a few days after the poet's funeral, Maderna wrote to his adoptive mother, Irma Manfredi, that he had finally found in *La sera fiesolana* from *Alcione* (1903) the poem he needed to compose outside of his coursework, his first art song for tenor and orchestra.[7]

---

2   See for example Carlo Bo, *Diario aperto e chiuso: 1932–1944* (Milan: Edizioni di Uomo, 1945), p. 253. On D'Annunzio's reception, see at least Niva Lorenzini, *D'Annunzio* (Palermo: Palumbo, 1993), pp. 79–156.

3   I allude to the imaginings, present in the *Libro*, about the relationship between D'Annunzio and Maderna's future Maestro, Gian Francesco Malipiero.

4   Notebook conserved among the manuscript texts at PSS-BMC. Unless otherwise stated, all the following citations come from here.

5   Alfredo Gargiulo, *Gabriele D'Annunzio: Studio critico* (Naples: Perrella, 1912), pp. 441 and 444.

6   Giuseppe De Robertis, "Il 'Libro Segreto,'" in *Omaggio a D'Annunzio*, ed. Giuseppe De Robertis and Enrico Falqui, *Letteratura: rivista trimestrale di letteratura contemporanea* 3 (March 1939), pp. 59–66: 65.

7   See Maderna's letter to Manfredi, dated 6 February 1938 (but certainly after the following 3 March, the day of D'Annunzio's funeral, as can be seen from the incipit), and also the next letters of 23 and 28 March 1938 (in "Per un ritratto di Bruno Maderna: estratti dalla corrispondenza," in Bruno Maderna, *Amore e curiosità: Scritti, frammenti e interviste sulla musica*, ed. Angela Ida De Benedictis, Michele Chiappini, and Benedetta Zucconi (Milan: il Saggiatore, 2020), pp. 543–638: 553–54). Several incomplete drafts of the short and full score for *La sera fiesolana* can be found in the composer's fonds at PSS.

Events presumably led him to draw from both the *fons iuventutis* of Italian chamber music of the early twentieth century, and from what was by now the exhausted poetic source of the regeneration of the "true poetry of true poets," advocated around the 1910s by Ildebrando Pizzetti in emulation of the "ultra-modern" French and German composers.[8] More precisely, Maderna, just like some of his predecessors in the 1920s, was gathering from "D'Annunzio's best"[9] (with the approval of the critics) rather than from *Chimera*, the musicians' favorite.[10]

The young man refers his adoptive mother to "pag. 26" of an unnamed copy of *Alcione* that was evidently present in the library at her home in Verona. Thus, he was himself reading *Alcione* in the widely disseminated edition of *Oleandro* (1931, 1933), not in the more prestigious National edition or in other sources. This is more significant on a biographical and cultural level than in terms of authorial variants, since a stable printed version of *La sera fiesolana* had been around since 1903.

La sera fiesolana is engraved in hendecasyllables combined with nine-, seven-, and five-syllable lines, plus a few with twelve and thirteen syllables.[11] Its "imaginary landscape" of "the purest serenity" satisfied two of the three typological characteristics that Maderna had indicated to his friend Policarpo Crosara some weeks before, in a letter asking him to send him a bucolic poem offering a sense of tranquility and written in lines with a "rather long structure (hendecasyllabic, couplets etc.)" and "short [ones], more or less like a sonnet."[12] However, a few weeks later, the project on D'Annunzio was dropped[13] for reasons that can be gleaned from Maderna's accounts of those days, in his own lucid – at times desperate – self-analysis and in the surviving musical sources. The latter, relating to the musical setting of the first five verses of the poem, document the difficulty he had in setting D'Annunzio's text with his technical and stylistic means. Particularly challenging was the "strophic writing" of *La sera fiesolana*, which tends to overcome any preestablished limits of rhythmic cadence, to achieve a sort of complete circle, inside of which everything is "free and extremely understated."[14] While Alfredo Casella had set the first verse in five fluid lines of syllabic recitative, with the first two in "half voice, almost murmuring,"[15] in Maderna's fragment the phrasing of the voice part, also syllabic and *"Legato – a mezza voce"* (in the drafts for the short score, → **EX. 1A**), then *fortissimo* (draft of the score), is shortened.[16]

---

8   Ildebrando Pizzetti, "La lirica vocale da camera" (1914), in idem, *Intermezzi critici* (Florence: Vallecchi, [1921]), pp. 163–72: 166.

9   Gargiulo, *Gabriele D'Annunzio* (see note 5), p. 441.

10   See Mila De Santis, "Aspetti della lirica da camera su testi di D'Annunzio," in *D'Annunzio musico immaginifico*, ed. Adriana Guarnieri, Fiamma Nicolodi, and Cesare Orselli (Florence: Olschki, 2008), pp. 215–51.

11   Gargiulo, *Gabriele D'Annunzio* (see note 5), pp. 412–13.

12   Letter of 28 January 1938, cited by Pozzi, "Classicismo Romano" (see note 1), p. 65.

13   See Maderna's letter to Manfredi, dated 29 November 1938 (in "Per un ritratto di Bruno Maderna" (see note 7), p. 556).

14   Adelia Noferi, *L'Alcyone nella storia della poesia d'annunziana* (Florence: Vallecchi, [1942]), p. 239.

15   Alfredo Casella, *La sera fiesolana: laude di Gabriele D'Annunzio musicata per canto e pianoforte* (Milan: Ricordi, 1924).

16   The text reads as follows: "Fresche le mie parole ne la sera / ti sien come il fruscio che fan le foglie / del gelso ne la man di chi le coglie / silenzioso e ancor s'attarda a l'opra lenta / su l'alta scala che s'annera." See the translation in John Woodhouse, *Gabriele D'Annunzio: Defiant Archangel* (New York: Oxford University Press, 1998), p. 207.

EX. 1A–C Bruno Maderna, *La sera fiesolana* (1938),
draft of unfinished short score,
pp. 3, 4, and n.n.; PSS-BMC.

EX. 2   Bruno Maderna, note in his "Diario – Annotazioni e pensieri"
(1938–39), col. 14, excerpt; PSS-BMC.

The apprentice composer stumbles when he moves away from the tried and tested harmonic sequences by taking paths already frequented by illustrious forerunners, but which were quite impracticable. The clearest example is found in the very place of his "shipwreck," where a surprising morphological study on the musical material (two "osmotic" aggregates of seven sounds, their intersections and complementarity) obviously struggles to develop (→ **EXX. 1B–C**). On 26 February 1938, Maderna's diary bears an important trace of the mental horizon in which this type of research could be inscribed: "When you want to create an atmosphere that you feel in your deepest soul, then you can use any procedure that seems most appropriate to you."[17]

However, a number of reasons prevented Maderna from finding the right conditions to carry out such a profound and lengthy reflection. One was his intransigent attitude toward his own work ("I did the first piece three times and I'm still not happy");[18] another was his confusion at the words of his teacher, Alessandro Bustini ("he told me that [*La sera fiesolana*] is difficult but something really beautiful can be done," "he says that I want to run before I can walk").[19] He was also held back by a reverential fear of Pizzetti ("I am a little in awe of him and I would like him to clearly see my qualities as a composer, which is why I am weighing up the impressionism in my 'Sera' so carefully");[20] and, last but not least, he was overburdened with schoolwork for his upcoming exams ("As long as Bustini keeps on giving me a fugue for homework every lesson, I won't be able to go on with the composition").[21] Not only did such a demanding lifestyle prevent him from

---

17   In "Diario – Annotazioni e pensieri" (see note 1), cols. 7–8.

18   Letter to Manfredi, 21 March 1938 (in "Per un ritratto di Bruno Maderna" (see note 7), pp. 553–54).

19   Quoted from the letters to Manfredi, dated 6 February [sic] 1938 (see note 7) and 21 March 1938 (see note 18). On the relationship between Maderna and Bustini see also Pozzi, "Classicismo Romano" (see note 1), and Angela Ida De Benedictis, "Bruno Maderna Orchestration of the Piano Sonata, op. 7, movt. 1," in *Ignition: Beethoven. Reception Documents from the Paul Sacher Foundation*, ed. Felix Meyer and Simon Obert (Woodbridge: The Boydell Press, 2020), pp. 35–39.

20   Letter to Manfredi, 12 May 1938 (in "Per un ritratto di Bruno Maderna" (see note 7), p. 554). Maderna's and Manfredi's acquaintance with Ildebrando Pizzetti is documented as starting in summer 1934 and mentioned in his letters to his adoptive mother until December 1939. See also Mario Baroni and Rossana Dalmonte, "Notizie sulla vita di Bruno Maderna," in *Documenti* (see note 1), pp. 7–69: 37–49.

21   Letter to Manfredi, dated 21 March 1938 (but see also the next one, dated 23 March 1938). Both in "Per un ritratto di Bruno Maderna" (see note 7), p. 554

dedicating the required thought to the "lyricism" and "the meter" of *La sera fiesolana*,[22] but he was also finding it hard to get out of the stylistic and technical deadlock in which he knowingly found himself. "It is extraordinary," he confessed in his diary entry for 5 April 1938 (→ **EX. 2**), "that I have a bent for static impressionism. Once I have found a happy idea, it is difficult for me to carry it through, and I almost always get entrapped in a sort of static-mystical and motionless feeling."[23]

Vincenzo Cardarelli (*Alba*)

In mid-March 1939, Bustini granted Maderna some leave to write a cycle of songs.[24] The first, "for alto voice and string orchestra,"[25] was ready two months later, in time for his class's recital.[26] The piece, the result of a brief but painful gestation, was a setting of *Alba*, a poem by the living writer, poet, and essayist Vincenzo Cardarelli, in its last published version (1936).[27] Inspiration for the second piece was, however, much harder to find (as we read in a letter to Manfredi, dated 30 June 1939), and his good intentions came to nothing. Then *Alba* fell into oblivion, only to reappear in the 1980s after the composer's death.[28]

The context and the circumstances that made Maderna choose to set Cardarelli's work to music are for the moment still rather vague. We have very few accounts of the composer's literary preferences during his time in Rome, and they certainly do not satisfy our thirst for more information on the matter: a letter from a friend recalls readings by Latin authors and discussions on "classics (Petronius etc.), philosophers, religion, music,

---

22   Letter to Manfredi, dated 23 March 1938 (see note 21).

23   "Diario – Annotazioni e pensieri" (see note 1). See also the letter of 19 January 1943 to Manfredi, in which Maderna points the finger at "Debussy," "impressionist music," and "the pedagogical system, still in vogue today in our conservatories" as being guilty of that kind of impasse. In "Per un ritratto di Bruno Maderna" (see note 7), pp. 572–73.

24   See the letter of 15 March 1939 to Manfredi; in "Per un ritratto di Bruno Maderna" (see note 7), pp. 557–58.

25   As on the title page of the fair copy of *Alba*, preserved at PSS-BMC. The string orchestra consists of vn 1, vn 2, va, vc, and db.

26   See the letters to Manfredi of 7 and 17 May 1939; in "Per un ritratto di Bruno Maderna" (see note 7), p. 559. In the letter to his adoptive mother, dated the following 5 June, Maderna writes that the song for string orchestra and contralto has been copied and is ready to be performed at the recital (which, he adds, "perhaps may not go ahead").

27   In *Poesie* (Rome: Edizioni di Novissima, 1936). The poem had previously appeared in a periodical (*L'Italiano*, 1927) and in two books, *Il sole a picco* (Bologna: L'Italiano, 1929) and *Giorni in piena* (Rome: Quaderni di Novissima, 1934).

28   The first mention is in G[iordano] Mo[ntecchi], *Alba*, "Catalogo ragionato delle opere," in *Documenti* (see note 20), p. 180. A few years later the work was included in the Edizioni Suvini Zerboni catalogue: Bruno Maderna, *Alba: lirica per voce di contralto ed orchestra, su parole di Vincenzo Cardarelli* (1937–40), ed. Giorgio Magnanensi (Milan: Suvini Zerboni, ©1997). On the basis of Maderna's letters, the exact year of composition (1939) was subsequently determined by Angela Ida De Benedictis; see her "Introduzione," in Bruno Maderna, *Concerto per pianoforte ed orchestra (1942)*, ed. Angela Ida De Benedictis (Milan: Suvini Zerboni, 2011), p. vi. For the list and description of existing music manuscripts, see the inventories at PSS-BMC and the critical apparatus in the aforementioned edition of *Alba*, pp. iv–viii. It should be noted that in the score the song moves between B_2 and G_4, a tessitura more appropriate to a mezzo-soprano, if not to a soprano, than to a contralto.

fiction, love!";[29] the pages of the aforementioned diary evoke "Foscolo's verses" together with the music of Debussy (night of 8 May 1938) and *The Idiot* from "the incomparable pen of Dostoevsky" (31 July). They also transcribe prose that has yet to be identified; contemporary letters to Manfredi record the purchase of "two volumes by Thomas Hardy" (8 February 1938), "a French book by Thomas Mann," and "a collection of novels by Huxley" (4 May); in yet another, we read of the request for a "Storia comparata delle Religioni" (comparative history of religion; 7 December 1937). His letters to his adoptive mother, usually crammed with facts, lack any information about his reading preferences: the only poets named are D'Annunzio and Aldo Palazzeschi (more on this later), while Cardarelli and his *Alba* are never mentioned even during the genesis of the piece.

Several facts disprove the claim that Maderna's composition teacher had been the one to suggest *Alba*. Maderna tells Manfredi, in his letter of 17 May 1939, that Bustini had indeed indicated a poem, but for the second piece of the cycle, after the completion of *Alba* and when the differences it had caused between Maestro and pupil had been temporarily set aside: "I am happy about my song [*Alba*], finally finished and approved by the Maestro. Now I have to do another one, a short one. The Maestro recommended a text by Palazzeschi to me" (hence my hypothesis that he had not done the same for *Alba*). Then, if we take a look at Bustini's vocal compositions, we can see that the Maestro's literary tastes were dated or close to safe, second- or third-rank contemporary authors.[30] In guessing which of Palazzeschi's poems he might have suggested for the second piece, a better place to look would be in school anthologies rather than in the most remarkable and fiery *L'Incendiario*. The poem had to be shorter than *Alba*, one that served to tame the student's audacity (*Rio Bo?*),[31] a futile corrective measure: "[...] I tried to do something good with Palazzeschi," Maderna complained, "but his findings are too dull and nothing worked."[32]

If it is true that the text of *La sera fiesolana* was Maderna's stumbling block in the completion of his first song, repentance after a failure cannot really justify the composer's choice of another poet (Cardarelli). And it certainly does not explain why he plumped for one of his poems in particular (*Alba*), other than its obvious differences with the D'Annunzian laud. In other words, it would be vainly tautological to try and explain this failure, repentance, and new choice by merely referring to the structure, syntax, meter, and rhythm of the poem *Alba* alone. Any attempt at an explanation must necessarily consider the work of many other poets who were around at the time and extraneous to the D'Annunzian constructions, and also analyze the actual correspondence between Maderna's music and Cardarelli's text. Finally, the completion of *Alba* in itself indicates, at the very most, an extrinsic convergence of a poetic text and the compositional means of a tenacious student.

---

29 Letter from Charles Spence (signed Carlo Spence), dated 3 May 1939, on letterhead paper from St. Gregory Seminary, Mount Washington, Cincinnati, Ohio. Spence, like Maderna, had lodged at the Casa S. Carlo in Corso Umberto I in Rome.

30 See Pozzi, "Classicismo Romano" (see note 1), p. 70.

31 See for example, *Rio Bo: lirica per una voce e pianoforte* by Annibale Bizzelli (Rome: Pélissier, 1929), dedicated "Al mio Maestro Alessandro Bustini" (To my Maestro Alessandro Bustini).

32 Letter to Manfredi, dated 30 June 1939; in "Per un ritratto di Bruno Maderna" (see note 7), p. 559.

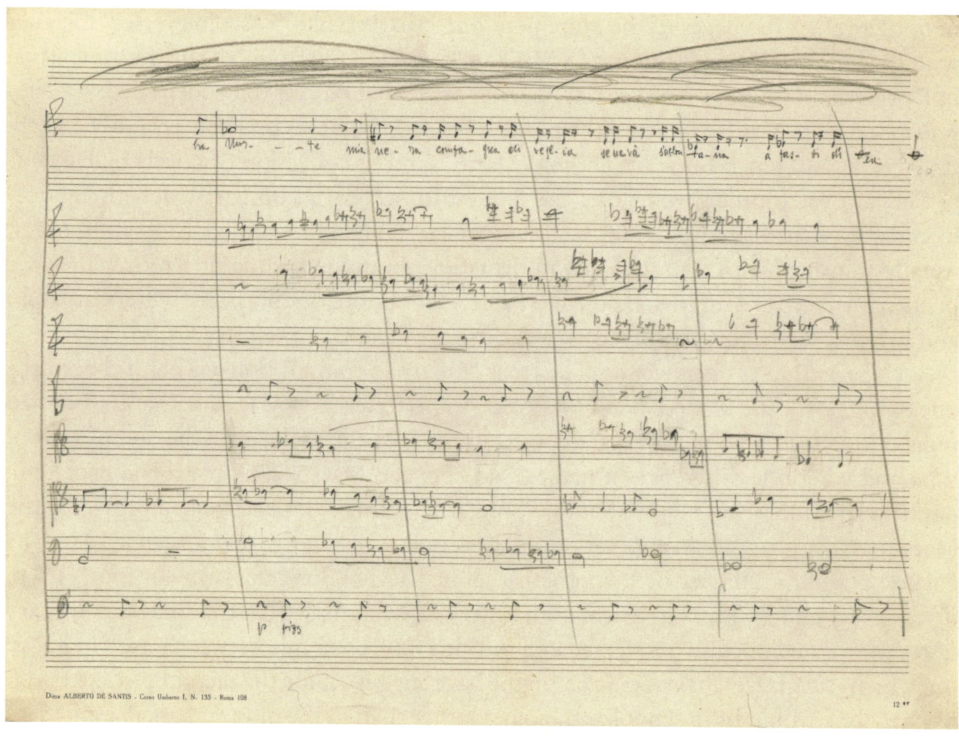

EX. 3   Bruno Maderna, *Alba* (1939), draft of bb. 50–55; PSS-BMC.

The properties of poetry and its setting to music call for painstaking observation, in terms of both the different metric and prosodic features of the text and as regards a non-homogeneous musical result. I shall just briefly mention two illustrative examples here.

1) It has been said that Maderna "does not feel tied to the rhythmic scansion of Cardarelli's verses" (an analysis, by the way, not lacking in errors in the metric calculation), "but that he prefers to extract images from them that he himself then subdivides or merges into different-length phrases."[33] And yet, in passages like the one at the end of *Lento con stanchezza* (bb. 50–56), "La morte mia nera / compagna di veglia, / se ne va, s'allontana / a passi di ladro" (two senarii, one septenary, and one senarius), it is all-too apparent that the linguistic structures (syntax and semantics) and the rhythmic-syllabic forms of the lines (the "amphibrach" in the senarii, the "anapest" in the septenary) generally correspond to the musical setting. A comparison with the stages prior to the definitive one, where the text is still grainy (see the eighth-note and sixteenth-note rests initially traced in the part of the song, → **EX. 3)** is most telling in this regard.

2) The differences that nevertheless occur between Cardarelli's verses and their setting should also be considered in the light of the creative process. In composing the

---

33   Rossana Dalmonte, "Prima della serie: Orientamenti stilistici di Maderna negli anni Quaranta: Le opere con testo poetico," in *Maderna e l'Italia musicale degli anni '40* (see note 1), pp. 129–39: 133.

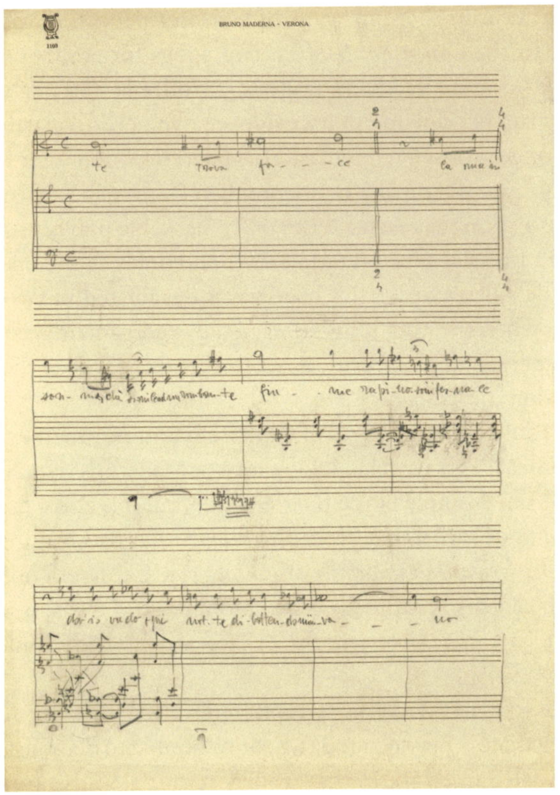

EX. 4   Bruno Maderna, *Alba* (1939), draft of bb. 16–24; PSS-BMC.

fourth line – a septenary ending with a proparoxytone, which Maderna elides with the next line ("Solo in te trova pace / *la mia insonnia ch'è simile^/ ad un rombante fiume*")[34] – the hiatus within the line imposed on "mia" and the rhythm of *"simile^ad un rom*bante" (with an imbalance on *"simi*le") depend on the reshaping of the passage. In fact, in the previous stages (→ **EX. 4**), *"la mia^in*sonnia" was set on *two* pitches (an upbeat melodic step) and *"simile^ad un rom*bante" was played in the space of a quarter note (triplet eighth note + two eighths), which gave an onomatopoeic rendering of the "image," an effect that remained in the instrumental parts of the final version.[35]

To explain Maderna's interest in the poet Cardarelli, scholars have to date either opted for existential causes[36] or environmental ones ("the Roman scene," where Cardarelli

---

34 The critical apparatus accompanying the edition of *Alba* edited by Magnanensi (see note 28) explicitly takes up the text of the poem from the 1948 edition (why?). Consequently Dalmonte (in "Prima della serie" (see note 33), p. 133) analyzes – and Pozzi (in "Classicismo Romano" (see note 1), p. 71) with fewer consequences transcribes – the later reading "l'insonnia mia ch'è simile," which was only set down *ne varietur* in the November 1942 edition of *Poesie*.

35 See also the transcriptions in the appendix to the edition of *Alba* (see note 28), p. 14.

36 See Rossana Dalmonte, "Scelte poetiche e letterarie," in *Studi su Bruno Maderna*, ed. Mario Baroni and Rossana Dalmonte (Milan: Suvini Zerboni, 1989), pp. 13–32: 16.

was a familiar figure). The latter causes are in want of a clearer definition, since they only appear in the reference to the *Colori del tempo*, "two songs for voice and piano" on Cardarelli's poems, composed and already published by Goffredo Petrassi, a former student of Bustini.[37] Pending further documentary evidence, we need to clarify that at that time Cardarelli was no longer considered a masterful poet, whatever later Maderna studies may say. In fact, the 1930s represent the moment when Cardarelli's career was *en route* toward the decline and isolation that even a series of "remarkable publishing events" failed to prevent.[38] Maderna's musical interpretation of *Alba* comes at the end of this intermediate decade – a decade when Cardarelli's poetry was devaluated in favor of Ungaretti's and Montale's works, when the poet himself reacted by reorganizing, collecting, and defending his work,[39] preparing a certain critical reassessment that paved the way for its wider and successful diffusion in the 1940s.[40]

The period offers us controversial images of Cardarelli and his poetry that bear little importance for our purposes unless we take a closer look at Maderna's response to the poem. *Alba* itself is a controversial example of the poet's work,[41] but it is also a prominent one: along with *Amore, Estiva* and *Adolescente* (from the *Prologhi*), it had featured in the celebrated anthology *Fiore della lirica italiana dalle origini a oggi*. Cardarelli opened the brief chapter on the twentieth century (Cardarelli, Saba, Montale, and Quasimodo), chosen as an example of "today's idea of lyric poetry in the strictest sense," "lofty," "universal," "dateless and placeless."[42]

It would be marvelous to place Maderna's reception of Cardarelli's poems within the literary field, to find the mediators between the two, or to be able to demonstrate that Maderna was that "stranger with a lively soul," that reader "with a sensitive intelligence and a recommended fast-moving heart," to whom the volume entitled *Specchio* was soon to be dedicated.[43] But the few available elements do allow us to reach some conclusions. First: with Cardarelli, Maderna set a poem that was enshrined in the Italian lyric tradition. And let us note *en passant* the short space in the *Fiore della lirica italiana* anthology between *Alba*, which opened the twentieth century, and, as it happens, D'Annunzio's *La sera fiesolana*, which brought the nineteenth century to a close.[44] Second: *Alba*'s score and

---

37 See Pozzi, "Classicismo Romano" (see note 1), p. 72. Maderna – let me add – had already met him in Venice in late August or early September 1938. See letter of 4 September 1938 to Manfredi (PSS-BMC).

38 See the "Introduzione" to Vincenzo Cardarelli, *Opere*, ed. Clelia Martignoni (Milan: Mondadori, 1981), pp. xi–xii.

39 See the "Prefazione" to Cardarelli, *Giorni in piena* (see note 27), p. 13.

40 In 1942 the Mondadori publishing house inaugurated the magnificent *Lo Specchio* poetry book series with the volume Vincenzo Cardarelli, *Poesie* ([Milan]: Mondadori, 1942).

41 See Giuseppe De Robertis, "Vincenzo Cardarelli, *Il sole a picco*. [...]," *Pegaso* 2, no. 2 (March 1930), pp. 371–74: 373, and, in contrast, Giansiro Ferrata, "Prefazione," in Cardarelli, *Poesie* (see note 40), p. 29.

42 Alfredo Gargiulo, "Sull'idea di lirica" and Enrico Falqui and Aldo Capasso, "Nota dei compilatori," in *Il fiore della lirica italiana dalle origini a oggi*, ed. Enrico Falqui and Aldo Capasso (Lanciano: Giuseppe Carrabba, 1933), p. vii and passim.

43 Ferrata, "Prefazione" (see note 41), p. 11.

44 This is not the late recognition of a previously unknown editorial source from which Maderna drew the texts of his first vocal lyrical pieces: the printed hypotext of his *La sera fiesolana* is known (see above); the *Alba* printed in *Fiore* is still that from *Sole a picco*.

its most successful passages show Maderna's penchant for this kind of poetry, while no other sources prove the young composer's acquaintance with other contemporary poets, not even ones with stable values, like Saba, Montale, and above all Cardarelli's "Roman" rival Giuseppe Ungaretti. Third: unlike Petrassi and his *Colori del tempo,* Maderna did not take *Alba* from a manuscript, a journal, or even from a prosometer, but from the entire collection of poems that Cardarelli had started to put together in the early 1930s.

This last remark goes beyond what is certainly an important finding as regards authorial variants. If Maderna read the *Poesie* in 1936, then he had presumably also read the preceding *Insonnia,* to then turn the page and find on the *verso Alba*'s unexpected, anaphoric apostrophe with its allocutive function. Thus, our analysis of this lyrical poem in music should be resumed from the exegesis of such a motif that was so fundamental to Cardarelli's production, and from the composer's drafts. And further indications can be found in Maderna's illuminating peritext that runs parallel to the work's gestation, not only in his letters, but also on the pages of his diary, which tell of doubts, difficulties, uncertainties, and the composer's inability to achieve "too lofty" musical ideals.[45]

Cenerentola, Ippolito

Two cantatas (*scènes lyriques*) composed in February–May 1940 as practice for the first part of the imminent diploma exam (→ **EXX. 5-6**) were also written in Rome.[46] The text of the first owes much to Maria Pezzè-Pascolato's libretto for Ermanno Wolf-Ferrari's *Cenerentola* (1900).[47] The other cantata came from a completely different source, that is, Ettore Romagnoli's translation of Euripides' *Ippolito.*[48]

---

45 See in particular the letters to Manfredi of 15 March, 23 April, and 3 May 1939 (in "Per un ritratto di Bruno Maderna" (see note 7), pp. 557–58), as well as the note dated 20 April 1939 in "Diario – Annotazioni e pensieri" (see note 1), this latter also transcribed in "Notizie sulla vita di Bruno Maderna," in *Documenti* (see note 1), pp. 48–49, with a comment that is no longer valid.

46 The chronology of their genesis can be seen once again from his correspondence with Irma Manfredi. See letters dated 22 February and 14 March 1940 (which show that Maderna was struggling with an opera scene, perhaps a first *Cenerentola,* which then got lost in the process) as well as 16 April and 10 May 1940 (for the completion of *Cenerentola* and the first short score for *Ippolito*). The last epistolary clues date back to 20 May of the same year ("I have to finish the orchestration of *Ippolito*"). See also in "Per un ritratto di Bruno Maderna" (see note 7), pp. 562–63.

47 See *Cenerentola: fiaba musicale in tre atti: azione scenica del maestro Ermanno Wolf-Ferrari, versi di Maria Pezzè-Pascolato* (Florence: Barbera, 1900). In the short score conserved in PSS-BMC, the beginning of the second act is set to music, then it is interrupted on the "Guarda" of the jester Nasturzio (p. 31), after which Prince Pallido's solo is radically cut, which also affects the subsequent exit of the royal couple (from "Non son triste, ma ignoro la gioia" to "Dimenticato / egli è dal ciel," pp. 29–31).

48 The thirty-three pages of the score (PSS-BMC) begin with the announcement of Phaedra's death ("Ahimè, ahimè! / Quanti siete qui presso, aiuto! Appesa / s'è la regina, di Tesèo la sposa") and end on the fourth verse of the chorus as they accompany her body into the palace ("Ahi, ahi, misera, o tua calamità! / Compiuta hai, perpetrata una tale opera / onde la casa tua sconvolta andrà. / Ahimè, [ahimè, con empio]"). The text used here comes from Euripides, *Le tragedie: Le supplici – Ercole – Ippolito* (Bologna: Zanichelli, 1928), in the series *I poeti greci tradotti da Ettore Romagnoli* (Euripides, *Tragedie* 3). The text transcribed by Maderna sometimes diverges from this edition in both spelling and punctuation, but not only. We thus still have to establish whether the composer used another edition, someone else's transcription, or just made some changes for musical needs.

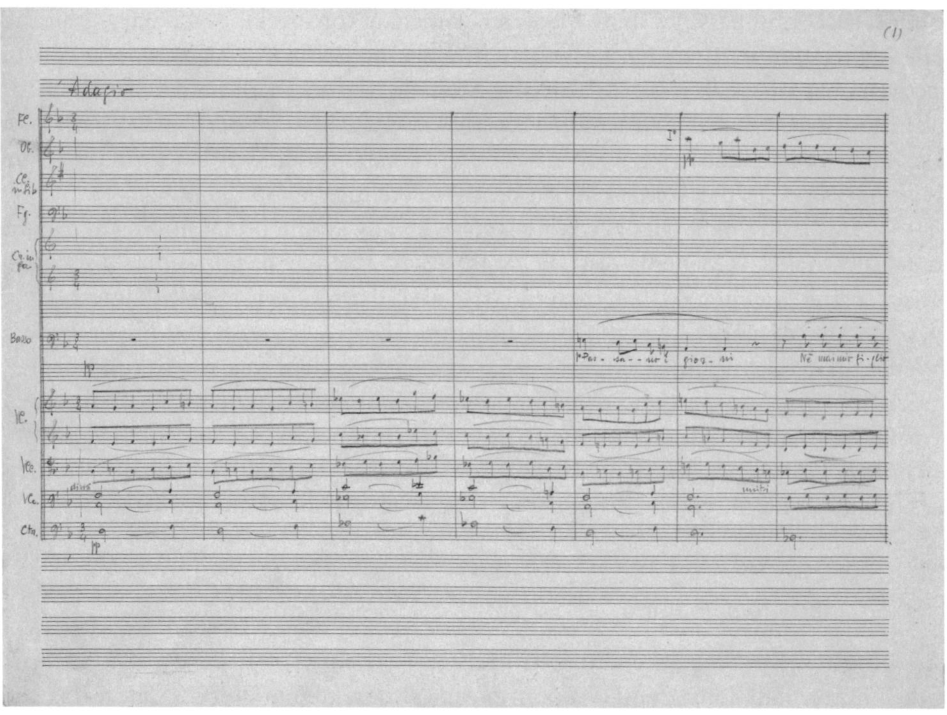

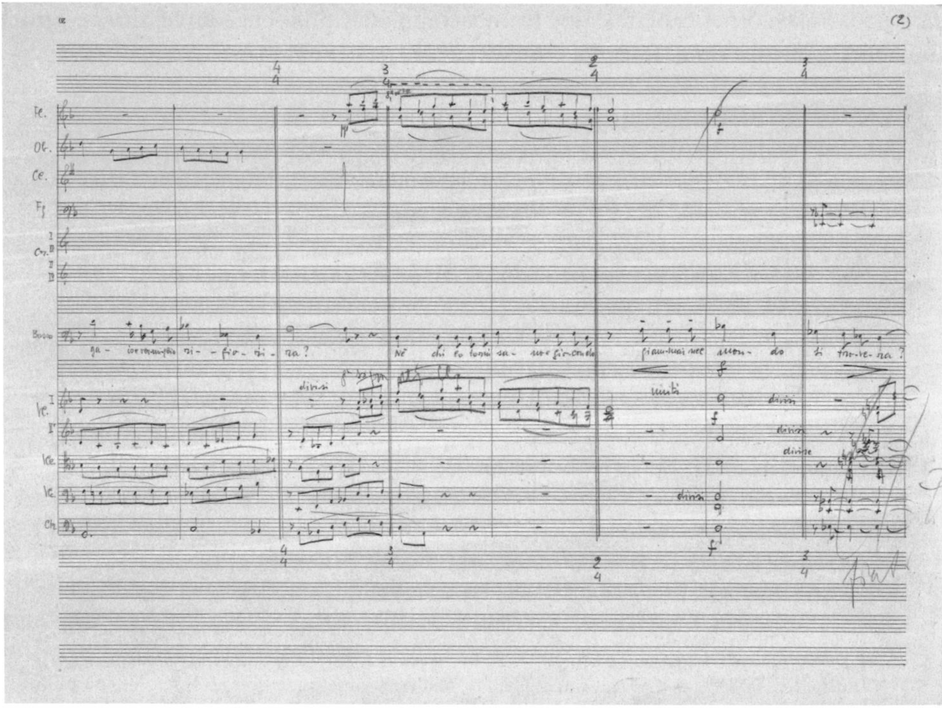

EX. 5A–B Bruno Maderna, *Cenerentola* (1940), autograph score
(incomplete) with allographic interventions, pp. 1–2; PSS-BMC.

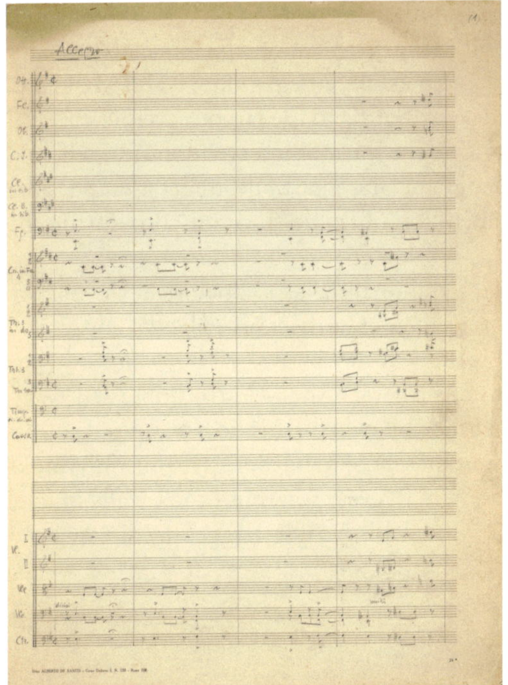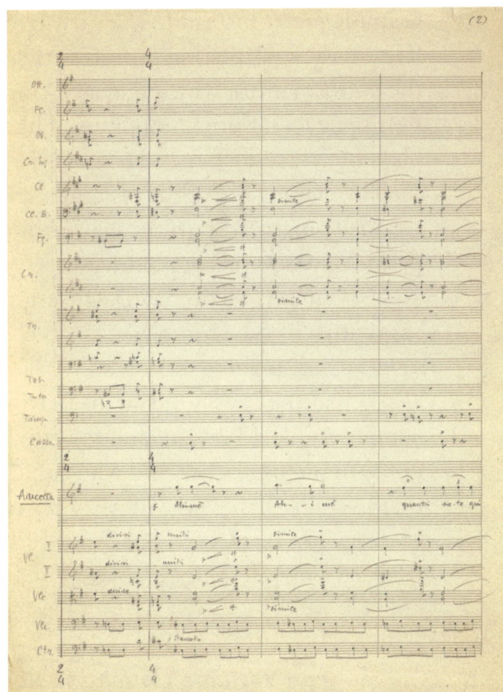

EX. 6A–B Bruno Maderna, *Ippolito* (1940), autograph score (incomplete), pp. 1–2; PSS-BMC.

The sources do not allow us to understand whether the texts were assigned by his composition teacher or whether Maderna chose them himself and, if so, whether they were on a list of indicated "study topics." The purely academic nature of writing the cantata on *Ippolito* is confirmed in his letter of 16 April 1940 to his adoptive mother, where he states that at first he did not have "the slightest idea what to do." However, his words may also hint at something else: although his literature tutor Aldo Pasoli and his readings of favorite classics might well have exposed Maderna to Romagnoli's translation of the "Greek poets," on this occasion, *Ippolito* was considered an imposition.[49]

The excerpts from *Cenerentola* and Euripides certainly complied with the educational objectives of the time, since the main aim of the *scène lyrique* was to acquaint the students with the greatest challenge in musical theater. They were required to provide the music for short plays or fragments of plays, usually written in verse, with two or more characters and on profane subjects. At the same time, however, both texts reflect specific trends, expectations, and contextual horizons that deserve further clarification in the future. For now, the best I can do is to illustrate a couple of points. Pezzè-Pascolato's poetry contained conventions of opera librettos of yesteryear. Romagnoli's well-known vilified versions, in barbarous meters or loose hendecasyllables (as in the fragment Maderna set

---

49 We have no proof that the Venetian Maria Pezzè-Pascolato (1869–1933) and "Brunetto" Grossato (Maderna) ever really met, let alone whether the composer had any interest in or fondness for her work.

to music), refer instead to the early twentieth-century revival of classical performances in Italy, to their adaptation for music theater, and to the composition of incidental music for the performances, which engaged composers such as Pizzetti, Zandonai, and Malipiero. Ever since 1914, Romagnoli himself had been contributing to the famous cycle of classical plays in Syracuse's Greek Theater, first by writing the musical interventions himself, and then by making use of the assiduous collaboration of Giuseppe Mulè, director of the Santa Cecilia Conservatory from 1925 until the Liberation of Rome, and thus also during the period of Maderna's apprenticeship.[50]

Finally, Maderna's manuscripts (Exx. 5 and 6) allow us to document the relative ease with which he completed the task and his feelings of satisfaction ("*Ippolito,* my second *scène lyrique,* is going quite well," "Maestro Bustini was very pleased with *Ippolito*").[51] They also reveal the causes of the underlying tensions between the Maestro, "obsessed" with composers like Mascagni and Puccini,[52] and the pupil, who, in his own way, tried at least not to upset his teacher, and who could not wait for school to be over: "He [Bustini] thinks that I want to make new music; I try to please him in every way, but I can't really imitate Mascagni or in any case make music like that. God willing, I'll finally get my diploma and be freed from all these miseries."[53]

Paul Verlaine (*Liriche su Verlaine*)

After a series of instrumental pieces, the war, and the *Requiem,* Maderna started setting poetry to music again with the three *Liriche su Verlaine* for soprano and piano. The exact date of the genesis of the work can be gleaned from the letters to his mother in the last two months of 1946. On 13 November, Maderna writes: "I've finished the composition of a song for soprano voice on Verlaine's words; I'll do two more and they'll be performed in Rome toward the end of December." On 24 November, he returned from a trip to the capital, where he had recorded the music for the film *Sangue a Ca' Foscari,* with plenty of news regarding film collaborations and concert projects, and with an exact date for the first audition: "They are going to perform my songs on Verlaine's text in Rome on 29 December." The work was then finished, as we learn from a later, undated letter, where he claims to have "finished the songs" and to have "printed them from the transparencies" so as to send them to Rome the next day.[54]

The rest of the story, pending new findings, is well known. The work may have featured in the composer's *curriculum vitae* in concert programs, but it is already missing from

---

50 See Mario Pintacuda, *Tragedia antica e musica d'oggi: la musica nelle rappresentazioni moderne dei tragici greci in Italia* (Cefalù: Misuraca, 1978), pp. 10–11.
51 Letters to Manfredi, dated 24 April and 10 May 1940; in "Per un ritratto di Bruno Maderna" (see note 7), pp. 562–63.
52 See the letter sent to Manfredi on 10 April 1940, during the gestation of *Cenerentola;* ibid., p. 562.
53 Letter sent to Manfredi on 24 April 1940, during the gestation of *Ippolito* (in ibid.).
54 These "songs" are undoubtedly the ones on Verlaine, seeing that in the same letter Maderna alludes to the music for the film *Il fabbro del convento – La rivolta dei cosacchi,* completed in the following months.

those of the late 1940s. The work was then performed and mentioned again in the mid-1980s.[55] In the late 1990s, it was released as a record for the first time, played on the basis of the only surviving source, which had a fair copy of the first and second songs and a draft of the third.[56]

Apart from the existence of an "autograph" on a transparency and its photomechanical reproduction, both of which are now missing,[57] Maderna's correspondence bears witness to periods of rapid elaboration and an unspecified Roman destination. The same documents, however, do not tell us why Maderna composed, in these circumstances, three songs for soprano and piano, and why he set Paul Verlaine and not another author to music. On this last point, however, clues or at least some suggestions come from the context, on account of Verlaine's public image and the circulation of his poetry around 1946.[58]

The years 1944–46 saw an unprecedented and remarkable boom in Italy of Verlaine editions and criticism. Such popularity was evidently favored by the ferment of postwar cultural revival and by the two important Verlainian anniversaries of the decade: the one-hundredth anniversary of his birth in 1944 and, above all, the fiftieth anniversary of his death in 1946.[59] Over these three years, great numbers of works by Verlaine came out in translation and in the original French, albeit still in limited or prestigious editions and in artist's books.

Between June and November 1946, the anniversary of his death was commemorated in numerous periodicals, celebrated by men of letters – poets, translators, critics – and artists from different backgrounds, who had all had some dealings with Paris in their lives. And they wrote from every angle with the common goal of redeeming Verlaine from indifference or disaffection or at least to allow him a discerning reappraisal. Of course, there is no evidence to justify the claim of a direct relationship between the fiftieth anniversary of Verlaine's death and the composition of Maderna's *Liriche su Verlaine,* but the following can be stated without fear of contradiction. First: the period of elaboration of the three songs in question coincided with the last months of the significant acme of Verlaine's fortune in Italy. Several leading figures who worked in or gravitated toward Venetian circles, the place where Maderna now lived, and who were close to Malipiero

---

55   See G[iordano] Mo[ntecchi], "Liriche su Verlaine," in "Catalogo ragionato delle opere" in *Documenti* (see note 1), p. 190.

56   See Bruno Maderna, *Liriche su Verlaine: per voce di soprano e pianoforte (1946–47),* ed. Benedetto Passannanti (Milan: Suvini Zerboni, 1997), with description of the manuscripts on pp. v–vi and viii–x. The recording is the one on Stradivarius CD 33547, 2002 (recorded in December 1998, with Alda Caiello accompanied by Maria Grazia Bellocchio); the CD booklet mentions an edition of the score from 1985, although the publisher has no (official) record of this. In any case, in bar 55 of *Sérénade,* Caiello either misreads the text or is reading from an erroneous transcription. See note 75.

57   If this deduction is correct, then Passannanti's hypotheses on the drafts and on the different degree of "completion" of the third piece with respect to the others become untenable; see Maderna, *Liriche su Verlaine* (see note 56), pp. vi–vii.

58   For further information on the following topics, see Paolo Dal Molin, "Le *Liriche su Verlaine* di Bruno Maderna: Disposizione, testo poetico, occasioni di un'opera giovanile e luoghi critici della sua fortuna postuma," *Philomusica on-line* 18 (2019) 1; http://riviste.paviauniversitypress.it/index.php /phi/article/view/2026 (consulted 24 June 2021).

59   See Antoine Fongaro, "Introduction," in idem, *Bibliographie de Verlaine en Italie* (Florence: Sansoni; Paris: Didier, 1976²), p. 41. See also Paolo Dal Molin, "Le *Liriche su Verlaine* di Bruno Maderna" (see note 58).

(Diego Valeri and Filippo De Pisis above all) had contributed to the poet's success. Second: compared to Cardarelli and his *Alba,* and to the other authors that Maderna set to music after 1946 (Quasimodo), Verlaine was an obligatory but obsolete poet from the past,[60] Debussy's favorite poet, a source of the outdated "Italian decadence" of Pascoli and above all D'Annunzio.[61] Third: in terms of the history of composition, setting Verlaine to music after the 1920s was a singular operation disconnected from any trend in vocal music.[62]

In their posthumous first edition, Maderna's *Liriche su Verlaine* open with a setting of *Green* entitled *Aquarelles.* The poem is in fact the first of the six *Aquarelles* from *Romances sans paroles* that had already been a favorite of Debussy, Fauré, Hahn, and many others, including Francesco Paolo Tosti (*Rêve*). *Sérénade* follows, from the earlier *Poèmes saturniens,* whose text inspired so many composers (Louis Vierne and Tony Aubin for example). The cycle closes with *Sagesse,* a title borrowed from Verlaine's *recueil* of the same name. In this case, Maderna did not work on pages that had already been set (by Ravel, Varèse, Stravinsky, Vierne, Hahn, Delius, Fauré, Vaughan Williams, Séverac, Le Flem, and Debussy), but used the opening poem of the second part ("Ô mon Dieu, vous m'avez blessé d'amour"), an object of hard-won admiration in literary circles, but the subject of very few and soon-to-be-forgotten compositions.

We do not know whether the three texts he set to music were taken from separate editions of each collection (unlikely) or from a "complete" edition of Verlaine's poetic works, or again from one of the various anthologies printed before 13 November 1946. Apart from the obvious errors and various differences in writing, it should be noted that Maderna certainly copied from a source that has the following two distinguishing features: "Ange" (*Sérénade*) is rightly written with a capital letter; lines 34 and 36 of *Sagesse II,i* have an "!" after "Hélas" and not "Hélas," (vv. 34 and 36) or "Hélas," (v. 34) and "Hélas!" (v. 36). Finally, the text for *Green* basically corresponds to the one appearing in the second and later printed editions, and not to the *editio princeps* wrongly indicated by the editor.[63]

The order of the three songs adopted in 1997 does not come from the sources, nor does it follow the chronology of Verlaine's works (the *Poèmes saturniens* are several years and three books earlier than the *Romances sans paroles*). In Maderna's manuscript, the three pieces are unnumbered and the autograph pagination (in pencil, above) starts again at the beginning of each melody, while the continuous one (in Indian ink, at the bottom of the page) is allographic and added later (→ **EXX. 7–9**). Then, the first page of *Sérénade* (Ex. 7) bears the subheading "for soprano voice and piano" and the wording "from *Poèmes saturniens* by Verlaine," thus citing the poet's name, unlike the other two cases. In other words, the paratext of the *Sérénade* is richer than those of the other two songs; both subheading and wording call to mind the expression Maderna used in the aforementioned

---

60   More about this in Italo Siciliano, "Morto due volte," *Fiera Letteraria* I, nos. 19–20 (15–22 August 1946), p. 5.

61   See for example Walter Binni, *La poetica del decadentismo italiano* (Florence: Sansoni, 1936), pp. 86–92.

62   See Ruth L. White, *Verlaine et les musiciens* (Paris: Librairie Minard, 1992), p. 125.

63   See Maderna, *Liriche su Verlaine* (see note 56), p. 1. Verlaine's reprinted text (ibid., p. xiv) is expressly based on the 1957 Gallimard edition (why?), except where Maderna's autograph version was deemed more appropriate.

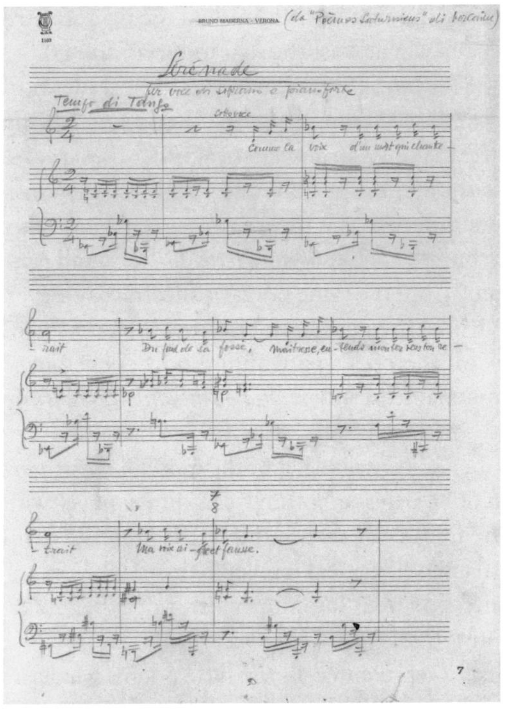

EX.7(↑) Bruno Maderna, *Liriche su Verlaine: Sérénade* (1946), autograph score, p. 1; PSS-BMC.

EX.8(↗) Bruno Maderna, *Liriche su Verlaine: Aquarelles* (1946), autograph score, p. 1; PSS-BMC.

EX.9(→) Bruno Maderna, *Liriche su Verlaine: Sagesse* (1946), autograph draft, p. 1; PSS-BMC.

letter to Manfredi of 13 November 1946, announcing that he had finished the first of three pieces on Verlaine, which suggests that *Sérénade* was at least the first to be composed.

Of course, the sequence *Aquarelles – Sérénade – Sagesse*, which is almost identical to the one found in the "catalogue raisonné" of 1985,[64] complies with criteria for drawing up an inventory: first the two fair copies of the melodies in alphabetical order (*Aquarelles, Sérénade*), then the *Sagesse* draft. However, although this is quite acceptable on the musical level, it barely overshadows a truly salient aspect of the three *Liriche su Verlaine* that distinguishes the work from, for example, Debussy's well-known *Ariettes oubliées* and *Fêtes galantes*. The texts set by Maderna do not come from the same poetry collection, nor even from a section within a collection, but are from three different books, which represent three or indeed *the* three crucial moments on the poet's path (Edmond Lepelletier).[65] This was the view that inspired the pages on Verlaine in *Autonomia ed eteronomia dell'arte* (1936), perhaps the most successful essay in the first "scientific" reception of the poet (Fongaro).[66] For Anceschi, Verlaine's most fundamental contribution to the cause of *poésie pure* essentially lies in *Sagesse*, where the tradition of French symbolism turns into a prayer with music as its "principle of independence." The music was that found in the *Romances sans paroles*, after the "transition" from the "harsh and self-critical intellectualism" (*Poèmes saturniens*) to the "more fluent, more lucid" confession, the "luminous mirror of experience," the "counterpoint of a cheerful autobiography" (*La Bonne Chanson*).[67]

Thus, (the) three Verlaine moments are represented in the lyric poems Maderna set to music by three pieces that are just as emblematic of the collection they belong to, as they are exceptional on the metric and/or strophic level: the stilted parody of the serenade, the classicizing *alborada* (Diego Valeri), and the *"poignante prière"* (Charles Morice) or *"prières dolentes et transies"* (Joris-Karl Huysmans) so notoriously stigmatized in Italy by Benedetto Croce.[68]

As we said before, no one knows whether Maderna was told to set these texts to music or whether he chose them himself while he was exploring Verlaine's works. On reading his most intimate papers that reveal his vices, doubts, and virtues, as well as a hard-fought faith that lends itself to a comparison with the sensual Catholicism of *Sagesse*, one might even be forgiven for thinking that he empathized with the poet.[69] And yet, a couple of glitches in metrics, prosody, and language indicate that the venture was somewhat impetuous. Still, neither hypothesis (Verlaine by assignment, or Verlaine by choice) contradicts the fact that the triptych illustrates the great poet's career, although who knows whether it sings its praises. In fact, each of the three *Liriche su Verlaine* are just as unique as each of the three poems and representative of the poet's different phases: a "degenerate" cabaret-style habanera, a stylistically spurious genuine *mélodie*, and an archaic-modernist hymn.

---

64   See above, note 55.

65   Edmond Lepelletier, *Paul Verlaine: sa vie – son œuvre* (Paris: Mercure de France, 1907), p. 242 (see also p. 241).

66   Luciano Anceschi, *Autonomia ed eteronomia dell'arte: sviluppo e teoria di un problema estetico* (Florence: Sansoni, 1936), pp. 154–80.

67   Ibid., pp. 155–57 and 160–61.

68   See his harsh words in the "Nota sul Verlaine," *La Critica* 60 (1942), pp. 164–172: 168.

69   Several pages of the aforementioned "Diario: Annotazioni – Pensieri" (see note 1) and his letters to the Capuchin friar Policarpo Crosara tell us more about this.

EX.10   Bruno Maderna, *Liriche su Verlaine: Aquarelles* (1946),
autograph score, p. 6 (bb. 44ff.); PSS-BMC.

Although the score has been around for about twenty years, neither musicologists nor musicians seem to have been queuing up to either analyze or perform it. It is easy to see why! Maderna has now mastered formal construction and its effects, and he no longer ends up in the blind alleys of "*static* impressionism" and "*motionless* mysticism,"[70] even where "counterpoint rules" do not apply.[71] But the music is extremely unrestrained and modular; the composer's talent and odd genius coexist in an unequal product. The analyst has to deal with the interpretive difficulties of a large amount of twentieth-century post-tonal repertoire, whose sound and gestures are on display. But, if one then takes away the composer's strategies, the coherence between compositional technique, reference system, and sound effect remains elusive.

For example, consider the moment of sweet, torpid calm after the "bonne tempête" ("*Dolcemente*") at the end of *Aquarelles* (bb. 44ff., → **EX. 10**). The components are clearly there for all to *see*. But one has to ask oneself how the hypnotic "compound" of

---

70 For the quotes see above, note 23 (my italics).
71 Letter from Maderna to Manfredi, dated 19 January 1943 (see note 23).

piano and voice in the first two occurrences, and then in the final resynchronized variant ("*a bocca chiusa*"), actually sounds to the listener. If it is modal, as it seems to be, what is or are the tonic(s)? Perhaps there is more than one answer, but invoking the "independence of the two parts"[72] does little to solve the problem: if anything, it may indicate a compositional premise. To such an extent that on the previous page of *Aquarelles* (bb. 36–43), where there is a glimpse of "the only moment of union" between voice and piano,[73] the answers to the same questions are to date both contradictory and unsatisfactory: "it is used for the vocal part," or "essentially a Phrygian scale, transposed on A, but lacking the E."[74] However, the voice does indeed dwell for a while on the notes of the tetrachord (D-C-B♭-A) and passes under different modal lights (at bb. 38_2–39_1, 39_2–40_1, and again at 40_2–41_1). When it gets to G (bb. 41_3–42_1), it becomes part of the "diatonic collection" with two flats. Finally, when it deploys all the notes of the hexachord (B♭-F-C-G-D-A), the last E to be heard is an E flat on the piano, while the natural E was previously there and will return afterwards in other harmonic fields.

Switching our attention elsewhere, we could examine the final two "barbaric" sequences of *Sagesse* (bb. 24–45) for their prominent octatonic harmony (stanza "Hélas! Vous, Dieu d'offrande et de pardon" and line "Hélas! Ce noir abîme de mon crime") and the high-level chromatic transformations of the "octophonic" line (8–2a) "Voici mes yeux luminaires d'erreur" (bb. 24–26 and 30–33), varied over "Dieu de terreur et Dieu de Sainteté" (8–5b).

The iteration of musical patterns certainly affects the text-music relationship of these Madernian experiments with French poetry and with Verlaine, too. The most obvious examples are certainly found in *Sagesse* and in *Sérénade*. In the latter, the lines flow over a sequence of vertically "ambiguous" chords by means of motivic variants and invariants, with frequent alienation effects on the sung text. The same rhythmic and intervallic profile (applied to various transposition levels) is imposed on the pentasyllable throughout the whole piece, with a melodic and expressive variation on the *clou* ("Mon Ange! ma Gouge"), and with just one exception ("Les nuits d'insomnie"). However, the model does not seem to fit perfectly with any of the lines and ends up corrupting the prosody of some segments preceding the ictus on the fifth syllable.

As far as the decasyllable is concerned, in cases of ambiguity, Maderna chooses between 4•6 and 6•4 ("Comme la voix • d'un mort qui chanterait" etc., but "Puis je louerai beaucoup, •comme il convient"); or he manipulates the 4•6 in various ways, opting for unforeseen alternatives ("Ouvre ton âme et ton ore • ille au son") or strongly emphasizing the second syllable ("Je *chan*terai tes yeux d'or et d'onyx" and "Puis *le* Lethé de ton sein, puis le Styx"); while nothing remains of the 4•6 to which "Dont le parfum opulent me revient" can be traced back. Musical grafting onto the decasyllables sometimes forces the structures of the text into a contrived execution. The paroxysm of this phenomenon is reached at the end of the fifth stanza, before the final refrain ("Et pour finir"). "Dont le

---

72 Dalmonte, "Prima della serie" (see note 33), p. 137.

73 Ibid.

74 Marina Giovanni, "Il linguaggio armonico del giovane Maderna," in *Bruno Maderna: Studi e testimonianze*, ed. Rossana Dalmonte and Marco Russo (Lucca: LIM, 2004), pp. 257–74: 267.

parfum opulent" (seven syllables) receives a melodic extension of the preceding "Puis je louerai beaucoup" (six syllables), before the repetition of "le parfum opulent me revient" without "Dont"; "anapestic" meter then takes precedence, even over the pentasyllable that follows (here lies the exception), splitting the monosyllabic *nuits* (nights) into *"nu-its"* (*sic*).[75]

Greek Lyric Poets

Two years after *Liriche su Verlaine*, Maderna composed *Tre liriche greche* for soprano, chamber choir and seven instruments on an anonymous *Canto mattutino*, Melanippides' *Le Danaidi*, and Ibycus' *Stellato*, which come from Salvatore Quasimodo's translation of *Lirici greci* (second edition, 1944). The triptych was the first of Maderna's works ever to be published.[76] The composer never conducted and perhaps knew nothing about the few performances that took place during his lifetime.[77] Historiographical issues have sparked the recent renewal of research interest in these works: *Tre liriche greche* are considered to be Maderna's first dodecaphonic work, and Quasimodo's *Lirici greci* figure among the major "literary events" of the 1940s in Italy,[78] with notable effects in the setting of (classical) poetry to music.[79]

There is no need to reexamine all these issues here, which would in any case be impossible. It is well known that the reception of the *Lirici greci* in Maderna's work, and likewise in that of Luigi Nono and Eunice Catunda, was mediated by the three cycles of melodies previously composed by Luigi Dallapiccola (1942–45) on the first edition of the collection (1940). This was a *sub specie artis* mediation, particularly through a "stricter dodecaphonic approach" that finally seemed to materialize "with the cycle of *Liriche greche*."[80]

Documents tell us that Nono and Maderna might have misunderstood the connection between text and music in Dallapiccola's triptych (*Cinque frammenti di Saffo*, *Sex Carmina Alcaei*, and *Due liriche di Anacreonte*). Neither of them initially grasped that there was a necessary and fundamental congruity for Dallapiccola between that "radical choice" of language for *Cinque frammenti di Saffo* back in 1942 ("I have extended some of

---

75 However, Maderna also splits "fru-its" at the beginning of *Aquarelles* (see Ex. 10). As compared to the autograph manuscript, the rhythmic profile of "je dirai le baiser" is wrong in the critical edition, as well as in Dalmonte, "Prima della serie" (see note 33), p. 138. Maderna subtly changes the rhythm of "d'un mort qui chanterait" / "monter vers ton retrait" / "pour toi cette chanson" / "à me martyriser," so that the stress is not on "*dirai.*"

76 The work is included in the Ars Viva Verlag catalogue, with copyright dated 1951.

77 See the essay by Maurizio Romito in this volume, p. 277. See also Bruno Maderna, *Tre liriche greche per piccolo coro, soprano solo e strumenti (1948)*, ed. Alberto Caprioli (Milan: Suvini Zerboni, 2002), pp. vii–viii. The work premiered in London on 5 March 1965 at the St. Pancras festival; see "Bruno Maderna's 'Greek Lyrics,'" *The Musical Times* 106, no. 1465 (March 1965), p. 186.

78 For more on the collection and its reception, see at least Niva Lorenzini, "Postfazione," in Salvatore Quasimodo, *Lirici greci*, ed. Niva Lorenzini (Milan: Oscar Mondadori, 2004), pp. 219–75 (first edition: 1985).

79 See Anna Scalfaro, *I "Lirici greci" di Quasimodo: un ventennio di recezione musicale* (Rome: Aracne, 2011).

80 Luigi Nono, "Luigi Dallapiccola and the *Sex Carmina Alcæi*" (ca. 1948), in *Nostalgia for the Future: Luigi Nono's Selected Writings and Interviews*, ed. Angela Ida De Benedictis and Veniero Rizzardi (Oakland: University of California Press, 2018) pp. 125–26: 125.

my dodecaphonic research beyond the limits of my previous work")[81] and "the knowledge of the *Lirici greci* volume, translated by Salvatore Quasimodo and published in 1940 by the Milanese publishing house Corrente."[82] They did not grasp the personal and epochal conjunction between the "radical choice" of musical language and the wish for "hellenische Heiterkeit" (Hellenic serenity) finally satisfied by Quasimodo's "sublime" and anti-rhetorical translation.[83] In fact, Nono understood from Dallapiccola's paraphrase that the latter wanted "to write music in contradiction with the text,"[84] while Maderna felt that Alcaeus' verse did not convey "the development in canonical form";[85] and, after all, while Nono was experimenting with the non-fragmentary but highly concentrated poetry of Ungaretti's *Allegria*, and about to try his hand at giving it a corresponding musical dimension (eight bars of *Sprechgesang* for the couplet of *Eterno*),[86] Maderna was grappling with composing the lengthy labyrinth of Franz Kafka's *The Trial* for the stage.[87]

However, traces of an indirect literary judgment via negation do emerge from this misunderstanding: Sappho's, Alcaeus', and Anacreon's lyric poems are considered different from the "contrapuntal nature of the utmost soundness" of Dallapiccola's music, from his "sense of architecture" – in short, from his "organic and logical impulse that finds its resolution in the dodecaphonic vision."[88] Or in his own words: "I chose a very 'vague' text," Dallapiccola replied to Nono, presumably quoting him, "*precisely* because I wanted to be able to write something 'very vague' while using the most precise contours [canons, etc.] that one can imagine."[89] Such traces signal at least some sense of the "alogical," "anti-syntactic," "random fragmentary state" of Greek lyric poetry, which favored the "encounter between Greek poetry and new poets."[90] And something else seems to emerge from the aforementioned letter when Nono talks about *Sex Carmina Alcaei* and suggests a correspondence between the "specific poetic quality of the text" (all six fragments) and the intervals of the only series considered in Hindemith's tensional perspective.[91] He might (also) have considered the "specific poetic quality of the text" as being suspended between the *enfance perdue* of ancient civilization and the contemporary unrest.

---

81   Letter of 19 July 1942 from Luigi Dallapiccola to Massimo Mila, published in Luigi Dallapiccola and Massimo Mila, *Tempus aedificandi: carteggio 1933–1975*, ed. Livio Aragona (Milan: Ricordi; Rome: Accademia Nazionale di Santa Cecilia, 2005), pp. 52–54: 53.

82   Luigi Dallapiccola, "A proposito delle *Due liriche di Anacreonte*" (1961), in idem, *Parole e musica*, ed. Fiamma Nicolodi (Milan: il Saggiatore, 1980), pp. 440–42: 441.

83   Ibid.

84   Letter of 16 November 1947 from Luigi Dallapiccola to Luigi Nono, quoted by Gianmario Borio, "L'influenza di Dallapiccola sui compositori italiani nel secondo dopoguerra," in *Dallapiccola: letture e prospettive*, ed. Mila De Santis (Milan: Ricordi; Lucca: LIM, 1997), pp. 357–87: 359.

85   Letter from Luigi Dallapiccola to Bruno Maderna, dated 27 June 1948, quoted by Maurizio Romito, "Lettere e scritti," in *Studi su Bruno Maderna* (see note 36), p. 57.

86   See Paolo Dal Molin, "'È giovane pieno d'intelligenza e di finezza': Luigi Nono e *L'Allegria* di Ungaretti," *Rivista Italiana di Musicologia* 49 (2014), pp. 177–210.

87   See the essay by Claudia Vincis in this volume, pp. 383–414.

88   Nono, "Luigi Dallapiccola and the *Sex Carmina Alcæi*" (see note 80), p. 125 and passim.

89   In his letter to Maderna (see note 85), Dallapiccola refers to the "stato d'animo assai indefinito dei versi" (the rather vague mood of the lines) of Alcaeus' third melody, *Già sulle rive dello Xanto ritornano i cavalli*.

90   Manara Valgimigli, "Poeti greci e Lirici nuovi," *Fiera Letteraria* 1, no. 8 (30 May 1946), pp. 1–2: 2. But for more on this point in particular see above all Luciano Anceschi's prefaces to the first two editions of Quasimodo's translation of the *Lirici greci* (1940 and 1944).

91   Nono, "Luigi Dallapiccola and the *Sex Carmina Alcæi*" (see note 80), p. 126.

Even more eloquent indications come to light if one compares the choices and handling of the *Lirici greci* in Dallapiccola's and Maderna's scores (and those of Nono and Catunda). In Dallapiccola's case, after writing a choral work on Romagnoli's translation of Alcaeus (*Estate*, 1932), he felt obliged to purposefully use a solo voice for Sappho's, Alcaeus', and Anacreon's melic monodies ("My reading of the *Lirici greci*, the poetic rethinking of Salvatore Quasimodo [...] prompted the idea of rethinking them in music, and above all melodically").[92] And this is a *single* voice, which is sustained by, but also swallowed up by, the instruments; a singing that is mindful of the prosody and of the comprehensibility of the text and thus differentiated by its character, dynamics, pacing, and expression, with prompt precision (where needed) and a refined and detailed literary style: from the "*pp* quasi parlato; semplice, ma insinuante" (*pp* almost spoken; simple, but insinuating) of *Cinque frammenti di Saffo, II*, to the "(torbido) mormorato" ((dense) murmured) of *Cinque frammenti di Saffo, V*, and so forth. This is how Dallapiccola gave an acoustic body to Quasimodo's translation, together with the reinvention of the "atmospheric" values of the ancient poetry that it conveyed.

Similar nuances, combined with just as many subtle variations of agogics and intensity, are missing in Maderna's *Tre liriche greche* (a mere handful of indications for 150 "vocal" beats/bars) and also in those by Catunda and Nono.

However, the mixed properties of Maderna's solo line (voice-flute in the first piece) and the prominence of a completely different type of musical setting, accompanied by the choice of choral lyrics by Melanippides and Ibycus, are what distinguishes Maderna from Dallapiccola. Maderna's choice of employing a collective-rhythmic setting, spoken or *recto tono* with chordal effects, deepens the distance between the two. And this distance reaches its maximum degree in Maderna's, Catunda's, and to some extent also Nono's vocal parts (in the first quatrain of *Ai Dioscuri*), who, through the repetition of words, dare to go where Dallapiccola never did, altering the poetic text in Alcaeus' sixth poem – "(O conchiglia marina) tu meravigli la mente dei fanciulli" – and above all, but for other purposes, Anacreon's verse.[93] In Maderna's *Danaidi*, the first two lines of Melanippides, but also the third and half of the next one, are caught up in a crowded sequence that progressively accumulates the units of meaning, replicating them. Thus there is the shrieking contrast, albeit musically mediated by the central beats, between the two parts of Quasimodo-Maderna's fragment of Melanippides, which illustrates the masculine-feminine duality of the Danaids: the composer renders their "addestramento" (training), verses 1–4 up to "selve" (forests), through a lively *caccia* for *Sprechchor* full of dynamic-spatial effects; the *détente*, with a sinuous monodic arabesque. Then in *Stellato*, he splits Ibycus' first line, which is multiplied along sixteen bars of Maderna's melody: the choir repeats "ardano" up to nine times, and five times out of six, the soloist suddenly utters "attraverso la notte" (always *piano* but clearer, more distinctive, as the other voices fade away) "beneath" the bundle of held syllables "ar-da-no" (*forte*, then *diminuendo*); then, while all the other voices are silent, the sopranos and contraltos each perform three or four melismas

---

92 See Dallapiccola, "A proposito delle *Due liriche di Anacreonte*" (see note 82), p. 442.

93 One can count the number of textual repetitions in the first two collections on one hand. They have a more circumscribed, non-structural function than in the musical setting of Anacreon.

"lungamente." To say that the first twenty-one bars and the following sustained trichord ("a bocca chiusa") translate and emphasize the semantics of Quasimodo's couplet would be an understatement.

Maderna expands the image, or should we say the presumed "original" image (since it is mediated by the translation), far beyond Dallapiccola's limits of the "sense of spring" to be contained in the music, and those of that "extremely undefined mood of the lines" to be developed. He also goes beyond the same skill that he shares with Dallapiccola of "giving the text a semantic and poetic depth that it might not even have."[94] And he does this, in the second and third pieces, at the cost of an increasing dismemberment of Quasimodo's translations. In fact, in the generation of polyvocal sequences, he treats the "words set in poetry" as re-adaptable matrices of transformable, mainly rhythmic, musical components with the side effect of altering the shape of the text. The poetic syntax of the fragments rewritten by Quasimodo is broken up in the horizontal and vertical, spatiotemporal iterations of the textual units; the word or the phrase remains, but becomes reverberated, obsessive, thickened, voluminous.

Due to the lack of counterevidence, I shall not elaborate on whether such a misrepresentation or betrayal – I believe – of Quasimodian values earns them an ill-begotten destiny. Would the most erudite earlier translations, with their metric molds, have held Maderna back from going his own way and therefore put a restraint on those passages that most deform Quasimodo's translations? I prefer instead to point out that this misrepresentation / betrayal is accompanied by a surprising, almost paradoxical fact. Like any translation into music, Maderna's compositions spring to life from the Italian metatext, in that they are based on it, or better, they rely on Quasimodo so much that, for example, the Danaids exercise *nude* (a characterization Quasimodo had deduced from the verb) and Ibycus' "stelle" (stars) become the subject of a hortatory subjunctive (obtained from a present participle), excluded from a simile.[95] And yet, Quasimodo's name *never* appears in the surviving papers of the Maderna-Nono-Catunda brotherhood: nor does it appear in the manuscripts of their "Greek lyrics" or even in the Ars Viva edition of Maderna's settings. Only the names of the Greek authors and Quasimodo's titles in Italian are found in the paratexts. A few years after their *editio princeps,* when all the controversy had died down, these *translated* Greek lyricists who had fueled Dallapiccola's inspiration could have seemed, to the young readers of the post-war period, the real Sappho, Alcaeus, Alcman… almost original and close at hand.[96]

---

94 Luciano Berio, "La traversata" (1995, ed. 1997), in idem, *Scritti sulla musica,* ed. Angela Ida De Benedictis (Turin: Einaudi, 2013), pp. 347–50: 349.

95 Filippo M. Pontani's translation reads "ardente, come nella notte lunga / pianeti rutilanti," in *I lirici greci* (Turin: Einaudi, 1969²), p. 309.

96 See Maderna's words in *Colloquio con Aldo Maranca* (1964), in Maderna, *Amore e curiosità* (see note 7), pp. 101–12.

Conclusions

This chapter abandons the standard biographical approach that has tended to interpret the literary tastes of Maderna through the prism of his presumed psychological and emotional needs at the time (a desire for respite, evasion, rebirth etc.). Indeed, many of these presumed needs closely resemble the generic labels typical of literature handbooks. For this reason, I have sought, wherever possible, to analyse Maderna's schoolworks, letters and early writings with reference to the contemporary cultural field, aiming to determine the positions and dispositions (and the circumstances) that presumably influenced the composer's textual choices.

Even the most cautious readers of the previous paragraphs may be tempted to view Maderna's poetic choices as 'aligned with' an Italian tradition of pure poetry that connects la Ronda with the 'new lyricists' and reaches back through them to Leopardi, the first Italian poets and the Greek lyricists. That, however, would be an error, because there is no evidence that the young composer actively adheres to *one* post-D'Annunzian line. Maderna's presumed indebtedness to *this* tradition of Italian poetry in fact derives from his school commentaries on poems by Carducci, Pascoli and D'Annunzio, his setting of Cardarelli's *Alba*, his allusions to his distaste for an unspecified poem by Palazzeschi, the conjecture that he was only occasionally interested in Verlaine, and, finally, the fact that he set translations by Quasimodo. These assertions and deductions do not constitute hard evidence, but are simply clues pointing toward complex socio-cultural dynamics that are reflected in Maderna's life, or what little we can understand about it from existing documents. Thus, I have tried to read the poetic choices Maderna made during his formative years as a reflection of his literary education, specific cultural landmarks of the time, the poetic trends then in vogue and their influence, even indirectly, through the vocal works of other composers (Dallapiccola's *Liriche greche*).

The same kind of approach can be applied to Maderna's completed and abandoned post-war settings of Kafka, Lorca (and Joyce).[97] While these works possess a literary dimension that is anchored in the cultural context and the publishing industry of the 1930s, they were also typical of a new synthesis between various other elements pursued by the composer at the time, some of which differed from those of the inter-war period. These include his attraction to both the texts of established modern foreign writers and the classics (such as Quasimodo's translations), their post-war collocation, the necessity of operating in Europe, the sense that a new international era had dawned – with its many apparently irreconcilable objectives ("remaking man," pushing him to "the ends of fruitful land," ...) – and the desire to give this era musical form.

---

97 See in particular Niva Lorenzini, "'Agglutinati all'oggi': musica e poesia alla svolta degli anni Cinquanta," in *Pour Bruno: Memorie e ricerche su Bruno Maderna,* ed. Rossana Dalmonte and Mario Baroni (Lucca: LIM, 2015), pp. 19–39, and the essay by Claudia Vincis in this volume, pp. 383–414.

CHRONOLOGY
BIBLIOGRAPHY
INDEX

Chronology of Bruno Maderna's Works
in collaboration with Maurizio Romito

This chronology lists Maderna's works published during his life or posthumously, together with the main information related to their world premiere. The list almost exclusively includes works deposited with a publisher that were not necessarily handed down in paper form (as in the case of *From A to Z* or other radio and electronic works). Only particular cases of any missing or unpublished compositions or opera versions, sometimes performed only once and never definitively fixed in the form of a score by the composer (for example, *Serenata IV*), are recorded. With rare exceptions, specific sectors of Madernian production such as music for cinema and television, incidental music for prose drama, music for use and radio background music are not taken into consideration here.[1]

The list includes Maderna's own works and his transcriptions of the works of others. Each of these two sections is ordered according to the year of composition of the pieces. Within the individual years, the compositions are listed chronologically respecting (where possible) the genetic succession of the individual works. If the date is uncertain, we have opted for the most indicative date of the entire compositional process, with specific reference to any dates present in the Maderna's autograph materials. The listing for each title also indicates: place and date of the world premiere (or of the first documented performance), together with the names of the performers and, where necessary, the type of event ("studio recording," "public performance"); the name of the publisher; reference to the year of publication or to the copyright of the reference edition.[2]

The list is by no means exhaustive but rather is designed to trace a global orientation of Maderna's creative path and to offer the reader a basis for the immediate comparison of some of the works cited in the essays gathered in this book. It is based on the "Chronology of works" found in *Amore e curiosità: Scritti, frammenti e interviste sulla musica*, ed. Angela Ida De Benedictis, Michele Chiappini and Benedetta Zucconi (Milan: il Saggiatore, 2020; pp. 831–40), revised and integrated with all the information about the first performances (dates and names of performers) by Maurizio Romito.[3] Thus, pending the publication of a complete and critical catalogue, this chronology represents the most up-to-date list in terms of dating, as well as one of the first attempts to account for the performance history of Maderna's works.

---

1 As regards this see *Catalogue des œuvres de Bruno Maderna*, in *à Bruno Maderna*, ed. Geneviève Mathon, Laurent Feneyrou, and Giordano Ferrari, vol. 2 (Paris: Basalte, 2009), pp. 565–86.

2 No distinction is made here between standard, critical or posthumous editions, nor are any reprints or subsequent editions taken into account.

3 We would like to thank Gabriele Bonomo (Edizioni Suvini Zerboni), Maria Pia Ferraris (Archivio Storico Ricordi), Claudia Mayer-Haase (Internationales Musikinstitut Darmstadt), and Mediateca RAI Torino for their support and kindness in answering our questions.

Works

1939

Alba, for contralto and string orchestra
(text: Vincenzo Cardarelli)
Reggello (Florence), 20 July 1991 – Lucia Rizzi –
cond. Aldo Bennici
ESZ[4] 1997

1942

Concerto for piano and orchestra
Venice, 22 June 1942 – Gino Gorini – cond. Ettore
Gracis
ESZ 2012

1942/1947[5]

*Introduzione e Passacaglia "Lauda Sion
Salvatorem,"* for orchestra
Florence, 3 April 1947 – cond. Maderna
ESZ 2005

1943–46

String Quartet
Venice, 16 October 1989 – Ex Novo Ensemble
Schott 1996

1945–46

Requiem, for 4 solo voices, 3 pianos, choir and
orchestra
Venice, 19 November 2009 – Carmela Remigio,
Veronica Simeoni, Mario Zeffiri, Simone Alberghini –
cond. Andrea Molino
ESZ 2011 (©2006)

1946

Concerto for piano and orchestra, transcription
for 2 pianos of the 1942 orchestral version
Venice, 19 May 2008 – Giovanni Mancuso, Debora
Petrina
ESZ (forthcoming)

Serenata per 11 strumenti
Venice, 21 September 1946 – cond. Maderna
missing

Liriche su Verlaine, for soprano and piano
(*Sérénade, Aquarelles, Sagesse*)[6]
Bonn, 16 March 1984 – Rita Heinen, Christian
de Bruyn
ESZ 1997

1947–48/1950–52/1955

Concerto for 2 pianos and instruments
1st version – Venice, 17 September 1948 – Gino
Gorini, Sergio Lorenzi – cond. Maderna
2nd version – Rome, RAI, 18 February 1950 – Gino
Gorini, Sergio Lorenzi – cond. Carlo Maria Giulini
3rd version – Cologne, NWDR, 5 March 1952
(studio recording) – Erika Frieser, Paul Traut – cond.
Maderna[7]
ESZ 2006

1948

Tre liriche greche, for soprano, chamber choir
and 7 instruments
(texts: Ibycus, Melanippides, anonymous)
Kansas City, 27 February 1959 – Freda Schell –
cond. Harold Decker
Ars Viva Verlag; then: ESZ 2002

1948–49

Composizione n. 1, for orchestra
Turin, RAI, 12 May 1950 – cond. Nino Sanzogno
ESZ 2007

1949

Fantasia e fuga, for 2 pianos
Darmstadt, 9 July 1949 – Carl Seemann,
Peter Stadlen
ESZ 2000

Il mio cuore è nel Sud, radio play
(text: Giuseppe Patroni Griffi)
1st broadcast: RAI, 11 March 1950
ESZ 2011 (©1995)

1949–50

Composizione n. 2, for orchestra
1st version – Darmstadt, 26 August 1950 – cond.
Hermann Scherchen
2nd version – Turin, RAI, 8 April 1952 (studio recording) – cond. Hermann Scherchen[8]
Heidelberg, SDR, 14 November 1952 (public performance) – cond. Maderna
ESZ 2006

1950

Studi per "Il Processo" di Franz Kafka, for speaker,
soprano and orchestra
Venice, 13 September 1950 – Ubaldo Lay, Ginevra
Vivante – cond. Hermann Scherchen
ESZ 2010

1951–52

Improvvisazione n. 1, for orchestra
Hamburg, NWDR, 18 February 1952 – cond. Maderna
Ars Viva Verlag 1952; then ESZ

---

4   The abbreviation ESZ refers to the publishing house
     Edizioni Suvini Zerboni (Milan).
5   The date placed after a slash always indicates a
     reworking of the work completed years later.
6   Order of pieces according to archival sources.

7   First broadcast, WDR, 27 Nobember 1952.
8   First broadcast, RAI, 19 July 1952.

1952
Musica su due dimensioni, for flute, cymbal and magnetic tape
Darmstadt, 21 July 1952 – Severino Gazzelloni, Romolo Grano
ESZ 2002

1953
Quattro lettere (Kranichsteiner Kammerkantate), for soprano, bass and chamber orchestra
(texts: Bruno Frittaion, anonymous, Franz Kafka, Antonio Gramsci)
Darmstadt, 30 July 1953 – Ilona Steingruber, Heinz Rehfuss – cond. Maderna
ESZ 2003

Improvvisazione n. 2, for orchestra
Heidelberg, SDR, 28 November 1953 – cond. Maderna
Ars Viva Verlag 1953; then ESZ

Divertimento in due tempi, for flute and piano
Bergamo, 6 June 1983 – Roberto Fabbriciani, Mauro Castellano
ESZ 1995

1953–54
Serenata: Komposition n. 3 (first version of *Serenata n. 2,* see below)
Paris, 10 April 1954 – cond. Hermann Scherchen
Ars Viva Verlag 1954

1954
Concerto for flute and orchestra
Darmstadt, 22 August 1954 – Severino Gazzelloni – cond. Ernest Bour
ESZ 1992

Composizione in tre tempi, for orchestra
Hamburg, NWDR, 8 December 1954 – cond. Maderna
ESZ 2008

Ritratto di città, radio play, with Luciano Berio
(text: Roberto Leydi)
1st broadcast: RAI, 20 May 1957 (partial, only final part)
RAI, 4 December 1971 (complete)
RAI[9]

Sequenze e strutture, for magnetic tape
Milan, 8 May 1956
ESZ

1955
Quartetto per archi in due tempi
Darmstadt, 1 June 1955 – Drolc-Quartett
ESZ 2009

1956
Notturno, for magnetic tape
Fonit (disc), 1956[10]
RAI, 20 May 1957 (radio broadcast)
Milan, 24 May 1957 (public performance)
ESZ

1956–57
Serenata n. 2, for 11 instruments
Cologne, WDR, 15 February 1957 (studio recording) – cond. Maderna[11]
Krefeld, 5 April 1957 (public performance) – cond. Maderna
ESZ 1957

1957
Syntaxis, for magnetic tape
RAI, 13 May 1957 (radio broadcast)
Milan, 24 May 1957 (public performance)
ESZ

Dark Rapture Crawl, for orchestra[12]
Rome, RAI, 2 December 1957 – cond. Maderna
ESZ 1959

1958
Continuo, for magnetic tape
Cologne, WDR, 25 March 1958
ESZ

Musica su due dimensioni, for flute and magnetic tape
Naples, RAI, 11 June 1958 – Severino Gazzelloni
ESZ 1960

1958–59
Concerto for piano and orchestra
Darmstadt, 2 September 1959 – David Tudor – cond. Maderna
ESZ 1960

1960
Dimensioni II. Invenzione su una voce, for magnetic tape
1st version, for voice and magnetic tape – Milan, 9 April 1960 – Cathy Berberian
2nd version, for magnetic tape – Paris, 13 June 1960
ESZ

---

9   First commercial edition of the original RAI production in *New Music on the Radio: Experiences at the Studio di Fonologia of the RAI, Milan 1954–1959,* ed. Veniero Rizzardi and Angela Ida De Benedictis (Rome: Cidim-ERI, 2000).

10   EP disc (Extendend Play) published as a supplement to the magazine *Elettronica,* V (1956) 3.
11   First broadcast, WDR, 21 October 1958.
12   First piece of the triptych *Divertimento* for orchestra (1957), followed by Luciano Berio's *Scat Rag* and *Rhumba-ramble.*

1961

Serenata III, for magnetic tape
Venice, 16 April 1961
ESZ

Serenata IV, for flute, instrumental ensemble and
magnetic tape
Darmstadt, 4 September 1961 – Severino Gazzelloni –
cond. Maderna
unpublished

Honeyrêves, for flute and piano
Darmstadt, 1961 – Severino Gazzelloni, Aloys
Kontarsky (studio recording, LP Time Records;
intermediate version)
Venice, 23 April 1962 – Severino Gazzelloni,
Frederic Rzewski (public performance; final version)
ESZ 1963

*Don Perlimplin, ovvero Il trionfo dell'amore e
dell'immaginazione,* radio play
(text: Federico García Lorca, translated by
Vittorio Bodini, adapted by Bruno Maderna)
1st broadcast: RAI, 12 August 1962
ESZ 1961[13]

1962

Le rire, for magnetic tape
1st version, for flute, marimba and tape – Berlin,
28 September 1964 – Karl-Bernhard Sebon,
Kurt Engel – cond. Maderna[14]
2nd version, for flute and magnetic tape –
Darmstadt, 21 August 1966 – Severino Gazzelloni
3rd version, for tape – Venice, 7 September 1966
ESZ

Konzert für Oboe und Kammerensemble
(Concerto for oboe and chamber ensemble)[15]
Hamburg, NDR, 24 October 1962 – Lothar Faber –
cond. Maderna
Bruzzichelli (now: Bèrben) 1963

1963

Dimensioni III, for orchestra, with a cadenza
for solo flute
1st version – Paris, 26 November 1963 – cond. Maderna
2nd version – Hannover, NDR, 25 January 1964 –
cond. Maderna
3rd version – s'-Hertogenbosch, 27 October 1964 –
Koos Verheul – cond. Maderna
ESZ 1965

Entropia I, for orchestra
Bruxelles, 17 May 1968 (as part of *Hyperion en
het geweld*)[16]
ESZ ©1968

Per Caterina, for violin and piano
Cremona, 24 October 1987 – Grazia Serradimigni,
Maria Grazia Bertocchi
ESZ 1983

1964

Dimensioni IV, for flute and chamber ensemble
Darmstadt, 23 July 1964 – Severino Gazzelloni –
cond. Maderna
unpublished

Hyperion, "lirica in forma di spettacolo" by
Bruno Maderna and Virginio Puecher
(text: Friedrich Hölderlin, with phonemes by
Hans Günter Helms)
Venice, 6 September 1964 – dir. Virginio Puecher,
cond. Maderna
ESZ

Aria, for soprano, flute and orchestra
(text: Friedrich Hölderlin)
Cologne, WDR, 16 November 1964 – Joan Carroll,
Severino Gazzelloni – cond. Maderna[17]
ESZ 1965

1965

Aulodia per Lothar, for oboe d'amore and guitar
ad libitum
Venice, 9 September 1965 – Lothar Faber, Alvaro
Company
ESZ 1977

---

13   First commercial edition of the original radio
      production in *Imagination at Play: The Prix Italia and
      Radiophonic Experimentation,* ed. Angela Ida De
      Benedictis and Maria Maddalena Novati
      (Milan: Die Schachtel/RAI Trade, 2012). A new edi-
      tion of the score was published by ESZ in 2001.

14   A fragment of *Le rire* had previously been used
      within the magnetic tape of *Komposition für Oboe,
      Kammerensemble und Tonband* (see note 15 below).

15   A preliminary version of the *Konzert* was performed
      in Darmstadt on July 15, 1962, with the title *Kom-
      position für Oboe, Kammerensemble und Tonband*
      (Lothar Faber – cond. Maderna). Even for the Ham-
      burg performance mentioned above in the text, the
      work still bore the title *Komposition für Oboe und
      Kammerensemble.*

16   This is a part of *Dimensioni III* used in *Hyperion
      en het geweld* with this title. Another part of *Dimen-
      sioni III* was used by Maderna, again in *Hyperion
      en het geweld,* with the title of *Entropia II* (unpub-
      lished). A third piece, entitled *Entropia III* (unpub-
      lished) was used in the *Suite aus der Oper "Hyper-
      ion,"* between the *Klage* and *Schicksalslied* episodes.

17   Performed, together with *Dimensioni III,* under the
      title of *"Dimensioni III* für Sopran, Flöte und Orches-
      ter ('Neufassung')."

Stele per Diotima, for orchestra
Hamburg, NDR, 19 Janaury 1966 – cond. Maderna
ESZ 1966

1966
Amanda, for chamber orchestra
Naples, 25 October 1966 – cond. Daniele Paris
ESZ 1967

1967
Widmung, for solo violin
Nürtingen, 27 October 1967 – Theo Olof
ESZ 1976

Concerto No. 2 for oboe and orchestra
Cologne, WDR, 10 November 1967 – Lothar Faber –
cond. Maderna
ESZ 1969

1968
Hyperion en het geweld, second stage version
of *Hyperion*
(text: Hugo Claus)
Brussels, 17 May 1968 – dir. Deryk Mendel, cond.
Maderna
ESZ

Hyperion – Orfeo dolente, third stage version of
Hyperion, interspersed with 5 "intermedi" of
Orfeo dolente by Domenico Belli (see below).
Bologna, 18 July 1968 – dir. Virginio Puecher,
cond. Maderna
ESZ

Serenade für Claudia, for violin and piano
Cremona, 24 October 1987 – Grazia Serradimigni,
Maria Grazia Bertocchi
ESZ 1983

1969
From A to Z, TV production
(text: Rebecca Rass)
1st broadcast: NTS, 2 April 1969
Ricordi

Quadrivium, for 4 percussionists and 4 orchestral
groups
Royan, 4 April 1969 – Bernard Balet, Jean-Pierre
Drouet, Gérard Lemaire, Diego Masson – cond.
Maderna
Ricordi 1970

Suite aus der Oper "Hyperion," for 2 flutes and
solo oboe (musette, ob. d'amore), speaker,
choir and orchestra (*Message, Solo, Psalm, Klage,
Schicksalslied*)
(texts: Wystan Hugh Auden, Friedrich Hölderlin,
Federico García Lorca)
Berlin, SFB-WDR, 13 May 1969 – ob.: Lothar Faber,
speak.: Peter Mosbacher – cond. Maderna
ESZ

Ritratto di Erasmo, radio play
(text and direction: Bruno Maderna)
1st broadcast: RAI, 31 March 1982
RAI[18]

Serenata per un satellite, for instruments *ad libitum*
Darmstadt, ESOC, 1 October 1969 – fl.: Angelika
Sweekhorst, ob.: Lothar Faber, vl.: Saschko Gawri-
loff, hrp.: Dagmar Busse, perc.: Hans Rossmann
Ricordi 1970

Gesti, for choir and orchestra
(text: Sappho)[19]
Vienna, 20 February 1970[20] – cond. Maderna
ESZ 2010

Serenata per Luisa, for 6 wind instruments
The Hague, end 1960s – musicians of Het Resi-
dentie-Orkest
ESZ 2020

1969–70
Concerto for violin and orchestra
1st version – Venice, 12 September 1969 – Theo Olof –
cond. Maderna
2nd version – Saarbrücken, SR, 28 May 1970 – Theo
Olof – cond. Maderna[21]
Ricordi 1969

1970
Grande Aulodia, for flute, oboe and orchestra
Rome, RAI, 7 February 1970 – Severino Gazzelloni,
Lothar Faber – cond. Maderna
Ricordi 1970

1970–71
Tempo libero I, for magnetic tape
1st version – Rimini, 21 September 1970
2nd version – Saarbrücken, SR, 19 April 1971 (studio
recording)[22]
Ricordi

Juilliard Serenade (*Tempo libero II*), for chamber
ensemble and magnetic tape *ad libitum*
New York, 31 January 1971 – cond. Maderna
Ricordi 1971

---

18 First commercial edition of the original RAI
    production in *Imagination at Play* (see note 13).
19 Hölderlin is incorrectly indicated as the author of
    the text on the cover of the published score.
20 Performed in Vienna as part of the last version of
    Hyperion.
21 Listed in the program as "Uraufführung der endgül-
    tigen Fassung" [world premiere of the final version].
22 First partial broadcast, SR, 24 May 1973.

1971
Pièce pour Ivry, for solo violin
Paris, 24 March 1971 – Ivry Gitlis
Ricordi 1976

Viola, for viola or viola d'amore
Florence, RAI, 27 October 1972 (studio recording) –
Aldo Bennici[23]
The Hague, 12 November 1972 (public perfor-
mance) – Aldo Bennici
Ricordi 1972

Solo, for oboe, musette, oboe d'amore, english horn
(1 performer)
Royan, 6 April 1971 – Lothar Faber
Ricordi 1972

Ausstrahlung, for female voice, flute and oboe, large
orchestra and magnetic tape
(texts: Dandin, Khayyam, Saadi, Rudaki, and other
Indian and Persian sacred texts)
Persepolis, 5 September 1971 – Cathy Berberian,
Koos Verheul, Lothar Faber – cond. Maderna
Ricordi 1988

Dialodia, for 2 flutes or 2 oboes or other instruments
Persepolis, 5 September 1971 (as part of *Ausstrah-
lung*)[24]
Como, 29 September 1973 – fl.: Patricia Dunkerley,
Donatella Gulli
Ricordi 1974

Y después, for 10 string guitar
New York, 1 December 1973 – Narciso Yepes
Ricordi 1973

1971–72
Venetian Journal, for solo tenor, small orchestra and
magnetic tape
(text: James Boswell)
New York, 12 March 1972 – Paul Sperry – cond.
Maderna
Ricordi 1974

1972
Aura, for orchestra
Chicago, 23 March 1972 – cond. Maderna
Ricordi 1973

Biogramma, for orchestra
Rochester (NY), 16 April 1972 – cond. Maderna
Ricordi 1973

Ages, radio play
(text: William Shakespeare, adapted by Giorgio
Pressburger)
1st broadcast: RAI, 28 September 1972
RAI[25]

Giardino religioso, for orchestra
Tanglewood, 8 August 1972 – cond. Maderna
Ricordi 1974

Ständchen für Tini, for violin and viola
Cremona, 24 October 1987 – Grazia Serradimigni,
Wim Janssen
ESZ 1983

1972–73
Satyricon, opera in 1 act
(text: Petronius, adapted by Bruno Maderna)
Scheveningen, 16 March 1973 – dir. Ian Strasfogel,
cond. Maderna
Salabert 1974

1973
Concerto No. 3 for oboe and orchestra
Amsterdam, 6 July 1973 – Han de Vries – cond.
Maderna
Salabert 1973

---

23   First broadcast, RAI, 28 February 1975.
24   The piece, in its entirety, is an integral part of
Ausstrahlung, together with *Solo.*

25   First commercial edition of the original sound recording in *Imagination at Play* (see note 13). In 1978
the Ricordi publishing house released a short choral
piece, entitled *All the world's a stage,* taken from
the materials for *Ages.*

Transcriptions

1947

Antonio Vivaldi, Concerto for violin, strings and harpsichord in C major, F. I n. 3 (RV 186)
Ricordi 1947

Antonio Vivaldi, Concerto for violin, strings and harpsichord in A major, F. I n. 5 (RV 352)
Ricordi 1947

Antonio Vivaldi, Concerto for violin, strings and harpsichord in D major, F. I n. 8 (RV 231)
Ricordi 1949

Antonio Vivaldi, Concerto in C major for violin, 2 strings choirs and two harpsichords *Per la SS. Assunzione di Maria Vergine,* F. I n. 13 (RV 581)
Venice, 3 October 1947 – Vittorio Brero – cond. Nino Sanzogno
Ricordi 1949

Antonio Vivaldi, Concerto in C minor for strings and harpsichord, F. XI n. 9 (RV 118)
Milan, 19 May 1952 – Herbert von Karajan
Ricordi 1949

Antonio Vivaldi, Concerto in C minor for strings and harpsichord, F. XI n. 8 (RV 120)
Venice, 4 October 1947 – Quartetto Ferro[26]
Ricordi 1949

1947–48

Antonio Vivaldi, *Beatus Vir,* Psalm 111 for solo voices, 2 mixed choirs (4 parts) and 2 orchestras (RV 597)
Venice, 17 September 1949 – Ginevra Vivante, Tommaso Spataro – cond. Angelo Ephrikian
Ricordi 1969 (score and reduction for voice and piano)

1948

Giovanni Battista Pergolesi, *Orfeo,* for soprano, woodwinds and strings
Venice, 29 September 1948 – Ginevra Vivante – cond. Hermann Scherchen
Ars Viva Verlag, n.d. [1952]

1948–50

Odhecaton (1501), for chamber orchestra
Paris, RTF, 25 January 1950 (selection) – cond. Maderna[27]
Ars Viva Verlag 1951 (but: 1952)

ca. 1951

Gustav Mahler, "Adagio" dalla X Sinfonia, for orchestra
ESZ (forthcoming)

1951–52

Tommaso Lodovico da Viadana, *Le Sinfonie* (*La Napoletana, la Venexiana, la Veronese, la Romana, la Mantovana*), for chamber orchestra
Zurich, SRG, 28 February 1952 – cond. Maderna
ESZ 1967

Giovanni Legrenzi, *La Basadonna,* for chamber orchestra
Munich, BR, 17 September 1952 – cond. Maderna
Ars Viva Verlag 1953, then ESZ

1952

Girolamo Frescobaldi, *Tre pezzi,* for chamber orchestra
Zurich, SRG, 7 October 1952 – cond. Maderna[28]
ESZ 1991

Unico Wilhelm von Wassenaer (previously attributed to Giovanni Battista Pergolesi), *Palestrina-Konzert (Concertino armonico n. 3),* for string orchestra
Stockholm, Radiotjänst, 20 December 1954 (studio recording) – cond. Maderna[29]
Ars Viva Verlag, n.d. [1952]

1961

Adam de la Halle, *Rondeaux,* for chamber orchestra
Tokyo, 22 April 1961 – cond. Maderna
ESZ (forthcoming)

1965

Franz Schubert, *Cinque danze,* for orchestra
Rome, RAI, 10 February 1965 – cond. Maderna
ESZ 1968

Giovanni Gabrieli, *In ecclesiis,* for large orchestra
Brussels, 10 October 1965 – cond. Maderna
ESZ 1966

---

26   Reduced version for string quartet.

27   The work – which includes 12 pieces from the collection published by Ottaviano Petrucci – has rarely been performed in its entirety. Amongst the very few complete performances, the one conducted by Luciano Berio stands out (Florence, 31 August 1985).
28   Performed under the title of *Tre ricercari per fiati.*
29   First broadcast, Radiotjänst, 4 May 1955.

1966
Josquin Desprez, *Magnificat quarti toni,* for mixed
choir and 3 instrumental groups
Leiden, 29 November 1966 – cond. Maderna
ESZ 1967

1967
Claudio Monteverdi, *Orfeo* (1607), "favola pastorale"
in 2 parts by Alessandro Striggio Jr.
Amsterdam, 17 June 1967 – dir. Raymond Rouleau,
cond. Maderna
ESZ 1967 (score and reduction for voice and piano)

1967–68
Music of Gaity, from *Fitzwilliam Virginal Book,* for
chamber orchestra
Delft, 24 April 1968 – cond. Maderna
Ricordi 1970

1968
Domenico Belli, *Orfeo dolente,* opera in 5 "intermedi"
Bologna, 18 July 1968 – dir. Virginio Puecher, cond.
Maderna
Ricordi 1969

1972
Giovanni Gabrieli, *Canzone a tre cori* ("12 voci"),
for orchestra
Tanglewood, 21 July 1972 – cond. Maderna[30]
Ricordi 1973

---

30 A different transcription of the piece had previously
been used in *Ritratto di Erasmo* (1969).

Selected Bibliography on Bruno Maderna

Presented here is a selection of monographs, miscellaneous volumes, and individual essays on Bruno Maderna from 1976 (the date of the first volume devoted to the composer after his death) to the present. The selection, the responsibility for which lies solely with the editor, does not include program notes, dissertations, critical or posthumous editions of Maderna's musical works published after 1973, or parts/chapters on Maderna's life and music within volumes/essays dedicated to more comprehensive or general themes.
The list is in chronological order.

Massimo Mila, *Maderna musicista europeo* (Turin: Einaudi, 1976); new edition 1999 (ed. Ulrich Mosch)

Luciano Berio, "Un inedito di Bruno Maderna," *Nuova Rivista Musicale Italiana* 12, no. 4 (1978), pp. 517–20

Horst Weber, "Form und Satztechnik in Bruno Maderna's Streichquartett," in *Miscellanea del Cinquantenario (Die Stellung der italienischen Avant-garde in der Entwicklung der neuen Musik. Symposium des Instituts für Wertungsforschung in Graz [1975])* (Milan: Suvini Zerboni, 1978), pp. 206–15

Anna Giubertoni, "Fonti poetiche dell'*Hyperion* di Bruno Maderna," *Nuova Rivista Musicale Italiana* 15, no. 2 (1981), pp. 197–205

Giordano Montecchi, "Bruno Maderna e la musica leggera," *Musica/Realtà,* no. 10 (1983), pp. 51–61

Maurizio Romito, "Il balletto *Das eiserne Zeitalter*," *Musica/Realtà,* no. 10 (1983) pp. 63–69

Bruno Maderna: Documenti, ed. Mario Baroni and Rossana Dalmonte (Milan: Suvini Zerboni, 1985); incl.:
• Raymond Fearn, "Maderna e l'Inghilterra," pp. 137–41
• Enzo Restagno, "L'ultimo Maderna dalla struttura all'evento," pp. 163–67
• Luigi Rognoni, "Memoria di Bruno Maderna negli anni Cinquanta," pp. 146–51

Studi su Bruno Maderna, ed. Mario Baroni and Rossana Dalmonte (Milan: Suvini Zerboni, 1989); incl.:
• Mario Baroni, "L'archetipo dell'aulos. Echi e reminiscenze melodiche," pp. 227–40
• Manfred Johann Böhlen, "Nell'incantesimo del numero. Il *Flötenkonzert* di Maderna," pp. 33–51
• Michela Garda, "Rilevamenti sulla ricezione della musica maderniana," pp. 74–94
• Francesca Magnani, "L'*Hyperion* di Maderna: quale poeta per quale canto," pp. 177–94
• Giordano Montecchi, "Il lavoro di precomposizione in *Serenata* n. 2," pp. 109–37
Maurizio Romito, "Lettere e scritti," pp. 52–73

Gianmario Borio, "La tecnica seriale in *Studi per 'Il Processo' di Franz Kafka* di Bruno Maderna," *Musica/Realtà,* no. 32 (1990), pp. 27–39

Raymond Fearn, *Bruno Maderna* (Chur: Harwood, 1990)

Laura Cosso, "La forma concerto in *Aulodia* di Bruno Maderna," *Nuova Rivista Musicale Italiana* 25, nos. 3–4 (1991), pp. 427–40

Luigi Pestalozza, "Maderna a Milano," in idem, *L'opposizione musicale: Scritti sulla musica del Novecento,* ed. Roberto Favaro (Milan: Feltrinelli, 1991), pp. 27–37

"Bruno Maderna," special issue of *I quaderni della civica scuola di musica,* nos. 21–22 (1992); incl.:
• Alvise Vidolin, "Avevamo nove oscillatori," pp. 13–22
• Giordano Montecchi, "*Continuo* di Bruno Maderna," pp. 43–53
• Joachim Noller, "*Musica su due dimensioni,* e l'unidimensionalità della musica nuova," pp. 65–69

Gianmario Borio and Veniero Rizzardi, "Die musikalische Einheit von Bruno Madernas *Hyperion*," in *Quellenstudien II: Zwölf Komponisten des 20. Jahrhunderts,* ed. F. Meyer (Winterthur: Amadeus, 1993), pp. 117–48

Nicola Verzina, "Concezione poetica e pensiero formale nel Maderna post-seriale: il *Konzert für Oboe un Kammerensemble* (1962–63)," *Studi Musicali,* 24, no. 1 (1995), pp. 131–59

Nicola Verzina, "Mutazioni storiche intorno a tre testi inediti di Bruno Maderna," *Studi musicali* 28, no. 2 (1999), pp. 495–527

Nicola Verzina, "Tecnica della mutazione e tecnica seriale in *Vier Briefe* (1953) di Bruno Maderna," *Rivista Italiana di Musicologia* 34, no. 2 (1999), pp. 309–45

Manfred Joh. Böhlen, *Die Solokonzerte Bruno Madernas: Fragment 1986–88* (Werl: mjbEDV 2000)

Malipiero Maderna 1973–1993, ed. Paolo Cattelan (Florence: Olschki, 2000); incl.:
  • Paolo Pinamonti, "Maderna dirige Malipiero," pp. 245–61
  • Mario Baroni, "Sull'opportunità di una ri-edizione critica delle opere di Bruno Maderna: Qualche considerazione di metodo critico," pp. 265–71
  • Susanna Pasticci, "Maderna verso il pensiero seriale: La *Fantasia e fuga per due pianoforti* (1949)," pp. 273–97
  • Paolo Cattelan, "Biografia di un concerto di Maderna: il *Concerto per due pianoforti e strumenti* (1947–1949)," pp. 299–333
  • Stefano Bellon, "Il *Concerto per due pianoforti e strumenti* di Bruno Maderna verso Darmstadt: un'analisi della partitura," pp. 335–54

Angela Ida De Benedictis, "'Qui forse una cadenza brillante': Viaggio nel *Venetian Journal* di Bruno Maderna," *Acta Musicologica,* 72, no. 1 (2000), pp. 63–105

Giordano Ferrari, *Les débuts du théâtre musical d'avant-garde en Italie. Berio, Evangelisti, Maderna* (Paris: L'Harmattan, 2000)

Maurizio Romito, "I commenti musicali di Bruno Maderna: radio, televisione, teatro," *Nuova Rivista Musicale Italiana* 34 (2000), no. 2, pp. 233–68, and ibid. 36 (2002), no. 1, pp. 79–98

Bruno Maderna and Wolfgang Steinecke, *Carteggio/ Briefwechsel,* ed. Rossana Dalmonte (Lucca: LIM, 2001)

Markus Fein, *Die musikalische Poetik Bruno Madernas: Zum "seriellen" Komponieren zwischen 1951 und 1955* (Frankfurt am Main: Lang, 2001)

Roberto Fabbi, "Cena sociale: *Satyricon* e il 'politico,'" *Musica/Realtà,* no. 67 (2002), pp. 83–100

Maurizio Romito, "Bruno Maderna alla RAI: Cronologia delle registrazioni e dei concerti: 1935–1973," *Nuova Rivista Musicale Italiana* 38, no. 1 (2003), pp. 89–126

Nicola Verzina, *Bruno Maderna: Étude historique et critique* (Paris: L'Harmattan, 2003)

Bruno Maderna: Studi e testimonianze, ed. Rossana Dalmonte and Marco Russo (Lucca: LIM, 2004); incl.:
  • Rossana Dalmonte, "Letture maderniane del *Processo* di Franz Kafka," pp. 9–40
  • Erika Schaller, "L'insegnamento di Bruno Maderna attraverso le fonti conservate presso l'Archivio Luigi Nono," pp. 107–16
  • Susana Pasticci, "'Una musica di facile ascolto': sulla *Composizione n. 2* di Bruno Maderna," pp. 117–47
  • Nicola Verzina, "Musica e impegno nella *Kranichsteiner Kammerkantate* (1953): il tema della libertà," pp. 199–25
  • Luca Conti, "Le *Tre liriche greche* di Maderna e la prima dodecafonia italiana," pp. 275–86
  • Leo Izzo, "Il commento sonoro realizzato da Bruno Maderna per il film *Le due verità*," pp. 299–41
  • Maurizio Romito, "Discografia," pp. 343–79

Angela Ida De Benedictis, "*Ritratto di Erasmo* di Bruno Maderna," *Musica/Realtà,* no. 73 (2004), pp. 152–82

Angela Ida De Benedictis, "Scritture e supporti nel Novecento: alcune riflessioni e un esempio (*Ausstrahlung* di Bruno Maderna)," in *La scrittura come rappresentazione del pensiero musicale,* ed. Gianmario Borio (Pisa: ETS, 2004), pp. 237–91

Christoph Neidhöfer, "Bruno Madernas flexibler Materialbegriff: Eine Analyse des *Divertimento in due tempi* (1953)," *Musik & Ästhetik* 9, no. 33 (2005), pp. 30–47

Susanna Pasticci, "Memorie di Petrucci a Venezia, quattro secoli dopo," in *Venezia 1501: Petrucci e la stampa musicale,* ed. Giulio Cattin and Patrizia della Vecchia (Venice: Edizioni Fondazioni Levi, 2005), pp. 683–738

Joachim Noller, "Maderna, la storia e la crisi della stampa musicale," in ibid., pp. 739–51

Claudia Vincis, "À propos de la nature modulable du *Satyricon* de Bruno Maderna: quelques notes sur la genèse du livret," in *L'opéra éclaté: La dramaturgie musicale entre 1969 et 1984,* ed. Giordano Ferrari (Paris: l'Harmattan, 2006), pp. 25–49

Leo Izzo, "Bruno Maderna e il Jazz," *Ring Shout: Rivista di Studi Musicali Afro-americani* 5/6 (2006/2007), pp. 5–46

à Bruno Maderna, ed. Geneviève Mathon, Laurent Feneyrou, and Giordano Ferrari, vol. I (Paris: Basalte 2007); incl.:
  • Geneviève Mathon, "À propos du *Satyricon*," pp. 69–86
  • Giordano Ferrari, "*Hyperion* les chemins du poête," pp. 89–121
  • Angela Ida De Benedictis, "*Ausstrahlung,* ou la textualité brisée d'un hymne à la vie," pp. 287–317

• Konrad Boehmer, "Retour à Maderna,"
pp. 341–53
• Laurent Feneyrou, "Bruno Maderna, musicien
de la vie," pp. 437–57
• Angela Ida De Benedictis and Giordano
Ferrari, "Bruno Maderna: Extraits de la correspondance choisis et annotés," pp. 459–517
• Stefano Bellon, "Maderna, entre improvisation
et jazz," pp. 522–33

Christoph Neidhöfer, "Bruno Maderna's Serial
Arrays," *Music Theory Online* 13, no. 1 (2007), 16 pp.
(https://mtosmt.org/issues/mto.07.13.1/mto.07.13.1
.neidhofer.pdf)

Esumazione di un Requiem, ed. Veniero Rizzardi
(Florence: Olschki, 2007)

Veniero Rizzardi, "Quasi perduto, quasi ritrovato:
Nota sulla riscoperta del giovanile *Concerto per
pianoforte* di Bruno Maderna," *Atti dell'Istituto Veneto
di Scienze, Lettere ed Arti* 166, nos. 1–2 (2007–08),
pp. 57–91

à Bruno Maderna, ed. Geneviève Mathon, Laurent
Feneyrou, and Giordano Ferrari, vol. 2 (Paris: Basalte
2009); incl.:
   • Alessandro Solbiati, "*Biogramma:* Projet et
   modalité de réalisation d'une *Weltanschauung,*"
   pp. 123–42
   • Frédéric Durieux, "*Quadrivium:* Une œuvre
   magistrale pour un art libéral," pp. 143–76
   • Laurent Feneyrou, "*Solo/tutti:* Introduction à
   cinq concertos de Bruno Maderna," pp. 179–228
   • Christoph Neidhöfer, "Vers un principe commun: Intégration de la hauteur et du rhythme
   dans le *Quartetto per archi in due tempi* (1955),"
   pp. 323–58
   • Angela Ida De Benedictis, "Bruno Maderna
   et le 'Studio di Fonologia' de la RAI de Milan,"
   pp. 389–421
   • Veniero Rizzardi and Nicola Scaldaferri, "*Musica su due dimensioni* (1952): Histoire, vicissitudes et importance d'une oeuvre (presque)
   absente," pp. 423–48
   • Nicola Scaldaferri, "De l'événement sonore
   au processus de composition: Analyse de
   Notturno," pp. 449–85
   • Claudia Vincis, "'Avec l'autorisation du Maître':
   Bruno Maderna et la musique ancienne: entre
   'reconstruction' et 'recréation,'" pp. 489–522
   • Gianfranco Vinay, "Maderna, chef d'orchestre
   humaniste," pp. 536–53

Antonio Rodà, "'Varianti d'autore': *Invenzioni su
una voce* di Bruno Maderna," *Musica/Tecnologia* 3
(2009), pp. 71–97

Anna Rita Addessi, "Auditive analysis of the
Quartetto per archi in due tempi (1955) by Bruno
Maderna," *Musicæ Scientiæ,* special issue (2010),
pp. 225–49

Susanna Pasticci, "La presenza del *Satyricon* sulla
scena culturale degli anni Settanta, da Maderna
a Pasolini," *Musica/Realtà,* no. 91 (2010), pp. 77–126

Egidio Pozzi, "Aspetti della multidimensionalità
formale e della relatività nella musica del Novecento: Il *Quartetto per archi in due tempi* di Bruno
Maderna," in *Con-scientia musica: Contrappunti
per Rossana Dalmonte e Mario Baroni,* ed. Anna Rita
Addessi, Ignazio Macchiarella, Massimo Privitera,
and Marco Russo (Lucca: LIM, 2010), pp. 149–93

Angela Ida De Benedictis, "Materiali parziali o
strutture fungibili? Nuove prospettive filologiche su
Honeyrêves, Don Perlimplin e *Serenata IV* di Bruno
Maderna," *Il Saggiatore Musicale* 18, nos. 1–2 (2011),
pp. 139–72

Veniero Rizzardi, "The Tone Row, Squared: Bruno
Maderna and the Birth of Serial Music in Italy,"
in *Rewriting Recent Music History: The Development
of Early Serialism 1947–1957,* ed. Mark Delaere
(Leuven and Walpole, MA: Peeters, 2011), pp. 45–66

Maderna e l'Italia musicale degli anni '40, ed.
Gabriele Bonomo and Fabio Zannoni (Milan: Suvini
Zerboni, 2012); incl.:
   • Raffaele Pozzi, "Classicismo Romano. Maderna
   allievo di Bustini," pp. 45–82
   • Veniero Rizzardi, "La scuola della nostalgia.
   Malipiero e Maderna (e Nono): Note da un
   apprendistato anomalo," pp. 83–96
   • Leo Izzo, "'Espressioni jazzistiche in un clima
   d'arte': La sintesi di Bruno Maderna," pp. 97–114
   • Mario Baroni, "Gli anni della guerra e la
   doppia versione di *Introduzione e Passacaglia,*"
   pp. 115–27
   • Rossana Dalmonte, "Prima della serie: Orientamenti stilistici di Maderna negli anni Quaranta:
   Le opere con testo poetico," pp. 129–39
   • Angela Ida De Benedictis, "Destini incrociati:
   sull'edizione del *Concerto per pianoforte ed
   orchestra* di Bruno Maderna (1942)," pp. 141–58

Giordano Ferrari, "Questa storia di Don Perlimplino era…" / "This story of Don Perlimplino was…,"
in *L'immaginazione in ascolto: Il Prix Italia e la
sperimentazione radiofonica / Imagination at Play:
The Prix Italia and Radiophonic Experimentation,*
bilingual ed. Angela Ida De Benedictis and Maria
Maddalena Novati (Milan: Rai Trade–Die Schachtel,
2012), pp. 25–34 (It.) and 217–26 (Eng.)

Maurizio Romito, "*Ritratto di Erasmo* di Bruno Maderna" / "*Ritratto di Erasmo* by Bruno Maderna," in ibid., pp. 35–68 (It.) and 227–60 (Eng.)

Claudia Vincis, "'*Totus mudus agit histrionem*,' Ages, invenzione radiofonica di Bruno Maderna e Giorgio Pressburger," / "'*Totus mudus agit histrionem*,' Ages, an Invention for Radio by Bruno Maderna and Giorgio Pressburger," in ibid., pp. 69–76 (It.) and 261–66 (Eng.)

Katrin und Stefan Keym, "Anmerkungen zum Problem der Literaturoper, zur offenen Form und zur Zitattechnik in Bruno Madernas *Satyricon*," *Res Facta Nova* 13 (2012), pp. 107–25

Delia Casadei, "Orality, Invisibility, and Laughter: Traces of Milan in Bruno Maderna and Virginio Puecher's *Hyperion* (1964)," *The Opera Quaterly* 30, no. 1 (2014), pp. 105–34

Daniel Moro Vallina, "Tradición y modernidad en la música serial de Bruno Maderna (1920–1973): Una aproximación a su producción de los años cincuenta," *Síneris: Revista de musicología* 20 (2014), 27 pp. (https://sineris.es/wp-content/uploads/2019/02/maderna.pdf)

Luca Cossettini and Angelo Orcalli, *L'invenzione della fonologia musicale: Saggi sulla musica elettronica sperimentale di Luciano Berio e Bruno Maderna* (Lucca: LIM, 2015)

Pour Bruno: Memorie e ricerche su Bruno Maderna, ed. Rossana Dalmonte and Mario Baroni (Lucca: LIM, 2015); incl.:
   • Mario Baroni, "Maderna negli anni Sessanta e lo stile *Hyperion*," pp. 59–127
   • Maurizio Romito, "Dediche e omaggi a Bruno Maderna (1973–2015)," pp. 251–367

Nicolò Palazzetti, "Italian harmony during the Second World War: Analysis of Bruno Maderna's First String Quartet," *Rivista di Analisi e Teoria Musicale* 21, no. 1 (2015), pp. 63–91

Angela Ida De Benedictis, "More than conducting, more than composing: Hermann Scherchen, Bruno Maderna, Luciano Berio," in *Komponieren & Dirigieren: Doppelbegabungen als Thema der Interpretationsgeschichte,* ed. Alexander Drčar and Wolfgang Gratzer (Freiburg im Breisgau et al.: Rombach, 2017), pp. 371–400

Daniele Badocco, "Bi-dimensional invention: Naming problems for *Dimensioni II/Invenzione su una voce* by Bruno Maderna," in *Sounds, Voices and Codes from the Twentieth Century: The Critical Editing of Music at MIRAGE,* ed. Luca Cossettini and Angelo Orcalli (Udine: Mirage, 2017), pp. 137–53

Luca Cossettini, "Towards an electronic 'global work': Author's transcription of *Dimensioni II/ Invenzione su una voce*," in ibid., pp. 155–70

Rossana Dalmonte, "Musical Borrowings in the Works of Bruno Maderna," in *The Dawn of Music Semiology: Essays in Honor of Jean-Jacques Nattiez,* ed. Jonathan Dunsby and Jonathan Goldman (Rochester: University of Rochester Press, 2017), pp. 119–38

Angela Ida De Benedictis, "The Beginning of the Studio di Fonologia Musicale and Bruno Maderna's *Notturno*," in *The Performance Practice of Electronic Music: The Studio di Fonologia years,* ed. Germán Toro-Pérez and Lucas Bennett (Bern et al.: Peter Lang, 2018), pp. 25–41

Paolo Dal Molin, "Le Liriche su Verlaine di Bruno Maderna: Disposizione, testo poetico, occasioni di un'opera giovanile e luoghi critici della sua fortuna postuma," *Philomusica on-line* 18 (2019) 1, 31 pp. (http://riviste.paviauniversitypress.it/index.php/phi/article/view/2026)

Maurizio Romito, "Da *Intolleranza 1960* a *Don Giovanni*," *Musica/Realtà,* no. 117 (2018), pp. 115–48 (I); ibid., no. 118 (2019), pp. 177–224 (II); ibid., no. 122 (2020), pp. 199–225 (Appendix, I); ibid., no. 123 (2020), pp. 197–233 (Appendix, II)

Mario Baroni and Rossana Dalmonte, *Bruno Maderna: La musica e la vita* (Lucca: LIM, 2020); Eng. transl.: *Bruno Maderna: His Life and Music* (Lanham et al.: Rowman & Littlefield, 2022)

Bruno Maderna, *Amore e curiosità: Scritti, interviste e frammenti sulla musica,* ed. Angela Ida De Benedictis, Michele Chiappini, and Benedetta Zucconi (Milan: il Saggiatore, 2020)

Index

§1. Index of Names and Titles (Musical Works)

Adorno, Theodor W., 204, 246
Alberghini, Simone, 444
Alcaeus, 350, 395, 436–38
Alcman, 438
Allorto, Riccardo, 47
Anacreon, 436–37
Anceschi, Luciano, 405, 432, 436
Anonymous (folk song)
  Fischia il vento, 373–74
  Bandiera rossa, 374
Arcaini, Ferruccio, 251
Arcalli, Franco ("Kim"), 183–84
Arenbergh, René van, 31
Arbasino, Alberto, 263
Arnheim, Gus (*see also* → § 2.4), 250, 271
Arrau, Claudio, 384
Ashkenazy, Vladimir, 286
Aubin, Tony, 430
  Six poèmes de Verlaine
    No. 1: *Sérénade,* 430
Auden, Wystan Hugh, 447
Auerbach, Eric, 66
Aulin, Ewa, 185

Babbitt, Milton, 321
Bacchiet, Nadia, 299
Bach, Johann Sebastian, 206–07, 210, 219, 230, 289
  Brandenburg Concertos, 289
  "Ricercar a 6" from the *Musical Offering* (arr. Anton Webern), 206–07, 210
Baden Powell de Aquino, Roberto, 184
Balet, Bernard, 447
Ballantine, Christopher, 241
Ballo, Ferdinando, 384–86, 389–90
Barberg, Rosmarie von, 27, 386, 415
Barouh, Pierre, 184
Barrault, Jean-Louis, 407
Barroso, Ary (*see also* → § 2.4), 250, 260, 273
Bartók, Béla, 21, 283, 295, 348, 358
Basso, Gianni, 265
Battagliola, Anania, 251
Bayer, Michael, 285
Becker, Howard Saul, 301
Beethoven, Ludwig van, 10, 141, 204, 215, 230, 280
  String Quartet No. 8 in e-Moll, op. 59 No. 2, 204
  String Quartet No. 15 in A minor, op. 132, 230
  Symphony No. 3 in E-flat major, op. 55 (*Eroica*), 230

Belli, Domenico (*see also* → § 2.3), 447, 450
Bellocchio, Maria Grazia, 429
Belt, Byron, 160
Benedetti, Arrigo, 390
Bennett, Earl, 296
Bennici, Aldo, 444, 448
Berg, Alban, 60, 174, 204, 288, 320, 410
  Lulu, 174
  Der Wein, 288
  String Quartet, op. 3, 204
Berberian, Catherine Anahid (Cathy), 37, 91–92, 112, 151, 252, 258, 272–73, 445, 448
Berio, Luciano, 10, 31, 144, 146, 161, 171, 181, 198, 200, 229, 246, 252, 261, 272–73, 279–80, 299–300, 335, 375, 445, 449
  Allez-hop, 252, 272
    Ora mi alzo, 252, 272–73
  Circles, 161
  Divertimento, 445
    Scat Rag, 445
    Rhumba-ramble, 445
  Epifanie, 279
  Passaggio, 300
  Nones, 198
  Ritratto di città (with Bruno Maderna), 445
Berlioz, Hector, 295, 340
Bernstein, Leonard, 284, 288
Bertocchi, Maria Grazia, 446–47
Bertola, Giulio, 336
Bertoni, Ferdinando, 223
Besthorn, Florian, 14
Betti, Laura, 245, 256, 262–68
Biamonte, Salvatore G., 247–48
Bianchini, Guido, 336
Birtwistle, Harrison, 35, 286, 307, 311
  Down by the Greenwood Side, 286, 307, 311
Bitter, Christof, 149–50, 152, 228
Bixio, Cesare Andrea, 250, 272
  Quanto sei bella Roma (canta se la vuoi cantà) (*see also* → § 2.4, *Fantasia su Roma*), 250, 272
Bizet, Georges
  Carmen, 37, 318
Bo, Carlo, 405
Bodini, Vittorio, 446
Boehmer, Konrad, 199, 210
Boito, Arrigo, 295
Bonagura, Enzo, 250, 272
Bonomo, Gabriele, 415, 443
Borella, Angelo Ramiro, 250, 274
Borio, Gianmario, 237–38, 394
Born, Sônia, 349
Boswell, James, 303, 323, 448
Boucourechliev, André, 117, 196

Boulez, Pierre, 10, 115–16, 144, 156, 200, 203–05, 210, 215–16, 280, 287–90, 299, 304, 335, 355
  Structure Ia, 115
  Third Piano Sonata, 116
Bour, Ernest, 445
Bove, Elisa Kadigia, 151
Brahms, Johannes, 292
  Symphony No. 1 in C minor, op. 68, 292
Brecht, Bertolt, 73, 251, 255–56, 261, 264, 266, 272
Breuer, Robert, 282
Brooks, Shelton (*see also* → § 2.4), 250, 271
Brown, Débria, 37, 299, 317–18
Brown, Earle, 117, 127–34, 135, 137, 215, 224, 280, 289, 291–92, 299, 313–15, 323
  Available Forms I, 117, 127–34, 135, 224, 292, 314–15
  Event: Synergy II, 289
  From Here, 280
  Synergy, 128
  Twenty-Five Pages, 128
Brown, Nacio Herb (Ignacio Herbert)
  (*see also* → § 2.4), 249–50, 274
Bruckner, Anton, 284, 288
  Symphony No. 7 in E major, WAB 107, 284
Bucchi, Valentino, 195, 345
  La dolce pena, 345
Busse, Dagmar, 447
Bustini, Alessandro, 335, 419–21, 424, 428

Cage, John, 115, 127, 151, 181, 280, 315
  First Construction in Metal, 115
Caiello, Alda, 429
Calandri, Max, 172
Calcagno, Giorgio, 227
Calder, Alexander, 315
Caldwell, Sarah, 277, 322
Calvino, Italo, 252, 272
Cantoni, Alberto, 31, 46
Cantoni, Remo, 405
Caocci, Duilio, 415
Caraël, Georges, 215, 218
Cardarelli, Vincenzo, 420–25, 430, 439, 444
Cardi, Guido, 390
Carducci, Giosuè, 415–16, 439
Cariaga, Daniel, 319
Carlson, Lenus, 286, 313
Carpi, Fiorenzo, 263
Carr, Bridget, 299
Carroll, Joan, 446
Carter, Elliott, 161, 306
  *Double Concerto for Harpischord and Piano
  with Two Chamber Orchestras,* 161
Casella, Alfredo, 417
  La sera fiesolana: laude di Gabriele D'Annunzio,
  417

Castellano, Mauro, 445
Castle, Joyce, 294, 299, 316
Catunda, Eunice, 349–52, 435, 437–38
Caudana, Mino, 248
Cederna, Camilla, 263
Ceroni, Athos, 251
Cestino, Giovanni, 141
Chailly, Luciano, 263
Chanfón, Carlos, 14, 357, 415
Chávez, Carlos, 386, 388
  La hija de Cólquide, 386
Chazalettes, Giulio, 28
Chiappini, Michele, 14, 266, 331, 383
Chopin, Frédéric, 284, 320
  Piano Concerto No. 2 in F minor, op. 21, 284
  Piano Sonata No. 2 in B-flat minor, op. 35
    Funeral March, 320
Ciceri, Carlo, 14
Claus, Hugo, 447
Clementi, Aldo, 251
Clifford, Gordon, 250
Coco, Julian, 185
Collaer, Paul, 354, 410
Company, Alvaro, 446
Compère, Loyset (*see also* → § 2.3), 206, 208
Contini, Ermanno, 407
Coppée, François, 9
Corbella, Maurizio, 247
Corgnati, Maurizio, 178, 180
Corsaro, Frank, 296
Cortese, Luigi, 386
Corti, Mario, 387
Cortis, Marcello, 261
Coward, Noël (*see also* → § 2.4), 249, 256–57, 273
Crivelli, Filippo, 263
Croce, Benedetto, 432
Crosara, Policarpo, 417
Cucchiara, Alfredo, 248
Cuppini, Gilberto ("Gil"), 265
Curtis, Alan, 294
Curtis-Smith, Curtis, 291

Daccò, Filippo, 251
Dahlhaus, Carl, 210, 238
Dal Fabbro, Beniamino, 393
Dalla Libera, Sandro, 336
Dallapiccola, Luigi, 174, 347–51, 374, 386, 391, 395, 435–39
  Canti di prigionia, 374
  Liriche greche, 351, 435, 439
    Cinque frammenti di Saffo, 435, 437
    Sex Carmina Alcaei, 349, 351, 435–36
    Due liriche di Anacreonte, 351, 435
  Il prigioniero, 374, 391
  Volo di notte, 174

Dall'Oglio, Renzo, 353, 356
Da Ponte, Lorenzo, 230, 239
Da Venezia, Gastone, 181
Dal Molin, Paolo, 14, 216, 383, 411
Dalmonte, Rossana, 27, 386, 388, 395–96, 409, 415, 423
d'Amico, Fedele, 263–64, 266
Dandin, 448
Daniels, Charles N., 250, 271
D'Annunzio, Gabriele, 415–17, 421, 424, 430, 439
Dasi, Gerardo Filiberto, 146, 152
Davies , Dennis Russell, 161, 289, 304
Davies, Sally, 14
De Benedictis, Angela Ida, 61, 125, 142, 146, 150, 158, 162, 178, 198, 211, 300, 303–04, 315, 359, 415, 420
de Bruyn, Christian, 444
Debussy, Claude, 219, 281, 287, 289–90, 335, 337, 358, 420–21, 430, 432
   Ariettes oubliées, 432
      Nos. 5 & 6: *Aquarelles – I. Green & II. Spleen,* 430
   Fêtes galantes, 432
   Jeux, 287, 289
   Trois mélodies de Paul Verlaine, 430
Decker, Harold, 277, 444
Decroupet, Pascal, 14, 375
de Curtis, Antonio (Totò), 178
de Groot, Roland, 33
de la Halle, Adam (*see also* → § 2.3), 449
De Landi, Margherita, 408
Delius, Frederick, 430
   Deux mélodies
      No. 2: *Le ciel est, par-dessus le toit,* 430
de Moraes, Vinícius, 184
De Pisis, Filippo, 430
de Pol, Henk van, 19, 29
de Poel, Piet Hein van, 22, 38, 60, 84, 310–11
de Roo, Hans, 22, 36, 39, 41, 306–08, 310–11, 314, 317
De Sica, Vittorio, 265, 266
Desormière, Roger, 351–52
de Vries, Han, 21, 448
Di Lazzaro, Eldo, 250, 272
   La Romanina (*see also* → § 2.4, *Fantasia su Roma*), 250, 272
Di Luzio, Ilaria, 19
Di Pietro, Rocco, 285–86, 299, 301, 304, 310–15, 321–23
Donadio, Attilio, 265
Donaldson, Walter (*see also* → § 2.4), 250, 274
Donati, Pino, 336
Domnick, Greta, 184
Domnick, Ottomar, 184
Dostoevsky, Fyodor Mikhailovich, 421
Drouet, Jean-Pierre, 447
Druckman, Jacob Raphael, 39, 290, 293, 323
   Incenters, 290
   Windows, 290, 294, 323

Drury, Stephen, 324
Dubin, Al, 249, 273
Dukas, Paul, 287
Dunkerley, Patricia, 448
"Duo Fasano" (*see* → Fasano, Delfina, and Fasano, Dina)

Engel, Kurt, 446
Ephrikian, Angelo, 386, 449
Erwin, Ralph (*see also* → § 2.4), 250, 274
Euripides, 425, 427

Fabbriciani, Roberto, 445
Faber, Lothar, 92, 353, 446–48
Fabris, Gastone, 353
Fanni, Sergio, 265
Fasano, Delfina, 250
Fasano, Dina, 250
Fauré, Gabriel, 430
   2 Mélodies, op. 83
      No. 1: *Prison (Le ciel est, par-dessus le toit)* [*Sagesse*], 430
   5 Mélodies "de Venise", op. 58
      No. 3: *Green,* 430
Fearn, Raymond, 317
Fellegara, Vittorio, 251
Felsenthal, Stefan, 42, 57
Fellini, Federico, 22, 311
Ferraris, Maria Pia, 141, 443
Ferrero, Mario, 181
Ferrero, Willy, 277
Fizdale, Robert, 383–84
Flaiano, Ennio, 263
Fortini, Franco, 263, 405, 407
Fortner, Wolfgang, 200
Foss, Lukas, 285, 305, 314
   Map: A Musical Game, 314
Fracci, Carla, 264
Frager, Malcolm, 287
Franco, Clare, 285
Frati, Enrico, 250, 274
Freed, Arthur, 249, 274
Frescobaldi, Girolamo (*see also* → § 2.3), 206–07, 215, 223, 449
Frieser, Erika, 444
Frittaion, Bruno, 333, 374, 445
Fromm, Paul, 161–62, 169, 286, 293–94, 301, 305–06, 322
Fruttero, Carlo, 180
Fuligno, Simone, 141

Gabrieli, Andrea (*see also* → § 2.3), 291
Gabrieli, Giovanni (*see also* → § 2.3), 224, 280, 283, 291–92, 449–50
  Canzoni et Sonate, 292
    Canzon XVI (*see also* → § 2.3 *Canzone a tre cori* [*Canzona a 12*]), 292
  Symphoniae sacrae, 291
    Exsultavit cor meum, 291
Gaipa, Ettore, 266
Galvani, Luigi, 40
Garda, Michela, 227
Garinei, Pietro, 250, 272
Gaslini, Giorgio, 22
  La cena di Joe Trimalchio, 22
Gawriloff, Saschko, 447
Gazzelloni, Severino, 92, 258, 263, 265, 268, 353, 445–47
Gershwin, George, 247
  Rhapsody in Blue, 247
Ghedini, Giorgio Federico, 392
  Billy Budd, 392
Gide, André, 407
Gijn, René van, 22, 310
Gill, Armando (*see* Testa, Michele)
Giovannini, Sandro, 250, 272
Gitlis, Ivry, 448
Giuffre, Jimmy, 255
Giulini, Carlo Maria, 336, 444
Glazer, Esther, 289
Gluck, Christoph Willibald, 60
Gold, Arthur, 383–84
Gorini, Gino, 336–37, 340, 388, 444
Götze, Werner, 213
Gounod, Charles, 295
Gozzi, Carlo, 258
Gracis, Ettore, 336, 388, 444
Graettinger, Robert F. ("Bob"), 268
Gramsci, Antonio, 333, 374, 445
Grano, Romolo, 353, 445
Gréco, Juliette, 247
Grossi, Pietro, 147
Grossato, Brunetto (*alias* Maderna, Bruno)
Grossato, Umberto, 245
Guadagnino, Luigi Maria, 393
Gulli, Donatella, 448

Haenen, Anne, 299, 301, 317–18
Hahn, Reynaldo, 430
  Mélodies (1er livre)
    No. 8: *Offrande* (Green), 430
    No. 16: *D'une prison* (*Le ciel est, par-dessus le toit*) [*Sagesse*], 430
Hammerich, Roy C., 283–84, 311–12
Hänggi-Stampfli, Sabine, 357

Hardy, Thomas, 421
Hartmann, Karl Amadeus, 348, 350–52, 356
Hangen, Bruce, 293–94
Heesemans, Jan, 33
Heg, Hans, 22, 310
Heinen, Rita, 444
Heiss, John, 299, 321
Helms, Hans Günter, 446
Henahan, Donal, 288, 318, 320, 323
Henck, Herbert, 203
Henze, Hans Werner, 60
Highstein, Ellen, 285
Hindemith, Paul, 204, 336–37, 343–44, 350–51, 358, 436
  Mathis der Maler, 343
    Engelkonzert, 343
Hines, Jerome, 295
Hocher, Barbara, 299
Hölderlin, Friedrich, 184, 446–47
Hoedeman, Wilhelmina, 32–33, 42
Holden, Poppy, 299, 301, 316–18
Holman, Bill, 182, 267
Holton, Robert, 162, 169
Horace (Quintus Horatius Flaccus), 66
Hübner, Herbert, 223, 352
Hulscher, Hans, 33
Hurney, Kate, 287
Huxley, Aldous, 421
Huysmans, Joris-Karl, 432

Ibycus, 435, 437–38, 444
Imam, James, 14
Ingarden, Roman, 218
Iser, Wolfgang, 218, 222
Isidore of Seville, 14
Israels, Charles ("Chuck"), 285
Ives, Charles, 168, 292–93, 295, 322–23
  Symphony No. 4, 295
  The Unanswered Question, 292–93, 322
Izzo, Leo, 14

Jacobson, Bernard, 289–90
Jaffé, Sula, 349
Janssen, Wim, 448
Jesenská, Milena, 333, 374
Joyce, James, 439

Kahn, Gustav Gerson ("Gus"), 250, 274
Kafka, Franz, 333, 374, 385–88, 391, 393–96, 405, 407, 409–11, 436, 439, 445
Kagel, Mauricio, 200
Kaletha, Holger, 238

Kant, Immanuel, 230
Karajan, Herbert von, 288, 449
Karchin, Louis, 285–86, 291, 324
Kassel, Matthias, 14
Keightley, Keir, 184
Kenton, Stan, 182, 268
Kerman, Joseph, 242
Kerner, Leighton, 294, 323
Khayyam, Omar, 448
Kirchner, Leon, 278
Klebe, Giselher, 196
Kleiber, Erich, 288
Klemperer, Otto, 288
Knussen, Oliver, 285–86
Koellreutter, Hans-Joachim, 349–50
Koenig, Gottfried Michael, 116
   Terminus, 116
Koepnick Maderna, Beate Christine, 31, 46, 162, 169, 231, 282, 340
Kohl, Jerome, 238
Kolisch, Rudolf, 203–04
Kontarsky, Aloys, 156, 203, 446
Koussevitzky, Natalie, 285
Koussevitzky, Serge, 285
Kramer, Gorni (*see also* → § 2.4), 250, 274
Kraut, Harry, 285, 305
Kubitzki, Anton Gronen, 410
Kunze, Stefan, 242
Kurosawa, Akira, 178

La Guardia, Fiorello, 280, 321
Lai, Francis, 184
La Pegna, Luigi, 390
Lay, Ubaldo, 388–89, 392, 408, 444
Lawergren, Bo, 319–20
   Triptych, 319–20
Lazzarini, Giulia, 262
Lecoq, Jacques, 264
Le Flem, Paul, 430
   D'une prison (Le ciel est, par-dessus le toit) *[Sagesse],* 430
Legrenzi, Giovanni (*see also* → § 2.3), 206, 210–14, 219, 223, 361
   Sonatas, op. 8, 210
     A Basadonna (arr. Gian Francesco Malipiero), 211–13, 218–19
Lehár, Franz, 251, 273
   Die lustige Witwe (*see also* → § 2.4 *Lehar*), 251, 273
Lelouch, Claude, 184
Leibniz, Gottfried Wilhelm von, 230
Leibowitz, René, 200
Leinsdorf, Erich, 284
Lemaire, Gérard, 447
Leonviola, Antonio, 178–80

Leopardi, Giacomo, 439
Leonardo da Vinci, 285
Lepelletier, Edmond, 432
Lerdahl, Alfred ("Fred"), 293, 323
   Chromorhythmos, 293, 323
Levy, Jonathan, 300, 303, 323
Levy, Marvin David, 290
   Trialogus, 290
Levinson, Gerald, 285–86
Leydi, Roberto, 246, 261–62, 265–66, 270, 445
Liberatore, Ugo, 181
Liberovici, Sergio, 261
Liebermann, Rolf, 348
Lifchitz, Max, 291
Ligeti, György, 33, 36, 306–07, 311, 316
   Aventures et Nouvelles Aventures, 33, 36, 306–07, 311, 316
Lini, Fermo, 251
Liszt, Franz, 288, 293
Locanto, Massimiliano, 237
Lodovici, Cesare Vico, 407
Lollobrigida, Gina, 185
Lord, Albert B., 143, 157
Lorca, Federico García, 183, 439, 446–47
Lorenzi, Sergio, 388, 444
Luter, Claude, 247
Lutyens, Elisabeth, 352

Macchi, Annamaria, 141
Machaut, Guillaume de, 280
Maderna, Andreas, 14
Maderna, Caterina, 14, 19
Maderna-Sieben, Claudia, 14, 19
Magnanensi, Giorgio, 423
Mahler Schindler, Alma, 220
Mahler, Gustav, 94, 215, 219–22, 286–87
   Symphony No. 2 in C minor, 94
   Symphony No. 5 in C-sharp minor, 286–87
   Symphony No. 10 in F-sharp major (*see also* → § 2.3), 219–22, 287
Malipiero, Gian Francesco, 204, 211–13, 219, 335–40, 342–45, 347–48, 352–53, 356, 358, 386, 390, 409, 416, 428–29
   Magister Josephus, 356
Malipiero, Riccardo, 195, 345, 347, 350, 392
   Piccolo concerto, 345
Mallarmé, Étienne (Stéphane), 9, 11
Malvano, Andrea, 249, 255, 273
Mancini, Umberto, 172
Mancuso, Giovanni, 444
Manfredi, Irma, 10, 92, 146, 297, 335–40, 344, 394, 396, 416–17, 419–21, 424–25, 428, 432–33
Mann, Thomas, 141, 421
Manning, Mary M., 299

Manzoni, Giacomo, 251, 261
Maranca, Aldo, 59, 200–01
Marcondes, Genny ("Gení"), 349
Marconi, Renzo, 147
Marinuzzi, Gino Jr., 247, 263
Martino, Donald, 320–21
  Notturno, 320
Masson, Diego, 447
Mayer-Haase, Claudia, 443
Mayhew, Billy, 274
  It's a Sin to Tell a Lie, 274
Maurri, Enzo, 252, 273
Mazzolini, Marco, 19, 87, 141
Mecenati, Ferrante, 384
Melanippides of Melos, 435, 437, 444
Mendel, Deryk, 447
Mendelssohn Bartholdy, Felix, 288
Mengelberg, Willem, 220, 288
Mennin, Peter, 281
Mercadante, Saverio, 281
  Il Giuramento, 281
Micheli, Giuseppe, 250, 272
Micheli, Renato, 250
Midana, Mario, 265
Migliacci, Franco, 272
Migliardi, Mario (*see also* → § 2.4), 247, 251, 273
Mignone, Carla (Milly), 262
Mila, Massimo, 84, 141, 201, 227–28, 241, 243, 246,
  261–62, 264, 266, 334, 340, 379, 392, 436
Milhaud, Darius, 60, 383–84, 386, 389
  Suite, op. 300 [*Concerto for two pianos and
  orchestra*], 383–84
Minescaut, Constant, 37, 54, 317
Miranda, Carmen, 260
Morehead, Philip, 299
Mitropoulos, Dimitri, 288
Modugno, Domenico (*see also* → § 2.4), 250, 272
Moles, Abraham, 146
Molino, Andrea, 444
Montale, Eugenio, 424–25
Montaigne, Michel de, 195–96
Monteverdi, Claudio (*see also* → § 2.3), 13, 34, 202,
  206–07, 215, 217, 223–24, 280, 294, 300, 315–16,
  323, 338, 450
  Il Combattimento di Tancredi e Clorinda
  (arr. Luciano Berio), 300
  Orfeo, 202
Moravia, Alberto, 263
Morice, Charles, 432
Morley, Christopher, 181
Morelli, Giovanni, 201, 356
Mosbacher, Peter, 447
Mosch, Ulrich, 144, 227

Mozart, Wolfgang Amadeus, 13, 36, 198–99, 227–43,
  280–81, 284, 286–87, 289, 292, 295–96, 302, 323
  La Clemenza di Tito, 229, 239–40, 281–82, 302,
  307–08
  Così fan tutte, 229, 239–40
  Don Giovanni, 198, 227–43, 295–96, 318
  Le nozze di Figaro, 241
  Piano Concerto No. 20 in D minor, K. 466, 286
  Symphony No. 31 in D major, K. 297 ("Paris"), 280
  Symphony No. 38 in D major, K. 504 ("Prague"),
  284, 289
  Symphony No. 41 in C major, K. 551 ("Jupiter"),
  230, 292
  "Vado, ma dove", K. 583, 282
  "Vorrei spiegarvi, oh Dio!", K. 418, 282
  Die Zauberflöte, K. 620, 316
Mulè, Giuseppe, 428
Munch, Charles, 284
Murray Schafer, Raymond, 289
  Requiems for the Party-Girl, 289

Nabokov, Nicolas, 339
Nash, Ogden, 268
Negri, Gino, 251
Neidhöfer, Christoph, 14
Neill, William, 39, 42, 57, 299, 301, 315–16, 318–20
Nicolai, Bruno, 262
Nono, Luigi, 10, 144, 151, 172, 204–05, 208, 211–16,
  224, 277–78, 283, 322, 332–35, 338, 343–45,
  348–56, 369, 374, 384, 386, 388, 411, 435–38
  Due liriche greche, 350, 435, 437–38
    Ai Dioscuri, 350
    La stella mattutina, 350
  Canti di vita e d'amore. Sul ponte di Hiroshima,
  224
  Contrappunto dialettico alla mente, 151
  Epitaffio per Federico García Lorca No. 1, 354, 374
  Intolleranza 1960, 277–78, 283, 322
  Musica-Manifesto n. 1, 151
  Prometeo, 345
  *Variazioni canoniche sulla serie dell'op. 41 di
  Arnold Schönberg,* 350, 352
  La victoire de Guernica, 354
  Y entonces comprendió, 151
Nonveiller, Roberto, 338
Norkin, Sam, 296
Novati, Maria Maddalena, 19, 245
Novis, Donald, 271

Oberer, Walter, 231
Obert, Simon, 14
Offenbach, Jacques, 307–08
   Croquefer, 307–08
Ohl, Herbert, 145–50, 152, 157
Olof, Theo, 184, 228, 447
Orchettini, Ribaldo, 454
Ötvös, Gabor, 231
Ozawa, Seiji, 291, 305

Pacuvio, Giulio, 407
Paderewski, Ignacy Jan, 295
   Piano Concerto in A minor, op. 17, 295
Palazzeschi, Aldo, 421, 439
Pannain, Guido, 384
Papetti, Fausto, 251
Paris, Daniele, 264, 447
Parry, Milman, 143
Pascoli, Giovanni, 415–16, 430, 439
Pasoli, Aldo, 427
Pasolini, Pier Paolo, 22, 263
Passannanti, Benedetto, 429
Pasticci, Susanna, 73, 354, 362, 366
Patroni Griffi, Giuseppe, 172–74, 258, 410
Pavese, Cesare, 181
Pecker Berio, Talia, 14
Pedrollo, Arrigo, 335
Penalva Santos, Alfonso, 349
Pennacchi, Renato, 147
Peragallo, Mario, 263
Pergolesi, Giovanni Battista (*see also* → § 2.3), 223, 449
Peri, Jacopo, 280
Pérotin (*see also* → § 2.3), 215, 224
Pestalozza, Luigi, 251, 261, 263
Petrassi, Goffredo, 424–25
   Colori del tempo, 424–25
Petrina, Debora, 444
Petronius Arbiter, 19, 22–23, 35, 37, 59, 61, 66, 285–86, 300, 302, 307, 309, 311–12, 317, 320, 420, 448
Petrucci, Ottaviano (*see also* → § 2.3), 206, 208, 354, 449
Pezzè-Pascolato, Maria, 425, 427
Pezzotta, Mario, 265
Piamonte, Guido, 390
Picasso, Pablo, 195–96
Piovesan, Alessandro, 173–74
Piscator, Erwin, 410–11
Pizzetti, Ildebrando, 335, 417, 419, 428
Pizzi, Nilla, 247
Poli, Liliana, 151
Polidoro, Gian Luigi, 22, 311
Pope, Conrad, 285

Porena, Boris, 261
Portaluppi, Piero, 181
Porter, Cole (*see also* → § 2.4), 250, 271–72
Pousseur, Henri, 117, 142, 153, 200, 282, 335
   Scambi, 117, 142, 153
Pozzi, Raffaele, 415
Pradella, Jonathan, 415
Pressburger, Giorgio, 448
Prokofiev, Sergei Sergeyevich, 334
Puecher, Virginio, 446–47, 450

Quasimodo, Salvatore, 351, 424, 430, 435–39
Questi, Giulio, 181, 183–84, 188

Radius, Emilio, 390, 392
Raeburn, Andrew, 291
Rascel, Renato, 250, 272
   Arrivederci Roma (*see also* → § 2.4, *Fantasia su Roma*), 250, 272
Rass, Rebecca, 447
Ratz, Erwin, 221
Ravel, Maurice, 224, 430
   Ma mère l'Oye, 224
   Un grand sommeil noir [*Sagesse*], 430
Rehfuss, Heinz, 445
Reiner, Fritz, 280
Remiglio, Carmela, 444
Resnais, Alan, 160
Respighi, Ottorino, 316
Ricaldone, Gian Domenico, 407
Rich, Alan, 289, 296
Rizzardi, Veniero, 14, 53, 141, 277
Robertazzi, Mario, 405
Rodríguez, Robert Xavier, 324
Rodziński, Artur, 288
Romagnoli, Ettore, 425, 427–28, 437
Romito, Maurizio, 14, 19, 35, 41, 249, 443
Rosen, David, 242
Rossi, Mario, 386
Rossini, Gioachino, 284
Rossmann, Hans, 447
Rotter, Fritz, 250, 274
Rouleau, Raymond, 450
Rudaki, 448
Rudel, Julius, 295, 320
Ruffini, Sandro, 407
Rugolo, Pete, 268
Russo, Bill, 268
   Egdon Heath, 268
Rzewski, Frederic, 446

Saadi of Shiraz, 448
Saba, Umberto, 424
Salabert, Erica, 37
Samama, Leo, 279
Samama, Sylvio, 36-37, 39, 41, 169, 231, 278-79, 281-83, 285, 287-89, 293, 302-06, 317, 322
Samara, Lena, 179
Sandbank, Miriam, 349
Sanguineti, Eduardo, 22, 61
Santa Cruz, Domingo, 384, 386
    Concerto for piano and orchestra, 384, 386
Sanzogno, Nino, 359, 361, 386, 408, 444, 449
Sappho, 436-38, 447
Sargeant, Winthrop, 288-89
Sartre, Jean-Paul, 9
Satie, Erik, 35, 307, 311
    Socrate, 307, 311
Scaldaferri, Nicola, 14
Scarlatti, Alessandro, 213, 223
Schaeffer, Pierre, 127, 159
Schat, Peter, 215
Schell, Freda, 444
Scherchen, Hermann, 206, 212, 219-20, 223, 283, 286, 288, 348-50, 352, 354-56, 383-86, 388-91, 409-10, 444-45, 449
Schiffer, Brigitte, 390
Schiffman, David, 278
Schippers, Thomas, 281
Schoenberg, Arnold, 21, 70, 174, 196-97, 203-05, 280, 282, 284, 287, 289-90, 303, 334, 343, 348, 350, 383-85, 389-92
    A Survivor from Warsaw, op. 46, 383, 389, 391-92, 410
    Violin Concerto, op. 36, 289
    Erwartung, op. 17, 70
    Kammersymphonie n. 1, op. 9 (Chamber Symphony), 284
    Moses und Aron, 384
    Phantasy, op. 47, 203
    Pierrot lunaire, op. 21, 282, 303
    Sechs kleine Klavierstücke, op. 19, 196
    Variations for Orchestra, op. 31, 280
    Verklärte Nacht (Transfigured Night), op. 4, 289-90
Schoenberg Nono, Nuria, 361
Schonberg, Harold C., 288-89, 296
Schubert, Franz (*see also* → § 2.3), 230, 279, 284, 287, 295, 449
    Marche Militaire, op. 51, no. 1, 279
    Symphony No. 2 in B♭ major, D 125, 284
    Symphony No. 9 in C major, D 944 ("The Great"), 295
Schucht, Julia, 333

Schuller, Gunther, 28, 161, 284-86, 291, 293, 301, 305-10, 313, 319, 321-22, 325
    Double Quintet, 286
    Five Bagatelles, 284
    Tre Invenzioni, 161, 293
Schutz, Alfred, 240
Schumann, Robert, 290, 293
    Symphony No. 2 in C major, op. 61, 293
    Violin Concerto in D minor, WoO 23, 293
Scliar, Ester, 349
Scodellari, Leda, 404
Searle, Humphrey, 352
Sebon, Karl-Bernhard, 446
Seemann, Carl, 444
Sergi, Antônio ("Totó"), 349
Sermonti, Vittorio, 258
Serradimigni, Grazia, 446-48
Sessions, Roger, 321
Séverac, Déodat de, 430
    Le ciel est, par-dessus le toit, 430
Severt, Marie, 41
Shakespeare, William, 343, 448
Shaw, Harold, 322
Shreffler, Anne C., 14, 141, 168
Shostakovich, Dmitri Dmitriyevich, 334
Sibaldi, Stefano, 248
Silver, Sheila, 324
Silverstein, Joseph, 277, 292
Silvestri, Franco, 250, 272
    Nannì ('Na gita a li Castelli) (see also → § 2.4, *Fantasia su Roma*), 250, 272
Simeoni, Veronica, 444
Sinatra, Frank, 248
Singer, Winnaretta (Princess Edmond de Polignac), 340
Sinopoli, Giuseppe, 89
Smalley, Denis, 117
Snyder, Louis, 319
Soffer, Sheldon, 39, 231, 278-79, 281-85, 287-89, 302-05, 307-08, 312, 322-23, 325
Solmi, Sergio, 338
Solti, Georg, 288
Sommi, Giorgio, 147
Souris, André, 351-52
Sousa, John Philip, 323
    Stars and Stripes Forever, 323
Spaak, Charles, 180
Spaini, Alberto, 396
Spence, Charles, 22, 421
Sperry, Paul, 36, 39, 289, 299-306, 316, 322-23, 448
Squarzina, Luigi, 264
Stadlen, Peter, 444
Staempfli, Edward, 408
Steinberg, Michael, 168, 278, 320
Steinberg, William, 279, 284

Steinecke, Wolfgang, 352, 379, 384, 410
Steingruber, Ilona, 445
Steuermann, Eduard, 203-04
Stiedry-Wagner, Erika, 282
Stockhausen, Karlheinz, 10, 115-16, 144, 200, 203, 280, 335
    Gesang der Jünglinge, 116
    Klavierstücke, 203
    Kontakte, 116
    Studie I, 115-16
Stone, George, 280, 343
Stout, Alan, 280
Strasfogel, Ian, 19, 27-28, 33-37, 39, 42, 51, 53, 285, 294, 299-301, 305, 307-14, 316-19, 321-22, 448
Strauss, Richard, 287
Strauss, Johann Jr., 287, 288
Stravinsky, Igor Fyodorovich, 204, 252, 279, 283, 287, 289-90, 292-93, 295, 303, 336, 348, 358, 386, 430
    La bonne chanson, op. 9 no. 2, 430
    Circus Polka, 279
    Concerto for piano and wind instruments, 290, 293
    Concerto in Es (*Dumbarton Oaks*), 289
    Histoire du Soldat, 303
    Jeu de Cartes [*A Card Game*], 283, 336
    Petrushka, 336
    Scherzo à la russe, 279
    Symphony of Psalms, 336
Strehler, Giorgio, 251, 261, 263, 266
Striggio, Alessandro Jr., 202, 450
Strongin, Theodore, 160
Sugar, Ladislao, 223
Svoboda, Josef, 277
Sweekhorst, Angelika, 447

Tartaglia, Antonio ("Toni"), 394-400, 402, 404-09, 412
Tartaglia, Franca, 396
Tartaglia, Gino, 396
Tartaglia, Raffaella, 387-88, 390, 396-97
Taxin, Ira, 324
Terry, Lilian, 262
Testa, Michele (Armando Gill) (*see also* → § 2.4), 250, 253-54, 274
Testi, Flavio, 54
Thomas, Michael Tilson, 285
Thomson, Virgil, 277, 339-41, 353
Tobias, Harry, 250, 271
Togliatti, Palmiro, 334
Togni, Camillo, 195, 345, 347
    Variazioni for piano and orchestra, 345
Toop, Richard, 315, 323
Toscanini, Arturo, 10, 277, 287-89, 296

Tosti, Francesco Paolo, 430
    Rêve, 430
Totò (*see* de Curtis, Antonio)
Traut, Paul, 444
Trintignant, Jean-Louis, 184-85
Tudor, David, 181, 203, 445
Turchi, Guido, 195, 336, 345
    Trio for flute, clarinet, and viola, 345

Ungaretti, Giuseppe, 424-25, 436

Valdambrini, Oscar, 265
Valenti, Sergio, 265
Valeri, Diego, 430, 432
Valli, Luca, 112
Vanoni, Ornella, 261
Varèse, Edgard, 430
    Un grand sommeil noir [*Sagesse*], 430
Vaughan Williams, Ralph, 430
    The Sky Above the Roof (Le ciel est, par-dessus le toit) [*Sagesse*], 430
Verdi, Giuseppe, 10, 66, 215, 287, 295, 340, 390
Verlaine, Paul, 428-30, 432, 434-35, 439
Verheul, Koos, 92, 446, 448
Verzina, Nicola, 373, 415
Viadana, Lodovico da (Lodovico Grossi) (*see also* → § 2.3), 206, 223, 449
Vierne, Louis, 430
    Spleens et Déstresses, op. 38
        No. 2: *Un grand sommeil noir,* 430
        No. 6: *Sérénade,* 430
Vincis, Claudia, 14, 33-34, 44, 415
Vidolin, Alvise, 95
Vigolo, Giorgio, 391-92
Vis, Lucas, 28-29, 31, 33-34, 41, 43-44, 47-48, 50-51, 285-86, 312, 318
Vivaldi, Antonio (*see also* → § 2.3), 223, 289, 338, 386, 449
    Concerto for 2 mandolins in G major, RV 532, 289
Vivante, Ginevra, 386, 388-89, 391-92, 444, 449
Vlijmen, Jan van, 280
    Serenata II, 280
Vogel, Wladimir, 350-352, 383-84, 386-87, 391
    Sieben Aspekte einer Zwölftonreihe (Sette aspetti di una serie dodecafonica), 383-84, 386, 391
    Thyl Claes, 352

Wagner, Richard, 10, 60, 199, 215, 242, 284, 287-88
    Wesendonck-Lieder, 288
Walter, Bruno, 288
Warren, Harry (*see also* → § 2.4), 249, 258-59, 273

Wassenaer, Unico Wilhelm van (*see also* → § 2.3),
223, 449
Waters, Emory, 285-86
Webern, Anton, 174, 196, 206-07, 210, 215, 286,
293-94, 312-13, 343, 348, 367, 379
Kinderstück, 286, 312-13
Six Bagatelles, op. 9, 196
Variations for orchestra, op. 30, 294, 343
Webster, James, 242
Weill, Kurt (*see also* → § 2.4), 60, 245-48, 251,
255-56, 261-62, 264-70, 272, 307
Aufstieg und Fall der Stadt Mahagonny, 265
Mahagonny Songspiel (stage production), 307,
309
Knickerbocker Holiday, 251, 265
Die Dreigroschenoper / Opera da tre soldi, 251,
255-56, 262-63, 265-66, 272
Seeräuber-Jenny (*Jenny delle spelonche*), 261
The Seven Deadly Sins (*I sette peccati capitali*),
264-65
Weinstock, Herbert, 216, 218
Wetters, Brent, 299
White, Claude, 285
Whiteman, Paul, 247
Wiener, Michael, 288
Wild, Earl, 284, 292-93, 295
Williams, Jan, 314
Willis, Thomas, 295
Wilson, Charles, 296
Wittgenstein, Ludwig, 216
Wolf-Ferrari, Ermanno, 425
Cenerentola, 425
Wuorinen, Charles, 285, 305

Yepes, Narciso, 297, 448

Zafred, Mario, 336
Zandonai, Riccardo, 428
Zeffiri, Mario, 444
Zanetti, Emilia, 387, 391, 393-94
Zanon, Sante, 336-37, 386
Zarlino, Gioseffo, 356
Ziani, Marc'Antonio (*see also* → § 2.3), 386
Zucconi, Benedetta, 14, 23, 26, 39, 331
Zuccheri, Marino, 40, 48, 150-51
Zukofsky, Paul, 289, 314, 319

§ 2. Index of Bruno Maderna's works

§ 2.1 Instrumental, Vocal, Stage and Electronic Music

Ages, 31, 125, 144, 172, 448
All the world's a stage, 448
Alba, 335, 420-25, 430, 439, 444
Amanda, 447
Aria, 446
Aulodia per Lothar, 446
Aura, 87, 89, 95, 97, 104, 117, 135-37, 144, 162, 281,
290, 297, 314, 331, 448
Ausstrahlung, 25, 55, 61-62, 87, 89-94, 97, 102-05,
107-08, 111-13, 123, 125-26, 135, 144, 162, 314-15,
375, 448
Biogramma, 87, 95, 97, 105, 109-10, 125, 162, 290,
295, 297, 331, 448
Cenerentola (unfinished), 425-28
Composizione in tre tempi, 354, 374, 445
Composizione n. 1 for orchestra, 174, 261, 351-52,
359-62, 408, 444
Composizione n. 2 for orchestra, 351, 359, 362-67,
375, 384-85, 444
Composizione n. 3 (unfinished), 410, 411
Concerto for 11 instruments (*see Serenata per
11 strumenti*)
Concerto for flute and orchestra, 445
Concerto for oboe and chamber ensemble (*Konzert
für Oboe and Kammerensemble*), 379, 446
Concerto for piano and orchestra (1942), 331, 336,
444
Concerto for piano and orchestra (1942), transcrip-
tion for two pianos (1946), 444
Concerto for piano and orchestra (1958-59), 445
Concerto for 2 pianos and instruments, 224, 283,
347-49, 351-52, 388, 444
Concerto for violin and orchestra, 158, 184, 189, 217,
228, 289, 293, 319, 344, 379, 447
Concerto No. 2 for oboe and orchestra, 379, 447
Concerto No. 3 for oboe and orchestra, 21, 41, 291,
331, 379, 448
Continuo, 445
Dialodia, 112, 448
Dimensioni II. Invenzione su una voce, 151, 445
Dimensioni III, 446
Dimensioni IV, 446
Divertimento, 445
Dark Rapture Crawl, 445
Divertimento in due tempi, 370, 374, 445
*Don Perlimplin, ovvero Il trionfo dell'amore e dell'
immaginazione,* 22, 40, 151, 172, 183, 189, 245, 258,
446

Entropia I, 446
Entropia II, 446
Entropia III, 446
Fantasia e Fuga for 2 pianos, 351–52, 444
From A to Z, 185, 443, 447
Improvvisazione n. 1 for orchestra, 351, 354, 444
Improvvisazione n. 2 for orchestra, 445
Introduzione e Passacaglia "Lauda Sion Salvatorem",
    336, 338, 444
Ippolito (unfinished), 425, 427–28
Gesti, 447
Giardino religioso, 2, 144, 161–63, 166–69, 286, 293,
    297, 306, 314, 319, 322, 448
Grande Aulodia, 87, 89, 91–92, 95, 97–106, 108, 112,
    352–53, 366, 447
Honeyrêves, 446
Hyperion, 72, 142, 184, 245, 282, 409, 446–47
Hyperion en het geweld, 446, 447
Hyperion – Orfeo dolente, 447
Liriche su Verlaine, 428–33, 435, 444
    Sérénade, 429–32, 434, 444
    Aquarelles, 430–35, 444
    Sagesse, 430–32, 434, 444
Juilliard Serenade (Tempo libero II), 25, 144–45, 150,
    153–56, 158–66, 281–82, 297, 302, 304, 308, 447
Musica su due dimensioni (1952), 143, 153, 332, 445
Musica su due dimensioni (1958), 160, 445
Musica per orchestra (see *Composizione n. 2*)
Notturno, 127, 200, 445
Per Caterina, 446
Piece pour Ivry, 144, 155, 448
Quadrivium, 87–89, 95–97, 104, 109, 118–19, 121–24,
    135, 144, 279, 281–82, 302, 314, 319, 447
Quartetto per archi in due tempi, 116, 375–79, 445
Quattro lettere (Kranichsteiner Kammerkantate),
    333, 368, 370–73, 411, 445
Requiem, 277, 283, 331, 338–45, 347, 353, 428, 444
Le Rire, 40, 446
Ritratto di città (with Luciano Berio), 151, 261, 445
Ritratto di Erasmo, 144, 291–92, 375, 447, 450
Satyricon, 12, 19–57, 59–84, 144, 245, 285–86, 289,
297, 299–302, 304–11, 313–23, 331, 448
Sequenze e strutture, 154, 445
La sera fiesolana (unfinished), 415–21, 424
Serenade für Claudia, 447
Serenata per Luisa, 447
Serenata per 11 strumenti, 195, 345, 388
Serenata per un satellite, 447
Serenata n. 2, 319, 445, 446
Serenata III, 446
Serenata IV, 443, 446
Solo, 112, 448
Ständchen für Tini, 448
Stele per Diotima, 447

Studi per "Il Processo" di Franz Kafka, 350–51,
    383–414, 444
Suite aus der Oper "Hyperion", 446–47
Syntaxis, 200, 445
String Quartet (1943-46), 338, 444
Tempo libero I, 144–46, 150–51, 154, 156, 159, 447
Tre liriche greche, 174, 277, 352, 375, 408, 435, 437,
    444
Venetian Journal, 23, 25, 36, 61–63, 105, 162, 289,
    297, 299–305, 315–316, 319–20, 322–23, 331, 366,
    448
Viola, 448
Y después, 298, 448
Widmung, 89, 184–89, 447

§ 2.2 Music for Film and Radio Productions

Film

Il fabbro del convento, 172, 428
Le due verità, 173, 178–80, 188
Lavoro a Ferrania, 146, 181
La morte ha fatto l'uovo, 181, 183–88
Opinione pubblica, 179–81, 183
Noi cannibali, 180
Sangue a Ca' Foscari, 172, 428

Radio Play

Aspetto Matilde, 251–52, 273
    Aspettare, 251–52, 271, 273
L'Augellino belverde, 258
Il cavallo di Troia, 179, 181–82, 188–89
Il mio cuore è nel Sud, 171–78, 183, 188,
    189, 245, 258, 388, 408, 410, 444

§ 2.3 Transcriptions of Early / Classical Music

Belli / Maderna
    Orfeo dolente, 447, 450
Compère / Maderna
    Nous sommes de l'ordre du Saint Babuyn,
    206–08, 210
de la Halle / Maderna
    Rondeaux, 449
Desprez / Maderna
    Magnificat quarti toni, 450

Frescobaldi / Maderna
   Tre pezzi, per orchestra da camera, 207, 223, 449
      Bergamasca, 206, 207
      Ricercare super La-Fa-Sol-La-Re, 206–07
Gabrieli, Andrea / Maderna
   La battaglia, 291
Gabrieli, Giovanni / Maderna
   Canzone a tre cori [*Canzona a 12*], 292, 450
   In ecclesiis, 280, 283, 449
   Ricercare del settimo tono, 224, 291, 292
Legrenzi / Maderna
   La Basadonna, 206, 210, 214, 449
   La Marinona, 213
   Totila, 361
Mahler / Maderna
   "Adagio" from the Symphony No. 10, 219–22, 449
Monteverdi / Maderna
   L'Incoronazione di Poppea (*The Coronation of
   Poppea*), 34, 294–95, 315–16
   Orfeo, 202, 450
   Sonata sopra Sancta Maria, 206–07, 224
Music of Gaity, 223, 281, 302, 450
Pergolesi / Maderna
   Orfeo, 449
Pérotin / Maderna
   Alle Psallite Alleluja/Haec dies, 224
Petrucci / Maderna
   Odhecaton, 206, 208, 218, 354, 449
Schubert / Maderna
   Cinque danze, 279, 287, 449
Viadana / Maderna
   Le Sinfonie, 449
      Mantovana, 449
      Napoletana, 449
      Romana, 206, 449
      Venexiana, 206, 449
      Veronese, 449
Vivaldi / Maderna
   Beatus Vir, Psalm 111, RV 597, 386, 449
   Violin Concerto in C major, F. I n. 3, RV 186, 449
   Violin Concerto in A major, F. I n. 5, RV 352, 449
   Violin Concerto in D major, F. I n. 8, RV 231, 449
   Violin Concerto in C major ("Per la SS. Assunzione
   di Maria Vergine"), F. I n. 13, RV 581, 386, 449
   Violin Concerto in C minor, F. XI n. 8, RV 120, 449
   Violin Concerto in C minor, F. XI n. 9, RV 118, 449
Wassenaer / Maderna
   Palestrina-Konzert (*Concertino armonico n. 3*),
   223, 449
Ziani / Maderna
   Il Sepolcro, 386

§ 2.4 Arrangements

Arnheim, Gus; Daniels, Charles N.; Tobias, Harry
   Sweet and Lovely, 250, 271
Barroso, Ary
   Bahia (Na baixa do sapateiro), 250, 260–61, 270,
   272–73
Brooks, Shelton
   The Darktown Strutters' Ball, 250, 271
Brown, Nacio Herb (Ignacio Herbert)
   Paradise, 250, 274
   You Are My Lucky Star, 249, 274
Coward, Noël
   Mad About the Boy, 249, 256–58, 273
Donaldson, Walter
   Yes Sir! That's My Baby (*Lola*), 250, 274
Erwin, Ralph
   Ich küsse Ihre Hand, Madame (*Signora mia gentil*),
   250, 274
Fantasia su Roma (*Roma Bbona*), 250, 271–72
   (*see also* → § 1. Bixio, Cesare Andrea; Di Lazzaro,
   Eldo; Rascel, Renato; Silvestri, Franco)
Kramer, Gorni
   Op! Op! Trotta cavallino, 250, 274
Lehar, 271, 273
   (*see also* → § 1. Lehár, Franz, *Die lustige Witwe*)
Migliardi, Mario
   Arianna, 251–52, 271, 273
Modugno, Domenico
   Nel blu, dipinto di blu, 250, 254–55, 272
Porter, Cole
   Begin the Beguine, 250, 271
   In the Still of the Night, 250, 272
Testa, Michele (Armando Gill)
   Come pioveva!..., 250, 252–54, 274
Warren, Harry
   I Only Have Eyes For You, 249, 258–59, 273
Weill / Maderna
   Aufstieg und Fall der Stadt Mahagonny, 265, 267
      Moon of Alabama, 265
      Wie man sich bettet, 265–67
   Das Berliner Requiem, 265
      La ragazza annegata, 265
   Die Dreigroschenoper / Opera da tre soldi, 251,
   255–56, 265–66, 272
      Ballade vom angenehmen Leben (*Ballata dell'
      agiatezza*), 265–66
      Barbara Song, 265–66
      Die Ballade von der sexuellen Hörigkeit (*Ballata
      della schiavitù sessuale*), 251, 255–56, 265–66,
      272
      Die Moritat von Mackie Messer, 251, 255–56,
      265–68, 272
      Jenny dei pirati [*Seeräuber-Jenny*], 265
      Salomon Song, 265

Die Zuhälterballade (Tango Ballade / Ballata del magnaccia), 251, 255, 265–66, 272
Happy End, 265
  Surabaya Johnny, 265
Knickerbocker Holiday, 265
  How Can You Tell an American, 265
  September Song, 265, 267
Maria Galante, 265
  Le grand lustucru, 265
  J'attends un navire, 265
One Touch of Venus, 265, 269
  Speak Low, That's Him, 265, 267–70
Der Silbersee, 265
  Lied der Fennimore, 265
The Seven Deadly Sins (I sette peccati capitali), 265
  Songs from the ballet, 265
Street Scene, 265
  Lonely House, 265